Lecture Notes in Computer Science

Lecture Notes in Computer Science

Lecture Notes in Computer Science

Edited by G. Goos and J. Hartmanis

375

J. L. A. van de Snepscheut (Ed.)

Mathematics of Program Construction

375th Anniversary of the Groningen University
International Conference
Groningen, The Netherlands, June 26–30, 1989
Proceedings

Springer-Verlag

Berlin Heidelberg New York London Paris Tokyo Hong Kong

CR Subject Classification (1987): B.7.1, C.1.2, C.2.4, D.1–2, F.3–4, G.4

ISBN 3-540-51305-1 Springer-Verlag Berlin Heidelberg New York
ISBN 0-387-51305-1 Springer-Verlag New York Berlin Heidelberg

Printing and binding: Druckhaus Beltz, Hemsbach/Bergstr.
2145/3140-543210 – Printed on acid-free paper

PREFACE

The papers in this volume were presented at the *Conference on Mathematics of Program Construction*, held June 26-30, 1989. The conference was organized by the Department of Computing Science, Groningen University, The Netherlands, at the occasion of the university's 375th anniversary.

The creative inspiration of the modern computer has led to the development of new mathematics, the *mathematics of program construction*. Initially concerned with the post hoc verification of computer programs, the mathematics have now matured to the point where they are actively being used for the discovery of elegant solutions to new programming problems. Initially concerned specifically with imperative programming, the application of mathematical methodologies is now established as an essential part of all programming paradigms —functional, logic and object-oriented programming, modularity and type structure etc. Initially concerned with software, the mathematics is also finding fruit in hardware design so that the traditional boundaries between the two disciplines have become blurred.

The varieties of *mathematics of program construction* are wide-ranging. They include calculi for the specification of sequential and concurrent programs, program transformation and analysis methodologies, and formal inference systems for the construction and analysis of programs. Such mathematics are characterised by an emphasis on calculation, by an unprecedented concern for notational issues, and by the strife for the utmost economy and clarity of presentation. Within the last few years we have seen enormous improvements in our ability to design programs and implementations. We are entering a period in which coherence must be the dominant goal so that the mathematics of specification, implementation and analysis become indispensable tools for the practising programmer.

The scientific program of MPC 1989 consisted of 6 invited lectures by distinguished researchers from industry and academia who presented their work and the insights they have gained from it. The program was complemented by 19 contributed papers selected by the program committee.

Acknowledgements

This conference represents the work of many individuals. The program committee members worked many long hours reviewing each of the submitted papers. The members of the organizing committee handled many organizational details to ensure a smoothly running conference. The authors of the invited and contributed papers deserve most of the credit, because their efforts to carry out research and report the results form the basis of the conference.

The conference has received sponsorship from the Department of Computing Science, Groningen; Koninklijke Nederlandse Academie van Wetenschappen; Nationale Faciliteit Informatica; Philips Research Laboratories; PTT Telematics Laboratory; and Shell Nederland B.V. The EATCS kindly supplied us with their mailing list.

Jan L.A. van de Snepscheut
Groningen, April 1989

PROGRAM COMMITTEE

ORGANIZING COMMITTEE

CONTENTS

Invited lectures

Contributed lectures

A FORMAL APPROACH TO LARGE SOFTWARE CONSTRUCTION

J.R. Abrial (Paris)

Is the rationalisation of SOFTWARE CONSTRUCTION the main preoccupation of informaticians today? In this paper, we present, briefly and informally, a number of results concerning the so called axiomatic answer to this question.

One of the recent trends of our discipline is to reduce the traditional distinction of the two main activities of software construction, namely specification and programming. This trend sometimes takes the form of "executable specifications" [14,19]; here, we adopt a somewhat different approach, that of "non necessarily executable programs".

In what follows, our intention is to show that the main concepts of specification (section 1) and those of programming (section 2) can be unified [15,16,17]. From this unification, a new activity, called design, will emerge (section 3); design is situated between specification and programming and its role is to ensure the systematic passage from one to the other [12,13,16,20].

1 SOFTWARE SPECIFICATION METHODOLOGY: MODELS

One of the important ideas of the axiomatic (model oriented) approach to software specification is to separate conceptually the specification of data from that of programs [13].

As a consequence, for specifying a piece of software, we shall adopt the following strategy: we define a MATHEMATICAL MODEL OF ITS DATA and also a corresponding ANIMATION of this model, animation specified under the form of a number of OPERATIONS whose eventual implementation will modify the data in question and, possibly, provide some results. Here is a pictorial representation of this approach.

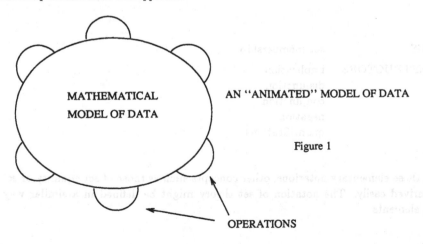

MATHEMATICAL MODEL OF DATA

AN "ANIMATED" MODEL OF DATA

Figure 1

OPERATIONS

At this level, no consideration about space or time efficiency should be taken into account: our only guideline will be that of formalising data in such a way that the specification of the operations can be written in a straightforward manner.

A piece of software specified in this way will be later used through one or several INTER-FACES activating the operations offered by the animated model. As a consequence, the programmer of one of these interfaces will have the ILLUSION to work directly at the level of the very abstract data as specified in the model; of course, this is only a working assumption: in practice, the operations effectively activated by the interface are ultimate REFINEMENTS of the specified operations, refinements done according to certain CHANGES OF VARIABLES (see section 3.3.2) whose role is to ensure that the data can be stored on conventional memories with full efficiency.

As a consequence, once the model has been agreed upon by the various concerned parties, the construction can proceed along two INDEPENDENT lines: first, the refinement of the specified operations; second, the development of various interfaces using these operations.

In the rest of this section, we study briefly the ways mathematical models of data can be defined (section 1.1), then we envisage their animation (section 1.2), and eventually their consistency (section 1.3). Finally, we consider the problem of building large models (section 1.4).

1.1 MATHEMATICAL MODEL OF DATA

Generally speaking, mathematical models are defined, first by listing their component VARIABLES, and second by writing down the relevant properties of these variables, properties which we call here the INVARIANT [13] of the model. Moreover, a model can be made more general by means of a number of, so called, GENERIC PARAMETERS, denoting given abstract sets which can be used freely in the invariant.

The invariant of a model is formalised using the full notation of FIRST ORDER LOGIC and that of SET THEORY. In this section, and in other dealing with similar notational questions, we briefly mention how such notations are defined in terms of a BASIS and various CONSTRUCTORS. For example, in the case of first order logic applied to set theory, we have the following elements

BASIS:	set membership
CONSTRUCTORS:	implication
	disjunction
	conjunction
	negation
	quantifications

From these elementary notations, other concepts such as those of set equality or set inclusion can be derived easily. The notation of set theory might be defined in a similar way from the following elements

BASIS: generic parameters

CONSTRUCTORS: cartesian product
                   power set
                   set comprehension

These set constructors can be combined in order to build more elaborate mathematical beings such as binary relations, partial or total functions, sequences, trees, and so on. We also suppose given the classical theory allowing us to define (primitive) recursive functions on inductively defined sets (i.e. natural numbers, finite sequences, finite trees, etc). For instance, arithmetical operations, as well as the classical operations on sequences and trees, can be defined in this way [1].

To summarise at this point, any formal expression with a rigorous mathematical definition is "permitted".

1.2 MODEL ANIMATION

As explained before, in order to animate a model, we SPECIFY a number of (possibly parameterised) OPERATIONS allowing us to modify the values of the variables of the model, and this while possibly providing also some results. Such modifications will be later physically realised by means of the execution of certain corresponding PROGRAMS.

Before proceeding, it seems important to make precise what we mean exactly by the term "program", and by the term "specification".

A PROGRAM,   defined on some global variables and providing some
             results, is the precise description of the way the
             values of these variables are MODIFIED and the values
             of these results are COMPUTED.

A SPECIFICATION (of program) is the precise description of a
             number of WISHFUL PROPERTIES that the variable
             modifications and result computations, as prescribed
             by the program, should enjoy.

As you can see, these definitions leave some room between a program and a specification: in particular, it should be clear that several distinct programs may correspond to the same specification. More precisely, a program is said to SATISFY its specification if the modifications and computations it prescribes enjoy the properties expressed in the specification.

Usually, this relation of "satisfaction", should not hold for all possible values of the variables of the model and parameters of the operation; this is so because, most of the time, only certain values of the variables and values of the parameters make sense for the operation in question. As a consequence, the specification of an operation has an attribute which is not shared by the program: this is the, so called, PRE-CONDITION [13], defining, in one way or another, the values of the variables and those of the parameters for which the operation is meaningful.

By analogy with the term pre-condition, we shall also use in what follows that of IN-CONDITION to qualify collectively the wishful properties as described in the specification of an operation. Finally, the term POST-CONDITION denotes a condition which must be verified by the values of the variables and by those of the results just after the operation execution.

To summarise at this point, the specification of an operation is defined by

> its pre-condition
> its in-condition

At least three different notational styles can be adopted to formalise the specification of an operation. In what follows, we shall adopt the last style. To simplify matters, we present these styles for operations without parameter and without result:

THE PREDICATIVE STYLE [11,12,13]

Let x denote the (collection of) variable of the model. The pre-condition is expressed as a FIRST ORDER PREDICATE in x: $pre(x)$; and the in-condition is expressed as a first order predicate in x and x': $in(x,x')$, where x' denotes, by convention, the collection of modified variables. In the sequel, we shall suppose that the in-condition is true when the precondition is false.

THE RELATIONAL STYLE [10]

Let V denote the set of values of the variables of the model. The pre-condition is expressed as a SUBSET of V: PRE; and the in-condition is expressed as a BINARY RELATION with source and destination V: IN. We suppose that the cartesian product of the complement of PRE and V is included in IN (this supposition is of the same nature as the one we have done for the predicative style). Obviously, the present style and the previous one are equivalent, formally

$$PRE = \{x \mid pre(x)\}$$
$$IN = \{x, x' \mid in(x, x')\}$$
$$pre(x) \Leftrightarrow x \in PRE$$
$$in(x, x') \Leftrightarrow x, x' \in IN$$

THE PROGRAMMING STYLE [2,15,16,17]

Here, pre- and in-conditions are integrated in a notation which looks like the INSTRUCTION part of a very small "programming" language. This notation is defined by means of the following basis and constructors

BASIS:	Multiple substitution
	Empty substitution
CONSTRUCTORS:	Pre-conditioning
	Guarding
	Bounded choice
	Unbounded choice

Multiple substitution is applied to some, or all, variables of the model. The constructors are generalisations, as well as simplifications, of the, so called, "guarded commands" of Dijkstra [6]. We collectively call theses constructors GENERALISED SUBSTITUTIONS. Here is a more precise description of the notation

$x, ..., y := E, ..., F$	Multiple substitution: x,...y are distinct variables, and E, ..., F are equally numbered set theoretic expressions.
$x := E \parallel ... \parallel y := F$	An alternative form for the previous notation (in section 1.4, we generalise this notation).
$skip$	Empty substitution.
$P \mid S$	Pre-conditionning: P is a first order predicate, and S is a generalised substitution.
$P \Longrightarrow S$	Guarding: P is a first order predicate, and S is a generalised substitution
$S \, [] \, T$	Bounded choice: S and T are two generalised substitutions.
$@z \bullet S$	Unbounded choice: z is a variable distinct from those of the model, and S is a generalised substitution.

In the sequel, we shall follow the convention that the binary operators $\mid$, $[]$, $\Longrightarrow$, $\parallel$, and $:=$, taken in that order, have an increasing syntactic priority.

Each generalised substitution S defines a PREDICATE TRANSFORMER (a predicate function) which associates to any post-condition R, the WEAKEST PRE-CONDITION, $[S]R$, ensuring that R holds just after the operation has taken place. When this is the case, then S is said to ESTABLISH R. Here are the (recursive) definitions of these predicate transformers applied to a post-condition R

$$[\,x,...,y:=E,...,F\,]R \quad \Leftrightarrow \quad \text{R with free occurences of x,...,y replaced}$$
$$\text{SIMULTANEOUSLY and respectively by E,...,F.}$$

$$[\,skip\,]R \quad \Leftrightarrow \quad R$$
$$[\,P\mid S\,]R \quad \Leftrightarrow \quad P \wedge [\,S\,]R$$
$$[\,P\Longrightarrow S\,]R \quad \Leftrightarrow \quad P \Rightarrow [\,S\,]R$$
$$[\,S\,[]\,T\,]R \quad \Leftrightarrow \quad [\,S\,]R \wedge [\,T\,]R$$
$$[\,@z \bullet S\,]R \quad \Leftrightarrow \quad \forall z \bullet [\,S\,]R \qquad \text{(where z is not free in R)}$$

We list now a number of very general properties of this notation. These properties will not be used directly in practice, only indirectly through their consequences.

The first property corresponds to the possibility for each element of the notation to be put in a NORMAL FORM: more precisely, one may show (by structural induction) that each generalised substitution S working with a (collection of) variable x can be put under the following form, where $A(x)$, $B(x,x')$ and $C(x)$ are three first order predicates

$$A(x) \mid @x' \bullet (B(x,x') \Longrightarrow x:=x') \;[]\; C(x) \Longrightarrow skip \qquad (1)$$

Notice that this formula contains all the features of the notation. From this result, we can deduce our second property exhibiting the following identity on generalised substitution

$$S = [\,S\,]true \mid @x' \bullet (\neg\,[\,S\,](x \neq x') \Longrightarrow x:=x') \qquad (2)$$

Finally, our last property shows that the predicative style depicted above and the present "programming" style ARE EQUIVALENT. More precisely, suppose we have a precondition $pre(x)$ and an in-condition $in(x,x')$ then the corresponding generalised substitution is

$$pre(x) \mid @x' \bullet (in(x,x') \Longrightarrow x:=x') \qquad (3)$$

Conversely, given a generalised substitution S, then the corresponding pre- and in-conditions are

$$pre(x) \quad \Leftrightarrow \quad [\,S\,]true$$
$$in(x,x') \quad \Leftrightarrow \quad \neg\,[\,S\,](x \neq x') \qquad (4)$$

1.3 MODEL CONSISTENCY

Once an animated model is defined, you may try to prove that it is consistent. This corresponds to two distinct concerns.

First, you might wish to prove that the model is not "empty". For this, we define a special operation, called the INITIALISATION, and prove that it establishes the invariant. This guarantees that the model is not empty, provided the initialisation is not contradictory; such a non-contradictory operation is said to be "feasible"; conversely, an operation establishing a contradiction is said to be "miraculous" [15,17].

Second, you might wish to verify that, under the assumption of its pre-condition, each operation PRESERVES THE INVARIANT. This invariant preservation proof obligation can obviously be defined as follows for an invariant $I(x)$ and for an operation defined with pre-condition $pre(x)$ and in-condition $in(x, x')$

$$I(x) \land pre(x) \Rightarrow \forall x' \bullet (in(x, x') \Rightarrow I(x')) \tag{5}$$

It can then be shown, using (2) and (4), that this statement is equivalent to the following formula in the "programming style"

$$I(x) \land [S] true \Rightarrow [S] I(x) \tag{6}$$

To summarize at this point, an animated model is made up of the following elements

its generic parameters
its variables
its invariant
its initialisation
its operations

1.4   BUILDING LARGE SPECIFICATIONS

When writing down specifications of real systems, one faces, sooner or later, the problem of the SIZE of our mathematical models and also that of the size of the corresponding consistency proofs. Obviously, we need a structuring mechanism allowing us to CONSTRUCT LARGE MODELS from smaller ones as well as to construct LARGE PROOFS from smaller ones. The main problem is the number of variables: a model with, say, up to 7 variables is manageable, whereas a model with more is not.

In this section, we show how such large specifications can be constructed from smaller ones. The rational for the proposed technique is to study FIRST how to simplify proofs and then to infer from this a technique to simplify the construction of large models.

As we have seen it in previous section, the general form of the invariant preservation proof obligation for a model with an invariant $I(x)$ and for an operation with pre-condition $pre(x)$ and in-condition $in(x, x')$ is

$$I(x) \land pre(x) \Rightarrow \forall x' \bullet (in(x, x') \Rightarrow I(x'))$$

Suppose now that our collection of variables is made of two DISJOINT sub-collections x and y; moreover, suppose that our invariant can be put under the conjuncted form $I1(x) \land I2(y)$ where y is not free in $I1(x)$ and x is not free in $I2(y)$; finally, suppose that our operation has a pre-condition of the form $pre1(x) \land pre2(y)$ and an in-condition of the form $in1(x, x') \land in2(y, y')$; then, the proof obligation for invariance preservation becomes

$$I1(x) \land I2(y) \land pre1(x) \land pre2(y)$$
$$\Rightarrow$$
$$\forall x', y' \bullet (in1(x, x') \land in2(y, y') \Rightarrow I1(x) \land I2(y))$$

But for these special forms of the invariant and pre- and in-conditions, we have more: it is easy to prove (using simple Predicate Calculus rules) that the previous large statement can be deduced from the following two smaller ones

$$I1(x) \land pre1(x) \Rightarrow \forall x' \bullet (in1(x, x') \Rightarrow I1(x))$$
$$I2(y) \land pre2(y) \Rightarrow \forall y' \bullet (in2(y, y') \Rightarrow I2(y))$$

This simple fact gives us a clue about the way we can structure large specifications: the idea is to PUT TOGETHER two (or more) animated models working on disjoint (collection of) variables; by the "putting together" of two models, we mean the concatenation of their variables and the conjunction of their invariants (notice that, while putting things together, we can also, at the same time, add some "gluing" invariant); concerning the operations, we can either take them as they are in their respective models, or we can strengthen their preconditions, or else we can combine two of them with "gards" and "choices", or finally and more importantly, we can combine two of them (taken in different models) by CONJUNCTING THEIR PRE- AND IN-CONDITIONS respectively.

Note that this latter combination of operations (conjuncting the pre- and in-conditions respectively) is in fact a GENERALISATION OF THE '||' OPERATOR we introduced previously (section 1.2) as a mere "syntactic sugar" for multiple substitution. We give now some more formal insights for supporting this informal remark. Let S and T be two generalised substitutions working with distinct variables and put under their normal form (1)

$$S = A(x) \mid @x' \bullet (B(x, x') \Longrightarrow x := x') \; [] \; C(x) \Longrightarrow skip$$
$$T = P(y) \mid @y' \bullet (Q(y, y') \Longrightarrow y := y') \; [] \; R(y) \Longrightarrow skip$$

Their "multiple" combination $S \parallel T$ is then defined as follows

$$S \parallel T = A(x) \land P(y) \mid \quad
\begin{aligned}
&@x', y' \bullet (B(x, x') \land Q(y, y') &&\Longrightarrow x, y := x', y') &&[]\\
&@x' \bullet (B(x, x') \land R(y) &&\Longrightarrow x := x') &&[]\\
&@y' \bullet (Q(y, y') \land C(x) &&\Longrightarrow y := y') &&[]\\
&C(x) \land R(y) &&\Longrightarrow skip
\end{aligned}$$

As you can see, the pre-condition of $S \parallel T$ is exactly, after (4), the conjunction of the pre-conditions of S and T, namely $A(x) \land P(y)$. And the in-conditions of $S \parallel T$ can be computed, again using (4), yielding

$$
\begin{aligned}
&B(x, x') \land Q(y, y') &&\lor\\
&B(x, x') \land R(y) \land y = y' &&\lor\\
&Q(y, y') \land C(x) \land x = x' &&\lor\\
&C(x) \land R(y) \land y = y' \land x = x'
\end{aligned}
$$

which can be simplified as follows

$$(B(x, x') \lor (C(x) \land x = x')) \land (Q(y, y') \lor (R(y) \land y = y'))$$

This latter formula is exactly the conjunction of the in-conditions of S and T taken individually: in conclusion, the proposed definition of the '‖' operator has indeed the property we wanted; however, this definition is not very useful in practice since we have to have two general substitutions transformed into their normal form in order to be able to put them together using the '‖' operator. Fortunately, from this very general definition, we can easily deduce the following quite intuitive (and, this time, very practical) laws

$$
\begin{aligned}
S \parallel T &= T \parallel S \\
S \parallel (T \parallel U) &= (S \parallel T) \parallel U \\
S \parallel skip &= S \\
S \parallel (P \mid T) &= P \mid (S \parallel T) \\
S \parallel (P \Longrightarrow T) &= P \Longrightarrow (S \parallel T) \qquad \text{(if } [\,S\,]true \text{ is } true) \\
S \parallel (T \,[]\, U) &= (S \parallel T) \,[]\, (S \parallel U) \\
S \parallel @z \bullet T &= @z.(S \parallel T) \qquad \text{(if } z \text{ not free in } S)
\end{aligned}
$$

Clearly, the very shape of these laws indicates that the '‖' operator is a mere NOTATIONAL CONVENIENCE which can always be eliminated: in other words, after "putting together" two operations by means of the '‖' operator, you can always mechanically eliminate all occurences of this operator.

Another very important property of this "multiple" operator is the following: given two generalised substitution S and T working on the two distinct (collections of) variables x and y respectively, and given two predicates $I(x)$ and $J(y)$ such that y is not free in $I(x)$ and x is not free in $J(y)$, then we have

$$
[\,S\,]I(x) \wedge [\,T\,]J(y) \Rightarrow [\,S \parallel T\,](I(x) \wedge J(y))
$$

As you can see, the proof of the "complex" statement $[\,S \parallel T\,](I(x) \wedge J(y))$ can be deduced from that of the two simpler statements $[\,S\,]I(x)$ and $[\,T\,]J(y)$; this is due to the fact that S and T are modifying two DISJOINT collections of variables and this is also due to the fact that the property to be established can be decomposed into the conjunction of two predicates working on these very disjoint collections respectively. Note finally that we obviously have the following results

$$
\begin{aligned}
[\,S\,]I &\Rightarrow [\,P \Longrightarrow S\,]I \\
[\,S\,]I \wedge [\,T\,]I &\Rightarrow [\,S \,[]\, T\,]I
\end{aligned}
$$

All this ensures that, whatever the way we combine the operations of our component models, then, when we put them together, the invariant preservation proofs done on each individual model are SUFFICIENT to ensure that the new operations preserve the new combined invariant. We have indeed achieve our goal: namely, that of using a SINGLE MECHANISM to simplify the construction of large models and at the same time to also simplify their consistency proofs. Figure 2 is a pictorial representation of this mechanism.

Note that the operations of the external model can "read" directly the data of the internal ones; however, they cannot modify these data directly: this has to be done indirectly through the operations offered by the internal models (as already explained, in doing so, the invariant preservation proofs performed in each internal model ensure the invariant preservation of the external model). We have here a laxist application of the so-called HIDING PRINCIPLE.

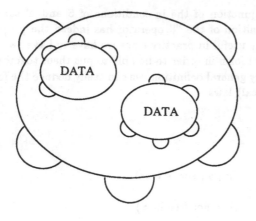

A MODEL BUILT

FROM TWO OTHERS

Figure 2

Note finally that these internal models can themselves have been built using the same approach.

Obviously, these internal models are just ARTEFACTS used to build larger models in a convenient manner. In constructing models in this way, the progressive COMPREHENSION of our future system goes from its heart towards its external boundaries: the system is understood by going AGAINST THE FLOW OF INFORMATIONS entering into it. You have to be aware of the fact that this does not mean that the future CONSTRUCTION of the system will necessarily follow the same structure (see section 3.3.3).

2 SOFTWARE CONSTRUCTION METHODOLOGY: MODULES

We turn now our attention to the other end of the spectrum, namely that of SOFTWARE CONSTRUCTION. In this section, our first intention is to analyse the main concepts at work in the programming of large softwares; then, we shall envisage the various ways these concepts might be put into practice.

The most important concept of programming in the large is, we believe, that of MODULE; this is a concept that receives various names in various programming contexts; for instance, it is sometimes called a "class" (SIMULA), or a "module" (MODULA), or a "package" (ADA), etc. This concept is important because it allows us to organize large softwares as independent pieces having well defined interfaces. This classical feature of programming will be defined here in a simple way by means of the following elements: its VARIABLES, its INITIALISATION and its SERVICES.

A large software system is generally made of several such modules, sometimes disposed next to each other, sometimes nested, more frequently organised in mixed structures. The "user" of a module is not allowed to "read" or "modify" directly its internal data, he can only do so through the offered services and this, provided, of course, the module has already been initialised. This is the, so-called, (full) HIDING PRINCIPLE.

Each service of a module might have two distinct effects, either to modify the internal variables of the module, or to produce one or several results (some services might combine both effects).

After choosing a programming language, you can build the various modules of a software system by DECLARING their variables and by PROGRAMMING their initialisation and services. We study now the corresponding features (i.e decalaration and programming); as you will see, we have only taken into account those mechanisms which, as experience shows, are sufficient in practice: their number is quite small and certainly present in every imperative programming language. In fact, we believe that the choice of a programming language is far less important than what people usually say; it is also our belief that this choice should be based on simplicity and efficiency criteria, rather than on "sophistication", as it is so often the case. One could also use a small part of an existing large programming language.

Declarations, traditionally, define the variables of a program by assigning them a TYPE which can be built after the following basis and constructors

BASIS: integer, real
CONSTRUCTORS: array on an integer interval
                    file

Significantly enough, we have no "record" type constructor and, may be more significantly, we have no "pointer" type constructor!

Following the programming language PASCAL terminology, the services of a module are either PROCEDURES (services with side effects and no result), or FUNCTIONS (services with results and sometimes with side-effects). These elements might be parameterised, and the actual parameters passed BY VALUE. Notice the absence of parameter passing "by name" or "by reference".

The programs corresponding to each procedure or function are written by means of an INSTRUCTION repertoire build from the following basis and constructors

BASIS: empty instruction
                    assignment of a variable of basic type
                    assignment of an array element of basic type
                    writing on a file
                    reading from a file
CONSTRUCTORS: conditional instruction
                    instruction defined by case
                    sequencing
                    loop

Both assignment instructions require the definition of some TYPED EXPRESSIONS elaborated after the following basis and constructors

BASIS:
    integer constant
    real constant
    variable

CONSTRUCTORS:
    array element
    arithmetic expressions
    file size
    type conversion (from real to integer and vice-versa)

Finally, all instruction constructors (but sequencing) require the definition of some BOOLEAN EXPRESSIONS elaborated from the following basis and constructors

BASIS:
    comparison of values of the same basic type

CONSTRUCTORS:
    boolean conjunction
    boolean disjunction
    boolean negation

3 SYNTHESIS OF MODELS AND MODULES

In this section, we intend to show how MODELS and MODULES can be unified. For this, we first analyse their analogies and differences (section 3.1), in order to unify them (section 3.2), and eventually study the systematic passage from one to the other (section 3.3).

3.1 ANALOGIES AND DIFFERENCES

It must be clear that a number of similarities already exist between models and modules: both of them are dealing with "variables"; both of them have an initialisation; moreover, invariants of models and declarations of module are very similar in nature; finally, operations of models and services of modules are also very close.

However, some notions, present in models, have no counterpart in modules; examples of these are: generic parameters, pre-conditions, guards, bounded and unbounded choices. Also, we had at our disposal in models the full generality of first order logic and that of set theory: obviously, such possibilities do not exist in programming languages.

Conversely, two programming concepts have no counterpart in models: namely, sequencing and loop. One might think that conditional instructions and instructions defined by case are also features not present in models; in fact, this is not the case since, as can be shown easily, these features can be formalised in terms of guards and bounded choice (also, clearly, assignements are formalised by simple substitutions).

Concerning the "types", it is clear that they can be formalised in set theory: for instance, the "integer" type can be formalised as a subset of the mathematical integers equipped with a biased arithmetic; likewise the type "real" can certainly be formalised in set theory; the "array on an interval" constructor can be formalised as a total function built on this interval; finally, "files" are simply formalised as finite sequences.

Expressions used in programming can be formalised by corresponding expressions in set theory. And boolean expressions are formalised by means of predicates of propositional logic using the simple logical connectives only (no quantification).

3.2 UNIFYING BOTH CONCEPTS: ABSTRACT MACHINES

Hence, as you can see from previous section, modules are almost models of a special form: "almost" however, since models have no sequencing nor loop. Let us add conceptually these features to models.

Such extended models are called ABSTRACT MACHINES.

Introducing sequencing and loop in models raises some theoretical difficulties in the case of loop. In fact, the "instructions" of our models have no reason to be continuous in general, because of unbounded non-determinism [7]. As a consequence, the classical techniques used to define the predicate transformer of loop do not work any more [6]. However, this predicate transformer for loop can be defined in another way [3,5,8]. The only counter-intuitive result is that some "loops" might "terminate" after a number of iterations which cannot be bounded by any natural number expression depending on the initial values of the variables. This is so, precisely, when the "body" of the loop has an unbounded non-determinism. In the Appendix, we formally define the loop.

3.3 FROM MODELS TO MODULES

In previous section, we have seen how the concepts of models and modules might be unified by that of abstract machine. In what follows, we shall still consider models and modules but in the following narrower sense:

A MODEL   is an abstract machine whose operation specifications
do not contain any sequencing or loop.

A MODULE   is an abstract machine with the following constraints:
first, its invariant implies that each variable belongs
to a set formalising a "type" ; second, its operations
only contain programming "instructions" dealing with
predicates formalising boolean expressions.

In this section, we shall see how we can go from a model to a module; such an activity is called "design" (section 3.3.1); we also study the practicalities of this activity, either by working on the data (section 3.3.2) or by working on the operations (section 3.3.3).

3.3.1 DESIGN

Design is a process realised by means of a finite sequence of steps. Each such step is associated with an abstract machine. You start with a model, and you reach eventually a module after encountering some intermediate abstract machines on the way.

MODEL   ABS. MCH. 1   ABS. MCH. *n*   MODULE

Two abstract machines, which are next to each other in this sequence, are related by a partial order relation called REFINEMENT; this relation generalises to abstract machines the informal definition of "satisfaction" already proposed in section 1.2.1. Two machines which are related by refinement have, of course, SIMILAR OPERATIONS, by this we mean: same name, same kind of (or no) parameters, same kind of (or no) results.

Informally speaking, an abstract machine M is said to be refined to another abstract machine N if every INTERFACE working with its own variables and invoking the operations of machines M or N (it does not matter which one since the "names" of these operations are the same) yields COMPARABLE RESULTS on its local variables, be it applied to the (previously initialised) machine M or to the (previously initialised) machine N. By "comparable results", we mean that those results provided non-deterministically by N are also results provided non-deterministically by M; however, the reverse is not true: M might provide some results that N does not; this is so, because N might be LESS NON-DETERMINISTIC than M.

This very general definition [10] is not very convenient in practice, however.

3.3.2 DATA REFINEMENT

In order to refine a machine we can, among other methods, proceed as follows: first, we do a CHANGE OF VARIABLE specified by means of a condition, called the "abstraction condition" [13], and linking the old and new variables; second, we propose a new machine working on the new variables only; third, we verify, as shown in a few moment, that the new machine refines the old one.

For a long time [13], people thought that this abstraction condition had to be functional and "surjective" from the new to the old variables; in other words, that all possible values of the variables of the old machine should be definable functionally in terms of that of the new machine; this is certainly the case when you do a "change of variable" in mathematics (for instance, in order to compute an integral formally). Recently [9,10,15], it has become clear that this constraint could be dropped, at the risk, of course, to "loose some information" in the new machine; but it does not matter if the information in question is not used in the definition of the operations of the old machine.

More precisely, let M be an abstract machine with the following elements

variable x
invariant $I(x)$
operation S (with pre-condition $P(x)$)

We suppose, of course, that this machine is "consistent" (see section 1.3); in other words, that, under both assumptions $I(x)$ and $P(x)$, each operation S establishes $I(x)$, formally

$$I(x) \wedge P(x) \Rightarrow [\, S\,] I(x)$$

The following elements are then proposed

variable y
change of variable $J(x, y)$
operation T

One should then prove that, under the three assumptions $P(x)$, $I(x)$, and $J(x, y)$, each new operation T establishes that the corresponding old operation S does not establishes the negation of $J(x, y)$ [9,18], formally

$$I(x) \wedge P(x) \wedge J(x, y) \Rightarrow [\, T\,]\neg\, [\, S\,]\neg\, J(x, y)$$

The double negation guarantees that the new operation T is less non-deterministic than the corresponding old one S. If this is so for all couples (S, T) of corresponding operations, then it can be shown [4] that N is an abstract machine refining M according to the informal definition given in section 3.3.1. Now, machine N can in turn be refined in a similar way, and so on.

3.3.3   OPERATION DECOMPOSITION

As experience shows, the refinement technique we have seen in previous section cannot be applied to many levels; this is so because, as the number of levels increases, the complexity of the invariant and that of the operations increases accordingly and, very soon, we face a situation which is difficult to master. We have then to use another technique, that of REFINEMENT BY PARTS, which will be explained informally in the remaining part of this section.

It is possible to show [4], that each instruction of our little repertoire is monotonic with respect to refinement; practically, this means that refining a compound instruction can be done by refining its component instructions. This gives us the clue to break down the dangerously inflating complexity alluded above: at some point, rather than refining directly a complex machine, we refine the elementary "parts" of its operations. Moreover, we group these parts in such a way that they form the operations of one (or several) new, or OFF THE SHELF, machine(s), on which the old machine is said to be IMPLEMENTED. Note that these new internal machines are aprehended only THROUGH THEIR SPECIFICATIONS (models). Here is a pictorial representation of this mechanism

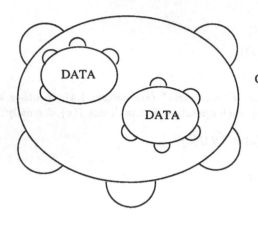

A MACHINE IMPLEMENTED

ON THE MODELS OF TWO OTHERS

Figure 3

As you can see, this picture is the same has the one of Figure 2 (section 1.4). But contrarily to what was done there for the building of large models by PUTTING TOGETHER smaller ones, here, in this mechanism of IMPLEMENTATION, the HIDING PRINCIPLE has to be applied in full; this time, an operation in the external machine cannot directly "read" datas of the internal models; this has to be done through the operations offered by the models: this is so, because we like to be able to later REFINE the inner models. Again, note that this decomposition has no reason to be the same as the one used in the putting together: the progressive COMPREHENSION of a system is distinct from its progressive CONSTRUCTION.

We are left now with a new simpler problem, namely that of refining the internal models; note that we may also use one of their refinements if these are already available. For refining the internal models, we may use the technique of previous section until, again, we reach a dangerously complex situation, in which case we use, again, the approach of this section, and so on.

This technique corresponds to a well known method consisting in organising large software systems in LAYERS. But, as is well known too, this method has a SERIOUS DRAWBACK: systems, programmed in this way, are notoriously slow because of the overhead due to layer crossing; in order to circumvent this difficulty, people usually cheat by breaking the opacity of the layers: in doing so, they simply violate the hiding principle; for example, in order to reach a "deep" operation, one "jumps" over several layers without paying the price of the intermediate operations whose only role might be just to "call" the next layer. This sort of manoeuvre is precisely the kind of dangerous practice which introduce gradually the chaos into an originally well designed system.

Here however, WE DO NOT FACE THIS DIFFICULTY for the layers we deal with are not program layers, they are layers of ABSTRACT MACHINES; in fact, the only operations which are effectively programmed are those operations made of programming instructions and possibly of calls to other operations; and quite often also, operations can be "programmed" as MACRO-INSTRUCTIONS, thus removing entirely the overhead in question.

4 CONCLUSION

In this short synthesis, we have shown that the theory of software construction exists and begins to be applied.

This theory has its own techniques which are quite different from those of the programming theory; in fact, we have not spoken of recursivity or algorithmics; on the other hand, we spoke of proofs.

The design of a software system might be nothing else but the proof of its construction.

ACKNOWLEDGMENTS

This work has been sponsored by British Petroleum. I would like to thank Ib Sorensen (from BP) and the members of his team for numerous and very helpful discussions. Also important were the technical contributions of the Programming Research Group of Oxford University, in particular those of Paul Gardiner. Finally, I like to thank Guy Laffitte and Jean Contensou, from INSEE (Paris).

References

[1] Abrial J.R. 1988 Formal Introduction to Set Notations.

[2] Abrial J.R. 1988 Abstract Machines: Basic Concepts

[3] Abrial J.R. 1988 Abstract Machines: Programming Concepts

[4] Abrial J.R. 1988 Abstract Machines: Refinement

[5] Boom H.J. 1982 A weaker precondition for loops. ACM TOPLAS 4

[6] Dijkstra E.W. 1976 A discipline of programming. (Prentice-Hall)

[7] Dijkstra E.W. 1982 The equivalence of bounded nondeterminacy and continuity. In Selected writings on computing: a personal perspective (Springer-Verlag)

[8] Dijkstra E.W. 1986 A simple fixpoint argument without the restriction to continuity. University of Austin, Texas

[9] Gries D. 1985 A new notion of encapsulation. SIGPLAN Notices July 1985

[10] He J. et al. 1986 Data refinement refined. PRG Oxford University

[11] Hehner E.C.R. 1984 Predicative programming part 1. Comm. ACM 27

[12] Hoare C.A.R. 1985 Programs are predicates. In Mathematical Logic and Programming Languages (Prentice-Hall)

[13] Jones C.B. 1986 Systematic software development using VDM. (Prentice-Hall)

[14] Kowalski R. 1985 The relation between logic programming and logic specification. In Mathematical Logic and Programming Languages (Prentice-Hall)

[15] Morgan C. 1986 The specification statement. PRG Oxford University

[16] Morris J.M. 1986 A theoretical basis for stepwise refinement and the programming calculus. University College, Dublin

[17] Nelson G. 1987 A generalization of Dijkstra's calculus. DEC Systems Research Center Palo Alto, California

[18] Robinson K. 1986 From specifications to programs. PRG Oxford University

[19] Turner D.A. 1985 Functional programs as executable specifications. In Mathematical Logic and Programming Languages (Prentice-Hall)

[20] Wirth N. 1971 Program development by stepwise refinement. Comm. ACM 14

A APPENDIX: Formal definitions of the sequencing and loop constructs

A.1 SEQUENCING

Given two generalised substitutions S and T and a post-condition R, we have the obvious following definition

$$[S; T]R \Leftrightarrow [S][T]R \tag{1}$$

A.2 LOOP

We use the "relational" style and the "programming" style at the same time. Given a generalised substitution S working with the (collection of) variable x, whose values are supposed to be members of a set V, we define the set $WLF(S)$ as follows

$$WLF(S) = \bigcap \{ s \mid s \subseteq V \wedge \{ x \mid [S](x \in s) \} \subseteq s \}$$

We now ASSUME that the expression $\{ x \mid [S](x \in s) \}$ is monotonic in s (we can verify that it is the case for all constructs S introduced so far, but, of course we do not know whether it is the case for the loop, whose very construction is done now, hence the "structural induction" hypothesis); as a consequence, we can then apply TARSKI's theorem telling us that $WLF(S)$ is the least fixpoint of the function associating with each subset s of V the set $\{ x \mid [S](x \in s) \}$; this yields

$$WLF(S) = \{ x \mid [S](x \in WLF(S)) \}$$

After applying the extensionality axiom, we obtain

$$x \in WLF(S) \Leftrightarrow [S](x \in WLF(S))$$

By defining the predicate $wlf(S)$ to be $x \in WLF(S)$, we obtain

$$wlf(S) \Leftrightarrow [S]wlf(S) \tag{2}$$

We now define the construct S^* by means of the following predicate transformer

$$[S^*]R \Leftrightarrow wlf(R \mid S) \tag{3}$$

(this definition is due to Paul Gardiner)

It can then be proved NOW that, under the "structural induction" hypothesis telling us that $\{ s \mid [S](x \in s) \}$ is monotonic in s, then $\{ s \mid [S^*](x \in s) \}$ is also monotonic in s. This results from the fact that $WLF(S)$ is a least fixpoint.

Finally, given a predicate P and a generalised substitution S, we define the construct **while** P **do** S **end** as follows

$$\text{while } P \text{ do } S \text{ end} = (P \Longrightarrow S)^*; (\neg P \Longrightarrow skip) \qquad (4)$$

We will eventually verify that this construct has the following well known loop "unfolding" property

$$
\begin{aligned}
\text{while } P \text{ do } S \text{ end} \quad = \quad &\textbf{if } P \textbf{ then} \\
&\quad S; \text{ while } P \text{ do } S \text{ end} \\
&\textbf{end}
\end{aligned}
$$

where the construct, **if** P **then** S **end**, is defined as follows

$$\text{if } P \text{ then } S \text{ end} = (P \Longrightarrow S \,[] \neg P \Longrightarrow skip) \qquad (5)$$

Here is the formal development

$$
\begin{aligned}
&[\textbf{ while } P \textbf{ do } S \textbf{ end }]R \\
\Leftrightarrow\quad &[(P \Longrightarrow S)^*; (\neg P \Longrightarrow skip)]R & (4) \\
\Leftrightarrow\quad &[(P \Longrightarrow S)^*][\neg P \Longrightarrow skip]R & (1) \\
\Leftrightarrow\quad &[(P \Longrightarrow S)^*](\neg P \Rightarrow R) \\
\Leftrightarrow\quad &wlf(\neg P \Rightarrow R \mid P \Longrightarrow S) & (3) \\
\Leftrightarrow\quad &[\neg P \Rightarrow R \mid P \Longrightarrow S]wlf(\neg P \Rightarrow R \mid P \Longrightarrow S) & (2) \\
\Leftrightarrow\quad &(\neg P \Rightarrow R) \wedge (P \Rightarrow [S][\textbf{ while } P \textbf{ do } S \textbf{ end }]R) \\
\Leftrightarrow\quad &[P \Longrightarrow (S; \textbf{ while } P \textbf{ do } S \textbf{ end }) [] \neg P \Longrightarrow skip]R \\
\Leftrightarrow\quad &[\textbf{ if } P \textbf{ then } S; \textbf{ while } P \textbf{ do } S \textbf{ end end }]R & (5)
\end{aligned}
$$

Since this result is valid whatever the post-condition R, we have eventually our desired goal

$$
\begin{aligned}
\text{while } P \text{ do } S \text{ end} \quad = \quad &\textbf{if } P \textbf{ then} \\
&\quad S; \text{ while } P \text{ do } S \text{ end} \\
&\textbf{end}
\end{aligned}
$$

Mathematics of Program Construction Applied to Analog Neural Networks

K. Mani Chandy
California Institute of Technology

Abstract

The mathematics of program construction has been developed over three decades to design correct digital programs in a systematic fashion. This mathematics has demonstrated its critical importance in the design of deterministic as well as nondeterministic programs, and in the design of both synchronous and self-timed circuits. This short note is to explore the use of this mathematics in the design of continuous systems such as analog neural networks.

A goal of this note is to explore the application of nondeterminism and asynchrony to analog systems.

1 Introduction

We are here to celebrate the 375th anniversary of Groningen University by celebrating the work of its faculty and students, particularly in the area on the mathematics of program construction. We are also here to felicitate the pioneers in this area [1,2,4]. I can think of no better way of participating in this ceremony, than to explore extensions of the methods of these pioneers to a new area.

This talk does not present completed work. My goal, in this talk, is to suggest that the mathematics of program construction may be useful in designing continuous systems (analog circuits) as well as digital computation systems. I will use neural networks [6] as an example of an analog system.

The definition of a neuron that I use is more general than that in the literature on neural networks; the literature focuses attention on neurons that can be constructed from operational amplifiers or light switches, or that exist in biological systems. I want to study continuous systems, and so I have not limited myself to neurons that can be constructed. Also, much of neural network research is devoted to how neural networks learn. This talk is not concerned with the learning behavior of neural networks.

Given a program specification, programmers propose properties that they want their programs to have, prove that all programs that have the proposed properties satisfy the specifications, and use heuristics to derive programs from the proposed properties. In this talk, we shall explore whether this approach can be applied to designing analog neural networks.

Differences between Analog and Digital Computation Some of the differences between analog neural networks and digital computers are outlined next:

1. Variables that appear in digital computer programs are discrete — they take on a bounded number of values determined by the word size. By contrast, it is helpful to consider neural networks in which signals (such as voltages and concentrations of chemicals) are continuous.

2. The execution of a digital computer program consists of a sequence of discrete atomic steps. For example the execution of a statement:
   x := x + 1,
   in a PASCAL program, is an atomic step. By contrast, the output signal of a neuron may change continuously as time progresses.

3. Noisy signals are not a problem in digital computers because the noise is much smaller than the signal levels used to represent the discrete values (i.e., 0 and 1) stored in the machine. By contrast, noise must be considered in designs of analog neural networks.

Does the mathematics of program construction transcend these differences?

The Value of Asynchrony and Nondeterminism Nondeterministic programs have been studied widely. An advantage of a nondeterministic program is that it may allow many possible computions, all of which are (required to be) proved correct. The particular computation that is executed may depend on the environment that the program interacts with. A goal is to design neural networks to be robust: the design of a neural network should produce correct results even if the value of a capacitance (for instance) varies from one implementation of the design to another. The attribute of robustness is particularly important for continuous systems. If we can formulate our designs of continuous systems in terms of nondeterminism, we may be able to capture an element of the robustness of the design. The issue of robustness is particularly important with respect to timing. So I want to explore with you, the possibility of using ideas from the pioneering work on self-timed circuits [7,8] to analog computations.

I shall try to use ideas from UNITY [3] to analog computations, because I am familiar with it, and because Misra's extensions of the UNITY theory to equational reasoning of nondeterministic systems [4] is very promising.

Overview A model of a neural network (or network, for short) is described in Section 2. This model attempts to apply ideas from asynchronous digital systems and self-timed digital circuits to analog neural networks. I am not certain that these ideas can be transferred from the digital to the analog domain, and the remainder of the paper is an exploration of whether this transfer of ideas across domains is useful. An extension of the UNITY logic, for proving the correctness of programs, to neural networks, is proposed in Section 3.

2 A Model of an Asynchronous Neural Network

My goal in this section is to propose an asynchronous nondeterministic model of analog neural networks. This model includes models of networks in the literature. As in the UNITY design method, I hope that we can design efficient analog networks by first designing nondeterministic networks, and by later refining our designs by making them more deterministic. In particular, I want to explore whether the UNITY model of a program as a set of atomic actions can be used in the context of a continuous system. We would like to think of a computation as an unbounded sequence of fair iterations of atomic actions from the set, and to use UNITY logic in reasoning about systems. The problem, of course, is that there is no atomicity, and indeed there is no (discrete) action in analog systems. This proposal is an attempt at overcoming this difficulty.

Definition of a Neuron   A *neuron* is:

1. a set of input signals, and

2. a single output signal that is not a member of the set of input signals, and

3. a continuous function from the set of input signals to the output signal.

(We restrict attention to ranges of signals that are bounded above and below; therefore, we may assume that all input signals to a network are bounded, and we have an obligation to prove that all output signals of neurons are also bounded. Most circuits with unbounded voltages burn out.)

A signal is a real number. A neuron with input-signal vector x, function f, and output signal y is represented by:

$$y \longleftarrow f(x)$$

Examples

Neuron R0: $y \longleftarrow x+1$.

Neuron R1: $x \longleftarrow w * y$.

Neuron R2: $x \longleftarrow w+y$.

A *network* is

1. a set of neurons in which no two neurons have the same output signal, and

2. a predicate on the initial values of signals.

Examples

Network W0: Set of neurons $\{R0\}$, initially $y < x$.

Network W1: Set of neurons $\{R0, R1\}$, initially $y > 0$.

The set of neurons $\{R0, R1, R2\}$ cannot form part of a network because neurons $R1$ and $R2$ have the same output signal x.

Graphical Representation A network is represented graphically by a bipartite graph with two kinds of vertices: neuron vertices (represented by circles) and signal vertices (represented by rectangles). Edges from signal vertices to neuron vertices represent inputs to neurons, and edges from neuron vertices to signal vertices represent outputs from neurons.

Notation This talk employs the following non-graphical representation of networks:

> **NETWORK** network-name
> **INITIALLY** predicate on signals
> **NEURONS** [list of neurons].
> Each neuron in the list is written as neuron-name: signal $\longleftarrow$ expression.

Example The following example defines the network $W1$, consisting of neurons $R0$ and $R1$.

NETWORK $W1$
INITIALLY $y > 0$
NEURONS

[$R0$: $y \longleftarrow x + 1$,
  $R1$: $x \longleftarrow w * y$
]

2.1 The Operation of a Network

The initial values of signals satisfy the predicate specified for the network. For instance, in network $W1$, initially y is positive, and x and w are arbitrary. The value of a neuron's output signal can change at any time according to the following rules: Consider a neuron, $y \longleftarrow f(x)$. The value of y can increase only if its current value is less than $f(x)$. The value of y can decrease only if its current value is greater than f(x). The value of y remains unchanged while its current value is equal to $f(x)$. In other words, if y changes, the rate of change of y has the same sign as $(f(x) - y)$. I assume that in all trajectories of a network, signals are differentiable functions of time. (Continuity is sufficient, but differentiability simplifies exposition a bit.)

Safety Rules for a Neuron $y \longleftarrow f(x)$

$((f(x) - y) > 0) \Rightarrow (dy/dt \geq 0)$.

$((f(x) - y) < 0 \Rightarrow dy/dt \leq 0$.

$(f(x) - y) = 0 \Rightarrow dy/dt = 0$.

A network is nondeterministic because the absolute value of the derivative of a signal with respect to time is not specified. For example, if $f(x)$ exceeds y, we know that dy/dt is nonnegative but we are not given the absolute value of dy/dt. In particular, the value of y can remain unchanged — i.e., $dy/dt = 0$ — even though $f(x)$ exceeds y.

The state of a network is given by the values of its variables. The state of a network with k variables is a point in k-space. We are interested in studying the trajectory of the network state, i.e., we are interested in studying how the network state changes with time. A nondeterministic network has many possible trajectories.

Example We shall derive a few properties of the following simple network.

NETWORK W3
INITIALLY $(x = 0) \land (y = 0)$
NEURONS

R0: $y \longleftarrow x + 1$,
R1: $x \longleftarrow y$

What are the possible trajectories of the network state? In all trajectories, at all times:

invariant $(x + 1) \geq y \geq x \geq 0$

because if $x + 1 = y$, from neuron R0, it follows that y cannot change, and from neuron R1 it follows that x can only increase; an increase in x while y remains unchanged results in $x + 1 > y$, and hence the condition $x + 1 \geq y$ is maintained. Similarly, if $y = x$, from neuron R0 it follows that y can only increase, and from neuron R1 it follows that x does not change; an increase in y while x remains unchanged results in $y > x$, and hence the condition $y \geq x$ is maintained.

(We can prove that, given any point (x, y) that satisfies $x + 1 \geq y \geq x$, there exists a trajectory that passes through that point.)

We conclude that x and y are monotone non-decreasing because: from neuron R1 and $y \geq x$ it follows that $dx/dt \geq 0$, and from neuron R0 and $x + 1 \geq y$ it follows that $dy/dt \geq 0$.

The reason for this little example is to demonstrate how some safety properties of networks can be derived. I want to suggest that ideas such as invariants may be useful in analog computation, though these ideas appear in a somewhat different guise than we are used to in programs.

2.2 Progress Properties

A network in which all neurons remain quiescent for ever is not interesting. Next, I propose progress properties of a neuron. Consider a neuron R: $y \longleftarrow f(x)$. Let X be a set of values of x and define $f(X)$ as follows:

$$f(X) = \{f(x) | x \in X\}.$$

Progress of the Computation of a Neuron   In a network containing neuron R, if x remains in X for ever, then eventually (i.e., within finite time) the value of y is in $f(X)$.

Informally speaking, the progress property is that the behavior of a neuron guarantees that eventually its output will catch up with its input.

Example   Consider the example network $W3$. For this network, x is always nonnegative. Let *noneg* be the set of nonnegative values, i.e.,

$$nonneg = \{x|x \geq 0\}$$

Define function f from the reals to the reals as:

$$f(x) = x + 1.$$

Thus, neuron $R0$ is:

$$y \longleftarrow f(x)$$

Then,

$$f(noneg) = \{y|y \geq 1\}.$$

Since x remains in *noneg* for ever, eventually the value of y becomes a member of $f(noneg)$, i.e., eventually $y \geq 1$.

In network $W3$, if $y \geq 1$ at some time, then $y \geq 1$ thereafter, because y is monotone nondecreasing. Define $gt1$ as

$$gt1 = \{y|y \geq 1\}.$$

Define function f from the reals to the reals as:

$$g(y) = y.$$

Thus neuron $R1$ is:

$$x \longleftarrow g(y)$$

Then,

$$g(gt1) = gt1.$$

We have shown that eventually the value of y is in $gt1$, and the value of y remains in $gt1$ thereafter. Hence eventually, the value of x becomes a member of $g(gt1)$, i.e., eventually, $x \geq 1$.

Using this argument, for all reals k, if $x \geq k$ then eventually $y \geq k+1$, and if $y \geq k+1$ then eventually $x \geq k+1$; hence if $x \geq k$ then eventually $x \geq k+1$.

By induction on natural numbers k, for all k, eventually, $y \geq k$, and $x \geq k$. Thus x and y grow without bound.

The purpose of this little example is to suggest that we can prove progress properties of these networks as well as safety properties. I think that ideas from temporal logic may be useful in analog circuits. The question, that I have not addressed, is that of extending the mathematics of program construction to this class of analog networks.

A neuron in a neural network is analogous to an assignment (an atomic state change) in UNITY. I would like to capture ideas of fairness in UNITY by constraining all neurons to satisfy the progress property. I want to capture the concept of a computation in UNITY (an infinite fair sequence of atomic actions) by a trajectory of the vector of signals of a neural network.

3 Applying the Mathematics of Programs

Let p and q be predicates on the state of the network. For example let:

$$p = (y \geq 2)$$
$$q = (x \geq 1).$$

3.1 Safety Properties

Define a relation *unless* between predicates on network states as follows: p *unless* q holds for a network W if and only if, for all times t, and for all trajectories of the network:

if p holds at time t then:

1. p holds forever after, or

2. there exists a time t' where $t' \geq t$ and q holds at t' and p holds for all times in the interval $[t, t')$.

Thus p *unless* q holds for a network if and only if, once p holds, it continues to hold forever, or p continues to hold until q holds.

Example For network $W3$:

$$(y \leq 2)\,unless\,(x \leq 1).$$

The only safety property used in UNITY is the *unless* relation, and this relation appears adequate for defining safety properties of continuous systems as well. A predicate p on the states of a network is defined to be *stable* as follows: p is stable if and only if once p holds it continues to hold forever after. Therefore p is stable if and only if:

$$p\,unless\,false.$$

An invariant is a stable property that holds initially.

How can we prove that $p\,unless\,q$ holds for a network? As in UNITY, $p\,unless\,q$ holds for a network if and only if it holds for all neurons in the network. In other words, to prove $p\,unless\,q$ for a network, our proof obligation is to consider each neuron R in the network, in turn, and prove $p\,unless\,q$ for a network consisting of the single neuron, R. Thus, universal quantification is used to prove safety properties.

How can we prove $p\,unless\,q$ for a network consisting of a single neuron? In UNITY we show that $p\,unless\,q$ holds for a statement s by demonstrating:

$$\{p \wedge \neg q\}s\{p \vee q\}$$

where $\{\,u\,\}\,s\,\{\,v\,\}$ is the Hoare-triple: i.e., if $\{u\}$ holds prior to the execution of s then the execution terminates and v holds upon termination.

Parenthetical Remark about Hoare Triples What is the analogy to the Hoare triple in analog computation? I propose an analogy below, but I do not find it useful. But I offer it anyhow, in the hope that you, the audience, can do better with the concept than I have. I shall not use Hoare triples later in the talk, and so this paragraph can be skipped.

Consider a neuron, R, defined by $y \longleftarrow f(x)$. We wish to prove $\{u\}R\{v\}$. Let the state of R at some point in a computation be (y_0, x_0). Assume that $y_0 \leq f(x_0)$. While x remains unchanged, y can become any value in the range $[y_0, f(x_0)]$. If u holds at (y_0, x_0), then we want v to hold for all points (y', x_0), where y' is in the interval $[y_0, f(x_0)]$.

Similarly, if $y_0 \geq f(x_0)$, and if u holds at (y_0, x_0), then we want v to hold for all points (y', x_0), where y' is in the interval $[f(x_0), y_0]$.

The Hoare triple in digital computation relates two states: the one before the atomic action and the one following the atomic action. The extension of the Hoare triple to analog computation relates a state S of a neuron, R, to all possible states that can be reached from S while the inputs of R remain unchanged.

Thus a possible definition of $\{u\}R\{v\}$ is:

for all points (y_0, x_0) such that u holds at the point: v holds at (y', x_0) for all y' between y_0 and $f(x_0)$.

A consequence of this definition of a triple $\{u\}R\{v\}$, where R is a neuron, is that $u \Rightarrow v$, because, if u holds then v holds even if R does not change state.

End of parenthetical remark

Proving 'Unless' Properties of a Neuron

Let us return to the problem of defining p *unless* q for a neuron R.

A trajectory of a neuron is its state as it varies with time. (The state is given by the values of the input and output signals.) Let Z be a trajectory of a neuron, and let $Z(t)$ be the state of the neuron at time t in trajectory Z. I propose the following definition for *unless*:

p *unless* q holds for a neuron R if and only if for all trajectories Z of R and all times t, if $p \wedge \neg q$ holds at $Z(t)$ then $p \vee q$ holds at $Z(t+)$, where $t+$ is an arbitrarily small value greater than t.

(Note: Time is unimportant in this definition; only the direction of the trajectory is relevant.)

Assume that $p \wedge \neg q$ is a closed set. (Otherwise, we have to introduce the concepts of *infimum* and *supremum*, and these do not add much insight into the problem.)

Consider a point (y_0, x_0) that satisfies $p \wedge \neg q$, but where point (y_0+, x_0) satisfies $\neg p \wedge \neg q$ where y_0+ is incrementally greater than y_0. We are required to prove that for all such points

$$y_0 \geq f(x_0)$$

where the neuron is defined by $y \longleftarrow f(x)$. The condition states that y cannot increase above y_0 while x remains at x_0, and therefore there is no trajectory that takes the system from a region in which $p \wedge \neg q$ holds to a region in which $\neg p \wedge \neg q$ holds, by increasing y.

Similarly, we are required to prove that there is no trajectory that takes the system from a region in which $p \wedge \neg q$ holds to a region in which $\neg p \wedge \neg q$ holds, by decreasing y.

3.2 Progress Properties

Define a relation $\rightsquigarrow$ (read leads-to), [5], between predicates of a network, as $p \rightsquigarrow q$ holds for a network if and only if for all trajectories Z of the network, if p holds at $Z(t)$ then there exists a t', where $t' \geq t$, such that q holds at $Z(t')$.

The Progress Property of a Neuron A neuron R, defined by $y \longleftarrow f(x)$, has the following property. Any network containing R, that has the safety property:

$$(x \in X) \wedge (y \notin f(X)) \, unless \, (x \in X) \wedge (y \in f(X))$$

where X is a set of values of x, also has the progress property:

$$(x \in X) \rightsquigarrow (y \in f(X)).$$

This property of neuron R is similar to the *ensures* property in UNITY logic. The only properties of neurons that we can use to prove progress properties of networks are the one just given, and that trajectories are continuous.

How can we use the property that trajectories are continuous? Let j be a constant. If a network has the safety property:

$$((x \in X) \wedge (y \leq j)) \, unless \, ((x \in X) \wedge (y > j))$$

and if

$$\forall y \in f(X) : y > j$$

then

$$((x \in X) \wedge (y \leq j)) \rightsquigarrow ((x \in X) \wedge (y > j))$$

A similar rule holds for decreasing y.

Let us attempt to prove $\rightsquigarrow$ properties by using metrics as in proofs of programs. Let M be a function from states of the network to the reals, where for all states S, $M(S) \geq 0$, and $M(S)$ is finite. We prove that for all nonnegative reals k:

$$p \wedge (M = k)unless(q \vee (M < k))$$

This guarantees that while $p \wedge \neg q$ holds, M does not increase. We need to demonstrate that, for each real value k, there exists a neuron that will ensure that if $p \wedge (M = k)$ holds then eventually $q \vee (M < k-\epsilon)$ holds, where ϵ is a positive constant. This guarantees, by induction, that eventually q holds. One way of doing this is to demonstrate, for each k, the existence of a neuron defined by $y \longleftarrow f(x)$, such that for all values of x for which $p \wedge (k \geq M \geq (k - \epsilon))$ holds, the points $(f(x), x)$ satisfy $q \vee (M < k - \epsilon)$.

Examples A conventional sorting network can be implemented as an analog neural network with analog (rather than digital) comparators. Eventually, the output of the sorting network will have the correct values.

One way of developing a class of sorting programs in UNITY is to start with the nondeterministic program: *(repeatedly) flip any out-of-order pair, until none remain.* This program cannot be implemented as an analog circuit because the operation of flipping a pair must be atomic for a correct program. We have not postulated a mechanism for inhibiting the operation of one neuron while another is changing the value of its output signal. (I note in passing, that inhibitory mechanisms exist in biological systems.)

Is it necessary that all analog neural networks be acyclic? No, there are useful networks that contain cycles; the problem with cycles, however, is feedback noise. Consider the all-points shortest path problem. We are given an array W, where $W[i, j]$ is the weight of the edge from vertex i to vertex j. (Assume that the graph is fully connected.) We are required to compute array D, where $D[i, j]$ is the length of the shortest path from vertex i to vertex j. One solution in UNITY is: Initially $D = W$. Repeatedly apply the rules:

$\forall\, i, j, k$ if $D[i, k] + D[k, j] < D[i, j]$
then $D[i, j] := D[i, k] + D[k, j]$
until $\forall\, i, j, k : D[i, k] + D[k, j] \geq D[i, j]$,

Suppose we implement each rule by an analog neuron. Neuron $R[i,j,k]$ has input signals $G[i,j], D[i,k], D[k,j]$, (where $G[i,j]$ is eventually the same as $D[i,j]$) and neuron $R[i,jk]$ has output signal $D[i,j]$; the output signal $D[i,j]$ is fed to another neuron that produces signal $G[i,j]$ — this neuron merely equates $G[i,j]$ to $D[i,j]$. (This artifice is because we do not allow an output signal of a neuron to also be its input signal. Thus, all memory is in feedback loops.) The values $D[i,j]$ and $G[i,j]$ vary continuously (rather than in discrete steps), and therefore an invariant of the network is that $D[i,j]$ is at least the length of the shortest path from i to j. The progress properties of the neurons guarantee that eventually $D[i,j]$ is the shortest path from i to j.

An invariant in the program is that $D[i,j]$ is the length of some path from vertex i to vertex j. This invariant does not hold for the analog computation. Only the weaker invariant that $D[i,j]$ is at least the length of some path from vertex i to vertex j, holds. Fortunately, the weaker invariant suffices.

A difficulty with the analog network is that if there is some noise that reduces the value of $D[i,j]$, this noise remains forever.

Another important example of cyclic analog networks is the Hopfield network. This network has been used to implement associative memory and for solving the traveling salesman problem (approximately). A Hopfield network is described by a set of differential equations, and the trajectory of the network is deterministic. But we can show that time is unimportant for the correctness of the Hopfield network, and a network of nondeterministic analog neurons will yield the correct answer.

A practical problem is that of detecting that a network has reached a steady- state. I think the use of nondeterminism allows us to get away from differential equations and precise time constants. We assume that the network has reached stable state after a 'sufficiently large' time has elapsed. Clearly, time plays an important role in biological information processing, but *precise* timing is not necessary; this suggests that nondeterministic analyses may be useful.

Conclusion   In this talk, I have attempted to show that the mathematics of program construction may be useful in understanding analog computations. This discussion is very exploratory. It is in the nature of a salute to the pioneers of the area of formal methods in programming. Their ideas seem to be so general, and suggest all kinds of interesting pathways to understanding all kinds of computations.

In this brief talk, I have only scratched the surface of what I think is an intriguing area. I am surprised by the number of problems for which analog computations suffice. I am also heartened by the generality of the mathematics of program construction.

Acknowledgement   This work was supported in part by the USA Defense Advanced Research Projects Agency, DARPA Number 6202, monitored by the Office of Naval Research, number N00014-87-K-0745.

I want to thank John Hopfield for interesting discussions about neural networks. The ideas about proofs here are from UNITY for which I want to thank Jayadev Misra.

References

[1] Dijkstra, E.W. *A Discipline of Programming*, Prentice Hall 1976.

[2] Hoare, C.A.R., *Communicating Sequential Processes*, Prentice-Hall 1984.

[3] Chandy, K.M., and J. Misra, *Parallel Program Design: A Foundation*, Addison-Wesley, 1988.

[4] Misra, J., 'Equational Reasoning of Nondeterministic Programs', Technical Report, Univ. Texas Austin, March 1989.

[5] Lamport, L., "Proving the Correctness of Multiprocess Programs", IEEE-TSE,3-2,March 1977.

[6] Hopfield, J., and D.W.Tank , 'Neural Computation of Decisions in Optimization Problems', Biological Cybernetics, 52, 141-152 (1985).

[7] Martin, A.J., 'Compiling Communicating Processes into Delay-Insensitive VLSI Circuits, Journal of Distributed Computing, 1:3, 1986.

[8] Seitz, C. 'System Timing', in *Introduction to VLSI Systems*, eds. C.Mead and L. Conway, Addison-Wesley 1980.

Termination is Timing

Eric C.R. Hehner

Department of Computer Science, University of Toronto, Toronto M5S 1A4 Canada

Summary   Termination is treated as a special case of timing, with the result that the logic of programming is simplified and generalized.

Introduction

Our formalism for the description of computation is divided into two parts: logic and timing. The logic is concerned with the question: what results do we get? The timing is concerned with the question: when do we get them? One possible answer to the latter question is: never, or as we may say, at time infinity. Thus we place termination within the timing part of our formalism. Nontermination is just the extreme case of taking a long time.

Specification

For now we ignore timing (and therefore also termination). We consider a specification of computer behavior to be a predicate in the initial values x, y, ... and final values x', y', ... of some variables. From any initial state $s = [x, y, ...]$, a computation satisfies a specification by delivering a final state $s' = [x', y', ...]$ that satisfies the predicate. A specification P is called *implementable* iff for every initial state s there is a satisfactory final state s' :

$$\forall s\ \exists s'\ P$$

For our specification language we will not be definitive or restrictive; we allow any well-defined predicate notations. To them we add the following four.

ok	=	$s'=s$
	=	$x'=x \wedge y'=y \wedge ...$
x:= e	=	ok(subst e for x)
	=	$x'=e \wedge y'=y \wedge ...$
if b then P else Q	=	$b \wedge P \vee \neg b \wedge Q$
	=	$(b \Rightarrow P) \wedge (\neg b \Rightarrow Q)$
P; Q	=	$\exists s''\ P(\text{subst } s'' \text{ for } s') \wedge Q(\text{subst } s'' \text{ for } s)$

The notation   ok   is the identity relation between pre- and poststate;   it specifies that the final values of all variables equal the corresponding initial values (it is sometimes called   skip).   In the assignment notation,   x   is any variable and   e   is any expression (we are ignoring questions of type and initialization).   The   **if**   notation requires a boolean expression   b   and two specifications   P   and   Q , and forms a new specification.   Finally, the sequential composition   P;Q   is just the   relational   composition   of specifications   P   and   Q.

Refinement

Specification   P   is *refined*   by specification   Q   iff all computer behavior satisfying   Q   also satisfies   P .   We denote this by   P:: Q   and define it formally as

P:: Q   ≡   ∀s ∀s' P⇐Q

Thus refinement simply means finding another specification that is everywhere equivalent or stronger.

> *Aside.* The *precondition* for   P   to be refined by   Q   is   ∀s' P⇐Q .   The *postcondition* for   P   to be refined by   Q   is   ∀s P⇐Q .   With these definitions we can relate our formalism to those formalisms based on pre- and postconditions.   But we do not pursue that here. *End of aside.*

Refinement is a partial ordering of specifications.   A function from specifications to specifications is called *monotonic*   if it respects the refinement ordering.   Thus, trivially, we have the

> Stepwise Refinement Theorem (refinement by steps):   If   f   is a monotonic function on specifications, and   P:: Q , then   fP:: fQ .

Another simple and very useful theorem is the

> Partwise Refinement Theorem (refinement by parts):   If   f   is a monotonic function on specifications, and   P:: fP   and   Q:: fQ , then (P∧Q):: f(P∧Q) .

Programs

A program is a specification of computer behavior; it is therefore a predicate in the initial and final state.   Not every specification is a program.   A program is an "implemented" specification, one that a computer can execute. To be so, it must be written in a restricted notation.   Let us take the following as our programming notations.

(a)   ok is a program.

(b)   If x is any variable and e is an "implemented" expression then x:= e is a program.

(c)   If b is an "implemented" boolean expression and P and Q are programs, then **if** b **then** P **else** Q is a program.

(d)   If P and Q are programs then P;Q is a program.

(e)   If P is an implementable specification and Q is a program such that P:: Q then P is a program.

In (b) and (c) we have not stated which expressions are "implemented"; that set will vary from one implementation to another. Likewise the programming notations (a) to (d) are not to be considered definitive, but only an example. Part (e) states that any implementable specification P is a program if a program Q is provided such that P:: Q . To execute P , just execute Q . The refinement acts as a procedure declaration; P acts as the procedure name, and Q as the procedure body; use of the name P acts as a call. Recursion is allowed; in part (e) we may use P as a program in order to obtain program Q.

Here is an example. Let x be an integer variable. The specification x'=0 says that the final value of variable x is zero. It becomes a program by refining it, which can be done in many ways. Here is one.

$$x'=0:: \textbf{if } x=0 \textbf{ then } ok \textbf{ else } (x:= x-1; \ x'=0)$$

In standard predicate notations, this refinement is

$$\forall x \ \forall x' \ \ x'=0 \ \Leftarrow \ x=0 \land x'=x \ \lor \ x{\neq}0 \land \exists x'' \ x''=x-1 \land x'=0$$

which is easily proven. (Helpful fact: x:= e; P = P(subst e for x).)

Timing

We have already seen the semantic formalism: it is similar to [2] but simplified by the omission of any consideration of termination. We now upgrade it from "partial correctness" to "total correctness" by adding a time variable. We do not change the formalism at all; the time variable is treated just like any other variable, as part of the state. Its interpretation as time is justified by the way we use it.

Let t be the initial time, i.e. the time at the start of execution; let t' be the final time, i.e. the time at the end of execution. To allow for nontermination we take the type of time to be a number system extended with ∞ . The number system we extend can be the naturals, or the integers, or the rationals, or the reals. The number ∞ is maximum

$$\forall t \ \ t{\leq}\infty$$

and it absorbs any addition

$$\infty + 1 = \infty$$

If t is time, it cannot decrease, therefore a specification P with time is implementable iff

$\forall s \; \exists s' \; P \wedge t' \geq t$

Time increases as a program is executed. There are many ways to measure time. We present just two: real time, and recursive time.

Real Time

Real time has the advantage of measuring the real execution time, and is useful in real-time programming. It has the disadvantage of requiring intimate knowledge of the implementation (machine and compiler).

To obtain the real execution time of a program, modify it as follows.
- Replace each assignment x:= e by

  t:= t+u; x:= e

  where u is the time required to evaluate and store e .
- Replace each conditional **if b then P else Q** by

  t:= t+v; **if b then P else Q**

  where v is the time required to evaluate b and branch.
- Replace each call P by

  t:= t+w; P

  where w is the time required for the call and return. For a call that is implemented "in-line", this time will be zero. For a "tail-recursion", it may be just the time for a branch. In general, it will be the time required to push a return address onto a stack and branch, plus the time to pop the return address and branch back.
- Each refined specification can include time. For example, let f be a function of the initial state s . Then

  t' = t + fs

  specifies that fs is the execution time,

  t' ≤ t + fs

  specifies that fs is an upper bound on the execution time, and

  t' ≥ t + fs

  specifies that fs is a lower bound on the execution time.

In our earlier example, suppose that the conditional, the assignment, and the call each take time 1. The refinement becomes

P:: t:= t+1; **if** x=0 **then** ok **else** (t:= t+1; x:= x-1; t:= t+1; P)

which is a theorem when

P = x'=0 ∧ (x≥0 ⇒ t'=t+3x+1) ∧ (x<0 ⇒ t'=∞)

Execution of this program always sets x to zero; when x starts with a nonnegative value, it takes time 3x+1 to do so; when x starts with a negative value, it takes infinite time. We shall see how to prove a similar example in a moment.

Recursive Time

To free ourselves from having to know implementation details, we allow any arbitrary scheme for inserting time increments $t := t+u$ into programs. Each scheme defines a new measure of time. In the recursive time measure,
- Each recursive call costs time 1.
- All else is free.

This measure neglects the time for "straight-line" and "branching" programs, charging only for loops.

In the recursive measure, our earlier example becomes

     P:: **if** x=0 **then** ok **else** (x:= x-1; t:= t+1; P)

which is a theorem when

     $P = x'=0 \land (x \geq 0 \Rightarrow t'=t+x) \land (x<0 \Rightarrow t'=\infty)$

As a second example, consider the refinement

     Q:: **if** x=1 **then** ok
            else if even x **then** (x:= x/2; t:= t+1; Q)
            else (x:= (x-1)/2; t:= t+1; Q)

where

     $Q = x'=1 \land (x \geq 1 \Rightarrow t' \leq t + lb\ x) \land (x<1 \Rightarrow t'=\infty)$

Execution of this program always sets x to one; when x starts with a positive value, it takes logarithmic time (lb = binary logarithm); when x starts nonpositive, it takes infinite time. The proof breaks into nine pieces: thanks to the theorem of refinement by parts, it is sufficient to verify the three conjuncts of Q separately; and for each there are three cases in the refinement. In detail, $\forall x \ \forall x' \ \forall t \ \forall t'$

     $x=1 \land x'=x \land t'=t \Rightarrow x'=1$
     $x \neq 1 \land$ even $x \land x'=1 \Rightarrow x'=1$
     $x \neq 1 \land$ odd $x \land x'=1 \Rightarrow x'=1$

     $x=1 \land x'=x \land t'=t \Rightarrow (x \geq 1 \Rightarrow t' \leq t + lb\ x)$
     $x \neq 1 \land$ even $x \land (x/2 \geq 1 \Rightarrow t' \leq t+1+lb(x/2)) \Rightarrow (x \geq 1 \Rightarrow t' \leq t + lb\ x)$
     $x \neq 1 \land$ odd $x \land ((x-1)/2 \geq 1 \Rightarrow t' \leq t+1+lb((x-1)/2)) \Rightarrow (x \geq 1 \Rightarrow t' \leq t + lb\ x)$

     $x=1 \land x'=x \land t'=t \Rightarrow (x<1 \Rightarrow t'=\infty)$
     $x \neq 1 \land$ even $x \land (x/2 < 1 \Rightarrow t'=\infty) \Rightarrow (x<1 \Rightarrow t'=\infty)$
     $x \neq 1 \land$ odd $x \land ((x-1)/2 < 1 \Rightarrow t'=\infty) \Rightarrow (x<1 \Rightarrow t'=\infty)$

Each is an easy exercise, which we leave to the reader. Note that the use of recursion does not require the proof to be an induction.

Variant

A standard way to prove termination is to find a variant (or bound function) for each loop. A variant is an expression over a well-founded set whose value decreases with each iteration. When the well-founded set is the natural numbers (a common choice), a variant is exactly a time bound according to the recursive time measure. We shall see in the section titled "A Void Obligation" why it is essential to recognize that a variant is a time bound, and to conclude that a computation terminates within some bound, rather than to conclude merely that it terminates.

Another common choice of well-founded set is based on lexicographic ordering. For any given program, the lexicographic ordering used to prove termination can be translated into a numeric ordering, and be seen as a time bound. To illustrate, suppose, for some program, that the pair [n, m] of naturals is decreased as follows: [n, m+1] decreases to [n, m] , and [n+1, 0] decreases to [n, fn] . Then we consider [n, m] as expressing a natural number, defined as follows.

$$[0, 0] = 0$$
$$[n, m+1] = [n, m] + 1$$
$$[n+1, 0] = [n, fn] + 1$$

Well-founded sets are unnecessary in our formalism; time can be an extended integer, rational, or real. Consider the following infinite loop.

$$R:: \ x:= x+1; \ R$$

We can, if we wish, use a measure of time in which each iteration costs half the time of the previous iteration.

$$R:: \ x:= x+1; \ t:= t+2^{-x}; \ R$$

is a theorem when $R = t'=t+2^{-x}$. The theory correctly tells us that the infinite iteration takes finite time. We are not advocating this time measure; we are simply showing the generality of the theory.

A Void Obligation

A customer arrives with the specification

(a) $x'=2$

He evidently wants a computation in which variable x has final value 2. I provide it in the usual way: I refine his specification by a program and execute it. The refinement I choose is

$$x'=2:: \ x'=2$$

and execution begins. The customer waits for his result, and after a time becomes impatient. I tell him to wait longer. After more time has passed, the customer sees the weakness in his specification and decides to strengthen it. He wants a computation that takes finite time, and specifies it thus:

(b) $x'=2 \land t'<\infty$

He says he does not care how long it takes, except that it must not take forever.   (We must reject (b) as unimplementable since   (b) $\land$ $t'\geq t$ is unsatisfiable for $t=\infty$, but for the sake of argument let us proceed.)   I can refine (b) with exactly the same construction as before! Including recursive time, my refinement is

$x'=2 \land t'<\infty::$ $t:= t+1;$ $x'=2 \land t'<\infty$

Execution begins. When the customer becomes restless I again tell him to wait longer. After a while he decides to change his specification again:

(c) $x'=2 \land t'=t$

He not only wants his result in finite time, he wants it instantly.   Now I must abandon my recursive construction, and I refine

$x'=2 \land t'=t::$ $x:= 2$

Execution provides the customer with the desired result at the desired time.

Under specification (a) the customer is entitled to complain about a computation if and only if it terminates in a state in which $x'\neq 2$. Under specification (b) he can complain about a computation if it delivers a final state in which $x'\neq 2$ or it takes forever. But of course there is never a time when he can complain that a computation has taken forever, so the circumstances in which he can complain that specification (b) has not been met are exactly the same as for specification (a).   It is therefore entirely appropriate that our theory allows the same refinement constructions for (b) as for (a).   Specification (c) gives a time bound, therefore more circumstances in which to complain, therefore fewer refinements.

I have argued elsewhere [3] that termination by itself is meaningless. Dijkstra has termed it a "void obligation" [1].   One might suggest that a time bound of a million years is also a void obligation, but the distinction is one of principle, not practicality.   A time bound is a line that divides shorter computations from longer ones.   There is no line dividing finite computations from infinite ones.

In the predicate transformer theory, the formula   wp(S, true)   is widely quoted as being the precondition for termination of (computations described by) program S . It is not. It is the precondition for the existence of a time bound [0]. To illustrate, consider S to be

    do x>0 → x:= x-1

      [] x<0 → "x≥0"

    od

where "x≥0" specifies that x takes a natural value.   Even if we allow

    wp("x≥0", true) = true

we find

wp(S, true) = 0≤x

In the theory presented in this paper, using the recursive time measure, we have

    S:: **if** x=0 **then** ok
        else if x>0 **then** (x:= x-1; t:= t+1; S)
        else (x'≥0 ∧ t'=t; t:= t+1; S)

when

    S = x'=0 ∧ (x≥0 ⇒ t'=t+x) ∧ (x<0 ⇒ t'>t)

When x<0 the most we can say about execution time is that it is positive.

Recursive Constructions

We have not introduced a loop programming notation; instead we have used recursive refinement. When convenient, we can refine "in-place". For example,

    x:= 5;
    (y'>x:: y:= x+1);
    z:= y

The middle line means what its left side says, hence the three lines together are equal to

    y' = z' > 5

Although we can see how y'>x is refined, we are not allowed to use that information and conclude z'=6 .

In-place refinement can, of course, be recursive, and thus serve as a loop. For example,

    x≥0 ⇒ y'=x! ∧ t'=t+x::
        y:= 1;
        (x≥0 ⇒ y'=y×x! ∧ t'=t+x::
            if x=0 **then** ok
            else (y:= y×x; x:= x-1; t:= t+1;
                    x≥0 ⇒ y'=y×x! ∧ t'=t+x))

A popular way to define the formal semantics of a loop construct is as a least fixed-point. An appropriate syntax would be

    identifier = program

where the identifier can be used within the program as a recursive call. (A fixed-point is a solution to such an equation, considering the identifier as the unknown. The least fixed-point is the weakest solution.) There are two difficulties.

We defined sequential composition as a connective between arbitrary specifications, not just programs. This is essential for programming in steps: we must be able to verify that P:: Q;R without referring to the refinements of Q and R . Similarly **if** applies to arbitrary specifications. For the same reason, we must define a loop construct, if we choose to have one, for all specifications:

    identifier = specification

Unfortunately, such equations do not always have solutions. Fortunately, we are not really interested in equality, but only in refinement. So we propose the syntax

    identifier:: specification

A solution to a refinement as called a pre-fixed-point. Since true is always a solution to a refinement, a pre-fixed-point always exists. But obviously we cannot be satisfied with the least pre-fixed-point as the semantics. The greatest (strongest) pre-fixed-point cannot be used either because it is often unimplementable, even when the specification is a program. How about the greatest implementable pre-fixed-point? Unfortunately, greatest implementable pre-fixed-points are not unique, even when the specification is a program.

The second difficulty is that a least fixed-point, or greatest implementable pre-fixed-point, is not always constructible. (With a constructive bias, I would complain that it does does not always exist.) Even when it is constructible, the construction process is problematic. One forms a (Kleene) sequence of predicates, then one takes the limit of the sequence as the solution. (The sequence starts with P_0 = true (without timing) or P_0 = t'≥t (with timing). Then P_{k+1} is formed by substituting P_k into the loop body in place of the unknown identifier.) Finding the "general member" requires an educated guess (induction hypothesis) and induction. The limit may not be expressible in the specification language. Due to discontinuity, the limit may not be a solution to the original problem. (It has been suggested [0] that the construction process should pass over any discontinuity, using the limit from one phase as the starting point for the next.)

In our approach, we ask a programmer to specify what he intends his loop to accomplish, and then to provide a refinement. We neatly avoid the Kleene sequence, the induction, the limit, and the continuity problem. Of course, these problems do not disappear, but we prefer to avoid them when possible.

Communication Timing

To our repertoire of programming notations we now add input c?x , output c!e , and parallel composition P||Q . Just as assignment is a predicate, so are input and output. Just as sequential composition is a predicate connective, so is parallel composition. We do not present the logic of concurrency and communication in this paper, but content ourselves with their timing. We move all consideration of deadlock and livelock from the logic to the timing, and that makes as great a simplification as did the movement of loop termination from the logic to the timing.

Parallel processes require separate timing variables. The time for the parallel composition is the maximum of the individual process times. Thus
       t0:= t;   t1:= t;
       (P0 (using t0)
       || P1 (using t1));
       t:= max t0 t1
is the general scheme.

Here is an example of two communicating processes.
       P; c!0; d?y; R || c?x; Q; d!1
The first process begins with a computation described by P , and then outputs a 0 on channel c . The second process begins with an input on channel c . Even if we decide that communication is free, we must still account for the time spent waiting for input. We therefore modify the program by placing a time increment before each input. For example, if
       t0'=t0+p:: P
       t1'=t1+q:: Q
then we modify the program as follows:
       P; c!0; t0:=t0+q; d?y; R || t1:=t1+p; c?x; Q; d!1
In general, the time increments in each process depend on the computation in the others.

It is sometimes reasonable to neglect the time required for a communication, as in the previous example. But it is not reasonable to neglect communication time when there are communication loops. Here is a simple deadlock to illustrate the point.
       c?x; d!2 || d?y; c!3
The logic (which we did not present) tells us that this program refines x'=3 ∧ y'=2 , but now we investigate "when". Inserting a wait before each input yields
       t0:= t0+u; c?x; d!2 || t1:= t1+v; d?y; c!3
On the left, input is awaited for time u ; then input is received and output is sent. We assign no time to the acts of input and output, so the output is sent at time t0+u . But we charge one time unit for transit, hence the output is available as input on the right after waiting time v = u+1 . By symmetry, we can also say u = v+1 . This pair of equations has a unique solution: u=∞, v=∞. The theory tells us that the wait is infinite.

If we had not charged for communication transit time, we would be solving u=v , and we would have to conclude that the communication could happen at any time. Assume that, after waiting time 100, an input is received on the left. Then the output can be sent at that same time (since we charge zero for the acts of input and output), and received on the right at that same time. And then the right side can send its output to the left at that same time, which justifies our original assumption. Of course, u=∞, v=∞ is also a solution. This "spontaneous" communication is unphysical, so communication loops, like refinement loops, should always include a charge for time.

Livelock is an infinite communication loop on a local (hidden) channel. Without a time variable, our logic treats livelock as though it were ok . With a time variable we find that livelock leaves all other variables unchanged (like ok) but takes infinite time (like deadlock). The infinite time results from the infinite loop (recursive measure), even if communication is free.

Time Dependence

Our examples have used the time variable as a ghost, or auxiliary variable, never affecting the course of a computation. But it can be used to affect the computation. Both
    x:= t
and
    if t < 1989:06:26:09:30:000 **then** ... **else** ...
are allowed, with no harm to the theory. We can look at the clock, but not reset it arbitrarily; all clock changes must correspond to the passage of time.

We may occasionally want to specify the passage of time. For example, we may want the computation to "wait until time w". Formally, this is
    t:= max t w
This specification is easily refined
    t:= max t w::
        if t≥w **then** ok **else** (t:= t+1; t:= max t w)
and we obtain a busy-wait loop. (For simplicity we have considered time to be integer-valued, and used the recursive time measure. For practicality perhaps we should use real-values and the real-time measure. The change is an easy exercise.)

Conclusion

We have a simple form of specification: a predicate in the initial and final values of some variables. And we have a simple notion of refinement: universally quantified implication. Without a time variable (or other termination indicator [3]), our logic would be more complicated. For example, sequential composition would be

P;Q   =   **if** P requires termination
            then relational composition of P and Q
            else P

in order to ensure "strictness" (we cannot have an infinite computation first, and then something more). But with a time variable, P;Q is just relational composition, and strictness is just the fact that $\infty + t = \infty$. Without time, input would be

c?x   =   **if** there is or will be a communication on channel c
            then assign it to x and advance the cursor
            else loop forever

With time, input is just an assignment and cursor advance, perhaps at time ∞.

The mathematics we need is just simple logic and arithmetic, with no special ordering or induction rules. In effect, our computational inductions are buried in the ordinary arithmetic on the time variable. We find it simpler to treat termination as a part of timing, and we find that timing is more easily understood and more useful than termination alone.

Acknowledgements

Je veux remercier mes amis à Grenoble, Nicolas Halbwachs, Daniel Pilaud, et John Plaice, qui m'ont enseigné que la récursion peut être contrôlée par le tic-tac d'une horloge. J'apprends lentement, mais j'apprends. I also thank IFIP Working Group 2.3, Theo Norvell, and Andrew Malton for criticism. Support is provided by a grant from the Natural Sciences and Engineering Research Council of Canada.

References

[0]   H.J. Boom: "A Weaker Precondition for Loops", ACM TOPLAS v.4 n.4 p.668-677 (1982)

[1]   E.W. Dijkstra: "Position Paper on Fairness", EWD1013 (October 1987)

[2]   E.C.R. Hehner, L.E. Gupta, A.J. Malton: "Predicative Methodology", Acta Informatica v.23 p.487-505 (1986)

[3]   E.C.R. Hehner, A.J. Malton: "Termination Conventions and Comparative Semantics", Acta Informatica, v.25, n.1, p.1-14 (1988)

Towards totally verified systems

David May and David Shepherd

INMOS Ltd., Bristol, U.K.

Abstract

With the increasing complexity and criticality of computer based systems it is important to verify the overall behaviour of the entire system. Much of the theoretical background needed for such a task is already available and could be used to implement totally verified systems. This paper sets out to show how a simple application could be verified. An application is implemented in a simple language and verified to be correct. This program is then compiled for a simple instruction set by a verified compiler. This instruction set is then implemented on a simple verified processor.

1 Introduction

Micro-processors are being used to perform increasing complex tasks as they become more powerful so that the ability to ensure correct design by traditional design techniques, centered around experimental testing, will become problematic. The use of formal design methods seems to offer a way out of this situation by providing a design methodology which prevents the introduction of errors into designs through the rigorous use of proof techniques to validate designs against specifications. Future systems will increasingly consist of processors running embedded programs along with specialised interface hardware. Due to this, it is important to address the problem of verifying mixed hardware and software systems.

A totally verified system will consist of a language, a program verifier for that language, a verified processor design and a verified compiler to compile the language into the processor instruction set. Previous research in the area of verification has only addressed certain areas of the system leaving other areas un-verified and thus compromising the security of the whole.

During the 1960s and 1970s considerable progress was made in modelling and reasoning about computer programs. A number of influential program verification systems were developed, including the Boyer-Moore theorem prover, Gypsy, AFFIRM, SDVS, LCF, m-EVES and NuPRL. Although some impressive proofs were done, the state-of-the-art in mechanized program verification is still limited to small programs (i.e. a few tens of pages of code). An example of the commercially significant application of formal methods to software is the development of the microcode for the IMS T800 transputer floating point unit. This example demonstrated that the use of formal verification is commercially advantageous.

During the late 1970s and 1980s new theories and formalisms to support software engineering emerged. These include CCS and CSP for concurrent programs, and VDM and Z for system specification. So far no theorem proving tools for these formalisms have been implemented, but some useful computer-based tools related to them have been developed (eg the 'B tool' for Z and the occam transformation system). However, these do not support the construction of machine checked proofs in an explicit logical calculus.

During the last ten years, methods for hardware verification by mechanized formal proof have developed rapidly. In some ways, this work has been more successful than software verification. There are two reasons for this: (i) the formal theories needed to model hardware are simpler than those needed for software, and (ii) hardware designs are often sufficiently small that their verification falls within the power of existing theorem proving tools. For example, the verification of a hardware multiplier could be commercially important, but the verification of a multiplication program is likely to be regarded as a toy problem by most software engineers. Various significant hardware verifications have been produced including the verification of the FM8501 microprocessor by Warren Hunt using the Boyer-Moore theorem prover [7] and the verification of aspects of the Viper microprocessor by Avra Cohn using the HOL system [3].

Over the next ten years it will be necessary to combine hardware and software verification techniques. Typical systems will consist of one or more processors running embedded programs interfaced to special purpose hardware all on a single device. Commercial considerations dictate that future designs must be competed quickly without error. As the complexity of devices increase there will be a need for more machine assistance in this process. For large designs, it will be essential to be able to check the design automatically in the same way that electronic design rule checking is currently performed automatically. For this reason, it is important to integrate verification tools with the existing CAD systems.

2   The simple language

The language we will consider in this paper will be extremely simple. Unnecessary complexity will be removed by considering only the core control structures of a language. All data will have the the same "type" although this will be interpreted according to context as integers, booleans etc.

The language will be based on a non-prioritised version of occam-1, and for even greater simplicity, concurrency will not initially be considered.

2.1 Syntax

The basic statements in the language are assignments and communications.

Skip	SKIP
Stop	STOP
Assignment	$Var := Exp$
Input	$Chan\ ?\ Var$
Output	$Chan\ !\ Exp$
Procedure call	$Name\ (\ Exp_0,\ ...\ ,\ Exp_n\ )$

Expressions are made up of the usual operations on variables and constants. All variables and constants will be fixed width bit strings which will be interpreted in the usual ways as booleans, numbers, integers etc. Modulo arithmetic and boolean operations are defined on these bit strings. For simplicity, there will be no concept of overflow errors — divide by zero will be defined to return an indeterminate result.

Programs are constructed from these basic processes by a small number of constructors. These are

Sequential composition	SEQ $(P_0,\ ...\ ,\ P_n)$
Conditional branching	IF $((b_0,P_0),\ ...\ ,\ (b_n,P_n))$
Iteration	WHILE (b,P)
Parallel composition	PAR $(P_0,\ ...\ ,\ P_n)$
Alternation	ALT $((g_0,P_0),\ ...\ ,\ (g_n,P_n))$

These are presented here in horizontal form for conciseness, and in a form that is ammenable to use by a theorem prover. In normal use the more traditional vertical format of occam programs would be used.

Declarations are used to define the scope of variables and channels and to introduce procedures.

Variable declaration	VAR $Var_0,\ ...\ ,\ Var_n$:
Channel declaration	CHAN $Chan_0,\ ...\ ,\ Chan_n$:
Procedure declaration	PROC($Param_0,\ ...\ ,\ Param_n$) P :

2.2 Semantics

To be able to verify the execution of programs in the language in the final system it is necessary to define the semantics of the language.

For the sequential part of the language this is fairly easy to define using traditional techniques. One point worth noting is that the semantics of procedure calls will be by the substitution of the procedure body at the call with suitable variable renamings.

The semantics of the concurrent part of the language poses more of a problem. A denotational semantics for occam has been produced [10]. Perhaps of more relevance is an operational semantics of an occam-like language viewed from a transputer-like implementation point of view [1]. This has shown how occam-like concurrency and communication can be formalised and this could provide a basis for correct implementation of the underlying constructs.

For simplicity, initially, we will not consider concurrency. The program will be a purely sequential process that interacts with it environment via an input and an output channel — rather like a UNIX filter. However, this "vestigal" communication will have semantics and implementations necessary to support the full communication so that the simplified implementation is a subset of the full implementation.

2.3 Program verification

As always the implemented system is only as strong as its weakest link. In particular having a "correct" implementation of a program is not much use if that program does not do what it is intended to do. For this reason it is necessary to verify the program against a higher level of specification. The intention here is to be able verify the program against an formal object whose correctness can be "tested".

Because we will have defined formal semantics for the language it will be possible to formally reason about programs in this language. Work has already been done in this area to produce a program verification system for a simple language [5]. The language subset outlined above is not much more complex than the simple language considered in that system so the possibility of mechanised verification has already been demonstrated.

3 The simple instruction set

The target instruction set will be based around the core instructions of the transputer. These will provide support for variable access, expression evaluation and procedure calling to enable the sequential parts of the language to be supported.

The users view of the machine will consist of an evaluation stack of 3 registers, an instruction pointer, a workspace pointer and the memory. The instruction set consists of instructions to move data between addresses in the workspace (the area of memory pointed to by the workspace pointer) and the evaluation stack, loading of constants and operations which combine the top elements of the evaluation stack. Program sequencing is supported by a jump instruction and a single conditional jump instruction.

Communication and concurrency will be handled in a similar manner to the current transputer with some simplification. Firstly, there is no notion of priority so that there will only be one scheduling queue and the need for high priority processes to interrupt low priority processes will be removed. Secondly the scheduling system can be simplified further by removing timeslicing. Timeslicing will be replaced by use of an explicit deschedule instruction. This will aid the treatment of concurrent programs as it will remove the need to argue about time which is inherent the definition of timeslicing as well as enabling explicit control over process scheduling in critical regions of programs.

The instruction set will be specified in terms of the programmers view of the machine state (i.e. registers, scheduling lists, etc), and the effect that the various instructions have on this state. In this way, given a machine state, it will be possible to reason about the future behaviour of the machine with respect to any external communication that it is able to perform.

4   Compiling programs

We now have defined the semantics of a simple language and of a simple instruction set. We are now in a position to construct a compiler to produce a machine code program equivalent to a given program.

To construct the compiler we need to know what we mean by this equivalence. The compiler is a function that takes a program and produces a machine state such that the behaviour of both are observationally equivalent. I.e. a function C such that:

$$\forall Prog \bullet \mathcal{B}_{prog}(Prog) = \mathcal{B}_{mach}(C(Prog))$$

where $\mathcal{B}_{prog}(Prog)$ is the behaviour of program $Prog$ and $\mathcal{B}_{mach}(M)$ is the behaviour of machine M. These behaviours are relations between initial states and resultant final states of observable variables.

Only silicon compilers produce machines as their output! A compiler for a general purpose machine produces executable code which causes the machine to be in the correct state when booted with that code. We will be compiling code for a target machine $\mathcal{M}$ which has a booting mechanism $\mathcal{BOOT}$ which takes a machine and a piece of executable code and returns the machine state that results from booting the machine with that code. For a transputer $\mathcal{BOOT}$ is implemented by sending a certain sequence of bytes down an input channel, however at this point we are not concerned with the actual mechanism of booting.

Given that we have the ability to boot a machine with code the compiler now only needs to produce this code. This code compiler C_{code} needs to be such that:

$$\forall Prog \bullet \mathcal{B}_{prog}(Prog) = \mathcal{B}_{mach}(\mathcal{BOOT}\ (\mathcal{M}, C_{code}(Prog)))$$

However, given the fact that we know the definition of the machine and the booting mechanism we can take one step back from the machine and reason about the behaviour of the code. So we need to construct C_{code} such that:

$$\forall Prog \bullet \mathcal{B}_{prog}(Prog) = \mathcal{B}_{code}(\mathcal{C}_{code}(Prog))$$

In reality, to make the proof of the compiler more ammenable to humans there will be an assembler hidden somewhere between $\mathcal{C}_{code}$ and the actual machine.

To construct the compiler we make use of the structure of the program. In fact, the compiler will be given as a recursive function on the structure of programs. Its correctness will be established by structural induction on all programs. This is accomplished by constructing the compiler inside the proof system as a series of rewriting rules and verifying that these functions satisfy the correctness conditions given above.

4.1 Compilation of SEQ

As the first example of compilation consider the case of the compilation of a sequential composition of two processes — the semantics of the language will allow the transformation of a sequence of processes into binary applications of the sequential constructor.

$$\mathcal{C}_{code}(\text{SEQ}(P, Q)) = append(\mathcal{C}_{code} P)(\mathcal{C}_{code} Q)$$

This will verified by a deriving a theorem that states that if two pieces of code $C1$ and $C2$ obey certain properties — notably that they can only exit through their last instruction (i.e. they cannot jump to a label external to themselves) then

$$\mathcal{B}_{code}(append \ C_1 \ C_2) = \mathcal{B}_{code} \ C_1; \mathcal{B}_{code} \ C_2$$

where ; is defined as sequential composition of behaviours. This then allows the derivation from the definition of sequential compilation of:

$$\mathcal{B}_{code}(\mathcal{C}_{code}(\text{SEQ}(P, Q))) = \mathcal{B}_{code}(\mathcal{C}_{code} P); \mathcal{B}_{code}(\mathcal{C}_{code} Q)$$

and this will be equal to

$$\mathcal{B}_{prog} P; \mathcal{B}_{prog} Q$$

by the structural induction hypothesis and this in turn will be equal to

$$\mathcal{B}_{prog}(\text{SEQ}(P, Q))$$

by the definition of ; on program behaviours.

4.2 Compilation of IF

A second example is the compilation of an IF statement. This is more complex as its execution is not compile time determined — the branch chosen depends on the run time conditions. A subsidiary compilation function C_{exp} is defined to compile an expression. It leaves the value of the expression in a register that can be used for testing — on a transputer this would be the top stack register **Areg**.

The semantics of the language enable all IFs to be transformed into binary IFs whose second component has a TRUE conditional. A (TRUE, STOP) branch is added to the end of each IF to catch total failures. Now the compilation of an IF of this form can be defined by:

$$C_{code}(\text{IF}((b, P), (\text{TRUE}, Q))) =$$
$$append(C_{exp}(b))\{cj\ label\}C_{code}(P)\{j\ endlab\}$$
$$\{label :\}C_{code}(Q)\{endlab :\}$$

where *label* and *endlab* are labels local to this block of code.

Similar arguments as were used in the proof of sequential composition can be used here. Using boolean cases on the portion of program from the cj onwards it can be shown the the code behaves as $C_{code}P$ if b holds and as $C_{code}Q$ otherwise.

4.3 Compilation of expressions and variables

The compilation of expressions is performed by implementing the algorithms given in [8] in the theorem prover as rewrites. These can be shown to correctly implement the evaluation of expressions.

To compile an expression it is first necessary to find out the number of registers required in its evaluation. The function *depth* defined below does this.

$$
\begin{aligned}
depth(constant) &= 1 \\
depth(variable) &= 1 \\
depth(e_1\ op\ e_2) &= \begin{cases} depth(e_1), & depth(e_1) > depth(e_2) \\ depth(e_2), & depth(e_1) < depth(e_2) \\ depth(e_1) + 1, & depth(e_1) = depth(e_2) \end{cases}
\end{aligned}
$$

$depth(e)$ is the depth of register stack needed to evaluate expression e. As on the machine there is only an evaluation stack of depth 3 it will be necessary to use temporary workspace locations when expressions have depth greater than 3. The compilation function C_{exp} can now be defined by

$$C_{exp}(e_1 \; op \; e_2)$$

$$= \begin{cases} C_{exp}(e_2); \; store \; temp; C_{exp}(e_1); \; load \; temp; \; OP, & depth(e_2) > depth(e_1) \\ & \wedge depth(e_1) > 2 \\ C_{exp}(e_2); C_{exp}(e_1); \; swap; \; OP, & depth(e_2) > depth(e_1) \\ & \wedge depth(e_1) \leq 2 \\ C_{exp}(e_1); C_{exp}(e_2); \; OP, & depth(e_2) \leq depth(e_1) \\ & \wedge depth(e_2) < 3 \\ C_{exp}(e_2); \; store \; temp; C_{exp}(e_1); \; load \; temp; \; OP, & otherwise \end{cases}$$

where OP is the instruction that implements the operation op.

Variables are handled as in transputer implementations of occam as locations in a local workspace. The compilation function needs to maintain a list of the order of these variables, and other data such as return addresses, in the local workspace so that C_{exp} can load the inner-most scoped value of each variable.

4.4 Assembly into machine code

The final stage of the compilation process is to assemble the compiler's output of assembly code into machine instructions. This type of procedure has already been performed in a formally verified environment by J Moore's Piton assembler for the FM8501 processor[9].

5 Design of a microcoded machine

We will implement the processor as a microcoded machine. The processor can be viewed as a collection of registers, a datapath, an arithmetic unit, a memory, and other elements which run a fixed program stored in the microcode ROM. In this way the machine can be defined as

$$\mathcal{M} = \mu\mathcal{M} \; \mu\mathcal{R}$$

where $\mu\mathcal{M}$ is a micromachine parameterized by its microcode ROM $\mu\mathcal{R}$.

We will define the micromachine $\mu\mathcal{M}$ to contain the necessary registers, datapaths, arithmetic and logical functions to support the instruction set defined above. Because the implementation of the instruction set is determined by the microcode ROM the micromachine will be to a large extent a "generic" machine. Most of the functions of the machine will be standard — for example it is likely that an adder will be required in the arithmetic unit. This enables this micromachine to be developed at the same time as the instruction set with the particular details of the instruction set being "customized" by the microcode. In fact, this view can be taken a stage further to allow a "generic" micromachine to be defined which is used to implement new instruction sets by defining new microcode ROMs. During the latter stages of development it is often possible to make changes in the capability of a processor by making changes to the microcode in a way that would not be possible if the underlying hardware had to be altered.

As before, we will give rigourous specifications of the micromachine $\mu\mathcal{M}$ and all its subcomponents and functions. These will enable the behaviour of the micromachine and microcode ROM to be reasoned about.

6   Implementation of instruction set in microcode

Work at INMOS on the IMS T800 showed how occam could be used in the design of microcode. The gap between a high level algorithm implementing an instruction and the low level description of what the microcode actually does can be bridged by using occam transformations to move from a high level occam implementation to another equivalent implementation that matched the micromachine functions. The occam transformation system [4] proved to be a useful tool in this process so we would like to be able to use it again in future work.

6.1   Occam transformations

The algebraic semantics of occam given in [10] consists of a set of laws which define the language constructs. The algebraic semantics has been shown to be consistent with the denotational semantics establishing the validity of these laws. These transformation laws enable a normal form for finite occam programs to be defined.

A transformation law can be used to transform one program into another whose observable behaviour is equivalent. Many transformation laws are "obviously true" and are regularly used by programmers - for example sequential composition of processes is associative

$$
\begin{array}{ccc}
\text{SEQ} & & \text{SEQ} \\
\quad \text{P} & & \quad \text{SEQ} \\
\quad \text{SEQ} & \equiv & \qquad \text{P} \\
\qquad \text{Q} & & \qquad \text{Q} \\
\qquad \text{R} & & \quad \text{R} \\
\end{array}
$$

This is the law *SEQ binassoc*. Others are more complex and include preconditions for validity but, with a bit of effort, can be seen to be true.

If a sequence of transformations can be found to transform one program into another then the two programs are known to be equivalent. If, in addition, one of these programs is known to be a correct implementation of a specification then the correctness of the other can be inferred.

6.1.1 An example transformation

As an example consider the following program fragment

```
SEQ
  X := A
  Y := Y + X
```

These two assignment statements can be merged into one multiple assignment statement. First the law *AS id* is used to add an identity assignment to each statement.

AS id $\underline{x}, \underline{y} := \underline{e}, \underline{y} \equiv \underline{x} := \underline{e}$

giving the program

```
SEQ
  X,Y := A,Y
  Y,X := Y + X,X
```

Next the law *AS perm* is applied to the second statement

AS perm $< x_i | i = 1..n >:=< e_i | i = 1..n >$

$$\equiv$$

$$< x_{\pi_i} | i = 1..n >:=< e_{\pi_i} | i = 1..n >$$
for any permutation π of $\{1..n\}$

giving

```
SEQ
  X,Y := A,Y
  X,Y := X,Y + X
```

Finally these two statements are merged by the law *SEQ comb*

SEQ comb $SEQ(\underline{x} := \underline{e}, \underline{x} := \underline{f}) \equiv \underline{x} := \underline{f}\,[\underline{e}/\underline{x}]$

giving

```
X,Y := A,Y + A
```

6.2 Occam representation of microcode

The conditional jump instruction can be specified at a high level in occam as being the program

```
CASE (OpCode)
  :
  CJ
    IF
      Areg = 0
        SEQ
          Iptr := Iptr + Oreg
          Areg, Breg := Breg, Creg
      TRUE
        SKIP
  :
```

This has the desired effect of popping the top value off the stack and taking the jump if it was FALSE (0) and doing nothing otherwise. The process described below will translate this into the program in Figure 1.

The shortcomings of the work performed on the IMS T800 [11] was that the correctness process only handled the middle of the design — the transformation from high level occam to low level "microcode occam". This left the reasoning about the correctness of the actual algorithm and the correctness of the underlying implementation of the micromachine to be done by other means. The correctness of the algorithms could be established by program proofs and by comparison with a correct floating point implementation produced by Geoff Barrett [2]. The correctness of the lower levels was left to traditional design techniques and the skill of the hardware design team.

6.3 Verification of microcode

In a verified system we need to tie up all the steps in the verification together. For this reason if we are going to use occam for the manipulation of microcode then we need to be able to verify occam against specifications. The programming language already outlined provides a basis for this as we will already have the need for occam-like program verification in another part of the system. This language, or perhaps a variant of it, can be used for the manipulation of the microcode. The transformation laws that are used in the transformation system can be verified to be consistent with these semantics so that equivalences derived from the transformation system have the same status as proofs of equivalence in the theorem prover.

```
SEQ
  CASE (OpCode)
    ⋮
    CJ
      μ-inst-ptr := cj.entry
    ⋮
  finished := FALSE
  ⋮
  WHILE (NOT finished)
    CASE (μ-inst-ptr)
      ⋮
      cj.entry
        SEQ
          AluResult := Areg - 0
          AluResultZero := (AluResult = 0)
          IF
            AluResultZero
              μ-inst-ptr := cj.false
            (NOT AluResultZero)
              μ-inst-ptr := cj.true
      cj.true
        finished := TRUE
      cj.false
        SEQ
          BregSlave := Breg
          AluResult := Iptr + Oreg
          Iptr := AluResult
          Areg := BregSlave
          Breg := Creg
          finished := TRUE
      ⋮
```

Figure 1: Low level occam representation of microcode

At this stage we have a machine specification M and a micromachine specification μM. We now need to derive μR such that:

$$M = \mu M \, \mu R$$

In this stage of refinement we are only concerned with the execution unit of the machine. Both M and μM contain a specification of an execution unit and other units.

$$M = M_{EXEC} \wedge M_{REST}$$

$$\mu M \, \mu R = (\mu M_{EXEC} \mu R) \wedge \mu M_{REST}$$

The execution unit executes a single instruction as a series of microcode steps operating on a datapath and signals back to the rest of the processor that it is ready for another on termination. The rest of the processor consists of modules such as the instruction sequencer and fetcher, the memory and the communication links etc.

We will assume that

$$\mu M_{REST} \Rightarrow M_{REST}$$

is established by a proof in the theorem prover. This proof should deal with objects that have much simpler behaviour than the execution unit and that can be manipulated in the theorem prover. The proof of the execution unit could in principle be done in the theorem prover but the use of a specialized tool, the occam transformation system, will reduce the amount of work needed.

To prove the implementation of the microcode we will derive a program P that is equivalent to the behaviour of the microcode. I.e. P is such that:

$$B_{mach} M_{EXEC} = B_{prog} P$$

Then using the transformation system we verify that this program is equivalent to another program Q of the form:

```
SEQ
  INIT -- set up microinstruction pointer
  WHILE (NOT finished)
    CASE ( microinstruction pointer)
      addr_i
        µINST_i
```

In this each $\mu INST$ is the low level occam code representing the microcode needed for the microinstruction at address $addr_i$. These pieces of code use the operations, registers, etc. that are available in μM_{EXEC}.

Because of the validation of transformations used in the transformation system by proof in the theorem prover we can now state

$$\mathcal{B}_{mach} M_{EXEC} = \mathcal{B}_{prog} Q$$

The execution unit of the microcode machine can be viewed as being a step function that is the execution of a single microinstruction contained in a microinstruction sequencer that continues to execute the step function until the instruction has been completed. This is reflected in the specification of μM_{EXEC} as

$$\mu M_{EXEC} \ \mu R = \mu M_{SEQ} \ \mu M_{STEP} \ \mu R$$

Here we have taken another step away from the details of the actual machine by using what will be a generic sequencer μM_{SEQ} that is parameterized by a step function μM_{STEP} and a microcode ROM μR.

We now produce a generic proof about microcode steppers. This states that if the effect of executing each branch in a program like Q is the same as executing the step function μM_{STEP} in the equivalent state, then the program Q is equivalent to the whole execution. I.e. that:

$$\forall addr_i \bullet (\mathcal{B}_{mach}(\mu M_{STEP} \ \mu R \ addr_i) = \mathcal{B}_{prog}(\mu INST_i))$$
$$\Rightarrow (\mathcal{B}_{mach}(\mu M_{SEQ} \ \mu M_{STEP} \ \mu R) = \mathcal{B}_{prog} \ Q)$$

The microcode ROM μR is generated automatically from the low level occam code in Q and this definition is then used to verify the execution of the step function μM_{STEP} against the low level occam code for each microinstruction. Once this has been done the theorem stated above is used to establish the correctness for the entire execution unit. This verification of the microcode ROM against the lowest level of occam removes the dangers of errors occurring due to deficiencies of the translation process. In particular it means that standard translation tools (such as sed, awk etc) can be used without the need to verify the correctness of their operation.

7   Implementing the micromachine

The remaining task is to implement the micromachine μM. At this level the machine is little more than a collection of registers, arithmetic units etc joined together by buses. Many of these objects can be taken out of a standard library of modules that is built up as designs progress.

As the design approaches the actual hardware the representations become closer to the Hardware Description Language (HDL).

Designs at INMOS have used an internally developed Hardware Description Language (HDL). This is a hierarchical language in which a device is designed in terms of modules. These modules, in turn, are designed in terms of sub-modules until, at the lowest level, primitive modules representing simple gates or transistors are used.

7.1 HDL specifications

An example of a (simple) portion of HDL is shown below

```
MODULE inverters2 (IN Input, OUT output)
  SIGNAL Internal {c=50fF}
    Internal = INV inv1 wp=6, lp=2, wn=6 ln=2 (Input)
    Internal = INV inv2 {wp=6, lp=2, wn=6, ln=2} (Internal)
END inverters2

MODULE inverters4 (IN ThisWay, OUT MidWay, ThatWay)
    inverters2 pair1 (IN ThisWay, OUT MidWay)
    inverters2 pair2 (IN MidWay,  OUT ThatWay)
END inverters4
```

In the HDL modules are defined and instanced in a similar manner to procedures and functions in a block structured programming language. In addition local wires can be declared with SIGNAL definitions like local variables. A module is instanced by

module-name instance-name {device parameters} (signal parameters)

The *module-name* specifies the module being used. The *instance- name* is a name given to this instance and is used by the simulator diagnostics. The *device parameters* allow the instance of the device to be characterized in terms of transistor sizes, forcing of outputs etc. The *signal parameters* specify what signals are used as inputs and outputs to this module instance. Certain primitive modules can be applied functionally in which case the output signal can be "assigned" to another signal — as in the use of the primitive inverter INV in the example.

Replicated sections of a design can be handled with a FOR construct.

7.2 Representing HDL in HOL

This hierarchical style of HDL specification can be very naturally represented in a HOL style specification. Each module is represented by a predicate stating the valid relationships between its inputs and outputs, local variables by existential quantification etc. For example the HDL given above could be specified by the HOL definitions below

```
inverters2 Input Output =
    ? Internal:signal .
        Internal = INV Input /\
        Output   = INV Internal

inverters4 ThisWay MidWay ThatWay =
    inverters2 ThisWay MidWay /\
    inverters2 MidWay  ThatWay
```

This example shows how the translation from HDL to HOL can be performed mechanically.

7.3 Proving HDL designs

The INMOS CAD system is currently being modified. One of the modifications will be to allow modules to contain a number of different "representations" – e.g. HDL, timing information, state machine. It is intended that one of these representations can be a HOL specification. In many cases this will be a formalisation of the boolean equations that a designer currently jots down on a piece of scrap paper while s/he derives the HDL.

At the lowest levels of design the primitive components, and some other basic modules, will be treated as "axiomatic" – their behaviours will be assumed to be in accordance with their specifications. When larger modules have been designed, it will be possible to obtain the HOL representations of the HDL specifications. These can then be shown to meet the specifications and the fact recorded in the design database. When a module is modified its correctness validation will be removed and the proof will have to be repeated. When a design, or portion of a design, is completed a validity checker can be run on it to ensure that all modules have been proved correct in the same way that connectivity checkers and electronic design rule checkers are currently used.

By recording proven validity in the design database, it should be possible to make small adjustments to a design at a late stage and know precisely which parts need to be reproven. In addition, if it is possible to record the proof strategies used in the past to prove components then much of this rechecking could be done automatically.

7.4 Correctness at the bottom level

All the work described above assumes that modules are well behaved boolean functions with well defined inputs and outputs. At the lowest levels of transistors etc this is not so. Many current techniques have used boolean logic enhanced with error and floating states. They also tend to use transistor models that are directional.

Recent work addresses the problems of CMOS design at a level where signals cannot be considered to be simply boolean values [6]. This method provides a design style for such combinatorial logic. This design style could be implemented inside HOL to handle the necessary proofs of correctness and consistency that are required.

8 Conclusions

This paper has described in a fairly superficial manner how a system can be implemented correctly. A simple language is defined with suitably clean semantics. This enables the behaviour of programs written in that language to be verified in a theorem prover against a higher level specification. The theorem prover is also used as the basis of a correct compiler. This compiler takes a program in the simple language and returns machine code that, when suitably booted into a machine, has equivalent behaviour to that of the program. This equivalence is determined by having rigorous semantics of the language and the instruction set. What the compiler does is to produce a machine code program which it can prove to be equivalent to the high level language program.

A processor is implemented to support the instruction set described above. This consists of a micromachine and a microcode ROM. A variant of the simple language is used to write the microcode so that the derived semantic properties can be used to ensure equivalence between specifications and microcode implementations. Transformation rules are validated for this language and a transformation system is used to simplify the equivalence proofs between programs in the language. In this way a microcode ROM can be produced that causes the microcode machine to correctly implement the machine specification.

The micromachine is decomposed into a hierarchy of HDL modules. The correctness of this decomposition and implementation is maintained by associating specifications with each module. As this design process progresses proofs are performed to ensure the correctness of the design. At the bottom level current design tools are used to ensure that the silicon layout correctly implements the bottom level of HDL.

The simplifying assumptions mentioned above, such as the restriction of the language to sequential programs, will enable this design process to be performed using current theory. In fact, each of the components (program verifier, compiler, processor) has already been done in a rigorous manner for small scale examples. The challenge here is to scale the process up to state of the art systems. In the area of concurrency there remains work to be done to embed recent theoretical work into mechanized systems.

Both of the steps above, scaling up to state of the art systems and the mechanisation of concurrency theory, will need foundations work in the theorem prover. Theories about the various types of objects that are used (e.g. n-bit words for processors, sets and bags for concurrency models, language components for compilers) will need to be developed. But as work progresses libraries of these preproved theories will become available so that just as in module libraries designers now take advantage of modules designed for previous devices in the future a theory library will be available of definitions and proofs used in previous work.

The capability to produce correct systems is already available. Current tools will provide most of the support that is needed — the problem is to some extent a matter of integrating these various tools into one consistent unit. However, there is still an immediate penalty in the need to develop the mechanical theories to handle the proofs that will be required. This will involve potential producers of correct systems to put investment into providing these foundations both by their own work in implementing current theory and by encouraging further research to produce the necessary theory in other areas such as concurrency.

References

[1] Barrett, G., *The Semantics and Implementation of occam*, Phd Thesis, Oxford Universtity, 1988.

[2] Barrett, G., *Formal methods applied to a floating point number system*, Oxford University Programming Research Group Technical Monograph PRG-58, 1987.

[3] Cohn, A., A proof of correctness of the Viper microprocessor: the first level, University of Cambridge Computer Laboratory Technical Report No. 104, 1987.

[4] Goldsmith,M., *The Oxford occam Transformation System (Version 0,1) – (Draft user documentation)*, Oxford University Programming Research Group, January 1988.

[5] Gordon, M.J.C., *Mechanizing programming logic in HOL*, University of Cambridge Computer Laboratory Technical Report No. 145, 1989.

[6] Hoare, C.A.R., *A calculus fot the derivation of c-mos switching circuits*, Draft April 1988.

[7] Hunt, W.A., *FM8501: A verified microprocessor*, Unversity of Texas at Austin Technical Report 47, 1985.

[8] INMOS, *The transputer instruction set manual — a compiler writer's guide*, Prentice Hall, 1988.

[9] Moore, J.S., *Verification of Piton assembler*, Computational Logic Incorporated, Austin, Texas.

[10] Roscoe, A.W., "Denotational semantics for occam" in *Proceedings for July 1984 Seminar on Concurrency*, Springer LNCS vol. 197, 1985.

[11] Shepherd, D.E., "The role of occam in the design of the IMS T800" in *Communicating Process Architecture*, Prentice Hall, 1988.

Constructing a calculus of programs

Lambert Meertens

CWI, Amsterdam & University of Utrecht

A large part of the effort in formal program developments is expended on repeating the same derivational patterns over and over again. The problem is compounded by notations that require many marks on paper for expressing one elementary concept, and 'administrative overhead', consisting of algorithmically uninteresting but technically necessary steps, like shuffling parts of an expression around without change in computational meaning, and the introduction of local auxiliary definitions for lack of a suitable notation for what is being defined. This can to a large extent be avoided by developing suitable theories, including a notation that is designed to increase the manipulability. After a reflexion on some of the issues, the more technical part of this paper is devoted to an attempt to construct a system of combinators that is better amenable to manipulation than the classical ones.

0. INTRODUCTION

Program construction is a mathematical activity. By 'mathematical activity' is not meant: the actual practice of professional mathematicians, but: establishing properties of formal objects with perfect certainty, that is, as a tautology. Often the property to be established is known, but the formal object that has to enjoy the property is only partially constructed. The programmer's task is to complete the construction. This constructive type of problem is not uncommon in general mathematics, but it is the pre-eminent type in programming. The formal objects concerned are expressions in some formal language. This includes both programs and (formal) specifications.

Programs can themselves be viewed as specifications, in two ways. One is the operational viewpoint: programs as specifying a process for some (abstract) machine. The notion of efficiency is intimately tied to this viewpoint: it is meaningless to discuss the efficiency of a program outside the context of a mapping to a process on a machine. Processes have 'observable' aspects (input and output to the outside world) and purely internal aspects, and the agreement is that (apart from efficiency) only the observable aspects count. This makes the notion of program optimisation meaningful.

We can also abstract from the internal process aspects by identifying observably equivalent processes, and consider the meaning of a program as a point in the resulting abstract space. We then obtain the 'declarative' viewpoint of programs as specifications. It is this viewpoint we are concerned with here. The notion of efficiency, although still a major pragmatic concern and a motive force in our design choices, is thereby moved out of the formal arena. The advantage is that we obtain a rich structure of relations between programs.

Consider what is needed for constructing a program: a formal language for expressing the specification as a formal object, a formal language for expressing programs, and rules that can be used to establish properties.

Let us assume that there are no *a priori* constraints on the formalisms. Can the resulting freedom be used to design formalisms that make the task of program construction easier?

1. ON THE NEED FOR POWERFUL THEORIES

No mathematician could do significant work on the basis of pure ZFC, pure predicate calculus, or pure lambda calculus. Instead, the starting point is a body of theories, with definitions, notations and theorems.

Likewise, for significant program development we need powerful theories, with definitions, notations and theorems that allow to capture large chunks of development in a single step.

Here is a simple example. Let f be a function on the naturals, with an inductive definition of the form:

$$f(0) = e \quad ,$$
$$f(n+1) = g(h(n), f(n)) \quad .$$

The value of $f(N)$ can be computed with the following iterative program, in which the result is the final value of the variable a:

```
|[ a: appropriate-type
 ; n: nat
 ; n := 0; a := e
 ; do n ≠ N →
       a := g(h(n), a); n := n + 1
 ; od
]|
```

A simple theorem, that has been rediscovered many times, is that under certain conditions the computation may also be arranged as follows:

```
|[ a: appropriate-type
 ; n: nat
 ; n := N; a := e
 ; do n ≠ 0 →
       n := n - 1; a := g(a, h(n))
 ; od
]|
```

There may be good reasons to prefer this computation schema. The conditions under which it applies are that g satisfies the functional equation

$$g(a, g(b, c)) = g(g(a, b), c)$$

and e is such that

$$g(e, a) = g(a, e) = a$$

for all a.

Most introductory programming texts do not mention this simple theorem. Should they? Its proof is straightforward enough, for example using standard techniques from DIJKSTRA & FEIJEN [3] The only aspect that possibly requires some inventiveness is the choice of the invariant, namely

$$g(a, f(n)) = f(N) \ .$$

It might, therefore, be argued that—since this fact can be derived on the spot when it applies—no theorem is needed here.

If carried to its extreme, this argument denies the value of having theorems at all. For example, it is not hard to derive the fact that

$$\frac{\mathrm{d}}{\mathrm{d}x} x^n = n \cdot x^{n-1}$$

when the need arises by applying standard techniques for computing limits. The strength of the Differential Calculus is of course that it is a *calculus*. It gives a method for computing a certain kind of limits by following a set of rules rather mechanically, using pattern matching and simple equational reasoning. This is only possible by virtue of a suitable notation geared towards these rules.

Coming back now to the simple theorem mentioned above, a possible reason for not formulating it explicitly is the lack of a suitable notation. As presented above, it takes up half a page. What is worse, the interesting part of it, from a calculus-oriented point of view, is not so much that there are two solutions to one problem, but that the two programs are equivalent under the given condition. It is not difficult to imagine that in a less abstract problem setting it would be hard to see by pattern matching that the theorem applies.

A formalism whose aim is to provide the kind of notation by which this and similar theorems can be formulated concisely, so that they can be applied as part of a calculus, was developed in [4, 1, 2]. The condition on g and e is precisely that they are the operation and identity element of a monoid. It is more pleasing then to denote g as an infix operator, say $\oplus$, which by the monoid properties is associative. The function f takes a natural as argument, but a slightly more general and abstract viewpoint is that the computation has the sequence

$$[h(0), h(1), \ldots, h(N-1)]$$

as its argument, and therefore *any* list. The function applied to this list 'reduces' it to a single value by combining the elements using the operation $\oplus$. A short notation for this function is

$$\oplus / \ ,$$

which is borrowed from APL but expresses in addition, when applied to a sequence, that its operation is that of a monoid, and thereby that there are many different orders in which the reduction can be computed.

For the two program schemas above, one in which the reduction is performed 'from left to right', and one in which the computation proceeds 'from right to left' (or in any case in the opposite direction), the operation is not required *per se* to be associative. It might even be the case that the two operands have different types, whereas they are of the same type for an associative operator. Concise notations for these two computation schemas are

$$\oplus\!\!\not\rightarrow_e \quad \text{and} \quad \oplus\!\!\not\leftarrow_e \ .$$

The theorem, formulated with the aid of this notation, is now:

$$\text{If } (\oplus, e) \text{ is a monoid, then } \oplus\!\!\not\rightarrow_e \ = \ \oplus\!\!\not\leftarrow_e \ .$$

The reader familiar with [1] or [2] will recognise this as (a mildly specialised version of) the Specialisation Lemma. The point is that in this form the theorem has the right characteristics to being useful as ingredient in a calculus.

It is not hard to understand why having theories is important. Given a significant piece of mathematical work, it is (theoretically) possible to make it entirely self-contained, theory-free so to say, by including definitions of all notations used, and statements and proofs of theorems invoked, and again definitions and proofs of notations and theorems used in there, down to some basic level. Theorems and notations that are used only occasionally, perhaps once, can be expanded in place. The result will not be pleasing. But this is how the work would look if we did not have theories to work from at our disposal. The prevailing situation in (formal) program construction is, unfortunately, not much better.

There is, therefore, reason for the hope that the currently often excessive length of rigorous formal program developments is not so much due to the need for rigour, but rather, at least to a large extent, to the lack of a suitable body of theories to build upon. The experience with our, thus far modest, formalism provides some evidence for this.

2. ALGORITHMICS ANONYMOUS

What now, precisely, are the characteristics that make this formalism suitable for doing program construction by calculation? One is that it is indeed modest. As the formalism is developed over time, more notation is added, and there is the constant need to be extremely careful here. Unchecked, it would explode into a flurry of special symbols.

The existing notations have been developed with an eye to conciseness of expression, taking account of what is actually often encountered. Conciseness is important for making the recording of the development steps less laborious, and also for making it possible in the first place to do the pattern matching needed to recognise the applicability of some rule.

A further advantage is that the need is diminished to *interrupt* the smooth, linear, development for doing an 'aside' sub-development. It is quite normal in a development to single out a subexpression of the main expression, derive an equivalent form for it, and substitute the result back. Whether and when this is done, and if so how, is a design choice in the presentation of the argument. The subdevelopment may precede the main development, perhaps as a lemma, or it may be a 'deferred justification'. In principle, it could be expanded in place. A good reason for not doing so may be the structuring of the argument. Especially if the context surrounding the subexpression is large, this device may increase readability by zooming in on the symbols where the action is. If, however, that context is mainly large because of the verbose notation, the interruption is more a matter of practical necessity than of choice.

Given a concise notation, the choice between singling-out versus having an uninterrupted, linear derivation, is up to the designer of the presentation, and it is a good thing to have this freedom. However, there are also cases where a separate subdevelopment is forced for purely technical reasons. This can be an annoying interruption of the argument. A further goal, therefore, of the formalism is to avoid this.

One important case where this phenomenon pops up is if recursively defined names are used. By 'name' here a single symbol is meant that refers to a definition elsewhere. In that sense, the expression '2+2', although denoting 4, is not a name for it. If a name has a recursive definition, this means that it is not possible to just replace the name by its definiens. The latter contains further occurrences of that name (by the definition of 'recursive definition'), and so the expression after substitution must—in contrast to what happens for non-recursive definitions—still be interpreted in the context of the original definition. Usually the well-foundedness of the recursion corresponds to a split in the definition into a base case and other cases, and this may generate then the need for a case analysis, another technical reason for an interruption. And, finally, recursive definitions often give rise to the need of a proof by induction, which cannot be done 'in place'.

The counterpart to this is if the *solution* to which a development leads requires, in the language used, a recursive definition, and thereby a name for the recursively defined part. Without some rather special mechanism, this also necessitates an aside in the development.

A theoretical solution is the use of a fixpoint combinator, but the 'theoretical' should be emphasised here; such a combinator is not particularly pleasant if it comes to calculating with it. The approach adopted in our formalism is to provide explicit notations for the solutions to the most frequent recursive definition patterns, and to give a set of laws to go with it. Above, we have seen the notation $\oplus/$; this is one such notation. The subexpression that before required a name, now can remain *anonymous*. This extremely simple stratagem buys us a good deal of calculational manipulability. It should, in fact, be familiar to every programmer. The 'while loop'

while p **do** S **od**

is an explicit anonymous notation for the solution to this recursive definition for W:

$$W \;=\; \textbf{if } p \textbf{ then } S\,;\, W \textbf{ fi} \;\; .$$

3. FURTHER CAUSES OF LABORIOUSNESS

Names are not by themselves bad, of course; attempts directed towards totally aban-
doning names lead to a tar pit. It is being forced to pick and use ephemeral names
for items that do not correspond to any abstraction worth naming, that is the cause
of much additional labour. After 'recursive' names, the next target is formed by
dummy (bound) variables, as in function definitions or lambda forms. The point
here is that a variable-free definition is at least potentially more manipulable. The
extra notation needed for denoting the dummy variables, and for delimiting the
scope, tends to get in the way of the easy manipulation. In our little formalism one
contribution here are the so-called sections; instead of writing something like

$$\lambda x : a \oplus x \quad ,$$

in which one operand is fixed, leaving a monadic function, the pithy notation

$$a \oplus$$

can be used. This saves us many, many marks on paper. The alternative in such
cases is hardly to use the lambda notation. Presently, if the existing devices for getting rid of dummy variables do not suffice, the best alternative is to interrupt the
development for a definition, like: "Putting

$$f x = a \oplus x \quad ,$$

we have ..." and so on. Again, introducing a name here is not necessarily bad; the
bad thing is being forced to it. One form of this that is all over the existing papers
using the current formalism occurs when an operator is needed, like in: "Putting

$$a \odot b = a \oplus (f b) \quad ,$$

we have ..." and so on. The interruption is forced in this case by the lack of an
explicit, closed-form expression for the solution $\odot$ of the functional identity
$a \odot b = a \oplus (f b)$.

What we need here are combinators that allow expressing that solution in terms
of components like $\oplus$ and f. The 'classical' combinators S and K will make anything variable-free, but they do not have the desirable manipulative properties. If it
is sometimes nice that 'there is only one thing you can do', these combinators virtu-
ally force us on a single development track: they act only at the head of a tree, and
most of the steps are just shuffling to get things up there. There is also the other
direction, in which combinators are not expanded but introduced, and here there are
usually too many possibilities, and no heuristics for choosing among these. Worst of
all, in proving the equivalence of two combinator expressions, the standard technique requires introducing dummy variables for unsatiated combinators.

The basic problem here is that the basic operation of the classical combinator
calculus (and also of the closely related lambda calculus) is application instead of
composition. Application has not a single property. Function composition is associative and has an identity element (if one believes in the 'generic' identity function).

Often seemingly minor notational issues make a huge difference. A well known example is the use of infix notation for associative operators. If much use of the associative property is made (and for function composition it is), the just sufficiently ambiguous infix notation

$$f \circ g \circ h$$

saves one calculation step for each case.

In [4] a notational suggestion was made, not followed in [1] and [2], for a further ambiguity-on-purpose. It is the device called 'apposition' there, to denote function *app*lication and com*position* in the same way. This saves us the trivial step in

$$f(g(x)) = (f \circ g)(x) \; .$$

There is a problematic aspect to this notational trick (dubbed, with another portmanteau, 'complication' by Bird): it requires knowing the types of the constituents to parse the train f-apposed-to-g-apposed-to-x. In a polymorphic context, it is in general impossible to guarantee that x will not be substantiated with a function, which would radically alter the meaning. So apposition is not so substitutive as is desirable.

4. Whither, apposition?

Apposition may perhaps be madness, but there is some curious (Dutch?) method to it. A close relative is the silent 'lifting' of operators to functions, another notational device in [4] that has not met with universal acclaim, whereby each operator $\oplus$ could be overloaded to also denote the operator $\hat{\oplus}$ such that

$$f \hat{\oplus} g = \lambda x : (f x) \oplus (g x) \; .$$

The relationship can be seen if we consider an operation that does not use its left operand. If the lifting is not denoted, the definition reads then: $\oplus$ applied to g is $\oplus$ composed with g. This suffers from the same problems as apposition does. The most irritating thing here is that these problems are real, but encountered rarely in practice (at least until now). The extra steps needed on giving this up are also real, and very frequent. One theoretically sound way of saving this device is to agree that also constants in the formalism are silently lifted to constant functions, so that '2', for example, is the name of the function

$$\lambda x : \text{``the successor of the successor of zero''} \; .$$

As the circumlocution in the body shows, we have lost the name for the number itself. This is not appealing; who wants to live with spurious identities like $2 \circ 3 = 2$?

There is something in common to many of the (usually minor) annoying problems in the use of the formalism. They all point in the direction of the need of a suitable system of combinators for making functions out of component functions without introducing extra names in the process. Composition should be the major method, and not application. Among the further desirable properties is that the system should not be opposed to a typing discipline. (The classical combinators do not permit any reasonable form of typing.) c Also, less effort should be needed for 'administrative' steps that serve to bring the 'data' in the expression to the spot where the action is (typically a substantial part of the work). In particular, the choice between the asymmetric 'Curried' view on the type of a function with two arguments, say

$$\alpha \rightarrow (\beta \rightarrow \gamma)$$

and the flat view

$$(\alpha \times \beta) \rightarrow \gamma$$

should be reasonably light-weight, and there should be no built-in bias for the first of the two for operators. Finally, it is desirable that functions can as easily and gracefully deliver a tuple as result as they will take it as an argument, facilitating composition.

The remainder of this paper is devoted to an attempt to construct such a set of combinators. The starting point is a type system that centres on functions taking (typed) tuples as arguments and giving tuples as result. The notion of combinator is next taken rather literally; it is examined how such functions can be combined, more or less as if they were wheeled in as physical boxes with output lines that can be connected to the input lines of other boxes.

5. A TYPE SYSTEM

We start with a typed universe of 'plain values', not containing tuples or functions. From the plain types we construct 'singleton types', 'tuple types' and 'function types', in a mutually recursive fashion. Greek letters, possibly adorned with subscripts, will serve as variables that stand for types. Specifically, σ, τ, υ and ω will be used for tuple types, and α, β and γ for singleton types.

Each function type is formed from an *out-type* (for the codomain) and an *in-type* (for the domain), both of which are tuple types. If σ and τ are two tuple types, then

$$\sigma \leftarrow \tau$$

denotes the function type with out-type σ and in-type τ. A more conventional notation would be $\tau \rightarrow \sigma$.

A tuple type is formed from a finite sequence of zero or more singleton types. Its *width* is defined to be the length of that sequence. Let a sequence be given of n singleton types α_i, $0 \leqslant i < n$. The corresponding tuple type has then width n. If $0 < n$, it is denoted by

$$\alpha_0, \alpha_1, \cdots, \alpha_{n-1} \ .$$

This resembles the n-ary operation $\_ \times \_ \times \cdots \times \_$ of the Cartesian product, but here the operation , is considered to be 2-ary and associative. For example,

$$\alpha, \beta, \gamma \quad ,$$

$$(\alpha, \beta), \gamma \quad ,$$

and

$$\alpha, (\beta, \gamma)$$

all denote the same tuple type. So if σ and τ are tuple types, then so is σ, τ. Its width is the sum of the widths of σ and τ. On purpose the notation does not distinguish between singleton types and tuple types of width 1. These are identified. We need a special notation for the (unique) tuple type of width 0, for which the symbol **1** will be used. Under the operation **,**, the tuple types form a monoid, with identity element **1** (so $\sigma, 1$ and $1, \sigma$ both denote the same type as σ).

Finally, the singleton types consist of the plain types, together with the function types.

Here is a BNF grammar for the 'type expressions' as described above, assuming a predefined metasyntactic variable ⟨plain type⟩:

⟨function type⟩ ::= (⟨tuple type⟩ ← ⟨tuple type⟩)

⟨tuple type⟩ ::= ⟨tuple type⟩,⟨tuple type⟩ | ⟨singleton type⟩ | 1

⟨singleton type⟩ ::= ⟨plain type⟩ | ⟨function type⟩

What this grammar does not express, of course, is that **,** is associative and has identity **1**.

The parentheses in the first syntax rule are needed to distinguish between, e.g., the function types

$$(\sigma \leftarrow (\tau \leftarrow \upsilon))$$

and

$$((\sigma \leftarrow \tau) \leftarrow \upsilon) \quad .$$

If no ambiguity can arise, these parentheses may be dropped. They also serve to distinguish between, e.g., the tuple type

$$\alpha, (\sigma \leftarrow \tau), \beta$$

and the function type

$$\alpha, \sigma \leftarrow \tau, \beta \quad ,$$

which is interpreted as $(\alpha, \sigma) \leftarrow (\tau, \beta)$.

The various new kinds of types are inhabited by values, exactly in the way that would be expected. So a value of type α, β, γ, for example, is a 3-tuple consisting of an α-, a β- and a γ-value. There is exactly one, not very interesting, value of type **1**. A function of type $\sigma \leftarrow \tau$ yields a σ-tuple when provided with a τ-tuple as argument. The width of σ is called the *out-width* of the function, and the width of τ its *in-width*. It is not assumed that functions are total.

The type system can be made polymorphic in a way that has become usual, with, for example, a generic identity function 'id' of the *polymorphic* type $\alpha \leftarrow \alpha$. However, such type polymorphism will only be exercised with the constraint that refinement of polymorphic types preserves the widths involved. As we shall see, it is essential that the out- and in-widths of functions denoted by expressions can be determined from those of the constituents, and the superposition of type polymorphism must not break this. We use the notation

$$\vec{\alpha}^n = \alpha_0, \alpha_1, \cdots, \alpha_{n-1}$$

for the unrestrained polymorphic type of width n. For each width n there is a different generic identity function

$$\text{id}_n: \vec{\alpha}^n \leftarrow \vec{\alpha}^n \quad,$$

and id_1 is usually abbreviated to just id.

6. THE FUNCTION WORLD

From now on we are only interested in functions. Here are some schematic pictures of functions:

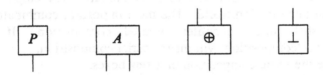

The functions are depicted as boxes. The argument tuple is fed into a box through the lines at the top, and the result tuple appears at the bottom. By convention, the flow in these schemas is always from high to low, so that there is no need to put arrowheads on the lines. The boxes are labelled with names for the functions. Let us consider them one by one.

The function P takes a singleton argument and delivers a singleton result.

The function A has in-width 0. Its argument is the uninteresting 0-tuple, which is the only inhabitant of the type 1. Since it carries no information, there is no need to show the 0 incoming lines more vividly. Functions with in-width 0 are called *sources*.

A source, like this function A, can be thought of as modelling a (constant) value in the function world. The result of A is a 2-tuple, or pair, of some type α, β. The type of A itself is then $\alpha, \beta \leftarrow 1$. The names of sources, that is, functions with in-type 1, will in general be taken from the initial part of the alphabet.

The function $\oplus$ has out-width 1 and in-width 2. As the example shows, the names of functions may be special symbols. Some more examples of symbol names are $+\!\!\!+$, $\odot$, $*$ and $/$. Functions with symbol names are also called 'operators'. Some of these symbols, like $+\!\!\!+$, denote by convention a specific function. For example, $+\!\!\!+$ stands for sequence concatenation; it has type $[\sigma] \leftarrow [\sigma], [\sigma]$. Others, like $\oplus$ and $\odot$, have no fixed meaning. They are true variables, just like P and A. The ordering of the incoming lines is significant. If the type of $\oplus$ is $\sigma \leftarrow \alpha, \beta,$

the α-value is supposed to be carried by the left in-line, and the β-value by the right in-line. Similarly, the out-lines of a box carry from left to right in order the single-ton values of which the output tuple is composed.

The last function can be called a terminator, or *sink*. It accepts a value but delivers no information. In general, a sink is any function whose out-type is $\mathbf{1}$. A sink is (up to polymorphic type refinement) fully determined by its in-width. The name of the unique sink of type $\mathbf{1} \leftarrow \alpha$, $\perp$, is thus chosen because of its graphical representation of the function as terminator. It bears no relationship to the bottom of a lattice. For the sink of in-width n we shall use the name $\perp_n$.

Not depicted above is $\perp_0$, the sink of in-width 0, the only sink that is also a source. This is the dullest function imaginable. It has some marginal theoretical interest though. Another name for this function is id_0.

7. SERIAL COMPOSITION

We want to have a set of *combinators* that form functions from given functions. For the purpose of combining functions, they are black boxes. A combinator cannot 'inspect' a function. From a mathematical point of view, a combinator is nothing but a higher-order function, but here these combinators are emphatically not con-sidered to live in our function world. The most important combinator is *serial com-position*. We shall also encounter parallel composition. If used without qualification, plain 'composition' will mean: serial composition.

Below we see the serial composition of a few boxes.

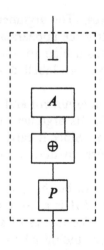

This composite will be expressed as $P \cdot \oplus \cdot A \cdot \perp$, in which $\cdot$ can be pro-nounced as 'dot'.

The purpose of the dashed box is to suggest that we can abstract from the details of the composition, and treat this as one new box:

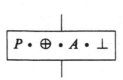

For the composite to be meaningful, the out-type of each box has to be compatible with the in-type of the box it interfaces to. In a polymorphic setting this may entail refining these types. It is understood then that the unifying type substitutions are consistently performed throughout the type of a box. In the schematic pictures it is always assumed that the components have types for which the whole combination is meaningful.

If P has out-width m and in-width n, then we have

$$P = \text{id}_m \bullet P = P \bullet \text{id}_n \quad .$$

In the schematic diagrams, a function id_n will not be shown explicitly as a box, but corresponds to any group of n adjacent collateral lines.

Thus far, it was tacitly assumed that the widths at each interface are equal. Such *balanced* serial composition is just the usual function composition. However, we will move on to a generalisation in which the widths do not have to balance. But first another form of composition is introduced.

8. PARALLEL COMPOSITION

The following picture depicts parallel composition:

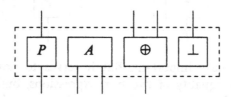

This parallel composite will be expressed as $P\|A\|\oplus\|\perp$, where $\|$ is pronounced 'para'. We may abstract as before:

The out-width of a parallel composite is the sum of the out-widths of the components, and likewise for the in-width.

Like serial composition, parallel composition is associative. There is also an identity element of $\|$, namely id_0. Two further simple laws relating identity functions and sinks to parallel composition are:

$$\text{id}_{m+n} \;=\; \text{id}_m\|\text{id}_n \quad,$$

and

$$\bot_{m+n} \;=\; \bot_m\|\bot_n \; .$$

We now come to a law relating serial and parallel composition. In a mixed expression, involving both the combinator $\|$ and the combinator $\bullet$, the first will take precedence. In fact, serial composition has the *lowest* priority of all combinators that will be introduced here. For the others no relative priorities are defined, and so parentheses will be needed to specify grouping in mixed expressions.

Now the promised law. If the compositions involved are balanced, the following law holds:

$$f\|F \bullet g\|G \;=\; (f \bullet g)\|(F \bullet G) \; .$$

(The requirement that the two compositions of the r.h.s are balanced is sufficient to guarantee balanced composition in the l.h.s.) In the terminology of [2], $\|$ *abides* with $\bullet$. The abide property is illustrated in the picture below:

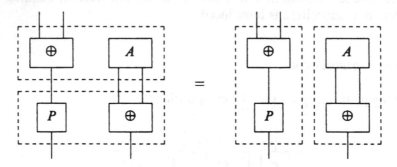

This law is not particularly important, but it serves to pose the question: What exactly do we mean by equality of two box expressions, built with (box) combinators? This could be defined in terms of a semantic domain involving functions, but a much simpler answer is possible: *Two box expressions are equal if the combinators specify networks with identical topologies between the component boxes.* This generates an algebra of boxes and combinators. If for certain boxes further properties are specified, for example, 'P is idempotent' (that is, $P \bullet P = P$), we can take the free algebra *modulo* these properties.

The box algebra is of course what we are interested in. There is some didactic advantage in the fact that various properties can be illustrated by diagrams, but proving complicated properties by pictures becomes laborious.

9. SERIAL COMPOSITION REVISITED

We shall now extend the definition of serial composition so as to allow *unbalanced* composition of boxes. This will be done by reducing it to balanced composition. The idea is the following: if the interfacing widths in a serial composition differ, the box with the deficit is 'stretched' to the required width by extending it to the right, by means of parallel composition, with an identity function whose width makes up the deficit. This can be defined more formally. Let the operation $\dot{-}$ between two naturals be defined by

$$m \dot{-} n \;=\; (m \uparrow n) - n \quad,$$

in which $\uparrow$ denotes the operation of taking the maximum of the two operands, and $-$ is conventional subtraction. It is immediate that

$$(m \dot{-} n) + n \;=\; (n \dot{-} m) + m \quad.$$

Also,

$$(m \dot{-} n) \downarrow (n \dot{-} m) \;=\; 0 \quad.$$

Let now P and Q be two functions, and let m be the in-width of P and n the out-width of Q. Then we define

$$P \bullet Q \;=\; (P \| \mathrm{id}_{n \dot{-} m}) \bullet (Q \| \mathrm{id}_{m \dot{-} n}) \quad.$$

The parallel composition with identity functions of the appropriate widths balances the composition in the r.h.s. If we apply this to a composition that was already balanced, the r.h.s. reduces to

$$(P \| \mathrm{id}_0) \bullet (Q \| \mathrm{id}_0) \quad,$$

which, since id_0 is the identity of $\|$, gives us back the l.h.s.. So the new definition extends the original meaning in a uniform way.

The diagram below shows this in action for each of the two ways in which a composition can be unbalanced. Here F has out-width 2 and in-width 4, whereas G has out-width 2 and in-width 1.

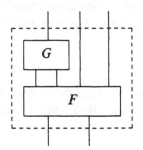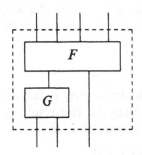

Note that the composite to the left resembles so-called 'partial parametrisation', especially if the box G is replaced by a source. In particular, it is the case that

$$F \bullet (A \| B) \;=\; (F \bullet A) \bullet B \quad,$$

provided at least that A is a source.

The important property making this more general form of serial composition useful is that this combinator is still associative. The composition combinator has an identity element, namely id_0, which was also the identity of parallel composition. (Note that $\mathrm{id} = \mathrm{id}_1$ is not an identity element, unless we restrict the domain of $\bullet$ to functions for which neither the in- nor the out-type is $\mathbf{1}$.)

There is a price to be paid for the additional flexibility afforded by the generalisation. It is the obligation to keep track of the widths. Quite a few of the laws involving composition have conditions on the widths concerned, for example of the pattern: 'provided that the in-width of P is at least the out-width of Q'. There is an opportunity for human errors here if the (usually boring) verification of such conditions is unduly omitted. In a mechanical system for providing assistance to reasoning with equalities of box expressions, the verification could be delegated to general type checking.

10. INPUT SHARING

The next combinator will allow several boxes to share their inputs. As a purely auxiliary group of generic functions we introduce first, for each natural n,

$$\Lambda_n\colon \vec{\alpha}^{\,n}, \vec{\alpha}^{\,n} \leftarrow \vec{\alpha}^{\,n} \quad,$$

which produces a $2n$-tuple from an n-tuple by joining two copies together. The following diagram shows Λ_3:

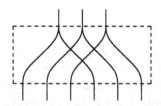

As before, we first define a balanced form of 'sharing', and extend the definition next to the general case. Let P and Q be functions with compatible in-types, which implies in particular that they have the same in-width. Let n be that in-width. Then we define

$$P\text{,}Q \;=\; (P\|Q)\bullet\Lambda_n \quad.$$

In words, the input to $P\text{,}Q$ is fed to both P and Q, and the output of $P\text{,}Q$ is then obtained by joining the two resulting output tuples. Both $(\mathrm{id}\|\bot)$ and $(\bot\|\mathrm{id})$ have out-width 1 and in-width 2, so

$$(\mathrm{id}\|\bot)\text{,}(\bot\|\mathrm{id})$$

has out-width 2 and in-width 2. It is easily seen (by 'proof by picture') to be id_2. If the two parallel composites are switched, thus:

$(\perp\|\text{id}),(\text{id}\|\perp)$,

we find again out-width 2 and in-width 2. This function switches the two components of a pair. It has polymorphic type

$\beta,\alpha \leftarrow \alpha,\beta$.

For the general case, in which the components do not have to have the same in-width, let m be the in-width of P and n that of Q. The requirement on the in-types becomes now that $P\|\text{id}_{n \dot{-} m}$ and $Q\|\text{id}_{m \dot{-} n}$ have compatible in-types. This amounts to compatibility of the first $m \downarrow n$ components of the two in-types. For serial composition, balance was achieved by stretching. Here we trim instead the input for the less demanding box to the required length. The function

$P\|\perp_{n \dot{-} m}$

has the same out-width as P, but in-width $m \uparrow n$. We define now for the case that $m \neq n$:

$P,Q = (P\|\perp_{n \dot{-} m}),(Q\|\perp_{m \dot{-} n})$.

As for the earlier combinators, , is associative and has identity id_0. The effect of , is illustrated by:

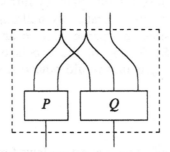

The line forked off to the left from the third in-line at the top is not shown; it would run into a $\perp$.

11. TYPE INFERENCE RULES

The following rules show how the type of a box expression built with $\cdot$, $\|$ and , can be deduced from the types of its components.

$$\frac{\begin{array}{ll} P: & \sigma \leftarrow \tau,\omega \\ Q: & \tau \leftarrow \upsilon \end{array}}{P \cdot Q : \sigma \leftarrow \upsilon,\omega} \qquad \frac{\begin{array}{ll} P: & \sigma \leftarrow \tau \\ Q: & \tau,\omega \leftarrow \upsilon \end{array}}{P \cdot Q : \sigma,\omega \leftarrow \upsilon}$$

$$P: \quad \sigma_0 \leftarrow \tau_0$$
$$Q: \quad \sigma_1 \leftarrow \tau_1$$
$$\overline{P \| Q : \sigma_0, \sigma_1 \leftarrow \tau_0, \tau_1}$$

$$P: \quad \sigma_0 \leftarrow \tau, \omega$$
$$Q: \quad \sigma_1 \leftarrow \tau$$
$$\overline{P, Q : \sigma_0, \sigma_1 \leftarrow \tau, \omega}$$

$$P: \quad \sigma_0 \leftarrow \tau$$
$$Q: \quad \sigma_1 \leftarrow \tau, \omega$$
$$\overline{P, Q : \sigma_0, \sigma_1 \leftarrow \tau, \omega}$$

For $\bullet$ and $,$ there are two rules, corresponding to the two ways of possible unbalance. For example, if we have

$$A: \sigma \leftarrow 1$$

$$P: \tau \leftarrow \upsilon$$

we can use the second rule for $\bullet$, with $(P, Q) := (A, P)$ and $(\sigma, \tau, \omega, \upsilon) := (\sigma, 1, \tau, \upsilon)$, to deduce

$$A \bullet P : \sigma, \tau \leftarrow \upsilon \quad .$$

If we compute the types of $A \| P$ and A, P, we find in both cases the same type.

It is possible to merge each of the rule pairs by introducing a (partial) tuple 'subtraction' operation, akin to $\div$ on naturals. By building up a small theory for this operation it becomes possible to prove, for example, that the expressions $(P \bullet Q) \bullet R$ and $P \bullet (Q \bullet R)$ (if any of the two is typable) have the same type without the extensive case analysis that would otherwise be required.

12. Laws

We sum up here, without proof, some important laws for the combinators $\bullet$, $\|$ and $,$. We need a convenient way to denote conditions on the laws.

The notation $P \preccurlyeq Q$ means: the in-width of P is at most the out-width of Q. Similarly, $P \succcurlyeq Q$ means that the in-width of P is at least the out-width of Q. Equality of these widths is denoted as $P \rightleftharpoons Q$. The composition in $P \bullet Q$ is balanced if and only if $P \rightleftharpoons Q$. Note that these relations are not transitive, and that $\rightleftharpoons$ is not reflexive. However,

$$(P \preccurlyeq Q) \wedge (P \succcurlyeq Q)$$

equivales

$$P \rightleftharpoons Q \quad .$$

If A occurs, it stands for a source. The letter denotes (implicitly) the condition $A \rightleftharpoons \mathrm{id}_0$.

    (L0) $\bullet$, $\|$ and $,$ are associative, with identity element id_0

    (L1) $\mathrm{id}_{m+n} = \mathrm{id}_m \| \mathrm{id}_n$

(L2) If $id_m \leqslant P$, then $id_m \cdot P = P$

(L3) If $P \geqslant id_n$, then $P \cdot id_n = P$

(L4) $\perp_{m+n} = \perp_m \| \perp_n$

(L5) If $id_0 \asymp P \asymp id_n$, then $P = \perp_n$

(L6) $A \cdot P = A\|P = A,P$

(L7) $P\|A = P,A$

(L8) $P \cdot \perp_n = \perp_n\|P$

(L9) If $p \asymp q$ and $P \asymp Q$, then $(p \cdot q)\|(P \cdot Q) = p\|P \cdot q\|Q$

(L10) If $P \asymp Q$, then $P \cdot Q\|R = (P \cdot Q)\|R = P\|R \cdot Q$

(L11) If $id_m \asymp P$, then $P\|Q = id_m\|Q \cdot P$

(L12) If $P \geqslant id_n$, then $\perp_n,P = P,\perp_n = P$

(L13) If $P \leqslant Q$, then $(P \cdot Q),R = P \cdot Q,R$

(L14) If in-width $P \leqslant$ in-width Q, then $P,(Q\|R) = (P,Q)\|R$

(L15) If $P \asymp R$ and $Q \asymp R$, then $P,Q \cdot R = (P \cdot R),(Q \cdot R)$

These laws do not constitute a carefully selected set; it would be interesting to create a nice (independent and complete) set of basic laws. The criterion for inclusion above was more practically inspired. For example, (L11) is essentially a variant of (L10). It is included because it is often applicable in this form, and saves us then one rather trivial step.

13. FORMULAE AND SECTIONS.

We introduce some special notations concerning operators, that is, functions denoted by special symbols (non-tags). Throughout this section the variable $\oplus$ stands for an operator with in-width $m+n$, and P and Q for functions with, respectively, out-width m and n. Furthermore, A and B denote sources, also with, respectively, out-width m and n. We define:

$$P \oplus Q = \oplus \cdot P,Q$$

$$P \oplus = \oplus \cdot P\|id_n$$

$$\oplus Q = \oplus \cdot id_m\|Q$$

All the compositions involved are balanced. The first form, in which two 'operands' are supplied, is called a 'formula'. The next two forms are a 'left section' and a 'right section'. If the expressions for the operands P or Q are not simple tags, they must be enclosed in parentheses to prevent ambiguities. This is also needed if they are themselves operators: does $\oplus \otimes$ mean $\otimes \cdot (\oplus\|id)$ or $\oplus \cdot (id\|\otimes)$? The first meaning can be specified by $(\oplus)\otimes$, and the second by $\oplus(\otimes)$. However, if $\oplus$ is an associative operator (see below), then the meaning of $(\oplus)\oplus$, and $\oplus(\oplus)$ is the same (and, as follows from (L16) below, equal to $\oplus \cdot \oplus$), and it is harmless then to drop the parentheses.

These special notations are useful for various reasons. In the first place, algebraic properties from the 'value world' are inherited in the function world. For example, in the usual definition of $\oplus: \sigma \leftarrow \sigma,\sigma$ being associative, namely

$$a\oplus(b\oplus c) = (a\oplus b)\oplus c \quad ,$$

the operands are assumed to range over all values of the type σ. Now this is equivalent to the property that

$$F\oplus(G\oplus H) = (F\oplus G)\oplus H \quad ,$$

where this time the operands range over all *functions* with out-type σ. Symmetry (commutativity) and idempotence are likewise inherited.

A second reason for having these notations is that they encode (implicitly) information about the widths. This makes it possible to formulate laws that can be applied without having to verify width conditions separately.

Here are some laws for formulae and sections with a source as operand.

(L16) $\quad A\oplus \quad = \quad \oplus \cdot A$

(L17) $\quad A\oplus Q \quad = \quad A\oplus \cdot Q$

(L18) $\quad P\oplus B \quad = \quad \oplus B \cdot P$

We show how these laws can be derived. For (L16):

$\qquad A\oplus$

$= \quad \{$ definition of left section $\}$

$\qquad \oplus \cdot A \| \mathrm{id}_n$

$= \quad \{$ (L6) $\}$

$\qquad \oplus \cdot A \cdot \mathrm{id}_n$

$= \quad \{$ (L0), (L2) $\}$

$\qquad \oplus \cdot A \quad .$

Now (L17) is easily derived:

$\qquad A\oplus Q$

$= \quad \{$ definition of formula $\}$

$\qquad \oplus \cdot A,Q$

$= \quad \{$ (L6) $\}$

$\qquad \oplus \cdot A \cdot Q$

$= \quad \{(L16)\}$

$\quad A \oplus \cdot Q \quad .$

For (L18) we have:

$\quad P \oplus B$

$= \quad \{\text{ definition of formula }\}$

$\quad \oplus \cdot P,B$

$= \quad \{(L7)\}$

$\quad \oplus \cdot P\|B$

$= \quad \{(L11)\}$

$\quad \oplus \cdot \text{id}_m\|B \cdot P$

$= \quad \{\text{ definition of right section }\}$

$\quad \oplus B \cdot P \quad .$

It is often desirable to have the mirrored version of an operator also available as an operator. Here we encounter a (not entirely unexpected) weakness of the tuple view adopted. What we want, basically, given an operator

$\quad \oplus: \sigma \leftarrow \tau,\upsilon \quad ,$

is to define a mirrored version

$\quad \widetilde{\oplus}: \sigma \leftarrow \upsilon,\tau \quad ,$

which is also an operator. However, the type former , leaves no seam when joining two tuple types, so it is not possible to define once and for all, for all operators, what the meaning of mirroring is. In many cases, however, the desired split in τ,υ is clear enough; often it will be in the middle, either because the in-type is of the form α,β, with width 2, or of the form σ,σ. In any case, we assume here that we know how the in-type of $\oplus$ should be split, namely into τ and υ, and that the width of τ is m and that of υ is n. Then, by definition,

$$\widetilde{\oplus} \;=\; (\perp_n\|\text{id}_m) \oplus (\text{id}_n\|\perp_m) \quad .$$

We have:

$$Q \,\widetilde{\oplus}\, P \;=\; P \oplus Q \quad ,$$

$$\widetilde{\oplus} P \;=\; P \oplus \quad ,$$

$$Q \,\widetilde{\oplus}\; \;=\; \oplus Q \quad .$$

14. LOCKING

We come now to a box construction that is less combinatorial in nature, called *locking*. Locking resembles lambda abstraction and 'quoting' (as in LISP), but also currying.

Let P be a function of type $\sigma \leftarrow \tau, \omega$, and let n denote the width of τ. Then we can 'lock' P, leaving in-type τ, by writing

$$\langle P \bullet ?_n \rangle : (\sigma \leftarrow \omega) \leftarrow \tau \quad .$$

The notation will shortly be explained, but first the meaning. This is a higher-order function; if fed with a τ-tuple, it produces a box (function) of type $\sigma \leftarrow \omega$. This box, when provided with an ω-tuple, yields that result that is produced by P when presented the τ-cum-ω-tuple in one go.

Now the notation. The $?_n$ is a *dummy*, or placeholder, for the τ-portion of the argument to P. Dummies are *only* allowed inside a $\langle \cdots \rangle$ form, called a locked expression, or for short a *lock*. *Within* that form, it is a box expression, formally typed

$$?_n : \vec{a}^n \leftarrow 1$$

(in which the polymorphic type may be refined to some more specific type like $\tau \leftarrow 1$ for P above). So a dummy is formally a source. We put further

$$?_{m+n} \;=\; ?_m \| ?_n \;=\; ?_m \bullet ?_n \;=\; ?_m, ?_n \quad ,$$

and use $?$ for $?_1$. Furthermore, $?_0 = \mathrm{id}_0$, and so it may be eliminated as being the identity of each of the combinators.

The information in the subscript n of $?_n$ is crucial. For example, if we have $P \colon \alpha \leftarrow \beta, \gamma$, we can form three different locks:

$$\langle P \rangle : \qquad (\alpha \leftarrow \beta, \gamma) \leftarrow 1 \quad ,$$
$$\langle P \bullet ? \rangle : \quad (\alpha \leftarrow \gamma) \leftarrow \beta \quad ,$$
$$\langle P \bullet ?_2 \rangle : \quad (\alpha \leftarrow 1) \leftarrow \beta, \gamma \quad .$$

The *scope* of a dummy is the body of the locked expression in which it occurs, with the exclusion of other locks therein contained. Within its scope, all the laws that apply to sources may be applied to a dummy, such as (L16), giving us

$$? \oplus \;=\; \oplus \bullet ? \quad ,$$

or (L10), giving

$$? \bullet ? \| P \;=\; (? \bullet ?) \| P \;=\; ? \| P \bullet ? \quad .$$

There are important constraints, though. The first is an injunction against swapping dummies. In particular, dummies must not trade places by the rules for a mirrored operator; for example,

$$F \;=\; \langle ? \oplus ? \rangle$$

has in general quite another meaning than

$$G = \langle ?\widetilde{\oplus}? \rangle \quad .$$

If $\oplus$ has type $\alpha \leftarrow \alpha, \beta$, then F would have type

$$(\alpha \leftarrow 1) \leftarrow \alpha, \beta \quad ,$$

whereas G would be typed

$$(\alpha \leftarrow 1) \leftarrow \beta, \alpha \quad .$$

The (L*)-laws given earlier are safe, however, *even if they appear to swap*. An example is provided by (L11), which can be instantiated to give

$$?_n \bullet P = \text{id}_n \| P \bullet ?_n \quad .$$

This allows us to shift dummies around, and it is valid even if P contains dummies. The explanation is that the dummy swap (if any) is only 'optically' present in the linearised box expression, and does not correspond to a swap in the topology of the network. For the human ease of application of rule (L19) given below, it is nevertheless helpful never to swap dummies, whether 'safe' or not.

A similar constraint must be exercised if algebraic properties of boxes are given, not only symmetry, but also having a zero, etc. For example, if for a given function P and given source C the property is known that

$$P \bullet A = C$$

for all sources A of in-width 1, this must not be used to simplify $P \bullet ?$ to C. A valid identity in this case is

$$P \bullet ? = C \bullet \bot \bullet ? \quad ,$$

in which the dummy, although 'sunk', is still visible. Like money, dummies may not be duplicated or embezzled. The (L*)-laws given earlier are also safe in this respect, with the exception of (L15) if the duplicated component contains dummies.

The following law allows moving a function across the boundary of a lock.

(L19) If P and R are dummy-free, and $\text{id}_m \rtimes R \rtimes \text{id}_n$, then

$$\langle P \bullet ?_m \bullet Q \rangle \bullet R = \langle P \bullet R \bullet ?_n \bullet Q \rangle \quad .$$

'Dummy-free' refers to dummies bound to the lock at this level; dummies of locked expressions contained within P or Q do not count. By combining this repeatedly with (L11), a bunch of functions can be moved across in one go. So as not to burden the exposition with excessive notation, here only the version with three functions is given, but the general pattern should be clear enough:

If all Pi and Ri are dummy-free, and $\text{id}_{mi} \rtimes Ri \rtimes \text{id}_{ni}$, then

$$\langle P0 \bullet ?_{m0} \bullet P1 \bullet ?_{m1} \bullet P2 \bullet ?_{m2} \bullet Q \rangle \bullet R0\|R1\|R2$$

$$=$$

$$\langle P0 \bullet R0 \bullet ?_{n0} \bullet P1 \bullet R1 \bullet ?_{n1} \bullet P2 \bullet R2 \bullet ?_{n2} \bullet Q \rangle \quad .$$

By supplying a source of the appropriate width, the body of a locked expression can be made dummy-free. If $P:\sigma \leftarrow \tau$ is dummy-free, then $\langle P \rangle$ has type $(\sigma \leftarrow \tau) \leftarrow 1$, so it is still a higher-order function. Something further is needed to set the locked function free.

15. Unlocking

Unlocking resembles application (or LISP eval), but also serves for uncurrying (when used in a left section). In this last aspect it is the counterpart of locking.

For each pair of naturals m and n we define a generic operator

$$@_{m,n}: \sigma \leftarrow (\sigma \leftarrow \omega), \omega \quad,$$

in which the width of σ is m, and that of ω is n. The semantics are apparent from the type. Note that the in-width of the operator is $n+1$.

Let Q be a function of type $(\sigma \leftarrow \omega) \leftarrow \tau$, and let m and n as before denote the widths of σ and ω. Then we can 'unlock' Q by writing

$$Q @_{m,n}: \sigma \leftarrow \tau, \omega \quad.$$

The information in the subscripts m and n of $@$ is also contained in the type of its left operand. If this information is known from the context, the subscripts may be dropped. The notation $Q @$ implies then that Q has out-width 1, its out-type being some function type. Note, however, that more information is needed here than just the in- and out-width of Q, in particular the in-width of its out-type. By repeated unlocking, this need to know the widths can go arbitrarily deep into the type.

The major relationship linking unlocking with locking is given by:

(L20) If P is dummy-free, and $P \preccurlyeq \mathrm{id}_n$, then

$$\langle P \bullet ?_n \rangle @ = P \quad.$$

We also have, so to speak, the converse of (L20), which allows us to express any higher-order function explicitly as a lock:

(L21) If Q has a function type as out-type, and in-width n, then

$$Q = \langle Q @ \bullet ?_n \rangle \quad.$$

16. Discussion

The objectives that had been set out at the start seem to have been achieved: the system is indeed centred around composition, is not opposed to typing, and has a relatively fair-handed treatment of, for example, both operand positions of an operator. The system comes with a rich (perhaps *too* rich) set of laws. If we use the names for values of the value world to name the corresponding sources in the function world, we get 'apposition' and 'lifting' for free, without the earlier semantic ambiguities.

A price is paid for all this—it is seldom that something really comes for free. In this case the price consists of conditions on most of the laws that are boring to verify.

The interest, if any, of this system is probably not in its theoretical properties. It has been constructed with a practical purpose in mind. The final judgment, therefore, must be how well it stands up in actual use. In particular, the question is if the additional convenience of the improved manipulability outweighs the inconvenience of the application conditions. As of now, the system has not yet been put to demanding tests. Some simple tests have been passed, but a lot more is needed before it can go into beta-test. The version presented here is not the first version; almost all notations, and several of the definitions, have undergone minor or sometimes dramatic changes since the inception of this line of research, and some combinators included at some time have been abandoned. In each case, the guiding principle has been to increase manipulability.

Several shortcomings are known that have not been pointed out. Some cherished notations of the formalism that served as the starting point, and also as a point of reference, do not fit in well. Most notable are the reduce notation, $\oplus/$, and the map notation, $f*$. The problem is that the operators $/$ and $*$ are not composed with, but applied to the (functional) operands. The notations introduced in this paper would require writing these as $\langle\oplus\rangle/$ and $\langle f\rangle*$, which is unacceptable. It is possible to introduce a special exemption here, which is kludgy, or to generalise this in some way, which unfortunately takes away some of the present simplicity of the system. Although in many cases less administrative overhead is needed than with any of several alternatives tried, and most of the time not even the surrogate variables provided by the dummies of a lock are needed, there are some examples where dummy variables do the job noticeably better than the anonymous ?-dummies used here. (A 'proof by picture' assigns essentially a name to the anonymous data, if only in the form of a pair of positions connected by a line on paper.)

Under the most liberal (semantic) definition of type-correctness, it is not decidable if an expression formed in this system can be typed. In each decidable typing discipline, some semantically unproblematic expressions are untypable. Without some restriction (as by a suitable typing), it is also undecidable if expressions are equivalent, and so there cannot be some canonical normal form. This is just as in the lambda calculus. It seems that next to locking and unlocking, also at least some duplicating Λ_n-function, possibly disguised as (id‖id), is a necessary ingredient for the undecidability results.

Acknowledgements

The work reported here could not have been done without the inspiration provided by the unrelenting criticism of Richard Bird, but also, and much more so, by the elegant way in which he forged some of my earlier stumbling approaches into fine tools. It should be clear, however, that he is entirely without blame concerning the combinatorial tricks perpetrated here. Further inspiration came from many people, including Jeroen Fokker, Maarten Fokkinga, Netty van Gasteren, Johan Jeuring,

Doaitse Swierstra, Nico Verwer, Jaap van der Woude, and Hans Zantema. The supportive context provided by the STOP project, sponsored by the Dutch National Facility for Informatics (NFI) and the Netherlands organization for scientific research (NWO), is gratefully acknowledged.

REFERENCES
1. R. S. BIRD. An introduction to the Theory of Lists. *Logic of Programming and Calculi of Discrete Design* (M. Broy, ed.) 5-42. NATO ASI Series Vol. F36, 1987. Springer-Verlag.
2. R. S. BIRD. *Lectures on Constructive Functional Programming*. Lecture notes, International Summer School on Constructive Methods in Computing Science, Marktoberdorff, 1988.
3. E. W. DIJKSTRA, W. H. J. FEIJEN. *A Method of Programming*. Addison-Wesley, 1988.
4. L. MEERTENS. Algorithmics—Towards programming as a mathematical activity. *Proc. CWI Symp. on Mathematics and Computer Science*, CWI Monographs Vol. 1 (J. W. de Bakker, M. Hazewinkel and J. K. Lenstra, eds.) 289 – 334, North-Holland, 1986.

SPECIFICATIONS OF CONCURRENTLY ACCESSED DATA*

Jayadev Misra
Department of Computer Sciences
The University of Texas at Austin
Austin, Texas 78712
(512) 471-9547
misra@cs.utexas.edu

1 Introduction

An object and its associated operations may be specified in many ways. One way is to give an abstract representation of the object data structure (viz., representing a queue by a sequence) and the effects of various operations on this abstract representation [3,4,5]. Another way [2] is to leave the representation aspects unspecified but to give a set of equations that relate the effects of various operations (the equations define a congruence relation in a term algebra). The common goal of a specification, however, is to serve as a legal document that spells out a contract between a user and an implementer: The user may assume no more about an object than what is specified and the implementer must satisfy the specification through his implementation.

We view specification not merely as a legal contract but additionally as a means (1) to deduce properties of a specified object, (2) to deduce properties of other objects in which the specified object is a component (i.e., inheritance of properties) and (3) to implement the object by stepwise refinement of its specification. Therefore we require that a specification not merely be formal but also be in a form that admits of effective manipulation. This requirement rules out many specification schemes in which a program fragment, in some high level language, is used as a specification; typically such program fragments cannot be manipulated effectively.

In many specification schemes it is assumed that (1) each operation on an object is deterministic (i.e., applying the operation to a given state of the object results in a unique next state and/or unique values being returned), (2) an operation once started always terminates in every state of the object, and (3) operations are not applied concurrently. In many cases of interest arising in

---

*Partially supported by ONR Contracts N00014-86-K-0763 and N00014-87-K-0510, by a fellowship from The John Simon Guggenheim Foundation, and by a grant from The University of Texas URI-FRA.

applications such as operating systems, process control systems and concurrent databases, these assumptions are rarely met.

The purpose of this paper is to propose a specification scheme which allows effective manipulations of specifications and admits of nondeterministic, nonterminating and concurrent operations on objects. The method is illustrated by studying one example—a first-in-first-out queue, or a *buffer*—in detail.

A buffer object acts as an intermediary between a producer and a consumer, temporarily storing the data items output by the producer and later delivering them to the consumer. The buffer object is required to (1) deliver data in the same order to the consumer as they were received from the producer, (2) receive data from the producer provided its internal buffer spaces are nonfull, and (3) upon demand, send data to the consumer provided its internal buffer spaces are nonempty. Requests from the producer and the consumer may be processed concurrently: The producer is delayed until there is some space in the buffer and the consumer is delayed until there is some data item in the buffer. Observe that a request from the producer, to add a data item to the buffer may not terminate if the buffer remains full forever, and similarly, a request from the consumer may not terminate if the buffer remains empty forever.

The specification mechanism is based on "UNITY logic" as in Chandy and Misra [1]. We give a brief description of the notation and the appropriate concepts of the logic in the next section. Specifications in this notation have proved to be surprisingly succinct; for the buffer example, the specification consists of the three properties given above plus the description of the assumed protocol for data production and consumption. The inference rules of UNITY logic can be applied to deduce properties from specifications and to prove correctness of implementations. For instance, in Section 4 we show that concatenations of two buffers of sizes M and N result in a buffer of size $M + N$.

We give a brief introduction to UNITY in Section 2 including all the notations and logic to understand this paper. We describe a buffer program informally and then formally using UNITY logic, in Section 3. We demonstrate the usefulness of this specification in Section 4 by showing that the concatenation of two buffers of sizes M and N implements a buffer of size $M + N$. (The proof is given in some detail to emphasize that such proofs need not be excessively long or tedious, as is often the case with formal proofs.) A refinement of this specification, as a first step toward an implementation, is proposed in Section 5. The refined specification is used to implement a program in Section 6; its correctness is obvious (in fact, it follows almost mechanically) from the refinement suggested in Section 5. We close with a brief summary in Section 7. Some of the proofs are in Appendices A and B.

2 A Brief Introduction to UNITY

A UNITY program consists of (1) declarations of variables, (2) a description of their initial values and (3) a finite set of statements. We shall not describe the program syntax except briefly in Section 6 of this paper because it is unnecessary for understanding this paper. However an operational description of the execution of a program is helpful in understanding the logical operators introduced later in this section.

An initial state of a program is a state in which all variables have their specified initial values (there can be several possible initial states if the initial values of some variables are not specified). In a step of program execution an arbitrary statement is selected and executed. Execution of every statement terminates in every program state. (This assumption is met in our model by restricting the statements to assignment statements only, where function calls, if any, must be guaranteed to terminate.) A program execution consists of an infinite number of steps in which each statement is executed infinitely often.

This program model captures many notions useful for programming such as: synchrony, by allowing several variable values to be modified by a single (atomic) statement; asynchrony, by specifying little about the order in which the individual statements are executed; processes communicating through shared variables, by partitioning the statements of the program into subsets and identifying a process with a subset; processes communicating via messages, by restricting the manner in which shared variables are accessed and modified, etc. We shall not describe these aspects of the model; however, it will become apparent from the buffer example that process networks can be described effectively within this model.

2.1 UNITY logic

Three logical operators, *unless*, *ensures*, and *leads-to*, are at the core of UNITY logic. Each of these is a binary relation on predicates; *unless* is used to describe the safety properties, and the other two to describe progress properties of a program.

Notation: Throughout this paper p, q, r denote predicates which may name program variables, bound variables and free variables (that are neither program variables nor bound variables). ▽

2.1.1 unless

For a given program

p *unless* q

denotes that once predicate p is true it remains true at least as long as q is not true. Formally (using Hoare's notation)

p *unless* q $\equiv$

$\langle$ for all statements s of the program :: $\{p \wedge \neg q\}$ s $\{p \vee q\}\rangle$

i.e., if $p \wedge \neg q$ holds prior to execution of any statement of the program then $p \vee q$ holds following the execution of the statement.

It follows from this definition that if p holds and q does not hold in a program state then in the next state either q holds, or $p \wedge \neg q$ holds; hence, by induction on the number of statement executions, $p \wedge \neg q$ continues to hold as long as q does not hold. Note that it is possible for $p \wedge \neg q$ to hold forever. Also note that if $\neg p \vee q$ holds in a state then p *unless* q does not tell us anything about future states.

Notation: We write $\langle \forall u :: P.u \rangle$ and $\langle \exists u :: P.u \rangle$ for universal quantification of u in $P.u$ and existential quantification of u in $P.u$, respectively. The dummy u could denote a variable, a statement in a program, or even a program. Any property having a free variable (i.e., a variable that is neither bound nor a program variable) is assumed to be universally quantified over all possible values of the variable. Thus,

$u = k$ *unless* $u > k$

where k is free, is a shorthand for

$\langle \forall k :: u = k$ *unless* $u > k \rangle$. ∇

Examples:

1. Integer variable u does not decrease.

   For all integer k:

   $u = k$ *unless* $u > k$

   or, $u \geq k$ *unless* *false*

2. A message is received (i.e., predicate $rcvd$ holds) only if it had been sent earlier (i.e., predicate $sent$ already holds).

   $\neg rcvd$ *unless* *sent* ∇

Example (Defining Auxiliary Variables)

Let u be an integer-valued variable and let v count the number of times u's value has been changed during the course of a program execution. The value of v is completely defined by initially $\quad v = 0$

$u = m \ \land \ v = n \quad unless \quad u \neq m \ \land \ v = n + 1$

The traditional way to define v, given a program in which u is a variable, is to augment the program text with the assignment,

$v \ := \ v + 1$

whenever u's value is changed; v is called an auxiliary variable. Our way of defining v, without appealing to the program text, is preferable because it provides a direct relationship between u and v which may be exploited in specifications and proofs. $\qquad\qquad\qquad\qquad\qquad\qquad \triangledown$

2.1.2 Stable, Invariant

Two special cases of *unless* are of importance. The predicate p *unless false*, from definition, denotes that p remains true forever once it becomes true; we write, "p is stable" as a shorthand for "p *unless false* ." If p holds in every initial state and p is stable then p holds in every state during any execution; we then say that "p is invariant."

2.1.3 ensures

For a given program,

$p \ ensures \ q$

implies that p *unless* q holds for the program and if p holds at any point in the execution of the program then q holds eventually. Formally,

$p \ ensures \ q \ \equiv$
$\qquad p \ unless \ q \ \land \ \langle \exists \ \text{statement} \ s \ :: \ \{p \ \land \ \neg q\} \ s \ \{q\} \rangle \ .$

It follows from this definition that once p is true it remains true at least as long as q is not true (from p *unless* q). Furthermore, from the rules of program execution, statement s will be executed sometime after p becomes true. If q is still false prior to the execution of s then $p \land \neg q$ holds and the execution of s establishes q.

2.1.4 leads-to

For a given program, p *leads-to* q, abbreviated as $p \mapsto q$, denotes that once p is true, q is or becomes true. Unlike *ensures*, p may not remain true until q becomes true. The relation *leads-to* is defined inductively by the following rules. The first rule is the basis for the inductive definition of *leads-to*. The second rule states that *leads-to* is a transitive relation. In the third rule, $p.m$, for different m, denote a set of predicates. This rule states that if every predicate in a set *leads-to* q then their disjunction also *leads-to* q.

(basis)

$$\frac{p \ \ ensures \ \ q}{p \ \mapsto \ q}$$

(transitivity)

$$\frac{p \ \mapsto \ q \ , \ q \ \mapsto \ r}{p \ \mapsto \ r}$$

(disjunction)

$$\frac{\langle \forall \ m \ :: \ p.m \ \mapsto \ q \rangle}{\langle \exists \ m \ :: \ p.m \rangle \ \mapsto \ q}$$

Notes on Inference Rules

We have explained the meaning of each logical operator in terms of program execution. However, neither the definitions nor our proofs make any mention of program execution. We use only the definitions, and a few rules derived from these definitions, in proofs; we believe that our proofs are succinct because we avoid operational arguments about program executions.

2.1.5 Derived Rules

The following rules for *unless* are used in this paper; for their proofs, see [1].

(consequence weakening)

$$\frac{p \ \ unless \ \ q \ , \ q \ \Rightarrow \ r}{p \ \ unless \ \ r}$$

(conjunction)

$$\frac{p \ \ unless \ \ q \ , \ p' \ \ unless \ \ q'}{p \ \wedge \ p' \ \ unless \ \ (p \ \wedge \ q') \ \vee \ (p' \ \wedge \ q) \ \vee \ (q \ \wedge \ q')}$$

The following rule and its corollaries appear in [6].

(general disjunction)

$$\frac{\langle \forall \ i \ :: \ p.i \ \ unless \ \ q.i \rangle}{\langle \exists \ i \ :: \ p.i \rangle \ \ unless \ \ \langle \forall \ i \ :: \ \neg p.i \ \vee \ q.i \rangle \ \wedge \ \langle \exists \ i \ :: \ q.i \rangle}$$

Corollary 1 (free variable elimination): Let u denote a set of program variables and k a free variable that does not appear in p or q.

$$\frac{p \wedge u = k \ \ unless \ \ q}{p \ \ unless \ \ q}$$

Corollary 2

$$\frac{p \wedge u = k \ \ unless \ \ p \wedge u \neq k}{p \ is \ stable}$$

We use the following results about *leads-to*.

(Implication)

$$\frac{p \Rightarrow q}{p \mapsto q}$$

Hence, using the transitivity of *leads-to*,

Corollary 3

$$\frac{p \Rightarrow p', \ p' \mapsto q', \ q' \Rightarrow q}{p \mapsto q}$$

The following rule allows us to deduce a progress property from another progress property and a safety property.

(PSP)

$$\frac{p \mapsto q, \ r \ \ unless \ b}{p \wedge r \mapsto (q \wedge r) \vee b}$$

2.1.6 Substitution Axiom

Substitution axiom allows us to replace an invariant by "true" and vice versa, in any predicate. Thus if I is an invariant and it is required to prove that

$$p \mapsto q \wedge I$$

it suffices to prove

$$p \mapsto q.$$

It is important to note that when several programs are composed (see Section 2.2) the invariant that can be substituted is an invariant of the composite program.

Due to the close relationship between invariants and theorems (or tautologies) we often write,

$$p$$

instead of

p is invariant.

2.2 Program Composition through *union*

Given two programs F, G, their *union*, written $F \parallel G$, is obtained by appending their codes together: the initial conditions of both F, G are satisfied in $F \parallel G$ (and hence, we assume that initial conditions of F, G are not contradictory) and the set of statements of $F \parallel G$ is the union of the statements of F and G.

Programs F, G may be thought of as executing asynchronously in $F \parallel G$. The union operator is useful for understanding process networks where each process may be viewed as a program and the entire network is their union; in this view, the buffer program, the producer, and the consumer are composed through the union operator to form a system.

The following theorem is fundamental for understanding union. It says that an *unless* property holds in $F \parallel G$ iff it holds in both F and G; an *ensures* property holds in $F \parallel G$ iff the corresponding *unless* property holds in both components and the *ensures* property holds in at least one component. (When there are multiple programs we write the program name with a property, such as p *unless* q in F.)

Union Theorem:

$$p \text{ } unless \text{ } q \quad \text{in } F \parallel G \equiv p \text{ } unless \text{ } q \quad \text{in } F \wedge p \text{ } unless \text{ } q \quad \text{in } G$$
$$p \text{ } ensures \text{ } q \text{ in } F \parallel G \equiv (p \text{ } unless \text{ } q \quad \text{in } F \wedge p \text{ } ensures \text{ } q \text{ in } G)$$
$$\vee \text{ } (p \text{ } ensures \text{ } q \quad \text{in } F \wedge p \text{ } unless \text{ } q \quad \text{in } G)$$

Corollary 1:

$$\frac{p \text{ } unless \text{ } q \text{ in } F \text{ , } p \text{ is stable } \text{in } G}{p \text{ } unless \text{ } q \quad \text{in } F \parallel G}$$

Corollary 2:

$$\frac{p \text{ } ensures \text{ } q \quad \text{in } F \text{ , } p \text{ is stable } \text{in } G}{p \text{ } ensures \text{ } q \quad \text{in } F \parallel G}$$

Note: If predicate p names only local variables of F (i.e., the variables that can be modified only in F) then p is stable in every other program G. $\qquad\qquad\qquad\qquad\qquad \triangledown$

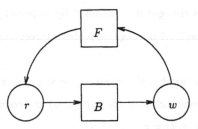

Figure 1: A Buffer Program B and its environment F

We shall also use properties of the following form in the specification of F, where P, Q are arbitrary properties. In the following, G is quantified over programs:

$$\langle \forall G :: (P \text{ in } G) \Rightarrow (Q \text{ in } F \,[\!] \, G) \rangle$$

This says that if P is a property of any program G then Q is a property of $F \,[\!] \, G$. This is a convenient way of specifying the properties of the environment with which F may be composed and the resulting properties of the composite program. This kind of specification will be crucial in describing a buffer, because the buffer program assumes certain properties of its environment.

3 The Buffer Program

A buffer program, B, reads data from a variable r and writes data into a variable w. The program runs asynchronously with another program, called F, which writes into r and reads from w. The communication structure is shown in Fig. 1.

The program F represents both the producer and the consumer. There might be multiple producers and consumers or even a single process that is both the producer and the consumer; the exact number is irrelevant for the specification of the buffer. The values that can be written into r, w are, again, irrelevant for specification. However we do postulate a special value, $\emptyset$, which is written into a variable to denote that it is "empty," i.e., it contains no useful data. The protocol for reading and writing is as follows. Program F writes into r only if $r = \emptyset$; only if $r \neq \emptyset$, program B reads a value from r and it may set r to $\emptyset$. Program B stores a value in w only if w is $\emptyset$; program F reads from w and it may set w to $\emptyset$ to indicate that it is ready to consume the next piece of data. (This is an informal description; the goal of the specification is to make this formal.)

3.1 Auxiliary Variables

For a program variable u, let $\bar{u}$ denote the sequence of all data items (non-$\emptyset$ values) written into u. The variable $\bar{u}$ is an auxiliary variable that is typically defined by augmenting the program text appropriately: Whenever u is changed $\bar{u}$ is modified by appending the (new) value of u to it. As shown in an example in Section 2.1.1 our logic provides a direct way of defining $\bar{u}$ without appealing to the program text.

In the following, d is a free variable of the same type as u, x is a free variable of the same type as $\bar{u}$ (i.e., x is any sequence of items each from the type of u) and concatenation operator for sequences is ";". By convention $(\emptyset; x) = (x; \emptyset) = x$.

Variable $\bar{u}$ is defined by

> initially $\quad \bar{u} = u$
>
> $\bar{u} = x \ \wedge \ u = d \ \ unless \ \ \bar{u} = x; u \ \wedge \ u \neq d$

To understand the relationship between u and $\bar{u}$ note that $\bar{u}$ remains unchanged as long as u is unchanged and $\bar{u}$ is changed by appending the (new) value of u to it whenever u is changed. Note that if $\emptyset$ is stored in u (i.e., data is consumed from u) then $\bar{u}$ remains unchanged (because $(x; u) = (x; \emptyset) = x$).

For the buffer example, we define $\bar{r}, \bar{w}$ analogously.

> initially $\quad (\bar{r}, \bar{w}) \ = (r, w)$ in $B \parallel F$ $\hspace{3cm}$ (A0)
>
> $\bar{r} = x \ \wedge \ r = d \quad unless \quad \bar{r} = x; r \ \wedge \ r \neq d \ $ in $B \parallel F$ $\hspace{1.5cm}$ (A1)
>
> $\bar{w} = y \ \wedge \ w = e \quad unless \quad \bar{w} = y; w \ \wedge \ w \neq e \ $ in $B \parallel F$ $\hspace{1.5cm}$ (A2)

These properties, A0,A1,A2, may be taken as axioms in a proof of $B \parallel F$.

3.2 Specification of a Buffer of Size N

A buffer of size N, $N \geq 1$, has $N - 1$ internal words for storage. (The reason for using $N - 1$, rather than N, is that with this definition concatenations of buffers of size M, N results in a buffer of size $M + N$.) For $N = 1$, the buffer program moves data from r to w directly.

Notation: All through this paper d, e, f refer to arbitrary data values and x, y denote sequences of these values. Define an ordering relation, $\prec$, among data values as follows:

> $\emptyset$ is "smaller than" all non-$\emptyset$ values, i.e.,
>
> $\quad d \prec e \ \equiv \ d = \emptyset \wedge e \neq \emptyset$ $\hspace{6cm}$ ∇

The properties P1 and P2, given below, state respectively that program B removes only non-$\emptyset$ data from r and it may set r to $\emptyset$, and it writes only non-$\emptyset$ data values in w provided $w = \emptyset$.

initially $w = \emptyset$ in B (P0)

$r = d$ *unless* $r \prec d$ in B (P1)

$w = e$ *unless* $e \prec w$ in B (P2)

Observe that setting d to $\emptyset$ in (P1) gives us (because $r \prec \emptyset \equiv false$),

$r = \emptyset$ is stable   in B

That is, B never changes r from $\emptyset$ to non-$\emptyset$. Similarly, we may deduce from (P2) that B never overwrites a non-$\emptyset$ value in w.

The next property, P3, says that (1) the sequence of data items stored in w by B is a prefix of the sequence supplied to it in r, (2) these two sequence lengths do not differ by more than N, the buffer size, (3) if the two sequences differ by less than N in length (i.e., internal buffer is nonfull) then data, if any, would be removed from r, (4) if more items have been supplied to B than have been produced then w is or will be set to a non-$\emptyset$ value. These properties, however, cannot hold if program F, with which B is composed, is uncooperative; for instance, if F overwrites a data value in r with another data value then B can never reproduce the overwritten value in w. Hence these properties—collectively called the conclusion for B, or $B.conc$—hold conditioned upon two properties of F—collectively called the hypothesis for B, or $B.hypo$—that F writes a value into r only if r is $\emptyset$ and F sets w only to $\emptyset$.

Notation: $|\bar{r}|, |\bar{w}|$ denote the lengths of $\bar{r}, \bar{w}$, respectively. $\triangledown$

The property (P3) is,

$\langle \forall F :: B.hypo$ in F $\Rightarrow$ $B.conc$ in $B \, [\!] \, F \rangle$ (P3)

where,

     $B.hypo$ :: $r = d$ *unless* $d \prec r$,

               $w = e$ *unless* $w \prec e$

and,

     $B.conc$ :: $\bar{w} \subseteq \bar{r}$,

               $|\bar{r}| \leq |\bar{w}| + N$,

               $|\bar{r}| < |\bar{w}| + N$ $\longmapsto$ $r = \emptyset$,

               $|\bar{r}| > |\bar{w}|$ $\longmapsto$ $w \neq \emptyset$

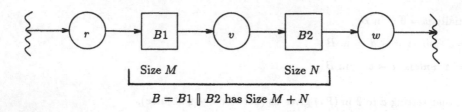

$$B = B1 \parallel B2 \text{ has Size } M + N$$

Figure 2: Concatenations of buffers $B1, B2$

Note that P3 is a property of program B. It says that if B is composed with *any* program F that satisfies $B.hypo$, then $B \parallel F$ satisfies $B.conc$. Also observe that $B.hypo$ is symmetric with (P1,P2), because the protocols for production and consumption by F are symmetric with those of B, with the roles of r, w interchanged.

This specification makes no commitment about the internal structure of the buffer program. For instance, the buffer program may choose to arrange its internal data in a number of possible ways— linear linked list/circular linked list/array of the appropriate length—and move data internally in various ways. Similarly, little assumption is made about the internal structure of F.

We derive some properties of a buffer in Appendix A.

4   Buffer Concatenation

Let $B1$ be a buffer of size M with input, output words, r and v, respectively, and $B2$ be a buffer of size N with input, output words v and w, respectively. We show that $B = B1 \parallel B2$ implements a buffer of size $M + N$ with input, output words r and w, respectively. The arrangement is shown pictorially in Fig. 2. Observe that r and w are different words (i.e., $B1, B2$ are not connected cyclically) and hence, r cannot be accessed by $B2$ nor can w be accessed by $B1$.

4.1   Proof of P0 for B

Trivially, from P0 of $B2$.

4.2   Proof of P1,P2 for B

We are given

$$r = d \quad unless \quad r \prec d \quad \text{in } B1 \qquad \text{(P1 for } B1)$$
$$v = f \quad unless \quad f \prec v \quad \text{in } B1 \qquad \text{(P2 for } B1)$$

.nd

$v = f$ *unless* $v \prec f$ in $B2$ (P1 for $B2$)

$w = e$ *unless* $e \prec w$ in $B2$ (P2 for $B2$)

We have to show, P1,P2 for B, where $B = B1 \,[\!]\, B2$:

$r = d$ *unless* $r \prec d$ in B (P1 for B)

$w = e$ *unless* $e \prec w$ in B (P2 for B)

We only show the proof of P1; P2's proof is nearly identical.

$r = d$ *unless* $r \prec d$ in $B1$, from P1 of $B1$

$r = d$ is stable   in $B2$, r is not accessible to $B2$

$r = d$ *unless* $r \prec d$ in $B1 \,[\!]\, B2$, Corollary 1 to union theorem (Sec. 2.2)

4.3   Proof of P3 for B

We are required to prove P3 for B assuming P3 for $B1$ and $B2$ (and also using P1,P2 for both $B1, B2$). More precisely, we have to show:

$$\langle \forall\, G \;::\; B1.hypo \quad \text{in } G \;\Rightarrow\; B1.conc \quad \text{in } B1 \,[\!]\, G \rangle$$

$$\wedge \; \langle \forall\, H \;::\; B2.hypo \quad \text{in } H \;\Rightarrow\; B2.conc \quad \text{in } B2 \,[\!]\, H \rangle$$

$$\Rightarrow \; \langle \forall\, F \;::\; B.hypo \quad \text{in } F \;\Rightarrow\; B.conc \quad \text{in } B \,[\!]\, F \rangle$$

Equivalently,

$$\langle \forall\, F \;::\; B.hypo \quad \text{in } F \;\wedge\; \langle \forall\, G \;::\; B1.hypo \quad \text{in } G \Rightarrow B1.conc \quad \text{in } B1 \,[\!]\, G \rangle$$

$$\wedge \; \langle \forall\, H \;::\; B2.hypo \quad \text{in } H \Rightarrow B2.conc \quad \text{in } B2 \,[\!]\, H \rangle$$

$$\Rightarrow \; B.conc \quad \text{in } B \,[\!]\, F \tag{1}$$

$$\rangle$$

The properties $B1.hypo$, $B1.conc$ (and similarly $B2.hypo$, $B2.conc$) are obtained from $B.hypo$, $B.conc$ of Section 3.2 by replacing w by v; these are shown below.

$B1.hypo \;::\; r = d$ *unless* $d \prec r$,

$\qquad\qquad v = f$ *unless* $v \prec f$,

$B1.conc \;::\; \bar{v} \subseteq \bar{r}$,

$\qquad\qquad |\bar{r}| \leq |\bar{v}| + M$,

$$|\bar{r}| < |\bar{v}| + M \;\mapsto\; r = \emptyset,$$
$$|\bar{r}| > |\bar{v}| \qquad\;\mapsto\; v \neq \emptyset$$
$$B2.hypo \;::\; v = f \;\; unless \;\; f \prec v,$$
$$w = e \;\; unless \;\; w \prec e$$
$$B2.conc \;::\; \bar{w} \subseteq \bar{v},$$
$$|\bar{v}| \le |\bar{w}| + N,$$
$$|\bar{v}| < |\bar{w}| + N \;\mapsto\; v = \emptyset,$$
$$|\bar{v}| > |\bar{w}| \qquad\;\mapsto\; w \neq \emptyset$$

The structure of the proof is as follows. Consider an arbitrary F and let $G = B2 \;\|\; F$ and $H = B1 \;\|\; F$ (because $B2 \;\|\; F$ is the environment for $B1$ and $B1 \;\|\; F$ for $B2$). We show,

$$B.hypo \quad \text{in } F \Rightarrow \; B1.hypo \quad \text{in } G \quad \text{and,} \tag{2}$$

$$B.hypo \quad \text{in } F \Rightarrow \; B2.hypo \quad \text{in } H \tag{3}$$

Hence, from the antecedent of (1), we may then assume $B1.conc$ in $B1 \;\|\; G$ and $B2.conc$ in $B2 \;\|\; H$. From the definitions of B, G, H, we have $B1 \;\|\; G = B2 \;\|\; H = B1 \;\|\; B2 \;\|\; F = B \;\|\; F$. Hence, we have $B1.conc$ in $B \;\|\; F$ and $B2.conc$ in $B \;\|\; F$. We will finally deduce,

$$B1.conc \quad \text{in } B \;\|\; F \;\wedge\; B2.conc \quad \text{in } B \;\|\; F \;\Rightarrow\; B.conc \quad \text{in } B \;\|\; F \tag{4}$$

Proof of (2)

The two proofs, corresponding to the two conjuncts in $B1.hypo$, are shown below.

Proof of $r = d \;\; unless \;\; d \prec r$ in G

$r = d \;\; unless \;\; d \prec r$ in F	, from $B.hypo$ in F
$r = d$ is stable in $B2$	, r is not accessed in $B2$
$r = d \;\; unless \;\; d \prec r$ in $B2 \;\|\; F$	, Corollary 1 to union theorem (Sec. 2.2) $\qquad\nabla$

Proof of $v = f \;\; unless \;\; v \prec f$ in G

$v = f \;\; unless \;\; v \prec f$ in $B2$	, property P2 of $B2$
$v = f$ is stable in F	, v is not accessed in F
$v = f \;\; unless \;\; v \prec f$ in $B2 \;\|\; F$	, Corollary 1 to union theorem (Sec. 2.2) $\qquad\nabla$

Proof of (3) is similar to proof of (2).

Proof of (4)

The proof has four parts, corresponding to the four conjuncts in $B.conc$. All properties are of $B \parallel F$.

Proof of $\bar{w} \subseteq \bar{r}$

$\bar{w} \subseteq \bar{v}$	, from $B2.conc$
$\bar{v} \subseteq \bar{r}$	, from $B1.conc$
$\bar{w} \subseteq \bar{r}$	, from the above two $\qquad\qquad\qquad \triangledown$

Proof of $|r| \leq |\bar{w}| + M + N$

$|\bar{r}| \leq |\bar{v}| + M$	, from $B1.conc$
$|\bar{v}| \leq |\bar{w}| + N$	, from $B2.conc$
$|\bar{r}| \leq |\bar{w}| + M + N$	, from the above two $\qquad\qquad \triangledown$

Proof of $|\bar{r}| < |\bar{w}| + M + N \;\mapsto\; r = \emptyset$

$|\bar{v}| < |\bar{w}| + N \;\mapsto\; v = \emptyset$

, from $B2.conc$

$v = \emptyset \;\mapsto\; r = \emptyset$

, from Lemma 5 of Appendix A

$|\bar{v}| < |\bar{w}| + N \;\mapsto\; r = \emptyset$

, transitivity on the above two

$|\bar{r}| < |\bar{v}| + M \;\mapsto\; r = \emptyset$

, from $B1.conc$

$|\bar{r}| < |\bar{v}| + M \;\vee\; |\bar{v}| < |\bar{w}| + N \;\mapsto\; r = \emptyset$

, disjunction on the above two

$|\bar{r}| < |\bar{w}| + M + N \;\Rightarrow\; |\bar{r}| < |\bar{v}| + M \;\vee\; |\bar{v}| < |\bar{w}| + N$

, seen easily by taking the contrapositive

$|\bar{r}| < |\bar{w}| + M + N \;\mapsto\; r = \emptyset$

, from the above two using implication rule for *leads-to* $\qquad \triangledown$

Proof of $|\bar{r}| < |\bar{w}| \;\mapsto\; w \neq \emptyset$

Similar to the above proof. $\qquad\qquad\qquad\qquad\qquad\qquad\qquad\qquad\qquad \triangledown$

5 A Refinement of the Specification

As a first step toward implementing a buffer, we propose a more refined (i.e., stronger) specification of a buffer. Our proof obligation then is to show that this proposed specification implies the specification given by properties P0,P1,P2,P3, of Section 3.2. In the next section we show a program that implements this refined specification. Because of the result of Section 4, any buffer of size N can be implemented by concatenating N buffers of size 1; hence we limit our refinement to $N = 1$.

For $N = 1$, the buffer program has no internal words for data storage (recall that there are $N - 1$ internal words for storage). Hence the only strategy for the buffer program is to move data from r to w when $w \neq \emptyset$. This is captured in the following specification.

$$\text{initially } w = \emptyset \quad \text{in } B \tag{R0}$$

$$(r, w) = (d, e) \quad \textit{unless} \quad (r, w) = (\emptyset, d) \wedge e \prec d \quad \text{in } B \tag{R1}$$

$$r \neq \emptyset \quad \textit{ensures} \quad w \neq \emptyset \quad \text{in } B \tag{R2}$$

Property R1 says that the pair (r, w) changes only if a non-$\emptyset$ data value is moved from r to w when the latter is $\emptyset$. The progress property, R2, says that if data can be moved—i.e., $r \neq \emptyset \wedge w = \emptyset$—then it will be moved.

Now we show that the refinement is correct, i.e. (R0,R1,R2) imply (P0,P1,P2,P3), given in Section 3.2.

5.1 Proofs of P0,P1,P2

Proof of (P0):   initially $w = \emptyset$ in B

Immediate from R0. $\triangledown$

Proof of (P1): $r = d$ *unless* $r \prec d$ in B

$r = d \wedge w = e$ *unless* $r \prec d$ in B

   , from R1 by weakening its consequence

$r = d$ *unless* $r \prec d$ in B

   , eliminating free variable e $\triangledown$

Proof of (P2): $w = e$ *unless* $e \prec w$ in B

$r = d \wedge w = e$ *unless* $e \prec w$ in B

   , from R1 by weakening its consequence

$w = e$ *unless* $e \prec w$ in B

   , eliminating free variable d $\triangledown$

.2 Proof of P3

he property P3 is of the form,

$$\langle \forall F :: B.hypo \quad \text{in } F \Rightarrow B.conc \text{ in } B \parallel F \rangle$$

'e prove P3 from (R0,R1,R2) by first proving (in Appendix B) that

$$\langle \forall F :: B.hypo \quad \text{in } F \wedge (\text{R0,R1}) \Rightarrow (\bar{r} = \bar{w}; r \text{ in } B \parallel F) \rangle \tag{P4}$$

hen we show that

$$\langle \forall F :: B.hypo \quad \text{in } F \wedge (\text{R2}) \wedge (\bar{r} = \bar{w}; r \text{ in } B \parallel F) \Rightarrow (B.conc \text{ in } B \parallel F) \rangle \tag{P5}$$

roof of P5

he proof consists of four parts; each part establishes one of the conjuncts in $B.conc$.

roof of $\bar{w} \subseteq \bar{r}$ in $B \parallel F$

Immediate from $\bar{r} = \bar{w}; r$ in $B \parallel F$ $\qquad\qquad\qquad\qquad\qquad\qquad\qquad\qquad \triangledown$

roof of $|\bar{r}| \leq |\bar{w}| + 1$ in $B \parallel F$

$\qquad |\bar{r}| = |\bar{w}| + |r|$ in $B \parallel F$, from $\bar{r} = \bar{w}; r$ in $B \parallel F$

$\qquad |\bar{r}| \leq |\bar{w}| + 1$ in $B \parallel F$, $|r| \leq 1$ $\qquad\qquad\qquad\qquad \triangledown$

he remaining proofs are for the progress properties appearing in $B.conc$:

$\quad |\bar{r}| < |\bar{w}| + 1 \;\mapsto\; r = \emptyset$ in $B \parallel F$ and,

$\quad |\bar{r}| > |\bar{w}| \qquad \mapsto\; w \neq \emptyset$ in $B \parallel F$

'sing the invariant—$\bar{r} = \bar{w}; r$ in $B \parallel F$—we simplify the left sides of the above progress properties

s follows:

$\quad |\bar{r}| < |\bar{w}| + 1 \equiv |\bar{r}| \leq |\bar{w}| \equiv r = \emptyset$ and,

$\quad |\bar{r}| > |\bar{w}| \quad \equiv r \neq \emptyset$

The first progress property is then,

$$r = \emptyset \;\mapsto\; r = \emptyset \quad \text{in } B \parallel F$$

·hich follows trivially by using the implication rule. The second progress property is

$$r \neq \emptyset \ \longmapsto \ w \neq \emptyset \ \text{in } B \parallel F$$

which follows from

$r \neq \emptyset$ is stable in F	, Lemma 4 of Appendix A
$r \neq \emptyset$ $ensures$ $w \neq \emptyset$ in B	, from (R2)
$r \neq \emptyset$ $ensures$ $w \neq \emptyset$ in $B \parallel F$	, Corollary 2 of Section 2.2
$r \neq \emptyset$ $\longmapsto$ $w \neq \emptyset$ in $B \parallel F$	, definition of $\longmapsto$

6 An Implementation

The specification of Section 5 can be implemented by a program whose only statement moves data from r to w provided $w = \emptyset$ (if $r = \emptyset$, the movement has no effect):

$$r, w := \emptyset, r \quad \text{if} \ \ w = \emptyset$$

The proof that this fragment has the properties (R1,R2) is immediate from the definition of $unless$ and $ensures$. The initial condition of this program is $w = \emptyset$, and hence (R0) is established.

An implementation for a buffer of size N, $N > 1$, is the union of N such statements: one statement each for moving data from a location to an adjacent location (closer to w) provided the latter is $\emptyset$. We show how this program may be expressed in the UNITY programming notation.

Rename the variables r and w to be $b[0]$ and $b[N]$, respectively. The internal buffer words are $b[1]$ through $b[N-1]$. In the following program we write $\langle \parallel i \ : \ 0 < i \leq N \ :: \ t(i) \rangle$ as a shorthand for $t(1) \parallel t(2) \ldots \parallel t(N)$, where $t(1)$, for instance, is obtained by replacing every occurrence of i by 1 in $t(i)$. The program specifies the initial values of $b[1]$ through $b[N]$ to be $\emptyset$ (in the part followed by **initially**). The statements of the program are given after **assign**; the generic statement shown moves $b[i-1]$ to $b[i]$ provided the latter is $\emptyset$.

Program $buffer$ {of N words, $N \geq 1$}

   initially $\langle \parallel i \ : \ 0 < i \leq N \ :: \ b[i] = \emptyset \rangle$

   assign $\langle \parallel i \ : \ 0 < i \leq N \ :: \ b[i-1], b[i] := \emptyset, b[i-1] \quad \text{if} \ \ b[i] = \emptyset \rangle$

end {$buffer$}

6.1 An Alternative Implementation

The implementation of the previous section is somewhat inefficient because every data item stored in r has to be stepped through all $(N-1)$ internal buffer words before it can appear in w. We propose an alternative implementation based on the well-known circular-list arrangement of the words in the buffer. The implementation is applicable for $N > 1$.

Let $c[0..N-1]$ be an array internal to the buffer program where data are to be stored; though there are N words in this array we shall store at most $N-1$ data items at any time. Let h, t ("head" and "tail") be indices to the array; data are stored consecutively in the array positions $h, h \oplus 1, \ldots \ominus 1$ (where $\oplus$ and $\ominus$ denote addition and subtraction mod N, respectively); $h = t$ denotes that there are no stored data items. The number of stored data items is then $t \ominus h$.

Program AB {Alternative Buffer for $N > 1$}

initially $t, h, w = 0, 0, \emptyset$ {buffer is empty initially}

assign

   {read a data item from r and add it to c provided $t \ominus h < N - 1$ and $r \neq \emptyset$}
   $c[t], t, r := r, t \oplus 1, \emptyset$ if $t \ominus h < N - 1 \wedge r \neq \emptyset$

[] {write a data item to w provided $w = \emptyset$ and $t \ominus h > 0$}
   $w, h := c[h], h \oplus 1$ if $t \ominus h > 0 \wedge w = \emptyset$

end {AB}

The proof obligation is to establish the properties $P0 - P3$ (of Section 3.2). For proving $P3$, first show that given $B.hypo$ in F, $\bar{r} = \bar{w}$; $c[h..t \ominus 1]$ is invariant in $AB \, [\!] \, F$ where $c[h..t \ominus 1]$ is the empty sequence if $h = t$ and otherwise it is the sequence $<< c[h], c[h \oplus 1] \ldots c[t \ominus 1] >>$.

7 Summary

Our specification of the buffer illustrates how some of the requirements described in the introduction are met. The specification is concise, and it can be manipulated easily. This allowed us to derive several properties of the buffer (Appendix A) and construct a proof of buffer concatenation (Section 4). Also refinement of the specification with the eventual goal of implementation seems feasible with this scheme.

Acknowledgment

It was a suggestion from Leslie Lamport which led me to study this problem and understand how auxiliary variables can be defined and effectively used. I am indebted to Ambuj Singh for simplifying my original version of property $P3$ (in Section 3.2); his work clearly reveals the importance of formal reasoning as I was unable to justify his simplification using intuitive arguments alone. Comments from the participants of the 9th International Summer School in Marktoberdorf, W. Germany, were most helpful; particular thanks go to Jan L. A. van de Snepscheut. Thorough and critical readings of the manuscript by Mani Chandy and Edgar Knapp have improved the presentation.

References

1. K. Mani Chandy and Jayadev Misra, *Parallel Program Design: A Foundation*, Addison-Wesley, Reading, Mass., 1988.

2. John Guttag, "Abstract Data Types and the Development of Data Structures," *Comm. of the ACM*, Vol. 20, No. 6, June 1977, pp. 396-404.

3. B. Hailpern, "Verifying Concurrent Processes Using Temporal Logic," Springer-Verlag, *Lecture notes in Computer Science 129*, 1982.

4. *Specification Case Studies*, Ian Hayes (ed.), Prentice-Hall International, Englewood Cliffs, N. J., 1987.

5. L. Lamport, "A Simple Approach to Specifying Concurrent Systems," *Digital Systems Research Center Report 15*, December 1986, 130 Lytton Avenue, Palo Alto, California 94301.

6. J. Misra, "General Conjunction and Disjunction Rules for *unless*," Notes on UNITY 01-88, University of Texas at Austin, 1988.

Appendix A: Some Properties of a Buffer

We derive a number of properties of a buffer B of size N, $N \geq 1$, from the specification (properties $P0, P1, P2, P3$) given in Section 3.2.

Lemma 0:

$$\bar{r} = x \ \land \ r = d \ \text{unless} \ \bar{r} = x; r \ \land \ r \neq d \ \text{in } B$$
$$\bar{w} = y \ \land \ w = e \ \text{unless} \ \bar{w} = y; w \ \land \ w \neq e \ \text{in } B$$

Proof: Use union theorem on $A1, A2$.　　　　　　　　　$\triangledown$

Lemma 1: $\bar{r} = x$ is stable　　in B

Proof: In the following proof all properties are of B.

$\bar{r} = x \ \land \ r = d \ \text{unless} \ \bar{r} = x; r \ \land \ r \neq d$	, from Lemma 0
$r = d \ \text{unless} \ r \prec d$	, from $P1$
$\bar{r} = x \ \land \ r = d \ \text{unless} \ \bar{r} = x; r \ \land \ r \prec d$	, conjunction of the above two
$\bar{r} = x \ \land \ r = d \ \text{unless} \ \bar{r} = x \ \land \ r \prec d$	, $r \prec d \Rightarrow r = \emptyset$
$\bar{r} = x \ \land \ r = d \ \text{unless} \ \bar{r} = x \ \land \ r \neq d$	, weakening the rhs of the above
$\bar{r} = x$ is stable	, Corollary 2 of Section 2.1.5

$\triangledown$

Lemma 2: $w = \emptyset \ \ unless \ \ |\bar{r}| < |\bar{w}| + N \quad$ in B

Proof: In the following proof all properties are of B

$\bar{w} = y \ \wedge \ w = e \ \ unless \ \ \bar{w} = y; w \ \wedge \ w \neq e \quad$, from Lemma 0

$\bar{w} = y \ \wedge \ w = \emptyset \ \ unless \ \ \bar{w} = y; w \ \wedge \ w \neq \emptyset \quad$, setting e to $\emptyset$ in the above

$\bar{w} = y \ \wedge \ w = \emptyset \ \ unless \ \ y \subset \bar{w} \quad$, weakening the rhs of the above

$\bar{r} = x$ is stable $\quad$, from Lemma 1

$(\bar{r}, \bar{w}) = (x, y) \ \wedge \ w = \emptyset \ \ unless \ \ \bar{r} = x \ \wedge \ y \subset \bar{w}$, conjunction of the above two

$|x| \leq |y| + N$ is stable $\quad$, x, y are free variables (see note below)

$(\bar{r}, \bar{w}) = (x, y) \ \wedge \ |x| \leq |y| + N \ \wedge \ w = \emptyset \ \ unless \ \ \bar{r} = x \ \wedge \ y \subset \bar{w} \ \wedge \ |x| \leq |y| + N$

, conjunction of the above two

$(\bar{r}, \bar{w}) = (x, y) \ \wedge \ |\bar{r}| \leq |\bar{w}| + N \ \wedge \ w = \emptyset \ \ unless \ \ |\bar{r}| < |\bar{w}| + N$

, rewriting the lhs and weakening the rhs

$(\bar{r}, \bar{w}) = (x, y) \ \wedge \ w = \emptyset \ \ unless \ \ |\bar{r}| < |\bar{w}| + N$

, using substitution axiom replace invariant $|\bar{r}| \leq |\bar{w}| + N$ by $true$

$w = \emptyset \ \ unless \ \ |\bar{r}| < |\bar{w}| + N$

, eliminating free variables x, y using Corollary 1 of Section 2.1.5 $\qquad \triangledown$

Note: Any predicate that names only free variables and constants is stable. This is because any such propety is a shorthand for a collection of properties, each one obtained by replacing the free variables by a set of their possible values; no such property is influenced by the program execution.

$\triangledown$

Lemma 3: Given $B.hypo$ in F

$w = \emptyset \ \ unless \ \ |\bar{r}| < |\bar{w}| + N \quad$ in $B \parallel F$

Proof:

$w = e \ \ unless \ \ w \prec e \ \text{ in } F \quad$, from $B.hypo$ in F

$w = \emptyset$ is stable in $F \quad$, setting e to $\emptyset$ in the above

$w = \emptyset \ \ unless \ \ |\bar{r}| < |\bar{w}| + N \ \text{ in } B \quad$, from Lemma 2

$w = \emptyset \ \ unless \ \ |\bar{r}| < |\bar{w}| + N \ \text{ in } B \parallel F \quad$, using Corollary 1 of Section 2.2 $\qquad \triangledown$

Lemma 4: Given $B.hypo$ in F

$r \neq \emptyset$ is stable in F

Proof: All properties in the following proof are of F.

$r = d \;\; unless \;\; d \prec r$, from $B.hypo$ in F

$d \neq \emptyset$ is stable   , d is a free variable (see Note in Lemma 2)

$r = d \;\land\; d \neq \emptyset \;\; unless \;\; d \prec r \;\land\; d \neq \emptyset$, conjunction of the above two

$r \neq \emptyset \;\land\; r = d$ is stable   , rewriting the lhs and the rhs

$r \neq \emptyset$ is stable

      , eliminating free variable d using Corollary 1 of Section 2.1.5 $\triangledown$

Lemma 5:   Given $B.hypo$ in F

    $w = \emptyset \;\; \mapsto \;\; r = \emptyset \;\;$ in $B \;[\!]\; F$

    $r \neq \emptyset \;\; \mapsto \;\; w \neq \emptyset \;\;$ in $B \;[\!]\; F$

Proof: We will prove only the first property; proof of the other one is similar. Since we have $B.hypo$ in F, we have $B.conc$ in $B \;[\!]\; F$ from $P3$. All properties are of $B \;[\!]\; F$ in the following proof.

$|\bar{r}| > |\bar{w}| \;\; \mapsto \;\; w \neq \emptyset$, from $B.conc$

$w = \emptyset \;\; unless \;\; |\bar{r}| < |\bar{w}| + N$, from Lemma 3

$w = \emptyset \;\land\; |\bar{r}| > |\bar{w}| \;\; \mapsto \;\; |\bar{r}| < |\bar{w}| + N$, PSP rule on the above two

$w = \emptyset \;\land\; |\bar{r}| = |\bar{w}| + N \;\Rightarrow\; w = \emptyset \;\land\; |\bar{r}| > |\bar{w}| \;$, $N \geq 1$

$w = \emptyset \;\land\; |\bar{r}| = |\bar{w}| + N \;\; \mapsto \;\; |\bar{r}| < |\bar{w}| + N$

      , using Corollary 3 of Section 2.1.5 on the above two

$w = \emptyset \;\land\; |\bar{r}| < |\bar{w}| + N \;\; \mapsto \;\; |\bar{r}| < |\bar{w}| + N$, implication rule

$w = \emptyset \;\land\; |\bar{r}| \leq |\bar{w}| + N \;\; \mapsto \;\; |\bar{r}| < |\bar{w}| + N$, disjunction on the above two

$w = \emptyset \;\; \mapsto \;\; |\bar{r}| < |\bar{w}| + N$

      , replace $|\bar{r}| \leq |\bar{w}| + N$ by $true$ using the substitution axiom

$|\bar{r}| < |\bar{w}| + N \;\; \mapsto \;\; r = \emptyset$, from $B.conc$

$w = \emptyset \;\; \mapsto \;\; r = \emptyset$, transitivity on the above two $\triangledown$

Appendix B: Proof of $P4$

To show that $\bar{r} = \bar{w}; r$ is invariant in $B \;[\!]\; F$, the proof obligations are,

    initially $\bar{r} = \bar{w}; r \;\;$ in $B \;[\!]\; F \;\;\;$ and,

    $\bar{r} = \bar{w}; r$ is stable $\;\;\;$ in $B \;[\!]\; F$

The initial condition can be seen from,

        initially $(\bar{r}, \bar{w}) = (r, w) \;\;\;$ in $B \;[\!]\; F \;\;\;$, from (A0) of Section 3.1

   and, initially $w = \emptyset \;\;\;$ in $B \;[\!]\; F$, from (R0) and the rule for union of B, F

Next we show that $\bar{r} = \bar{w}; r$ is stable   in $B \parallel F$.

Proof of $\bar{r} = \bar{w}; r$ is stable   in $B \parallel F$

$r = d$ unless $d \prec r$ in F

   , from $B.hypo$ in F

$w = e$ unless $w \prec e$ in F

   , from $B.hypo$ in F

$(r, w) = (d, e)$ unless $(d, w) \prec (r, e)$ in F

   , conjunction of the above two; $(d, w) \prec (r, e)$ stands for

   $(d = r \wedge w \prec e) \vee (d \prec r \wedge w = e) \vee (d \prec r \wedge w \prec e)$

$(r, w) = (d, e)$ unless $r \prec d \wedge e \prec w \wedge w = d$ in B

   , from (R1)

$(r, w) = (d, e)$ unless

$(d, w) \prec (r, e)$	$\{1.1\}$
$\vee (r \prec d \wedge e \prec w \wedge w = d)$	$\{1.2\}$
in $B \parallel F$	(1)

   , weakening the right sides of the above two and applying the union theorem

Next use the properties (A1,A2) of Section 3.1 and form their conjunction to get:

$(\bar{r}, \bar{w}) = (x, y) \wedge (r, w) = (d, e)$ unless

$[(\bar{r}, \bar{w}) = (x, \ y; w) \wedge r = d \wedge w \neq e]$	$\{2.1\}$
$\vee [(\bar{r}, \bar{w}) = (x; r, \ y) \wedge r \neq d \wedge w = e]$	$\{2.2\}$
$\vee [(\bar{r}, \bar{w}) = (x; r, \ y; w) \wedge r \neq d \wedge w \neq e]$	$\{2.3\}$
in $B \parallel F$	(2)

Next form the conjunction of (1) and (2). Observe that every disjunct in the right side of (1) and (2) imply $(r, w) \neq (d, e)$, and therefore, conjunctions of these with the left sides of (2) and (1), respectively, result in *false*.

$(\bar{r}, \bar{w}) = (x, y) \wedge (r, w) = (d, e)$ unless

$[(\bar{r}, \bar{w}) = (x, \ y; w) \wedge r = d \wedge w \prec e]$	$\{3.1, \text{from } 1.1 \wedge 2.1\}$
$\vee [(\bar{r}, \bar{w}) = (x; r, \ y) \wedge d \prec r \wedge w = e]$	$\{3.2, \text{from } 1.1 \wedge 2.2\}$
$\vee [(\bar{r}, \bar{w}) = (x; r, \ y; w) \wedge d \prec r \wedge w \prec e]$	$\{3.3, \text{from } 1.1 \wedge 2.3\}$
$\vee [(\bar{r}, \bar{w}) = (x; r, \ y; w) \wedge r \prec d \wedge e \prec w \wedge w = d]$	$\{3.4, \text{from } 1.2 \wedge 2.3\}$
in $B \parallel F$	(3)

We next set the free variable x to $y; d$ in (3). The terms in the right side may be weakened to yield

$$\bar{r} = \bar{w}; r \ \wedge \ (\bar{w}, r, w) = (y, d, e) \quad unless \quad \bar{r} = \bar{w}; r \ \wedge \ (\bar{w}, r, w) \neq (y, d, e) \quad \text{in } B \parallel F$$

$$\bar{r} = \bar{w}; r \text{ is stable} \quad \text{in } B \parallel F \qquad \text{, Corollary 2 of Section 2.1.5} \qquad \triangledown$$

Stepwise Refinement of Action Systems

R.J.R. Back   K. Sere

Åbo Akademi University, Department of Computer Science

Lemminkäisenkatu 14, SF-20520 Turku, Finland

April 1 , 1989

Abstract

A method for the formal development of provably correct parallel algorithms by stepwise refinement is presented. The entire derivation procedure is carried out in the context of purely sequential programs. The resulting parallel algorithms can be efficiently executed on different architectures. The methodology is illustrated by showing the main derivation steps in a construction of a parallel algorithm for matrix multiplication.

1 Introduction

Stepwise refinement is one of the main methods for systematic construction of sequential programs: a high level specification of a program is transformed by a sequence of correctness preserving transformations into an executable and efficient program that satisfies the original specification. The *refinement calculus* is a formalization of the stepwise refinement approach. It was first described in [Back78, Back80] and has been further elaborated in [Back88a, Morgan88, Morris87].

The *action system* formalism for parallel and distributed computations was introduced in [BaKu83] and is further developed in e.g. [BaKu88]. The behaviour of parallel and distributed programs is described in terms of the actions which processes in the system carry out in co-operating with each other. Several actions can be executed in parallel, as long as the actions do not have any variables in common. The actions are atomic: if an action is chosen for execution, it is executed to completion without any interference from the other actions in the system.

Atomicity guarantees that a parallel execution of an action system gives the same results as a sequential and nondeterministic execution. This allows us to use the sequential refinement calculus to construct parallel action systems by stepwise refinements. We can start our derivation from a more or less sequential algorithm and successively increase the degree of parallelism in it, while preserving the correctness of the algorithm. Parallelism is introduced by merging action systems and refining the atomicity of actions [Back88b].

The refinement calculus is based on the assumption that the notion of correctness we want to preserve is total correctness. The refinement relation is not bound to the choice of this specific notion of correctness, but much of the methods developed and the theory is specific to this choice. Total correctness is the appropriate correctness notion for *parallel algorithms*. These programs differ from sequential algorithms only in that they are executed in parallel, by co-operation of many processes. They are intended to terminate, and only the final results are of interest. The refinement calculus and the action system formalism together provide a powerful and uniform method for deriving parallel algorithms by stepwise refinement.

The action system approach is the topic of section 2. A classification of action systems based on the characteristics which allow their efficient implementation on different machine architectures is also briefly discussed there. The refinement calculus for statements and actions is presented in section 3. In section 4 we describe the methods needed to increase parallelism in action systems. These methods are illustrated by the derivation of a nontrivial parallel algorithm for matrix multiplication in section 5. We end with some concluding remarks in section 6.

2 Action systems

An *action system* $\mathcal{A}$ is a collection of *actions* $\{A_1, \ldots, A_m\}$ on some set of *state variables* $x = \{x_1, \ldots, x_n\}$. Each variable is associated with some domain of values. The set of possible assignments of values to the state variables constitutes the *state space* Σ. Each action A_i is of the form $g_i \rightarrow S_i$, where the *guard* g_i is a boolean condition and the *body* S_i a sequential, possibly nondeterministic statement on the state variables. An *initialization statement* S_0 assigns initial values to the variables x.

An action system describes the state space of a system and the possible actions that can be executed in the system. The way in which the actions are executed depends on the evaluation mechanism that we postulate for the system. The simplest evaluation mechanism is *sequential*: the behaviour of the action system $\mathcal{A}$ is that of the guarded iteration statement

$$S_0; \ \textbf{do } A_1 [] \ldots [] A_m \ \textbf{od}$$

on the state variables x [Dijkstra76], i.e. actions are executed sequentially with nondeterministic choices when more than one action is enabled.

The following is a sorting program for exchange sort, described as an action system:

[*var x.1, ..., x.n is integer;*
$x.1, \ldots, x.n := X.1, \ldots, X.n;$
do $x.1 > x.2 \rightarrow x.1, x.2 := x.2, x.1$
$\ldots$

[] $x.(n-1) > x.n \rightarrow x.(n-1), x.n := x.n, x.(n-1)$
od]

This program will sort n integers $X.1, \ldots, X.n$ in ascending order. We can look upon this program as an action system with an initialization statement and $n-1$ sorting actions. The program terminates in a state where the array x is a permutation of the original array X and $x.i \leq x.(i+1)$ for $i = 1, \ldots, n-1$.

Action systems can also be executed in *parallel*. We consider here two different ways of parallel execution: *concurrent action system* and *distributed action system*. In the concurrent execution model the *actions* are partitioned among the processes. This gives us a shared variable model for communication and synchronization. Each action is assigned to some specific process. A variable that is referenced by at least two different actions in two different processes is *shared*, while a variable that is referenced only by actions in one process is *private* to that process. The actions are executed in parallel, with the restriction that all actions are *atomic*: two actions that share a common variable may not execute at the same time.

In the *distributed action system* the *variables* (rather than the actions) are partitioned among the processes. This results in a distributed execution model where all variables are local and processes synchronize and communicate by a generalized handshaking mechanism. Each variable is assigned to a unique process. An action is *shared*, if it refers to variables in two or more processes and private if it only refers to variables in one process. A shared action is assumed to be executed jointly by all the processes sharing this action. The processes are therefore synchronized for execution of such an action. Shared actions also provide communication between processes: a variable in one process may be updated in a way that depends on the values of variables in other processes involved in the shared action. The actions are executed in parallel, again with the restriction enforced by atomicity: no two actions involving a common process may execute simultaneously. This implies that no two actions refering to a common variable may execute in parallel.

The example sorting program becomes a concurrent action system if we assign each of the $n-1$ actions to a process of its own. The variables $x.2, \ldots, x.(n-1)$ are then shared by two processes each, while $x.1$ and $x.n$ are private. The program becomes a distributed action system if we assign each element of the array x to a process of its own. Each action in the system is then shared by exactly two processes. In both cases, actions that do not have any variables $x.i$ in common can execute in parallel.

Classification of distributed action systems The distributed action systems can be divided into subclasses, depending on the way in which they are implementable on different kinds of distributed architectures. Let $\mathcal{A}$ be an action system with initialization S_0, actions $A = \{A_1, \ldots, A_m\}$ and state variables $x = \{x_1, \ldots, x_n\}$. We will identify a *process* with a subset of state variables x. Let $p = \{p_1, \ldots, p_k\}$ be a partitioning of x into processes, i.e. $p_i \subset x$ for each i, $x = \cup p$ and $p_i \cap p_j = \emptyset$ for any i, j, $i \neq j$. The action A_i (or action guard g, action body S) is said to *involve* process p_j if A_i (or g, S) refers to some variable in p_j.

An action A_i is of *degree n* if it involves n processes. An action system is of *degree n* if each of its actions is of at most degree n. The usual message passing models for parallel programming, such as Ada and CSP/Occam, correspond to action systems of degree 2. Synchronous broadcasting among N processes, e.g. to execute the same program on different processes in lock-step, corresponds to a system with degree N. The distributed sorting algorithm is of degree 2.

An action A_i is *decentralized*, if its guard g_i is a boolean combination of *primitive guards* $g_i^{\,1}, \ldots, g_i^{\,r}$, each of which only involves a single process. An action system is *decentralized*, if each of its actions is decentralized. The processes can in such a system determine the truth of primitive guards by only inspecting their own local variables. The

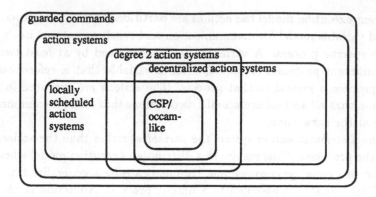

Figure 1: A classification of distributed action systems.

enabledness of an action is thus determined in a distributed fashion. The actual scheduling of actions for execution may be done in a centralized or distributed fashion.

A process p involved in action A_i is *committed* to the action if, whenever action A_i is enabled, no other action in $\mathcal{A}$ that p is involved in can be enabled. An action A_i is *locally scheduled* in $\mathcal{A}$, if at most one uncommitted process is involved in the action (the uncommitted action is then called a *scheduler* for the action). The action system $\mathcal{A}$ is *locally scheduled* if each of its actions is locally scheduled. In such a system, we do not need any expensive agreement protocols to decide which of the possibly conflicting enabled actions should be executed, because the scheduler of each action can make this decision for itself, without danger of deadlock. The local scheduling condition is enforced in e.g. CSP/Occam by disallowing output guards and in Ada by the asymmetric treatment of callers and callees.

The different classes of action systems are illustrated in Figure 1. We see that a programming language such as Occam forms a subset of decentralized and locally scheduled action systems of degree 2. It is only a subset, because it only permits an assignment statement as the body of a communication action, with the additional restriction that the variables in one of the processes may only be read and the variables in the other process may only be written.

Action systems generalize the communication mechanisms usually found in programming languages for parallel and distributed programming. Parallel implementations of action systems require some additional mechanism to enforce atomicity and to schedule the execution of actions. In [BaKu83] it is shown how decentralized action systems of degree 2 can be implemented in CSP with output guards. Efficient algorithms to implement decentralized action systems of any degree on broadcasting networks are presented in [BaHaKu85, BaKu88]. In a forthcoming paper [BaSe88b] we show how decentralized and locally scheduled action systems of any degree can be efficiently implemented in Occam [INMOS84], which does not permit output guards.

Programming with action systems   The use of action systems permits the design of the logical behaviour of a system to be separated from the issue of how the system is to be implemented. The latter is seen as a design decision that does affect the way in which he action system is built, but is not reflected in the logical behaviour of the system. The decision whether the action system is to be executed in a sequential, concurrent or distributed fashion can be postponed to a later stage, when the logical behaviour of the action system has been designed. The construction of the program is thus done within a single unifying framework.

The stepwise refinement of action systems would start with a specification of the intended behavious of the system, in the form of a sequential statement. The goal is to construct an action system that fits into one of the classes described above, with a specific target architecture in mind. The required parallel action system is constructed by making small refinements in the original statement, until an action system satisfying the requirements has been constructed.

3   Refinement calculus

We restrict ourselves to the language of guarded commands [Dijkstra76], with some extensions. We have two different syntactic categories, *statements* and *actions*, which we define as follows. A *statement* S is defined as

$$
\begin{array}{lll}
S ::= & x := x'.Q & \textit{(nondeterministic assignment)} \\
 & | \ \ \{Q\} & \textit{(assert statement)} \\
 & | \ \ S_1; \ \ldots; S_n & \textit{(sequential composition)} \\
 & | \ \ [A_1[] \ldots []A_n] & \textit{(conditional composition)} \\
 & | \ \ \star[A_1[] \ldots []A_n] & \textit{(iterative composition)} \\
 & | \ \ [var \ x_1 : T_1; \ \ldots; x_n : T_n; S] & \textit{(block with local variables)} \ .
\end{array}
$$

Here $A_1, \ldots, A_n$ are actions, x and x' are (lists of) variables and Q is a predicate. We write $(i : 1..n : S_i)$ for $S_1; \ \ldots; S_n$ and similarly $[i : 1..n : A_i]$, $\star[i : 1..n : A_i]$ and $var \ x.i : T_i, i : 1..n; S]$ for the other constructs.

The *nondeterministic assignment statement* $x := x'.Q$ [Back80] permits specifications to be treated as statements. It assigns to the variables x some values x' that make the condition Q true. The statement aborts, if this is not possible. The *assert statement* $\{Q\}$ acts as *skip*, if the condition Q holds in the initial state. If the condition Q does not hold in the initial state, then the effect is the same as *abort*. The other statements have their usual meanings. The *(multiple) assignment statement* $x_1, \ldots, x_n := e_1, \ldots, e_n$ is a special case of the nondeterministic assignment statement, definied as $x_1, \ldots, x_n := x'_1, \ldots, x'_n.(x'_1 = e_1 \wedge \ldots \wedge x'_n = e_1)$. We write it as $\| \ i : 1..n : x_i := e_i \ \|$.

An *action* (or guarded command) A is of the form

$$ A ::= g \rightarrow S $$

where g is a boolean condition (the *guard*) and S is a statement (the *body*). We will write gA for the guard of action A and bA for the body of action A.

An *action system* $\mathcal{A}$ is simply a statement of the form

$$ [var \ y_i : T_i, i : 1..m; \ S_0; \ \star[i : 1..n : A_i]] $$

where $A_1, \ldots, A_n$ are actions. The variables $y_1, \ldots y_m$ are local to the action system, while other variables referenced in the system are global.

The *weakest precondition* $\text{wp}(S, R)$ for *statement* S to establish postcondition R is definied in the usual way[Dijkstra76], with the adaptions needed for the unbounded nondeterminism introduced by the nondeterministic assignment statement [Back88a]. The weakest precondition for an *action* $A = g \to S$ to establish postcondition R is definied as

$$\text{wp}(g \to S, R) = (g \Rightarrow \text{wp}(S, R)).$$

The weakest precondition for a finite sequence $A_1; A_2; \ldots A_k$ of actions to establish postcondition R is definied in the same way as for statements,

$$\text{wp}(A_1; A_2; \ldots A_k, R) = \text{wp}(A_1, \text{wp}(A_2; \ldots A_k, R)), k > 1.$$

Observe that the law of excluded miracle, $\text{wp}(S, false) = false$, does not necessarily hold for actions [Back88b, Morgan88, Morris87]. As an example, we have that $\text{wp}(false \to skip, false) = true$. Also, the continuity property need not hold, as the nondeterminism may be unbounded. The other healthiness properties of [Dijkstra76] are valid.

3.1 Refinement of statements and actions

Let S and S' be sequential statements. Statement S is said to be *refined* by the statement S', denoted $S \leq S'$, if for every postcondition R,

$$\text{wp}(S, R) \Rightarrow \text{wp}(S', R).$$

Refinement captures the notion of statement S' preserving the correctness of statement S. More precisely, $S \leq S'$ holds if and only if $P\langle S \rangle Q \Rightarrow P\langle S' \rangle Q$ for every precondition P and postcondition Q, where $P\langle S \rangle Q$ stands for the total correctness of S w.r.t. P and Q. Hence, if S is totally correct with respect to a given P and Q and $S \leq S'$, then S' will also be totally correct with respect to P and Q.

We say that the statements S and S' are *(refinement) equivalent*, denoted $S \equiv S'$, if $S \leq S'$ and $S' \leq S$.

The refinement relation is reflexive and transitive, i.e. it is a preorder. The statement constructors are also monotonic with respect to the refinement relation, i.e. $T \leq T' \Rightarrow S(T) \leq S(T')$ for any statement S in which T occurs as a substatement $(S = S(T))$. The refinement relation becomes a partial order if we identify statements with their associated predicate transformers.

The refinement relation provides a formalization of the stepwise refinement method for program construction. One starts with an initial high level specification/program statement S_0, and constructs a sequence of successive refinements of this, $S_0 \leq S_1 \leq \ldots \leq S_{n-1} \leq S_n$. By transitivity, the last version S_n will then be a refinement of the original program S_0. An individual refinement step may consist of replacing some substatement T of $S_i(T)$ by its refinement T'. The resulting statement $S_{i+1} = S_i(T')$ will then be a refinement of S_i by monotonicity. The refinement relation and its use in program derivation is studied in more detail in [Back80, Back88a, Morgan88, Morris87].

Refinement between actions is defined in the same way as refinement between statements, i.e. an action A is *refined by* an action A', $A \leq A'$, if

$$\mathrm{wp}(A, R) \Rightarrow \mathrm{wp}(A', R)$$

for any postcondition R. The notion of total correctness can be directly extended to actions: we define $P\langle A\rangle Q$ to hold if $P \Rightarrow wp(A, Q)$ (A *establishes* Q *when* P). This is equivalent to $P \wedge gA \Rightarrow wp(bA, Q)$.

Observe that even if refinement of statements is monotonic, as stated above, action systems are *not* necesserily monotonic with respect to refinement of actions, i.e. $g_i \rightarrow S_i \leq g_i' \rightarrow S_i'$ need not imply $S_0; \star[\ldots []g_i \rightarrow S_i \ldots] \leq S_0; \star[\ldots []g_i' \rightarrow S_i' \ldots]$ (unless $g_i = g_i'$).

The refinement relation is quite strong, and we are therefore often faced with a situation where $S(T) \leq S(T')$ does in fact hold, but $T \leq T'$ does not hold. This means that the replacement of T by T' is correct in the specific context $S(\cdot)$ considered, even if it is not correct in every context. *Context dependent* replacements of this kind can be established correct by the following method [Back80, Back88a]: We prove

(1) $S(T) \leq S(\{Q\}; T)$ (*context introduction*) and

(2) $\{Q\}; T \leq T'$ (*refinement in context*).

By monotonicity and transitivity we then have that $S(T) \leq S(T')$. The first step introduces information about the context in the form of an assert statement at the appropriate place, the second step uses this information.

Note that we are always permitted to remove any context assertion, i.e. $S[\{Q\}; T] \leq S[T]$ is always valid (because $\{Q\}; T \leq T$ is always valid).

3.2 Properties of actions

We define below some properties of actions that will be useful in describing transformation rules for action systems, especially those by which parallelism is increased.

The way in which actions can enable and disable each other is captured by the following definitions.

Q *is invariant over* A	$=$	$Q\langle A\rangle Q$,
A *cannot enable* B	$=$	$\neg gB\langle A\rangle \neg gB$,
A *must enable* B	$=$	$\neg gB\langle A\rangle gB$,
A *cannot disable* B	$=$	$gB\langle A\rangle gB$,
A *must disable* B	$=$	$gB\langle A\rangle \neg gB$,
A *cannot precede* B	$=$	$true\langle A\rangle \neg gB$
A *disables itself*	$=$	$true\langle A\rangle \neg gA$,
A *excludes* B	$=$	$gA \Rightarrow \neg gB$.

The assertions can in all these cases be qualified to hold when some precondition Q holds initially; e.g. A *cannot disable* B *when* Q stands e.g. for $Q \Rightarrow gB\langle A\rangle gB$. Q is *invariant over* $\star[i : A_i]$ if Q is invariant over each A_i. The last property is generalized to sets of actions: $\{A_1, \ldots, A_m\}$ *excludes* $\{B_1, \ldots, B_n\}$, if $\vee gA_i \Rightarrow \neg \vee gB_i$.

Another important set of properties has to do with commutativity of actions. We say that A *commutes with* B if $A; B \leq B; A$. One can show that this is the case if and only if

(i) A cannot disable B and

(ii) B cannot enable A and

(iii) $\{gA \wedge gB\}; bA; bB \leq bB; bA$.

A sufficient condition for two actions A and B to commute is that there are no read-write conflicts for the variables that they access: none of the variables written by A is read or written by B and vice versa.

4 Stepwise refinement of action systems

Because action systems are just a special kind of sequential statements, we can use the refinement calculus as such for stepwise refinement of action systems. However, the goal is to transform a more or less sequential algorithm or algorithm specification into an action system that can be executed in a highly parallel fashion, so we need special refinement rules to introduce parallelism into the execution. These do not necessarily make much sense with a strictly sequential execution (they often make the execution less efficient), but become important when considering a parallel execution.

To change a sequential statement into an action system, which is just a simple kind of loop, we need to transform the statement into a form where the iteration construct is at the outermost level, preceeded by some loop initialization. We therefore need

(i) methods for transforming sequential statements directly into iterative constructs, and

(ii) methods for combining iterative substatements into a single iterative construct.

These permit us to change parts of a sequential statement into iterative constructs, and then gradually move the iterations outwards through the statement until we get an action system.

The above rules do not necessarily introduce any real parallelism in the resulting action system. For this we also need

(iii) methods for changing variables in substatements.

These will make it possible to change the way in which the program state is represented by variables in the system, in order to replace a centralized representation by a distributed one. Typically we replace a single variable by a number of variables, one for each process. These new variables hold the same information as the original variable, but permit the information to be accessed in a distributed fashion. This makes the processes less dependent of each other, so that more activity can go on in parallel.

We also need general rules and methods for massaging a program into a form where the above methods can be applied, and also for improving the efficiency of the program in general. These are not specific to the construction of action systems but apply to any kind of statements. Especially important are rules by which we can assert something about the context of substatements to be refined and general rules for changing the control structure of statements. We do not consider these here in any more detail. Rules for context introduction are described in detail in [Back88a], while the rules for changing control structures are often straightforward and usually easy to check.

4.1 Constructing and merging loops

The first three rules tell us when a statement can be directly transformed into a loop:

Rule 1 (*Making a loop directly*)

$$\{Q\}; S \leq \star[b \rightarrow S]$$

provided that

(i) $Q \Rightarrow b$ and

(ii) $b \rightarrow S$ disables itself.

Thus, a sufficient condition for directly turning a statement into a loop is that the guard holds initially and is disabled by the statement itself. This guarantees that the statement is executed exactly once in the loop.

Rule 2 (*Changing a sequence to a loop*)

$$\{Q\}; (i : 1..n : S_i) \leq \star[i : 1..n : b_i \rightarrow S_i]$$

provided that

(i) $Q \Rightarrow b_1$,

(ii) $b_i \rightarrow S_i$ enables $b_{i+1} \rightarrow S_{i+1}$, for $i = 1, \ldots, n-1$,

(iii) $b_n \rightarrow S_n$ establishes $\neg \lor b_i$ and

(iv) $b_i \rightarrow S_i$ excludes all other actions $b_j \rightarrow S_j$, $j \neq i$.

This rule will change a sequence to a loop. However, exactly the same statements are executed as before and in the same order. In particular, there is no parallelism in the execution of the statements, as they exclude each other. Observe that Rule 1 is a special case of Rule 2 ($n = 1$).

Rule 3 (*Changing a conditional to a loop*)

$$\{Q\}; [i : 1..n : b_i \rightarrow S_i] \leq \star[i : 1..n : b_i \rightarrow S_i]$$

provided that

(i) $b_i \rightarrow S_i$ establishes $\neg \lor b_i$ when Q, for every $i = 1, \ldots, n$.

Changing a conditional into a loop is thus always permitted, if every action disables all the actions of the conditional statement.

Rule 4 (*Merging a sequence of loops*)

$$\star[i : A_i]; \; \star[j : B_j] \leq \star[i : A_i \; [] \; j : B_j]$$

provided that

(i) for every i,j, B_j cannot enable or disable A_i,

(ii) for every i,j, either B_i cannot precede A_j or A_j commutes with B_i and

(iii) $\star[j : B_j]$ terminates when $\vee g A_i$.

This rule does introduce more parallelism in the execution of a action system. We have initially a situation where the execution of two loops must be done in sequence: the actions of the second loop may not start before all the actions of the first loop have become disabled. The rule permits the execution of the actions from the two loops to be overlapped, provided the essential sequential constraints are preserved.

Rule 5 (*Merging a conditional composition of loops*)

$$\{Q\}; [b_1 \rightarrow S_1; \; \star[i : A_i] \; [] \; b_2 \rightarrow S_2; \; \star[j : B_j]]$$
$$\leq \; \star[b_1 \rightarrow S_1 \; [] \; b_2 \rightarrow S_2 \; [] \; i : A_i \; [] \; j : B_j]$$

provided that

(i) $Q \Rightarrow b_1 \vee b_2$,

(ii) $b_1 \rightarrow S_1$ and $b_2 \rightarrow S_2$ exclude $\{i : A_i\}$ and $\{j : B_j\}$,

(iii) $b_1 \rightarrow S_1$ and $\{i : A_i\}$ cannot enable $b_1 \rightarrow S_1$ or $b_2 \rightarrow S_2$ or $\{j : B_j\}$.

(iv) $b_2 \rightarrow S_2$ and $\{j : B_j\}$ cannot enable $b_1 \rightarrow S_1$ or $b_2 \rightarrow S_2$ or $\{i : A_i\}$.

This rule permits us to create a single action system from a conditional composition of action systems. The replacement can be made provided that the actual execution of the systems preserves the original distinction between the two action systems.

Rule 6 (*Merging nested loops*)

$$\{Q\}; \; \star[b_0 \rightarrow S_0; \; \star[i : A_i] \; [] \; j : B_j]$$
$$\leq \; \star[b_0 \rightarrow S_0 \; [] \; i : 1..n : A_i \; [] \; j : B_j]$$

provided that

(i) $Q \Rightarrow \neg(\vee i : 1..n : g A_i)$,

(ii) $\{j : B_j\}$ cannot enable or disable $\{i : 1..n : A_i\}$,

(iii) $A_0 = b_0 \rightarrow S_0$ is excluded by $\{i : 1..n : A_i\}$ and

(iv) the actions in $\{j : B_j\}$ that are not excluded by $\{i : 0..n : A_i\}$ can be partitioned into left movers $\{k : L_k\}$ and right movers $\{h : R_h\}$, such that

(a) for each $i = 0,\ldots,n$ and k, either A_i cannot precede L_k or L_k commutes with A_i,

(b) for each $i = 0, \ldots, n$ and h, either R_h cannot precede A_i or A_i commutes with R_k,

(c) for each k and h, either R_h cannot precede L_k or L_k commutes with R_h and

(d) $\star[h : R_h]$ terminates when $(\vee i : 0..n : gA_i)$.

The last rule shows us how to refine the atomicity of an action. Initially we have a loop where one of the action bodies is in fact an action system. However, only the outermost actions can be executed in parallel, so the inner action system is executed sequentially, as one big action. The rule shows us under what conditions we are permitted to merge the two loops into a single loop, where the inner actions are executed interleaved with the actions of the outer loop. This means that the inner action system is not executed atomically anymore, but that its execution may overlap with execution of actions from the outer loop. This method of refining atomicity is studied in detail in [Back88b].

The above rules are all stated without considering possible invariants that may hold for the actions involved. These invariants are very important in practice, because many reasonable refinements turn out to hold only because some specific invariant holds. However, we can always take these invariants into account by e.g. temporarily adding them to the guards, prove the required conditions with these strengthened guards, and then later remove the invariants again from the guards.

The following rule can be used to change the guards of an iteration statement.

Rule 7 (*Changing guards in loops*)

$$\{Q\}; \; \star[i : b_i \rightarrow S_i] \equiv \{Q\}; \; \star[i : b_i' \rightarrow S_i]$$

provided that

(i) $Q \wedge b_i \Leftrightarrow Q \wedge b_i'$ for every i and

(ii) Q is invariant of $\star[i : b_i \rightarrow S_i]$.

In particular, we have that

$$\{Q\}; \; \star[i : b_i \rightarrow S_i] \equiv \{Q\}; \; \star[i : b_i \wedge I \rightarrow \{b_i \wedge I\}; S_i]$$

when I is an invariant of the loop, so we may add the invariant to each of the guards. Furthermore, the invariant and the guard may be added as a context assertion for the body of the action. In the other direction, we may remove a common conjunct from all the guards if we can show that this conjunct is, in fact, an invariant of the loop (a context assertion again may always be removed).

4.2   Changing variables

The other important class of refinement rules for parallelization involve changing the way in which the program state is represented by variables. We need this e.g. to change a scalar variable into an array for loop parallelization. This again models the replication of a variable across a collection of processes, so that each process can work with its own copy of the variable, with readings and updates taking place in parallel when possible.

We can add assignment statements to a new variable x anywhere in a statement S, if x is made into a local variable:

Rule 8 (*Adding auxilliary variables*)

$$S \equiv [var\ x;\ S[x := h_1/skip^1, \ldots, x := h_n/skip^n]]$$

provided that

(i) S does not contain any occurrence of x.

Here $skip^1, \ldots, skip^n$ denote different occurrences of the $skip$ statement in S. This refinement equivalence can be proved correct in the weakest precondition calculus by structural induction.

Assume that we have initially a statement $[var\ x;\ S]$ and we want to replace the variables x with some other variables y, changing S to S' accordingly, such that

$$[var\ x;\ S] \leq [var\ y;\ S'].$$

(In essence, we are changing the data representation in this statement). We can achieve this by the following sequence of steps:

(1) *Introduce new variables* y. Let $S_1 = S[y_1 := e_1/skip^1, \ldots, y_n := e_n/skip^n]$. Applying rule 8 and monotonicity of refinement, we have

$$[var\ x;\ S] \equiv [var\ x;\ [var\ y;\ S_1]].$$

(2) *Introduce context assertion relating* x *and* y. Let $Q_1, \ldots, Q_k$ be assertions on x and y, and assume that context introduction gives us

$$S_1 \leq S_1[\{Q_1\};\ T_1/T_1, \ldots, \{Q_k\};\ T_k/T_k],$$

where $T_1, \ldots, T_k$ are substatements of S_1 that refer to the variables in x.

(3) *Replace statements on* x *with statements on* y. Let $T_1', \ldots, T_k'$ be statements that do not refer to variables in x, and assume that we can show that

$$\{Q_1\};\ T_1 \leq T_1'$$
$$\vdots$$
$$\{Q_k\};\ T_k \leq T_k'.$$

By transitivity of refinement, we now have

$$S_1 \leq S_1[T_1'/T_1, \ldots, T_k'/T_k] = S_2$$

(4) *Remove old variables* x. Assume that all the remaining occurrences of x are now in assignments to variables in x, i.e.

$$S_2 = S_2'[x := h_1/skip^1, \ldots, x := h_m/skip^m]$$

where S_2' does not contain any occurrences of x.

Applying rule 8 again then gives us

$$
\begin{aligned}
[var\ x;\ [var\ y;\ S_1]] \ &\leq\ [var\ x;\ [var\ y;\ S_2]] \\
&\equiv\ [var\ y;\ [var\ x;\ S_2]] \\
&\equiv\ [var\ y;\ [var\ x;\ S_2'[x := h/skip^1, \ldots, x := h_m/skip^m]]] \\
&\equiv\ [var\ y;\ S_2'].
\end{aligned}
$$

Transitivity of refinement then gives us the desired result

$$[var\ x;\ S] \leq [var\ y;\ S_2'].$$

5 Example derivation: Matrix multiplication

In this section we show the main refinement steps in the construction of a parallel and distributed algorithm for matrix multiplication.

We are interested in performing the multiplication

$$C = A \cdot B$$

where C, A and B are $N \times N$ matrices. We assume that the target architecture consists of N processors configured in a ring. Each processor has a local memory and there is no global memory. Processor i can participate in two–process shared actions with its two neighbours. The intention is that process i should store row i from A, B and C, and that the updating of the rows in C could proceed in parallel. Our task is to design a decentralized and locally scheduled action system of degree 2 for matrix multiplication, to be implemented on this architecture.

Let us start by deriving an alternative definition of matrix multiplication that is more suitable for parallelization. For $i, j = 1, \ldots, N$, we have

$$
\begin{aligned}
C_{i,j} \ &=\ \sum_{k=1}^{N} A_{i,k} \cdot B_{k,j} \\
&=\ \sum_{k=1}^{i-1} A_{i,k} \cdot B_{k,j} + \sum_{k=i}^{N} A_{i,k} \cdot B_{k,j} \\
&=\ \sum_{k=i}^{N} A_{i,k} \cdot B_{k,j} + \sum_{k=1}^{i-1} A_{i,k} \cdot B_{k,j} \\
&=\ \sum_{k'=0}^{N-i} A_{i,i+k'} \cdot B_{i+k',j} + \sum_{k'=N-i+1}^{N-1} A_{i,i+k'-N} \cdot B_{i+k'-N,j} \\
&=\ \sum_{k'=0}^{N-i} A_{i,r(i,k')} \cdot B_{r(i,k')j} + \sum_{k'=N-i+1}^{N-1} A_{i,r(i,k')} \cdot B_{r(i,k')j} \\
&\qquad \text{where } r(i, k') = (i + k' - 1)\, mod\, N + 1 \\
&=\ \sum_{k'=0}^{N-1} A_{i,r(i,k')} \cdot B_{r(i,k')j}
\end{aligned}
$$

Hence, we can compute the value of $C_{i,j}$ by

$C.i.j:=0;\ (k:\ 0..N\text{-}1:\ C.i.j:=\ C.i.j+\ A.i.r(i,k)\star B.r(i,k).j)$

This gives us our initial algorithm for matrix multiplication:

[*function* $r(i,k) = (i+k\text{-}1)\ mod\ N + 1;$ (S0)
$(i:1..N:(j:1..N:\ C.i.j:=\ 0));$
$(k:\ 0..N\text{-}1:$
      $(i:1..N:\ (j:1..N:\ C.i.j:=\ C.i.j+\ A.i.r(i,k)\star B.r(i,k).j)))]$

We compute here all elements $C.i.j$ at the same time for a specific $k = 0,\ldots,N-1$. This is permitted because the computations of the different elements $C.i.j$ are independent of each other. (The index calculations would be slightly simpler if the array indexing was from $0,\ldots,N-1$, but our choice does not complicte the successive derivations so we keep it this way).

We will in the sequel usually not explicitly state that a specific program version is a refinement of another version. Instead, we adopt the convention that successively numbered versions are refinements, i.e. $Si \leq S(i+1)$. The same holds for versions on a nested level, i.e. $Si.j \leq Si.(j+1)$ and so on.

5.1   Shifting the B matrix

Our first refinements are intended to localize the matrix multiplications that have to be done, so that each multiplication only concerns elements with the same row index. In the final architecture all elements with the same row index will be stored in the same processor, so that each multiplication becomes an internal action of a processor.

We will achieve this by rotating the B matrix cyclically after each iteration of k. The transformations below are an example of the method for changing variables described in the previous section. When describing operations on the element of the matrices we often refer to the entire matrix or to a row of a matrix. Let us first add an auxilliary matrix B' to the program, together with assignments to it:

[*function* $r(i,k) = (i+k\text{-}1)\ mod\ N + 1;$ (S1)
var $B'.i.j$ *is integer, i: 1..N, j: 1..N;*
$C:=\ 0;\ B':=\ B;$
$(k:\ 0..N\text{-}1:\ \{Q1\};$
      $(i:1..N:(j:1..N:\ C.i.j:=\ C.i.j+\ A.i.r(i,k)\star B.r(i,k).j));\ \ll S1.1\gg$
      $\|i:1..N:B'.i:=B'.r(i,1)\ \|);\ \{Q2\}\ ]$

We have $S0 \leq S1$, by rule 8. We use above the notation $\ll S1.1 \gg$ to name a substatement in the program (it refers to the immediately preceeding substatement plus the eventual context assertion). Similarly, when writing a context assertion in the program, we say that the context assertion in question can be inserted at the place indicated.

We can show that $Q1$ holds at the place indicated,

$$Q1 = (\forall i : 1..N : (\forall j : 1..N : B'.i.j = B.r(i,k).j)).$$

Hence, we may use B' instead of B for updating C:

$$(i:1..N:(j:1..N: C.i.j:= C.i.j+ A.i.r(i,k)*B'.i.j)) \qquad (S1.2)$$

We can also show that upon termination the B' matrix has been restored to B, i.e.

$$Q2 = (B' = B)$$

holds. We may therefore use B directly in the computation, instead of B' and remove B':

> [*function r(i,k) = (i+k-1) mod N + 1;*   (S2)
> *C:= 0;*
> *(k: 0..N-1:*
>   *(i:1..N:(j:1..N: C.i.j:= C.i.j+ A.i.r(i,k) ⋆ B.i.j));*
>   *‖i:1..N: B.i:=B.r(i,1) ‖ ≪ S2.1 ≫*
>)]

Next we replace the parallel shift $S2.1$ of the B-matrix by a sequential shift:

> [*function r(i,k) = (i+k-1) mod N + 1;*   (S3)
> *function q(i) = (i+1) mod (N+1);*
> *var B.0.j is integer, j: 1..N;*
> *C:= 0;*
> *(k: 0..N-1:*
>   *(i:1..N:(j:1..N: C.i.j:= C.i.j+ A.i.r(i,k) ⋆ B.i.j));*
>   *(i:0..N:(j:1..N: B.i:=B.q(i)))≪ S3.1 ≫*
>)]

The sequential shift $S3.1$ uses the auxilliary function $q(i) = (i + 1) mod(N + 1)$. We also needed to introduce new local variabels $B.0.j$, $j = 1, \ldots, N$, as temporary storage for the cyclic shifting.

Introducing some abbreviations for future convenience, we then have the following version of matrix multiplication:

> [*function r(i,k) = (i+k-1) mod N + 1;*   (S4)
> *function q(i) = (i+1) mod (N+1);*
> *var B.0.j is integer, j: 1..N;*
> *procedure zeroC =(i:1..N:(j:1..N: C.i.j:= 0));*
> *procedure mult.i.k =*
>   *(j:1..N: C.i.j:= C.i.j+ A.i.r(i,k) ⋆ B.i.j), i:1..N, k:0..N-1;*
> *procedure shift.i = (j:1..N: B.i.j:=B.q(i).j), i:0..N;*
> *zeroC;*
> *(k: 0..N-1:*
>   *(i:1..N: mult.i.k); (i:0..N: shift.i)) ≪ S4.1 ≫]*

The notation indicates that we have e.g. $N + 1$ different versions of the shift-procedure, shift.0, \ldots, shift.N.

5.2 Parallelizing the multiplications within a cycle

The multiplications within each cycle are now done in a strictly sequential manner, although they affect disjoint rows. Our next task is to parallelize these. In the sequel, we will focus on the main loop $S4.1$, taking this as the basis for further refinements:

$$(k:\ 0..N\text{-}1: \hspace{6cm} (S4.1)$$
$$(i:1..N:\ mult.i.k);$$
$$(i:0..N:\ shift.i))$$

Let us first move the first shifting operation, $shift.0$, to precede the multiplications:

$$(k:0..N\text{-}1: \hspace{6cm} (S4.2)$$
$$shift.0;$$
$$(i:\ 1..N:\ mult.i.k);\ \ll S4.2.1 \gg$$
$$(i:\ 1..N:\ shift.i))$$

The operation $shift.0$ commutes with each $mult.i.k$ operation because there are no read-write conflicts: the $shift.0$ opeation reads variables $B.1$ and writes variables $B.0$ while the $mult.i.k$ operation reads $C.i, A.i.k, B.i, i = 1, \ldots, N$ and writes $C.i, i = 1, \ldots, N$. This refinement is carried out, because the operation $shift.0$ differs from the other shift-operations.

We add new variables $h.i$ to $S4.2.1$, to keep track of which multiplications already have been done:

$$[var\ h.i\ is\ boolean,\ i:1..N; \hspace{4cm} (S4.2.2)$$
$$(i:\ 1..N:\ h.i:=\ true);$$
$$(i:\ 1..N:\ mult.i.k;\ h.i:=\ false)\ \ll S4.2.2.1 \gg];$$

Next we change the first two multiplications in $S4.2.2.1$ into loops:

$$\star\ [h.1\ \rightarrow\ mult.1.k;\ h.1:=\ false]; \hspace{3cm} (S4.2.2.2)$$
$$\star\ [h.2\ \rightarrow\ mult.2.k;\ h.2:=\ false];$$
$$(i:\ 3..N:\ mult.i.k;\ h.i:=\ false);$$

These are permitted by rule 1, because the actions are initilly enabled ($h.1 = h.2 = true$ initially) and they disable themselves.

We can now merge the two loops into one:

$$\star\ [h.1\ \rightarrow\ mult.1.k;\ h.1:=\ false \hspace{3cm} (S4.2.2.3)$$
$$[]h.2\ \rightarrow\ mult.2.k;\ h.2:=\ false];$$
$$(i:\ 3..N:\ mult.i.k;\ h.i:=\ false);$$

The merge is permitted by rule 4: (1) $mult.2.k$ cannot disable or enable $mult.1.k$, (2) $mult.1.k$ and $mult.2.k$ commute (because they affect different rows) and (3) the second loop must terminate.

The other multiplications can then also be merged into this loop, one by one, by the same reasoning. This gives us:

$\star$ [i: 1..N: h.i $\rightarrow$ mult.i.k; h.i:= false];   (S4.2.2.4)

Hence we have derived the following refinement of statement S4.2:

(k:0..N-1:   (S4.3)
    shift.0;
    [var h.i is boolean, i:1..N;
    (i: 1..N: h.i:= true);
    $\star$[i: 1..N: h.i $\rightarrow$ mult.i.k; h.i:= false]];
    (i: 1..N: shift.i))

All multiplications within a cycle can now be done in parallel.

5.3 Merging shift operations with multiplications

Our next task is to move the shift-operations into the multiplication loop. We are trying to make the whole cycle into a single action system, so the sequential composition of multiplications and shifts must be removed from the cycle.

We first add new variables m.i and assignments to these, to keep track of which shift operations already have been done:

[var h.i is boolean,:1..N; var m.i is boolean, i:0..N;   (S4.4)
(k:0..N-1:
    shift.0; (i: 1..N: h.i:= true); (i: 0..N: m.i:= false); m.1:= true;
    $\star$ [i: 1..N: h.i $\rightarrow$ mult.i.k; h.i:= false]]; {Q3};
    (i: 1..N: shift.i; m.i,m.q(i):= false, true)
)]

We have also moved the declarations outwards, to the beginning of the block. Assertion Q3 holds after the multiplication loop,

$$Q3 = (\forall i : 1..N : \neg h.i) \land m.1.$$

We then make shift.1 into a loop:

[var h.i is boolean, i:1..N; var m.i is boolean, i:0..N;   (S4.5)
(k:0..N-1:
    shift.0; (i: 1..N: h.i:= true); (i: 0..N: m.i:= false); m.1:= true;
    $\star$ [i: 1..N: h.i $\rightarrow$ mult.i.k; h.i:= false];
    $\star$ [m.1 $\land$ $\neg$h.1$\rightarrow$ shift.1; m.1,m.2:= false, true];
    (i: 2..N: shift.i; m.i,m.q(i):= false, true)
)]

This is permitted, because (1) the action disables itself and (2) the action is initially enabled, by assertion Q3 and the initialization of m.1

The shift.1 operation is then merged with the preceeding loop:

[*var h.i is boolean, i:1..N; var m.i is boolean, i:0..N;*   *(S4.6)*
 (k:0..N-1:
     shift.0; (i: 1..N: h.i:= true); (i: 0..N: m.i:= false); m.1:= true;
     ⋆ *[i: 1..N: h.i → mult.i.k; h.i:= false*
     []m.1 ∧ ¬h.1→ shift.1; m.1,m.2:= false, true];
     (i: 2..N: shift.i; m.i,m.q(i):= false, true)
)]

This is permitted by rule 4, because

1. *shift*.1 does not disable or enable any multiplication,

2. *shift*.1 commutes with every *mult.i.k*, $i \neq 1$, while for $i = 1$, *shift*.1 cannot precede *mult*.1.*k*, as

$$m.1 \wedge \neg h.1 \Rightarrow wp(shift.1; m.1, m.2 := false, true, \neg h.1) = \neg h.1$$

and

3. the *shift*.1 loop terminates.

The rest of the *shift.i* actions can then also be merged one by one into the multiplication loop:

[*var h.i is boolean, i:1..N; var m.i is boolean, i:0..N;*   *(S4.7)*
 (k:0..N-1:
     shift.0; (i: 1..N: h.i:= true); (i: 0..N: m.i:= false); m.1:= true;
     ⋆ *[i: 1..N: h.i → mult.i.k; h.i:= false*
     []i:1..N: m.i ∧ ¬h.i→ shift.i; m.i,m.q(i):= false, true];
)]

The *shift.i* operations do not interfere with the multiplication actions, for $i = 1, \ldots, N$, by the same reasoning as above. We also need to show that *shift.i* does not interfere with the operations $shift.1, \ldots, shift.(i-1)$ already added to the loop. This is seen as follows:

1. *shift.i* does not enable or disable $shift.j$, $1 \leq j < i$.

2. *shift.i* cannot precede $shift.j$, $j < i$, because

$$m.i \wedge \neg h.i \Rightarrow wp(shift.i; m.i, m.q(i) := false, true, \neg m.j \vee h.j) = \neg m.j \vee h.j$$

This again is valid because

$$Q4 = (\forall i : 0..N : m.i \Rightarrow (\forall j : 0..N : j \neq i \Rightarrow \neg m.j))$$

is invariant of all the actions in the loop where $shift.1, \ldots, shift.(i-1)$ have been inserted, and is also an invariant of the action with *shift.i*.

The variables *m.i* simulate here a token that is passed from process to the next in the ring, to guarantee that the shift operations are done in the correct order.

5.4   Move cycle initialization inside loop

Next we make also the initialization of each cycle into an action of the multiplication loop. We first add variables *iter.i*, to keep count on the number of iterations already done and to prevent successive cycles from being mixed up:

> [*var h.i is boolean, i:1..N; var m.i is boolean, i:0..N;*   (S4.8)
> *var iter.i is integer, i:0..N;*
> (*i: 0..N: iter.i:= 0*);
> (*k:0..N-1: {Q5}*;
>   *shift.0;* (*i: 1..N: h.i, m.i:= true, false*);
>   *m.0,m.1:= false,true; iter.0:= iter.0+1; {Q6}*;
>   ⋆ [*i: 1..N: h.i* → *mult.i.k; h.i:= false*
>   []*i: 1..N: m.i* ∧ ¬*h.i*→ *shift.i; m.i,m.q(i),iter.i:− false, true,iter.i+1*]
>)]

The assertion Q5 holds at the indicated place,

$$Q5 = (\forall i : 0..N : iter.i = k).$$

Thus the iteration counters are in step whenever the next cycle is about to start.

The assertion $Q6$ is an invariant of the loop,

$$Q6 \; = \; (\forall i : 1..N : h.i \Rightarrow iter.i = k) \land$$
$$(\forall i : 1..N : m.i \Rightarrow (\forall j : i..N : iter.i = k) \land (\forall j : 0..i-1 : iter.j = k+1))$$

Because of it, we can add the assertion $iter.i = k$ to the guards of the loop, by rule 7:

> [*var h.i is boolean, i:1..N; var m.i is boolean, i:0..N;*   (S4.9)
> *var iter.i is integer, i:0..N;*
> (*i: 0..N: iter.i:= 0*);
> (*k:0..N-1:*
>   *shift.0;* (*i: 1..N: h.i, m.i:= true, false*);
>   *m.0,m.1:= false,true; iter.0:= iter.0+1;*
>   ⋆ [*i: 1..N: h.i* ∧ *iter.i = k*→ *mult.i.k; h.i:= false*
>   []*i: 1..N: m.i* ∧ ¬*h.i* ∧ *iter.i = k*→
>   *shift.i; m.i,m.q(i),iter.i:= false, true,iter.i+1*]
>)]

We can then set the variables *h.i* to true in the *shift.i* actions and also replace reference to k in *mult.i.k* by *iter.i*:

> [*var h.i is boolean, i:1..N; var m.i is boolean, i:0..N;*   (S4.10)
> *var iter.i is integer, i:0..N;*
> (*i: 0..N: iter.i:= 0*);
> (*k:0..N-1:*
>   *shift.0;* (*i: 1..N: h.i, m.i:= true, false*);
>   *m.0,m.1:= false,true; iter.0:= iter.0+1;*

$$\star \ [i\colon 1..N\colon h.i \wedge iter.i = k \rightarrow mult.i.(iter.i); \ h.i := false$$
$$[]i\colon 1..N\colon m.i \wedge \neg h.i \wedge iter.i = k \rightarrow$$
$$shift.i; \ m.i, m.q(i), iter.i, h.i := false, \ true, iter.i+1, true \ ]; \{Q7\}$$
$$)]$$

The change of k to $iter.i$ is justified by the guard. The updating of $h.i$ is justified because $iter.i$ is set to $k+1$ at the same time, so the multiplication actions do not become enabled anew in this cycle.

Assertion $Q7$ will now hold at the indicated place,

$$Q7 = (\forall i : 1..N : h.i \wedge \neg m.i) \wedge m.0$$

Hence we can remove the initializations between the cycles as unnecessary. The initialization of the first cycle is moved to the beginning of the program. We add initial assignments to $m.0$ and $m.1$, to get into step with the situation after the next iteration:

$$[var \ h.i \ is \ boolean, \ i{:}1..N; \ var \ m.i \ is \ boolean, \ i{:}0..N; \qquad (S4.11)$$
$$var \ iter.i \ is \ integer, \ i{:}0..N;$$
$$(i\colon 0..N\colon iter.i := 0); \ (i\colon 1..N\colon h.i, \ m.i := true, \ false); \ m.0 := true;$$
$$(k{:}0..N{-}1\colon$$
$$\quad (shift.0; \ m.0, \ m.1 := false, true; \ iter.0 := iter.0 + 1 \ll S4.11.1 \gg;$$
$$\quad \star \ [i\colon 1..N\colon h.i \wedge iter.i = k \rightarrow mult.i.(iter.i); \ h.i := false$$
$$\quad []i\colon 1..N\colon m.i \wedge \neg h.i \wedge iter.i = k \rightarrow$$
$$\qquad shift.i; \ m.i, m.q(i), iter.i, h.i := false, \ true, iter.i+1, true \ ]$$
$$)]$$

The statement $S4.11.1$ can now be changed into a loop

$$\star \ [\ m.0 \wedge iter.0 = k \rightarrow \qquad\qquad (S4.11.2)$$
$$\quad shift.0; \ m.0, \ m.1 := false, true; \ iter.0 := iter.0 + 1]$$

and merged with the loop following it, to get:

$$[var \ h.i \ is \ boolean, \ i{:}1..N; \ var \ m.i \ is \ boolean, \ i{:}0..N; \qquad (S4.12)$$
$$var \ iter.i \ is \ integer, \ i{:}0..N;$$
$$(i\colon 0..N\colon iter.i := 0); \ (i\colon 1..N\colon h.i, \ m.i := true, \ false); \ m.0 := true;$$
$$(k{:}0..N{-}1\colon$$
$$\quad \star \ [\ m.0 \wedge iter.0 = k \rightarrow$$
$$\qquad shift.0; \ m.0, \ m.1 := false, true; \ iter.0 := iter.0 + 1$$
$$\quad []i\colon 1..N\colon h.i \wedge iter.i = k \rightarrow mult.i.(iter.i); \ h.i := false$$
$$\quad []i\colon 1..N\colon m.i \wedge \neg h.i \wedge iter.i = k \rightarrow$$
$$\qquad shift.i; \ m.i, m.q(i), iter.i, h.i := false, \ true, iter.i+1, true \ ]$$
$$)]$$

This is again justified by rule 4. We omit the details of the proof here.

5.5   Change outer iteration into loop

We are now ready for the final steps, where we change the whole sequence of cycles into a single action system. We can again use rule 4, merging all actions into a single loop, in the same way as was done above. This gives us

[var h.i is boolean, i:1..N; var m.i is boolean, i:0..N;   (S4.13)
var iter.i is integer, i:0..N;
(i: 0..N: iter.i:= 0); (i: 1..N: h.i, m.i:= true, false); m.0:= true;
$\star$ [k:0..N-1: m.0 $\wedge$ iter.0 = k$\rightarrow$
             shift.0; m.0, m.1:= false,true; iter.0:= iter.0+1
[]k:0..N-1, i: 1..N: h.i $\wedge$ iter.i = k$\rightarrow$ mult.i.(iter.i); h.i:= false
[]k:0..N-1, i: 1..N: m.i $\wedge$ $\neg$h.i $\wedge$ iter.i = k$\rightarrow$
             shift.i; m.i,m.q(i),iter.i,h.i:= false, true,iter.i+1,true]
)]

The justification of this step is similar to the preceding ones (although somewhat tedious).

We can now combine all those actions that have the same body into a single action with this same body, but with the disjunction of all the action guards as its guard:

[var h.i is boolean, i:0..N; var m.i is boolean, i:0..N;   (S4.14)
var iter.i is integer, i:0..N;
(i: 1..N: iter.i, h.i, m.i:= 0,true, false); iter.0,h.0,m.0:= 0,false,true;
$\star$ [i: 1..N: h.i $\wedge$ iter.i < N$\rightarrow$ mult.i.(iter.i); h.i:= false
[]i: 0..N: m.i $\wedge$ $\neg$h.i $\wedge$ iter.i < N$\rightarrow$
             shift.i; m.i,m.q(i),iter.i,h.i:= false, true,iter.i+1,i $\neq$ 0]
)]

This follows from the fact that

$$(\vee k : 0..N - 1 : m.0 \wedge iter.0 = k) \Leftrightarrow m.0 \wedge iter.0 < N$$

(in combination with the loop invariant $iter.i \geq 0$) and similarly for the other actions. We have also massaged the shift-actions a little bit, so that they also all have the same body.

5.6   Final version

The final version of our algorithm is now as follows:

[function r(i,k) = (i+k-1) mod N + 1;   (S5)
function q(i) = (i+1) mod (N+1);
var B.0.j is integer, j: 1..N;
var h.i is boolean, m.i is boolean, iter.i is integer, i:0..N;
procedure zeroC = (i:1..N:(j:1..N: C.i.j:= 0));
procedure mult.i =
        (j:1..N: C.i.j:= C.i.j+ A.i.r(i,iter.i) $\star$ B.i.j), i:1..N;
procedure shift.i =

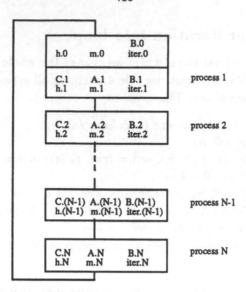

Figure 2: The structure of the parallel program.

$(j:1..N: B.i.j:=B.q(i).j)$, $i:0..N$;
zeroC;
$(i: 1..N: iter.i, h.i, m.i:= 0,true, false)$; $iter.0, h.0, m.0:= 0, false, true$;
$\star$ [$i: 1..N: h.i \wedge iter.i < N \rightarrow mult.i$; $h.i:= false$
    [] $i: 0..N: m.i \wedge \neg h.i \wedge iter.i < N \rightarrow$
            $shift.i$; $m.i,m.q(i),iter.i,h.i:= false, true,iter.i+1,i \neq 0$]
)]

We can implement this program on either $N+1$ or N processors, depending on whether we want to allocate a separate processor to the variables with index 0. In both cases the resulting program is obviously decentralized and has only one and two-process actions, the latter involving only neighbours in the ring. The only action with two processes is $shift.i$ for $i \geq 1$. This action will involve processes $p.i$ and $p.(i + 1)$. If we choose $p.i$ to be a committer in this action, then no other action in which $p.i$ is involved can be enabled at the same time as $shift.i$ is enabled. Hence, the system is locally scheduled, as required.

The process structure is shown in Figure 2. All multiplications can be done in parallel in the program. The shift-operations can proceed simultaneously with the multiplications, moving the m-token around the processor ring, but only one $shift.i$ operation may be in progress at a time. Multiplications from two successive cycles can be in progress at the same time. The only synchronization is that the next row of the B matrix may not be shifted into a processor before the previous row has been used for the multiplication.

6 Concluding remarks

The refinement calculus and the action system formalism has been combined into a formal method for the stepwise construction of parallel algorithms. The combination gives us a methodology where the entire derivation of such systems can be done in the context of purely sequential programs.

In [BaSe88a] a detailed case study of the method was carried out: a parallel and distributed algorithm for solving linear systems of equations was constructed by stepwise refinement, starting from the original sequential Gaussian elimination algorithm. The study showed that the main body of the derivation could be done using only a few transformation rules and methods, by which the parallelism in the algorithm was increased step by step. In this derivation the atomicity refinement rule (rule 6) played an equally central role as the rule for merging loops has played in the derivation of the matrix algorithm above.

Stepwise refinement of parallel programs is also studied in [ChMi88] with the UNITY approach. UNITY programs are very similar to action systems, although their actions are restricted to conditional, deterministic assignment statements. The approach to refinement is also different from ours: the specification of the program is refined instead of refining the program text as we do here. Another approach to the construction of totally correct parallel programs is presented in [LaSi79]. Commutativity as a tool in verifying correctness of parallel programs is also emphasized in [Lengauer82] and [Lipton75].

Acknowledgements

The work reported here was supported by the Academy of Finland, the Ministry of Education in Finland and the FINSOFT III program sponsored by the Technology Development Centre of Finland. We would like to thank Jochum von Wright for helpful discussions on the topics treated here.

References

[Back78]   R.J.R. Back, *On the Correctness of Refinement in Program Development*, Ph.D. thesis, Report A–1978-4, Department of Computer Science, University of Helsinki, 1978.

[Back80]   R.J.R. Back, *Correctness Preserving Program Refinements: Proof Theory and Applications*, Mathematical Center Tracts 131, Mathematical Centre, Amsterdam 1980.

[Back88a]   R.J.R. Back, A Calculus of Refinements for Program Derivations,*Acta Informatica*, Vol 25, 1988, pp. 593–624, Springer–Verlag.

[Back88b]   R.J.R. Back, Refining Atomicity in Parallel Algorithms, *Åbo Akademi, Reports on computer science and mathematics*, Ser. A, No 57,1988. To appear in PARLE Conference on Parallel Architectures and Languages Europe, Eindhoven, the Netherlands, June 12–16, 1989.

[BaHaKu85] R.J.R. Back, E. Hartikainen and R. Kurki-Suonio, Multi-process handshaking on broadcasting networks, *Åbo Akademi, Reports on computer science and mathematics*, Ser. A, No 42,1985.

[BaKu83]   R.J.R. Back and R. Kurki-Suonio, Decentralization of process nets with centralized control, *2nd ACM SIGACT-SIGOPS Symp. on Principles of Distributed Computing*, Montreal, Canada, August 1983, pp. 131–142.

[BaKu88]   R.J.R. Back and R. Kurki-Suonio, Distributed Co–operation with Action Systems, *ACM Transactions on Programming Languages and Systems 10*, October 1988, pp.513–554.

[BaSe88a]   R.J.R. Back and K. Sere, An exercise in deriving parallel algorithms: Gaussian elimination, *Åbo Akademi, Reports on computer science and mathematics*, Ser. A, No 65,1988.

[BaSe88b]   R.J.R. Back and K. Sere, An Implementation of Action Systems in occam, Åbo Akademi, in preparation.

[ChMi88]   K.M. Chandy and J. Misra, *Parallel Program Design: A Foundation*, Addison–Wesley, 1988.

[Dijkstra76] E.W. Dijkstra, *A Discipline of Programming*, Prentice–Hall International, 1976.

[Hoare78]   C.A.R. Hoare, Communicating sequential processes, *CACM*, Vol 21, No 8, August 1978, pp. 666–677.

[INMOS84]   INMOS Ltd., *occam Programming Manual*, Prentice–Hall International, 1984.

[LaSi79]   A. van Lamsweerde and M. Sintzoff, Formal Derivation of Strongly Correct Concurrent Programs, *Acta Informatica*, Vol 12, 1979, pp. 1–31, Springer–Verlag.

[Lengauer82] C. Lengauer, A Methodology for Programming with Concurrency: The Formalism, *Science of Computer Programming 2*, 1982, pp. 19–52, North–Holland.

[Lipton75]   R.J. Lipton, Reduction: A Method of Proving Properties of Parallel Programs, *CACM*, Vol 18, No 12, December 1975, pp. 717–721.

[Morgan88]   C. Morgan, The Specification Statement, *ACM Transactions on Programming Languages and Systems*, Vol 10, No 3, July 1988, pp. 403–419.

[Morris87]   J.M. Morris, A Theoretical Basis for Stepwise Refinement and the Programming Calculus, *Science of Computer Programming 9*, 1987, pp. 287–306, North–Holland.

[Wright88]   J. von Wright, A Derivation of a Parallel Matrix Multiplication Algorithm, Åbo Akademi, manuscript.

A Lattice-theoretical Basis for a Specification Language

R.J.R. Back *   J. von Wright [†]

Abstract

A very basic lattice-based language of commands, based on the primitive operations of substitution and test for equality, is constructed. This base language
permits unbounded nondeterminism, demonic and angelic nondeterminism and is
extended to permit miracles also. It is shown to be complete, in the sense that
all monotonic predicate transformers can be constructed in it. The base language
provides a unifying framework for various specification languages; we show how two
Dijkstra-style specification languages can be embedded in the base language.

1 Introduction

The weakest precondition calculus of [Dijkstra76] identifies the meaning of a program
statement with its weakest precondition predicate transformer. Dijkstra's "healthiness
conditions" state that these predicate transformers for executable program statements
are strict (Law of excluded miracle), monotonic, conjunctive (and-distributive) and continuous (or-continuous).

Extensions to the Dijkstra-style programming language that drop some of the healthiness conditions have subsequently been used to allow treatment of specifications, parallel
programs and data refinement. [Back78, Back80] introduces weakest preconditions for
specifications. Unbounded determinism is permitted, thus dropping the continuity condition. Further, a refinement relation on statements is introduced, such that S is refined
by S' iff

$$\forall Q.(\mathrm{wp}_S(Q) \Rightarrow \mathrm{wp}_{S'}(Q))$$

where wp_S is the weakest precondition predicate transformer for S. In [Hehner84, Mor-
ris87] statements are identified with predicate transformers, an approach which also we
follow in this paper. Thus we write $S(Q)$ for $\mathrm{wp}_S(Q)$. In [deBakker80, Nelson87] the
weakest precondition calculus is extended to cover partial state transformers, i.e. nonstrict statements. [Morgan88b] and [Morris87] write specifications as pre-postcondition
pairs, also allowing miracles (nonstrict statements). The actions of [Back88a], used to

---

*Åbo Akademi, Department of Computer Science, Lemminkäisenkatu 14, SF-20520 Turku, Finland
[†]Swedish School of Economics and Business Education, Biblioteksgatan 16, SF-65100 Vasa, Finland

model parallel programs, are also nonstrict. In [GaMo88] a conjunction operation on statements is defined, such that the resulting statements are not conjunctive. The same holds for the angelic basic statement of [Back88b]. Generalized specification languages are also considered in [Hesselink88]. Thus, in going from a pure programming language to a specification language, we see that most of the original healthiness conditions have been questioned, in order to gain expressive power. In this sense a specification language is truly more general than a programming language, for which all the original healthiness conditions are well motivated.

In [Morris87] it is noted that the monotonic predicate transformers form a lattice, with the partial order corresponding to the refinement ordering of statements. This is indirectly noted also in [GaMo88], where the operators ∥ (choice) and + (conjunction) on statements correspond to the lattice operators meet and join on predicate transformers. Similar operators, written ∩ and ∪, are introduced in [HHH87].

In this paper we show how simple specification languages can be constructed within the complete lattice of monotonic predicate transformers, using only very simple primitive statements and functional (sequential) composition in addition to meets and joins.

In section 2 we define the lattice-based language *Cmd*, which has a substitution command and a test command as primitives. In section 3 we show that our language is complete, in the sense that all strict monotonic predicate transformers can be constructed within it. In section 4, a lattice-based language *Cmd⁰*, which is dual to *Cmd*, is constructed. This language permits miraculous (non-strict) statements. We also combine these two languages into a single lattice-based theory which covers all monotonic predicate transformers. In sections 5 and 6 we show how statements of two more conventional languages with assignments, conditional composition and recursion, but also permitting unbounded determinism, angelic and demonic nondeterminism and miracles, can be constructed within *Cmd*.

Prerequisites We assume the concepts of partial orders and lattices (complete, distributive and boolean lattices) are familiar, as presented in e.g. [Birkhoff61,Grätzer78], as well as the weakest precondition technique of [Dijkstra76].

In the following we assume that L is a lattice. We say that K is a complete sublattice of L if all meets and joins in K yield the same result as when taken in L. We will make use of the *pointwise extended* partial order on the set $[K \to L]$ of functions from a set K to a lattice L, defined by

$$f \leq g \quad \stackrel{\text{def}}{=} \quad \forall x.(f(x) \leq g(x))$$

We assume that *Var* is a countable set of *program variables*, with typical element u and typical list of distinct elements v. Sometimes we will need to consider all the elements of *Var* as a list, which we will then denote V. Further we assume a flat domain D of values, with typical element c and typical list of elements d. A *state* is a (total) function from *Var* to D. We assume that there are no undefined values. The set of all states is called the *state space* and is denoted Σ, with typical element σ. A *(semantic) substitution* in Σ is defined in the following way: $\sigma[c/u]$ is the state which differs from σ only in that it assigns the value c to the variable u.

Let *Bool* be the complete lattice of truth values for a two-valued logic, $Bool = \{ff, tt\}$, ordered so that $ff < tt$ (the implication ordering). A *predicate* is a total function from Σ to *Bool*. We denote the set of all predicates *Pred* with typical elements P and Q. Pointwise extension of the partial order on *Bool*,

$$P \leq Q \stackrel{\text{def}}{=} \forall \sigma.(P(\sigma) \leq Q(\sigma))$$

makes *Pred* a complete boolean lattice (we can interpret $P \leq Q$ as "P implies Q"and meet (join) as logical conjunction (disjunction) of predicates). The bottom element of *Pred* is the predicate *false* and the top element is the predicate *true*.

Substitutions in Σ are extended to *Pred* in a natural way. The predicate $P[d/v]$ assigns to any state σ the same truth value as P assigns to $\sigma[d/v]$.

We say that a *predicate P depends on the variable u* if there exist values c_1 and c_2 such that $P[c_1/u] \neq P[c_2/u]$. The set of variables that the predicate P depends on is denoted $Var(P)$.

Assume that v is a list of distinct variables and that $\{Q_d\}$ is a set of predicates indexed by the set of all lists of values from D of the same length as v. We use the following notations for *qualified meets* (and the corresponding notations for joins): $\bigwedge_{d:P[d/v]} Q_d$ (or simply $\bigwedge_{d:P} Q$) means taking the meet over all lists d of elements from D such that $P[d/v] = true$, thus

$$\bigwedge_{d:P[d/v]} Q_d \stackrel{\text{def}}{=} \bigwedge \{Q_d | d \text{ a list} \wedge P[d/v] = true\}$$

$$\bigvee_{d:P[d/v]} Q_d \stackrel{\text{def}}{=} \bigvee \{Q_d | d \text{ a list} \wedge P[d/v] = true\}$$

Then $\bigwedge_{d:true}$ is the same as $\bigwedge_d$, the meet over all lists d of appropriate length, and $\bigvee_{d:true}$ is the same as $\bigvee_d$. The length of the list d is assumed to be clear from the context.

Quantified predicates are defined as follows:

$$\forall v.P \stackrel{\text{def}}{=} \bigwedge_d P[d/v]$$

$$\exists v.P \stackrel{\text{def}}{=} \bigvee_d P[d/v]$$

Given these definitions, we can treat predicates predicates much in the same way as we treat ordinary first-order formulas. In particular, substitution distributes over connectives and quantifications.

The lattice of predicate transformers *Predicate transformers* are total functions from *Pred* to *Pred*. The set of all predicate transformers is denoted *Ptran*, with typical element S. *Ptran* is a complete boolean lattice with the pointwise extended partial order from *Pred*:

$$S \leq S' \stackrel{\text{def}}{=} \forall P.(S(P) \leq S'(P))$$

This ordering is equivalent to the *refinement ordering* of [Back78,Back80]. It is also used in [Morris87] and [GaMo88]. The bottom element, called **abort**, maps every predicate to *false* and the top element, called **magic**, maps every predicate to *true*.

We write $S_1; S_2$ for the functional composition (here called *sequential composition*) of two predicate transformers S_1 and S_2. Thus $(S_1; S_2)(P) = S_1(S_2(P))$.

We denote the sublattice of predicate transformers that are both strict and monotonic *SMtran*. *SMtran* is a complete lattice and all meets and joins, except $\bigwedge \emptyset$, yield the same result when taken in *SMtran* as when taken in *Ptran*.

Predicate transformers interpreted as statements We interpret monotonic predicate transformers as statements, identifying statements with their weakest precondition predicate transformers. The intuitive meaning of the statement S, identified with the predicates transformer S, is the following (see [Dijkstra76]): The statement S is guaranteed to terminate in a state in which P holds if and only if it is executed in an initial state in which the predicate $S(P)$ holds (where P is an arbitrary predicate). Thus, for example, a statement (predicate transformer) that maps *true* to *true* is guaranteed to terminate for all initial states. The statement **abort** maps *true* to *false*. Thus it cannot terminate. The statement **magic**, on the other hand, maps *false* to *true*. Since the predicate *false* does not hold in any state, this means that **magic** achieves the impossible; we say it is *miraculous*. Miraculous statements cannot be implemented, but they can be useful in program development [Morgan88a, Morgan88b]. In this respect they resemble imaginary numbers.

2 A lattice-based specification language

In this section we construct a lattice of commands. These commands will form a sublattice of *Ptran*.

As noted above, u denotes a program variable and v a list of distinct program variables, while c denotes a value from D and d a list of values from D. As a basis for our specification language we introduce two primitive commands, the *(multiple) substitution command* $\langle d/v \rangle$ and the *(single, strict) test command* $\langle u = c \rangle$ defined by

$$\langle d/v \rangle(Q) \stackrel{\text{def}}{=} Q[d/v]$$
$$\langle u = c \rangle(Q) \stackrel{\text{def}}{=} (u = c) \wedge Q$$

for all predicates Q. All multiple tests can be defined as the meet of the component tests. On the other hand, only finite substitutions can be constructed using single substitutions (by sequential composition); thus we could use the single substitution command as primitive if we restricted ourselves to only finite substitutions.

Starting from the primitive commands we generate new commands by applying three command constructors: sequential composition, meet and join. These constructors have the same meaning as in the lattice of predicate transformers. Thus, commands are defined by

$$
\begin{array}{llll}
S & ::= & \langle d/v \rangle & (substitution\ command) \\
& | & \langle u = c \rangle & (test\ command) \\
& | & S_1; S_2 & (sequential\ composition) \\
& | & \bigwedge_{i \in I} S_i & (meet) \\
& | & \bigvee_{i \in I} S_i & (join)
\end{array}
$$

where S, S_1, S_2 and S_i are commands and I is any index set. We follow the convention that the constructor ";" binds tighter than "$\wedge$", which in turn binds tighter than "$\vee$". The commands thus generated form a complete sublattice of $SMtran$ which we call Cmd. We refer to it as the *base language*. This language permits both demonic and angelic nondeterminism, the former introduced by the meet and the latter by the join operator. It also permits unbounded nondeterminism, since arbitrary meets and joins are permitted,

Let us look at a few example commands. Assume that P is a predicate and v is a list of variables with $Var(P) \subseteq v$. Then

$$(\bigvee_{d:P} \langle v = d \rangle)(Q) \quad = \quad P \wedge Q \tag{1}$$

$$(\bigwedge_{d:P} \langle d/v \rangle)(Q) \quad = \quad \forall v.(P \Rightarrow Q), \text{ if } P \neq false \tag{2}$$

$$(\bigvee_{d:P} \langle d/v \rangle)(Q) \quad = \quad \exists v.(P \wedge Q) \tag{3}$$

where d in the meets $\bigwedge_{d:P}$ and the joins $\bigvee_{d:P}$ ranges over all lists such that $P[d/v] = true$. If $P = false$ then $\bigwedge_{d:P} \langle d/v \rangle$ degenerates to $\bigwedge \emptyset$, the top element of Cmd (see (7) below). As special cases of the above, with $P = true$, we have

$$(\bigvee_{d} \langle v = d \rangle)(Q) \quad = \quad Q \tag{4}$$

$$(\bigwedge_{d} \langle d/v \rangle)(Q) \quad = \quad \forall v.Q \tag{5}$$

$$(\bigvee_{d} \langle d/v \rangle)(Q) \quad = \quad \exists v.Q \tag{6}$$

The above commands can be used as building blocks when constructing other commands,

The bottom element of Cmd is **abort**, generated as $\bigvee \emptyset$. The top element is **choose**, defined by

$$\textbf{choose } (Q) \quad \overset{\text{def}}{=} \quad \exists V.Q \quad = \quad \begin{cases} true & \text{if } Q \neq false \\ false & \text{if } Q = false \end{cases} \tag{7}$$

(recall that V is a list containing all program variables). This is obviously the greatest possible strict predicate transformer. The command **choose** is constructed as $\bigvee_d \langle d/V \rangle$ (or as $\bigwedge \emptyset$), it is an extreme angelic command which succeeds always when it is possible.

The classical healthiness axioms state that the wp predicate transformers are strict (i.e. satisfy the Law of Excluded Miracle), monotonic and conjunctive. Statements that are disjunctive but not conjunctive are considered in [GaMo88, Back88b].

The commands of Cmd are easily shown to be both strict and monotonic. Simple counterexamples show that the commands of Cmd are generally neither conjunctive nor disjunctive. However, the primitive commands are both conjunctive and disjunctive. Furthermore, sequential composition preserves both conjunctivity and disjunctivity, while meets (and least upper bounds of ascending sequences) preserve conjunctivity and joins (and greatest lower bounds of descending sequences) preserve disjunctivity.

We summarize the main results concerning the base language.

THEOREM 1 *The language Cmd is a complete sublattice of SMtran, with top element* **choose** *and bottom element* **abort**. *Its primitive commands are conjunctive and disjunctive. Conjunctivity is preserved by sequential composition and meets, while disjunctivity is preserved by sequential composition and joins.*

Intuitive interpretation of the base language commands The substitution command $\langle d/v \rangle$ is interpretated as assigning the values d to the variables v, leaving the rest of the state unchanged (it always terminates). The test command $\langle u = c \rangle$ terminates without changing the state if the value of the variable u in the initial state is c, otherwise it aborts.

Sequential composition has its usual interpretation. The meet $S_1 \wedge S_2$ is interpreted as a demonic choice between the two commands S_1 and S_2. Thus, for $S_1 \wedge S_2$ to establish some condition P we require that both S_1 and S_2 establish P. The join $S_1 \vee S_2$, on the other hand, is interpreted as an angelic choice between S_1 and S_2. For $S_1 \vee S_2$ to establish some condition P it is enough that either S_1 or S_2 establishes P.

3 Completeness of the language

In this section we show that $Cmd = SMtran$, i.e. that all strict monotonic predicate transformers can be generated within Cmd.

We first define the concept of base for a lattice. A subset B of a lattice L is a $\vee$-*base* (or just *base*) for L if every element of L can be written as a join of elements in B (note that the bottom element of a complete lattice can be written as the empty join).

A base for *Pred* is formed by the one-state predicates $\{b_\sigma | \sigma \in \Sigma\}$, where b_σ is defined by

$$b_\sigma(\sigma') = \begin{cases} tt & \text{if } \sigma' = \sigma \\ ff & \text{otherwise} \end{cases}$$

Using this base, any predicate P can be written as

$$P = \bigvee_{\sigma : P(\sigma)} b_\sigma$$

A base for *SMtran* is the set of predicate transformers $\{G_{P,\sigma} | false \neq P \in Pred, \sigma \in \Sigma\}$ where $G_{P,\sigma}$ is defined by

$$G_{P,\sigma}(Q) = \begin{cases} b_\sigma & \text{if } P \leq Q \\ false & \text{otherwise} \end{cases} \tag{8}$$

$G_{P,\sigma}$ is a command which establishes P (and, by monotonicity, all predicates implied by P) when executed in the initial state σ and aborts otherwise. The condition $P \neq false$ in (8) makes every $G_{P,\sigma}$ strict.

We now state the completeness theorem.

THEOREM 2 *Any strict monotonic predicate transformer S can be generated within our base language Cmd. In fact,*

$$S = \bigvee_{P \in Pred} \bigvee_{\sigma : S(P)(\sigma)} (\langle V = \sigma(V) \rangle; \bigwedge_{d : P} \langle d/V \rangle)$$

Proof Let V be the list of all variables in Var and consider an arbitrary $G_{P,\sigma}$. Then

$$((V = \sigma(V)); \bigwedge_{d:P} \langle d/V \rangle)(Q)$$
$= $ [definitions of constructors and primitive commands]
$$(V = \sigma(V)) \wedge \bigwedge_{d:P} Q[d/V]$$
$= $ [rewriting]
$$b_\sigma \wedge \forall V.(P \Rightarrow Q)$$
$= $ [definition of $G_{p,\sigma}$]
$$G_{p,\sigma}(Q)$$

for every predicate Q. Thus

$$G_{P,\sigma} = \langle V = \sigma(V) \rangle; \bigwedge_{d:P} \langle d/V \rangle$$

Since every element of a base of $SMtran$ can be constructed, this means that every strict monotonic predicate transformer can be generated within Cmd, i.e. the language is complete. The actual construction is done by taking the join over the appropriate members of the base. $\square$

4 A dual language with miracles

The base language Cmd does not permit miracles (nonstrict commands). In this section we consider a command lattice Cmd^0, which is dual to Cmd and which contains miraculous commands.

For every predicate transformers S we define its *dual* S^0 by

$$S^0(Q) \stackrel{\text{def}}{=} \neg S(\neg Q) \tag{9}$$

for all predicates Q. The following properties hold:

$$\begin{aligned}
(S^0)^0 &= S \\
S \text{ monotonic} &\Leftrightarrow S^0 \text{ monotonic} \\
S_1 \leq S_2 &\Leftrightarrow S_2^0 \leq S_1^0 \\
(S_1 \wedge S_2)^0 &= S_1^0 \vee S_2^0 \\
(S_1 \vee S_2)^0 &= S_1^0 \wedge S_2^0
\end{aligned}$$

We define $Cmd^0 = \{S^0 | S \in Cmd\}$. Then from the above properties it follows that Cmd^0 is a complete lattice and that $(Cmd^0, \geq)$ is isomorphic with $(Cmd, \leq)$. By calculating duals we get the following results. Cmd^0 consists of all the monotonic predicate transformers that are strict with respect to *true*. It contains miracles (commands that are not strict with respect to *false*), these are the duals of possibly nonterminating commands in Cmd. On the other hand, all commands in Cmd^0 are always terminating (since they are strict with respect to *true*).

The top element of Cmd^0 is **magic**, which is constructed as $\bigwedge \emptyset$ (dual to the construction of **abort** in Cmd). The bottom element is **fail**, defined by

$$\textbf{fail } (Q) \overset{\text{def}}{=} \forall V.Q \; = \; \begin{cases} \textit{true} & \text{if } Q = \textit{true} \\ \textit{false} & \text{if } Q \neq \textit{true} \end{cases}$$

By (6), **fail** is constructed as $\bigwedge_d \langle d/V \rangle$ (or as $\bigvee \emptyset$). The command **fail** is the dual of **choose**, it avoids to produce the required final state whenever it is possible without aborting.

As primitive commands in Cmd^0, we take the duals of the primitive commands in Cmd. The substitution command is its own dual, while the dual of the test command is the *miraculous test command* $\langle u \approx c \rangle$, defined by

$$\langle u \approx c \rangle (Q) \overset{\text{def}}{=} (u = c) \Rightarrow Q$$

We summarize the features of the dual language Cmd^0.

THEOREM 3 *The language Cmd^0 contains all the predicate transformers that are monotonic and strict with respect to true. Cmd^0 is dually isomorphic with Cmd with bottom element* **fail** *and top element* **magic**, *and all monotonic predicate transformers that are strict with respect to true can be generated within Cmd^0.*

In order to show that all monotonic predicate transformers that are strict with respect to *true* can be generated within Cmd^0, we use the dual of the construction in section 3 to generate all predicate transformers in the $\wedge$-base $\{G^0_{P,\sigma} | false \neq P \in Pred, \sigma \in \Sigma\}$.

Combining the two languages Since the test command $\langle u \approx c \rangle$ is miraculous, it cannot be generated within Cmd. Conversely, the test command $\langle u = c \rangle$ cannot be generated within Cmd^0, since it is possibly nonterminating. However, adding the single command **magic** to Cmd is sufficient to get all the commands in Cmd^0; we have

$$\langle u \approx c \rangle \; = \; \bigvee_{c':c' \neq c} (\langle u = c' \rangle; \textbf{magic }) \vee \bigvee_{c'} \langle u = c' \rangle$$

Note that by (4), the second conjunct is $\bigvee_{c'} \langle u = c' \rangle = \textbf{skip }$.

In fact, adding the **magic** command to Cmd makes it possible to construct *all* monotonic predicate transformers. To show this, we first note that adding the predicate transformers $\{G_{false,\sigma} | \sigma \in \Sigma\}$ to the $\vee$-base of $SMtran$ yields a $\vee$-base for all the monotonic predicate transformers. Since

$$G_{false,\sigma} \; = \; \{b_\sigma\}; \textbf{magic}$$

we can construct all elements of this base.

Adding **abort** to Cmd^0 is again sufficient to get all the commands in Cmd (and, in fact, all monotonic predicate transformers):

$$\langle u = c \rangle \; = \; \bigwedge_{c':c' \neq c} (\langle u \approx c' \rangle; \textbf{abort }) \wedge \bigwedge_{c'} \langle u \approx c' \rangle$$

Again note the second conjunct, $\bigwedge_{c'} \langle u \approx c' \rangle = \textbf{skip }$ (so **skip** is its own dual).

Thus we have the following result.

COROLLARY 1 *Adding the* **magic** *command to Cmd (or, dually, adding the* **abort** *command to Cmd^o) yields a language within which all monotonic predicate transformers can be generated. This can also be done by taking the substitution command and the ordinary as well as the miraculous test command as primitive commands in the langauge.*

We call the combined language with primitive commands $\langle d/v \rangle$, $\langle u = c \rangle$ and $\langle u \approx c \rangle$ and constructors ";", "$\wedge$" and "$\vee$", the *extended base language*, denoted Cmd^+. Note that in Cmd^+, $\bigwedge \emptyset = $ **magic** and $\bigvee \emptyset = $ **abort** .

We also note that the intersection $Cmd \cap Cmd^o$ is the complete lattice consisting of all the strict and always terminating commands.

5 Derivation of a simple language in the command lattice

The base languages constructed in the previous sections are infinitary, in the sense that they permit arbitrary meets and joins of commands. The definition of commands as predicate transformers is highly semantic, since predicates are considered to be functions from Σ to *Bool*.

In this section we consider a finitary specification language with a syntactic notion of predicates. The language is an extension of the language of guarded commands of [Dijkstra76]. We identify the statements of this language with their weakest precondition predicate transformers. Our aim is to show how this language can be embedded in the base language *Cmd*.

Our starting point is a modified version of the language of [Back88b] (subsequently called the *specification language*, denoted *Stat*). This language permits input-output-specifications to be embedded as statements in a program. It permits both demonic and angelic nondeterminism, but not miracles. The nondeterminism of a statement can be unbounded. Ordinary program statements form a sublanguage of *Stat*. The statements of *Stat* are defined by

$$
\begin{array}{lll}
S & ::= & v := v'.P & \text{(\emph{demonic assignment statement})} \\
& | & \overline{v := v'.P} & \text{(\emph{angelic assignment statement})} \\
& | & [\textbf{var } v; S] & \text{(\emph{block})} \\
& | & X & \text{(\emph{statement variable})} \\
& | & S_1; S_2 & \text{(\emph{sequential composition})} \\
& | & \textbf{if } b_1 \rightarrow S_1 [\!] b_2 \rightarrow S_2 \textbf{ fi} & \text{(\emph{conditional composition})} \\
& | & \mu X.T & \text{(\emph{recursive composition})}
\end{array}
$$

Here v is a list of variables, b_1 and b_2 are predicate formulas and S_1 and S_2 are statements. T is a *statement with a statement variable*, i.e. an expression built up from primitive statements, constructors and the statement variable X. In the assignment statements, v' is a list of *auxiliary variables* (i.e. variables not belonging to *Var*), and P is a predicate formula which may refer to the auxiliary variables in v'.

Semantic and syntactic predicates Since the base language *Cmd* treats predicates as semantic objects and we now consider a language where predicates are syntactic objects we must be careful.

To avoid confusion, we refer to syntactic predicates as *predicate formulas*. Assume that every value d in D has a name d (so that every value can be considered a term). It is then easy to show that a predicate formula P, which refers only to variables in *Var*, has a straighforward meaning as a predicate in *Pred*. Furthermore, this meaning function is preserved by connectives, quantifications and substitution of values d for variables v.

However, we note that predicate formulas may refer to *auxiliary variables*, not belonging to *Var*. Such formulas do not correspond to predicates in *Pred* unless the auxiliary variables have been removed by substitution or bound by quantification.

Meaning of the statements in the specification language The effect of the demonic assignment statement is to assign values nondeterministically to the variables v so that the condition P becomes established (unbounded nondeterminism is permitted). The angelic assignment statement is similar, but executed with angelic nondeterminism. Formally we give the following meanings to the statements of *Stat*:

$$(v := v'.P)(Q) \overset{\text{def}}{=} \exists v'.P \wedge \forall v'.(P \Rightarrow Q[v'/v])$$
$$\overline{(v := v'.P)}(Q) \overset{\text{def}}{=} \exists v'.(P \wedge Q[v'/v])$$
$$([\mathbf{var}\ v; S])(Q) \overset{\text{def}}{=} \forall v.S(\forall v.Q)$$
$$(S_1; S_2)(Q) \overset{\text{def}}{=} S_1(S_2(Q))$$
$$(\mathbf{if}\ b_1 \to S_1 [\!] b_2 \to S_2\ \mathbf{fi}\ )(Q) \overset{\text{def}}{=} (b_1 \vee b_2) \wedge (b_1 \Rightarrow S_1(Q)) \wedge (b_2 \Rightarrow S_2(Q))$$

for all predicate formulas Q.

The definition of the meaning of the block statement [**var** $v; S$] above is somewhat different from the corresponding definitions used in e.g. [Back80, Morris87, GaMo88]. The reason for this is that we want the statements to be defined for all predicate formulas referring to variables in *Var*. Thus, the local variables of our block construct exist outside the block, but their values are undefined.

The meaning of the recursive composition $\mu X.T(X)$ is defined as the least fixpoint (the existence of which is guaranteed by the results in [Tarski55]) of the monotonic function $\lambda X.T(X)$ on the lattice of predicate transformers (similar definitions have been used in e.g. [Hehner79, Park80, DiGa86]). We assume that the logic is sufficiently expressive, so that these least fixpoints also can be expressed as predicate formulas, see [Hehner79, Back87].

The demonic assignment statement for an empty list ϵ of variables (the *assert statement*) is written $\{P\}$ instead of $\epsilon := \epsilon.P$. Special cases are **skip** $= \{true\}$ and **abort** $= \{false\}$. The ordinary *multiple assignment statement* $v := e$ can be defined as the demonic assignment $v := v'.(v' = e)$. Thus

$$\{P\}(Q) = P \wedge Q$$
$$(v := e)(Q) = Q[e/v]$$

A game theoretic interpretation of the specification language The intuitive interpretation of statements defined as predicate transformers has to be somewhat extended to cover the angelic assignment statement. The nondeterminism of the demonic assignment statement is demonic, i.e. $(v := v'.P)(Q)$ holds in a state σ_0 if and only if all possible executions of $v := v'.P$ in initial state σ_0 lead to final states where Q holds. On the other hand, the nondeterminism of the angelic assignment statement is angelic, i.e. $(\overline{v := v'.P})(Q)$ holds in a state σ_0 if and only if there exists a possible execution of $v := v'.P$ in initial state σ_0 which leads to a final state where Q holds. The execution of a statement in the specification language can be interpreted as a game between the system (the demon) and the user (the angel). The demon chooses the values in the demonic assignment statement and the angel chooses the values in the angelic assignment statement. Also, the demon chooses the branch of the conditional composition in the case when both branches are enabled. Assume that the statement S is executed in the initial state σ_0. The angel tries to make the execution terminate is a state where Q holds, whereas the demon tries to prevent this. The state σ_0 belongs to the weakest precondition of S to establich Q, so $S(Q)$ holds in σ_0, iff the angel has a *winning strategy*, i.e. no matter what choices the demon makes, the angel can force the execution to terminate in a final state where Q holds.

Construction of the specification language statements in the base language We now show how the statements of *Stat* can be constructed within the base language *Cmd*. The proofs are straightforward using the definitions.

In order to construct the demonic assignment statement we first construct the *demonic update statement* $v.P$, defined by

$$(v.P)(Q) \stackrel{\text{def}}{=} \exists v.P \wedge \forall v.(P \Rightarrow Q)$$

Assume v is a list of variables and P is a predicate formula. We first consider the special case when $Var(P) \subseteq v$. Then

$$v.P = (\bigvee_{d:P} \langle d/v \rangle); \textbf{choose} \wedge \bigwedge_{d:P} \langle d/v \rangle \tag{10}$$

The two conjuncts here correspond to the two conjuncts in the definition of $(v.P)(Q)$. Note that since the specification language statements are defined only for predicate formulas, the base language construction in (10) should be interpreted as restricted to those predicates which correspond to some predicate formula.

Now consider the general case when v and P are arbitrary. Let w be the list of variables that P refers to and which are not in v. For all list of values d of appropriate length, $P[d/w]$ then refers only to variables in Var, and $v.P[d/w]$ is a demonic update statement of the kind considered in (10). The construction of the general case is then

$$v.P = \bigvee_d (\langle w = d \rangle; v.P[d/w]) \tag{11}$$

(the disjunction over d is needed to find the value of w in the state). Using (11), the nondeterministic assignment statement is constructed as

$$(v := v'.P) = \bigvee_d (\langle v = d \rangle; v.P[d, v/v, v']) \tag{12}$$

where this time the correct initial values of v are found by the disjunction. In a similar way, the angelic assignment statement is constructed as

$$\overline{(v := v'.P)} \ = \ \bigvee_d (\langle v = d \rangle; \overline{v.P[d, v/v, v']}) \tag{13}$$

using the *angelic update statement* $\overline{v.P}$ defined by

$$\overline{v.P} \ = \ \bigvee_{d:P} \langle d/v \rangle$$

when $Var(P) \subseteq v$, and in the general case as

$$\overline{v.P} \ = \ \bigvee_d (\langle w = d \rangle; \overline{v.P[d/w]})$$

where the list w consists of all the variables that P refers to and which are not in v.

The block statement is constructed as

$$[\mathbf{var}\ v; S] \ = \ (\bigwedge_d \langle d/v \rangle); S; (\bigwedge_d \langle d/v \rangle)$$

By definition, sequential composition in *Stat* is the same as sequential composition in *Cmd*.

Before we construct the conditional composition we note that by (1), the assert statement $\{P\}$ can be constructed as $\bigvee_{d:P} \langle v = d \rangle$. Using this, we have

$$\mathbf{if}\ b_1 \to S_1 \| b_2 \to S_2 \mathbf{fi} \ = \ \{b_1 \vee b_2\}; (((\{\neg b_1\}; \mathbf{choose}\ \vee\ S_1) \wedge (\{\neg b_2\}; \mathbf{choose}\ \vee\ S_2))$$

A similar construction is used in [Hesselink88].

Finally, we consider recursion. First assume that $T(X)$ is an expression built from the symbol X, the primitive statements, sequential composition, meet and join, but no recursive composition. Then if X is replaced by any statement S of *Cmd*, the result $T(S)$ will be another statement of *Cmd*. Since the statement constructors are monotonic in their arguments, $T(X)$ as a function of X is a monotonic function from *Cmd* to *Cmd*. Since *Cmd* is a complete lattice, T has a least fixpoint in *Cmd*. This least fixpoint equals $\mu X.T(X)$.

This definition is generalized by an inductive argument to the case when the expression $T(X)$ contains recursive composition. Note that there is no need to introduce an explicit recursion constructor into the base language, as $\mu X.T(X)$ is just used as an abbreviation for a statement that already has a representation in terms of the primitive statements and the three given constructors sequential composition, meet and join.

We summarize the constructions above in the following theorem, which states that *Stat* can be embedded in *Cmd*.

THEOREM 4 *All statements of the specification language Stat can be constructed within the base language Cmd.*

As an example, let us look at the simple assignment statement $u := u + 1$. Using the construction of the demonic assignment statement we get (after simplifications)

$$u := u + 1 \;=\; \bigvee_{c} (\langle u = c \rangle; \langle c + 1/u \rangle)$$

We can consider the substitution command $\langle c+1/u \rangle$ as the updating while the test command in combination with the join finds the correct value to be incremented. [GaMo88] uses their conjunction statement (corresponding to our join) in the same way to avoid having to mention the initial value of a variable in the postcondition.

6 Derivation of a language with miracles

In this section we introduce a specification language, denoted $Stat^+$, which extends the language of section 5 by permitting miraculous statements. This language is syntactic and finitary (although permitting unbounded nondeterminism), in the same way as $Stat$. In addition, it is self-dual, in the sense that the dual of every statement in $Stat^+$ is also in $Stat^+$.

We call this language *the extended specification language* and denote it $Stat^+$. The statements of $Stat^+$ are defined by

$$
\begin{array}{llll}
S & ::= & v :\approx v'.P & (\textit{demonic, miraculous assignment statement}) \\
  & | & \overline{v := v'.P} & (\textit{angelic, strict assignment statement}) \\
  & | & X & (\textit{statement variable}) \\
  & | & S_1; S_2 & (\textit{sequential composition}) \\
  & | & S_1 \wedge S_2 & (\textit{meet; demonic composition}) \\
  & | & S_1 \vee S_2 & (\textit{join; angelic composition}) \\
  & | & \mu X.T & (\textit{least fixpoint composition}) \\
  & | & \nu X.T & (\textit{greatest fixpoint composition})
\end{array}
$$

Note that we do not define the block or the conditional composition. We shall see later how these can be defined using the other constructs.

Meaning of the statements The angelic assignment statement and sequential composition have the same meanings as in $Stat$, while meet and join have the same meanings as in the base language.

The meaning of the demonic miraculous assignment statement is given by

$$(v :\approx v'.P)(Q) \;\stackrel{\text{def}}{=}\; \forall v'.(P \Rightarrow Q[v'/v])$$

Thus the demonic miraculous assignment statement of $Stat^+$ is similar to its strict counterpart, the demonic assignment statement of $Stat$, but it succeeds miraculously where its strict counterpart aborts.

The fixpoint compositions are given the following meanings: $\mu X.T(X)$ is the least and $\nu X.T(X)$ the greatest fixpoint of the monotonic function $\lambda X.T(X)$ on the complete lattice of predicate transformers. The existence of a least as well as a greatest fixpoint is guaranteed by the results of [Tarski55]. The least fixpoint composition in $Stat^+$ is the same as the recursive composition in $Stat$.

All statements of $Stat^+$ are monotonic and all statement constructors are monotonic with respect to substatement replacement.

The demonic miraculous assignment statement nondeterministically assigns values v' to the variables v, establishing the condition P. If this is not possible, the statement succeeds miraculously. The angelic strict assignment statement and the sequential composition have the same intuitive interpretation as in $Stat$. Meet and join have the same intuitive interpretation as in the base language Cmd.

Duals in the extended specification language Let the duality operator $()^0$ have the same meaning as in section 4, i.e. defined by (9). For every statement in $Stat^+$, we can construct its dual as follows :

$$(v :\approx v'.P)^0 = \overline{v := v'.P}$$
$$(S_1; S_2)^0 = S_1^0; S_2^0$$
$$(S_1 \wedge S_2)^0 = S_1^0 \vee S_2^0$$
$$(\mu X.T(X))^0 = \nu X.T^0(X)$$

where $T^0(X)$ is the statement with statement variable defined by

$$T^0(S) \stackrel{\text{def}}{=} (T(S^0))^0$$

for all statements S.

Thus the statement language has a strong sense of duality; every statement has a dual which is simple to construct. Note that we do not include the duality operator as a real statement constructor in $Stat^+$. It has the disadvantage of not being monotonic with respect to substatement replacement, Furthermore, the above result shows that it is not needed.

Derived statements Within the extended specification language $Stat^+$ we now define *derived statements*, i.e. statements defined in terms of other, already defined, statements. Let ϵ be the empty list and let P be an arbitrary predicate formula. Then we define the *assert statement* $\{P\}$ and its dual, the *guard statement* $P \to$ by

$$\{P\} \stackrel{\text{def}}{=} \overline{\epsilon := \epsilon.P}$$
$$P \to \stackrel{\text{def}}{=} \epsilon :\approx \epsilon.P$$

(the guard statement has been introduced in [Hesselink88]). This gives the following meanings:

$$\{P\}(Q) = P \wedge Q$$
$$(P \to)(Q) = P \Rightarrow Q$$

As special cases, we have $\{false\} = \textbf{abort}$ and $(true \rightarrow) = \textbf{magic}$ (note that $Stat^+$ is a lattice with a top and a bottom element, though it is not complete).

The *guarded statement* $P \rightarrow S$ can now be considered to be an abbreviation for the composition $(P \rightarrow); S$. Thus,

$$(P \rightarrow S)(Q) \;=\; P \Rightarrow S(Q)$$

which corresponds to the definitions given in [Nelson87, Morgan88a, Back88a]. Note that the dual of $P \rightarrow S$ is $\{P\}; S$, which has the similar abbreviation $\{P\}S$.

The *demonic strict assignment statement* (i.e. the demonic assignment statement of the original specification language $Stat$) is now defined as

$$v := v'.P \;\overset{\text{def}}{=}\; \overline{v := v'.P}; \textbf{magic} \;\wedge\; v :\approx v'.P$$

Dually we can define the *angelic miraculous assignment statement* as

$$\overline{v :\approx v'.P} \;\overset{\text{def}}{=}\; v :\approx v'.P; \textbf{abort} \;\vee\; \overline{v := v'.P}$$

Using the demonic strict assignment statement we can define the ordinary multiple assignment statement using the same construction as in $Stat$.

We now show that the block statement and the conditional composition, as defined in the original specification language, can be defined in terms of other statements in the extended specification language.

The block statement is defined as

$$[\textbf{var } v; S] \;\overset{\text{def}}{=}\; v := v.true; S; v := v.true$$

This definition also shows the intuitive meaning of our block construct; the value of v is undefined when entering the block as well as when leaving it.

The (demonic) conditional composition is defined as

$$\textbf{if } b_1 \rightarrow S_1 [\!] b_2 \rightarrow S_2 \textbf{ fi} \;\overset{\text{def}}{=}\; \{b_1 \vee b_2\}; ((b_1 \rightarrow S_1) \wedge (b_2 \rightarrow S_2))$$

Identifying the symbol $[\!]$ with $\wedge$ (both standing for a demonic choice) we could instead have defined **if** ... **fi** as a constructor, using the definition of [Nelson87, Morgan88b],

$$(\textbf{if } S \textbf{ fi })(Q) \;=\; \neg S(false) \wedge S(Q) \qquad (14)$$

permitting S to be any statement. However, this definition is compatible with the above definition of conditional composition only when S_1 and S_2 are strict. Furthermore, the constructor **if** ... **fi** is not monotonic with respect to substatement replacement. This limits its usefulness in program development, as pointed out by [Morgan88b]. Since all constructors of our extended base language Cmd^+ are monotonic in their substatements, this also means that that the constructor **if** ... **fi** could not be defined using the commands and constructors of the extended base language. Hence, we will *not* accept (14) as a definition.

We define a second conditional composition;

$$\textbf{if } b_1 \rightarrow S_1 \Diamond b_2 \rightarrow S_2 \textbf{ fi} \;\overset{\text{def}}{=}\; \{b_1 \vee b_2\}; (b_1 \rightarrow S_1 \;\vee\; b_2 \rightarrow S_2)$$

This is the *angelic conditional composition*. When executed in a state where both b_1 and b_2 holds, it makes an angelic choice between S_1 and S_2. In all other states it acts like the ordinary conditional composition.

When there is only one alternative, the two conditional compositions coincide, we define

$$\textbf{if } b \to S \textbf{ fi } \stackrel{\text{def}}{=} \{b\}; S$$

Construction of the statements of $Stat^+$ in Cmd^+ We now show how all the statements in the extended specification language $Stat^+$ can be constructed within the extended base language Cmd^+. The angelic strict assignment statement is constructed as in section 5. Sequential composition, meet and join are the same as the corresponding constructors in Cmd^+.

From the duality shown above it follows that the construction of the demonic miraculous assignment statement is the dual of the construction (13) of the angelic strict assignment statement. Thus

$$v :\approx v'.P \;=\; \bigwedge_d ((v \approx d); (v \sim P[d, v/v, v']))$$

using the *demonic miraculous update statement* $v \sim P$, constructed as

$$v \sim P \;=\; \bigwedge_{d:P} \langle d/v \rangle$$

when $Var(P) \subseteq v$, and in the general case as

$$v \sim P \;=\; \bigwedge_d ((w \approx d); v \sim P[d/w])$$

where the list w consists of all the variables that P refers to and which are not in v.

Since every monotonic predicate transformer can be constructed in Cmd^+, all fixpoint statements have a construction i Cmd^+.

All the derived statements of $Stat^+$ have been defined using the primitive statements and the three basic constructors. Thus the constructions in Cmd^+ of the two primitive statements can be used to construct the derived statements. In particular,

$$\{P\} \;=\; \bigvee_{d:P} \langle v = d \rangle$$

$$P \to \;=\; \bigwedge_{d:P} \langle v \approx d \rangle$$

We summarize our results concerning the extended specification language $Stat^+$.

THEOREM 5 *The language $Stat^+$ is an extension of the specification language $Stat$. Every statement of $Stat^+$ has a dual in $Stat^+$ and all statements of $Stat^+$ can be constructed in the extended base language Cmd^+.*

7 Conclusion

We have shown how every strict monotonic predicate transformer can be constructed starting from a very basic set of primitive statements together with the lattice-theoretic constructors meet and join and sequential composition. This lattice-theoretical base language was shown to be complete, in the sense that all strict monotonic predicate transformers can be constructed within it. We showed how a change in the definition of one of the primitive statements gives rise to a dual statement lattice which permits miracles but not nontermination. We also showed how to combine these two statement lattices into a single extended base language which permits both nonterminating and miraculous statements.

The weakest precondition predicate transformers for the statements of a quite general specification language, permitting both demonic and angelic nondeterminism, were then constructed.

Finally we defined a general specification language with a self-dual nature, permitting both demonic and angelic nondeterminism as well as strict and miraculous statements, and showed how the statements of this language can be constructed using the extended base language.

Acknowledgements

We have benefited greatly from discussions with Carroll Morgan, John Tucker and Viking Högnäs. This research was funded by the Academy of Finland and the Finsoft III research project by Tekes.

References

[Back78] R.J.R. Back, *On the correctness of refinement steps in program development* (Ph.D. thesis), Report A-1978-4, Dept. of Computer Science, University of Helsinki, 1978.

[Back80] R.J.R. Back, *Correctness Preserving Program Refinements: Proof Theory and Applications*, Mathematical Centre Tracts 131, Mathematical Centre, Amsterdam 1980.

[Back87] R.J.R. Back, *A Calculus of Refinements for Program Derivations*, Acta Informatica, Vol. 25, No. 6, 593–624 (1988).

[Back88a] R.J.R. Back, *Refining Atomicity in Parallel Algorithms*, Reports on Computer Science and Mathematics 57, Åbo Akademi 1988, (to appear in *Conference on Parallel Architectures and Languages Europe 1989*).

[Back88b] R.J.R. Back, *Changing Data Representation in the Refinement Calculus*, Hawaii International Conference on System Sciences 1989 (also available as *Data Refinement in the Refinement Calculus*, Reports on Computer Science and Mathematics 68, Åbo Akademi 1988).

[deBakker80] J. de Bakker, *Mathematical Theory of Program Correctness*, Prentice-Hall 1980.

[Birkhoff61] G. Birkhoff, *Lattice Theory*, American Mathematical Society, Providence, RI, 1961.

[Dijkstra76] E.W. Dijkstra, *A Discipline of Programming*, Prentice Hall 1976.

[DiGa86] E.W. Dijkstra, A.J.M. van Gasteren, *A Simple Fixpoint without the Restriction to Continuity*, Acta Informatica Vol. 23, 1–7 (1986).

[GaMo88] P. Gardiner, C. Morgan, *Data Refinement of Predicate Transformers*, Manuscrip 1988.

[Grätzer78] G. Grätzer, *General Lattice Theory*, Birkhuser Verlag, Basel, 1978.

[Hehner79] E. Hehner, **do** considered **od** : *A Contribution to the Programming Calculus*, Acta Informatica Vol. 11, 287–304 (1979).

[Hehner84] E. Hehner, *The Logic of Programming*, Prentice-Hall 1984.

[Hesselink88] W.H. Hesselink, *An algebraic calculus of commands*, CS8808, Department of Mathematics and Computer Science, University of Groningen, 1988.

[HHH87] C.A.R. Hoare, I.J. Hayes, J. He, C.C. Morgan, A.W. Roscoe, J.W. Sanders, I.H. Sorensen, J.M. Spivey and A. Surfin, *Laws of Programming*, Communications of the ACM, Vol. 30, No. 8, 672–686 (August 1987).

[Morgan88a] C. Morgan, *Data Refinement by Miracles*, Information Processing Letters 26, 243–246 (January 1988).

[Morgan88b] C. Morgan, *The Specification Statement*, ACM TOPLAS, Vol. 10, No 3, 403–419 (1988).

[MoGa88] C. Morgan, P. Gardiner, *Data Refinement by Calculation*, Manuscript 1988.

[Morris87] J. Morris, *A Theoretical Basis for Stepwise Refinement and the Programming Calculus*, Science of Programming, 9, 287–306 (1987).

[Nelson87] G. Nelson, *A Generalization of Dijkstra's Calculus*, Tech. Rep 16, Digital Systems Research Center, Palo Alto, Calif., (April 1987).

[Park80] D. Park, *On the Semantics of Fair Parallelism*, Lecture Notes in Computer Science 86, 504–526, Springer 1980.

[Tarski55] A. Tarski, *A Lattice Theoretical Fixed Point Theorem and its Applications*, Pacific J. Math. 5, 285–309 (1955).

Transformational programming and forests

A. Bijlsma
Eindhoven University of Technology
Department of Mathematics and Computing Science
P.O. Box 513, 5600 MB Eindhoven, The Netherlands

Introduction

In an earlier paper [0], we introduced the concept of <u>constructs</u>. These may
be regarded as a common generalization of finite and infinite sequences,
finite and infinite bags, trees of arbitrary arity and forests. In this paper
we attempt to show how constructs may be used as an alternative foundation for
the transformational programming method proposed by Bird [1] and Meertens [2].
In our view, the main advantage of such an approach would be the fact that
generally applicable operations like "map" and "reduce" can be given a simple
definition at the level of constructs, so that the need for referring to
polymorphism or type hierarchies disappears. The later sections of this paper
introduce an operator on constructs that generalizes both "map" and "reduce"
and may be used to express in a succinct way many properties of trees and
forests. In the last sections it is shown how the properties of this operator
can be exploited to transform some specifications involving trees and forests
into efficient functional programs.

Constructs

In this section we list some facts about constructs. Proofs are omitted,
but can be found in [0].

Consider mappings from (partially) ordered sets to arbitrary sets. Two such
mappings, say $f \in A \rightarrow X$ and $g \in B \rightarrow Y$, are called equivalent if there
exist an isomorphism σ of A onto B such that $f = g \circ \sigma$. (Note that
this implies $X = Y$). With every mapping f we associate an object $C(f)$ in
such a way that $C(f) = C(g)$ if and only if f and g are equivalent; the
objects $C(f)$ are called <u>constructs</u>.

A finite sequence is a construct, say $C(f)$ with $f \in A \rightarrow X$, such that f
is surjective and A is a finite, linearly ordered set. In case A is the
set $\{1, 2, ..., n\}$ with its usual ordering, it is common practice to denote
$C(f)$ by $\langle f(1), f(2), ..., f(n) \rangle$. Every finite sequence can be written as

$\langle x_1, x_2, \ldots, x_n \rangle$ in precisely one way.

A bag is a construct, say $C(f)$ with $f \in A \to X$, such that f is surjective and A is discretely ordered. In case A is the set $\{1, 2, \ldots, n\}$ with the discrete ordering, we shall denote $C(f)$ by $[f(1), f(2), \ldots, f(n)]$. Every finite bag can be written as $[x_1, x_2, \ldots, x_n]$. The elements $x_1, x_2, \ldots, x_n$ are uniquely determined but for permutations. Two bags, say $C(f)$ and $C(g)$ with $f \in A \to X$ and $g \in B \to Y$, are equal if and only if $X = Y$ and, for all x in X,

$$(\underline{N} \ i: \ i \in A: \ f(i) = x) = (\underline{N} \ j: \ j \in B: \ g(j) = x) \quad .$$

For a construct $C(f)$ with $f \in A \to X$ and a mapping $g \in X \to Y$ we define

$$g*(C(f)) = C(g \circ f) \quad .$$

For instance, if C0 is the infinite bag that contains every integer value twice, and g is the mapping defined by $g(x) = 2x + 1$, then $g*(C0)$ is the infinite bag that contains every odd integer value twice. (In [1] and [2] the symbol $*$ was introduced for finite sequences and finite bags separately. The pronunciation of $*$ is variously reported as "map" [1] or "applied to all" [2].)

Let X be any set and let A be the ordered set obtained by ordering X discretely. The construct $C(id_A)$ is called the <u>set construct</u> of X : it is a bag in which every element of X occurs precisely once. Conversely, for any construct, say $C(f)$ with $f \in A \to X$, we define its <u>base set</u> to be im f . Then, for any set X, the base set of the set construct of X is again X ; in this sense there is a natural correspondence between sets and set constructs. We shall exploit this correspondence in the following way: if f is some mapping from constructs to constructs and X is a set, we denote by $f(X)$ the base set of the image under f of the set construct of X . For instance, if Z is the set of integers and g is defined on Z by $g(x) = x^2$, then $g*(Z)$ is the set of natural numbers.

Let A and B be ordered sets. The <u>concatenation</u> of A and B, denoted $A ++ B$, is the set

$$(0) \qquad \{(0, a) \mid a \in A\} \cup \{(1, b) \mid b \in B\} \quad ,$$

rdered in such a way that

$$(i0, c0) \leq_{A++B} (i1, c1)$$
$$\equiv (i0 = 0 \wedge i1 = 1)$$
$$\vee (i0 = i1 = 0 \wedge c0 \leq_A c1) \vee (i0 = i1 = 1 \wedge c0 \leq_B c1) \quad.$$

onsider constructs $C(f)$ and $C(g)$, where $f \in A \rightarrow X$ and $g \in B \rightarrow Y$. The
oncatenation of $C(f)$ and $C(g)$, denoted $C(f) ++ C(g)$, is the construct
(h) , where $h \in (A ++ B) \rightarrow X \cup Y$ is defined by

1) $\qquad h(0, a) = f(a) \wedge h(1, b) = g(b)$

or $a \in A$, $b \in B$. Thus

$$\langle 1, 2, 5 \rangle ++ \langle 5, 3, 0 \rangle = \langle 1, 2, 5, 5, 3, 0 \rangle$$

nd $\langle 1, 2, 5 \rangle ++ [2, 2]$ is the partially ordered construct

Concatenation of constructs reduces to the normal concatenation operator
hen the constructs are sequences. There is also an operation on constructs
hat generalizes the normal operator on bags:
Let A and B be ordered sets. The sum of A and B , denoted $A + B$,
s the set (0), ordered in such a way that

$$(i0, c0) \leq_{A+B} (i1, ci)$$
$$\equiv (i0 = i1 = 0 \wedge c0 \leq_A c1) \vee (i0 = i1 = 1 \wedge c0 \leq_B c1) \quad.$$

onsider constructs $C(f)$ and $C(g)$, where $f \in A \rightarrow X$ and $g \in B \rightarrow Y$. The
um of $C(f)$ and $C(g)$, denoted $C(f) + C(g)$, is the construct $C(h)$,
here $h \in (A + B) \rightarrow X \cup Y$ is defined by (1).

We shall call a construct $C(f)$, with $f \in A \to X$, <u>empty</u> if A is empty. It follows that there is only one empty construct, namely $\{\emptyset\}$.

We shall call a nonempty construct <u>irreducible</u> if it cannot be written as the concatenation or sum of nonempty constructs. Clearly, every finite nonempty construct may be built from irreducible constructs with the operators ++ and + . The question naturally occurs whether this decomposition is in some sense unique. Obviously, it cannot be completely unique, since both ++ and + are associative and + is commutative (as operators between constructs; they are so up to isomorphism as operators between ordered sets). Therefore, we must allow rearrangement of terms and introduction of parentheses that exploit these properties; for instance, [2] + ([1] + [0]) = [0] + [1] + [2] . However, apart from this the decomposition turns out to be unique.

Let A be an ordered set. The relation $(<_A)$ is defined on A by

$$a \;(<_A)\; b \equiv a <_A b \wedge \neg \;(\underline{E}\; x: x \in A: a <_A x <_A b) \quad .$$

If a and b satisfy $a \;(<_A)\; b$, we say that a is a <u>predecessor</u> of b , and that b is a <u>successor</u> of a .

An ordered set A is called <u>tree-like</u> if A is finite and there exists an r in A such that for all a in A ,

$$(\underline{N}\; x: x \in A: x \;(<_A)\; a) = \underline{if}\; a = r \to 0 \;\|\; a \neq r \to 1 \;\underline{fi} \quad .$$

If such an r exists, it is obviously unique; we call it the <u>root</u> of A . In a tree-like ordered set, the root is the least element.

A <u>tree</u> is a construct $C(f)$, say with $f \in A \to X$, such that A is tree-like and f is surjective. For example, let A denote the set of words of length at most 2 over the alphabet $\{0, 1, 2\}$. For words t and u we let $t \leq_A u$ mean that t is a prefix of u . Define f on A as the sum of the numerical values of the symbols in a word. Then $C(f)$ is the ternary tree

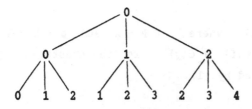

te that the left-right ordering of the successors of any given node is
urely arbitrary: interchanging, for instance, the leftmost 0 and 1 on the
ottom row would not change C(f) . Note also that this tree could equally
ell have been described with the aid of the operators ++ and + , since it
s exactly equal to

$$
\begin{array}{l}
[0] \;++\;(\quad([0]\;++\;([0]\;+\;[1]\;+\;[2]))\\
\qquad\quad+\;([1]\;++\;([1]\;+\;[2]\;+\;[3]))\\
\qquad\quad+\;([2]\;++\;([2]\;+\;[3]\;+\;[4]))\\
\qquad\quad)\quad.
\end{array}
$$

n fact, every tree may be built from singleton bags with the operators ++
nd + . As singleton bags are obviously irreducible, it follows from the
bove that this decomposition is essentially unique.

(It is not true that every finite construct can be decomposed into
ingleton bags. As a counterexample, consider the ordered set A consisting
f {2, 3, 6, 9} with the divisibility ordering. If f is the identity
unction on A , then C(f) is neither a concatenation nor a sum.)

A sum of trees will be called a <u>forest</u>. Then forests have the following
roperties: every finite sequence, finite bag, or tree is a forest. The sum
f any two forests is again a forest. The concatenation of a singleton bag and
 forest is a tree. Every forest may be built from singleton bags by means of
he operators ++ and + in such a way that the left hand operand of ++ is
lways a singleton bag.

In the rest of this paper, we let X denote an arbitrary set and we let
o(X) denote the set of all nonempty constructs that can be built from
ingleton bags over X by means of ++ and + , and Fo(X) the set of all
onempty forests among these. Due to the essential uniqueness of the canonical
ecomposition, we may define functions on Co(X) by describing their values
n singleton bags and their behaviour under ++ and + .

DEFINITION. Let \$ denote a commutative, associative operator on X . Then
/ is the X-valued function on Co(X) that satisfies

$/([x]) = x$ for all x in X ,
$/(C0 ++ C1) = $/(C0) \$ $/(C1)$ for all $C0$, $C1$ in $Co(X)$,
$/(C0 + C1) = $/(C0) \$ $/(C1)$ for all $C0$, $C1$ in $Co(X)$.

(In [1] and [2] the symbol / was introduced for finite sequences and finite bags separately. The pronunciation is "reduce" [1] or "inserted in" [2].)   ∎

Thus, if · denotes multiplication in Z , then

$\cdot/(\langle 2, 3, 5\rangle) = \cdot/([2] ++ [3] ++ [5]) = 2 \cdot 3 \cdot 5 = 30$;
$\cdot/([2, 3, 5]) = \cdot/([2] + [3] + [5]) = 2 \cdot 3 \cdot 5 = 30$;
$\cdot/(\langle 2, 3\rangle ++ [2, 3, 5])$
$= \cdot/([2] ++ [3] ++ ([2] + [3] + [5])) = 2 \cdot 3 \cdot 2 \cdot 3 \cdot 5 = 180$.

It is worth mentioning that, for $f \in X \to Y$, the mapping $f*$ introduced earlier may be defined on $Co(X)$ by

$f*([x]) = [f(x)]$ for all x in X ,
$f*(C0 ++ C1) = f*(C0) ++ f*(C1)$ for all $C0$, $C1$ in $Co(X)$,
$f*(C0 + C1) = f*(C0) + f*(C1)$ for all $C0$, $C1$ in $Co(X)$.

A generalization of the Bird-Meertens symbols

Comparison of the formulae given for $/ and $f*$ on $Co(X)$ immediately leads to the following common generalization, which turns out to be well suited for expressing various properties of trees and forests.

DEFINITION. Let X and Y be sets; assume $f \in X \to Y$. Let $0 and $1 be associative operators on Y such that $1 is also commutative. Then $(f, $0, $1)!$ denotes the mapping $F \in Co(X) \to Y$ that satisfies

$F([x]) = f(x)$ for $x \in X$,
$F(C0 ++ C1) = F(C0) \$0 F(C1)$ for $C0, C1 \in Co(X)$,
$F(C0 + C1) = F(C0) \$1 F(C1)$ for $C0, C1 \in Co(X)$.   ∎

EXAMPLES. (a) $([\blacksquare], ++, +)! = id_{Co(X)}$.

(b) $(id_x, \$1, \$1)! = \$1/$. For instance, $(id_x, +, +)!(C)$ is the sum of all values in C , and $(id_x, \underline{max}, \underline{max})!(C)$ is the maximum of all values in .

(c) $([\blacksquare] \circ f, ++, +)! = f*$. Together, (b) and (c) justify our claim that is a generalization of $/$ and $*$.

(d) For $p \in X \to Bool$ we define

$$\tilde{p}(x) = \underline{if}\ p(x) \to [x] \parallel \neg\ p(x) \to []\ \underline{fi}\ .$$

hen $(\tilde{p}, ++, +)!(C)$ is obtained from C by leaving out all values that do ot satisfy p . For instance, if $p = even$, applying $(\tilde{p}, ++, +)!$ to the ree

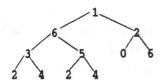

ields the forest

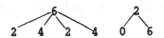

eneralizing a notation introduced by Bird and Meertens for sequences and ags, we propose to write $(\tilde{p}, ++, +)! = p^\triangleleft$.

(e) Note that $(f, \$0, \$1)! = (id_Y, \$0, \$1)! \circ f*$. Hence, at the price of lightly longer formulae, we might have limited the new notation to the case here f is the identity mapping.

(f) $([\blacksquare], +, +)!(C)$ is the bag of elements of C . For instance, if C is he tree in Example (d), then $([\blacksquare], +, +)!(C)$ is the bag $[0, 1, 2, 2, 2, 3,$, 4, 5, 6, 6].

(g) $(1, +, +)!(C)$ is the number of values in C .

In the examples that follow, we assume C to be a forest. A root path of is the sequence of values occurring on a path from a root to a leaf of C .

(h) The number $(1, +, \underline{max})!(C)$ is the height of C , i.e., the maximal umber of nodes on any root path. Similarly, $(id_x, +, \underline{max})!(C)$ is the maximal sum of the values on any root path.

(i) $(1, +, \underline{min})!(C)$ is the minimal number of nodes on any root path and $(id_x, +, \underline{min})!(C)$ is the minimal sum of the values on any root path.

(j) $(1, \underline{max}, +)!(C)$ is the number of leaves in C .

(k) $(1, \underline{min}, +)!(C)$ is the number of roots in C .

(l) Let the operator $\leftarrow$ be defined on X by $a \leftarrow b = a$. Then $(id_x, \leftarrow, +)!(C)$ denotes the sum of the values in the roots of C .

(m) Similarly, if $\rightarrow$ is defined by $a \rightarrow b = b$, then $(id_x, \rightarrow, +)!(C)$ denotes the sum of the values in the leaves of C .

(n) $(1, \rightarrow, +)!(C)$ is the number of leaves in C (cf. (j)).

(o) $(1, \leftarrow, +)!(C)$ is the number of roots in C (cf. (k)).

(p) $([\blacksquare], \rightarrow, +)!(C)$ is the bag consisting of the values in the leaves of C . Similarly, $([\blacksquare], \leftarrow, +)!(C)$ is the bag consisting of the values in the roots of C .

(q) $(id_x, \leftarrow, \underline{max})!(C)$ is the maximum value in any root of C . Similarly, $(id_x, \rightarrow, \underline{min})!(C)$ is the minimum value in any leaf of C .

(r) $(\{\blacksquare\}, \cup, \cup)!(C)$ is the set of all values in C .

(s) $(\{\blacksquare\}, \rightarrow, \cup)!(C)$ is the set of values in the leaves of C .

(t) $(\{\blacksquare\}, \cap, \cup)!(C)$ is the set of values x with the property that there exists a root path of C containing only the value x .

(u) $(\{\blacksquare\}, \cup, \cap)!(C)$ is the set of values that occur on all root paths of C .

(v) For $x \in X$, we define

$$\chi_x(y) = \underline{if}\ y = x \rightarrow 1\ \|\ y \neq x \rightarrow 0\ \underline{fi} \quad .$$

Then $(\chi_x, +, +)!(C)$ is the number of times that x occurs in C .

(w) $(\chi_x, \rightarrow, +)!(C)$ is the number of times that x occurs in a leaf of C . Replacing $\rightarrow$ by $\leftarrow$ gives the same thing for a root.

(x) Let $\uparrow$ be a commutative, associative operator on the set of finite sequences over X such that $S \uparrow T \in \{S, T\}$ and

$$\#(S \uparrow T) = (\#S)\ \underline{max}\ (\#T) \quad ,$$

where $\#S$ denotes the length of a sequence S . (The existence of such an operator follows from the axiom of choice.) Then $([\blacksquare], ++, \uparrow)!(C)$ is a root th of maximal length.

(y) $([\blacksquare], \leftarrow, \uparrow)!(C)$ is a singleton bag containing a root value of C .
milarly, $([\blacksquare], \rightarrow, \uparrow)!(C)$ contains a leaf value.

(z) Let $\bullet$ denote a commutative, associative operator on the set of finite
quences over   X   such that $S \bullet T \in \{S ++ T, T ++ S\}$ for all S and T .
gain, such an operator exists by the axiom of choice.) Then $([\blacksquare], ++, \bullet)!C$
 a pre-order traversal of C .

The following property of the symbol ! can be used to transform specific-
ions into efficient functional programs.

THEOREM. Let £0 , £1 be associative operators on X and let \$0 , \$1 be
sociative operators on   Y . Assume that £1 and \$1 are commutative and
at $f \in X \rightarrow Y$ satisfies

) $f(x0\ £0\ x1) = f(x0)\ \$0\ f(x1)$,
       $f(x0\ £1\ x1) = f(x0)\ \$1\ f(x1)$

r all x0, x1 in X . Then, for $g \in W \rightarrow X$,

) $(f \circ g, \$0, \$1)! = f \circ (g, £0, £1)!$.

PROOF. By induction on the canonical decomposition of the argument. Base:

        $(f \circ (g, £0, £1)!)([w])$
    = {definition of ! }
        $f(g(w))$
    = {definition of ! }
        $(f \circ g, \$0, \$1)!([w])$.

Step: assume both functions yield the same value when applied to   C0 , and
so when applied to C1 . Then

        $(f \circ (g, £0, £1)!)(C0 ++ C1)$
    = {definition of ! }
        $f((g, £0, £1)!(C0)\ £0\ (g, £0, £1)!(C1))$

```
       = {(2)}
         f((g, £0, £1)!(C0)) $0 f((g, £0, £1)!(C1))
       = {induction hypothesis}
         (f ° g, $0, $1)!(C0) $0 (f ° g, $0, $1)!(C1)
       = {definition of  ! }
         (f ° g, $0, $1)!(C0 ++ C1)            .
```

Repeating this derivation with ++ , £0 , $0 replaced by + , £1 , $1
completes the induction step.   ∎

In the canonical decomposition of constructs in   Fo(X) , the left hand
operand of   ++   is always a singleton bag. Hence, on   Fo(X) a slightly
stronger version of the theorem holds: equality (2) need only be satisfied for
x0 ∈ im g , not necessarily for all x0 ∈ X . It is in fact this stronger
version of the theorem that we shall apply.

An application: unique values on root paths

In Example (t) of the previous section, it was stated without proof that
for any forest   C the value of ({■}, ∩, ∪)!(C) is the set of all x with
the property that there exists a root path in C that contains only   x . In
this section, we shall derive this formula from a formal definition of root
paths.

Informally, we defined a root path as the sequence of values occurring on a
path from a root to a leaf. In order to formalize this, an inductive definition seems appropriate. Clearly the only root path of [x]   is   [x] , and a
root path of C0 + C1 is either a root path of C0 or one of C1 . But which
are the root paths of C0 ++ C1 ? These are of the form P0 ++ P1 , where P0
is a root path of C0 and P1 is a root path of C1. Let us define, for sets
S0 , S1 of constructs,

```
       S0 +++ S1 = {P0 ++ P1 | P0 ∈ S0 ∧ P1 ∈ S1}          .
```

Now the set of root paths of C0 ++ C1   can be found from the sets of root
paths of   C0 and C1 respectively by applying the operator   +++ . Hence the
set of root paths of a forest C may be formally defined as

4) $(\{[\blacksquare]\}, +++, \cup)!(C)$

here $\{[\blacksquare]\}$ is the mapping that has value $\{[x]\}$ in x .

Next we investigate the meaning of the phrase "construct CO contains only
he value x ". Put CO = C(f) , where $f \in A \to X$; we shall then take the
hrase to mean that   im f = $\{x\}$. This, however, may be transformed as
ollows:

$$im\ f = \{x\}$$
$$= \{\ CO \in Co(X)\ ,\ hence\ \ A \neq \emptyset\ \}$$
$$(\underline{A}\ a: a \in A: f(a) = x)$$
$$= \{\}$$
$$(\underline{A}\ a: a \in A: x \in \{f(a)\})$$
$$= \{definition\ of\ \cap\ \}$$
$$x \in \cap/(C(\{\blacksquare\} \circ f))$$
$$= \{definition\ of\ *\ \}$$
$$x \in (\cap/ \circ \{\blacksquare\}*)(C(f))\qquad .$$

ence the phrase "construct CO contains only x " may also be rendered by

5) $x \in (\cap/ \circ \{\blacksquare\}*)(CO)$.

traightforwardly combining (4) and (5), we find that the set of all x   with
he property that there exists a root path in C that contains only x   is

$$\{x \mid (\underline{E}\ P: P \in (\{[\blacksquare]\}, +++, \cup)!(C): x \in (\cap/ \circ \{\blacksquare\}*)(P))\}$$
$$= \{definition\ of\ \cup\ \}$$
$$\{x \mid x \in \cup/(\{(\cap/ \circ \{\blacksquare\}*)(P) \mid P \in (\{[\blacksquare]\}, +++, \cup)!(C)\})\}$$
$$= \{\}$$
$$\cup/(\{(\cap/ \circ \{\blacksquare\}*)(P) \mid P \in (\{[\blacksquare]\}, +++, \cup)!(C)\})$$
$$= \{definition\ of\ *\ \}$$
$$(\cup/ \circ (\cap/ \circ \{\blacksquare\}*)*)(\{P \mid P \in (\{[\blacksquare]\}, +++, \cup)!(C)\})$$
$$= \{\}$$

6) $(\cup/ \circ (\cap/ \circ \{\blacksquare\}*)* \circ (\{[\blacksquare]\}, +++, \cup)!)(C)$.

his may be regarded as an inefficient functional program or a specification;

by means of the (strengthened) theorem of the previous section, we shall transform it into the more efficient program $(\{■\}, ∩, ∪)!(C)$.

The shape of (6) suggests that we apply the theorem with

$$f, £0, £1:= ∪/ ° (∩/ ° \{■\}*)*, +++, ∪ \quad .$$

Next we determine which choice to make for $0 and $1 . Now for any S0 and S1 such that S0 is a singleton set, say {P} ,

      f(S0 +++ S1)

 = {definitions of f and +++ }

    (∪/ ° (∩/ ° {■}*)*)({P0 ++ P1 | P0 ∈ S0 ∧ P1∈ S1})

 = {definition of * }

    ∪/({(∩/ ° {■}*)(P0 ++ P1) | P0 ∈ S0 ∧ P1 ∈ S1})

 = { * distributes over ++ }

    ∪/({∩/({■}*(P0) ++ {■}*(P1)) | P0 ∈ S0 ∧ P1 ∈ S1})

 = {∩/(C0 ++ C1) = ∩/(C0) ∩ ∩/(C1)}

    ∪/({∩/({■}*(P0)) ∩ ∩/({■}*(P1)) | P0 ∈ S0 ∧ P1 ∈ S1})

 = {S0 = {P}}

    ∪/({∩/({■}*(P)) ∩ ∩/({■}*(P1)) | P1 ∈ S1})

 = {definition of * }

    (∪/ ° (∩/({■}*(P)) ∩)*)({∩/({■}*(P1)) | P1 ∈ S1})

 = { ∩ distributes over ∪ }

    ∩/({■}*(P)) ∩ ∪/({∩/({■}*(P1)) | P1 ∈ S1})

 = {S0 = {P}}

    (∪/ ° (∩/ ° {■}*)*)(S0) ∩ (∪/ ° (∩/ ° {■}*)*)(S1)

 = {definition of f }

    f(S0) ∩ f(S1)   .

As it is easy to see that

    f(S0 ∪ S1) = f(S0) ∪ f(S1)   ,

we can now use the theorem to rewrite (6) in the form

(7)   (∪/ ° (∩/ ° {■}*)* ° {[■]}, ∩, ∪)!(C)   .

owever,

$$(\cup/ \circ (\cap/ \circ \{\blacksquare\}*)* \circ \{[\blacksquare]\})(x)$$

= {definition of $\{[\blacksquare]\}$ }

$$(\cup/ \circ (\cap/ \circ \{\blacksquare\}*)*)(\{[x]\})$$

= {definition of $*$ }

$$\cup/(\{(\cap/ \circ \{\blacksquare\}*)([x])\})$$

= {definition of $*$ }

$$\cup/(\{(\cap/(\{[x]\})\})$$

= {definition of $/$ }

$$\cup/(\{\{x\}\})$$

= {definition of $/$ }

$$\{x\}$$

= {definition of $\{\blacksquare\}$ }

$$\{\blacksquare\}(x) \qquad .$$

herefore

$$\cup/ \circ (\cap/ \circ \{\blacksquare\}*)* \circ \{[\blacksquare]\} = \{\blacksquare\}$$

nd so (7) reduces to

$$(\{\blacksquare\}, \cap, \cup)!(C)$$

as promised.

Another application: the maximal sum of a subtree

The concept of a nonempty subtree (of a forest) may be defined recursively as follows. The only nonempty subtree of $[x]$ is $[x]$ itself. A subtree of $[x] ++ C1$ is either a subtree of $C1$ or the tree $[x] ++ C1$. A subtree of $C0 + C1$ is either a subtree of $C0$ or one of $C1$. Hence, the set of all nonempty subtrees of a forest C over Z is $St(C)$, where $St \in Fo(Z) \to P(Fo(Z))$ is defined by

$$St([x]) = \{[x]\} \quad ,$$
$$St(C0 \mathbin{++} C1) = \{C0 \mathbin{++} C1\} \cup St(C1) \quad ,$$
$$St(C0 + C1) = St(C0) \cup St(C1) \quad .$$

The definition of St is not one of the sort that can be denoted by $!$, since the right hand side of the second line mentions $C0$ and $C1$, not just $St(C0)$ and $St(C1)$. Note that this is an essential objection, since St is not injective: a forest consisting of two copies of a tree has the same set of subtrees as that tree itself. However, there is a way out of this difficulty: we "strengthen the invariant" by computing the pair $(C, St(C))$ rather than just $St(C)$. Define $£0$, $£1$ on $(Fo(Z) \times P(Fo(Z)))$ by

$$(C0, S0) \; £0 \; (C1, S1) = (C0 \mathbin{++} C1, \{C0 \mathbin{++} C1\} \cup S1) \quad ,$$
$$(C0, S0) \; £1 \; (C1, S1) = (C0 + C1, S0 \cup S1)$$

and $g \in Z \to (Fo(Z) \times P(Fo(Z)))$ by

$$g(x) = ([x], \{[x]\}) \quad ;$$

then the above calculation shows that

$$(g, £0, £1)!(C) = (C, St(C))$$

for any C in $Fo(Z)$. Hence

(8) $\qquad St = snd \circ (g, £0, £1)! \quad ,$

where $snd(x, y) = y$.

Now let us consider the task of computing the maximal sum of any nonempty subtree of a given forest C. With the aid of (8) this may be written as

(9) $\qquad (\underline{max} \circ +/* \circ snd \circ (g, £0, £1)!)(C) \quad .$

Again, (9) may be viewed as a specification or an inefficient program and it is our task to transform it into an equivalent but more useful expression. The shape of (9) suggest that we apply the theorem with f:= <u>max</u> ° +/* ° snd   .

---

now determine the proper choice for $0 and $1 .Under the hypothesis that
0, S0) ∈ im g , hence for some x ∈ Z both C0 = [x] and S0 = {[x]} , we
ve

    f((C0, S0) £0 (C1, S1))

= {definitions of f and £0 }

    (<u>max</u>/ ° +/* ° snd)(C0 ++ C1, {C0 ++ C1} ∪ S1)

= {definition of snd }

    (<u>max</u>/ ° +/*)({C0 ++ C1} ∪ S1)

= {definition of * }

    <u>max</u>/({+/(C0 ++ C1)} ∪ +/*(S1))

= {+/(C0 ++ C1) = +/(C0) + +/(C1) , by the definition of / }

    <u>max</u>/{+/(C0) + +/(C1)} ∪ +/*(S1))

= {<u>max</u>/(A ∪ B) = <u>max</u>/(A) <u>max</u> <u>max</u>/(B) , by the definition of / }

    <u>max</u>/({+/(C0) + +/(C1)}) <u>max</u> <u>max</u>/(+/*(S1))

= { C0 = [x] , by hypothesis}

    (x + +/(C1)) <u>max</u> <u>max</u>/(+/*(S1))

= { S0 = {[x]} , by hypothesis}

    (<u>max</u>/(+/*(S0)) + +/(C1)) <u>max</u> <u>max</u>/(+/*(S1))

= {definition of f }

    (f(C0, S0) + +/(C1)) <u>max</u> f(C1, S1)   .

he application of the theorem presents problems since we do not succeed in
xpressing +/(C1) in terms of f(C0, S0) and f(C1, S1) . Once again, the
olution comes from "strengthening the invariant" and computing

    F(C, S) = (+/(C), f(C, S))

nstead of f(C, S) . This is sufficient for the original problem, since (9)
s equal to

    (snd ° F ° (g, £0, £1)!)(C)   .

From the above calculation it follows that if we define $0 on Z × Z by

$$(x0, y0) \ \$0 \ (x1, y1) = (x0 + x1, (y0 + x1) \ \underline{max} \ y1) \ ,$$

we have (under the hypothesis mentioned)

$$F((C0, S0) \ £0 \ (C1, S1)) = F(C0, S0) \ \$0 \ F(C1, S1) \quad .$$

Moreover,

$$f((C0, S0) \ £1 \ (C1, S1))$$
= {definitions of f and £1 }
$$(\underline{max} \ / \ ° \ +/* \ ° \ snd)(C0 + C1, S0 \cup S1)$$
= {definition of snd }
$$(\underline{max}/ \ ° \ +/*)(S0 \cup S1)$$
= { * distributes over ∪ }
$$\underline{max}/(+/*(S0) \ \cup \ +/*(S1))$$
= { $\underline{max}/(A \cup B) = \underline{max}/(A) \ \underline{max} \ \underline{max}/(B)$, by the definition of / }
$$(\underline{max}/ \ ° \ +/*)(S0) \ \underline{max} \ (\underline{max}/ \ ° \ +/*)(S1)$$
= {definition of f }
$$f(C0, S0) \ \underline{max} \ f(C1, S1) \quad .$$

Hence, if we define $1 on Z × Z by

$$(x0, y0) \ \$1 \ (x1, y1) = (x0 + x1, y0 \ \underline{max} \ y1) \quad ,$$

we have

$$F((C0, S0) \ £1 \ (C1, S1)) = F(C0, S0) \ \$1 \ F(C1, S1) \quad .$$

Application of the (strengthened) theorem now gives

$$F \ ° \ (g, £0, £1)! = (F \ ° \ g, \$0, \$1)! \quad .$$

For any $x \in Z$ we have

```
   (F ° g)(x)
=  {definitions of  F  and  g }
   (+/[x], (max/ ° +/* ° snd)([x], {[x]}))
=  {definitions of  /  and  snd }
   (x, (max/ ° +/*)({[x]}))
=  {definition of  * }
   (x, max/({+/([x])}))
=  {definition of  / }
   (x, x)     .
```

gathering together our results, we find that the maximal sum of any nonempty subtree of C is (snd ° (H, \$0, \$1)!)(C) , where

```
H(x) = (x, x)      ,
(x0, y0) $0 (x1, y1) = (x0 + x1, (y0 + x1) max y1)      ,
(x0, y0) $1 (x1, y1) = (x0 + x1, y0 max y1)        .
```

References

[0]   A. Bijlsma, A unified approach to sequences, bags, and trees. Computing Science Notes 88/13. Eindhoven University of Technology, 1988.

[1]   R.S. Bird, An introduction to the theory of lists; in: M. Broy (ed.), Logic of programming and calculi of discrete design (lecture notes international summer school, Marktoberdorf, 1986). NATO Adv. Sci. Inst. Ser. F, 36. Springer-Verlag, Berlin, 1987.

[2]   L. Meertens, Algorithmics: towards programming as a mathematical activity; in: J.W. de Bakker, M. Hazewinkel, J.K. Lenstra (eds.), Mathematics and computer science. North Holland, Amsterdam, 1986.

Networks of Communicating Processes
and
Their (De-)Composition

Wei Chen
Department of Computer Science
Washington University
St. Louis, MO

Jan Tijmen Udding
Department of Mathematics and Computing Science
Groningen University
Groningen, The Netherlands

Tom Verhoeff
Department of Mathematics and Computing Science
Eindhoven University of Technology
Eindhoven, The Netherlands

Abstract

In this paper we sketch a general framework within which a study of networks of processes can be conducted. It is based upon the mathematical technique to abstract from irrelevant detail. We start out with a large class of objects and some operations upon them. Depending upon a correctness criterion to be imposed, some of these objects turn out to be equivalent. The resulting space of equivalence classes and operations upon them is, under certain conditions, the (fully) abstract space of interest for that particular correctness concern.

We use this approach to study networks for which we assume the communications to be asymmetric and asynchronous. We impose the correctness criterion of absence of computation interference. The resulting abstract space turns out to be the space of delay-insensitive specifications. As operator we study composition of networks. The composition operator on the resulting space is shown to have a surprisingly simple factorization property, the prove of which turns out to be very simple due to the approach taken.

0 Introduction

In this paper we study networks of communicating processes. The communications between processes are asymmetric, that is, for each communication there is an initiating party which sends a signal to other parties regardless of their readiness. We study both synchronous (all parties complete their parts of the communication at the same step) and asynchronous (each party is free to complete its part of the communication at its own convenience) communications. The overall goal is to model computations implemented as electrical circuits—where communications are typically asynchronous—in a mathematical way, so we can derive programs to be implemented as circuits in the same way as we derive computer programs. Since most concurrent programming languages are based upon synchronous symmetric communication primitives (and rightfully so!), it is important to establish a semantically consistent link between synchronous and asynchronous based communication primitives.

The approach we take to this problem is quite general and widely applicable when modeling the operation of systems. We start out from a large class of primitive objects. The kind of the objects we consider is discussed in the next section. Some of these objects are just as "good" as other objects for implementing a particular specification. A well-known example of such an ordering of objects is the one induced by non-determinism. Removing non-determinism yields a program which is at least as good as the original one. In general, a certain correctness concern induces an ordering on the objects under consideration. We call two objects equivalent if either of the two is as good as the other one. This induces equivalence classes of objects that cannot be distinguished under that particular correctness concern. In this way each correctness concern induces a (fully abstract) space of equivalence classes. We illustrate this approach by choosing absence of computation interference as our correctness concern. Absence of computation interference means that no signal will arrive at a process when that process is not ready for it according to its specification.

For this particular correctness concern it turns out that the induced equivalence classes yield an obvious way to define a denotational semantics of parallel composition. It is shown to have properties such as monotonicity, associativity, and continuity. More importantly, we show how composition can be used to mechanically decompose a given specification into smaller ones, the composition of which satisfies the original specification. Roughly speaking, if the composition of an unknown component X and a given component M is to satisfy a certain specification S, then it is good enough too look for X's satisfying the composition of S and the "inverse" of M. This is very similar to the situation in sequential programming where, given an invariant of a repetition and a statement establishing a step towards termination, the specification of the rest of the body of the repetition can be computed.

The authors believe that similar, but more powerful, algebraic laws will hold when other correctness concerns, such as progress, are taken into consideration.

Overview

In Section 1 we describe the formal model. It introduces a space of processes and a space of process networks together with a network composition operator. For the closed networks we define two operational semantics—one for synchronous and one for asynchronous communication—and a related correctness concern. This induces two natural satisfaction relations on the space of networks. To each satisfaction relation corresponds a notion of equivalence for networks.

Section 2 studies the space of networks under the equivalence relation based on asynchronous communication and its correctness concern. The major result is that each network is equivalent to a network consisting of single process. This result is used in Section 3 to give a fully abstract denotational semantics for the composition of processes. We show that composition has certain interesting properties. We also present a factorization theorem that can be used for decomposition.

Finally, in Section 4 we comment on our approach and briefly compare it to that of others.

1 Networks of communicating processes

In this section we define our primitive objects and the operations on them, and we give a mechanistic appreciation so as to provide the reader with some intuition behind the definitions. We emphasize that this intuition is unnecessary, and can even be dangerous, once the formal basis of our objects and operations has been given. We only want to sustain the claim that the purely mathematical game that we are playing may have some practical significance.

1.0 Structure of systems

The objects we wish to study are networks of communicating processes, also called systems. We are only interested in the external behavior of a process. Externally, a process in a network communicates with another process by sending signals to and receiving signals from that process via so-called *links*. The set of links via which processes can communicate with one another is called Σ. Each sending and each receiving of a signal constitutes an *event*. These events are atomic actions, that is, there is no notion of overlapping events. The event "sending a signal" onto a certain link is denoted by the name of the link followed by an exclamation mark. The event "receiving a signal" on a certain link is denoted by the name of the link followed by a query mark.

We characterize a process by the set of events it can engage in, called its alphabet, and in what order those events may occur, which is captured by its trace set. We formalize these concepts in the following way.

Definition 0   A *directed* symbol is an element of $\Omega = \Sigma \times \{?, !\}$. A directed symbol is called an input symbol when its second component is '?' and an output symbol otherwise.
□

We have called the elements of Ω directed symbols rather than symbols, since the elements of Σ are often referred to as symbols in the literature. However, in the sequel the only set of interest is Ω. Therefore, we say symbol in the sequel when we mean directed symbol.

Definition 1   The *reflection* of symbol a, denoted by $\tilde{a}$, is the symbol that is equal to a in its first component and differs from a in its second component. The reflection of set A of symbols, denoted by $\tilde{A}$, is the set of reflected symbols of A.   □

Thus, by reflection an input symbol becomes an output symbol and vice versa.

Definition 2   For set A of symbols, iA denotes the set of input symbols of A and oA denotes the set of output symbols of A.   □

As said earlier, we characterize the way in which a process communicates with other processes by specifying the symbols it can send and receive. This determines how processes in a network "hook up" to one another. We call this set of symbols the *alphabet* of a process. We assume our links to be unidirectional, which means that a process can use a particular link either for sending or for receiving. Hence, an alphabet cannot just be any subset of Ω, but it is subject to the following restriction.

Definition 3   An *alphabet* A is any subset of Ω such that $A \cap \widetilde{A} = \emptyset$.   □

Thus, the symbols of an alphabet differ in their first components. Next we formalize the way in which we specify the sequences of events that a process may engage in.

Definition 4   A *trace* is a finite-length sequence of symbols. The empty trace is denoted by ε. The reflection of trace t, denoted by $\tilde{t}$, is the trace obtained by reflecting all symbols of t. Trace s is called a *prefix* of trace t when $(\exists u :: su = t)$, where juxtaposition of traces denotes concatenation. The *length* of trace t, denoted by $\ell(t)$, is the number of symbols in t. The *number of occurrences* of symbol a in trace t is denoted by $\#_a t$.   □

A trace may be viewed as denoting a sequence of events, which have either occurred, when that trace describes a certain history, or can occur, when that trace specifies an allowed behavior of a process.

Definition 5   A *trace set* is a set of traces. A trace set is called *prefix-closed* when it contains all the prefixes of its traces. The reflection of trace set T, denoted by $\widetilde{T}$, is the set of all reflected traces of T.   □

A trace set specifies the possible sequences of events that a process may engage in. During the operation of a process specified by trace set T, there is a trace t of events engaged in thus far. We characterize a process by a directed trace structure.

Definition 6   A *directed trace structure*, or DTS, is a pair consisting of an alphabet and a prefix-closed trace set over that alphabet. For DTS S we denote its alphabet by aS and its trace set by tS. As a pair, DTS S is sometimes written as $\langle aS, tS \rangle$. The input alphabet of S, denoted by iS, is $i(aS)$ and the output alphabet, denoted by oS, is $o(aS)$. The reflection of S, denoted by $\widetilde{S}$, has alphabet $(aS)^\sim$ and trace set $(tS)^\sim$.

The DTS $CHAOS$ is defined as $\langle \emptyset, \emptyset \rangle$. The space of all DTSs is denoted by $\mathcal{DTS}$ and the subspace of all DTSs with alphabet A is denoted by $\mathcal{DTS}(A)$.   □

So far for single processes. As said earlier, we want to study networks of processes. A network is a set of processes in which each link is used by at most two processes. At most one process can send signals on a certain link and at most one process can receive signals from that link. Links that are used by exactly one process allow communications of the network with the "outside world", which is usually just another network. The latter network can be viewed as an environment of the former. Throughout this paper we refer to a formal network as a system. We also introduce an operator on systems to model their parallel composition in an operational sense.

Definition 7 A *system* X is a set of DTSs with pairwise disjoint alphabets, that is,

$$(\forall S, T : S \in X \wedge T \in X \wedge S \neq T : \mathrm{a}S \cap \mathrm{a}T = \emptyset).$$

Let A be the set of symbols $(\bigcup S : S \in X : \mathrm{a}S)$, called the system's *symbol set*. The sets $\mathrm{i}A$, $\mathrm{o}A$, and $A \setminus \tilde{A}$ are alphabets. These are called the *input*, *output*, and *external* alphabets of X respectively and they are denoted by $\mathrm{i}X$, $\mathrm{o}X$, and $\mathrm{e}X$ respectively. System X is called *closed* when $A = \tilde{A}$. The *pattern* of X, denoted by $\mathrm{p}X$, is the set of alphabets of the elements of X.

Notice that the union of two systems with disjoint symbol sets is a system. We do not consider the set of *internal* symbols $A \cap \tilde{A}$ to be an attribute of a system. That is, we do not distinguish systems that are equal modulo renaming of internal symbols. We assume that in all cases we can rename internal symbols to fresh ones.

The *operational parallel composition* of systems X and Y with disjoint external alphabets is denoted by $X \uplus Y$. Let X' and Y' be systems obtained from X and Y by renaming their internal symbols such that the symbol sets of X' and Y' are disjoint. This renaming is possible because $\mathrm{e}X \cap \mathrm{e}Y = \emptyset$. We now define $X \uplus Y = X' \cup Y'$. This is a proper definition, i.e. independent of the chosen renaming, because the names of internal symbols are immaterial. In fact, we will assume, whenever we write $X \uplus Y$, that the symbol sets of X and Y are disjoint.

The space of all systems is denoted by $\mathcal{SYS}$. □

The empty set is a system and for DTS S the singleton $\{S\}$ is also a system. The external alphabet of the composite of systems X and Y satisfies

$$\mathrm{e}(X \uplus Y) = (\mathrm{e}X \cup \mathrm{e}Y) \setminus (\mathrm{e}X \cup \mathrm{e}Y)^{\sim}$$

and the symbols in $\mathrm{e}X \cap \widetilde{\mathrm{e}Y}$ and $\widetilde{\mathrm{e}X} \cap \mathrm{e}Y$ have become internal in the composite. For DTSs S and T we have that $\{S, T\}$ forms a system if and only if the singleton systems $\{S\}$ and $\{T\}$ are composable, and in that case we have

$$\{S\} \uplus \{T\} = \{S, T\}.$$

A closed system has no external links and all communications take place internally. The pattern of a system specifies how the components are connected to one another.

1.1 Operation of systems

The previous section sufficiently describes the objects we want to study. In the next paragraphs we define how systems operate. As far as operation is concerned we consider closed systems only, since an open system always operates in some context, together with which it forms a closed system.

The key notion is that of the state of a system, which is given by the sequence of events that each component has communicated thus far. Subsequently, we define how a closed system moves from one state to the next, describing the operation of a system as a labeled transition system.

Definition 8 For system X a *system state* v, or *state* for short, is a mapping from $\mathrm{p}X$ to Ω^* such that $(\forall A : A \in \mathrm{p}X : v.A \in A^*)$. The set of all states on X is denoted by $\mathrm{v}X$. The length of state v, denoted by $\ell(v)$, is the sum of the lengths of the individual traces of v. For state v on system X and for some $S \in X$ we denote by $v(aS : +a)$ the state that differs from v only on aS, where it has the value $(v.aS)a$. Similarly, for $S \in X$ and $T \in X$, $S \neq T$, we denote by $v(aS, aT : +a, +b)$ the state that differs from v only in aS and aT. In aS it has the value $(v.aS)a$ and in aT the value $(v.aT)b$. With $\#_a v$ we denote $(\mathbf{SUM}\, S : S \in X : \#_a v.aS)$. A state v on system X is called *safe* when $(\forall S : S \in X : v.aS \in tS)$. $\qquad\square$

Notice that the length of a state may be infinite even if all individual traces have finite lengths, viz. if the system is infinite.

> **Notational convention**: A mapping can be viewed as a set of pairs. The first element in the pair is an element of the domain of the mapping, the second element is the image under that mapping. Therefore, if X and Y are systems with disjoint symbol sets and if state $x \in vX$ and state $y \in vY$, then $x \cup y$ is a state on $X \cup Y$. By Definition 7 the elements of the domain of a state are disjoint alphabets. By Definition 8 we have for any pair, say (aS, s), that $s \in (aS)^*$, which implies that the pair is determined by s if $s \neq \varepsilon$. Using this property we denote a state by the set of second elements of its pairs.

The operation of a closed system is described as moving from state to state according to some rules, which we discuss later, starting in the initial state. This is the state in which none of the components has sent or received any signals.

Definition 9   The *initial* state of system X is the state v on X such that $(\forall A : A \in pX : v.A = \varepsilon)$. A state on a system is called *reachable* if it can be reached from the initial state by a succession of moves according to the rules. $\qquad\square$

We distinguish two different sets of rules to move from one state to the next. The first set of rules is called the synchronous game and the other one is called the asynchronous game.

The synchronous game resembles CSP in the sense that sending and receiving are one event. It differs from CSP in the sense that there is an asymmetry between sending and receiving. The sender of a signal is the cause for this event to take place. In the asynchronous game sending a signal and receiving it are two distinct events. The only restriction is that receiving a signal is preceded by sending it. In the next two definitions we characterize a successor relation on states both for the synchronous and for the asynchronous game. This successor relation determines how a system may evolve starting in its initial state.

Definition 10   *Synchronous Game*
For v and w states on a closed system X we call w a successor of v when

$$(\exists S, T, a \;\; : S \in X \land T \in X \land a \in oS \land \tilde{a} \in iT \land (v.aS)a \in tS$$
$$: w = v(S, T : +a, +\tilde{a})).$$

$\qquad\square$

In words, w is a successor of v when w differs from v in two places, aS and aT. In these places the traces of w are the ones of v extended with a symbol a in one place and its reflection in the other one. That symbol is such that S can send it, i.e. the trace of S generated in this game thus far, being $v.aS$, can be extended with a according to

$t S$. Moreover, the pattern of the system is such that T is the component to receive that signal, i.e. $\tilde{a} \in iT$. It is important to notice that these two events can take place if the sending end can produce that symbol according to its specification. The receiving end need not be ready for the reception, which may cause the resulting trace not to belong to the corresponding trace set. Due to the prefix-closedness of the trace sets under consideration, if a trace associated with a component does not belong to the trace set of that component then no extension of that trace will belong to that trace set either. Therefore, a component that has received an input which it could not according to its trace set, will in this game never send another signal. We come back to this phenomenon later.

Definition 11 *Asynchronous Game*

For v and w states on a closed system X we say that w is a successor of v when it is either an output successor or an input successor of v. It is an *output successor* of v when

$$(\exists S, a : S \in X \wedge a \in oS \wedge (v.aS)a \in tS : w = v(S : +a)).$$

It is an *input successor* of v when

$$(\exists S, a : S \in X \wedge a \in iS \wedge \#_{\tilde{a}} v > \#_a v.aS : w = v(S : +a)).$$

□

In the asynchronous game a symbol can be sent under the same conditions as in the synchronous game. Reception of that symbol, however, is now a distinct event. For an input event to take place there should have been sent more symbols on the corresponding link than have been received thus far.

1.2   The Correctness Concern

For two systems X and Y we want to define when X is at least as "good" as Y, denoted by $X \, \mathbf{sat} \, Y$. If X is viewed as implementation and Y as specification, one usually says "X satisfies Y". We will, however, not explicitly distinguish systems that serve as implementation or as specification.

The measure of goodness depends on the correctness criteria that are taken into consideration. We capture a correctness concern by a predicate $P(X, U)$, where X is the system under consideration and system U can be viewed as (testing) environment of X. $P(X, U)$ holds if and only if X has "no problems" with U.

Definition 12   For correctness concern P and for systems X and Y of DTSs we say that X satisfies Y, denoted by $X \, \mathbf{sat} \, Y$, when

$$(\forall U : P(Y, U) : P(X, U)),$$

where U ranges over the space of systems.   □

Property 0   The relation **sat** is a pre-order, that is, it is reflexive and transitive.   □

Generally, $P(X, U)$ is the conjunction of a number of predicates. One of these predicates will always be that $X \uplus U$ defines a closed system, i.e. $eX = \widetilde{eU}$, so that modules and environments "hook up" to one another correctly. Throughout the rest of the paper we choose as our additional correctness concern that the closed system $X \uplus U$ has absence of computation interference, which is defined in the following way.

Definition 13   Closed system X is said to have *absence of computation interference* when all reachable states are safe. We denote the predicate that X is closed and has absence of computation interference by **nsi** X when playing the synchronous game and by **nai** X when playing the asynchronous game.   □

Thus, $P(X, U) \equiv \mathbf{nai}\, X \uplus U$ in the asynchronous game. Notice that whether there is computation interference does not depend on the names of the internal symbols of the closed system.

A system has computation interference, when a move can extend a trace in a reachable state with an input symbol while the resulting trace is not a member of the corresponding DTS's trace set. We note that the situation of computation interference is undesirable, because then our formalism is no longer a valid model for the behavior of electrical circuits. The games, however, are always well defined. We have arbitrarily chosen for some behavior once there is computation interference, viz. the interfered process will no longer be able to send outputs.

Property 1   A closed system X has absence of computation interference in the synchronous game when the initial state is safe and when for all safe reachable states v

$$(\forall S, T, a : S, T \in X \land \tilde{a} \in oS \land a \in iT : (v.S)\tilde{a} \in tS \Rightarrow (v.T)a \in tT).$$

It has absence of computation interference in the asynchronous game when the initial state is safe and when for all safe reachable states v

$$(\forall T, a : T \in X \land a \in iT : \#_{\tilde{a}}v > \#_a v.T \Rightarrow (v.T)a \in tT).$$

□

We can confine ourselves in this property to the *safe* reachable states since any non-initial unsafe reachable state can only be reached by a transition from a safe to an unsafe state. Notice that if a closed system has absence of computation interference in the asynchronous game, then it has absence of computation interference in the synchronous game. Notice also that any system containing a DTS with empty trace set has computation interference, since the initial state is not safe.

Given the **sat**-relation we can define an equivalence relation on the space of all systems. We call two systems equivalent when no environment can distinguish the two. This equivalence is called testing equivalence in [3].

Definition 14   Two systems X and Y of DTSs are called equivalent, denoted by $X \mathbf{equ}\, Y$, when $X \mathbf{sat}\, Y \land Y \mathbf{sat}\, X$.   □

Property 2   Relation **equ** is an equivalence relation and for systems X and Y we have

$$X \mathbf{equ}\, Y \equiv (\forall U :: P(X, U) \equiv P(Y, U)).$$

In fact, **equ** is even a congruence relation on the space $\langle \mathcal{SYS}, \mathbf{sat}, \uplus \rangle$. That is, for systems X, X', Y, and Y' such that $X \mathbf{equ}\, X'$ and $Y \mathbf{equ}\, Y'$ we have

$$X \mathbf{sat}\, Y \quad \equiv \quad X' \mathbf{sat}\, Y',$$
$$X \uplus Y \quad \mathbf{equ} \quad X' \uplus Y'.$$

Proof That equ is an equivalence relation is obvious. We show the two congruence conditions. Assuming X **sat** Y we derive X' **sat** Y' by computing for arbitrary environment Z:

$$\text{nai}\, Y' \uplus Z$$
$$= \quad \{\, Y \text{ equ } Y' \,\}$$
$$\text{nai}\, Y \uplus Z$$
$$\Rightarrow \quad \{\, X \text{ sat } Y \,\}$$
$$\text{nai}\, X \uplus Z$$
$$= \quad \{\, X \text{ equ } X' \,\}$$
$$\text{nai}\, X' \uplus Z$$

Symmetry does the rest. Furthermore, we derive for arbitrary environment Z:

$$\text{nai}\, X \uplus Y \uplus Z$$
$$= \quad \{\, X \text{ equ } X' \,\}$$
$$\text{nai}\, X' \uplus Y \uplus Z$$
$$= \quad \{\, Y \text{ equ } Y' \,\}$$
$$\text{nai}\, X' \uplus Y' \uplus Z$$

Thus, we have $X \uplus Y$ equ $X' \uplus Y'$. □

The following relation on DTSs turns out to be important.

Definition 15 We define the relation $\sqsubseteq$ on $\mathcal{DTS}$ by

$$S \sqsubseteq T \equiv (\forall U : \mathbf{nsi}\{T, U\} : \mathbf{nsi}\{S, U\}),$$

for DTSs S and T (U also ranges over $\mathcal{DTS}$). □

Notice the resemblance to the synchronous **sat** relation, which uses arbitrary systems as environments, instead of singletons. Actually, synchronous **sat** and $\sqsubseteq$ are the same relation, but we do not prove that in this paper. We quote the following results from [7].

Theorem 0 For DTSs S and T we have

$$S \sqsubseteq T \equiv (\mathbf{a}S = \mathbf{a}T \vee \mathbf{t}T = \emptyset) \wedge (\varepsilon \in \mathbf{t}T \Rightarrow \varepsilon \in \mathbf{t}S) \wedge$$
$$(\forall s, a \quad : \quad s \in \mathbf{t}S \cap \mathbf{t}T$$
$$\quad : \quad (a \in \mathbf{o}A \wedge sa \in \mathbf{t}S \Rightarrow sa \in \mathbf{t}T)$$
$$\quad \wedge \quad (a \in \mathbf{i}A \wedge sa \in \mathbf{t}T \Rightarrow sa \in \mathbf{t}S)).$$

□

The relation $\sqsubseteq$ is not a partial order on $\mathcal{DTS}$. It lacks antisymmetry, since we have $S \sqsubseteq T$ for any DTSs S and T with $\mathbf{t}T = \emptyset$, also if $\mathbf{a}S \neq \mathbf{a}T$ and $\mathbf{t}S =$. The abundance of DTSs with empty trace set is the only "problem". If we leave out all but one, say $CHAOS$, of these, then $\sqsubseteq$ is a partial order. We also have

Theorem 1 The space $\langle \mathcal{DTS}(A), \sqsubseteq \rangle$ is a complete lattice, with $\langle A, \emptyset \rangle$ as top and $\langle A, \mathbf{i}(A)^* \rangle$ as bottom. □

Furthermore, we have the following duality property.

Property 3   For DTSs S and T with non-empty trace sets we have

$$S \sqsubseteq T \equiv \tilde{T} \sqsubseteq \tilde{S}.$$

□

Theorem 2   For $X \subseteq \mathcal{DTS}(A)$ such that $\langle A, \emptyset \rangle \notin X$ we can characterize the trace set of the least upper bound of X, $t(\sqcup X)$, as follows.

- $\varepsilon \in t(\sqcup X)$
- for trace s and symbols $a \in iA$ and $p \in oA$

$$sa \in t(\sqcup X) \quad \equiv \quad s \in t(\sqcup X) \wedge (\forall S : S \in X \wedge s \in tS : sa \in tS)$$
$$sp \in t(\sqcup X) \quad \equiv \quad s \in t(\sqcup X) \wedge (\exists S : S \in X \wedge s \in tS : sp \in tS)$$

If $\langle A, \emptyset \rangle \in X$ then the least upper bound of X is the top $\langle A, \emptyset \rangle$.   □

Property 4   For $X \subseteq \mathcal{DTS}(A)$ we have $t(\sqcup X) \subseteq (\bigcup S : S \in X : tS)$.   □

2   Analysis of the Space of Systems

In this section we study the space $\langle \mathcal{SYS}, \mathbf{sat} \rangle$ under the equivalence relation based on the asynchronous game. The composition operator $\uplus$ will be treated in the next section. Throughout the rest of the paper equ stands for this asynchronous equivalence. Thus, we are interested in $\langle \mathcal{SYS}, \mathbf{sat} \rangle / \mathbf{equ}$. Our goal is to find a simpler isomorphic space. We show that $\langle \mathcal{DTS}, \sqsubseteq \rangle$ contains such an isomorphic subspace. We do so by exhibiting a homomorphism $[\cdot]$ from $\langle \mathcal{SYS}, \mathbf{sat} \rangle$ into $\langle \mathcal{DTS}, \sqsubseteq \rangle$ satisfying the condition

$$X \, \mathbf{equ} \, Y \equiv [X] = [Y],$$

for all systems X and Y. This condition expresses that $[\cdot]$ exactly identifies equivalent systems. That $[\cdot]$ is a homomorphism means, as you may know, that it satisfies $X \, \mathbf{sat} \, Y \equiv [X] \sqsubseteq [Y]$. We will see that this already implies the above condition on $[\cdot]$, because $\sqsubseteq$ is a partial order on the image space under $[\cdot]$. The desired result now follows from the Homomorphism Theorem. We will also explicitly characterize the image space $\mathcal{DI}$ of $[\cdot]$.

The definition of the homomorphism is based on the following non-trivial property: Each system of DTSs is equivalent to a suitable system consisting of a single DTS. We will even show that each equ-equivalence class of systems contains a very special singleton system. The DTS member of that special equivalent singleton system serves as image under the homomorphism. We now give the construction of this singleton system and we define the space of delay-insensitive DTSs that will turn out to be the subspace of images.

Definition 16   For system X, its set of *friends*, denoted by $FR(X)$, is defined by

$$FR(X) = \{U : U \in \mathcal{DTS} \wedge \mathbf{nai}\{U\} \uplus X : U\}.$$

Notice that all friends of system X have the same external alphabet, viz. $\widetilde{eX}$, and that they have non-empty trace sets. DTS $[X]$ is defined by

$$[X] = \begin{cases} CHAOS & \text{if } FR(X) = \emptyset \\ (\sqcup FR(X))^{\sim} & \text{if } FR(X) \neq \emptyset \end{cases}$$

The space $\mathcal{DI}$ of delay-insensitive DTSs is defined by

$$\mathcal{DI} = \{S : S \in \mathcal{DTS} \wedge \mathbf{nai}\{S, \widetilde{S}\} : S\} \cup \{CHAOS\}.$$

$\square$

It is instructive to verify that $FR(\emptyset) = \{\langle \emptyset, \{\varepsilon\}\rangle\}$ and, hence, $[\emptyset] = \langle \emptyset, \{\varepsilon\}\rangle$. Notice that $\langle \mathcal{DI}, \sqsubseteq \rangle$ is a poset. Notice also, if we have proved $[\cdot]$ to be a homomorphism, that **sat** and $\sqsubseteq$ coincide on $\mathcal{DI}$, i.e. for $S \in \mathcal{DI}$ and $T \in \mathcal{DI}$ we have $\{S\}\,\mathbf{sat}\,\{T\} \equiv S \sqsubseteq T$.

We make the following claims:

(a) $X\,\mathbf{equ}\{[X]\}$,

(b) $[X] \in \mathcal{DI}$,

(c) $[\{S\}] = S$ for all $S \in \mathcal{DI}$.

The latter two claims express that $\mathcal{DI}$ is the image space of $[\cdot]$. Assuming these claims and monotonicity of **nai** (see below) to hold for a moment, we can show that $[\cdot]$ satisfies the requirements mentioned earlier, viz. that it is a homomorphism which exactly identifies equivalent systems. First, to see that it is a homomorphism we prove two implications separately.

$\quad X\,\mathbf{sat}\,Y$
$=\quad \{$ definition of **sat** $\}$
$\quad \{Z : \mathbf{nai}\,X \uplus Z : Z\} \supseteq \{Z : \mathbf{nai}\,Y \uplus Z : Z\}$
$\Rightarrow\quad \{$ set theory and definition of $FR(X)$ $\}$
$\quad FR(X) \supseteq FR(Y)$
$\Rightarrow\quad \{$ definition of $[\cdot]$ and $\sqsubseteq$, using Property 3 $\}$
$\quad [X] \sqsubseteq [Y]$

Assuming $[X] \sqsubseteq [Y]$ we derive $X\,\mathbf{sat}\,Y$ by computing for environment Z:

$\quad \mathbf{nai}\,Y \uplus Z$
$=\quad \{\ Y\,\mathbf{equ}\{[Y]\}$ according to claim (a) $\}$
$\quad \mathbf{nai}\{[Y]\} \uplus Z$
$\Rightarrow\quad \{$ monotonicity of **nai** (Theorem 3 below), using $[X] \sqsubseteq [Y]$ $\}$
$\quad \mathbf{nai}\{[X]\} \uplus Z$
$=\quad \{\ X\,\mathbf{equ}\{[X]\}$ according to claim (b) $\}$
$\quad \mathbf{nai}\,X \uplus Z$

Second, to see that $[\cdot]$ exactly identifies equivalent systems, it is sufficient to notice that $[\cdot]$ is a homomorphism and that $\sqsubseteq$ is a partial order on $\mathcal{DI}$, especially that it is antisymmetric.

The next subsection is devoted to the proofs of claims (a) through (c).

2.0 Proving the claims

Our first goal is claim (a). The case of a friendless system is dealt with in

Lemma 0   For system X we have

$$X \, \text{equ}\{CHAOS\} \equiv [X] = CHAOS.$$

Hence, if $FR(X) = \emptyset$, then

$$X \, \text{equ}\{[X]\}.$$

Proof   We derive

$X \, \text{equ}\{CHAOS\}$

=   { Property 2 }

$(\forall Y :: \text{nai}\, X \uplus Y \equiv \text{nai}\{CHAOS\} \uplus Y)$

=   { empty trace set implies computation interference; predicate calculus }

$(\forall Y :: \neg\, \text{nai}\, X \uplus Y)$

=   { see Note below }

$(\forall U :: \neg\, \text{nai}\, X \uplus \{U\})$

=   { definition of $FR(X)$ }

$FR(X) = \emptyset$

=   { definition of $[X]$ }

$[X] = CHAOS$

Note: Because every singleton system is a system, we have the implication downwards. The implication upwards follows from the fact that if X has computation interference with $\{(\widetilde{eX}, (\widetilde{oX})^*)\}$ then it has interference with any system.   □

The other case, in which $FR(X) \neq \emptyset$, is proved by separately establishing $X \, \text{sat}\{[X]\}$ (Thm. 5) and $\{[X]\} \, \text{sat}\, X$ (Thm. 6). For the former we need monotonicity (Thm. 3) and continuity (Thm. 4) of **nai** with respect to $\sqsubseteq$, and a form of transitivity of **nai** (Lemma 3).

The following two Theorems express monotonicity and a form of upward continuity of **nai** with respect to $\sqsubseteq$. More precisely, we consider for system X the boolean-valued function which maps DTS S into $\text{nai}\{S\} \uplus X$. On the booleans we take the order $\Leftarrow$, for which universal quantification corresponds to taking the least upper bound. First, however, we need a lemma on reachability.

Lemma 1   For DTSs S and T, such that $S \sqsubseteq T$, and for system X, such that $\text{nai}\{T\} \uplus X$, we have

$$v \text{ is reachable in } \{S\} \uplus X \Rightarrow v \text{ is reachable in } \{T\} \uplus X.$$

Proof   Omitted, see [0].   □

Theorem 3   *Monotonicity of* **nai**
For system X and for DTSs S and T we have

$$S \sqsubseteq T \;\Rightarrow\; (\mathbf{nai}\{S\} \uplus X \Leftarrow \mathbf{nai}\{T\} \uplus X).$$

Proof We assume $S \sqsubseteq T$ and

$$\mathbf{nai}\{T\} \uplus X \tag{0}$$

and prove $\mathbf{nai}\{S\} \uplus X$. We have to show that every reachable state v is safe in $\{S\} \uplus X$. First we show that we can confine our considerations to $v.aS$ by proving that $(\forall U : U \in X : v.aU \in tU)$ for any reachable state v in $\{S\} \uplus X$. We derive

$\qquad v$ is reachable in $\{S\} \uplus X$

$\Rightarrow \qquad \{$ Lemma 1 $\}$

$\qquad v$ is reachable in $\{T\} \uplus X$

$\Rightarrow \qquad \{$ (0) $\}$

$\qquad v$ is safe in $\{T\} \uplus X$

$\Rightarrow \qquad \{$ definition of safety $\}$

$\qquad (\forall U : U \in X : v.aU \in tU)$

Hence, the remaining proof obligation is to show that $v.aS \in tS$ for every reachable state v in $\{S\} \uplus X$. We prove this by induction on the length of $v.aS$.

Base:

$\qquad$ true

$= \qquad \{$ (0), rules of the game $\}$

$\qquad \varepsilon \in tT$

$\Rightarrow \qquad \{\; S \sqsubseteq T$, using Theorem 0 $\}$

$\qquad \varepsilon \in tS$

Step: Any reachable state in which the component on aS is not the empty trace has come about by making a transition from reachable state v to $v(aS : +a)$ in $\{S\} \uplus X$ for some symbol $a \in aS$. Therefore, we assume that

$$v \text{ and } v(aS : +a) \text{ are reachable in } \{S\} \uplus X. \tag{1}$$

for some $a \in aS$. We show that $(v.aS)a \in tS$ given that

$$v.aS \in tS. \tag{2}$$

If $a \in oS$ then $(v.aS)a \in tS$ by the rules of the game. Therefore, assume that

$$a \in iS. \tag{3}$$

We derive

$\qquad$ true

$= \qquad \{$ (1) $\}$

$\qquad v(aS : +a)$ is reachable in $\{S\} \uplus X$

$\Rightarrow \qquad \{$ Lemma 1 $\}$

$\qquad v(aS : +a)$ is reachable in $\{T\} \uplus X$

$\Rightarrow \quad \{ \text{ nai}\{T\} \uplus X \text{ on account of } (0), \text{ using } \mathbf{a}S = \mathbf{a}T \}$

$(v.\mathbf{a}S)a \in \mathbf{t}T$

$= \quad \{ (3) \text{ and } (2) \}$

$(v.\mathbf{a}S)a \in \mathbf{t}T \wedge v.\mathbf{a}S \in \mathbf{t}S \wedge a \in \mathbf{i}S$

$\Rightarrow \quad \{ S \sqsubseteq T \text{ by assumption, using Theorem 0 } \}$

$(v.\mathbf{a}S)a \in \mathbf{t}S$

$\square$

Theorem 4 *Upward Continuity of* **nai**

For system X and non-empty set Z of DTSs with the same alphabet, we have

$$\mathbf{nai}\{\sqcup Z\} \uplus X \equiv (\forall U : U \in Z : \mathbf{nai}\{U\} \uplus X).$$

Proof Notice that the least upper bound of such Z exists. The implication from left to right follows immediately from the monotonicity of **nai**. We now concentrate on the implication from right to left. Assume the right-hand side and define E as $\sqcup Z$, that is, as the least upper bound of Z. We show that $\mathbf{nai}\{E\} \uplus X$ holds.

Since $Z \neq \emptyset$ we know that $\varepsilon \in \mathbf{t}E$ and that all components of X contain ε. Therefore, the initial state in $\{E\} \uplus X$ is safe, and reachable by definition. Next we assume

$$v \text{ is safe and reachable in } \{E\} \uplus X \tag{0}$$

and prove that any successor of v in $\{E\} \uplus X$ is safe in $\{E\} \uplus X$. This then proves $\mathbf{nai}\{E\} \uplus X$.

Output successors of a safe and reachable state are safe by the rules of the game. Hence, we confine our attention to input successors of v in $\{E\} \uplus X$. On account of Property 4 we infer that $\mathbf{t}E \subseteq (\bigcup U : U \in Z : \mathbf{t}U)$. Hence, we may assume $S \in Z$ to be such that

$$\mathbf{nai}\{S\} \uplus X \wedge v \text{ is reachable in } \{S\} \uplus X. \tag{1}$$

Input successors of v are solely determined by v and the pattern on which the game is played. Therefore, using (0) and (1), we infer that any input successor of v in $\{E\} \uplus X$ is reachable and safe in $\{S\} \uplus X$. Hence, if an input successor of v is the result of a move of a component of X then that successor is safe in $\{E\} \uplus X$. If an input successor of v is the result of a move of E then

$$v(E : +a) \text{ is and input successor of } v \text{ in } \{E\} \uplus X \tag{2}$$

for some

$$a \in \mathbf{i}E. \tag{3}$$

It remains to be proven that $(v.\mathbf{a}E)a \in \mathbf{t}E$. We derive

true

$= \quad \{ v(E : +a) \text{ is reachable and safe in any game } \{U\} \uplus X \text{ whenever } U \in Z, \text{ and } v.\mathbf{a}E \in \mathbf{t}U \text{ on account of } (0), (2), \text{ and the rules of the game } \}$

$(\forall U : U \in Z \wedge v.\mathbf{a}E \in \mathbf{t}U : (v.\mathbf{a}E)a \in \mathbf{t}U)$

$\Rightarrow$ { $v.aE \in tE$ on account of (0), $a \in iE$ on account of (3), and $E = \sqcup Z$, using Theorem 2 }

    $(v.aE)a \in tE$

□

Continuity has an important consequence:

Corollary 0   For system X such that $FR(X) \neq \emptyset$ we have $\mathbf{nai}\{[\![X]\!]^\sim\} \uplus X$.   □

Lemma 2   Let E be a DTS and let X and Y be systems such that $\mathbf{nai}\{E\} \uplus X$ and $\mathbf{nai}\{\widetilde{E}\} \uplus Y$. Then we have for states x on X and y on Y such that $x \cup y$ is reachable in $X \uplus Y$:

$(\exists s : s \in tE : \quad \{s\} \cup x$ is reachable in $\{E\} \uplus X \wedge$
                         $\{\widetilde{s}\} \cup y$ is reachable in $\{\widetilde{E}\} \uplus Y$).

Proof   Omitted, see [0].   □

Lemma 3   For DTS E and systems X and Y such that $\mathbf{nai}\{E\} \uplus X$ and $\mathbf{nai}\{\widetilde{E}\} \uplus Y$ we have $\mathbf{nai}\, X \uplus Y$.

Proof   It is obvious that $X \uplus Y$ is a closed system if $\mathbf{nai}\{E\} \uplus X$ and $\mathbf{nai}\{\widetilde{E}\} \uplus Y$. Let x be a state on X and let y be a state on Y such that $x \cup y$ is reachable in $X \uplus Y$. On account of Lemma 2 we may assume $s \in tE$ to be such that $\{s\} \cup x$ is reachable in $\{E\} \uplus X$ and such that $\{\widetilde{s}\} \cup y$ is reachable in $\{\widetilde{E}\} \uplus Y$. Since $\mathbf{nai}\{E\} \uplus X$ and $\mathbf{nai}\{\widetilde{E}\} \uplus Y$ we conclude that x is safe in X and that y is safe in Y. Hence, $x \cup y$ is safe in $X \uplus Y$.   □

Theorem 5   For system X such that $FR(X) \neq \emptyset$, we have

    $X \,\mathbf{sat}\{[\![X]\!]\}$.

Proof   For environment Y we derive

    $\mathbf{nai}\{[\![X]\!]\} \uplus Y$
$=$ { Corollary 0, using $FR(X) \neq \emptyset$ }
    $\mathbf{nai}\{[\![X]\!]^\sim\} \uplus X \wedge \mathbf{nai}\{[\![X]\!]\} \uplus Y$
$\Rightarrow$ { Lemma 3 }
    $\mathbf{nai}\, X \uplus Y$

□

Our next aim is to establish $\{[\![X]\!]\} \,\mathbf{sat}\, X$ if $FR(X) \neq \emptyset$. We need three lemmata. Lemma 4 considers the interference-free closed system $X \uplus \{[\![X]\!]^\sim\}$ (Corr. 0) and it says that all input extensions of traces in $[\![X]\!]^\sim$ are really needed to avoid computation interference. Lemma 5 expresses a form of transitivity of reachability and it can be viewed as a converse of Lemma 2. Finally, Lemma 6 gives a condition under which the trace set of a DTS in a system can be extended without introducing interference.

Lemma 4   For system X such that $FR(X) \neq \emptyset$ we have

$(\forall s : s \in t[X]^\sim : (\exists x : x \text{ on } X : \{s\} \cup x \text{ is reachable in } \{[X]^\sim\} \uplus X)).$

Proof   Omitted, see [0].   □

Lemma 5   Let E be a DTS and let X and Y be systems. For t a trace in E and for x a state on X and for y a state on Y such that $y \cup \{\tilde{t}\}$ is reachable in $Y \uplus \{\widetilde{E}\}$ and $\{t\} \cup x$ is reachable in $\{E\} \uplus X$ we have that $y \cup x$ is reachable in $Y \uplus X$.

Proof   Omitted, see [0].   □

Lemma 6   Let E be a DTS and let X and Y be systems such that **nai**$\{E\} \uplus X$ and **nai** $X \uplus Y$. For trace t in tE, for symbol $a \in oE$, and for state y on Y such that $\{\tilde{t}\tilde{a}\} \cup y$ is reachable in $\{\widetilde{E}\} \uplus Y$ we have **nai**$\{F\} \uplus X$, where $aF = aE$ and $tF = tE \cup \{ta\}(iE)^*$. Furthermore, if $F \sqsubseteq E$ then $ta \in tE$.

Proof   Omitted, see [0].   □

Theorem 6   For system X such that $FR(X) \neq \emptyset$, we have

   $\{[X]\} \text{ sat } X.$

Proof   Let $E = [X]$. Assuming **nai** $X \uplus Y$ we prove **nai**$\{E\} \uplus Y$. Let trace s over aE and state y on Y be such that

   $\{s\} \cup y$ is reachable in $E \uplus Y.$ (0)

We show that $\{s\} \cup y$ is safe in $\{E\} \uplus Y$. First we show that y is safe in Y if $s \in tE$.
   In case $s \in tE$ we may assume state x on X to be such that

   $\{\tilde{s}\} \cup x$ is reachable in $\{\widetilde{E}\} \uplus X$ (1)

on account of Lemma 4. From (0), (1) and Lemma 5 we conclude that $x \cup y$ is reachable in $X \uplus Y$. Since we have **nai** $X \uplus Y$ by assumption, we have that y is safe in Y.
   The only remaining proof obligation is to show that s in (0) is an element of tE. Since $\varepsilon \in tE$ this is the case initially and output moves of E do not violate this. Hence, we have to show if, in addition to (0), $s \in tE$ and $\{sa\} \cup y$ is a successor of $\{s\} \cup y$ in $\{E\} \uplus Y$ for some $a \in iE$ then $sa \in tE$. This follows immediately from Lemma 6 since we have **nai**$\{\widetilde{E}\} \uplus X$ on account of Corollary 0, and $a \in iE = \tilde{a} \in o\widetilde{E}$ and $\widetilde{E}$ is an upper bound so that $sa \in tE$.   □

This finally takes care of claim (a):

Theorem 7   For system X we have

   $X \text{ equ} \{[X]\}.$

Proof   In case $FR(X) = \emptyset$ then the equivalence follows from Lemma 0. In case $FR(X) \neq \emptyset$ the equivalence follows from Theorems 5 and 6.   □

We now get the proof for claim (b) almost for free:

Theorem 8 For system X such that $FR(X) \neq \emptyset$, we have $\mathbf{nai}\{[X], [X]^\frown\}$. Therefore, for any system X we have $[X] \in \mathcal{DI}$.

Proof On account of Corollary 0 we know $\mathbf{nai}\{[X]^\frown\} \uplus X$ if $FR(X) \neq \emptyset$. Choosing in Theorem 6 $\{[X]\}$ for Y yields the result desired. Hence, in this case $[X] \in \mathcal{DI}$. Otherwise, if $FR(X) = \emptyset$, then by definition $[X] \in \mathcal{DI}$. □

In order to prove claim (c) we need one more lemma:

Lemma 7 For DTSs U and S we have

$$\mathbf{nai}\{U, S\} \Rightarrow U \sqsubseteq \tilde{S}.$$

Proof Omitted, see [0]. □

Theorem 9 For DTSs S and T in $\mathcal{DI}$ we have

$$\{S\}\,\mathbf{equ}\{T\} \;\Rightarrow\; S = T.$$

Therefore, we also have

$$[\![\{S\}]\!] = S.$$

Proof We derive for DTSs S and T such that $\{S\}\,\mathbf{equ}\{T\}$:

$\quad S \in \mathcal{DI}$
$= \quad \{ \text{ definition of } \mathcal{DI} \,\}$
$\quad \mathbf{nai}\{S, \tilde{S}\} \vee S = CHAOS$
$\Rightarrow \quad \{ \{S\}\,\mathbf{equ}\{T\} \text{ assumed } \}$
$\quad \mathbf{nai}\{T, \tilde{S}\} \vee S = CHAOS$
$\Rightarrow \quad \{ \text{ Lemma 7 and Theorem 0 } \}$
$\quad T \sqsubseteq S$

Similarly, if $T \in \mathcal{DI}$ we have $S \sqsubseteq T$. The first result now follows from antisymmetry of $\sqsubseteq$ on $\mathcal{DI}$. For the second result we derive for $S \in \mathcal{DI}$:

$\quad \text{true}$
$= \quad \{ \text{ Theorem 7 } \}$
$\quad \{[\![\{S\}]\!]\}\,\mathbf{equ}\{S\}$
$\Rightarrow \quad \{ \text{ Theorem 8, } S \in \mathcal{DI}, \text{ and above result } \}$
$\quad [\![\{S\}]\!] = S$

□

This takes care of claims (a) through (c).

2.1 More results

Now that we have these main results it becomes fairly straightforward to prove other properties, without digging into the operational semantics over and over again. We give three examples.

Property 5 For systems X and Y we have

$$X \operatorname{sat} Y \equiv (\forall U : \mathbf{nai}\{U\} \uplus Y : \mathbf{nai}\{U\} \uplus X),$$

where U ranges over $\mathcal{DI}$.

Proof The implication from left to right follows from the definition of **sat**. Assuming the right-hand side we derive for environment Z:

$$\mathbf{nai}\, Y \uplus Z$$
$$= \quad \{ \text{ Theorem 7 } \}$$
$$\mathbf{nai}\, Y \uplus \{[Z]\}$$
$$\Rightarrow \quad \{ \text{ assumption, using that } [Z] \in \mathcal{DI} \}$$
$$\mathbf{nai}\, X \uplus \{[Z]\}$$
$$= \quad \{ \text{ Theorem 7 } \}$$
$$\mathbf{nai}\, X \uplus Z$$

$\square$

Property 6 For DTSs S and U such that $S \in \mathcal{DI} \setminus \{CHAOS\}$, i.e. $\mathbf{nai}\{S, \widetilde{S}\}$, we have

$$\mathbf{nai}\{U, S\} \equiv U \sqsubseteq \widetilde{S}.$$

Proof Applying Theorem 3 with $\{S\}$ for X to $\mathbf{nai}\{S, \widetilde{S}\}$ we find $U \sqsubseteq \widetilde{S} \Rightarrow \mathbf{nai}\{S, U\}$. The other implication follows immediately from Lemma 7. $\square$

Property 7 For systems X and Y with $[Y] \neq CHAOS$ we have

$$\mathbf{nai}\, X \uplus Y \equiv [X] \sqsubseteq [Y]^{\sim}.$$

Proof We derive

$$\mathbf{nai}\, X \uplus Y$$
$$= \quad \{ \text{ Theorem 7 } \}$$
$$\mathbf{nai}\{[X], [Y]\}$$
$$= \quad \{ \text{ Property 6, using Theorem 8 and } [Y] \neq CHAOS \}$$
$$[X] \sqsubseteq [Y]^{\sim}$$

$\square$

3 Composition and Decomposition

In this section we study $\langle \mathcal{SYS}, \uplus \rangle$ under the congruence **equ**. We define a denotational parallel composition operator $\|$ for DTSs and show that $\langle \mathcal{SYS}, \uplus \rangle / \mathbf{equ}$ is isomorphic to $\langle \mathcal{DI}, \| \rangle$. We do this with the mapping $[\![\cdot]\!]$ from the previous section, which is also a homomorphism in this setting. We also prove a number of other properties of composition.

Theorem 7 shows that system $\{S, T\}$ is equivalent to the system consisting of singleton system $\{[\![\{S, T\}]\!]\}$. It is obvious now how to define parallel composition.

Definition 17   The parallel composition of DTSs S and T with disjoint alphabets, denoted by $S \| T$, is defined as $[\![\{S, T\}]\!]$. □

Property 8   For DTSs S and T we have $\{S \| T\}\, \mathbf{equ}\, \{S, T\}$. □

That $[\![\cdot]\!]$ is a homomorphism is now readily shown. Considering systems X and Y, and DTS U we derive

$$[\![X \uplus Y]\!] = [\![X]\!] \, \| \, [\![Y]\!]$$
$$= \quad \{ \text{ definition of } \| \ \}$$
$$[\![X \uplus Y]\!] = [\![\{[\![X]\!], [\![Y]\!]\}]\!]$$
$$= \quad \{ \ [\![\cdot]\!] \text{ precisely identifies equivalent systems } \}$$
$$X \uplus Y \ \mathbf{equ}\, \{[\![X]\!], [\![Y]\!]\}$$
$$= \quad \{ \text{ property of } \uplus \text{ for 2-process systems } \}$$
$$X \uplus Y \ \mathbf{equ}\, \{[\![X]\!]\} \uplus \{[\![Y]\!]\}$$
$$= \quad \{ \text{ Theorem 7 and } \mathbf{equ} \text{ is a congruence on account of Property 2 } \}$$
$$\text{true}$$

Composition has all the desired properties as we show in the next couple of theorems.

Theorem 10 $\|$ is monotonic under **sat** and under $\sqsubseteq$.

Proof   Since **sat** and $\sqsubseteq$ coincide on $\mathcal{DI}$ it suffices to prove this theorem only for **sat**. Let $\{S\}\, \mathbf{sat}\, \{T\}$. We show that $\{S \| U\}\, \mathbf{sat}\, \{T \| U\}$ for any DTS U. This boils down to showing that for all systems V $\mathbf{nai}\{T \| U\} \uplus V \Rightarrow \mathbf{nai}\{S \| U\} \uplus V$ by the definition of **sat**. We derive

$$\mathbf{nai}\{T \| U\} \uplus V$$
$$= \quad \{ \text{ Property 8 } \}$$
$$\mathbf{nai}\{T, U\} \uplus V$$
$$\Rightarrow \quad \{ \ S\, \mathbf{sat}\, T, \text{ definition of } \mathbf{sat} \ \}$$
$$\mathbf{nai}\{S, U\} \uplus V$$
$$= \quad \{ \text{ Property 8 } \}$$
$$\mathbf{nai}\{S \| U\} \uplus V$$

□

Theorem 11   Parallel composition is associative if the external alphabets are pairwise disjoint.

Proof

$$S \,\|\, (T \,\|\, U)$$
$$= \quad \{ \text{ definition of } \| \}$$
$$[\![\{ S, (T \,\|\, U) \}]\!]$$
$$= \quad \{ \text{ Property 8, using that the alphabets of } S, T, \text{ and } U \text{ are disjoint } \}$$
$$[\![\{ S, T, U \}]\!]$$

Symmetry does the rest. □

Theorem 12 For any alphabet A we have that $\|$ is continuous with respect to $\sqcup$ on $\mathcal{DTS}(A)$.

Proof Let $Z \subseteq DTS(A)$ and let P be a DTS. On account of the monotonicity of $\|$ with respect to $\sqsubseteq$ we have $S \sqsubseteq \sqcup Z \Rightarrow P \,\|\, S \sqsubseteq P \,\|\, \sqcup Z$ for any S. Therefore, $P \,\|\, \sqcup Z$ is an upper bound of $\{ S : S \in Z : P \,\|\, S \}$. Left to prove is that it is the least upper bound. We derive

$$(\forall S : S \in Z : P \,\|\, S \sqsubseteq T)$$
$$\Rightarrow \quad \{ \text{ Theorem 3 applied to } \{ P \,\|\, S, (P \,\|\, S)^\frown \} \}$$
$$(\forall S : S \in Z : \mathbf{nai}\{ P \,\|\, S, \widetilde{T} \})$$
$$= \quad \{ \text{ Property 8, using that } \mathbf{nai} \text{ for a DTS and the composition of two DTSs holds}$$
$$\qquad \text{ only if the alphabets of these DTSs are disjoint } \}$$
$$(\forall S : S \in Z : \mathbf{nai}\{ S, P \,\|\, \widetilde{T} \})$$
$$\Rightarrow \quad \{ \text{ Lemma 7 } \}$$
$$(\forall S : S \in Z : S \sqsubseteq (P \,\|\, \widetilde{T})^\frown)$$
$$\Rightarrow \quad \{ \text{ definition of least upper bound } \}$$
$$\sqcup Z \sqsubseteq (P \,\|\, \widetilde{T})^\frown$$
$$\Rightarrow \quad \{ \text{ Theorem 3 applied to } \{ P \,\|\, \widetilde{T}, (P \,\|\, \widetilde{T})^\frown \} \}$$
$$\mathbf{nai}\{ \sqcup Z, P \,\|\, \widetilde{T} \}$$
$$= \quad \{ \text{ Property 8, using that } \mathbf{nai} \text{ for a DTS and the composition of two DTSs holds}$$
$$\qquad \text{ only if the alphabets of these DTSs are disjoint } \}$$
$$\mathbf{nai}\{ P \,\|\, \sqcup Z, \widetilde{T} \}$$
$$\Rightarrow \quad \{ \text{ Lemma 7 } \}$$
$$P \,\|\, \sqcup Z \sqsubseteq T$$

□

Finally, we prove a factorization theorem. In practice we often encounter the problem, given a specification S and part M of its implementation, to find the rest of the implementation. Hence, we are asked to find a specification such that any X, satisfying that specification, composed with M satisfies S. The following theorem states that the specification $(M \,\|\, \widetilde{S})^\frown$ is the strongest specification with that property on the space $\mathcal{DI}$. For practical reasons we do not state the theorem for DTSs in $\mathcal{DI}$ only, but generalize it to arbitrary DTSs. In practice we will not always be given the $\mathcal{DI}$-representative but an arbitrary member of its class. Although we could, the following theorem shows that it is not always necessary to compute the $\mathcal{DI}$-representative first.

Theorem 13 *Factorization Theorem*

For DTSs S, M, and X such that $M \parallel \widetilde{S} \neq CHAOS$ we have

$$X \sqsubseteq (M \parallel \widetilde{S})^{\sim} \Rightarrow X \parallel M \sqsubseteq S,$$

and if $S \in \mathcal{DI}$ then we have an equivalence.

Proof Notice that both the left-hand and the right-hand side of the implication imply that the alphabets of X, M, and $\widetilde{S}$ are disjoint, given that $M \parallel \widetilde{S} \neq CHAOS$. We derive

$$X \sqsubseteq (M \parallel \widetilde{S})^{\sim}$$
$$= \quad \{ \text{ Property 6, using } (M \parallel \widetilde{S})^{\sim} \in \mathcal{DI} \setminus \{CHAOS\} \}$$
$$\text{nai}\{X, M \parallel \widetilde{S}\}$$
$$= \quad \{ \text{ Property 8, using that the alphabets of } X, M, \text{ and } \widetilde{S} \text{ are disjoint } \}$$
$$\text{nai}\{X \parallel M, \widetilde{S}\}$$
$$\Rightarrow \quad \{ \text{ Lemma 7 } \}$$
$$X \parallel M \sqsubseteq S$$

Assuming $S \in \mathcal{DI}$ the last step is an equivalence for the following reason. If $S = CHAOS$, then we would also have $(M \parallel \widetilde{S})^{\sim} = CHAOS$. Thus, from the assumptions follows $S \neq CHAOS$. In the last step we can now apply Property 6. □

4 Concluding Remarks

In this section we discuss various aspects of the work reported in this paper. We relate it to some other work in this area and mention ongoing and future research.

This work starts out from an operational semantics of networks of processes. We strongly believe that this is the right point of departure to get a handle on a formal and total definition of a process. On the one hand, these semantics can be viewed as a first abstraction of the operation of electrical circuits. This means that it is reasonable to assume that these formal networks of processes can indeed be implemented. On the other hand, it is formal and yet rich enough to be mathematically tractable. Using mathematical techniques we can abstract from detail which is irrelevant for a particular correctness concern. This correctness concern fully determines the corresponding denotational model. The only freedom left is the choice of that correctness concern. It is much easier to choose such a correctness concern than it is to come up with the corresponding denotational model.

As opposed to [5], where a similar approach is taken for undirected and synchronous communications, we have not introduced a process syntax, which we believe to be a separate issue. In [1] a similar denotational space of synchronously communicating processes is defined, but no operational model is introduced. We expect our approach to be particularly useful when incorporating certain liveness properties. Rather than having to come up with a denotational model—for which we have an overwhelming number of possibilities—we have to come up with a correctness concern at the operational level, where the number of reasonable choices is easily seen to be quite limited. As in [3] we have the notion of testing equivalence. Our approach differs in the sense that the distinction between process and experimenter vanishes.

Towards a Calculus of Data Refinement

Wei Chen
Department of Computer Science
Washington University
St. Louis, MO 63130

Jan Tijmen Udding
Department of Mathematics and Computing Science
Groningen University
Groningen, The Netherlands

Abstract

In this paper we lay a foundation for a calculus of data refinement. We introduce the concept of conditional data refinement which enables us to incorporate contextual information in a refinement step. We give a number of its properties and show in several examples how data refinement can be used in practice.

0   Introduction

The method of stepwise refinement has long been recognized as an effective method in program construction, cf. [2,3,14]. Deriving a program from its specification we usually go through a number of intermediate programs, the next one being a refinement of the previous one. We are inclined to use objects that are abstract and mathematically familiar as the first step towards the ultimate program. In later stages of construction, those *abstract* objects are replaced with their *concrete* implementations. Usually this process is considered to take place on a single state space on which all programs operate. We call this type of refinement *algorithmic* refinement. Much work has been done to formalize the process of its application and to demonstrate its validity as a program construction technique, e.g. in [0,8,10,11].

Quite often, however, it turns out that these intermediate programs actually do not operate on the same state space. For example, an abstract program may operate on a set where a concrete program operates on the implementation of this set, which may involve list or array variables. Hence, not only programs are refined but also the data on which they operate. We call this technique *data* refinement. A correctness criterion for data refinement was suggested a long time ago by Hoare [6] and has recently been further developed by Gries, Morgan and Prins [5,7]. In this paper we formally characterize data refinement and investigate its various features.

Although inspired by [5,7], we start out with what we consider to be a more natural definition of data refinement by viewing it as a generalization of algorithmic refinement. We show that this definition is equivalent to the one in [5]. Data refinement is useful in practice only if it can be applied as a program derivation technique. For that to be the case data refinement must have properties such as monotonicity and semi-transitivity. The former reduces data refinement on programs to that on their components. The latter enables us to divide data refinement into stages. We define these properties formally and show that data refinement meets these requirements.

Underlying the idea of this (unconditional) data refinement is the concept that a concrete program can replace an abstract program under *all* circumstances. In program derivation, however, we usually need a concrete program that can replace the original program only in a *specific* context. It is not difficult to find examples of programs for which obviously correct refinements cannot be proved correct using the concept of unconditional refinement. Therefore, we extend the notion of data refinement to *conditional* data refinement. We show that conditional data refinement has similar properties as unconditional data refinement.

The paper is organized as follows. The first section introduces notions we need in this paper. The second section formally characterizes data refinement. The subsequent section is on monotonicity and semi-transitivity of data refinement. Then in the next two sections we discuss conditional data refinement and its properties. Some small examples are presented in order to demonstrate the concepts. In the second to last section we show that conditional data refinement can be a powerful tool for program development. Finally, some concluding remarks are made.

1   Preliminaries

We specify a program M by its weakest precondition with respect to a postcondition R, which is denoted by $wp(M, R)$ as in [3]. It represents the set of all states such that execution of M started in any one of them is guaranteed to terminate in a state satisfying R. The collection of program variables of a program is referred to as that program's *state* variable. Execution of a program corresponds to a sequence of value changes on its state variable. Usually, M is "generic" in the sense that non-program variables may also appear. Values of these variables are fixed in the properties discussed in this paper.

The universal quantification of a predicate P over all *program* variables is denoted by $[P]$. We use F to denote the predicate that is false everywhere and T to denote the one that is true everywhere. According to the above operational appreciation of wp, we assume that wp observes the following laws.

Law of the excluded miracle: $[\neg wp(M, F)]$.

Law of $\wedge$-distributivity: $[wp(M, (\forall x :: R)) = (\forall x :: wp(M, R))]$
    when dummy variable x does not appear in M.

Law of $\lor$-distributivity: $[(\exists x :: wp(M, R)) \Rightarrow wp(M, (\exists x :: R))]$
   when dummy variable x does not appear in M.

Law of monotonicity: $[Q \Rightarrow R] \Rightarrow [wp(M, Q) \Rightarrow wp(M, R)]$.

Law of $\land$-independence: $[wp(M, Q \land R) = wp(M, Q) \land R]$
   when none of the program variables of M appear free in R.

Law of $\lor$-independence: $[wp(M, Q \lor R) = wp(M, Q) \lor (wp(M, T) \land R)]$
   when none of the program variables of M appear free in R.

In the above, the laws of monotonicity and $\lor$-distributivity can be derived from the law of $\land$-distributivity. None of our results depend on the law of the excluded miracle, which might be helpful for further extensions, e.g. incorporating recursion.

We impose the usual syntactic restriction on $wp(M, R)$ that a free variable of it be a variable of M or a free variable of R. Thus, free variables of $wp(M, R)$ can only be inherited from variables of M and free variables of R. For the sake of convenience, we assume that two programs in data refinement operate on two *name-disjoint* state spaces. The word independence is used to express name-disjointness.

Definition 0   A number of programs is *independent* of one another if no program variable of any program occurs in any of the other programs. A predicate is *independent* of a program if none of the program variables appear free in the predicate.   □

Obviously, two independent programs operate on name-disjoint state spaces. A program may have non-program variables. Therefore, two independent programs may have common non-program variables.

We use Dijkstra's guarded command language [3] for our programs. We adopt his definitions for wp of the various constructs, except for the repetitive construct for which we use Park's formulation [13], i.e. $wp(\mathbf{do}, R)$ is the strongest solution of

$$X : [X = (\forall i :: B_i \Rightarrow wp(S_i, X)) \land ((\exists i :: B_i) \lor R)]$$

where **do** is an abbreviation of the repetitive construct in which $B_i \rightarrow S_i$ is the ith guarded command. Similarly, with **if** we denote the alternative construct in which $B_i \rightarrow S_i$ is the ith guarded command.

This definition of $wp(\mathbf{do}, R)$ allows unbounded nondeterminism, which often occurs in an abstract program. We use the following theorems in the sequel.

Theorem 0   For R a predicate $wp(\mathbf{do}, R)$ exists and it is also the strongest solution of

$$X : [(\forall i :: B_i \Rightarrow wp(S_i, X)) \land ((\exists i :: B_i) \lor R) \Rightarrow X].$$

Proof   This is an instance of the Knaster-Tarski fixed point theorem. A proof can be found in [4].   □

Simple predicate calculus yields the following theorem.

Theorem 1   For predicate R we have $[wp(\text{do}, R) = wp(\text{do}, R \wedge (\forall i :: \neg B_i))]$.   □

2   Characterization of data refinement

Algorithmic refinement of one program Sa into another program Sc means that every result of Sa is also a possible result of Sc. Formally, it means $[wp(Sa, R) \Rightarrow wp(Sc, R)]$ holds for any R. (See, e.g. [8].) Algorithmic refinement can also be considered to take place between two independent programs. We choose a relation that renames program variables of Sc such that Sa and Sc become independent and let Sc' be the correspondingly renamed program. Now algorithmic refinement means that the renaming of any result of Sc' is a possible result of Sa. Suppose that the state variable of Sc (and thus of Sa) is a and that it is renamed to c. Then we can express the algorithmic refinement in a different way as $[wp(Sa, R) \Rightarrow wp(Sc', R_c^a)_a^c]$ for any R on the state space of Sa. Predicate calculus establishes its equivalence to

$$[(a = c) \Rightarrow (Ra = Rc)] \Rightarrow [(a = c) \Rightarrow (wp(Sa, Ra) \Rightarrow wp(Sc', Rc))]$$

for any Ra on the state space of Sa and Rc on the state space of Sc'. Data refinement can be viewed as a generalization of this formula. The one-to-one correspondence between the two state variables is replaced by an arbitrary relation, called a *coupling* invariant.

Definition 1   A program Sa is *data-refined* to another independent program Sc under a predicate I, denoted by $Sa \sqsubseteq_I Sc$, when

$$[I \Rightarrow (Ra = Rc)] \Rightarrow [I \Rightarrow (wp(Sa, Ra) \Rightarrow wp(Sc, Rc))]$$

for any predicates Ra independent of Sc and Rc independent of Sa.   □

We adopt the following convention in the definitions and properties of this paper. Sa, Sb and Sc are programs of state variables a, b, and c, respectively. Also, when quantifying, dummies a, b, and c will range over the state spaces of Sa, Sb, and Sc respectively. With if_a we denote the alternative construct over state variable a with $Ba_i \rightarrow Sa_i$ as its ith guarded command. A similar convention applies to if_c, do_a and do_c. Programs over state variables a, b, and c are assumed to be independent of one another.

Gries, Morgan and Prins[5,7], following Hoare[6], start from another point of view by requiring the execution of Sa and Sc to maintain I. They observe that Sc is allowed to be more deterministic than Sa. So the best one can expect is that after execution of Sc, execution of Sa can possibly terminate in a state satisfying I if it ever terminates. Formally, this is expressed as

$$[I \wedge wp(Sa, T) \Rightarrow wp(Sc, \neg wp(Sa, \neg I))].$$

It turns out that the above formulation is equivalent to Definition 1. The following theorem gives five equivalent characterizations of data refinement.

Theorem 2   The following five formulations are equivalent.

(i) $[I \wedge wp(Sa, T) \Rightarrow wp(Sc, \neg wp(Sa, \neg I))]$

(ii) $[I \Rightarrow (Ra = Rc)] \Rightarrow [I \wedge wp(Sa, Ra) \Rightarrow wp(Sc, Rc)]$
     for any Ra independent of Sc and Rc independent of Sa

(iii) $[I \wedge Ra \Rightarrow Rc] \Rightarrow [I \wedge wp(Sa, Ra) \Rightarrow wp(Sc, Rc)]$
     for any Ra independent of Sc and Rc independent of Sa

(iv) $[I \wedge wp(Sa, (\forall c :: I \Rightarrow Rc)) \Rightarrow wp(Sc, Rc)]$
     for any Rc independent of Sa

(v) $[I \wedge wp(Sa, Ra) \Rightarrow wp(Sc, (\exists a :: I \wedge Ra))]$
     for any Ra independent of Sc.

$\square$

Originally, we studied the first three characterizations. We expanded our result to the current setting after Carroll Morgan [9] recently informed us of his new characterization, which is essentially the fifth one above. The theorem is a special case of a more general theorem, which we state and prove in a later section about conditional data refinement. Among the above five characterizations, (i) often acts as the proof rule, (iii) is used to derive properties, while (iv) and (v) are two special forms of (iii).

Example 0   With Theorem 2(i), we can show that $a := a + 1 \sqsubseteq_{c = even(a)} c := \neg c$ and that $c := \neg c \sqsubseteq_{c = even(a)} a := a + 1$.

$\square$

Example 1   The statement $a :\in S$ assigns an arbitrary element of a non-empty bag S to a, i.e.

$$wp(a :\in S, R) = (S \neq \emptyset \wedge (\forall a : a \in S : R)).$$

Let $B[m..n]$ be an array of integers. Then $a :\in S \sqsubseteq_{a = c \wedge S = (i : m \leq i \leq n : B.i)} c := B[m]$ because

$$wp(c := B[m], \neg wp(a :\in S, \neg(a = c \wedge S = (i : m \leq i \leq n : B.i))))$$

$=$ { definition of $wp(a :\in S, ?)$ and calculus }

$$wp(c := B[m], S = \emptyset \vee (\exists a : a \in S : a = c \wedge S = (i : m \leq i \leq n : B.i)))$$

$=$ { calculus }

$$wp(c := B[m], S = \emptyset \vee (c \in S \wedge S = (i : m \leq i \leq n : B.i)))$$

$= \quad \{ \text{definition of assignment} \}$

$m \leq n \wedge (S = \emptyset \vee (B[m] \in S \wedge S = \langle i : m \leq i \leq n : B.i \rangle))$

$\Leftarrow \quad \{ \text{calculus} \}$

$a = c \wedge S = \langle i : m \leq i \leq n : B.i \rangle \wedge wp(a :\in S, T).$

Similarly, $a :\in S \sqsubseteq_{a=c \wedge S=\langle i:m \leq i \leq n:B.i \rangle} c := B[n]$. If we further assume that $m \leq n$ then

$\qquad a :\in S \sqsubseteq_{a=c \wedge \langle i:m \leq i \leq n:B.i \rangle \subseteq S} c := B[m]$.

If S is infinite then $a :\in S$ exhibits unbounded nondeterminism. $\qquad \square$

3 Monotonicity and semi-transitivity in data refinement

Data refinement induces a relation on programs and program constructs can be viewed as operators on programs. It is clear that we want to carry' out data refinement of a program by data-refining its components, since this is common practice in reality. This means that we have to show our program constructs to be monotonic with respect to data refinement. The following three theorems show that sequential composition, alternative and repetitive constructs are monotonic. Again, we postpone their proofs to the next sections where we discuss similar properties for conditional data refinement.

We use the following abbreviations for predicates I, R and Q

$\qquad (R \Rightarrow_I Q) = [I \wedge R \Rightarrow Q]$ and $(R =_I Q) = [I \Rightarrow (R = Q)]$.

Theorem 3 $\qquad Sa_0 \sqsubseteq_I Sc_0 \wedge Sa_1 \sqsubseteq_I Sc_1 \Rightarrow Sa_0 ; Sa_1 \sqsubseteq_I Sc_0 ; Sc_1.$ $\qquad \square$

Actually, given the left hand side of the implication we can for reasons of symmetry conclude that $Sa_1 ; Sa_0 \sqsubseteq_I Sc_1 ; Sc_0$. This freedom limits the applicability of the theorem in practice.

Example 2 Let X be a constant integer array containing at least one element $X[0]$. Then

$\qquad m := 0; a := X[0] \sqsubseteq_{m=n \wedge a=c} n := 0; c := X[n]$.

However, this cannot be justified by Theorem 3, because then we would also have

$\qquad a := X[0]; m := 0 \sqsubseteq_{m=n \wedge a=c} c := X[n]; n := 0$

which is not true. Variable n may have an initial value differing from 0. $\qquad \square$

For simplicity, we assume in the sequel that the guarded commands of $\mathbf{if}_a$ ($\mathbf{do}_a$) and $\mathbf{if}_c$ ($\mathbf{do}_c$) have equal index sets.

Theorem 4

$$\frac{(\exists i :: Ba_i) \Rightarrow_I (\exists i :: Bc_i), (\forall i :: Ba_i \Leftarrow_I Bc_i), (\forall i :: Sa_i \sqsubseteq_I Sc_i)}{\mathbf{if}_a \sqsubseteq_I \mathbf{if}_c}.$$

$\square$

The theorem indicates that the nondeterminism of $\mathbf{if}_a$ can be removed by strengthening a guard. The following example, which is essentially algorithmic refinement, demonstrates this.

Example 3 It is obvious that

$$
\begin{array}{ccc}
x \leq y \vee y \leq x & \Rightarrow_{x=u \wedge y=v} & u \leq v \vee v < u \\
(x \leq y \Leftarrow_{x=u \wedge y=v} u \leq v) & \wedge & (y \leq x \Leftarrow_{x=u \wedge y=v} v < u) \\
(x := y \sqsubseteq_{x=u \wedge y=v} u := v) & \wedge & (y := x \sqsubseteq_{x=u \wedge y=v} v := u)
\end{array}
$$

By Theorem 4, we have

$$
\begin{array}{llll}
\mathbf{if} & x \leq y & \rightarrow & x := y \\
[] & y \leq x & \rightarrow & y := x \\
\mathbf{fi} & & &
\end{array}
\quad \sqsubseteq_{x=u \wedge y=v} \quad
\begin{array}{llll}
\mathbf{if} & u \leq v & \rightarrow & u := v \\
[] & v < u & \rightarrow & v := u \\
\mathbf{fi} & & &
\end{array}
$$

$\square$

Theorem 5 $(\forall i :: Ba_i =_I Bc_i) \wedge (\forall i :: Sa_i \sqsubseteq_I Sc_i) \Rightarrow \mathbf{do}_a \sqsubseteq_I \mathbf{do}_c$. $\square$

The applicability of Theorems 4 and 5 is also limited, for example, they do not exploit information of guards. Actually, there are more general results than stated in the above theorems, which don't require the guarded command sets of two programs to be identically indexed. Since we don't need these results in this paper we omit their discussion.

Now we turn to semi-transitivity in data refinement. In algorithmic refinement it is well known that if Sc refines Sb and Sb refines Sa, then Sc refines Sa. This means that algorithmic refinements can be carried out in a number of stages. In data refinement the coupling invariants are likely to differ in each step, which means that we use different orderings in each step. Therefore, we do not expect general transitivity to hold. Important is that data refinement can also be carried out in a number of stages. For example, we first refine one set into its implementation and then another set into its implementation. The overall effect is that we have refined the two sets into their implementations. As another example, we may first refine a set into a heap and subsequently into its array representation. The overall effect is that the set is refined into an array representation. The following theorem, which we call semi-transitivity, shows that it is indeed possible to do so in data refinement.

Theorem 6 For I_0 independent of Sc and I_1 independent of Sa

$$Sa \sqsubseteq_{I_0} Sb \sqsubseteq_{I_1} Sc \Rightarrow Sa \sqsubseteq_{(\exists b :: I_0 \wedge I_1)} Sc$$

Proof Using Theorem 2(iii) we have to prove that for any Ra independent of Sc and Rc independent of Sa

$$[(\exists b :: I_0 \wedge I_1) \wedge Ra \Rightarrow Rc] \Rightarrow [(\exists b :: I_0 \wedge I_1) \wedge wp(Sa, Ra) \Rightarrow wp(Sc, Rc)].$$

Note that we can always rename the state variable of Sb such that it is independent of Ra and Rc. By renaming I_0, I_1, and Sb correspondingly, the value of the left hand side of the implication in the premise does not change and neither does the right hand side. Therefore, we assume Sb to be independent of Ra and Rc.

$[(\exists b :: I_0 \wedge I_1) \wedge Ra \Rightarrow Rc]$

$=$ { calculus, using that Ra and Rc are independent of Sb }

$[I_0 \wedge I_1 \wedge Ra \Rightarrow Rc]$

$=$ { calculus, using that I_1 and Rc are independent of Sa }

$[I_1 \wedge (\exists a :: I_0 \wedge Ra) \Rightarrow Rc]$

$\Rightarrow$ { $Sb \sqsubseteq_{I_1} Sc$, using Theorem 2(iii) and $(\exists a :: I_0 \wedge Ra)$ is independent of Sc }

$[I_1 \wedge wp(Sb, (\exists a :: I_0 \wedge Ra)) \Rightarrow wp(Sc, Rc)]$

$\Rightarrow$ { $Sa \sqsubseteq_{I_0} Sb$, using Theorem 2(v) and Ra is independent of Sb }

$[I_1 \wedge I_0 \wedge wp(Sa, Ra) \Rightarrow wp(Sc, Rc)]$

$=$ { calculus, using that Ra and Rc are independent of Sb }

$[(\exists b :: I_0 \wedge I_1) \wedge wp(Sa, Ra) \Rightarrow wp(Sc, Rc)].$

□

Example 4 From Example 0 we have $b_0 := b_0 + 1 \sqsubseteq_{c_0 = even(b_0)} c_0 := \neg c_0$. Then, if we consider B and m as constants, we have

$$b_0, b_1 := b_0 + 1, B[m] \sqsubseteq_{c_0 = even(b_0) \wedge b_1 = c_1} c_0, c_1 := \neg c_0, B[m].$$

Similarly, from Example 1, we deduce, viewing S, B, m, and n as constants

$$a_0 := a_0 + 1; a_1 :\in S \sqsubseteq_{a_0 = b_0 \wedge a_1 = b_1 \wedge S = (i:m \leq i \leq n:B[i])} b_0, b_1 := b_0 + 1, B[m].$$

By Theorem 6 we can conclude after simplification of the existential quantification in the coupling invariant

$$a_0 := a_0 + 1; a_1 :\in S \sqsubseteq_{c_0 = even(a_0) \wedge a_1 = c_1 \wedge S = (I:m \leq i \leq n:B[i])} c_0, c_1 := \neg c_0, B[m].$$

This demonstrates how semi-transitivity provides a means of decomposing a complex refinement into several simpler ones.

□

4 Conditional data refinement

The obvious ordering that data refinement induces upon programs is not yet fine enough for our purpose. It is quite often the case that a program component can be refined to a desired program component only because of the context it is placed in. In isolation that refinement need not be valid. This has been noted in [0] for algorithmic refinement and in [7] for data refinement. Usually, the contextual information of a program is expressed in its pre- and postcondition. We introduce in our framework a pair of auxiliary predicates for the same purpose. In this way we can express some precondition of Sc in refining Sa to Sc. In return we allow the postcondition of Sc to be strengthened by an additional predicate.

Definition 2 A program Sa is data-refined to another independent program Sc under a predicate I, *conditionally* upon predicates Q_0 and Q_1, denoted by $Sa \sqsubseteq_{(Q_0)I(Q_1)} Sc$, when

$$[I \Rightarrow (Ra = Rc)] \Rightarrow [I \Rightarrow (Q_0 \wedge wp(Sa, Ra) \Rightarrow wp(Sc, Q_1 \wedge Rc))]$$

for any predicates Ra independent of Sc and Rc independent of Sa. □

With this definition of refinement there is no need for the introduction of miracles. Hence, neither is there any need to eliminate miracles after each refinement step as opposed to [7]. Note that when taking Q_0 and Q_1 to be T, we obtain the previous ordering. We adopt the following abbreviations.

$$Sa \sqsubseteq_{(Q_0)I} Sc = Sa \sqsubseteq_{(Q_0)I(T)} Sc \text{ and } Sa \sqsubseteq_{I(Q_1)} Sc = Sa \sqsubseteq_{(T)I(Q_1)} Sc.$$

We rephrase Theorem 2 more generally with these auxiliary predicates in Theorem 9. Before doing so we prove a number of useful lemmata and theorems. The proofs of the lemmata can be found in [1].

Lemma 0 If $[I \wedge Q_0 \wedge wp(Sa, T) \Rightarrow wp(Sc, Q_1 \wedge \neg wp(Sa, \neg I))]$ and $[I \wedge Ra \Rightarrow Rc]$, then

$$[I \wedge Q_0 \wedge wp(Sa, Ra) \Rightarrow wp(Sc, Q_1 \wedge Rc)]$$

for Ra independent of Sc and Rc independent of Sa. □

In the following lemma and theorem we use the dot to denote function application. For predicate P and state variable a we mean by $P.a$ the predicate in which the program variables of a in P are fixed by the values of a. Function application is left-associative.

Lemma 1 Let Xa be a state of Sa and let I be a predicate. We define

$$Rc = \neg wp(Sa, \neg I).Xa \text{ and } Ra = (\forall c :: I \Rightarrow Rc)$$

Then (i) $wp(Sa, T).Xa \Rightarrow wp(Sa, Ra).Xa$ and (ii) $[I \wedge Ra \Rightarrow Rc]$. □

Theorem 7 $[I \wedge Q_0 \wedge wp(Sa, T) \Rightarrow wp(Sc, Q_1 \wedge \neg wp(Sa, \neg I))]$ holds exactly when $[I \wedge Ra \Rightarrow Rc] \Rightarrow [I \wedge Q_0 \wedge wp(Sa, Ra) \Rightarrow wp(Sc, Q_1 \wedge Rc)]$ for any Ra independent of Sc and Rc independent of Sa.

Proof The only-if part follows directly from Lemma 0. For the if part, consider arbitrary states Xa of Sa and Xc of Sc, and take Ra and Rc to be such as defined in Lemma 1. Then by Lemma 1(ii) and the assumption, we have

$$[I \wedge Q_0 \wedge wp(Sa, Ra) \Rightarrow wp(Sc, Q_1 \wedge Rc)]. \tag{0}$$

Hence,

$(I \wedge Q_0 \wedge wp(Sa, T)).Xa.Xc$

= { function application }

$I.Xa.Xc \wedge Q_0.Xa.Xc \wedge wp(Sa, T).Xa.Xc$

⇒ { Lemma 1(i), using that Sa and Sc are independent }

$I.Xa.Xc \wedge Q_0.Xa.Xc \wedge wp(Sa, Ra).Xa.Xc$

⇒ { calculus, using (0) }

$wp(Sc, Q_1 \wedge Rc).Xa.Xc$

⇒ { definition of Rc, using the independence of Sa and Sc }

$wp(Sc, Q_1 \wedge \neg wp(Sa, \neg I)).Xa.Xc.$

□

Instead of defining Ra using a universal quantification we can also define Ra using an existential quantification. The next two lemmata result if we take the existential rather than the universal quantification. The proofs are similar to the proofs of Lemma 1 and Theorem 7.

Lemma 2 Let Xa be a state of Sa and let I be a predicate. If we define

$$Rc \; = \; \neg wp(Sa, \neg I).Xa \quad \text{and} \quad Ra \; = \; (\exists c :: I \Rightarrow Rc)$$

then (i) $wp(Sa, T).Xa \Rightarrow wp(Sa, Ra).Xa$ and (ii) $[I \Rightarrow (Rc \Rightarrow Ra)]$. □

Lemma 3 $[I \wedge Q_0 \wedge wp(Sa, T) \Rightarrow wp(Sc, Q_1 \wedge \neg wp(Sa, \neg I))]$ holds if $[I \wedge Rc \Rightarrow Ra] \Rightarrow [I \wedge Q_0 \wedge wp(Sa, Ra) \Rightarrow wp(Sc, Q_1 \wedge Rc)]$ for any Ra independent of Sc and Rc independent of Sa. □

By combining Theorem 7 and Lemma 3 we conclude

Theorem 8 $Sa \sqsubseteq_{(Q_0)I(Q_1)} Sc$ holds exactly when
$$[I \wedge Q_0 \wedge wp(Sa, T) \Rightarrow wp(Sc, Q_1 \wedge \neg wp(Sa, \neg I))] \text{ holds.}$$ □

Now we formulate and prove the generalization of Theorem 2.

Theorem 9 The following five formulations of data refinement are equivalent.

(i) $[I \wedge Q_0 \wedge wp(Sa, T) \Rightarrow wp(Sc, Q_1 \wedge \neg wp(Sa, \neg I))]$

(ii) $[I \Rightarrow (Ra = Rc)] \Rightarrow [I \wedge Q_0 \wedge wp(Sa, Ra) \Rightarrow wp(Sc, Q_1 \wedge Rc)]$
    for any Ra independent of Sc and Rc independent of Sa

(iii) $[I \wedge Ra \Rightarrow Rc] \Rightarrow [I \wedge Q_0 \wedge wp(Sa, Ra) \Rightarrow wp(Sc, Q_1 \wedge Rc)]$
    for any Ra independent of Sc and Rc independent of Sa

(iv) $[I \wedge Q_0 \wedge wp(Sa, (\forall c :: I \Rightarrow Rc)) \Rightarrow wp(Sc, Q_1 \wedge Rc)]$
    for any Rc independent of Sa

(v) $[I \wedge Q_0 \wedge wp(Sa, Ra) \Rightarrow wp(Sc, Q_1 \wedge (\exists a :: I \wedge Ra))]$
    for any Ra independent of Sc.

Proof The equivalence of the first three has been shown in Theorems 7 and 8. It suffices to prove that (iii) implies (iv), that (iv) implies (v), and finally that (v) implies (iii).

(iii) $\Rightarrow$ (iv): Given an Rc, define $Ra = (\forall c :: I \Rightarrow Rc)$. By predicate calculus, $[I \wedge Ra \Rightarrow Rc]$. Hence, with (iii) $[I \wedge Q_0 \wedge wp(Sa, (\forall c :: I \Rightarrow Rc)) \Rightarrow wp(Sc, Q_1 \wedge Rc)]$.

(iv) $\Rightarrow$ (v): Given an Ra, define $Rc = (\exists a :: I \wedge Ra)$. Then

    true

=   { calculus, using the definition of Rc }

    $[I \wedge Ra \Rightarrow Rc]$

$\Rightarrow$ { calculus, using that Ra is independent of Sc }

    $[Ra \Rightarrow (\forall c :: I \Rightarrow Rc)]$

$\Rightarrow$ { monotonicity of wp }

    $[wp(Sa, Ra) \Rightarrow wp(Sa, (\forall c :: I \Rightarrow Rc))]$

$\Rightarrow$ { calculus, using (iv) }

    $[I \wedge Q_0 \wedge wp(Sa, Ra) \Rightarrow wp(Sc, Q_1 \wedge Rc)]$

$\Rightarrow$ { definition of Rc }

    $[I \wedge Q_0 \wedge wp(Sa, Ra) \Rightarrow wp(Sc, Q_1 \wedge (\exists a :: I \wedge Ra))]$

(v) $\Rightarrow$ (iii): We derive

$[I \wedge Ra \Rightarrow Rc]$

$\Rightarrow$ { calculus, using that Rc is independent of Sa }

$[Q_1 \wedge (\exists a :: I \wedge Ra) \Rightarrow Q_1 \wedge Rc]$

$\Rightarrow$ { monotonocity of wp }

$[wp(Sc, Q_1 \wedge (\exists a :: I \wedge Ra)) \Rightarrow wp(Sc, Q_1 \wedge Rc)]$

$\Rightarrow$ { calculus, using (v) }

$[I \wedge Q_0 \wedge wp(Sa, Ra) \Rightarrow wp(Sc, Q_1 \wedge Rc)].$

□

As said earlier, Theorem 2 is a special case of this theorem by taking T for Q_0 and Q_1.

Example 5   The last part of Example 1 is actually a conditional refinement

$$a :\in S \ \sqsubseteq_{(m \leq n)a=c \wedge (i:m \leq i \leq n:B.i) \subseteq S} \ c := B[m]. $$

□

5   Properties of conditional data refinement

Since the monotonic properties (Theorems 3-5) discussed in a previous section do not exploit any contextual information, their applicability is limited as demonstrated in Example 2. The following three theorems are stronger version of the earlier ones.

Theorem 10   For Q_1 and Q_2 independent of Sa_0 we have

$$\frac{Sa_0 \sqsubseteq_{(Q_0)I(Q_1)} Sc_0, \ Sa_1 \sqsubseteq_{(Q_1)I(Q_2)} Sc_1}{Sa_0; Sa_1 \sqsubseteq_{(Q_0)I(Q_2)} Sc_0; Sc_1}.$$

Proof   For an Rc independent of $Sa_0; Sa_1$ and an Ra independent of $Sc_0; Sc_1$, we derive

$[I \wedge Ra \Rightarrow Rc]$

$\Rightarrow$ { $Sa_1 \sqsubseteq_{(Q_1)I(Q_2)} Sc_1$, using Theorem 9(iii) }

$[I \wedge Q_1 \wedge wp(Sa_1, Ra) \Rightarrow wp(Sc_1, Q_2 \wedge Rc)]$

$=$ { calculus }

$[I \wedge wp(Sa_1, Ra) \Rightarrow (\neg Q_1 \vee wp(Sc_1, Q_2 \wedge Rc))]$

$\Rightarrow$ { $Sa_0 \sqsubseteq_{(Q_0)I(Q_1)} Sc_0$, using Theorem 9(iii) and Q_1 and Q_2 are independent of Sa_0 }

$[I \wedge Q_0 \wedge wp(Sa_0, wp(Sa_1, Ra)) \Rightarrow wp(Sc_0, Q_1 \wedge wp(Sc_1, Q_2 \wedge Rc))]$

$\Rightarrow$ { definition of sequential composition and monotonicity of wp }

$[I \wedge Q_0 \wedge wp(Sa_0; Sa_1, Ra) \Rightarrow wp(Sc_0; Sc_1, Q_2 \wedge Rc)].$

Hence, by Theorem 9(iii) we have that $Sa_0; Sa_1 \sqsubseteq_{(Q_0)I(Q_2)} Sc_0; Sc_1.$ □

Theorem 3 is a special case of this theorem by taking Q_0, Q_1, and Q_2 to be T. We thus have proved Theorem 3.

Example 6 Now we can justify the refinement in Example 2 as follows. We first show that

$$m := 0 \sqsubseteq_{m=n \wedge a=c(n=0)} n := 0 \text{ and } a := X[0] \sqsubseteq_{(n=0)m=n \wedge a=c} c := X[n].$$

Then by the above theorem, we conclude

$$m := 0; a := X[0] \sqsubseteq_{m=n \wedge a=c} n := 0; c := X[n].$$

□

In order to avoid having to state the index sets of the guarded commands of $\textbf{if}_a$ and $\textbf{if}_c$ we assume, as in the previous sections, that $\textbf{if}_a$ and $\textbf{if}_c$ have equal index sets. By being explicit about the index sets one can prove a somewhat stronger theorem. A similar remark can be made for the repetition.

Theorem 11

$$\frac{(\exists i :: Ba_i) \Rightarrow_{R_0 \wedge I} (\exists i :: Bc_i), \; (\forall i :: Ba_i \Leftarrow_{R_0 \wedge I} Bc_i), \; (\forall i :: Sa_i \sqsubseteq_{(Q_i)I(R_1)} Sc_i)}{\textbf{if}_a \sqsubseteq_{(R_0 \wedge (\forall i :: Bc_i \Rightarrow Q_i))I(R_1)} \textbf{if}_c}.$$

Proof We assume $[I \wedge Ra \Rightarrow Rc]$ for Ra independent of $\textbf{if}_c$ and Rc independent of $\textbf{if}_a$. Then it is sufficient to prove, on account of Theorem 9(iii),

$$[I \wedge R_0 \wedge (\forall i :: Bc_i \Rightarrow Q_i) \wedge wp(\textbf{if}_a, Ra) \Rightarrow wp(\textbf{if}_c, R_1 \wedge Rc)].$$

We achieve this in two steps, using the definition of wp for the alternative construct.
Step 0 : We prove $[I \wedge R_0 \wedge (\forall i :: Bc_i \Rightarrow Q_i) \wedge wp(\textbf{if}_a, Ra) \Rightarrow (\exists i :: Bc_i)].$

$\qquad I \wedge R_0 \wedge (\forall i :: Bc_i \Rightarrow Q_i) \wedge wp(\textbf{if}_a, Ra)$

$\Rightarrow \quad \{ \text{ calculus } \}$

$\qquad I \wedge R_0 \wedge wp(\textbf{if}_a, Ra)$

$\Rightarrow \quad \{ \text{ definition of } wp(\textbf{if}_a, Ra) \}$

$\qquad I \wedge R_0 \wedge (\exists i :: Ba_i)$

$\Rightarrow \quad \{ \text{ first premise } \}$

$(\exists i :: Bc_i)$

Step 1 : We prove $[I \wedge R_0 \wedge (\forall i :: Bc_i \Rightarrow Q_i) \wedge wp(\mathbf{if}_a, Ra) \wedge Bc_j \Rightarrow wp(Sc_j, R_1 \wedge Rc))]$ for any j in the index set of the guarded commands of $\mathbf{if}_c$.

$I \wedge R_0 \wedge (\forall i :: Bc_i \Rightarrow Q_i) \wedge wp(\mathbf{if}_a, Ra) \wedge Bc_j$

$\Rightarrow \quad \{ \text{ calculus } \}$

$I \wedge R_0 \wedge wp(\mathbf{if}_a, Ra) \wedge Bc_j \wedge Q_j$

$\Rightarrow \quad \{ \text{ second premise } \}$

$I \wedge wp(\mathbf{if}_a, Ra) \wedge Ba_j \wedge Q_j$

$\Rightarrow \quad \{ \text{ definition of } wp(\mathbf{if}_a, Ra) \}$

$I \wedge wp(Sa_j, Ra) \wedge Q_j$

$\Rightarrow \quad \{ \text{ third premise, using Theorem 9(iii) and the assumption } [I \wedge Ra \Rightarrow Rc] \}$

$wp(Sc_j, R_1 \wedge Rc)$

$\square$

Theorem 4 is a special case of the above theorem by taking the Q_i's and R_i's to be T.

Theorem 12 For La independent of $\mathbf{do}_c$ we have

$$\frac{(\forall i::(Ba_i =_{La \wedge I} Bc_i) \wedge (Ba_i \Rightarrow_{La \wedge I} Q_i) \wedge (Sa_i \sqsubseteq_{(Q_i)I} Sc_i) \wedge (wp(Sa_i, T) \Rightarrow_{La \wedge Ba_i} wp(Sa_i, La)))}{\mathbf{do}_a \sqsubseteq_{(La)I((\forall i::\neg Bc_i) \wedge (\exists a::I \wedge La))} \mathbf{do}_c}.$$

Proof In addition to the premises we assume $[I \wedge Ra \Rightarrow Rc]$ for Ra independent of $\mathbf{do}_c$ and Rc independent of $\mathbf{do}_a$. On account of Theorem 9(iii) we have to prove

$$[I \wedge La \wedge wp(\mathbf{do}_a, Ra) \Rightarrow wp(\mathbf{do}_c, (\forall i :: \neg Bc_i) \wedge (\exists a :: I \wedge La) \wedge Rc)]$$

We abbreviate $wp(\mathbf{do}_c, (\exists a :: I \wedge La) \wedge Rc)$ to Xc and $(\forall c :: I \wedge La \Rightarrow Xc)$ to Xa. First we massage our proof obligation as follows.

$[I \wedge La \wedge wp(\mathbf{do}_a, Ra) \Rightarrow wp(\mathbf{do}_c, (\forall i :: \neg Bc_i) \wedge (\exists a :: I \wedge La) \wedge Rc)]$

$= \quad \{ \text{ Theorem 1 and definition of } Xc \}$

$[I \wedge La \wedge wp(\mathbf{do}_a, Ra) \Rightarrow Xc]$

$= \quad \{ \text{ definition of } Xa, \text{ using that } \mathbf{do}_c \text{ is independent of } \mathbf{do}_a \text{ and } Ra \}$

$[wp(\mathbf{do}_a, Ra) \Rightarrow Xa]$

$\Leftarrow \quad \{ \text{ Theorem 0, } wp(\mathbf{do}_a, Ra) \text{ being the strongest solution of that equation } \}$

$[(\forall i :: Ba_i \Rightarrow wp(Sa_i, Xa)) \wedge (Ra \vee (\exists i :: Ba_i)) \Rightarrow Xa]$

$=$ { definition of Xa, using that $\mathbf{do}_c$ is independent of $\mathbf{do}_a$ and Ra }

$\qquad [I \wedge La \wedge (\forall i :: Ba_i \Rightarrow wp(Sa_i, Xa)) \wedge (Ra \vee (\exists i :: Ba_i)) \Rightarrow Xc]$.

This is our new proof obligation. The following is a list of simple facts, the proofs of which are omitted.

0. $[La \wedge Xa \Rightarrow (\forall c :: I \Rightarrow Xc)]$, by definition of Xa.

1. $[(\forall i :: I \wedge La \wedge \neg Ba_i \Rightarrow \neg Bc_i)]$, by the first premise.

2. $[I \wedge La \wedge (Ra \vee (\exists i :: Ba_i)) \Rightarrow (Rc \wedge (\exists a :: I \wedge La)) \vee (\exists i :: Bc_i)]$, by the first premise and the assumption $[I \wedge Ra \Rightarrow Rc]$.

3. $[(\forall i :: I \wedge Q_i \wedge wp(Sa_i, (\forall c :: I \Rightarrow Xc)) \Rightarrow wp(Sc_i, Xc))]$, by Theorem 9(iv) and the third premise.

4. $[(\forall i :: Bc_i \Rightarrow wp(Sc_i, Xc)) \wedge (Rc \wedge (\exists a :: I \wedge La) \vee (\exists i :: Bc_i)) \Rightarrow Xc]$, by the definition of Xc and Theorem 0.

We start the derivation from the second premise.

$\qquad [(\forall i :: I \wedge La \wedge Ba_i \Rightarrow Q_i)]$

$\Rightarrow$ { fact (3) }

$\qquad [(\forall i :: I \wedge La \wedge Ba_i \wedge wp(Sa_i, (\forall c :: I \Rightarrow Xc)) \Rightarrow wp(Sc_i, Xc))]$

$\Rightarrow$ { fact (0), monotonicity of wp }

$\qquad [(\forall i :: I \wedge La \wedge Ba_i \wedge wp(Sa_i, Xa \wedge La) \Rightarrow wp(Sc_i, Xc))]$

$\Rightarrow$ { fourth premise, $\wedge$-distributivity of wp }

$\qquad [(\forall i :: I \wedge La \wedge Ba_i \wedge wp(Sa_i, Xa) \Rightarrow wp(Sc_i, Xc))]$

$=$ { first premise }

$\qquad [(\forall i :: I \wedge La \wedge wp(Sa_i, Xa) \Rightarrow (Bc_i \Rightarrow wp(Sc_i, Xc)))]$

$\Rightarrow$ { fact (1) }

$\qquad [(\forall i :: I \wedge La \wedge (Ba_i \Rightarrow wp(Sa_i, Xa)) \Rightarrow (Bc_i \Rightarrow wp(Sc_i, Xc)))]$.

$\Rightarrow$ { calculus }

$\qquad [I \wedge La \wedge (\forall i :: Ba_i \Rightarrow wp(Sa_i, Xa)) \Rightarrow (\forall i :: Bc_i \Rightarrow wp(Sc_i, Xc))]$

$\Rightarrow$ { facts (2) and (4) }

$\qquad [I \wedge La \wedge (\forall i :: Ba_i \Rightarrow wp(Sa_i, Xa)) \wedge (Ra \vee (\exists i :: Ba_i)) \Rightarrow Xc]$.

$\square$

Note that La is essentially a loop invariant of $\mathbf{do}_a$. Theorem 5 is a special case of this theorem by taking La and the Q_i's to be T. Another special case, which turns out to be quite useful in practice, because it does take the guards into account but remains relatively simple, results by taking La to be T and the Q_i's to be the Bc_i's.

Corollary 0 $(\forall i :: Ba_i =_I Bc_i) \wedge (\forall i :: Sa_i \sqsubseteq_{(Bc_i)I} Sc_i) \Rightarrow \mathbf{do}_a \sqsubseteq_I \mathbf{do}_c.$ $\square$

Example 7   Consider the following program that sums up a bag S of N values. We assume N to be a constant.

$$sum, summed := 0, \emptyset;$$
$$\mathbf{do}\ summed \neq S \rightarrow$$
$$\qquad x :\in (S \backslash summed); \quad sum := sum + x; \quad summed := summed \cup \{x\}$$
$$\mathbf{od}$$

Now assume that S is represented by an array A ranging from 0 up to N. Then we can perform this summation by adding its elements one by one in increasing order of their indices. We propose the following coupling invariant I

$$0 \leq n \leq N \wedge sum = w \wedge x = y \wedge$$
$$summed = \langle i : 0 \leq i < n : A[i] \rangle \wedge S = \langle i : 0 \leq i < N : A[i] \rangle$$

Then we can prove the following refinements using Theorem 9(i)

$sum, summed := 0, \emptyset$	$\sqsubseteq_I$	$w := n := 0$
$summed \neq S$	$=_I$	$n \neq N$
$x :\in (S \backslash summed)$	$\sqsubseteq_{(n \neq N)I(n \neq N \wedge y = A[n])}$	$y := A[n]$
$sum := sum + x$	$\sqsubseteq_{(n \neq N \wedge y = A[n])I(n \neq N \wedge y = A[n])}$	$w := w + y$
$summed := summed \cup \{x\}$	$\sqsubseteq_{(n \neq N \wedge y = A[n])I}$	$n := n + 1.$

Hence, by Theorem 10 and Corollary 0, we conclude

$sum, summed := 0, \emptyset;$		$w := n := 0;$
$\mathbf{do}\ summed \neq S \rightarrow$		$\mathbf{do}\ n \neq N \rightarrow$
$\quad x :\in (S \backslash summed);$		$\quad y := A[n];$
$\quad sum := sum + x;$	$\sqsubseteq_I$	$\quad w := w + y;$
$\quad summed := summed \cup \{x\}$		$\quad n := n + 1$
$\mathbf{od}$		$\mathbf{od}$

This refinement cannot be shown correct with unconditional refinement, as has been argued in [7]. However, rather than introducing miracles for the refinement and later on eliminating them we prove the individual refinement steps to be correct in the appropriate contexts. $\square$

Theorems 10 through 12 are the fundamental theorems of conditional data refinement. Our aim is to develop a calculus of data refinement and these theorems are too big for easy manipulation. Therefore, we need additional laws that make these theorems more easily applicable. We find a quite similar situation in the wp-calculus. In addition to the axioms for the language constructs there are a number of laws for easier manipulation. In the rest of this section we give a number of these laws for data refinement. They provide a first step towards a calculus of data refinement.

In many cases, we use simpler contextual information when performing a refinement and later on we incorporate the entire context into the refinement. This calls for properties that allow us to weaken and strengthen auxiliary predicates. We state three of these properties, which can easily be proved.

Law of consequence:
$$\frac{[R_0 \Rightarrow Q_0], \; Sa \sqsubseteq_{(Q_0)I(Q_1)} Sc, \; [Q_1 \Rightarrow R_1]}{Sa \sqsubseteq_{(R_0)I(R_1)} Sc}.$$

Law of conjunction:
$$\frac{Sa \sqsubseteq_{(Q_0)I(Q_1)} Sc, \; Sa \sqsubseteq_{(R_0)I(R_1)} Sc}{Sa \sqsubseteq_{(Q_0 \wedge R_0)I(Q_1 \wedge R_1)} Sc}.$$

Law of disjunction:
$$\frac{Sa \sqsubseteq_{(Q_0)I(Q_1)} Sc, \; Sa \sqsubseteq_{(R_0)I(R_1)} Sc}{Sa \sqsubseteq_{(Q_0 \vee R_0)I(Q_1 \vee R_1)} Sc}.$$

These laws allow one to use simpler contextual information than actually available. A second category of laws allows us to combine, or decompose, coupling invariants. Sometimes a refinement is most easily performed by distinguishing several cases. For this purpose we have the following property.

Property 0 $Sa \sqsubseteq_{(Q_0)I(Q_1)} Sc \wedge Sa \sqsubseteq_{(Q_0)J(Q_1)} Sc \Rightarrow Sa \sqsubseteq_{(Q_0)I \vee J(Q_1)} Sc.$ $\qquad\square$

The last property in this section provides a means of incremental refinement by taking the deterministic part of the coupling invariant apart. Theorem 9(i) is easier to apply if we can remove the two negations which are the result of allowing Sa to be more nondeterministic than Sc.

Property 1 $\dfrac{[I \wedge J \wedge Q_0 \wedge wp(Sa,T) \Rightarrow wp(Sc, Q_1 \wedge wp(Sa,I))], Sa \sqsubseteq_{(R_0 \wedge I)J(R_1)} Sc}{Sa \sqsubseteq_{(Q_0 \wedge R_0)I \wedge J(Q_1 \wedge R_1)} Sc}.$ $\qquad\square$

The first condition is in general stronger than a refinement. It does not allow Sc to restrict the nondeterminism of Sa. A special case of this property, which is obtained by assuming I to be independent of Sa and Sc and by taking $Q_0 = R_0$ and $Q_1 = R_1$, is often used.

Corollary 1 For I independent of Sa and Sc we have
$$Sa \sqsubseteq_{(Q_0 \wedge I)J(Q_1)} Sc \Rightarrow Sa \sqsubseteq_{(Q_0)I \wedge J(Q_1)} Sc. \qquad\square$$

6 Program construction by data refinement

In this section we argue that data refinement can be a powerful technique for program derivation. The following theorem shows that data refinement is correctness preserving in some sense. Given a pre- and a postcondition of the abstract program, it provides a pre- and postcondition of the concrete program.

Theorem 13   For Q_1 independent of Sa and Q_3 independent of Sc,

$$Sa \sqsubseteq_{(Q_0)I(Q_1)} Sc \wedge \{Q_2\} Sa \{Q_3\} \Rightarrow \{(\exists a :: I \wedge Q_0 \wedge Q_2)\} Sc \{(\exists a :: I \wedge Q_1 \wedge Q_3)\}.$$

Proof   We assume $\{Q_2\} Sa \{Q_3\}$ and derive

$$Sa \sqsubseteq_{(Q_0)I(Q_1)} Sc$$

$\Rightarrow$ { Theorem 9(v), using that Q_3 is independent of Sc }

$$[I \wedge Q_0 \wedge wp(Sa, Q_3) \Rightarrow wp(Sc, Q_1 \wedge (\exists a :: I \wedge Q_3))]$$

$\Rightarrow$ { assumption $\{Q_2\} Sa \{Q_3\}$, definition of a Hoare triple }

$$[I \wedge Q_0 \wedge Q_2 \Rightarrow wp(Sc, Q_1 \wedge (\exists a :: I \wedge Q_3))]$$

$=$ { calculus, using that Q_1 is independent of Sa }

$$[(\exists a :: I \wedge Q_0 \wedge Q_2) \Rightarrow wp(Sc, (\exists a :: I \wedge Q_1 \wedge Q_3))]$$

$=$ { definition of a Hoare triple }

$$\{(\exists a :: I \wedge Q_0 \wedge Q_2)\} Sc \{(\exists a :: I \wedge Q_1 \wedge Q_3)\}.$$

$\square$

In the case of algorithmic refinement a dual property holds, viz. that $\{Q_2\} Sa \{Q_3\}$ implies $\{Q_2\} Sc \{Q_3\}$ if Sc refines Sa. In data refinement, however, going from Sa to Sc we have to take the coupling invariant I into account. This theorem is referred to as a suitability condition in [5]. One might expect the theorem to hold without the existential quantification in the right hand side of the implication. The following example shows that this is not the case.

Example 8   It is obvious that $\{ T \} x := 1 \{x = 1\}$ and that $x := 1 \sqsubseteq_T skip$. But we do not have $\{ T \} skip \{x = 1\}$.

By Theorem 13, we can only assert that $\{(\exists x :: T)\} skip \{(\exists x :: x = 1)\}$, which fortunately is a tautology. $\square$

Theorem 13 can also be used to generalize a well-known theorem [12, formula (3.7)] about elimination of auxiliary variables into

Generalization   Let v be an auxiliary variable in S' and S is obtained from S' by deleting all assignments to v. Then

$$\{Q\} S' \{R\} \Rightarrow \{ (\exists v :: Q) \} S \{ (\exists v :: R) \}.$$

We can choose the coupling invariant I in Theorem 13 to be a simple renaming of the program variables other than v. Then assignments to v can be refined to *skip* while all other statements are renamed according to I. $\square$

The following three theorems state that data refinement preserves the program correctness through the program constructs. Their proofs, which use Theorem 13 and the properties of data refinement, are left to the interested reader.

Theorem 14 (sq-rule) For Q_1 independent of Sa_0 and Q_2 independent of Sa_1,

$$\frac{\{Q_0\}\, Sa_0\, \{Q_1\}\,;\; Sa_1\, \{Q_2\},\; Sa_0 \sqsubseteq_{(Q_0)I} Sc_0,\; Sa_1 \sqsubseteq_{(Q_1)I} Sc_1}{\{(\exists a :: I \wedge Q_0)\}\, Sc_0\, \{(\exists a :: I \wedge Q_1)\}\,;\; Sc_1\, \{(\exists a :: I \wedge Q_2)\}}.$$

$\square$

Theorem 15 (if-rule) For Q_1 independent of $\mathbf{if}_c$,

$$\frac{\{Q_0\}\, \mathbf{if}\, [\!| i :: Ba_i \rightarrow \{Q_0 \wedge Ba_i\}\, Sa_i\, \{Q_1\}\, \mathbf{fi},\; (\exists i :: Ba_i) \Rightarrow_{Q_0 \wedge I} (\exists i :: Bc_i)}{\{(\exists a :: I \wedge Q_0)\}\, \mathbf{if}\, [\!| i :: Bc_i \rightarrow \{(\exists a :: I \wedge Q_0) \wedge Bc_i\}\, Sc_i\, \{(\exists a :: I \wedge Q_1)\}\, \mathbf{fi}}.$$

$\square$

Theorem 16 (do-rule) For La independent of $\mathbf{do}_c$, let Lc denote $(\exists a :: I \wedge La)$. Then

$$\frac{(\forall i :: Ba_i =_{La \wedge I} Bc_i),\; (\forall i :: Sa_i \sqsubseteq_{(Bc_i \wedge La)I} Sc_i),}{\{Lc\}\, \mathbf{do}\, [\!| i :: Ba_i \rightarrow \{La \wedge Ba_i\}\, Sa_i\, \{La\}\;\; \mathbf{od}\, \{(\forall i :: \neg Ba_i) \wedge La\}}{\{Lc\}\, \mathbf{do}\, [\!| i :: Bc_i \rightarrow \{Lc \wedge Bc_i\}\, Sc_i\, \{Lc\}\;\; \mathbf{od}\, \{(\forall i :: \neg Bc_i) \wedge Lc\}}.$$

$\square$

In the above three theorems, we see that assertions proved of the abstract programs can be carried over to the refined programs. We conclude this section with a somewhat larger example.

Example 9 Given an integer constant N, $N \geq 0$, whose cubic root we want to approximate under the restriction that we are to use only addition and shifting. More precisely, we are to construct a program S, such that

$$\{N \geq 0\}\, S\, \{x^3 \leq N < (x+1)^3\}$$

Using standard techniques, choosing invariant

$$P:\quad x^3 \leq N < (x+2^n)^3 \wedge n \geq 0$$

for the main repetition the following program can readily be derived.

$\{\,N \geq 0\,\}$
$x, n := 0, 0;$
$\textbf{do } 2^{3n} \leq N \;\rightarrow\; n := n + 1 \textbf{ od};$
$\{\text{ loop invariant} : P\,\}$
$\textbf{do } n \neq 0 \;\rightarrow\; n := n - 1;$
$\qquad \textbf{if } \;(x + 2^n)^3 \leq N \;\;\rightarrow\;\; x := x + 2^n$
$\qquad \|\quad (x + 2^n)^3 > N \;\;\rightarrow\;\; skip$
$\qquad \textbf{fi}$
$\textbf{od}$
$\{\, x^3 \leq N < (x + 2^n)^3 \wedge n = 0;\ \text{hence},\ x^3 \leq N < (x + 1)^3 \,\}$

The above program needs operations that are not allowed. We refine the above program to one which uses only addition and shifting. This technique is sometimes called coordinate transformation, cf. [3, page 61-65], but it can be viewed as a special case of data refinement. To this end, we observe that

$$(x + y)^3 = x^3 + 3x^2 y + 3xy^2 + y^3$$

Therefore, we introduce concrete variables a, b, c, and d in the following coupling invariant

$$I : \quad a = x^3 \wedge b = 3x^2 2^n \wedge c = x 2^{2n} \wedge d = 2^{3n}$$

We use $c = x 2^{2n}$ rather than $c = 3x 2^{2n}$, since x is the value the program should yield when $n = 0$. The following refinements hold.

$$
\begin{array}{lll}
x, n := 0, 0 & \sqsubseteq_I & a, b, c, d := 0, 0, 0, 1 \\
2^{3n} \leq N & =_I & d \leq N \\
n := n + 1 & \sqsubseteq_I & b, c, d := 2 * b, 4 * c, 8 * d \\
n \neq 0 & =_I & d \neq 1 \\
n := n - 1 & \sqsubseteq_I & b, c, d := b/2, c/4, d/8 \\
(x + 2^n)^3 \leq N & =_I & a + b + 3 * c + d \leq N \\
x := x + 2^n & \sqsubseteq_I & a, b, c := \; a + b + 3 * c + d, \\
& & \qquad\quad b + 6 * c + 3 * d, \\
& & \qquad\quad c + d
\end{array}
$$

By Theorems 14 through 16 we come to the following program.

$\{\,(\exists x, n :: I \wedge N \geq 0)\,\}$
$a, b, c, d := 0, 0, 0, 1;$
$\textbf{do } d \leq N \;\rightarrow\; b, c, d := 2 * b, 4 * c, 8 * d \textbf{ od};$
$\{\text{ loop invariant} : (\exists x, n :: I \wedge P)\,\}$
$\textbf{do } d \neq 1 \;\rightarrow\; b, c, d := b/2, c/4, d/8;$
$\qquad \textbf{if } \; a + b + 3 * c + d \leq N \;\;\rightarrow\;\; a, b, c := \; a + b + 3 * c + d,$
$\qquad\qquad\qquad\qquad\qquad\qquad\qquad\qquad\qquad\qquad\quad b + 6 * c + 3 * d,$
$\qquad\qquad\qquad\qquad\qquad\qquad\qquad\qquad\qquad\qquad\quad c + d$
$\qquad \|\quad a + b + 3 * c + d > N \;\;\rightarrow\;\; skip$
$\qquad \textbf{fi}$
$\textbf{od}$
$\{\, d = 1 \wedge (\exists x, n :: I \wedge P)\,\}$

It is clear that the precondition can be weakened to $N \geq 0$ and the postcondition to $c^3 \leq N < (c+1)^3$. The loop invariant is equivalent to

$$b^3 = 27a^2 d \wedge c^3 = ad^2 \wedge a \leq N < a+b+3c+d \wedge (\exists x :: a = x^3) \wedge (\exists i : i \geq 0 : d = 8^i).$$

$\square$

7 Conclusion

We have formally characterized the concept of data refinement and studied its various properties. Our characterization can be viewed as a straightforward generalization of algorithmic refinement. We have shown that it is equivalent to all currently known characterizations of data refinement. Moreover, we have proved that data refinement has indispensable properties such as monotonicity and semi-transitivity.

It has been noticed, cf. [0,7], that this (unconditional) type of data refinement is not powerful enough for practical purposes. Therefore, we have introduced the concept of conditional data refinement, which allows us to incorporate contextual information in a refinement step. Yet, it still enables us to prove an abstract program correct at the abstract level independently of possible implementations. Also conditional data refinement turns out to have nice algebraic properties, a number of which we have investigated in this paper.

We are still working on more general laws and properties of conditional data refinement so as to develop it into a sound technique in program derivation. As a first step we have related in this paper data refinement and program correctness and we have demonstrated in what way the correctness of a concrete program follows from the correctness of its corresponding abstract program. For the sake of convenience we have required a program and its refinement to operate on name-disjoint state spaces. Usually, a refinement is performed on just a part of the state space and it is clear that we should relax this requirement to make data refinement useful in practice. Another, more important and difficult issue here is how to find a refining program and its coupling invariant given an abstract program. We strongly believe that they should be developed together and that we should find heuristics for doing so. We have a similar situation when developing an abstract program. A program and its proof are developed hand in hand.

8 Acknowledgement

We thank Carroll Morgan for mentioning a version of Theorem 0, which reminded us of an effective approach to treat repetitive constructs with unbounded nondeterminism. Moreover, we gratefully acknowledge the financial support from the Department of Computer Science at Washington University in Saint Louis, made possible by its chairman Jerome R. Cox, Jr.

References

[0] Back R.J.R.: "A calculus of refinements for program derivations", *Acta Informatica* **25**, pp 593-624, 1988.

[1] Chen, W. and Udding, J.T., "Towards a Calculus of Data Refinement", Computing Science Notes CS8902, Dept. of Mathematics and Computing Science, Groningen University, Groningen, The Netherlands, 1989.

[2] Dahl, O.-J., Dijkstra, E.W. and Hoare, C.A.R.: *Structured Programming*, Academic Press, London and New York, 1972.

[3] Dijkstra, E.W.: *A Discipline of Programming*, Prentice-Hall, Englewood Cliffs, NJ, 1976.

[4] Dijkstra, E.W.: "Extreme solutions of equation(draft of ch.5)", EWD 912, UT at Austin, Texas, 1985.

[5] Gries, D. and Prins, J.: "A new notion of encapsulation", **in**: Proceedings of Symposium on Language Issues in Programming Environments, pp 131-139, *SIGPLAN* June 1985.

[6] Hoare, C.A.R.: "Proof of correctness and data representations", *Acta Informatica* **1**, pp 271-281, 1972.

[7] Morgan, C.C.: "Data refinement by miracles", *IPL* **26**, pp 243-246, 1987/88.

[8] Morgan, C.C.: "The specification statement", *ACM TOPLAS* **10**, pp 403-419, 1988.

[9] Morgan, C.C.: Personal communication, September 1988.

[10] Morgan, C.C. and Robinson, K.: "Specification statements and refinement", *IBM J. Res. Develop.* **31**, pp 546-555, 1987.

[11] Morris, J.M.: "A theoretical basis for stepwise refinement and the programming calculus", *Sci. of Comp. Prog.* **9**, pp 287-306, 1987.

[12] Owicki S. and Gries D.: "An axiomatic proof technique for parallel programs", *Acta Informatica* **6**, pp 319-340, 1976.

[13] Park, D.: "On the semantics of fair parallelism", **in**: *Abstract Software Specification*, LNCS 86, pp 504-526, 1980.

[14] Wirth, N.: "Program development by stepwise refinement", *CACM* **14**, pp 221-227, 1971.

Stepwise Refinement and Concurrency: A Small Exercise[1]

E. Pascal Gribomont

Philips Research Laboratory, Brussels

Abstract. A simple methodology for the design of concurrent programs is illustrated by a short example. This methodology formalizes the classical concept of "stepwise refinement".

1 Introduction

The concept of *invariant* is the most adequate tool for the formal design of programs. An invariant is a relation between the variables and the control points of the program, which is respected by every statement of the program. If an invariant is true at the initial state of a computation, then it remains true throughout the computation. Invariants can be represented by first order logic formulas.

The adequacy of the notion of invariant relies on two properties. First, it is usually easy to check whether some formula is an invariant or not; second, many interesting properties of programs can be summarized into an invariant of this program.

It is therefore convenient, from the design point of view, to consider a program only in association with an invariant of it [14,20]. This association is a principle of programming methodology.

Both programs and invariants can be big objects; as a consequence, they are often designed in several steps. In the "top-down" approach the steps are *refinements*, that is, roughly speaking, the replacement of an abstract statement of a program by some block of statements, more oriented towards an implementation. The block has to satisfy some constraints, in such a way that the replacement does not endanger the global specification of the whole program; the adaptation of the invariant reflects the satisfaction of the constraints. No attempt is done for now to give a formal definition of the concept of a refinement; we give only an elementary example.

The triple

$$\{x = x_0\}\ S\ \{f = x_0!\},$$

where x_0 denotes a natural number, can be viewed as the specification of a program S (x and f are program variables). Here is a sequence of programs correct with respect to this specification; every program (but the last one) is more abstract than its successor.

$$S_0 ::= \quad f := x!$$

$$S_1 ::= \quad y := 1;\ \{x = x_0 \wedge y = 1\}$$
$$(y, x) := (x!, 0);\ \{x = 0 \wedge y = x_0!\}$$
$$f := y$$

$$S_2 ::= \quad y := 1;\ \{x = x_0 \wedge y = 1\}$$
$$\text{while } x > 0 \text{ do } \{0 < x \le x_0 \wedge y * x! = x_0!\}$$
$$(y, x) := (y * x, x - 1);$$
$$\{x = 0 \wedge y = x_0!\}$$
$$f := y$$

[1] Supported in part by the ESPRIT project ATES.

$$S_3 ::= \quad y := 1; \ \{x = x_0 \wedge y = 1\}$$
$$\text{while } x > 0 \text{ do } \{0 < x \leq x_0 \wedge y * x! = x_0!\}$$
$$\qquad y := y * x; \ \{0 < x \leq x_0 \wedge y * (x - 1)! = x_0!\}$$
$$\qquad x := x - 1;$$
$$\{x = 0 \wedge y = x_0!\}$$
$$f := y$$

Comment. As usual in structured sequential programming, control points are implicit. In parallel programming, however, it appears that explicit labelling can be convenient [26,29]. With self-explaining notation, the first element (S_0, I_0) of the sequence could be denoted

$$S_0 ::= \quad \{(\ell_0, \ f := x, \ \ell_e)\},$$
$$I_0 ::= \quad (at \ \ell_0 \supset x = x_0) \wedge (at \ \ell_e \supset f = x_0!).$$

A refinement implies a local change in the program and a local change in the invariant; these changes can be trivial (step from S_2 to S_3 for instance), or involve a less evident algorithmic idea (step from S_1 to S_2).

The concept of stepwise refinement is especially useful for parallel programming; most of the proofs reported in the literature make use of it, in one way or another (see e.g. [16,26,1,6,7]). In this paper, we demonstrate on a small example a simple and general framework to deal with stepwise refinement in concurrency. A semantic-based language is presented in section 2, the method is outlined in section 3, the special case of sequential decomposition is introduced in section 4 and section 5 is devoted to an example. Comparison with related work is done in section 6.

2 A language

Transitions systems are generally found adequate to represent concurrent programs [24,38,7], and their semantics is clear and well-known. The language used here will be the formalism of transition systems, as studied in [37], except that labels, or control points, will be allowed; as usual, assignments are used to specify the relations associated with the transitions.

A *structured transition system*, or an STS, is a triple $S = (\mathcal{P}, \mathcal{M}, \mathcal{T})$ where $\mathcal{P}$ is a set of *(formal) processes*, $\mathcal{M}$ is a *memory* and $\mathcal{T}$ is a set of *transitions*. A process is a set of *labels*, or *control points* (processes are pairwise disjoint) and the memory is a set of (typed) variables. A transition has a *type*, which is the set of processes *involved* by the transition. Transitions specify modifications of the system state; a transition $T = (L, C \longrightarrow A, M)$ is described by an *origin* L, a *condition* C, an *assignment* A and an *extremity* M. The condition is interpreted as a predicate on the memory state. The assignment specifies a transformation of the memory state. The origin and the extremity of a transition both contain exactly one control point of each process involved by the transition. The execution of a transition is possible only when each involved process is at the control point specified by the origin and when the condition is satisfied. After the execution of the transition, each involved process is at the control point specified by the extremity (non-involved processes are at the same control point before and after the execution of the transition). Furthermore, the memory state has been transformed according to the assignment.

Comment. The transition $(L, C \longrightarrow A, M)$ will sometimes be noted $(L \to M)$, when there is no risk of confusion.

The formalism of structured transition systems can be viewed as a lexical version of the classical (and graphical) formalism of flowcharts, slightly generalized. The generalization is the possibility to represent actions involving more than one process.

As an example, let us now consider the representation in STS of a simple concurrent algorithm (it is a variant of the algorithm presented in CSP in [15]).

Variables are x and y (integers), and S and T (sets of integers). Informally speaking, the small elements are transferred to S and the large elements are transferred to T, while maintaining the size of the sets.

$\mathcal{P} = \{P_s, P_t\}$,

where $P_s = \{l_0, l_1, l_2, l_4, l_5\}$ and $P_t = \{m_1, m_2, m_3, m_4, m_5\}$.

$\mathcal{M} = \{S, T, x, y\}$

where $\text{type}(S) = \text{type}(T) = set\ of\ int$ and $\text{type}(x) = \text{type}(y) = int$.

$\mathcal{T} = \{(l_0, max(S) \neq x \longrightarrow x := max(S), l_1),$
$(l_1 m_1, y := x, l_2 m_2),$
$(l_2, S := S \setminus \{x\}, l_4),$
$(m_2, T := T \cup \{y\}, m_3),$
$(m_3, y := min(T), m_4),$
$(l_4 m_4, x := y, l_5 m_5),$
$(l_5, S := S \cup \{x\}, l_0),$
$(m_5, T := T \setminus \{y\}, m_1)\}$.

The initial conditions are formalized into the following assertion:

$$S_0 \neq \emptyset \wedge x = +\infty \wedge S_0 \cap T_0 = \emptyset \wedge at\ l_0 \wedge at\ m_1 \wedge S = S_0 \wedge T = T_0,$$

The corresponding final conditions are formalized into

$$S \cup T = S_0 \cup T_0 \wedge less(S, T) \wedge |S| = |S_0| \wedge |T| = |T_0|,$$

where the predicate $less(A, B)$ means that every member of A is less than every member of B.

Place predicates, like "at l_2", are introduced, with their usual meaning; an expression like "at $l_3 m_1$" is used for $(at\ l_3 \wedge at\ m_1)$. With this notation, a transition $(L, C \to S, M)$ can be executed only in a state satisfying the formula $(at\ L \wedge C)$; after the execution, $at\ M$ is true. Otherwise, labelled transitions behave like usual transitions [37].

If A is a formula and if $at\ L$ is a place predicate, the formula $A_{[at\ L]}$ is obtained by "making $at\ L$ true in A".[2] Here is an example about the system introduced above.

$A =_{def} [(at\ \ell_5 \vee at\ m_3) \supset x = y] \wedge [at\ \ell_0 m_1 \supset S \cup T = S_0 \cup T_0],$

$A_{[at\ m_1]} = [(at\ \ell_5 \vee false) \supset x = y] \wedge [at\ \ell_0 \supset S \cup T = S_0 \cup T_0],$
$= (at\ \ell_5 \supset x = y) \wedge (at\ \ell_0 \supset S \cup T = S_0 \cup T_0).$

Comment. Formula A is an invariance property of the system.

The formal reasoning tool for programs and their invariants is adapted from classical Hoare's logic and from the liberal version of Dijkstra's programming calculus [21,14,13]. The notion of a Hoare triple for a transition is introduced by the rule

$$\{P\}\,(L, C \to A, M)\,\{Q\} \quad =_{def} \quad \{P_{[at\ L]} \wedge C\}\,A\,\{Q_{[at\ M]}\}. \tag{1}$$

A formula I is an invariant of the system $\mathcal{S} = (\mathcal{P}, \mathcal{M}, \mathcal{T})$ if and only if $\{I\}\,T\,\{I\}$ holds for all $T \in \mathcal{T}$.

The liberal version of Dijkstra's programming calculus can be introduced as follows. Let us consider the triple $\{P\}\,S\,\{Q\}$. If S and Q are fixed, the set pre of formulas P such that the triple is true admits the weakest element $\bigvee pre$, which is denoted $wlp[S; Q]$ (weakest liberal precondition); similarly, if P and S are fixed, the set $post$ of formulas Q such that the triple is true admits the strongest element $\bigwedge post$, which is denoted $slp[P; S]$ (strongest liberal postcondition).[3]

---

[2] More precisely, if $L = \ell_1 \ldots \ell_n$, where $\ell_1 \in P_1, \ldots, \ell_n \in P_n$, then $A_{[at\ L]}$ is obtained from A as follows. Each place predicate $at\ \ell$ occurring in A is replaced by $true$ if there exists an i such that $\ell = \ell_i$, by $false$ if there exists an i such that $\ell \in P_i \setminus \{\ell_i\}$, by $at\ \ell$ (no change) otherwise.

[3] A formula A is *stronger* than a formula B if the formula $(A \supset B)$ is valid.

The "l" in slp and wlp stands for "liberal"; this means that termination is not guaranteed. In fact, the formulas $\{P\}\,S\,\{Q\}$, $(P \supset wlp[S;Q])$ and $(slp[P;S] \supset Q)$ are equivalent. This equivalence leads to the following relations:

$$
\begin{aligned}
wlp[(C \longrightarrow A); Q] &\equiv (C \supset wlp[A;Q]), \\
slp[P; (C \longrightarrow A)] &\equiv slp[(P \wedge C); A].
\end{aligned}
\tag{2}
$$

Let us observe that these relations are not true for the classical predicate transformers wp and sp; for instance, with Dijkstra's notation, $wp[\text{if } C \longrightarrow A \text{ fi}; Q]$ reduces to $(C \wedge wp[A;Q])$. Furthermore, the formula $wlp[S;true]$ is identically true, whereas the formula $wp[S;true]$ is true for a state s_0 if and only if all computations of S whose initial state is s_0 terminate. If S is a (multiple) assignment which never fails, then $wp[S;Q] = wlp[S;Q]$ for all Q.

3 Outline of a methodology

We propose an incremental design method for parallel programs or, more exactly, for ordered pairs (System, Invariant). When a pair (S, I) is fixed, only computations of S whose initial state satisfies the invariant I are considered.

3.1 A correctness criterion for refinements

In the context of structured transition systems, the stepwise refinement method consists in repeatedly replacing some transitions of the system in hand by some new transitions, until a satisfactory system is obtained. The designer is like a traveler: he (or she) must know where he is, where he goes, and what he has to keep with him during the travel. More precisely, the designer must know the relevant properties of the old version of the system, he must know how to modify this version to obtain the new one, and also which properties of the old version have to be preserved in the new version (if these properties are not preserved, the new version is declared unsatisfactory, and rejected; another refinement can be attempted).

In this paper, the relevant properties of the old version are formalized into an invariant I. The intended modification is formalized into a set of old transitions and a set of new transitions (old transitions are tentatively replaced by new transitions). The properties to be preserved are formalized into a *refinement condition* E: the invariant I of the old version must be true in every state where the refinement condition is true. More concisely, the formula $(E \supset I)$ must still be an invariance property of the new version.

This formalization of the problem is somewhat restrictive, because only invariance properties are considered. However, many important properties of concurrent systems, including partial correctness and mutual exclusion, are still within the scope of the method.

3.2 A formal framework for refinements

The replacement must satisfy *syntactic* constraints, which simply express that the new transitions can evoke only existing labels and variables. If the designer intends to introduce new processes, labels and variables, preliminary transformations are needed.

A refinement is also subject to *semantical* constraints. These constraints are stated by the designer (explicitly or not). Most of the time, the designer intends to increase the efficiency of the system, without destroying the essential properties of the initial version.

A *preliminary transformation* consists of a transformation of a pair (S, I) into another pair (S', I'), where the system S' is obtained from the system S by applying (once or more) some of the following transformations:

1. a process P containing a single label ℓ is added in $\mathcal{P}$;

2. a new label m is added into an already existing process;

3. a new variable x is added to the memory.

Preliminary transformations do not deeply alter the system, since the transitions are not modified. In the first case, the new invariant I' can be $(I \wedge at\ \ell)$; in the second case, we have $I' = (I \wedge \neg at\ m)$ (for no transition evokes m) and, in the third case, I' can be $(I \wedge P(x))$ if an initial condition holds for x (as no transition can alter x, this initial condition is also an invariance property).

The concept of refinement can now be formalized.

A *refinement* for (S, I) is a tuple $R = (O_R, N_R, E, J)$ where $O_R \subset T$ is a set of transitions to be replaced by a set N_R of new transitions. The formula E is a part of I which discriminates between "old" transitions and "new" ones, in the following sense: the execution of an old transition $\tau \in T$ cannot change the truthvalue of E, while the execution of a new transition $\tau \in N_R$ can. Formula J is a new piece of invariant. More formally, R is a refinement if

- O_R is a subset of T;

- N_R is a set of new transitions;

- the *refinement condition* E is a formula satisfying the following requirements:
  - $(I \supset E)$;
  - $\{\neg E\}\, T\, \{\neg E\}$, for all $T \in T$;

- the formula $I' =_{def} [(E \supset I) \wedge (\neg E \supset J)]$ is an invariant of the transition system $\{\mathcal{P}, \mathcal{M}, T'\}$, where $T' = (T \setminus O_r) \cup N_r$.

Let S' be the transition system $\{\mathcal{P}, \mathcal{M}, T'\}$; the pair (S', I') is the *R-refined version* of (S, I). Let us note that $(I \wedge E)$ and $\neg E$ are both invariants of the initial system S, whereas I' is an invariant of the refined system S'.

The notion of refinement is intuitively simple. A computation of S' contains two kinds of states: "old states", for which E is true, and which can belong to a computation of S, and "new states", for which E is false. The old states satisfy I and the new ones satisfy J. The invariance requirement about I' can be rewritten as the following set of triples:

$$
\begin{array}{llr}
1. & \{I \wedge E\}\, T\, \{E \supset I\}, & T \in N_R, \\
2. & \{I \wedge E\}\, T\, \{\neg E \supset J\}, & T \in N_R, \\
3. & \{J \wedge \neg E\}\, T\, \{E \supset I\}, & T \in N_R, \\
4. & \{J \wedge \neg E\}\, T\, \{\neg E \supset J\}, & T \in T'.
\end{array}
\tag{3}
$$

Let us observe that the unknown assertion J does not occur in the constraints of group 1, occurs only once in the constraints of groups 2 and 3, and occurs twice in the constraints of group 4.

A refinement R is a *simple refinement* if O_R contains only one transition. Otherwise, it is a *multiple refinement*. A multiple refinement can always be viewed as a sequence of simple refinements.

Comment. The link between the initial and the refined versions of the system is the fact that the formula $(E \supset I)$ is an invariance property of both versions. It is the responsibility of the designer to ensure that this formula is strong enough to imply the specified invariance properties of the system (mutual exclusion, freeness of deadlock, partial correctness, and so on). As a consequence, the invariant I will always be chosen as strong as possible, whereas the refinement condition E will be chosen as weak as possible. The choice $E =_{def} I$, for instance, is not appropriate, because no connection is established between the initial and the refined versions.

3.3 From informal to formal refinement

In this paper, formal programming means programming with invariants. However, the notion of refinement also exists in informal programming, as an ordered pair (O_R, N_R). The additional components E and J are meant to act as a filter, that allows the designer to reject "bad" informal refinements. It is the responsibility of the designer to summarize the specifications of the initial version into an invariant I; indeed, the fact that some informal refinement can be extended into a formal refinement depends on the choice of I. In our opinion, it is adequate to leave this responsibility to the designer; in fact, one can argue, first, that the invariant is an adequate tool to express the semantics of systems (as far as only invariance properties are considered) and, second, that the designer is not entitled to write and modify programs without stating explicitly their semantics.

Another responsibility left to the designer is to "guess" which informal refinement (O_R, N_R) is likely to be both useful and correct, i.e., extendable into a formal refinement (O_R, N_R, E, J); the set of constraints (3) provides only the a posteriori verification. As the number of informal refinements can be infinite, we would like to provide some help in this matter.

There are many kinds of useful informal refinements, but the *sequential decomposition* is by far the most frequent one. Informally speaking, the sequential decomposition consists in replacing a single transition, involving a single process, by an ordered set of transitions, involving only the same process. From the sequential point of view, O_R and N_R are strictly equivalent, but, due to interference with the other processes of the system, the old version of the system and the new one may behave differently; the difference may be acceptable or not. (The old version is often called to be *coarser-grained* than the new one, which is *finer-grained* than the old one.)

Let us recall briefly an elementary example of this well-known phenomenon. With classical notation, we have

$$\{x = 0\} \; < x := x + 1 > \; \| \; < x := x + 1 > \; \{x = 2\}$$

but we have not

$$\{x = 0\} \; (a := x; a := a + 1; x := a) \; \| \; (a := x; a := a + 1; x := a) \; \{x = 2\},$$

although the triple $\{x = x_0\} \, S \, \{x = x_0 + 1\}$ holds for both $S =_{def} x := x + 1$ and $S =_{def} (a := x; a := a + 1; x := a)$.
Sequential decomposition is considered in more detail in section 4.

3.4 Incremental design method

Let $((S_n, I_n) \; : \; n = 0, \ldots, r)$ be a sequence such that, for all $n < r$, the pair (S_{n+1}, I_{n+1}) is obtained from the pair (S_n, I_n) by the refinement (O_n, N_n, E_n, J_n) (maybe preceded by some preliminary transformation). The formula

$$\left(\bigwedge_{i=0}^{n-1} E_i \right) \supset I_0$$

is an invariance property of the system S_n, since it is a logical consequence of its invariant I_n; this is proved easily by induction on n.

Provided that the refinements conditions E_n and the initial invariant I_0 are well-chosen, this formula will guarantee the correctness of the last system S_r, with respect to some interesting invariance property. Furthermore, provided that the informal refinements (O_n, N_n) are well chosen, the last version will be efficiently implementable.

4 Sequential decomposition

In this section, the most usual kind of refinement is investigated in more details. Informally speaking, the *sequential decomposition* consists in replacing some statements, considered as atomic, by blocks of more elementary statements; this increases the *grain of parallelism*. In this paper, it is supposed that the replacing blocks are sequences. Furthermore, we restrict to the case where all transitions involve a single process (this is true in the shared memory framework).

The simplest case is the replacement of a single transition by two new transitions. This case will be considered first.

4.1 Simple sequential decomposition in STS

Let $S = (P, M, T)$ be a structured transition system where $P = \{P_0, P_1, \ldots\}$, with $P_0 = \{a_1, \ldots, a_n\}$, and let I be an invariant of S. We suppose that T contains a transition

$$T = (a_i, C \longrightarrow A, a_j)$$

One can attempt to "split" this transition, that is, to replace it by the new transitions

$$T_1 = (a_i, C_1 \longrightarrow A_1, a_x),$$
$$T_2 = (a_x, C_2 \longrightarrow A_2, a_j).$$

where a_x is a new label and where C_1, C_2, A_1 and A_2 satisfy the *compatibility requirements* given below.

> For all P, Q such that the triple $\{P\} C \longrightarrow A \{Q\}$ holds, there exists a formula R such that both triples $\{P\} C_1 \longrightarrow A_1 \{R\}$ and $\{R\} C_2 \longrightarrow A_2 \{Q\}$ hold.

The validity of such a replacement must be checked carefully (invalid sequential decomposition is one of the most frequent mistakes in parallel programming). A preliminary transformation is needed, consisting in the addition of the new label a_x. This leads to the pair (S_1, I_1) where

$$P_1 = \{P_0 \cup \{a_x\}, P_1, \ldots\},$$
$$M_1 = M \cup \{\ldots\},$$
$$T_1 = T;$$
$$I_1 = (I \wedge \neg at\, a_x).$$

If new variables are evoked in T_1 and T_2, they are added to the memory. As a_x is a new label, not referred in any (old) transition, $at\, a_x$ is always false.

The sequential decomposition is now defined as the ordered pair $(\{T\}, \{T_1, T_2\})$. Before dealing with the validation problem, let us recall briefly why the sequential decomposition is useful.

4.2 Usefulness of sequential decomposition

The implementation of a coarse-grained system requires special devices like semaphore, test-and-set, critical region, and so on, to ensure that the statements of the transitions are executed without interference. The efficiency of a system usually depends on the grain of parallelism. The best case occurs when the grain corresponds to the elementary actions whose atomicity is provided by the hardware.

The designer has two responsibilities in this context. First, the critical regions of the program must be clearly identified (classically, they are surrounded by angle brackets); second, the size of these regions must be as small as possible. In the abstract language STS, each transition is a critical region. If the designer suspects that a transition is "too big" to be conveniently implemented as such, a sequential decomposition has to be attempted.

It is well-known that the grain of parallelism is critical only when processes share memory; when processes communicate by message passing, the grain of action does not matter (except for communication statements).

In the framework of shared memory, some theorems exist to know whether the sequential decomposition can endanger the properties of a system (see e.g. [35] for more detail). These theorems guarantee the validity of sequential decomposition, provided that some constraints are satisfied. We will now consider the validation problem for the simple sequential decomposition.

4.3 Validation of sequential decomposition

With the notation introduced above, the data of the problem are an old version (S_1, I_1) and a sequential decomposition $(\{T\}, \{T_1, T_2\})$; the target is a refinement condition E and an assertion J, which would guarantee that the attempted sequential decomposition is a formal refinement.

A natural candidate for the refinement condition is $E = \neg at\ a_x$. This choice clearly satisfies the requirements: first, E is a logical consequence of the invariant I_1 and, second, no old transition can switch E from false to true.[4]

The refinement itself can now be defined as the tuple

$$R =_{def} (\{T\}, \{T_1, T_2\}, \neg at\ a_x, J).$$

The formula J must satisfy the system (3), which can be rewritten into

2. $\{I\}\ T_1\ \{J\}$,
3. $\{J\}\ T_2\ \{I\}$,
4. $\{J\}\ \tau\ \{J\}$, $\tau \notin \{T_1, T_2\}$,

and then into

2. $slp[I_{1[at\ a_i]};\ (C_1 \longrightarrow A_1)] \supset J$,
3. $J \supset wlp[(C_2 \longrightarrow A_2); I_{1[at\ a_j]}]$,
4. $\{J\}\ \tau\ \{J\}$, $\tau \notin \{T_1, T_2\}$,

Due to the compatibility requirements, the constraints of group 1 are always satisfied and have been omitted. The group 2 and 3 define a Boolean lattice C within which an adequate J must be selected. Due to the compatibility requirements, C is never empty. The group 4 is a set of interaction requirements; these conditions cannot usually be solved explicitly, since J occurs twice in each of them.

The selection procedure is, in principle, very simple: select repeatedly members of C and try them against the interaction requirements, until a solution is found. The problem is that C can be infinite, and that the existence of a solution is not guaranteed. Fortunately, the experience shows that, when a solution exists, either the strongest possible choice, or the weakest one, is often adequate. When a solution has been found, the new system $S_2 = (\mathcal{P}_2, \mathcal{M}_2, \mathcal{T}_2)$ and the new invariant I_2 are adopted, where

$$\mathcal{P}_2 = \mathcal{P}_1 = \{\{a_1, \ldots, a_n, a_x\}, P_1, \ldots\},$$
$$\mathcal{M}_2 = \mathcal{M}_1,$$
$$\mathcal{T}_2 = (\mathcal{T}_1 \setminus \{T\}) \cup \{T_1, T_2\};$$
$$I_2 = [(\neg at\ a_x \supset I_1) \wedge (at\ a_x \supset J)].$$

---

[4]This choice is called "natural" only because it always satisfies the requirements; in specific cases, other candidates could be considered.

If no solution is found, the sequential decomposition should be rejected. In both cases, further refinements can be attempted.

Comment. Constraints of groups 2 and 3 are *sequentiality constraints*; they involve only the new transitions and do not take into account the interactions due to the transitions involving other processes. The proposed strategy is rather natural. A refinement is considered first in isolation, and then with respect to the whole system.

Comment. The formula J is relevant in I_2 only when $at\ a_x$ holds; as a consequence, it is not a restriction to consider only the case $J \equiv J_{[at\ a_x]}$.

4.4 Multiple sequential decomposition

The sequential decomposition is the replacement of one transition by two transitions. This can be generalized in two ways. First, the set of new transitions can contain more than two elements.[5] Second, more than one old transition can be replaced by a set of new transitions (but we suppose that the replaced transitions involve distinct processes; practical experience shows that the simultaneous replacement of several transitions involving the same process is not interesting).

The starting point for a multiple sequential refinement is a pair (system, invariant) (S_0, I_0), where

$$\mathcal{P}_0 = \{P_1, \ldots, P_n, Q_0, \ldots, Q_m\},$$
$$\mathcal{M}_0 = \mathcal{M},$$
$$\mathcal{T}_0 = \mathcal{T}.$$

The informal refinement consists in replacing, for each process P_i, a transition T_i involving P_i by a set of new transitions $\{T_i^0, \ldots, T_i^{k(i)}\}$ of the same type $\{P_i\}$. A preliminary transformation is needed to introduce new labels and (possibly) new variables. The result of this transformation is

$$\mathcal{P}_1 = \{P_1', \ldots, P_n', Q_0, \ldots, Q_m\},$$
$$\mathcal{M}_1 = \mathcal{M} \cup \{\ldots\},$$
$$\mathcal{T}_1 = \mathcal{T},$$
$$I_1 = (I_0 \wedge \bigwedge_{i=1}^{n} \bigwedge_{j=1}^{k(i)} \neg at\ a_i^j),$$

where $P_i' = P_i \cup A_i$, with $A_i = \{a_i^1, \ldots, a_i^{k(i)}\}$, for all $i = 1, \ldots, n$.

Let $i \in \{1, \ldots, n\}$ and let $k(i) = k$. If the old transition T_i has the form

$$T_i = (b_i,\ C \longrightarrow A,\ c_i),$$

then the new transitions are

$$T_i^0 = (b_i,\ C_0 \longrightarrow A_0,\ a_i^1),$$
$$T_i^j = (a_i^j,\ C_j \longrightarrow A_j,\ a_i^{j+1}),\ j = 1, \ldots, k-1,$$
$$T_i^k = (a_i^k,\ C_k \longrightarrow A_k,\ c_i).$$

The compatibility requirements associated with the new transitions are as follows. For all P, Q such that the triple $\{P\}T_i\{Q\}$ holds, formulas $R_j : j = 1, \ldots, k-1$ exist such that the $k+1$ triples $\{P\}T_i^0\{R_1\}$, $\{R_j\}T_i^j\{R_{j+1}\}$ ($j = 1, \ldots, k-1$) and $\{R_k\}T_i^k\{Q\}$ hold. Similar sets of requirements hold for $i = 1, \ldots, n$.

The system S_2 is obtained from the system S_1 by replacing $\mathcal{T}_1 = \mathcal{T}$ by

$$\mathcal{T}_2 = (\mathcal{T} \setminus \{T_1, \ldots, T_n\}) \cup \{T_1^0, \ldots, T_1^{k(1)}\} \cup \cdots \cup \{T_n^0, \ldots, T_n^{k(n)}\}.$$

---

[5] For instance, when the double assignment $(u, v) := (v, u)$ is replaced by the sequence $t := u,\ u := v,\ v := t$, three new transitions (and a new variable, and two new labels) are needed.

4.5 Validation (general case)

The invariant of S_2 will be

$$I_2 =_{def} [(E \supset I_1) \wedge (\neg E \supset J)],$$

where

$$E =_{def} \bigwedge_{i=1}^{n} \bigwedge_{j=1}^{k(i)} \neg at\ a_i^j.$$

A convenient notation is introduced now about the refined system S_2: the new place predicate $at\ a_i^0$ is defined as the formula $(\neg at\ a_i^1 \wedge \cdots \wedge \neg a_i^{k(i)})$. As a consequence, the assertion $at\ a_i^0 + at\ a_i^1 + \cdots + at\ a_i^{k(i)} = 1$ is an invariance property (and an invariant) of the system S_2. The invariant I_2 can be rewritten more specifically as

$$I_2 \equiv \bigwedge_{i_1=0}^{k(1)} \cdots \bigwedge_{i_n=0}^{k(n)} [at\ a_1^{i_1} \ldots a_n^{i_n} \supset J(a_1^{i_1}, \ldots, a_n^{i_n})],$$

where $J(a_1^0, \ldots, a_n^0)$ reduces to I_1 (or I_0).

As usual, the unknown assertions $J(a_1^{i_1}, \ldots, a_n^{i_n})$ are determined by the set of constraints given below:

$$\{I_2\}\ \tau\ \{I_2\}\ , \text{ for all } \tau \in \mathcal{T}_2. \tag{4}$$

Every transition involves only one process. It is convenient to distinguish transitions involving a process $\pi \in \{P_1', \ldots, P_n'\}$ and transitions involving a process $\pi \in \{Q_0, \ldots, Q_m\}$. The P_1'-part of the system (4) can be rewritten into

$$\{J(a_1^0, a_2^{i_2}, \ldots, a_n^{i_n})\}\ \tau\ \{J(a_1^0, a_2^{i_2}, \ldots, a_n^{i_n})\}\ ,\quad \tau \in \mathcal{T} \setminus \{T_1\}\ ,\quad type(\tau) = P_1'$$
$$\{J(b_1, a_2^{i_2}, \ldots, a_n^{i_n})\}\ (b_1 \rightarrow a_1^1)\ \{J(a_1^1, a_2^{i_2}, \ldots, a_n^{i_n})\}\ ,$$
$$\{J(a_1^j, a_2^{i_2}, \ldots, a_n^{i_n})\}\ (a_1^j \rightarrow a_1^{j+1})\ \{J(a_1^{j+1}, a_2^{i_2}, \ldots, a_n^{i_n})\}\ ,\quad j = 1, \ldots, k(1) - 1 \tag{5}$$
$$\{J(a_1^{k(1)}, a_2^{i_2}, \ldots, a_n^{i_n})\}\ (a_1^{k(1)} \rightarrow c_1)\ \{J(c_1, a_2^{i_2}, \ldots, a_n^{i_n})\}\ ,$$
$$[\text{for all } 0 \leq i_2 \leq k(2),\ \ldots,\ 0 \leq i_n \leq k(n)]$$

The P_i'-parts of the system are obtained similarly for $i = 2, \ldots, n$. The Q_0-part of the system is

$$\{J(a_1^{i_1}, \ldots, a_n^{i_n})\}\ \tau\ \{J(a_1^{i_1}, \ldots, a_n^{i_n})\}\ ,\ \tau \in \mathcal{T}_1\ ,\ type(\tau) = Q_0\ ,$$
$$[\text{for all } 0 \leq i_2 \leq k(2),\ \ldots,\ 0 \leq i_n \leq k(n)]. \tag{6}$$

The Q_j'-parts of the system are obtained similarly for $j = 1, \ldots, m$.

Generally, the set of constraints (5, 6) is too complex to be solved explicitly. The experience shows that multiple refinements are better to be replaced by sequences of simple refinements, except when $\{P_1, \ldots, P_n\}$ is a family of symmetric processes. In this case, it is indicated to maintain the symmetry and, therefore, to split similar transitions involving symmetric processes at the same time. This case is considered in the next paragraph.

4.6 Validation (symmetric case)

The pair (S_0, I_0) introduced in the previous paragraph is *symmetric* in the index set $\{1, \ldots, n\}$ if every permutation of this set preserves the pair (system, invariant).

Comment. This definition implies that distinct index sets are disjoint. The usual notation does not respect this condition, because index sets often are initial segments of the natural (or positive) integers. However, we can consider that disjoint copies of the integers are available. For instance, we suppose that the index sets $\{1, \ldots, n\}$, used for the P-processes, and $\{0, \ldots, m\}$, used for the Q-processes, are disjoint.

A (simple) sequential decomposition would destroy the symmetry, since it involves the addition of a label into one process. In order to maintain the symmetry, only multiple sequential decompositions, preserving the symmetry, will be considered.

Let us suppose that (S_r, I_r), $r = 0, 1, 2$, are symmetric in the index set $\{1, \ldots, n\}$ used for the P-processes and let k be the common value of $k(1) = \cdots = k(n)$. The symmetry induces some simplification into the computation of the n-dimensional array $[J(a_1^{i_1}, \ldots, a_n^{i_n})]$ but, except in some specific cases (not considered here), the direct computation is still fastidious.

In the case of symmetric systems, it is often possible to avoid both the destruction of the symmetry and the fastidious computation connected with a multiple refinement.

Let $A = \{1, \ldots, n\}$ be the index set and let (O, N) be a multiple decomposition, symmetric with respect to A. The *ith projection* (O_i, N_i) is the simple decomposition obtained by considering only the ith part of (O, N), that is, by modifying only the transition involving P_i. More precisely, we have $O_i = \{T_i\}$ and $N_i = \{T_i^0, \ldots, T_i^k\}$. The new assertions

$$J(a_1^0, \ldots, a_{i-1}^0, a_i^j, a_{i+1}^0, \ldots, a_n^0), \ j = 1, \ldots, k$$

are determined by the usual method for simple refinements.

An "educated guess" is made to find a general expression $J(a_1^{i_1}, \ldots, a_n^{i_n})$, which reduces to $J(a_1^0, \ldots, a_{i-1}^0, a_i^j, a_{i+1}^0, \ldots, a_n^0)$ when $i_r = 0$ for all $r \neq i$, and $i_r = j$ for $r = i$.

This provisional form is checked against the system of constraints developed in the previous paragraph. In case of success, the provisional form is adopted; in case of failure, another guess can be attempted.

Other forms of symmetry can appear in a system; the notion of projection can still be used in this case. For instance, if a refinement consists in the introduction of n symmetric variables $h_1, \ldots, h_n$ in a system, then the kth projection of this refinement will be obtained by omitting all of these variables except h_k (an example is given in the next section).

Comment. The sequential decomposition is the most usual kind of refinement but other kinds of refinements can be presented in a similar way. When performing a refinement, the critical step is the discovery of an adequate refinement condition. This will also be illustrated in the next section.

5 An example

5.1 Introduction

The program considered in this section has been written and proven by E.W. Dijkstra in [17]. The program and its proof have been presented again in [5] by E. Best, together with another proof.

Dijkstra's proof required the introduction of a family of Boolean values which was the minimal solution of a set of Boolean equations. This proof illustrates the interplay between Mathematics and Programming, and shows that program proving, as Euclidean geometry, requires a special form of creativity; this creativity is well assisted by formal tools (see [17,18]).

In Best's proof, the discovery of the invariant has taken place in successive approximations. Each approximation arose "quite naturally from an analysis of the failure of the preceding formulas".

As a matter of fact, both the program and the invariant can be obtained in an incremental and systematic way. The method proposed here is not intended to provide a substitute for the skill often needed in programming; more modestly, it allows the designer to make his or her ideas clear and precise, and to verify their validity in a formal and systematic way.

The sequel of this section goes on as follows. In the next paragraph, the problem is described and a first version of the program is derived in a straightforward way. The second step of the design consists of a "creative refinement", that is, a refinement which is not simply a sequential decomposition. This transformation is explained informally and its correctness is proved by adaptation of the invariant. As this refinement has induced multiple assignments, a series of sequential decompositions have to be considered. Each of them gives rise to a further adaptation of the invariant.

5.2 The problem and its toy solution

Let $y = f(y)$ be a fixpoint equation in some n-dimensional space. Under some hypotheses which are not introduced here, such an equation can be solved by selecting an adequate initial value $\hat{y}$ for y and then repeating assignments like $y_i := f_i(y)$, where $y = (y_1, \ldots, y_n)$ and $f(y) = (f_1(y), \ldots, f_n(y))$, until the difference between y and $f(y)$ becomes negligible. (This condition is denoted $y \simeq f(y)$ and is supposed to be equivalent to $\forall i [y_i \simeq f_i(y)]$.) A simple sequential nondeterministic program for this problem is

$$
\begin{aligned}
\textbf{do} \quad & y_1 \not\simeq f_1(y) \longrightarrow y_1 := f_1(y)\,; \\
\square \quad & y_2 \not\simeq f_2(y) \longrightarrow y_2 := f_2(y)\,; \\
\cdots \quad & \cdots \qquad\qquad \cdots \\
\square \quad & y_n \not\simeq f_n(y) \longrightarrow y_n := f_n(y) \\
\textbf{od} &
\end{aligned}
$$

A distributed implementation of this sequential nondeterministic algorithm is obtained immediately, by associating each guarded command with a process. This leads to the pair system-invariant (S_0, I_0) given below.

$$
\begin{aligned}
\mathcal{P}_0 &= \{P_1, \ldots, P_n\}, \text{ where } P_i = \{\ell^i_n\}, \text{ for all } i = 1, \ldots, n\,, \\
\mathcal{M}_0 &= \{y_i : i = 1, \ldots, n\}\,, \\
\mathcal{T}_0 &= \{(\ell^i_n,\ y_i \not\simeq f_i(y) \longrightarrow y_i := f_i(y)\,,\ \ell^i_n) : i = 1, \ldots, n\}\,; \\
I_0 &= true\,.
\end{aligned}
$$

Comments. The unique label of process P_i has been called ℓ^i_n (instead of ℓ^i, for instance), because this notation will appear to be convenient in the sequel.
Except stated otherwise, $\forall i\, A$ stands for $\forall i [1 \leq i \leq n \supset A]$; similarly, $\exists i\, A$ stands for $\exists i [1 \leq i \leq n \wedge A]$.

5.3 A creative refinement

The simple system S_0 is not satisfactory, since no mechanism for detecting distributed termination is provided; when a process, say P_i, is suspended because the condition $y_i \simeq f_i(y)$ is satisfied, nothing indicates whether the ith transition will still be executed later or not. A solution [17] consists in the addition of variables,[6] called $h_1, \ldots, h_n$, such that h_i indicates that a further execution of the transition $(\ell^i_n \to \ell^i_n)$ is needed. Initially, all the h_i's are true; a

---

[6]This is the crucial point of the design.

h_i becomes false only when the corresponding relation $y_i \simeq f_i(y)$ is true. The termination condition will be $\neg \exists j \, h_j$.

A preliminary transformation is used to introduce the new variables into the memory. The new system S_1 and its invariant are given by

$$
\begin{aligned}
P_1 &= P_0, \\
M_1 &= \{y_i, h_i : i = 1, \ldots, n\}, \\
T_1 &= T_0; \\
I_1 &= \forall i \, h_i.
\end{aligned}
$$

Comment. As all h_i are initially true and never altered, $\forall i \, h_i$ is an invariant of the system.

The refinement itself is a more creative transformation; it will consists in implementing the intended role of the new variables. This role is formalized as follows.

- As the termination condition is $\neg \exists j \, h_j$, the common guard of the transitions becomes $\exists j \, h_j$.

- If $y_i \not\simeq f_i(y)$, then the assignment $y_i := f_i(y)$ must be executed; furthermore, as this assignment is likely to destroy some or all the relations $y_j \simeq f_j(y)$, for all $j \neq i$, the assignment $h_j := true$ has to be executed, for all $j \neq i$.

- If $y_i \simeq f_i(y)$, then the execution of the assignment $y_i := f_i(y)$ is not needed; as a consequence, the assignment $h_i := false$ is executed.

As a result, the transition

$$(\ell_n^i, \; y_i \not\simeq f_i(y) \; \longrightarrow \; y_i := f_i(y), \; \ell_n^i)$$

is replaced, for all i, by

$$(\ell_n^i, \; \exists j \, h_j \; \longrightarrow \; A_i, \; \ell_n^i),$$

where A_i is the assignment

$$
\begin{pmatrix}
y_i \\
h_1 \\
\vdots \\
h_{i-1} \\
h_i \\
h_{i+1} \\
\vdots \\
h_n
\end{pmatrix}
:= \quad \text{if } y_i \simeq f_i(y) \quad \text{then} \quad
\begin{pmatrix}
y_i \\
h_1 \\
\vdots \\
h_{i-1} \\
false \\
h_{i+1} \\
\vdots \\
h_n
\end{pmatrix}
\quad \text{else} \quad
\begin{pmatrix}
f_i(y) \\
true \\
\vdots \\
true \\
h_i \\
true \\
\vdots \\
true
\end{pmatrix} .
$$

Comment. In the "else" part of this assignment, we can replace "h_i" by "$true$" without risk. We do that for the sake of uniformity.

As the "if-then-else" notation is not convenient, we will avoid it by replacing the transition by two transitions: one for the "then" part and the other for the "else" part. This modification is only notational and does not alter the semantics of the system. The new transitions are

$$(\ell_n^i, \; \exists j \, h_j \wedge y_i \simeq f_i(y) \; \longrightarrow \; h_i := false, \; \ell_n^i),$$
$$(\ell_n^i, \; \exists j \, h_j \wedge y_i \not\simeq f_i(y) \; \longrightarrow \; (y_i, h_1, \ldots, h_n) := (f_i(y), true, \ldots, true), \; \ell_n^i).$$

This system transformation has to be validated by an adaptation of the invariant. Clearly enough, such an adaptation is needed, since the formula I_1 is no longer an invariant of the transformed system. As mentioned in paragraph 4.6, the easiest way to obtain an adequate invariant is to consider first the case of the kth projection of the refinement, where k is a fixed element of $\{1, \ldots, n\}$. The kth projection of the attempted refinement is concerned only with h_k. The variables h_i, $i \neq k$, are never assigned and keep their common initial value $true$; as a result, the guard $\exists i \, h_i$ reduces to $true$ and is omitted. The refined version S_2 is given below.

$$
\begin{aligned}
\mathcal{P}_2 = \mathcal{P}_1 = \ & \{\{\ell_n^i\} : i = 1, \ldots, n\}, \\
\mathcal{M}_2 = \mathcal{M}_1 = \ & \{y_i, h_i : i = 1, \ldots, n\}, \\
\mathcal{T}_2 = \ & \{(\ell_n^i, \ y_i \not\simeq f_i(y) \longrightarrow (y_i, h_k) := (f_i(y), true), \ \ell_n^i) : \\
& i = 1, \ldots, k-1, k+1, \ldots, n\} \\
\cup \ & \{(\ell_n^k, \ y_k \simeq f_k(y) \longrightarrow h_k := false, \ \ell_n^k), \\
& \ (\ell_n^k, \ y_k \not\simeq f_k(y) \longrightarrow (y_k, h_k) := (f_k(y), true), \ \ell_n^k)\}.
\end{aligned}
$$

This refinement is not a sequential decomposition. As a consequence, the first task is to select a refinement condition E, before looking for an invariant $I_2 =_{def} [(E \supset I_1) \wedge (\neg E \supset J)]$. In the present case, this is rather easy. As the refinement introduces the role of h_k, the refinement condition will involve h_k. Furthermore, the formal requirements (§ 3.2) about E are

- $\forall i \, h_i \supset E$;
- $\{\neg E\} \, T \, \{\neg E\}$, for all old transitions.

The second requirement vanishes, since there is no old transition.

Obviously, a simple acceptable choice for E is h_k itself; as no old transition can alter h_k, the second requirement is trivially satisfied, and so is the first one.

The form of the new invariant I_2 will be

$$
\begin{aligned}
I_2 \ & \equiv \ [(E \supset I_1) \wedge (\neg E \supset J)] && \text{definition}, \\
& \equiv \ [(h_k \supset \forall i \, h_i) \wedge (\neg h_k \supset J)] && \text{substitution}, \\
& \equiv \ [(\forall i \neq k) \, h_i \wedge (h_k \supset h_k) \wedge (\neg h_k \supset J)] && h_i \text{ is never assigned for } i \neq k, \\
& \equiv \ [(\forall i \neq k) \, h_i \wedge (h_k \vee J)] && \text{simplification}.
\end{aligned}
$$

The system of constraints (3, §3.2) is

1. $\{\forall i \, h_i\} \, T \, \{h_k \supset \forall i \, h_i\}$, $\qquad T \in N_R$,
2. $\{\forall i \, h_i\} \, T \, \{h_k \vee J\}$, $\qquad T \in N_R$,
3. $\{\neg h_k \wedge J\} \, T \, \{h_k \supset \forall i \, h_i\}$, $\qquad T \in N_R$,
4. $\{\neg h_k \wedge J\} \, T \, \{h_k \vee J\}$, $\qquad T \in T'$.

Comment. In this case, $T' = N_R = \mathcal{T}_2$ since all old transitions have been altered.

As the h_i, $i \neq k$, are never accessed, the formula $(\forall i \neq k) \, h_i$ is an invariant of the new system and is therefore always true; this induces some simplification of the set of constraints, which is rewritten into

1. $\{h_k\} \, T \, \{true\}$, $\qquad T \in \mathcal{T}_2$,
2. $\{h_k\} \, T \, \{h_k \vee J\}$, $\qquad T \in \mathcal{T}_2$,
3. $\{\neg h_k \wedge J\} \, T \, \{true\}$, $\qquad T \in \mathcal{T}_2$,
4. $\{\neg h_k \wedge J\} \, T \, \{h_k \vee J\}$, $\qquad T \in \mathcal{T}_2$.

Groups 1 and 3 are always satisfied and can be omitted. Groups 2 and 4 are explicited into

2a. $\{h_k\}\ y_i \not\simeq f_i(y) \longrightarrow (y_i, h_k) := (f_i(y), true)\ \{h_k \vee J\}$, for all $i \neq k$;

2b. $\{h_k\}\ y_k \simeq f_k(y) \longrightarrow h_k := false\ \{h_k \vee J\}$;

2c. $\{h_k\}\ y_k \simeq f_k(y) \longrightarrow (y_k, h_k) := (f_k(y), true)\ \{h_k \vee J\}$;

4a. $\{\neg h_k \wedge J\}\ y_i \not\simeq f_i(y) \longrightarrow (y_i, h_k) := (f_i(y), true)\ \{h_k \vee J\}$, for all $i \neq k$;

4b. $\{\neg h_k \wedge J\}\ y_k \simeq f_k(y) \longrightarrow h_k := false\ \{h_k \vee J\}$;

4c. $\{\neg h_k \wedge J\}\ y_k \simeq f_k(y) \longrightarrow (y_k, h_k) := (f_k(y), true)\ \{h_k \vee J\}$;

Groups 2a, 2c, 4a and 4c are satisfied for any choice of J; the two remaining constraints are rewritten into

2b. $[y_k \simeq f_k(y) \wedge \neg h_k] \supset J$,

4b. $\{\neg h_k \wedge J \wedge y_k \simeq f_k(y)\}\ h_k := false\ \{J\}$.

Obviously, the choice $J =_{def} true$ is formally acceptable but, as mentioned earlier, we are interested in as strong invariants as possible. The strongest possible choice, given by constraint 2b, is $J =_{def} [y_k \simeq f_k(y) \wedge \neg h_k]$; as this choice also satisfies 4b, it can be adopted. The new invariant will be

$$I_2 \equiv [(\forall i \neq k)\, h_i \wedge (h_k \vee J)],$$
$$\equiv [(\forall i \neq k)\, h_i \wedge (h_k \vee [y_k \simeq f_k(y) \wedge \neg h_k])],$$
$$\equiv [(\forall i \neq k)\, h_i \wedge (h_k \vee y_k \simeq f_k(y))].$$

Comment. Let us observe that the invariant simply expresses in a formal way the intended meaning of the new variable h_k: it has to be true as long as the kth component of the identity $y \simeq f(y)$ is not reached. This is a rather usual phenomenon: the set of constraints has to be solved, but an educated guess can spare much symbolic computation.

The full multiple refinement can now be considered. Let the system S_3 be the result of this transformation.

$$\mathcal{P}_3 = \{\{\ell_n^i\} : i = 1, \ldots, n\},$$
$$\mathcal{M}_3 = \{y_i, h_i : i = 1, \ldots, n\},$$
$$\mathcal{T}_3 = \{(\ell_n^i, \exists j\, h_j \wedge y_i \simeq f_i(y) \longrightarrow h_i := false, \ell_n^i),$$
$$(\ell_n^i, \exists j\, h_j \wedge y_i \not\simeq f_i(y) \longrightarrow (y_i, h_1, \ldots, h_n) := (f_i(y), true, \ldots, true), \ell_n^i) :$$
$$i = 1, \ldots, n\},$$

The invariant I_2 has been obtained from the invariant I_1 by replacing the old assertion h_k by the new assertion $(h_k \vee y_k \simeq f_k(y))$. Hopefully, the invariant I_3 will be obtained by a similar replacement, applied to the assertions h_i, $i \neq k$. This leads to

$$I_3 =_{def} \forall i\, [h_i \vee y_i \simeq f_i(y)].$$

The validity of this invariant is checked in a straightforward way, and the crucial step of the design is completed.

Comment. It appears now that the weak choice $J =_{def} true$ is not acceptable, because it leads to $I_3 \equiv true$, which is useless.

5.4 Towards a fine-grained version

The version S_3 is more satisfactory than the version S_0, from the point of view of termination detection. Unfortunately, this transformation has induced conditional multiple assignments, which have to be executed like atomic statements. It is indicated to decompose these multiple assignments into sequences of more elementary statements; these transformations do not require creativity.

First multiple sequential decomposition.

The multiple assignments

$$(y_i, h_1, \ldots, h_n) := (f_i(y), true, \ldots, true)\,,\ i = 1, \ldots, n\,,$$

are tentatively replaced by the sequences

$$y_i := f_i(y);\ (h_1, \ldots, h_n) := (true, \ldots, true)\,,\ i = 1, \ldots, n\,.$$

As a first step, only the kth projection of this refinement is considered. The preliminary transformation consists in the introduction of a new label ℓ_0^k in process $\{\ell_n^k\}$. The refinement itself is the replacement given above, restricted to $i = k$. This leads to the system S_4 given below.

$$
\begin{aligned}
\mathcal{P}_4 =&\ \{\{\ell_n^i\} : i = 1, \ldots, k-1, k+1, \ldots, n\} \cup \{\{\ell_n^k, \ell_0^k\}\}\,,\\
\mathcal{M}_4 =&\ \{y_i, h_i : i = 1, \ldots, n\}\,,\\
\mathcal{T}_4 =&\quad \{(\ell_n^i,\ \exists j\, h_j \wedge y_i \simeq f_i(y)\ \longrightarrow\ h_i := false,\ \ell_n^i)\,,\\
&\quad\ (\ell_n^i,\ \exists j\, h_j \wedge y_i \not\simeq f_i(y)\ \longrightarrow\ (y_i, h_1, \ldots, h_n) := (f_i(y), true, \ldots, true),\ \ell_n^i)\ :\\
&\quad\ i = 1, \ldots, k-1, k+1, \ldots, n\}\\
&\cup \{(\ell_n^k,\ \exists j\, h_j \wedge y_k \simeq f_k(y)\ \longrightarrow\ h_k := false,\ \ell_n^k)\,,\\
&\quad\ (\ell_n^k,\ \exists j\, h_j \wedge y_k \not\simeq f_k(y)\ \longrightarrow\ y_k := f_k(y),\ \ell_0^k)\,,\\
&\quad\ (\ell_0^k,\ (h_1, \ldots, h_n) := (true, \ldots, true),\ \ell_n^k)\}\,,\\
\mathcal{I}_4 =&\ [(at\ \ell_n^k \supset I_3) \wedge (at\ \ell_0^k \supset J)]\,.
\end{aligned}
$$

The set of constraints is stated easily and reduces to

1. $true$,
2. $(\forall i [h_i \vee y_i \simeq f_i(y)] \wedge \exists j\, h_j \wedge y_k \simeq f_k(y)) \supset J$,
3. $J \supset true$,
4. $\{J\}\, (\ell_n^i \to \ell_n^i)\, \{J\}$, for all $i \neq k$.

The strongest possible choice, given by constraint 2, appears to be not respected by constraints of group 4. Fortunately, the weakest choice, given by constraint 3, is acceptable here. As a result, we select

$$I_4 =_{def} (at\ \ell_n^k \supset \forall i [h_i \vee y_i \simeq f_i(y)])\,.$$

The second step consists in completing the multiple refinement (the replacement done for k is now done for all $i = 1, \ldots, n$). This leads to the system S_5 given below.

$$
\begin{aligned}
\mathcal{P}_5 =&\ \{\{\ell_n^i, \ell_0^i\} : i = 1, \ldots, n\}\,,\\
\mathcal{M}_5 =&\ \{y_i, h_i : i = 1, \ldots, n\}\,,\\
\mathcal{T}_5 =&\ \{(\ell_n^i,\ \exists j\, h_j \wedge y_i \simeq f_i(y)\ \longrightarrow\ h_i := false,\ \ell_n^i)\,,\\
&\quad\ (\ell_n^i,\ \exists j\, h_j \wedge y_i \not\simeq f_i(y)\ \longrightarrow\ y_i := f_i(y),\ \ell_0^i)\,,\\
&\quad\ (\ell_0^i,\ (h_1, \ldots, h_n) := (true, \ldots, true),\ \ell_n^i)\ :\\
&\quad\ i = 1, \ldots, n\}\,,\\
\mathcal{I}_5 =&\ (at\, (\ell_n^1 \ldots \ell_n^m) \supset \forall i [h_i \vee y_i \simeq f_i(y)])\,.
\end{aligned}
$$

Second multiple sequential decomposition.

Further sequential decomposition is possible; the next refinement will be the replacement of the multiple assignment $(h_1, \ldots, h_n) := (true, \ldots, true)$ by a sequence of n simple assignments.

As a first step, the transition

$$(\ell_0^k,\ (h_1, \ldots, h_n) := (true, \ldots, true),\ \ell_n^k)$$

is replaced by the new transitions

$$(\ell_0^k, (h_1, \ldots, h_r) := (true, \ldots, true), \ell_r^k),$$
$$(\ell_r^k, (h_{r+1}, \ldots, h_n) := (true, \ldots, true), \ell_n^k),$$

where k and r are arbitrary elements of $\{1, \ldots, n\}$. (As a preliminary transformation, a new label ℓ_r^k is added to the process $\{\ell_0^k, \ell_n^k\}$.) This refinement results in a system S_6 whose invariant will be

$$I_6 =_{def} \quad [at\,(\ell_n^1 \ldots \ell_n^{k-1} \ell_n^k \ell_n^{k+1} \ldots \ell_n^m) \supset \forall i (h_i \vee y_i \simeq f_i(y))]$$
$$\wedge \quad [at\,(\ell_n^1 \ldots \ell_n^{k-1} \ell_r^k \ell_n^{k+1} \ldots \ell_n^m) \supset J].$$

The usual technique leads to select $J =_{def} (\forall i \le r)(h_i \vee y_i \simeq f_i(y))$.

As a second step, we consider the insertion of the new labels ℓ_j^k, for $j \neq r$, and the corresponding refinement of the statement $(h_1, \ldots, h_n) := (true, \ldots, true)$ into a sequence of n assignments instead of two; this leads to a system S_7, whose invariant is easily found to be

$$I_7 =_{def} \quad [at\,(\ell_n^1 \ldots \ell_n^{k-1} \ell_1^k \ell_n^{k+1} \ldots \ell_n^m) \supset (h_1 \vee y_1 \simeq f_1(y))]$$
$$\vdots \qquad\qquad \vdots \qquad\qquad \vdots$$
$$\wedge \quad [at\,(\ell_n^1 \ldots \ell_n^{k-1} \ell_r^k \ell_n^{k+1} \ldots \ell_n^m) \supset (\forall i \le r)(h_i \vee y_i \simeq f_i(y))]$$
$$\vdots \qquad\qquad \vdots \qquad\qquad \vdots$$
$$\wedge \quad [at\,(\ell_n^1 \ldots \ell_n^{k-1} \ell_n^k \ell_n^{k+1} \ldots \ell_n^m) \supset \forall i (h_i \vee y_i \simeq f_i(y))].$$

which is rewritten into

$$I_7 =_{def} \forall r\,[at\,(\ell_n^1 \ldots \ell_n^{k-1} \ell_r^k \ell_n^{k+1} \ldots \ell_n^m) \supset (\forall i \le r)(h_i \vee y_i \simeq f_i(y))].$$

The third step consists in applying the preceding steps to all i; this results into the system S_8 given below.

$$\mathcal{P}_8 = \{\{\ell_j^i : j = 0, \ldots, n\} : i = 1, \ldots, n\},$$
$$\mathcal{M}_8 = \{y_i, h_i : i = 1, \ldots, n\},$$
$$\mathcal{T}_8 = \{(\ell_n^i, \exists j\, h_j \wedge y_i \simeq f_i(y) \longrightarrow h_i := false, \ell_n^i),$$
$$(\ell_n^i, \exists j\, h_j \wedge y_i \not\simeq f_i(y) \longrightarrow y_i := f_i(y), \ell_0^i),$$
$$(\ell_{j-1}^i, h_j := true, \ell_j^i) : j = 1, \ldots, n :$$
$$i = 1, \ldots, n\}$$

The invariant of this system will be

$$I_8 =_{def} \forall j_1 \cdots \forall j_n\,[at\,(\ell_{j_1}^1, \ell_{j_2}^2, \ldots, \ell_{j_n}^m) \supset J(j_1, j_2, \ldots, j_n)],$$

where the j_k's can take any value in $\{1, \ldots, n\}$. The expressions $J(j_1, j_2, \ldots, j_n)$ must be generalized from the knowledge inherited from I_7: $J(j_1, \ldots, j_n)$ reduces to $(\forall i \le r)(h_i \vee y_i \simeq f_i(y))$ when all the j_i's are n except one of them whose value is r. An appropriate generalization is

$$J(j_1, j_2, \ldots, j_n) =_{def} (\forall i \le \inf(j_1, \ldots, j_n))(h_i \vee y_i \simeq f_i(y)).$$

This choice is shown to be appropriate by direct verification of the constraints listed below.

$$\{J(j_1, \ldots, j_{k-1}, u-1, j_{k+1}, \ldots, j_n)\}\, h_u := true\, \{J(j_1, \ldots, j_{k-1}, u, j_{k+1}, \ldots, j_n)\}$$
$$\{J(j_1, \ldots, j_{k-1}, n, j_{k+1}, \ldots, j_n) \wedge \exists l\, h_l \wedge y_k \simeq f_k(y)\}\, h_k := false\, \{J(j_1, \ldots, j_{k-1}, n, j_{k+1}, \ldots, j_n)\}$$
$$\{J(j_1, \ldots, j_{k-1}, n, j_{k+1}, \ldots, j_n) \wedge \exists l\, h_l \wedge y_k \not\simeq f_k(y)\}\, y_k := f_k(y)\, \{J(j_1, \ldots, j_{k-1}, 0, j_{k+1}, \ldots, j_n)\}$$

Third multiple sequential decomposition.

As a further refinement, we consider the possibility to test the termination condition (about $h_1, \ldots, h_n$) and the condition about y in distinct transitions. Here is only the result.

$$
\begin{aligned}
\mathcal{P}_9 =\ & \{\{\ell_j^i : j = 0, \ldots, n+1\} : i = 1, \ldots, n\}, \\
\mathcal{M}_9 =\ & \{y_i, h_i : i = 1, \ldots, n\}, \\
\mathcal{T}_9 =\ & \{(\ell_n^i, \exists j\, h_j \longrightarrow skip, \ell_{n+1}^i), \\
& \quad (\ell_{n+1}^i, y_i \simeq f_i(y) \longrightarrow h_i := false, \ell_n^i), \\
& \quad (\ell_{n+1}^i, y_i \not\simeq f_i(y) \longrightarrow y_i := f_i(y), \ell_0^i), \\
& \quad (\ell_{j-1}^i, h_j := true, \ell_j^i) : j = 1, \ldots, n\ : \\
& \quad i = 1, \ldots, n\}, \\
\mathcal{I}_9 =\ & \forall j_1 \cdots \forall j_n\, (\, at(\ell_{j_1}^1 \ldots \ell_{j_n}^n) \supset [\forall i \le \inf(n, j_1, \ldots, j_n)\,(h_i \vee y_i \simeq f_i(y))]).
\end{aligned}
$$

Comment. The index set for the j_i is now $\{1, \ldots, n+1\}$ instead of $\{1, \ldots, n\}$.

Further refinements could be attempted.

6 Related work and further work

We have attempted to formalize the methodology of stepwise refinement, but the work has been completed only for the most elementary kind of refinement, i.e., the sequential decomposition.

Several authors have considered more elaborate kinds of refinements. The problem of *decentralization* is defined and investigated in [3] (see also [4]). Roughly speaking, a system is decentralized when it can be implemented as a set of communicating sequential processes. In particular, all transitions involve one or two processes and each variable x belongs to a process P, which means that x can be evoked only in transitions involving P. Furthermore, the condition of a transition involving two processes is restricted in such a way that "each process can determine by itself whether to participate in an action or not". These requirements are rather restrictive and are usually not satisfied by arbitrary systems. However, the stepwise refinement technique can be used to transform an arbitrary system into a decentralized one; the refinements are not trivial and creativity is needed. For instance, decentralized systems for mutual exclusions are definitely more complex then centralized ones [36]. The transformation of arbitrary systems into decentralized ones is worth further investigation, especially to identify the step(s) where creativity is needed.

Decentralized systems can be further refined, for instance to check whether the synchronous communication scheme can be replaced by an asynchronous one; this problem is considered in [19]. In the framework of asynchronous distributed systems, the notion of refinement has been introduced in [30]; a general formalism is presented which allows to model a system at several level of detail. A related approach, evoked in [26], consists in proving a high-level version of a system, and then establishing that a lower-level version is a faithful implementation of it. The notion of state function, introduced in the same paper, allows to formalize the effect of sequential decomposition on the invariant. Let us also recall that many formal proofs of parallel algorithms have been obtained by variants of the stepwise refinement method [16,1,6].

The notions of stepwise refinement and data refinement have received much attention in the area of sequential programming. Some relevant papers and books are [14,20,33,2,31,32]. In our opinion, the results obtained in the sequential framework should also be obtained in the concurrent framework. An important step in this direction is [7].

The formal tools used in this paper (transition systems, predicate transformers, Hoare logic) have also been the subject of many papers. Some references have already been mentioned; additional ones are [25,27] and [10], where a variant of Hoare logic is introduced and investigated. The variant used in this paper is simpler, since the formalism of structured transition systems is simpler than the usual programming languages. Several papers and books already mentioned are also devoted to predicate transformers (several systems of notation are used); varieties of the operator wlp are presented in [34]. Predicate transformers in the framework of (classical) transition systems are presented in [37].

The notion of structured transition system is obtained, first, from the classical flowchart notation and, second, from the formalism of transition system presented in [37]. From the theoretical point of view, the introduction of labels and processes is not needed and, even from a more practical point of view, these concepts are not mandatory, as demonstrated in [7]. However, labels are often more convenient than auxiliary variables in concurrent programming (see e.g. [29]). In our opinion, this is especially true in the framework of stepwise refinement, since labels and place predicates have a prominent role for sequential decomposition. As an illustration, one can try to rewrite some pairs (system, invariant) presented in section 5 in a classical programming notation, e.g. the notation introduced in [35]. In most cases, this translation requires the introduction of adequate "program counters".

In the present paper, a method is proposed to check whether an informal refinement can be extended into a formal (correct) refinement, but no general decision criterion is given. More precisely, the failure of the method does not necessarily imply that no formal refinement exists. The method can be made complete if fixpoint operators are used. Appropriate fixpoint operators have been introduced by several authors; see e.g. [38,8,28]. As our ultimate purpose is the design of an interactive system for the development of concurrent programs, we have avoided the introduction of fixpoint operators, which cannot always be computed explicitly (even when special approximation methods are used; see [9,11]). The usefulness of fixpoint operators in the context of stepwise refinement can be summarized as follows. If (S, I) is a pair (system, invariant) and if S' is obtained from S by an informal refinement, then the strongest invariant I' of S' is the solution of a fixpoint equation. Provided that this equation can be explicitly solved, one can see whether I' is strong enough to guarantee some specified invariance property.

7 Conclusion

The usual concept of stepwise refinement has proved very useful in the area of parallel programs design. However, due to the lack of formality of this concept, proofs based on it appear rather subtle. More precisely, the reader of such proofs is convinced of the validity of the applied refinements, but may wonder how the author has distinguished valid refinements from non-valid ones, when designing the program and the proof.

The solution proposed here is: do not try to guess whether some possible refinement is valid or not; just write down the corresponding set of constraints and try to solve it. The refinement is valid if this simple procedure succeeds. In this paper, only the most elementary kind of refinement has been considered, but many refinements used in parallel programming can be formalized as the sequential decomposition.

Last, it is important to note that the systems of constraints induced by tentative refinements can be large, but the solving procedure can be partly mechanized.

References

[1] K.R. APT, "Correctness Proofs of Distributed Termination Algorithms", ACM Toplas, vol. 8, pp. 388-405, 1986

[2] R.J.R. BACK, "A Calculus of Refinements for Program Derivations", Acta Informatica, vol. 25, pp. 593-624, 1988

[3] R.J.R. BACK and R. KURKI-SUONIO, "Decentralization of Process Nets with Centralized Control", Proc. 2nd ACM Symp. on Principles of Distributed Computing, pp. 131-142, 1983

[4] R.J.R. BACK and R. KURKI-SUONIO, "Distributed Cooperation with Action Systems", ACM Toplas, vol. 10, pp. 513-554, 1988

[5] E. BEST, "A Note on the Proof of a Concurrent Program", IPL, vol. 9, pp. 103-104, 1979

[6] M. CHANDY and J. MISRA, "An Example of Stepwise Refinement of Distributed Programs: Quiescence Detection", ACM Toplas, vol. 8, pp. 326-343, 1986

[7] M. CHANDY and J. MISRA, "Parallel Program Design: A Foundation", Addison-Wesley, 1988.

[8] E.M. CLARKE, "Synthesis of Resource Invariants for Concurrent Programs", ACM Toplas, vol. 2, pp. 338-358, 1980

[9] P. COUSOT and R. COUSOT, "Abstract interpretation: a unified lattice model for static analysis of programs by construction or approximation of fixpoints", Proc. 4th ACM Symp. on Principles of Programming Languages, pp. 238-252, 1977

[10] P. COUSOT and R. COUSOT, "A Language Independent Proof of the Soundness and Completeness of Generalized Hoare Logic", Information and Computation, vol. 80, pp. 165-191, 1989

[11] P. COUSOT and N. HALBWACHS, "Automatic discovery of linear restraints among variables of a program", Proc. 5th ACM Symp. on Principles of Programming Languages, pp. 84-96, 1978

[12] J.W. de BAKKER and L.G.L.T. MEERTENS, "On the completeness of the inductive assertion method", JCSS, vol. 11, pp. 323-357, 1975

[13] J.W. de BAKKER, "Mathematical Theory of Program Correctness", Prentice Hall, New Jersey, 1980

[14] E.W. DIJKSTRA, "A discipline of programming", Prentice Hall, New Jersey, 1976

[15] E.W. DIJKSTRA, "A correctness proof for networks of communicating processes: a small exercise", EWD 607, Burroughs, The Netherlands, 1977

[16] E.W. DIJKSTRA and al., "On-the-Fly Garbage Collection: An Exercise in Cooperation", CACM, vol. 21, pp. 966-975, 1978

[17] E.W. DIJKSTRA, "Finding the Correctness Proof of a Concurrent Program", LNCS, vol. 69, pp. 24-34, 1979

[18] E.W. DIJKSTRA, "On the Interplay between Mathematics and Programming", LNCS, vol. 69, pp. 35-46, 1979

[19] E.P. GRIBOMONT, "From synchronous to asynchronous communication", Workshop BCS-FACS on Specification and Verification of Concurrent Systems (Stirling, Scotland, 1988), to appear in "FACS Workshop Series", vol 1, 1989

[20] D. GRIES, "The Science of Programming", Springer-Verlag, Berlin, 1981

[21] C.A.R. HOARE, "An axiomatic basis for computer programming", CACM, vol. 12, pp. 576-583, 1969

[22] C.A.R. HOARE, "Communicating Sequential Processes", CACM, vol. 21, pp. 666-677, 1978

[23] C.A.R. HOARE, "Communicating Sequential Processes", Prentice-Hall, 1985

[24] R.M. KELLER, "Formal Verification of Parallel Programs", CACM, vol. 19, pp. 371-384, 1976

[25] L. LAMPORT, "The 'Hoare Logic' of Concurrent Programs", Acta Informatica, vol. 14, pp. 21-37, 1980

[26] L. LAMPORT, "An Assertional Correctness Proof of a Distributed Algorithm", Science of Computer Programming, vol. 2, pp. 175-206, 1983

[27] L. LAMPORT and F.B. SCHNEIDER, "The 'Hoare Logic' of CSP, and All That", ACM Toplas, vol. 6, pp. 281-296, 1984

[28] L. LAMPORT, "win and sin: Predicate Transformers for Concurrency", DEC SRC Report 17, 1987

[29] L. LAMPORT, "Control Predicates are Better than Dummy Variables for Reasoning about Program Control", ACM Toplas, vol. 10, pp. 267-281, 1988

[30] N.A. LYNCH and M.R. TUTTLE, "Hierarchical Correctness Proofs for Distributed Algorithms", Proc. 6th ACM Symp. on Principles of Distributed Computing, pp. 137-151, 1987

[31] C. MORGAN, "The Specification Statement", ACM Toplas, vol. 10, pp. 403-419, 1988

[32] C. MORGAN, "Auxiliary variables in data refinement", IPL, vol. 29, pp. 293-296, 1988

[33] J. MORRIS, "A theoretical basis for stepwise refinement and the programming calculus", Science of Computer Programming, vol. 9, pp. 287-306, 1987

[34] J.M. MORRIS, "Varieties of weakest liberal preconditions", IPL, vol. 25, pp. 207-210, 1987

[35] S. OWICKI and D. GRIES, "An Axiomatic Proof Technique for Parallel programs", Acta Informatica, vol. 6, pp 319-340, 1976

[36] M. RAYNAL, "Algorithms for Mutual Exclusion", North Oxford Academic, 1986

[37] J. SIFAKIS, "A unified approach for studying the properties of transition systems", TCS, vol. 18, pp. 227-259, 1982

[38] A. van LAMSWEERDE and M. SINTZOFF, "Formal derivation of strongly correct concurrent programs", Acta Informatica, vol. 12, pp. 1-31, 1979

Deriving Mixed Evaluation from Standard Evaluation for a Simple Functional Language

JOHN HANNAN and DALE MILLER

Department of Computer and Information Science
University of Pennsylvania
Philadelphia, PA 19104-6389 USA

We demonstrate how a specification for the standard evaluation of a simple functional programming language can be systematically extended to a specification for mixed evaluation. Using techniques inspired by natural semantics we specify a standard evaluator by a set of inference rules. The evaluation of programs is then performed by a restricted kind of theorem proving in this logic. We then describe a systematic method for extending the proof system for standard evaluation to a new proof system that provides greater flexibility in treating bound variables in the object-level functional programs. We demonstrate how this extended proof system provides the capabilities of a mixed evaluator and how correctness with respect to standard evaluation can be proved in a simple and direct manner. The current work focuses only on a primitive notion of mixed evaluation for a simple functional programming language, but we believe that our methods will extend to more sophisticated kinds of evaluations and richer languages.

1   Introduction

The formal derivation and correctness of program analysis tools play a central role in many programming language research efforts. In this paper we focus on evaluators for programming languages. We shall use natural deduction techniques to specify and derive evaluators for a simple functional language. With a natural deduction theorem prover, one constructs formal proofs of propositions using a particular set of inference rules. If we encode programs as terms then we can build propositions expressing relationships between programs. A proof system can then axiomatize such relationships. This approach to program analysis shares much with the work on structural operational semantics [19] and natural semantics [12].

Since what we shall call "mixed evaluation" is related to the terms "partial evaluation" and "mixed computation," we provide a brief description of our use of these terms. *Standard evaluation* refers to a conventional notion of evaluation or interpretation of functional programs. *Partial evaluation* is a systematic method of constructing an efficient program based on a given program and a part of its input [3]. In general terms, it can be described as follows. Let f be some functional program of two arguments x and y and consider the application $f(c, y)$ for some constant (known) value c and variable (unknown) value y. We wish to construct a new functional program f_c such that $f_c(y) = f(c, y)$ for all values of y, such that for any value of y, computing $f_c(y)$ should be easier (or faster) than computing $f(c, y)$. Such improvement is possible by "compiling" the information that $x = c$ in f into the definition of f_c.

Mixed evaluation, also called *symbolic evaluation* in [5], is the process of evaluating expressions, which may contain free variables (i.e., not bound to any values), to some canonical form. This process must deal with the proper treatment of the interaction of known and unknown (symbolic) values and hence the adjective "mixed." The key task of mixed evaluation is making *maximal use* of the partial information or performing as much computation in advance *as possible*. Unfortunately, there are languages for which no evaluation strategy can perform such maximal compiling [10]. We would, however, like to produce mixed evaluators that are capable of a reasonable level of performance.

The importance of mixed evaluation was elucidated by Futamura [3] when he described the construction of compiled programs, compilers, and compiler generators via mixed evaluation. Thus mixed evaluation is a means for understanding and constructing a wide range of translation tools. *But where do mixed evaluators come from?* In particular, can mixed evaluators be formally derived from standard evaluators? Few research efforts have addressed the formal construction of mixed evaluators using principled techniques. We address this question by demonstrating how, for a simple functional programming language, a specification for mixed evaluation can be derived from a specification for standard evaluation.

The remainder of this paper is organized as follows. In Section 2 we introduce a simple functional programming language, giving both a concrete and an abstract syntax. Following this we specify a standard evaluator for this language in Section 3. In Section 4 we use the signature of the functional program's abstract syntax to construct a mixed evaluator and in Section 5 we prove a form of its correctness. Issues of implementation are discussed in Section 6. Summary comments and a description of related work are provided in Section 7.

2 Abstract Syntax as Lambda Terms

We introduce a simple functional programming language for which we shall specify two evaluators in subsequent sections. There is strong connection between the choice of *abstract syntax* for the formal representation of functional programs and the complexity of the presentation of these evaluators. An appropriate choice of abstract syntax will

$$C : tm \qquad\qquad\qquad lamb : (tm \rightarrow tm) \rightarrow tm$$
$$if : tm \rightarrow tm \rightarrow tm \rightarrow tm \qquad let : (tm \rightarrow tm) \rightarrow tm \rightarrow tm$$
$$@ : tm \rightarrow tm \rightarrow tm \qquad\qquad fix : (tm \rightarrow tm) \rightarrow tm$$

FIGURE 1

Typed Constants of E

ater facilitate our specification of simple and declarative evaluators. It is this simple
and declarative aspects of one evaluator (for standard evaluation) that will permit it to
•e simply and automatically enhanced to yield another evaluator (for mixed evaluation).

We distinguish between *concrete syntax*, which provides a convenient human-readable
•resentation for programs, and abstract syntax. Let E be the functional language whose
concrete syntax is defined by the following grammar:

$$E \quad ::= \quad C \mid x \mid \text{ if } E \text{ then } E \text{ else } E \mid (E\ E) \mid$$
$$\lambda x.E \mid \text{ let } x = E \text{ in } E \mid \text{ fix } x.E$$

The symbol C ranges over primitive constants that are assumed to be the integers and
•ooleans.

We now define an abstract syntax for the programs of E. We shall view an evaluator
.s a (meta-)program that manipulates terms denoting E-programs. Thus we must define
he set of terms and a method for encoding E-programs into such terms. We shall use
imply typed λ-terms as the representation language. To define our abstract syntax for
E we begin by introducing the base type tm and a set of typed constants that we shall
ıse to construct terms denoting E-programs. (See Figure 1.) Notice that the constants
amb, *let* and *fix* are second-order, that is, they each require a functional argument of
ype $tm \rightarrow tm$. In the examples that follow, M will be used as a second-order variable
•f this meta-type and e_i and α_i will be meta-variables of type tm.

Using the new constants of Figure 1 we can build up λ-terms forming an abstract
•yntax for E as follows. For constants and variables in the concrete syntax we introduce
.ssociated constants and variables of type tm to the abstract syntax. For the if statement
we introduce the new constant if such that if the three terms e_1, e_2, e_3 are of type tm,
hen $(if\ e_1\ e_2\ e_3)$ is a term of type tm. Application is made explicit with the infix
•perator '@' so that $e_1 @ e_2$ represents the expression denoted by the term e_1 applied to
e_2. For lambda abstraction we introduce the constructor *lamb* that takes a meta-level
.bstraction of the form $\lambda x.e$, in which x and e are of meta-type tm, and produces a
•erm of type tm. For example, the concrete syntax for lambda abstraction is $\lambda x.E$ while
ts abstract syntax form is $(lamb\ \lambda x.e)$ (in which e is the abstract syntax form of E).
Similar to *lamb*, the *let* construct uses a meta-term M of the form $\lambda x.e$ to represent the
•inding of an identifier. Thus the concrete syntax let $x = E_1$ in E_2 is given by the
.bstract term $(let\ \lambda x.e_2\ e_1)$ in which e_1 and e_2 are the abstract syntax forms of E_1 and

E_2, respectively. To represent the recursive fix construct we introduce the *fix* constant, which again uses an explicit abstraction to capture the binding. An example of this construction is given below.

The language E shall also contain several constants denoting lists and primitive operations on list. That is, we shall assume that E also contains the constants *cons, nil, car, cdr,* and *null* all at primitive type *tm*. Given this typing scheme, to apply the constant *null* to an argument, say *e*, we must write (*null@e*). It is possible to provide *null* with the type *tm* → *tm* and to write this application as simply (*null tm*). For most aspects of this paper, this choice of typing for these primitive constants will not make a significant difference. We shall, however, adopt the convention that those functions that do not correspond to special forms in ML will be denoted with the simple type *tm*.

We will not discuss any primitive operations on integers or booleans in this paper. They are, of course, important to have in the full language but including them here is neither difficult nor illuminating. In the following and subsequent examples, we systematically drop the apply "@" operator in order to make examples more readable. Consider the following expression that defines the append function and then applies it to two lists.

> let app = (fix f.λk.λl.(if (empty k) then l else (cons (hd k) (f (tl k) l))))
> in (app [1] [2]).

The corresponding term in the abstract syntax is

> (*let* λ*app* (*app* (*cons* 1 *nil*) (*cons* 2 *nil*))
>   (*fix* λ*f*(*lamb* λ*k*(*lamb* λ*l*(*if* (*empty k*) *l* (*cons* (*hd k*) (*f* (*tl k*) *l*)))))))).

Note how the four bindings in the concrete syntax (**app, f, k, l**) are translated into explicit λ-abstractions in the abstract syntax.

We shall assume that the reader is familiar with the notions of β-conversion and β-normal form for simply typed λ-terms. For discussions on the motivation and advantages of using simply typed λ-terms to encode functional programs, see [7, 8, 11, 13, 18].

3   Standard Evaluation

We now present an evaluator for E, which we shall call the standard evaluator for E to distinguish it from a second evaluator defined later. We shall divide the description of this evaluator into two parts. The *declarative* aspects of it shall be presented using a proof system similar in style to structural operational semantics and natural semantics [12, 19]. Computing will be equated to finding proofs in this proof system. The *control* aspects of this evaluator, that is, the search strategy used to find proofs, shall be particularly simple for the standard evaluator. Control of our second evaluator will be much more difficult. Logic programming provides a good setting for relating these different aspects of evaluators. A particularly relevant logic programming language is discussed in Section 6.

To represent the proposition that a given program evaluates to a particular value, we

$$c \longrightarrow c \tag{1}$$

$$\frac{e_1 \longrightarrow true \qquad e_2 \longrightarrow \alpha}{(if\ e_1\ e_2\ e_3) \longrightarrow \alpha} \qquad \frac{e_1 \longrightarrow false \qquad e_3 \longrightarrow \alpha}{(if\ e_1\ e_2\ e_3) \longrightarrow \alpha} \tag{2a, 2b}$$

$$(lamb\ M) \longrightarrow (lamb\ M) \tag{3}$$

$$\frac{e_1 \longrightarrow (lamb\ M) \qquad e_2 \longrightarrow \alpha_2 \qquad (M\ \alpha_2) \longrightarrow \alpha}{(e_1 @ e_2) \longrightarrow \alpha} \tag{4}$$

$$\frac{e_2 \longrightarrow \alpha_2 \qquad (M\ \alpha_2) \longrightarrow \alpha}{(let\ M\ e_2) \longrightarrow \alpha} \qquad \frac{(M\ (fix\ M)) \longrightarrow \alpha}{(fix\ M) \longrightarrow \alpha} \tag{5, 6}$$

FIGURE 2

nference Rules for the Standard Evaluator for E

need to add to our term language a new type o for proposition, and a binary, infix constant $\longrightarrow$ of type $tm \rightarrow tm \rightarrow o$. The basic propositions for both evaluators we consider will, therefore, be of the form $e \longrightarrow e'$ where e and e' are both closed λ-terms denoting expressions of E. If this proposition is provable then we shall say that e evaluates to e'. Since evaluation is represented as a relation, a given program may "evaluate" to more than one value. While this is not true of the standard evaluator (see Proposition 3.1), it will be true of our second evaluator.

The declarative aspects of the standard evaluator are given by inference rules provided in Figure 2. Proofs using these rules are defined in the usual, natural deduction fashion with only the following difference. Whenever an inference rule involves a formula of the form (Me) where M is a term of type $tm \rightarrow tm$ and of the form $\lambda x\ t$, then we shall assume that this non-β-normal term is an abbreviation for the term that results from substituting e for the free occurrences of variable x in the term t. Notice that if M and e are β-normal terms of E, then the result of this substitution is again a β-normal term of E. That is, no new redexes are introduced by substitution. For this reason, we shall generally limit ourselves to considering only proofs in which all terms from E are in β-normal form. The non-β-normal terms appearing in the inference rules for $lamb$, fix, and @ are intended as a shorthand for β-normal terms.

If the proposition $e \longrightarrow e'$ has a proof using only the inference rules in Figures 2 and 3 then we shall write $\vdash_{se} e \longrightarrow e'$ and refer to the resulting proof as an se-proof. Notice that any such proof does not use two structural aspects of general natural deduction proofs: arguments from hypotheses and critical variables (eigen-variables). Our second

$$nil \longrightarrow nil \qquad\qquad \frac{e_1 \longrightarrow \alpha_1 \qquad e_2 \longrightarrow \alpha_2}{(cons\ e_1\ e_2) \longrightarrow (cons\ \alpha_1\ \alpha_2)}$$

$$\frac{e \longrightarrow (cons\ \alpha_1\ \alpha_2)}{(car\ e) \longrightarrow \alpha_1} \qquad\qquad \frac{e \longrightarrow (cons\ \alpha_1\ \alpha_2)}{(cdr\ e) \longrightarrow \alpha_2}$$

$$\frac{e \longrightarrow nil}{(null\ e) \longrightarrow true} \qquad\qquad \frac{e \longrightarrow (cons\ \alpha_1\ \alpha_2)}{(null\ e) \longrightarrow false}$$

FIGURE 3
Additional Inference Rules for Some Primitive Constants

interpreter, however, will make use of both of these aspects of natural deduction proofs.

The first rule in Figure 2 specifies that the constants of E evaluate to themselves. The next two rules treat the *if* expression in a natural way: the conditional part, e_1, must evaluate to *true* or *false* for a proof to be found. Rule (3) states that object-level λ-abstractions also evaluate to themselves. In the rule for application (4), meta-level substitution correctly captures the notion of function application (with a call-by-value semantics). In terms of our encoding at the abstract syntax level, this rule simply states that @ $\circ$ *lamb* is the identity function of terms of type $(tm \to tm)$. Similar comments apply to the rule for *let* (5). In the rule for recursion (6), the fixed point operator is given the obvious unfolding meaning. This again makes explicit use of substitution at the meta-level since the meta-term M is applied to the term $(fix\ M)$. The result of this substitution replaces recursive calls with the body of the recursive program, namely $(fix\ M)$. Static scoping is ensured with this specification because substitution, as a means of propagating binding information, guarantees that the abstracted identifiers are replaced with their associated value prior to evaluating abstractions. Thus we shall not need closures for manipulating abstractions.

Recall that we included in E some primitive constants for manipulating lists. The inference rules for specifying the behavior of the standard evaluator for these additional constants are given in Figure 3.

Given some closed expression e, we can think of the evaluation of e as the process of finding a proof of the proposition $\vdash_e e \to e'$, for some expression e'. It is easy to see from the inference rules, that the only terms e' for which a proposition of the form $e \to e'$ has a proof are either integers, boolean constants, object-level lambda expressions, or nested lists of such objects. We shall refer to such terms as (*proper*) *values* and use α to denote such terms. Note that we have not supplied an explicit evaluation ordering to either the inference rules or the propositions in a premise. Thus one should think of nondeterministically searching for a proof via these inference rules. An actual implementation, however, must make some commitment.

The following proposition about the standard evaluator is easily proved.

PROPOSITION 3.1 Given a closed λ-term e of type tm, there is at most one proof of a proposition of the form $e \longrightarrow \alpha$, where α is some term.

We say that e *has a value* if there is a proof of $e \longrightarrow \alpha$ for some term α. By virtue of the above proposition, we may say that if e has a value, it has a unique value, i.e. the α such that $e \longrightarrow \alpha$ is provable. Notice that we shall not insist that all functional programs of E have values. An object-level, ML-style typing scheme could be used to remove certain programs that do not have values. Of course, other programs may fail to have values since they never terminate. We shall not identify such non-terminating programs with the "undefined value" as is often done in denotational semantics.

By virtue of Proposition 3.1, it is possible to use theorem proving or logic programming techniques to turn the proof system specification of an evaluator into an actual implementation. For example, all the inference rules for constructing se-proofs can be represented as Horn clauses over a language where first-order terms are replaced by simply typed λ-terms. For example, inference rule (4) could be written as the Horn clause

$$\forall e_1, e_2, \alpha, \alpha_2, M [e_1 \longrightarrow (lamb\ M)\ \&\ e_2 \longrightarrow \alpha_2\ \&\ (M \alpha_2) \longrightarrow \alpha \Rightarrow (e_1 @ e_2) \longrightarrow \alpha].$$

Here, conjunction is denoted by the logical constant & of type $o \rightarrow o \rightarrow o$. Determining that e has a value is equivalent to proving that the formula $\exists \alpha (e \longrightarrow \alpha)$ has a proof from Horn clauses that result from translating the inference rules of the evaluator. As is well known, if such proofs can be found, it can be assumed that they contain the witness for this existential, which would, of course, be the value of e. Because the rules for standard evaluation have a very regular structure, a very naive control strategy, such as the depth-first control of Prolog, would serve to find values whenever they exist. Thus, when we refer to standard evaluation as an actual, deterministic process, we shall think of it as this kind of Prolog-like execution.

Evaluation of this kind can be viewed as a kind of one-way rewriting. In this evaluator, however, rewriting always takes place at the top-most level of an expression. Rewriting could be attempted on proper subexpressions of a given expression, although this would be problematic if the subexpression was inside the scope of an object-level abstraction. Notice that this evaluator deals with object-level abstractions in one of two ways: it either treats it as essentially "quoted," as in the case of *lamb*, or it removes it by substituting a value in for it, as in the case of @, *let*, and *fix*.

Computing inside an abstraction has at least two problems. The first is that of correctly evaluating an expression containing an abstracted variable: the evaluator currently only deals with expressions whose top-level symbol is a constant declared in Section 2. A reasonable method for solving this problem is to specify that when an abstracted variable is encountered, it should evaluate to itself, that is, it should be treated as a "quoted" expression. The challenge here is to see how a proof system might support such a treatment of abstracted variables. The second problem of rewriting within an abstraction is that generally the result of such rewriting will not be a proper value. Consider, for example, the expression

$$(lamb\ \lambda x(if\ (null\ x)\ e_1\ e_2)).$$

Applying the standard evaluator to the expressions e_1 and e_2 would yield proper values if their evaluation was independent of any value assigned to x. So assume that e_1 and e_2 evaluate to the expressions α_1 and α_2, respectively. Further evaluation of the *if* expression is impossible as the value of $(null\ x)$ is dependent on having a known value for x. We can only reduce the above expression to

$$(lamb\ \lambda x(if\ (null\ x)\ \alpha_1\ \alpha_2)).$$

Thus, we must deal with "improper" or generalized values. As this example illustrates, an *if* statement can be rewritten in three different ways: Figure 2 provides two ways and the third way replaces an *if* statement with another *if* statment where its arguments may have been rewritten. This last observation reveals a cost in doing a more liberal rewriting of terms: evaluation may become more non-deterministic.

In the next section, we specify an extension to standard evaluation that is capable of systematically descending into abstractions and correctly handling abstracted variables.

4   Mixed Evaluation

The notion of descending into an abstraction to perform rewrites is often referred to as *mixed evaluation* since evaluation must be done not only on terms of E but also on terms containing abstracted variables and these are often treated as *symbolic* values. Thus, computations on "real" and symbolic values must be mixed together.

To obtain a *mixed evaluator* for E we first specify its proof system, which will be obtained by adding proof rules to those for the standard evaluator. As the discussion from the last section indicates, we should add the following inference figure to the standard evaluator.

$$\frac{e_1 \longrightarrow e_1' \qquad e_2 \longrightarrow e_2' \qquad e_3 \longrightarrow e_3'}{(if\ e_1\ e_2\ e_3) \longrightarrow (if\ e_1'\ e_2'\ e_3')}$$

Thus, an *if*-expression can "mix-evaluate" to another *if*-expression if their corresponding arguments "mix-evaluate." Notice again that the above inference rule can be written as a Horn clause.

The kinds of inference rules we have presented so far (those equivalent to Horn clauses) do not provide a natural setting for dealing with the mixed evaluation of expressions, such as $(lamb\ M)$, that contain abstractions. To handle such expressions we consider two additional meta-logical constants and the natural deduction inference rules for introducing them. Implication, written as $\Rightarrow$, is a constant of type $o \rightarrow o \rightarrow o$. Also, for every type τ built up exclusively from tm and $\rightarrow$, universal quantification at type τ will be denoted by the constant $\forall_\tau$ of type $(\tau \rightarrow o) \rightarrow o$. Quantification will be written as $\forall_\tau(\lambda x\ A)$ or more simply as $\forall_\tau x\ A$. Furthermore, we shall generally drop the type subscript when its value can be determined from context.

To prove propositions using these two new connectives, we introduce the following two introduction rules given by Gentzen [4] and Prawitz [20].

$$
\begin{array}{c}
(A_1) \\
\vdots \\
A_2 \\
\hline
A_1 \Rightarrow A_2
\end{array} \; (\Rightarrow I)
\qquad\qquad
\frac{A[x \mapsto c]}{\forall_\tau x \, A} \; (\forall I)
$$

Here, c is a constant of type τ that must not occur in the formula $\forall x \, A$ or in any undischarged assumptions of this rule. Here, of course, $[x \mapsto c]$ denotes the operation of substituting c for free occurrences of x. Given our convention regarding non-β-normal formulas from Section 3, this rule could be simply written as

$$
\frac{(Bc)}{\forall_\tau B} \; (\forall I)
$$

Here, B would be an abstraction of the form $\tau \rightarrow o$.

Both of these inference rules provide a kind of hypothetical or scoping construction in proofs. Implication introduction allows a new formula to be assumed and discharged while universal introduction allows a new constant to be introduced and discharged. Both an assumed formula and an introduced constant have very specific scopes.

Given these extensions to our proof system, we claim that the following inference rule specifies a natural mix evaluation strategy for object-level λ-abstractions.

$$
\frac{\forall x \forall y \; (x \longrightarrow y \; \Rightarrow \; ((M \, x) \longrightarrow (M' \, y)))}{(lamb \, M) \longrightarrow (lamb \, M')}
$$

To understand this rule, let us examine a simpler rule. Consider an inference rule whose premise is of the form

$$
\forall x (A_1 \; \Rightarrow \; A_2).
$$

To construct a proof of this formula we first select a new constant, c, not occurring in A_1, A_2, or any undischarged hypothesis, and substitute it for the bound variable x. Then we assume the formula $A_1[x \mapsto c]$. This assumption will generally denote some property about this newly introduced constant. Finally, from this new assumption, we attempt to prove the formula $A_2[x \mapsto c]$. If a proof can be found, then we discharge the assumption $A_1[x \mapsto c]$ and the constant c.

Given this operational interpretation of universal and implicational propositions, the rule for the mixed evaluation of $(lamb \, M)$ can be read operationally as follows: if from the assumption that c mix-evaluates to d, where c and d are two new constants, it follows that Mc mix-evaluates to $M'd$, then we can conclude that $(lamb \, M)$ mix-evaluates to $(lamb \, M')$. Thus, let M be of the form $\lambda z \, t$. This inference rule can be interpreted as replacing the bound variable z in t with a new constant that will "name" that bound variable. This new name, the constant c, is also assumed to have a value, the new constant d. A value is then sought for the expression $t[z \mapsto c]$. This value, say s, will contain occurrences of d but not c. The abstraction M' is then the result of abstracting d out of s, that is, it would be the term $\lambda z \, s[d \mapsto z]$.

$$\frac{e_1 \longrightarrow e_1' \qquad e_2 \longrightarrow e_2' \qquad e_3 \longrightarrow e_3'}{(if \ e_1 \ e_2 \ e_3) \longrightarrow (if \ e_1' \ e_2' \ e_3')} \tag{2c}$$

$$\frac{\forall x \forall y \ (x \longrightarrow y \ \Rightarrow \ ((M \ x) \longrightarrow (M' \ y)))}{(lamb \ M) \longrightarrow (lamb \ M')} \qquad \frac{e_1 \longrightarrow e_1' \qquad e_2 \longrightarrow e_2'}{(e_1 @ e_2) \longrightarrow (e_1' @ e_2')} \tag{3a, 4a}$$

$$\frac{e_2 \longrightarrow e_2' \qquad \forall x \forall y \ (x \longrightarrow y \ \Rightarrow \ ((M \ x) \longrightarrow (M' \ y)))}{(let \ M \ e_2) \longrightarrow (let \ M' \ e_2')} \tag{5a}$$

$$\frac{\forall x \forall y \ (x \longrightarrow y \ \Rightarrow \ ((M \ x) \longrightarrow (M' \ y)))}{(fix \ M) \longrightarrow (fix \ M')} \tag{6a}$$

FIGURE 4
Inference Rules for the Mixed Evaluator for E

Figure 4 contains all the inference rules that are needed to extend the proof system for standard evaluation into the proof system for mixed evaluation. Note that since we have constructed this proof system by augmenting the one for standard evaluation, $\vdash_{se} (e \longrightarrow \alpha)$ implies $\vdash_{mix} (e \longrightarrow \alpha)$, where $\vdash_{mix}$ denotes provability in the extended proof system. The converse is not true, however, and for a given e there may now be many e' such that $\vdash_{mix} e \longrightarrow e'$. Also notice that mix evaluation is *reflexive*, that is, for all terms $e \in E$, $\vdash_{mix} e \longrightarrow e$.

The similarity of the rules in Figure 4 suggest that they can be explained or generated via some uniform technique. This is, indeed, the case. Before presenting such a transformation, we note that there is an alternative presentation of inference figures.

As was mentioned in Section 3, the inference rules in that section could be identified naturally with Horn clauses of the meta logic. The inference rules in this section can also be naturally identified with formulas, but they will not generally be Horn clauses. For example, the inference figure above for object-level λ-abstractions can be written as the formula

$$\forall M \forall M' [\forall x \forall y (x \longrightarrow y \Rightarrow (Mx) \longrightarrow (M'y)) \Rightarrow (lamb \ M) \longrightarrow (lamb \ M')],$$

which is not a Horn clause because of the implication and universal quantifier in the antecedent. The class of formulas that is necessary here to capture the inference rules described in this section can be described as follows. Let A be a syntactic variable denoting atomic formulas of the meta-logic, that is, formulas of the form $e \longrightarrow e'$. The required class of formulas is then defined as the range of the syntactic variable L that is defined as

$$L ::= A \mid L_1 \wedge L_2 \mid L_1 \Rightarrow L_2 \mid \forall_\tau x \ L.$$

Such formulas form a subset of the hereditary Harrop formulas investigated in [14] where it is shown that in an intuitionistic proof system, these formulas can give rise to an operational interpretation similar to Horn clauses: logic programming can be naturally interpreted in hereditary Harrop formulas. The class of L-formulas is very similar to the language used for the specification of logics in the Isabelle theorem prover [17].

Given this relation between inference rules and formulas, we shall describe a syntactic transformation on constants of E that will yield the L-formulas that encode the inference rules of Figure 4. Let t and s be terms of E that are both of type τ. The following two clauses define by recursion on simple types the three place function $[t \longrightarrow s : \tau]$, which returns L-formulas.

- $[t \longrightarrow s : \tau \rightarrow \sigma] := \forall x \forall y ([x \longrightarrow y : \tau] \Rightarrow [tx \longrightarrow sy : \sigma])$.

- $[t \longrightarrow s : tm] := t \longrightarrow s$.

The inference rules in Figure 4 are exactly those rules that translate into the formulas denoted by $[c \longrightarrow c : \tau]$ in which c is some constant of type τ of E. These rules for mixed evaluation are therefore derived independently of standard evaluation: they only depend on the constants of the abstract syntax of E. If E were enriched with new language features then the abstract syntax would be extended with new constants. The above translation, applied to these constants, would yield an appropriate collection of mixed evaluation clauses for these new features.

Now let us consider an example of mixed evaluation. Let A be an abbreviation of the append function given by the term

$$(fix\ \lambda f(lamb\ \lambda x(lamb\ \lambda y(if\ (null\ x)\ y\ (cons\ (car\ x)\ (f\ (cdr\ x)\ y)))))).$$

Now suppose we try to show that there exists some α such that $\vdash_{se} (A @ (cons\ 1\ nil)) \longrightarrow \alpha$. It is not hard to see that the only possible value for α is

$$(lamb\ \lambda y(if\ (null\ (cons\ 1\ nil))\ y\ (cons\ (car\ (cons\ 1\ nil))\ (A\ (cdr\ (cons\ 1\ nil))\ y)))).$$

No further evaluation is possible.

Now consider showing $\vdash_{mix} (A @ (cons\ 1\ nil)) \longrightarrow \alpha$ for some α. The additional rules of the $\vdash_{mix}$ proof system provide for further simplification of this expression. In particular, the partial instantiation of a list structure often provides enough information for the evaluation of some functions [5], e.g., the function $null$ applied to the "cons" of any two expressions that have values is always false. Clearly we can have the same value for α as above. Further evaluation, however, is also possible, yielding $(lamb\ \lambda y(cons\ 1\ y))$.

In this section we have concentrated exclusively on the declarative aspects of mixed evaluation. Of course, for an actual implementation of a mixed evaluator, the control aspects must also be addressed. Obviously, control of this evaluator is much more complex than for the standard evaluator since Proposition 3.1 does not hold for the extended proof system. For the rest of this paper, we shall assume that the mixed evaluator is a kind of non-deterministic program. The issue of imposing particular search strategies on it is beyond the scope of this paper.

5 Correctness of Mixed Evaluation

We constructed a proof system for mixed evaluation by extending the one for the standard evaluation of E. Given this intimate connection between the two systems we are able to express and prove a form of correctness for mixed evaluation directly in terms of standard evaluation. We want the mix system to preserve the values of expressions given by the standard evaluator. This notion of correctness is stated by the following theorem.

THEOREM 5.1 (Partial Correctness of Mixed Evaluation) For all $e, e', \alpha \in E$, if $\vdash_{\text{mix}} e \longrightarrow e'$ and $\vdash_{\text{se}} e \longrightarrow \alpha$ then there exists some value α' such that $\vdash_{\text{se}} e' \longrightarrow \alpha'$ and $\vdash_{\text{mix}} \alpha \longrightarrow \alpha'$.

Graphically, this relation among terms is depicted by the following commuting diagram:

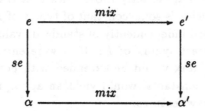

An outline for the proof of this theorem is as follows. Assume $\vdash_{\text{mix}} e \longrightarrow e'$ and $\vdash_{\text{se}} e \longrightarrow \alpha$ for $e, e', \alpha \in E$. The proof proceeds by induction on the structure of the se-proof of $e \longrightarrow \alpha$ and then by case analysis on the last inference rule for the mix-proof of $e \longrightarrow e'$. At each point, it is possible to build the unique value α' such that $\vdash_{\text{se}} e' \longrightarrow \alpha'$ and to construct a proof that $\vdash_{\text{mix}} \alpha \longrightarrow \alpha'$. The inductive cases involving abstractions and substitution at the meta-level need to make use of the normalization theorem for intuitionistic logic [20] and uniform proof result for hereditary Harrop formulas [14].

Notice, however, that Theorem 5.1 states that mix preserves values only in the forward direction. An analogous statement for the reverse direction does not hold, i.e., for some expressions e, e' such that $\vdash_{\text{mix}} e \longrightarrow e'$, e' may have a value while e has none. As an example, consider the expression $e = (lamb\ \lambda x.true)@(fix\ \lambda x.x)$. It is easy to show that

$$\vdash_{\text{mix}} (lamb\ \lambda x.true)@(fix\ \lambda x.x) \longrightarrow true$$

while $(lamb\ \lambda x.true)@(fix\ \lambda x.x)$ has no value. This example illustrates the interaction of mixed and eager evaluation. The standard evaluator of Section 3 uses an eager evaluation strategy, i.e., arguments are evaluated before being used. (In a lazy evaluation strategy an argument is not evaluated until later, if ever.) In particular, in each of the following inference rules for standard evaluation

$$\frac{e_1 \longrightarrow (lamb\ M) \quad e_2 \longrightarrow \alpha_2 \quad (M\ \alpha_2) \longrightarrow \alpha}{(e_1@e_2) \longrightarrow \alpha} \qquad \frac{e_2 \longrightarrow \alpha_2 \quad (M\ \alpha_2) \longrightarrow \alpha}{(let\ M\ e_2) \longrightarrow \alpha} \qquad (4,5)$$

he argument e_2 is evaluated before it is used. But notice that these two rules, in the context of mixed evaluation, become more flexible. Recall the observation that our mixed evaluation was reflexive in that any expression can mix-evaluate to itself. Hence, the following two instances of these rules are derivable from the *mix* set of inference rules.

$$\frac{e_1\longrightarrow(lamb\ M)\quad e_2\longrightarrow e_2\quad (M\ e_2)\longrightarrow\alpha}{(e_1@e_2)\longrightarrow\alpha}\qquad\frac{e_2\longrightarrow e_2\quad (M\ e_2)\longrightarrow\alpha}{(let\ M\ e_2)\longrightarrow\alpha}$$

for some given e_1, e_2, M, α. But these are effectively the inference rules that one uses (instead of the two above) for standard evaluation employing a lazy evaluation strategy, namely,

$$\frac{e_1\longrightarrow(lamb\ M)\quad (M\ e_2)\longrightarrow\alpha}{(e_1@e_2)\longrightarrow\alpha}\qquad\frac{(M\ e_2)\longrightarrow\alpha}{(let\ M\ e_2)\longrightarrow\alpha}\qquad (4',5')$$

in which arguments are not evaluated first. We can conclude that our mixed evaluator includes not only "eager" evaluation but also "lazy" evaluation. We conjecture the following relationship between lazy evaluation and mixed evaluation.

CONJECTURE 5.2 Let se' be the proof system obtained by replacing rules 4 and 5 in Figure 2 by the rules $4'$ and $5'$ given above and let $\vdash_{se'}$ refer to provability in this new proof system. Then the following hold:

(i) For all $e, e', \alpha \in E$, if $\vdash_{mix} e\longrightarrow e'$ and $\vdash_{se'} e\longrightarrow\alpha$ then there exists some value α' such that $\vdash_{se'} e'\longrightarrow\alpha'$ and $\vdash_{mix} \alpha\longrightarrow\alpha'$.

(ii) For all $e, e', \alpha' \in E$, if $\vdash_{mix} e\longrightarrow e'$ and $\vdash_{se'} e'\longrightarrow\alpha'$ then there exists some value α such that $\vdash_{se'} e\longrightarrow\alpha$ and $\vdash_{mix} \alpha\longrightarrow\alpha'$.

In other words, if e mix-evaluates to e' then e has a value if and only if e' has a value (in the se' system) and these values are also connected by mix evaluation.

The general discussion of correctness in this section has been greatly simplified by two features of our standard and mixed evaluation. First, the lack of explicit environments for manipulating bound variables in our specifications reduces the overall complexity of our proof systems and (meta) proofs about those systems. Second, the values for both our evaluation systems are a subset of the language of expressions, namely E. Thus we can manipulate these values just as regular expressions in the language. For specifications that include, for example, closures as values, such uniform treatment is not easily obtained.

6   Implementation of the Meta-Logic

In Sections 3 and 4, we claimed that techniques found in logic programming can be used to provide implementations of our evaluators. In this section, we elaborate a bit more on this claim.

One way to provide implementations of standard and mix evaluation is to embedded them into Prolog-like systems. Such systems must, however, extend conventional Prolog [22] in, at least, the following directions.

- The collection of hereditary Harrop formulas (or the subset of L-formulas) must be supported. Prolog supports Horn clauses, which are a proper subset of hereditary Harrop formulas.

- First-order terms must be replaced with the more general notion of simply typed λ-terms.

- Unification of simply typed λ-terms must be supported to some degree. In particular, the equality of λ-terms must be determined up to α-conversion and head level β-contraction.

- Unification must also be modified to deal with the appearance of constants introduced to prove universally quantified formulas. In particular, any free or "logical" variables, say x, present when such a new constant, say c, is introduced must be constrained so that any term that instantiates x must not contain an occurrence of c.

The higher-order logic programming language λProlog [15] contains all of these extensions to conventional Prolog. Aspects of the formal foundations for λProlog can be found in [14]. The proof systems and examples in this paper were developed and tested using a prototype implementation of this language.

As we mentioned in Section 3, the depth-first search strategy of Prolog (and also of λProlog) is adequate for providing an implementation of a standard evaluator. Controlling mixed evaluation, however, is much more difficult. For this task there is probably not one correct notion of what *should* be the *unique* result of mixed evaluation. More likely, different control strategies for mixed evaluation will be needed for different applications. Thus the depth-first control mechanisms of λProlog would not be particularly useful. Instead, a collection of high-level tactics and tacticals [6] could be employed to structure the search for proofs. Tactical and tactics can be implemented directly in λProlog [2] or in a secondary language, such as ML [17].

7 Summary and Related Work

We have shown how an elementary specification for mixed evaluation can be derived from a specification for standard evaluation. By encoding programs as simply typed λ-terms and specifying evaluation via inference rules akin to structural operational semantics, we demonstrated a natural method of extending standard evaluation with additional inference rules derived from the signature of E, the abstract syntax of a simple functional programming language. As this signature contains constants of second-order types, this extension led to inference rules that require hypothetical and scoping constructions. Such rules, fortunately, can be given a simple operational interpretation and can be naturally implemented using logic programming techniques.

Of course, the mixed evaluator that we derive provides only a "core" set of mixed evaluation rules. For example, our method is not rich enough to provide mixed evaluation rules that can simplify an expression like $max(max(x,1),x)$ to just $max(1,x)$ (given a typical definition for max) since this evaluation requires the additional information that max is both commutative and associative. This information is additional in the sense that a standard evaluator does not need it. The application of such auxiliary information is commonly found in compilers that perform such tasks as constant folding. Future work will attempt to capture this kind of auxiliary information.

The current paper provides only syntactic results concerning different forms of evaluation. We hope to extend this work to a semantic characterization that provides a natural connection between our standard and mixed evaluation systems. One promising approach uses logical relations [21]. These are relations defined over the type structure of simply typed λ-terms and they have been used to study both the syntax and semantics of the simply typed λ-calculus. The similarity between our construction of new inference rules (based on the types of constants) and the definition of logical relations is striking, but subtle differences between the two remain. We would, however, like to characterize evaluation in terms of logical relations and give semantic proofs for the soundness of mixed evaluation. Logical relations may well provide a convenient and powerful mechanism for characterizing and understanding mixed evaluation.

The use of natural deduction as a framework for evaluating programs has been studied by several others [1, 12, 19] and has been called structural operational semantics [19] and natural semantics [12]. More specifically, the discussion of mixed evaluation in the context of natural deduction or inference rules is also found in [9]. However, in that work a language independent philosophy is taken and mixed evaluation is an operation over proof trees, using a pruning-like method. A set of heuristics is developed to guide the manipulation of these proof trees. This approach is more general than ours in that it is for a specific meta-language (TYPOL) rather than for a specific object-language. Our approach, however, attempts to derive mixed evaluation automatically.

The idea of deriving mixed evaluation as an enrichment of standard evaluation was suggested by Heering with what he calls "automatic partial ω-enrichment" [10]. This technique attempts to extend mechanically standard evaluation to mixed evaluation via a set of *enrichment rules*. Our approach appears to be an instance of these kinds of enrichment rules.

Finally, our work shares much in spirit with the automatic binding time analysis of [16]. In that work the authors present a two-level λ-calculus for distinguishing between compile-time and run-time computations. Constructions such as application and abstraction (of λ-terms) are annotated with binding information, identifying them as occurring either early (at compile-time) or late (at run-time). They describe an algorithm which, given partial binding information, computes the "best" complete binding information. The notion of best refers roughly to performing as much computation as possible at compile-time. Their ability to identify and perform computations at compile-time is similar to our ability to perform computations over terms containing symbolic values.

Acknowledgements: The first author is supported in part by a fellowship from the Corporate Research and Architecture Group, Digital Equipment Corporation, Maynard, MA USA. Both authors are supported in part by grants NSF CCR-87-05596, ONR N00014-88-K-0633, and DARPA N00014-85-K-0018.

References

[1] R. Burstall and Furio Honsell. A natural deduction treatment of operational semantics. In *Foundations of Software Technology and Theoretical Computer Science*, pages 250–269, Springer-Verlag LNCS, Vol. 338, 1988.

[2] A. Felty and D. Miller. Specifying theorem provers in a higher-order logic programming language. In *Proceedings of the Ninth International Conference on Automated Deduction*, 1988.

[3] Y. Futamura. Partial evaluation of computation process – an approach to a compiler-compiler. *Computer, Systems, Controls*, 2(5):45–50, 1971.

[4] G. Gentzen. Investigations into logical deduction. In M. Szabo, editor, *The Collected Papers of Gerhard Gentzen*, pages 68–131, North-Holland Publishing Co., 1969.

[5] F. Giannotti, A. Matteucci, D. Pedreschi, and F. Turini. Symbolic evaluation with structural recursive symbolic constants. *Science of Computer Programming*, 9(2):161–177, 1987.

[6] Michael J. Gordon, Arthur J. Milner, and Christopher P. Wadsworth. *Edinburgh LCF: A Mechanised Logic of Computation*. Volume 78 of *Lecture Notes in Computer Science*, Springer-Verlag, 1979.

[7] J. Hannan and D. Miller. A meta-logic for functional programming. In M. Rogers and H. Abramson, editors, *Proceedings of the META88 Workshop*, MIT Press, 1989. (to appear).

[8] J. Hannan and D. Miller. Uses of higher-order unification for implementing program transformers. In K. Bowen and R. Kowalski, editors, *Fifth International Conference and Symposium on Logic Programming*, MIT Press, 1988. Also available as University of Pennsylvania Technical Report MS-CIS-88-46.

[9] L. Hascoët. Partial evaluation with inference rules. *New Generation Computing*, 6(2–3):187–209, 1988.

[10] J. Heering. Partial evaluation and ω-completeness of algebraic specifications. *Theoretical Computer Science*, 43:149–167, 1986.

[11] G. Huet and B. Lang. Proving and applying program transformations expressed with second-order logic. *Acta Informatica*, 11:31–55, 1978.

12] G. Kahn. Natural semantics. In *Proceedings of the Symposium on Theoretical Aspects of Computer Science*, pages 22–39, Springer-Verlag LNCS, Vol. 247, 1987.

13] D. Miller and G. Nadathur. A logic programming approach to manipulating formulas and programs. In *Proceedings of the IEEE Fourth Symposium on Logic Programming*, IEEE Press, 1987.

14] D. Miller, G. Nadathur, F. Pfenning, and A. Scedrov. Uniform proofs as a foundation for logic programming. To appear in the *Annals of Pure and Applied Logic*.

15] G. Nadathur and D. Miller. An overview of λProlog. In K. Bowen and R. Kowalski, editors, *Fifth International Conference and Symposium on Logic Programming*, MIT Press, 1988.

16] H. Nielson and F. Nielson. Automatic binding time analysis for a typed λ-calculus. *Science of Computer Programming*, 10(2):139–176, 1988.

17] L. Paulson. The foundation of a generic theorem prover. (To appear in the *Journal of Automated Reasoning*).

18] F. Pfenning and C. Elliot. Higher-order abstract syntax. In *Proceedings of the ACM-SIGPLAN Conference on Programming Language Design and Implementation*, 1988.

19] G. Plotkin. *A Structural Approach to Operational Semantics*. DAIMI FN-19, Aarhus University, Aarhus, Denmark, September 1981.

20] Dag Prawitz. *Natural Deduction*. Almqvist & Wiksell, Uppsala, 1965.

21] R. Statman. Logical relations and the typed λ-calculus. *Information and Control*, 65:85–97, 1985.

22] L. Sterling and E. Shapiro. *The Art of Prolog: Advanced Programming Techniques*. MIT Press, Cambridge, MA, 1986.

REALIZABILITY MODELS FOR PROGRAM CONSTRUCTION

Martin C. Henson
University of Essex, Wivenhoe Park,
Colchester, Essex, England

0 Abstract

In this paper we investigate the design of realizability interpretations for program development in extensions to the constructive and intensional set theory TK [Henson 88]. These realizability interpretations express the idea that a program meets a specification. We explore a variety of topics including, unwanted data, polymorphism, data abstraction, types and typechecking, conditional assertions, let assertions, pattern directed invocation and recursion equations. Our aim is to ensure that, when constructive reasoning is harnessed for the derivation of programs from proofs of specifications, the programs we obtain are expressed in a natural way.

1 Introduction

In this paper we investigate the design of realizability interpretations for program development in extensions to the constructive and intensional set theory TK [Henson 88].

In an intuitionistic theory the construction implicit in a proof can be made explicit. This observation goes a long way towards explaining the explosion of interest in the use of such theories to provide *models for program development*; a project which involves the identification of specifications with assertions, and programs with the explicit constructions obtained from the proofs of these specifications. A number of theories have been employed for this purpose, notably NuPRL [Constable 86], Martin-Lof's Type Theory (MLTT) [Martin-Lof 82] [Backhouse 88], Feferman's T_0 [Beeson 86] [Hayashi 87], Beeson's polymorphic set theories ZFR and IZFR [Beeson 88] and Henson and Turner's theory TK [Henson 88] [Henson 89]. Underpinning all these theories, historically if not explicitly, is a relationship between terms and formulae: the notion of *realizability* [Kleene 45], and this is the vehicle by which proof objects (programs) are obtained from derivations.

Much of the recent research in this area, particularly that which is based on Martin-Lof's theory, concerns itself with the ameleoration of a problem: there is a mismatch between proof objects and programs (see [Backhouse 87] for example). Within Martin-Lof's paradigm the available research proceeds by extending the theory with new propositional forms. This approach is taken because the rules of this theory come equipped with proof objects and so the relationship between programs and proofs is fixed. We have argued elsewhere [Henson 88] that most of these extensions seem incoherent because they undermine the desiderata of Martin-Lof's theory (in particular the notion of "completely presented set").

Our approach has been to develop a theory based at the outset on desiderata derived from a reflection on our computational intuitions and predilections. We have kept the relationship between proof objects and propositions (which gives rise to programs from derivations) separate from the logical rules. It is then possible to investigate the analogy between proof objects and programs in a principled way; the principle being a notion of *soundness* (proposition 2.4 below).

Our theory has more in common with Feferman's theories than Martin-Lof's. It is therefore closer to the work of Hayashi than that of Backhouse or Constable. Hayashi's PX system is an especially restricted version of Feferman's T_0 in which the original term language of T_0 (combinatory algebra) is supplanted by the programming language LISP. We do not define a theory based immediately upon a useable programming language; rather we view our theory TK as standing in relation to useable programming logics rather as the lambda calculus stands in relation to useable programming languages. That is, we expect to use TK to provide a semantic interpretation of various programming logics just as the lambda calculus provides models for various programming languages. In this paper we shall not provide a formal interpretation for any particular programming logic within TK but rather just explore a number of dimensions along which a relationship between programs and specifications (a PSR) can be designed and to illustrate how such designs tackle the mismatching problem outlined above.

The paper follows the following plan. In the next section we provide a brief introduction to TK and we review the basic ideas of realizability theory. Section three, the main section of the paper, is devoted to the exploration of nine distinct issues concerning the relationship between programs and specifications and how various options can be expressed and accommodated. Section four contains our concluding remarks.

2 Propaedeutic

2.1 The language of the theory TK

The theory consists of a language of terms, sets and formulae. The term language consists of the untyped lambda notation extended with constants, abstractions over the types, and types as objects:

$t \in TERMS; \quad t \rightarrow x \mid c \mid \lambda x.t \mid \lambda X.T \mid (t\,t) \mid T$

Using well known techniques we can enrich the infrastructure of terms with pairs, conditionals, boolean constants and so on. We will do this extensively without further elaboration.

Sets are called types or kinds. Although both classify *objects* of the theory the kinds also classify those objects which are constructed from types.

$T \in TYPES; \quad T \rightarrow X \mid \{x \mid \Phi'\} \mid \Xi(T,T(X))$
$K \in KINDS; \quad K \rightarrow T \mid \{x \mid \Phi\}$

Sets can be formed from properties by comprehension and by (monotone) induction. Comprehension supports the introduction of well known type constructions, such as sums, products, function spaces, polymorphisms and data abstractions. Inductive generation allows us to satisfy certain recursive type definitions.

Atomic formulae consist of membership, equality, definedness, failure and absurdity assertions:

$\alpha \in ATOMS; \quad \alpha \rightarrow t \in T \mid t \in K \mid t = t \mid t\downarrow \mid fail \mid \perp$

Those involving just equality, definedness, failure and absurdity we call the *simple* atoms. We explain the role of the atom *fail* in 3.8.

We can then close off the assertions in the normal way, although we include quantifiers over types as well as objects.

$\Phi \in WFFS; \Phi \rightarrow \alpha \mid \Phi \wedge \Phi \mid \Phi \vee \Phi \mid \Phi \rightarrow \Phi \mid (\forall x)\Phi \mid (\exists x)\Phi \mid (\forall X)\Phi \mid (\exists X)\Phi$

The set *WFF'* over which Φ ranges is that subset of *WFF* which includes no element involving a bound type variable (by quantification).

This completes the presentation of the basic language of the theory.

2.2 The rule system of TK

The logical apparatus of TK falls into two parts. First we have the ordinary rules of intuitionistic predicate logic. Secondly we have the logic of terms and of sets. The axioms for terms are essentially those for a *partial lambda calculus*, again we refer the reader to our earlier work for the details. Those for sets we now provide:

$$\frac{z \in \{x \mid \Phi\}}{\Phi(z)} \quad (\{\}\text{-}Elim) \qquad\qquad \frac{\Phi(z)}{z \in \{x \mid \Phi\}} \quad (\{\}\text{-}Intro)$$

$$\frac{z \in A}{z \in \Xi(A,B(X))} \quad (\Xi\text{-}Intro(i)) \qquad\qquad \frac{z \in B(\Xi(A,B(X)))}{z \in \Xi(A,B(X))} \quad (\Xi\text{-}Intro(ii))$$

$$\frac{(\forall z \in \Xi(A,B(X)))(z \in B(\{w \mid \psi(w)\}) \Rightarrow \psi(z))}{(\forall z \in \Xi(A,B(X)))\psi(z)} \quad (\Xi\text{-}Elim)$$

For the purposes of the logical apparatus $B(X)$ is a type expression, B, which is monotone in its distinguished free type variable, X. Inductive types satisfy the following equation (where $\equiv$ denotes *extensional* equality):

Theorem 2.1

$$\Xi(A,B(X)) \equiv A \cup B(\Xi(A,B(X)))$$

proof ($\subseteq$)by Ξ-induction ($\supseteq$)by Ξ-closure.∎

2.3 Realizability

Ideally we wish to establish a two place relation between programs and specifications which holds just in case the program meets the specification (we shall refer to such "Program/Specification Relationships" as PSR's in the sequel). The basis for a PSR is the notion of realizability. In particular we are interested in the following general schema for specifications:

$$SPECIFICATION: (\forall x)(\Phi(x) \Rightarrow (\exists y)(\psi(x,y)))$$

where Φ is a pre-condition and ψ is a post-condition over the input datum x and output datum y.

The technique of realizability was originally introduced [Kleene 45] to capture formally the constructive meaning of the logical operations. To each formula, Φ, we associate another, written (meta-notationally) "$e \, \rho \, \Phi$", which is to be read "e realizes Φ" or more provocatively, but very roughly: "e is a program which meets the specification Φ". The idea is that the translation makes the constructive character of assertions explicit. Usually formulae of the form "$e \, \rho \, \Phi$" are formulae within the same theory so the interpretation is internal.

Before we move on, we need to make a few technical remarks. The free variables of $e \, \rho \, \Phi$ are those of Φ in addition to e (which is not free in Φ) although we shall see that, in general, there may be a reinterpretation of the free variables implicit in the transition from Φ to $e \, \rho \, \Phi$. We shall take it that ρ binds more tightly in expressions than the binary logical connectives but less tightly than quantifiers and membership (note, however, that expressions of the form $e \, \rho \, \Phi$ are meta-notation). The standard definition of abstract realizability, for first order intuitionistic predicate logic (IL), runs as follows:

Definition 2.2

$$
\begin{array}{lll}
e \, \rho \, \Phi & is & \Phi \ (atomic\ \Phi) \\
e \, \rho \, (\Phi \wedge \psi) & is & (fst\ e) \, \rho \, \Phi \wedge (snd\ e) \, \rho \, \psi \\
e \, \rho \, (\Phi \vee \psi) & is & (fst\ e){=}true \wedge (snd\ e) \, \rho \, \Phi \vee (snd\ e){=}false \wedge (snd\ e) \, \rho \, \psi \\
e \, \rho \, (\Phi \Rightarrow \psi) & is & (\forall x)(x \, \rho \, \Phi \Rightarrow (e\,x){\downarrow} \wedge (e\,x) \, \rho \, \psi) \\
e \, \rho \, \forall x \Phi & is & (\forall x)((e\,x){\downarrow} \wedge (e\,x) \, \rho \, \Phi) \\
e \, \rho \, \exists x \Phi & is & (snd\ e) \, \rho \, \Phi((fst\ e)) \ ∎
\end{array}
$$

Lemma 2.3   Commutativity of realizability with substitution

$$e \rho \ (\Phi[x\leftarrow z]) \ \leftrightarrow \ (e \rho \ \Phi)[x\leftarrow z] \ \blacksquare$$

The seductive similarity between realizability and the notion that a program meets a speicification seems, however, to break down in the existential case. Our intuitions suggest that *(fst e)* is the value which corresponds to the object that meets the specification $\exists x \Phi$. This is just the first of a number of senses in which realizability and a PSR part conceptual company and the observation provides at least some motivation for the *design* of interpretations for PSR's. Indeed this very point has given rise to considerable reserach within the MLTT paradigm and has lead to various notions of "sub-typing" (see [Backhouse 88] for much discussion on the more general topic of "information loss")

Proposition 2.4 (soundness of realizability)

If TK $\vdash \Phi$ then there is a term t such that TK $\vdash t\!\downarrow \wedge t \rho \ \Phi$

proof By induction on the length of the derivation $\vdash \Phi$. We will outline cases from this proof in 3.6 and 3.9 below. $\blacksquare$

There are two avenues which have to be explored. First of all, definition 2.1 and proposition 2.4 concern IL and we shall need to extend the definition to cover TK. Secondly, the comment above regarding existentials suggests that basic realizability is not a PSR so we shall be inclined to provide alternative definitions which are. However, we shall need some measure of success in both enterprises and this is provided by (appropriate reformulations of) the soundness theorem above: as we reformulate the relation ρ we shall require that it still satisfies the equivalent to proposition 2.4: that is, every satisfiable specification leads to a program which meets it.

3 Designing PSR's

In this, the main section of the paper, we shall examine a variety of issues in programming language design (for example type checking and pattern matching) and show how these can be incorporated within the definition of a PSR.

There are a number of slightly different senses in which standard realizability fails to be a PSR. One such concerns the structure of the assertions themselves. Taking this point seriously amounts to accepting that, of course, the standard connectives of our logic do not constitute a *specification language* any more than a Turing machine provides a sensible model of a *programming language*. Feferman has used the terms *adequate* and *accordance* in this regard [Feferman 79]. A theory T is adequate for a body of informal mathematics M if every concept and result can be expressed within the theory. The theory is in accordance with the informal mathematics if, essentially, it does not go beyond what is required for the exposition of M. Although our theory is adequate it is not (again using Feferman's classification) *directly* adequate. Rather it is only *indirectly* adequate (like the theory of Turing machines) for it is necessary to show how a wide variety of phenomena are justifiable in the theory. In a sense an indirectly adequate theory preserves only the *extensional* properties of M whilst a fully adequate sytem preserves the *intensional* properties too (cf. Beeson's remark that Peano arithmetic does not support the Euclid algorithm for greatest common divisor [Beeson 86]). The assertion language of TK is only indirectly adequate in this sense. The design of a PSR involves the creation of directly adequate facilities for specification and programming, the connection between these two and the interpretation of all this within the underlying theory TK.

We shall begin this project with a rather fundamental flaw in the realizability interpretation given in section 2 which seems to be independent of any programming notation and specification structure whatsoever.

3.1 Q-realizability and "Star"-types

There is another sense, related to the one mentioned in 2.4, in which standard realizability and any proposed PSR differ. Suppose the proposition, Φ, in the preamble to proposition 2.4, has the form $\exists x \psi$, for some x and ψ. We should like to be sure that not only is $t\!\downarrow$ and $t \rho \Phi$ but also that $\psi(t)$. This is easy to justify: our schema for specification utilises existential formulae in connection with post-conditions; presumably we should insist that the witness, t, *actually satisfies the post-condition*! Unfortunately this cannot be established for the definition of realizability we have given. This property (one of a number known in constructive mathematics as *existence properties*) can be satisfied by an alternative definition of realizability, which then provides a notion closer in intent to our computational intuitions.

Definition 3.1

$$
\begin{array}{lll}
e \rho \ \Phi & is & \Phi \ (atomic \ \Phi) \\
e \rho \ (\Phi \wedge \psi) & is & (fst \ e) \rho \ \Phi \wedge (snd \ e) \rho \ \psi \\
e \rho \ (\Phi \vee \psi) & is & (fst \ e)=true \wedge (snd \ e) \rho \ \Phi \wedge \Phi \vee \\
& & (snd \ e)=false \wedge (snd \ e) \rho \ \psi \wedge \psi \\
e \rho \ (\Phi \Rightarrow \psi) & is & (\forall x)(\Phi \wedge x \rho \ \Phi \Rightarrow (e \ x)\!\downarrow \wedge (e \ x) \rho \ \psi) \\
e \rho \ \forall x \Phi & is & (\forall x)((e \ x)\!\downarrow \wedge (e \ x) \rho \ \Phi) \\
e \rho \ \exists x \Phi & is & \Phi((fst \ e)) \wedge (snd \ e) \rho \ \Phi((fst \ e)) \ \blacksquare
\end{array}
$$

With this we can prove:

Proposition 3.2

If $TK \vdash \exists x \Phi$ then there is a term t such that $TK \vdash t\!\downarrow \wedge \Phi(t)$

proof a simple consequence of soundness. $\blacksquare$

In fact, we have not moved much from the historical development: this definition, known as Q-realizability is also due to Kleene ([Kleene 71] is an excellent account, by that author, of a number of approaches including Q-realizability). Q-realizability also allows us to solve the problem of 2.3, concerning existentials, by means of the following proposition:

Proposition 3.3 Program Extraction

If $TK \vdash (\forall x)(\Phi(x) \Rightarrow (\exists y)(\psi(x,y)))$ where $\Phi(x)$ is safe, then for some closed term t, $TK \vdash (\forall x)(\Phi(x) \Rightarrow (t \ x)\!\downarrow \wedge \psi(x, (t \ x)))$.

proof This is the axiom AC_{safe} (Axiom of choice for safe formulae). We will discuss safety in 3.5 below. For the proof see [Beeson 86] for example. $\blacksquare$

This analysis, however, is still expository for it concerns only IL and we need to extend it to TK. If we simply take the above and extend it to the second order quantifiers by analogy with the first order cases (we will discuss this in detail in 3.3 and 3.4 below):

$$
\begin{array}{lll}
e \rho \ \forall X \Phi & is & (\forall X)((e \ X)\!\downarrow \wedge (e \ X) \rho \ \Phi) \\
e \rho \ \exists X \Phi & is & (\exists X)((fst \ e)=X \wedge (snd \ e) \rho \ \Phi)
\end{array}
$$

then we might expect to have made progress. In fact the resulting interpretation is not sound for reasons similar to those for T_0 in [Feferman 79]. That is, the (full) axiom of choice would then be a consequence of TK but TK+AC is inconsisitent. The reason for this concerns the definition of realizability for the atomic assertions. The solution is based on a technique due, originally, to Kreisel and Troelstra [Kreisel 70]. This suggests that to each type T we associate a type T^* and take:

$e \rho \ x {\in} T \quad is \quad <e,x> {\in} T^*$

The task is to define T^* for each T in a way which makes this sound. For comprehension types this is easy:

$$\{x \mid \Phi\}^* = \{<e,x> \mid e \rho \ \Phi\} \ (more\ exactly: \{z \mid (\exists u)(\exists x)(u \rho \ \Phi)\})$$

and, in fact, is only introduced for long enough to observe that realizability for membership in these types reduces immediately to:

$$e \rho \ z {\in} \{x \mid \Phi\} \quad is \quad e \rho \ \Phi[x {\leftarrow} z]$$

The story for inductive types is (much) more complex. Intuitively the type $\Xi(A,B(X))^*$ consists of pairs $<e,x>$ and each e is evidence explaining why x is an element of $\Xi(A,B(X))$. If $x {\in} A$ then $<e,x> {\in} A^*$; but if not then e will be a summary of all the evidence supporting the membership of each of the predecessors of x in $\Xi(A,B(X))$. We have to omit the technical details in the current context.

The case where the type expression is a variable is rather interesting. According to the definition above we have it that:

$$e \rho \ x {\in} X \quad is \quad <e,x> {\in} X^*$$

but how do we define a suitable translation here? In fact we can let X^* be a fresh variable. Indeed under the *original* definition of realizability we can allow X^* to be X itself with the consequent change of interpretation captured by a modification of lemma 2.3:

Lemma 3.4 Commutativity of realizability with substitution

$$e \rho \ (\Phi[x {\leftarrow} z][X {\leftarrow} Z]) \quad (e \rho \ \Phi)[x {\leftarrow} z][X {\leftarrow} Z^*] \ \blacksquare$$

In the Q-realizability variation we have to allow X^* to be fresh since the free variables of $e \rho \ \Phi$ are e, x, X and X^* if the free variables of Φ are x and X, as any simple example demonstrates. Thus the lemma in this case is:

Lemma 3.5 Commutativity of Q-realizability with substitution

$$e \rho \ (\Phi[x {\leftarrow} z][X {\leftarrow} Z]) \quad (e \rho \ \Phi)[x {\leftarrow} z][X {\leftarrow} Z][X^* {\leftarrow} Z^*] \ \blacksquare$$

With these changes to the realizability of atomic assertions involving membership in place we can prove a soundness result for Q-realizability for TK.

The deliberations of this section have been of a technical nature and are not based upon any of our programming intuitions or requirements. Nevertheless they are important for a proper understanding of those modifications which are. It is to these we now turn.

3.2 Unwanted witnesses

A problem which arises almost immediately one begins to entertain the use of realizability as a PSR is that certain objects appear in programs which are unwanted in some sense. This is most clearly evident in work using MLTT (see for example [Backhouse 88] [Abbas 87] or [Nordstrom 87]) and we shall elaborate this a little in section 4. One way in which these objects arise concerns certain very simple atomic assertions. These are often crucial parts of the specification but are not intended to give rise to objects within an putative program for the specification. It is possible to design these out of our PSR by isolating them in certain contexts in which they may occur. In TK atomic assertion are of two kinds, membership within types, and the simple atoms. As we discussed above, realizability for these is defined as follows:

$e \rho \; \Phi \qquad$ is $\quad \Phi \;$ *(for Φ simple atomic)*
$e \rho \; t{\in}T \qquad$ is $\quad <e,t>{\in}T^*$

Now we ensure that when simple atoms occur in conjunctions and they do not give rise to an object in the program:

$e \rho \; (\Phi \wedge \psi) \qquad$ is $\quad \Phi \wedge e \rho \; \psi \;$ *(for Φ simple atomic)*
$e \rho \; (\Phi \wedge \psi) \qquad$ is $\quad e \rho \; \Phi \wedge \psi \;$ *(for ψ simple atomic)*

Both of these alterations are easily shown to be sound. However this is still rather limited in scope. One common form of conjunction is $t{\in}T \wedge \psi$ (for example: $(\exists x{\in}T)\psi$ is syntactic sugar for $(\exists x)(x{\in}T \wedge \psi)$) and as it stands an object which realizes this conjunction will be a pair the *fst* component of which realizes that the witness for x belongs to the correct type. In many cases we may not wish the objects our programs manipulate to explicitly represent typing information (in compile time typed languages), but our alterations to conjunction above do not help here. We proceed from the observation that simple atoms are in a certain sense *self-realizing*. We make this general notion precise by means of:

Definition 3.6

Φ *is self-realizing if, and only if:*

i) $e \rho \; \Phi \rightarrow \Phi$
ii) $\Phi(x) \rightarrow t(x) \rho \; \Phi \;$ *(for some term t)* ∎

We can now explore the extent of this property beyond the simple atoms. It turns out that those formulae which make no existential assertion (so that includes disjunctions) are self realizing. Moreover, we may extend the notion to the types too and obtain a characterisation of certain simple types for which membership is self realizing. Consider the following syntactic classes of formulae and types:

Definition 3.7

The predicates safe(Φ) (Φ *is safe) and* safe(T) (T *is safe) are defined as follows:*

$safe(^{\perp})$
$safe(t{\downarrow})$
$safe(t = t')$
$safe(T) \rightarrow safe(t{\in}T)$
$safe(\Phi) \wedge safe(\psi) \rightarrow safe(\Phi \wedge \psi)$
$safe(\psi) \rightarrow safe(\Phi \rightarrow \psi)$
$safe(\Phi) \rightarrow safe((\forall x)\Phi)$
$safe(\Phi) \rightarrow safe(\{x \mid \Phi\})$
$safe(T) \wedge (\forall X)(safe(X) \rightarrow safe(B(X))) \rightarrow safe(\Xi(T,B(X)))$ ∎

It is now possible to show that:

Proposition 3.8

i)   If safe(Φ) then Φ is self-realizing
ii) If safe(T) then $x{\in}T$ is self-realizing

proof For this formulation we require soundness of Q-realizability and proceed, in both cases by induction on the structure of formulae. Safe formulae are close to the following classes of formulae found in related literature: negative, alomst negative [Beeson 85], Harrop [Dummett 77], essentially $(\vee, \exists)$-free [Feferman 79], type zero [Hayashi 87]. ∎

As a result of this we can reformulate realizability with the following clauses:

$$
\begin{array}{lll}
e \, \rho \, \Phi & is & \Phi \;\; (for\ safe(\Phi)) \\
e \, \rho \, (\Phi \wedge \psi) & is & \Phi \wedge e \, \rho \, \psi \;\; (for\ safe(\Phi)) \\
e \, \rho \, (\Phi \wedge \psi) & is & e \, \rho \, \Phi \wedge \psi \;\; (for\ safe(\psi))
\end{array}
$$

Notice that, for example, $t \in T \wedge \psi$ will succumb now, providing that T is safe. In fact, the types we use in programming languages to build data structures are all safe. More exactly, we have the following proposition:

Proposition 3.9

i) $safe(T) \wedge safe(S) \Rightarrow safe(T \otimes S)$ *(cartesian product)*

ii) $safe(T) \wedge safe(S) \Rightarrow safe(T \oplus S)$ *(disjoint union)*

iii) $safe(T) \wedge safe(S) \Rightarrow safe(T \rightarrow S)$ *(function space)*

iv) $safe(T) \wedge (\forall X)(safe(X) \Rightarrow safe(B(X))) \Rightarrow safe(\Xi(T,B(X)))$ ∎

We take proposition 3.9 as evidence to support the fact that in TK types and assertions are distinct (as opposed to MLTT in which there is an isomorphism between types and assertions): Data types are, in the precise sense indicated, simpler than propositional types in general. In TK then we might rather have employed the slogan "the homomorphism between propositions and types". This is covered in more detail in [Henson 88].

We shall see in 3.5 and 3.6 some examples of how these ideas can be used to supress unwanted objects.

3.3 Polymorphism

The natural expression of polymorphism, at the level of specifications, utilises higher order universal quantification. A schema for polymorphic specification might be:

POLYMORPHIC SPECIFICATION: $(\forall X)((\forall x)(\Phi(X,x) \Rightarrow (\exists y)(\psi(X,x,y))))$

which suggests that we can find a solution to the basic specification schema for all types, X.

There are two possible approaches to extend realizability to the universal quantifier over types. These correspond to two notions of polymorphism which have been referred to [Leivant 83] as the *type abstraction* approach [Reynolds 74] and the *type quantification* approach [McQueen 82]. For type abstraction we mirror, exactly, quantification at the object level. We refer to this as the *Kleene approach*:

$$e \, \rho \, \forall X \Phi \quad is \quad (\forall X)((e\,X)\!\downarrow \wedge \, (e\,X) \, \rho \, \Phi)$$

Let us consider the intuitive meaning of such assertions. The universal assertion is claiming that e is a program which satisfies Φ for all types. e is thus a polymorphic object. Note that under this interpretation e must take a type as an argument and then meet the specification Φ. So we are introducing terms which resemble those of the second order lambda calculus; for example a polymorphic specification of the form given above leads to programs of the form: $e = \lambda X.\lambda x.\lambda z.d$ where $\psi(X,x,(e\,X\,x\,z))$ whenever $z \, \rho \, \Phi(X,x)$.

The type quantification approach to polymorphism is that adopted in languages like Miranda[TM]

[Turner 85]. Terms are no longer uniquely typed for we supress the explicit type abstraction at the object level. This suggests:

$$e \; \rho \; \forall X\Phi \quad is \quad (\forall X)(e \; \rho \; \Phi)$$

Note how the type information remains in the assertion and, in this case, does not appear in the realizer e. We call this the *Kreisel-Troelstra approach* [Kreisel 70] because they adopted a similar definition for realizing second order quantification in the theory HAS of "Heyting arithmetic with species". In this case the program which arises for our polymorphic specification has the form: $e = \lambda x.z.d$ where $\psi(X,x,(e \; x \; z))$ whenever $z \; \rho \; \Phi(X,x)$.

So, if we are thinking about the design of a PSR for PEBBLE [Burstall 84] we should adopt the Kleene approach whereas the Kreisel-Troelstra approach to realizability seems more in line with the (rather more numerous) languages which are in some sense congruent to the programming notation and polymorphic types of Miranda.

3.4 Data abstraction

Abstract data types are rendered in theories such as TK via the higher order existential type [Mitchell 85]. A typical formulation for such a structure might be:

$$ABSTRACT \; DATA\text{-}TYPES: \; (\exists X \exists f_1 \in T_1(X)...\exists f_n \in T_n(X))\Phi$$

in which $\Phi \leftrightarrow true$, if we consider simple anarchic algebras and, in other cases, Φ will be the conjunction of a number of "axioms" for the f_i.

There are similar options open to us for the realization of the higher order existential formulae. The first (the Kleene approach) is to mirror the clause for object level existentials:

$$e \; \rho \; \exists X\Phi \quad is \quad (\exists X)(X=(fst \; e) \wedge (snd \; e) \; \rho \; \Phi)$$

It is necessary to adopt the existential quantification on the right hand side because *(fst e)* is a term and not a type (syntactically); consequently *(fst e)* cannot itself be substituted for X in Φ. This mimics the unmodified object level existential and not the Q-realizability formulation. But presumably we do wish it to be the case that for a given type T for X we do actually have some algebra. This assertion amounts to a Q-realizability variant:

$$e \; \rho \; \exists X\Phi \quad is \quad (\exists X)(X=(fst \; e) \wedge \Phi \wedge (snd \; e) \; \rho \; \Phi)$$

Perhaps surprisingly, this clause, unlike the similar one at the object level, is already consonant with our intuitions of a PSR: *(fst e)* is a type and *(snd e)* is a collection of operations (satisfying any axioms specified). This definition gives rise, in a very natural way, to a universe of algebras of the sort described by the formula Φ. Specifically we define:

$$\Sigma_{kleene}X.\Phi = \{ <X,z> \mid z \; \rho \; \Phi \wedge \Phi \}$$

More formally this is given by the comprehension term:

$$\Sigma_{kleene}X.\Phi = \{ w \mid (\exists X)(\exists z)(w=<z,X> \wedge z \; \rho \; \Phi \wedge \Phi \}$$

which we stress because it becomes clear that this is a *kind* and not a type.

The second possibility (the Kreisel-Troelstra approach) is to take:

$$e \; \rho \; \exists X\Phi \quad is \quad (\exists X)(e \; \rho \; \Phi)$$

In this case the type remains squarely within the assertion structure and not the program object. Thus the object *e* here plays the role of *(snd e)* in the alternative Kleene approach. In this case the corresponding universe of types is given by:

$$\Sigma_{kreisel}X.\Phi = \{w \mid (\exists X)(w \rho \ \Phi)\}$$

In order to evaluate these possibilities we consider a simple example. Suppose we take the classic example: sorting. The naive polymorphic specification is too strong:

$$(\forall X)((\forall x)(x \in List(X) \rightarrow (\exists y)(y \in List(X) \wedge sorted(X,y) \wedge perm(X,x,y))))$$

because arbitrary types will not have an ordering relation. We can of course specify a universe of acceptable types utilising the higher order existential type. First we consider a type $\Sigma X.\Phi$ where Φ postulates the existence of a binary relation on *X* which is a total ordering. This becomes our universe for the specification. If $\Sigma X.\Phi$ is given its Kleene interpretation we may make the following definition:

$$(\forall w)(w \in \Sigma_{kleene}X.\Phi \rightarrow ((\forall x)(x \in List(fst(w)) \rightarrow$$
$$(\exists y)(y \in List(fst \ w)) \wedge sorted((fst \ w),(snd \ w),y) \wedge perm((fst \ w),x,y))))$$

which, anticipating 3.8, may be written more perspicuously:

$$(\forall <X,r> \in \Sigma_{kleene}X.\Phi)((\forall x)(x \in List(X) \rightarrow (\exists y)(y \in List(X)) \wedge sorted(X,r,y) \wedge perm(X,x,y)))$$

This seems quite appropriate. If we interpret $\Sigma X.\Phi$ as $\Sigma_{kreisel}X.\Phi$ then it is not obvious how we can instantiate the type constructor *List* with a suitable type for the relation *r* without resorting to a rather ugly device:

$$(\forall r \in \Sigma_{kreisel}X.\Phi)(\exists Y)(r \rho \ \Phi[X \leftarrow Y] \rightarrow$$
$$((\forall x)(x \in List(Y) \rightarrow (\exists y)(y \in List(Y)) \wedge sorted(Y,r,y) \wedge perm(Y,x,y))))$$

That is, we recover the type information supressed in the universe $\Sigma_{kreisel}X.\Phi$. So evidently the adoption of the Kleene Q-realizability clause for abstract data types seems most appropriate for a PSR.

3.5 Types and Typechecking

Often the precondition in a specification amounts to restriction on type. Here is the example from the previous section written slightly differently:

$$(\forall <X,r> \in \Sigma_{kleene}X.\Phi)(\forall x \in List(X))(\exists y \in List(X))(sorted(X,r,y) \wedge perm(X,x,y))$$

This example demonstrates how such pre-conditions can be presented neatly by the use of syntactic sugar for bounded quantification. These are unpacked in the obvious way. However, there are certain important consequences of allowing the realizability to proceed via this unpacking. Consider the following schematic bounded quantification and its realization:

$$e \rho \ (\forall x \in T)\Phi \ is \ e \rho \ (\forall x)(x \in T \rightarrow \Phi) \ is \ (\forall x)((e \ x) \rho \ (x \in T \rightarrow \Phi)) \ is$$
$$(\forall x)((\forall z)(z \rho \ (x \in T) \rightarrow (e \ x \ z) \rho \ \Phi))$$

We combine this with a little currying to obtain the following definition of realizability for bounded quantification:

$$e \rho \ (\forall x \in T)\Phi \ \ is \ \ (\forall x)((\forall z)(z \rho \ (x \in T) \rightarrow (e <x, z>) \rho \ \Phi))$$

Note that the realizing function e is supplied with a pair consisting of an arbitrary object together with information as to its type (in T). In programming terms this standard interpretation corresponds to a run-time typed programming language in which each value comes equipped with its type. This might be appropriate if we wished to design a constructive set theory for, say, an object oriented language.

For languages like Miranda this would be entirely inappropriate. In this case we do not expect programs to manipulate objects tagged with their types. This can be acheived by making an alternative definition for bounded quantification:

$$e \, \rho \, (\forall x \in T)\Phi \quad is \quad (\forall x \in T)((e \, x) \, \rho \, \Phi)$$

In this case the typing remains in the assertion structure. We have to be a little careful here because, as it stands, this adjustment to realizability is not sound since AC can now be derived and this contradicts the consistency of TK. However, if we restrict the above to *safe* types the reinterpretation is sound:

$$e \, \rho \, (\forall x \in T)\Phi \quad is \quad (\forall x \in T)((e \, x) \, \rho \, \Phi) \, (for \, safe(T))$$

Even this may be too strong, for safe types include certain object level dependent types and allowing these might lead to a situation in which the type regime admitted in this clause leads to undecidable typechecking. We may wish to restrict the situation further and allow the reinterpretation only for certain 'simple' types . This would be important for Miranda but not for, say, PEBBLE (in which typechecking is not decidable).

This section illustrates another example in which there appears to be a conceptual advantage in isolating a language of data types from the more general and complex language of types which arise from treating propositions as types.

3.6 Conditional assertions

The disjunction is not as useful a specificational device as the closely related notion of conditionals. We now introduce a *conditional assertion* similar (though not equivalent) to one introduced in [Hayashi 87]. These are written by "$t \to \Phi, \psi$" where t is a term and Φ and ψ are formulae (we will also write "$\delta \to \Phi, \psi$" when δ is decidable). There are two (equivalent) interpretations of these assertions:

$$t \to \Phi, \psi \quad \leftrightarrow \quad (t=true \wedge \Phi) \vee (t=false \wedge \psi) \qquad (\vee\text{-}presentation)$$
$$t \to \Phi, \psi \quad \leftrightarrow \quad t \in Bool \wedge (t=true \to \Phi) \wedge (t=false \to \psi) \, (\wedge\text{-}presentation)$$

The motivation for considering these assertions is that they provide a specificational analogue to a programming device: the conditional expression, which is usually written: $t_1 \to t_2, t_3$ where the t_i are terms. Thus a specification of the form $t \to \Phi, \psi$ can be thought of as an intermediate assertion in which part of the program (t) is already evident but where the alternatives Φ and ψ are still pure specifications. We might hope that there is a smooth passage from assertions of this kind to conditional programs. However this passage will be by no means smooth if we adopt a PSR in which $e \, \rho \, t \to \Phi, \psi$ just in case e realizes one of the two syntactic unpackings given above. For example if we take:

$$e \, \rho \, t \to \Phi, \psi \quad is \quad e \, \rho \, (t=true \wedge \Phi) \vee (t=false \wedge \psi)$$

then e will have the form $<b,z>$ where b is *true* and $z \, \rho \, \Phi$ or where b is *false* and $z \, \rho \, \psi$. Note that e does not have the form $<b,<y,z>>$ where $y \, \rho \, t=true$ (or $t=false$) for the reasons outlined in 3.2. The alternative presentation is no better; there $(e \, x) \, \rho \, \Phi$ if $x \, \rho \, t=true$ (or $(e \, x) \, \rho \, \psi$ if $x \, \rho \, t=false$). However we can adopt the following definition of realizability:

$e \, \rho \; t \rightarrow \Phi, \psi \;$ *is* $\; t \rightarrow e \, \rho \; \Phi, e \, \rho \; \psi$

and this is much more useful as the following proposition demonstrates. First we note that the two unpackings give rise to four derived rules for the conditional assertion (two introduction rules and two elimination rules). This follows the development in [Hayashi 87] although in that case the rules are not independent and the situation is very complicated. We consider just one case for exposition.

Proposition 3.10

The following rule for → - elimination (∨-presentation) is sound:

$$[t{=}true \wedge \Phi] \qquad [t{=}false \wedge \psi]$$

$$\frac{t \rightarrow \Phi, \psi \quad \eta \qquad\qquad \eta}{\eta}$$

proof This is just one of the cases of proposition 2.4. Suppose, by hypothesis, that $t_1 \, \rho \; t \rightarrow \Phi, \psi$, that $t_2(z_1) \, \rho \; \eta$ whenever $z_1 \, \rho \; t{=}true \wedge \Phi$ and that $t_3(z_2) \, \rho \; \eta$ whenever $z_2 \, \rho \; t{=}false \wedge \psi$. By the definition of realizability for conditional assertions we have: $t \rightarrow t_1 \, \rho \; \Phi, t_1 \, \rho \; \psi$. Note that if $z_1 \, \rho$ $t{=}true \wedge \Phi$ then we have: $t{=}true \wedge z_1 \, \rho \; \Phi$ (similarly for z_2). So then we can conclude that $t \rightarrow t_2(t_1)$, $t_3(t_1) \, \rho \; \eta$ ■

So the realizability interpretation above does indeeed reflect an intuitive notion of *specification refinement* in which the overall structure (a conditional form) is maintained. We shall find that these assertions are particularly useful in 3.8 when we consider pattern directed invocation.

3.7 Let assertions

One extension to the assertion language which we have found useful, and which we use in particular in our earlier work are the "let assertions". Hayashi [Hayashi 87] also considered assertions of this sort but here the interpretation is rather more general. In the assertion: "*let p = x in Φ*" we take p to be a *pattern* in the sense this is used in a number of functional programming languages. To be exact we assume that patterns over a type T are built up from variables, constants, bracketing and data construction in a standard way, together with a binary union over patterns which is introduced purely for technical purposes:

Definition 3.11

The grammar of patterns:

$$p \rightarrow (p) \mid D \, p^* \mid x \mid c \mid p \cup p$$
$$p^* \rightarrow p \, \{ p \}^* \quad ■$$

where D is a data-constructor. To facilitate the definition of let assertions we define a binary relation between terms and patterns which holds just in case the term has the structure of the pattern.

Definition 3.12

   The matching relation:

   $t \sim x$
   $t \sim c$ $\leftrightarrow t = c$
   $t \sim (p)$ $\leftrightarrow t \sim p$
   $t \sim D\,p^* \leftrightarrow (\exists v^*)(v^* \sim p^* \wedge t = (D\,v^*))$ ∎

in which v^* is a tuple and $v^* \sim p^*$ is the obvious conjunction. This relation is decidable. We say that two patterns are *T-equivalent* providing that they match against precisely the same elements of the type *T*. For example, the patterns x and $[] \cup (a{:}l)$ are *List*-equivalent since in both cases the patterns match against the entire type *List*.

Before we go on we need some technical apparatus to cope with substitution into formulae in the presence of patterns. By $\Phi(p)$ we mean that Φ has the free variables of p free. The formula $\Phi(x/p)$ is formed from $\Phi(p)$ by substituting appropriate components of x for the free variables of p in an obvious way. If $x \sim p$ then $\Phi(p \leftarrow t)$, the notion of substituting a suitable term for a pattern, can then be defined so that it satisfies: $\Phi(p \leftarrow t) = \Phi(x/p)(x \leftarrow t)$. A simple example: $\Phi(<x_1,x_2>) = x_1 \in A \wedge x_2 \in B$ Then, $\Phi(x/<x_1,x_2>) = (fst\ x) \in A \wedge (snd\ x) \in B$ and $\Phi(<x_1,x_2> \leftarrow <a,b>) = \Phi(x/<x_1,x_2>)(x \leftarrow <a,b>) = a \in A \wedge b \in B$.

We can now unpack let assertions:

   $let\ p = x\ in\ \Phi \leftrightarrow (\exists x)(x \sim p \wedge \Phi(x/p))$

There are two derived rules for introducing and eliminating let-assertion formulae which are easy to construct from the unpacking provided above. As before it is possible to provide a realizability interpretation independently of the syntactic unpacking given above; we define:

   $e\,\rho\ let\ p = x\ in\ \Phi\ is\ let\ p = x\ in\ e\,\rho\ \Phi$

Although we do not have the space to provide the reasoning explicitly, we can now ensure that let expressions are obtained from proofs which involve instances of the let assertion elimination rule just as we did for the conditional assertions in the previous section.

3.8 Pattern directed invocation

Modern functional programming languages, among others, allow for pattern directed invocation. In line with the development of the previous two sections we allow pattern directed quantification in the assertion language. We extend lambda abstraction to patterns in the standard way:

Definition 3.13

   Pattern directed lambda terms:

   $\lambda x.t$ *is*   *as usual*
   $\lambda c.t$ *is* $M\,c\,t$
   $\lambda D\,p^*.t$ *is* $D!\ (\lambda p^*.t)$
   $\lambda (p).t$ *is* $\lambda p.t$
   $\lambda p\,p^*.t$ *is* $\lambda p.\lambda p^*.t$ ∎

where $D!$ is the combinator which "undoes" the constructor D: that is, $D!\,f\,(D\,v_1 \dots v_n) = f\,v_1 \dots v_n$; $D!\,f\,z = F$ otherwise.

If $f = \lambda p.t$ then we shall also write this, as is standard, by the equation: $f\,p = t$ (see 3.9 for an example).

Now we use the relation defined in 3.7 in order to define universal quantification over a pattern:

$(\forall p \in T)\Phi$ is $(\forall x \in T)(x \sim p \to \Phi(x/p), fail)$

where *fail* asserts failure: we take realizability of *fail* to be: $e \rho \; fail$ is $e=F \wedge fail$ (F is Turner's failure combinator). Now how do we realize these assertions? Perhaps surprisingly, in this case we do realize this via the syntactic unpacking. This leads to:

$e \rho \; (\forall p \in T)\Phi \leftrightarrow (\forall x \in T)((e\,x)\!\downarrow \wedge x \sim p \to (e\,x) \rho \; \Phi(x/p), (e\,x) \rho \; fail)$

which is rather intuitive (we assume here that, at most, *safe(T)*). The rules for introducing and eliminating these quantifiers are derived in a straightforward manner from their definition. Briefly, $(\forall p \in T)\Phi$ is introduced from the assumptions $\Phi(p\leftarrow t)$, $t \in T$ and $t \sim p$; the soundness of realizability can be extended easily since $\lambda p.e$ will realize the conclusion if $e(p\leftarrow t)$ realizes $\Phi(p\leftarrow t)$. $(\forall p \in T)\Phi$ is eliminated with the usual extra assumption that $t \in T$ to yield $t \sim p \to \Phi(p\leftarrow t)$, *fail* as conclusion. If e realizes that $(\forall p \in T)\Phi$ and $t \in T$ then $(e\,t)$ realizes the conclusion. Finally, note that $(\forall p \in T)\Phi$ and $(\forall p' \in T)\Phi$ are equivalent providing that p and p' are T-equivalent.

3.9 Recursion equations

The work of the previous section will provide us in many cases with, in some sense, incomplete functions. For example, if $e \rho \; (\forall p \in T)\Phi$ then $(e\,x)\!\downarrow$ for all $x \in T$ but $(e\,x)$ is only useful when x conforms to p. In pattern directed languages one is inclined to provide a number of incomplete functions of this kind which taken together provide a complete (non *fail*) function. We will use the notation $e_1 \mathbf{|} \; e_2$ for a pair of such incomplete functions. This is to be understood in the term language via Turner's T combinator.

$e_1 \mathbf{|} \; e_2$ is $T\,e_1\,e_2$

Alternatively we can read $\mathbf{|}$ as the equivalent 'bar' operator introduced in [Peyton-Jones 87]. For systems involving more than two clauses we can always write $e_1 \mathbf{|} \; e_2 \mathbf{|} \; e_3$ which can be understood to mean $e_1 \mathbf{|} \; (e_2 \mathbf{|} \; e_3)$. The bar binds more tightly than the logical connectives.

Now we can prove the following theorem:

Proposition 3.14

$e = e_1 \mathbf{|} \; e_2 \wedge e_1 \rho \; (\forall p_1 \in X)\Phi \wedge e_2 \rho \; (\forall p_2 \in X)\Phi \to e \rho \; (\forall p_1 \cup p_2 \in X)\Phi$ ∎

This device is most useful in connection with the elimination rule for inductive types. This rule gives rise, via the soundness of realizability, to recursively defined functions. We shall not tackle the general case for TK in this section because of certain technical complications regarding the type functor B in $\Xi(A,B(X))$ (see [Henson 88b] for more detail) and we will concentrate on a simple special case: the natural numbers. Our analysis relies crucially on the above, and on the material of 3.5 and 3.8.

The introduction rules are, as usual:

$$\frac{}{0 \in N} \; (i) \qquad \frac{n \in N}{succ(n) \in N} \; (ii)$$

and the elimination rule of 2.2 simplifies to:

$$\frac{\psi(0) \qquad (\forall n)(n \in \{succ\} \otimes N \wedge \psi((snd\ n)) \rightarrow \psi(n))}{(\forall n)(n \in N \rightarrow \psi(n))}$$

We will write elements $<succ,n>$ of the type $\{succ\} \otimes N$ as $succ(n)$ as usual. The rule can be rewritten by a logically equivalent rule which uses pattern directed and bounded quantification.

$$\frac{(\forall 0)\psi(0) \qquad (\forall succ(n) \in N)(\psi(n) \rightarrow \psi(succ(n)))}{(\forall n \in N)(\psi(n))}$$

We can now provide a sketch of how the soundness proof for realizability for inductive data types is proven.

Suppose that, by hypothesis, we have $t_1 \rho\ \psi(0)$ and $t_2 \rho\ (\forall n \in \{succ\} \otimes N)(\psi((snd\ n)) \rightarrow \psi(n))$. Then we see that: $\lambda 0.t_1 \rho\ (\forall 0)\psi(0)$ and $\lambda\ succ(m).t_2\ succ(n)\ (f\ n) \rho\ (\forall succ(n) \in N)(\psi(n) \rightarrow \psi(succ(n)))$ provided that $(f\ n) \rho\ \psi(n)$. Now we need a function *nrec* so that:

$$nrec\ t_1\ t_2\ n \rho\ \psi(n), for\ all\ n \in N$$

We shall claim that this is satisfied if *nrec* is defined to be:

$$nrec\ t_1\ t_2 = \lambda 0.t_1 \mathbf{|}\ \lambda\ succ(m).t_2\ succ(m)\ (nrec\ t_1\ t_2\ m)$$

This is established by N-induction: base case: we need to show that *nrec* $t_1\ t_2\ 0 \rho\ \psi(0)$ but by definition this amounts to $t_1 \rho\ \psi(0)$ which we know. Induction case: *nrec* $t_1\ t_2\ succ(n) \rho\ \psi(succ(n))$ will follow providing that: $t_2\ succ(n)\ (nrec\ t_1\ t_2\ n) \rho\ \psi(succ(n))$ and this will following immediately providing that: *nrec* $t_1\ t_2\ n \rho\ \psi(n)$, but this we have *ex hypothesi*. By proposition 3.14 and the fact that $0 \cup succ(m)$ is a pattern N-equivalent to n the proof is complete. Written out more perspicuously nrec is:

$$nrec\ t_1\ t_2\ 0 \qquad = t_1$$
$$nrec\ t_1\ t_2\ succ(m) = t_2\ succ(m)\ (nrec\ t_1\ t_2\ m)$$

4 Conclusions and final comments

The aim of this paper has been to explore a variety of opportunities for overcoming the mismatch between programs and proofs in the context of the constructive and intensional theory TK. Indeed we have gone further: not only do we avoid particularly inappropriate proof objects we actually design for desirable program forms. In MLTT the proof objects are rather low level, essentially a typed lambda calculus. We have shown how it is possible to arrange that the proof objects correspond immediately to higher level expressions. In particular, in 3.9 we saw how to extract pattern directed equations in the Miranda style from proofs of numerical induction. The material of 3.9 can be generalised for the general notion of inductive type which TK supports. The analysis, for safe inductive types, can be found in [Henson 88b].

Our approach has been to put forward modified realizability interpretations for similarly modified infrastructure built onto the term language and onto the assertion language of the theory. These modifications are not arbitrary and can only be made in a principled fashion. In this case the principle at stake is that the modifications should be *sound*. The consequence of soundness is that constructive proofs lead to well defined programs which meet their specification. Our approach should be compared to work with a similar motivation which is, and has been, carried out for program development in MLTT where new types with more reasonable properties are investigated.

One distinctive feature of TK, in comparison to MLTT, is the seperation of propositions from types. We began this research with the intuition that there was an important conceptual distinction between programming data types and those more adventurous types which arise from regarding propositions as types and that this distinction might be lost in the parsimony of MLTT. We now feel vindicated: programming data types seem to be simple in a technical sense and this we termed *safe* in section 3.2. These types are in a precise sense trivial or at least the evidence that elements belong to them is. This allows us to omit this information in certain cases, for example, in bounded quatification.

Another distinctive feature of the theory is its *intensionality*, in particular the intensionality implicit in realizability. For example a realizer of Φ does not necessarily realize ψ even if Φ and ψ are logically equivalent (consider for example the realizers of the assertions $\Phi \wedge \psi$ and $\psi \wedge \Phi$). So realizers are sensitive, not only to the logical force of the assertions but to the *way in which they are presented to us*. One interesting consequence of this is a precise sense in which theories such as TK fail to be directly adequate (Feferman's sense) for the activity which they attempt to formalise. For example in TK although we can account for bounded quantification (via the obvious interpretation using unbounded quantification and implication) we cannot *isolate* the instances for the purposes of providing an alternative realizability interpretation since this requires an intensional distinction whereas the interpretation above just accounts for the logical force of bounded quantification: the extensional property. These intensional distinctions can only be achieved if there is an explicit concept in the theory, which is made available by explicit syntax. The same argument holds true for let-assertions and for conditional assertions among others. So although TK may be an adequate basis for accounting for certain general properties of programming logics (for example showing that they are consistent via an explicit semantics) it is not in *itself* adequate for the practice of program development. That degree of adequacy can only be achieved by providing certain intensional properties: particular ways of writing things down and some of these devices have been expored in this paper. We feel that an excessively parsimonious approach to the design of constructive theories may be appropriate for the analysis of the foundations of constructive mathematics but is not appropriate for the practice of program development. This was a major motivation behind the development of TK and is the focus of our critique of the use of MLTT in this area.

5 Acknowledgements

I should like to thank Ray Turner with whom TK was developed for useful conversations. The research reported here was funded by the Science and Engineering Council of the United Kingdom, grant number: GR/F/02809.

6 References

[Abbas 87] Abbas, A., **Programming with types and rules in Martin-Lof's theory of types**, Ph.D. thesis, London University, 1987

[Backhouse 87] Backhouse, R., **Overcoming the mismatch between programs and proofs**, Proc. workshop on programming logic, pp 116-122, Marstrand, June 1987.

[Backhouse 88] Backhouse, R., *et al*, **Do-it-yourself type theory**, tech. rep. CS 8811, Dept. Maths. and computing science, University of Gronigen, 1988; to appear: Formal aspects of computing, 1989.

[Beeson 85] Beeson, M. J., **Foundations of constructive mathematics**, Springer Verlag, 1985

[Beeson 86] Beeson, M. J., **Proving programs and programming proofs**, Logic, Methodology and Philosophy of Science VII, North Holland, pp 51-82, 1986

[Beeson 88] Beeson, M. J., **Towards a computation system based on set theory**, tech. rep., Dept. Maths. and Computer Sciences, San Jose state University, 1988

272

[Burstall 84] Burstall, R. and Lampson, B., **A kernel language for abstract data types and modules,** Symp. on semantics of data types, LNCS Vol. 173, pp 1- 50, Springer, 1984

[Constable 86] Constable, R. *et al*, **Implementing mathematics with the NuPRL proof development system,** Prentice Hall, 1986

[Dummett 77] Dummett, M., **Elements of Intuitionism,** Clarendon Press, Oxford, 1977

[Feferman 79] Feferman, S., **Constructive theories of functions and classes,** Logic Coll. '78., pp 159-224, North Holland, 1979

[Hayashi 87] Hayashi, S. and Nakano, H., **The PX system - a computational logic,** Publications of the Research Institute for Mathematical Sciences, Kyoto University, Tokyo, 1987

[Henson 88a]   Henson, M. C. and Turner, R., **A constructive set theory for program development,** Proc. 8th conf. on FST & TCS, LNCS vol. 338, Springer, pp 329-347, 1988

[Henson 88b]   Henson, M. C., **Transformational programming, type simulations and intensional set theory,** submitted to: ACM trans. prog. lang. and sys., also: Tech. Rep. CSM-121 Dept. Computer Science, University of Essex, October, 1988

[Henson 89]   Henson, M. C., **Program development in the constructive set theory TK,** To appear: Formal Aspects of Computing, 1989

[Kleene 45] Kleene, S. C., **On the interpretation of intuitionistic number theory,** J. symb. logic, 10, pp 109-124, 1945

[Kleene 71] Kleene, S. C., **Realizability: a retrospective survey,** Proc.   Cambridge summer school in mathematical logic, pp 95-113, 1971

[Kreisel 70] Kreisel, G. and Troelstra, A., **Formal systems for some branches of intuitionistic analysis,** Annals of math. logic., Vol. 1, pp 229-387, 1970

[Leivant 83] Leivant, D., **Polymorphic type inference,** Proc. 10th ACM symp. on principles of programming languages, 1983

[McQueen 82] McQueen, D. and Sethi, R., **A semantic model of types for applicative programming languages,** Proc. ACM symp. LISP and functional programming, pp 243-252, 1982

[Martin-Lof 82]   Martin-Lof, P., **Constructive mathematics and computer programming,** Logic, methodology and philosophy of science VI, North Holland, 1982

[Mitchell 85] Mitchell, J. and Plotkin, G., **Abstract types have existential type,** Proc. 12th ACM conf. on principles of programming languages, pp 37-51, 1985

[Nordstrom 87]   Nordstrom, B., **Terminating general recursion,** Tech. rep., University of Goteborg, Programming methodology group, 1987

[Reynolds 74] Reynolds, J. C., **Towards a theory of type structures,** Proc. programming symposium, LNCS Vol. 19, Springer, 1974

[Turner 85] Turner, D. A., **Miranda™: a non strict functional language with polymorphic types,** Proc. conf. on functional programming and computer architecture, LNCS Vol. 201, pp 445-472, 1985 ™ Miranda is a trademark of Research Software Limited.

Initialisation with a final value, an exercise in program transformation

Wim H. Hesselink, March 1989

Rijksuniversiteit Groningen, Department of Computing Science
P.O. Box 800, 9700 AV Groningen, The Netherlands

0. Introduction

In an environment with input and three program variables p, q and r, we consider a command S given by

0) $S = [\![\text{ read}(p)$
          ; **while** $b(p, q)$ **do**
          $[\![\quad q := f(p, q)$
          ; $\quad r := g(p, r)$
          ; $\quad$ read$(p)]\!]$
          $]\!]$

where b, f and g are expressions in two variables. The problem is to extend command S by initialising variable r with the final value of q.

This problem often occurs in programming. In principle, it is always there when input is read in two passes. For us the original occurrence was the problem to read a string of decimal digits and to store the represented natural number n in a stack of 5–digit numbers $m(k)$, in such a way that $n = \sum(k :: m(k) \times 10^{5 \times k})$. In this case, q is the number of digits read, modulo 5, and r is the triple that consists of the decimal position of the current digit, the current accumulated 5–digit number, and the stack.

As noted above, the abstract problem can be solved by using two passes over the input. That solution is not elegant. Moreover, for interactive programs we can hardly expect the user to give the same input twice. Another solution is to build a separate data structure to store the input. We shall derive a third solution, which uses a recursive procedure with both value and procedural parameters instead of a separate data structure. We do not claim that our solution is efficient. The only claim is that it has a certain elegance. One could say that the task of building an appropriate data structure is delegated to the compiler.

Usually such solutions are obtained by operational reasoning and formal proofs are omitted. Our objective is to present a derivation together with a proof of correctness. The derivation is based on techniques of program transformation as developed in [H0], [H1] and [H2]. Apart from one big theorem of [H2], however, the present note is independent.

The main purpose of this note is to serve as a test for our formal ability to manipulate procedures, recursion and parameters.

1. Relational semantics

We use relational semantics for the formalisation of the problem specification. Let St be the state space. Let ∞ be a symbol not in St and let Stt be the union of St with the singleton set that contains ∞. Any command c is characterised by a relation $[\![c]\!]$ between St and Stt. The interpretation is as follows. For states $s, t \in St$:

(1) $\qquad s[\![c]\!]\, t \;\equiv\;$ execution of c may transform s into t,

$\qquad\quad s[\![c]\!]\infty \;\equiv\;$ execution of c starting in s need not terminate.

We define equivalence ($\cong$) of commands c and d by

(2) $\qquad c \cong d \;\equiv\; (\forall s \in St, t \in Stt :: s[\![c]\!]\, t \;\equiv\; s[\![d]\!]\, t)$.

We use the program constructors composition (;), choice ($[\!]$), guards (?) and assertions (!) in the same way as in [H0] and [H1]. In relational semantics these constructors are defined as follows. For commands c and d and elements $s \in St$ and $t \in Stt$ we have

(3) $\qquad s[\![c\, ;\, d]\!]\, t \;\equiv\; (\exists u \in St :: s[\![c]\!]\, u \wedge u[\![d]\!]\, t) \;\vee\; (s[\![c]\!]\infty \wedge t = \infty)$,

(4) $\qquad s[\![c\,[\!]\, d]\!]\, t \;\equiv\; s[\![c]\!]\, t \vee s[\![d]\!]\, t$.

We generalise (4) to unbounded choice (cf. [H0]). For a family $(i \in I :: c.i)$ of commands we introduce a choice command $([\!]\, i \in I :: c.i)$ with

(5) $\qquad s[\![([\!]\, i \in I :: c.i)]\!]\, t \;\equiv\; (\exists i \in I :: s[\![c.i]\!]\, t)$.

For any boolean function b on St we have a guard command $?b$ and an assertion command $!b$ given by

(6) $\qquad s[\![?b]\!]\, t \;\equiv\; b.s \wedge s = t$,

$\qquad\quad s[\![!b]\!]\, t \;\equiv\; (b.s \wedge s = t) \vee (\neg b.s \wedge t = \infty)$.

The standard commands $skip$, $fail$ and $abort$ are defined by

(7) $\qquad skip = ?true = !true$,

$\qquad\quad fail = ?false \quad,\quad abort = !false$.

Assertions are used only occasionally. Guards, however, are very important, especially in combination with the choice operator. For example, the conditional combination is constructed by

(8) $\qquad$ **if** b **then** c **else** d **fi** $\cong (?b\, ;\, c\,[\!]\, ?\neg b\, ;\, d)$.

If $f : St \to V$ is a function and $v \in V$, we define the boolean function $(f = v)$ on St by

(9) $\qquad (f = v).s \;\equiv\; (f.s = v)$.

A procedure p with an input parameter v of type V is regarded as a family $(v \in V :: p.v)$ of commands $p.v$. A call of procedure p with actual parameter f is the command

(10) $\qquad ([\!]\, v \in V :: ?(f = v)\, ;\, p.v)$.

Notice that in (8) and (10) the guards immediately follow a choice operator and that the disjunction of the guards is the constant boolean function $true$. This fact is important for the implementability of these constructions. We note in particular that

(11) $\qquad ([\!]\, v \in V :: ?(f = v)) \;\cong\; skip$.

2. The formal specification

For the moment we abstract from the form of command S as given by (0). So, we let S be an arbitrary, possibly nondeterminate command. Let q and r be state variables. What does it mean to extend command S by initialising variable r by the final value of q? Our answer is that we want to construct an implementable command T that for all states $s, t \in St$ satisfies

$$\text{(12)} \qquad s[\![T]\!]t \;\equiv\; s[\![r := q.t\,;\, S]\!]t, \quad \text{and}$$
$$s[\![T]\!]\infty \;\equiv\; (\exists v :: s[\![r := v\,;\, S]\!]\infty)$$

where $q.t$ is the value of variable q in state t. In the second alternative, nontermination of T is allowed if there is some initial value of r such that S need not terminate. This choice can be justified by the observation that (according to (0)) termination of S is independent of the initial value of r. In order to get a more convenient version of (12), we observe that for any $s \in St$ and $t \in Stt$

$$\begin{aligned}
&\quad \text{(12)}\\
&\equiv \quad \{\text{as given}\}\\
&\quad (\exists v :: s[\![r := v\,;\, S]\!]t \wedge (t = \infty \vee q.t = v))\\
&\equiv \quad \{\text{(9) and (6)}\}\\
&\quad (\exists v :: s[\![r := v\,;\, S]\!]t \wedge (t = \infty \vee t[\![\,?(q = v)]\!]t))\\
&\equiv \quad \{\text{a somewhat lengthy calculation using (6) and (3)}\}\\
&\quad (\exists v :: s[\![r := v\,;\, S\,;\; ?(q = v)]\!]t)\\
&\equiv \quad \{\text{(5)}\}\\
&\quad s[\![\,(\,[\!|\,v :: r := v\,;\, S\,;\; ?(q = v))\,]\!]t.
\end{aligned}$$

Therefore, specification (12) is equivalent to

$$\text{(13)} \qquad T \;\cong\; (\,[\!|\,v :: r := v\,;\, S\,;\; ?(q = v)).$$

This is a nice specification of T, but it is not yet implementable, for it uses guards that are not at implementable positions, and an unbounded choice. The righthand side of (13) is like a procedure call where the input parameter v is to be determined upon termination of the call.

We claim that specification (13) is implied by

$$\text{(14)} \qquad (\forall v :: T\,;\; ?(q = v) \;\cong\; r := v\,;\, S\,;\; ?(q = v)).$$

This is proved by calculation of the righthand side of (13):

$$\begin{aligned}
&\quad (\,[\!|\,v :: r := v\,;\, S\,;\; ?(q = v))\\
&\cong \quad \{\text{(14)}\}\\
&\quad (\,[\!|\,v :: T\,;\; ?(q = v))\\
&\cong \quad \{\text{distributive law (17) below}\}\\
&\quad T\,;\,(\,[\!|\,v :: ?(q = v))\\
&\cong \quad \{\text{(11)}\}\\
&\quad T.
\end{aligned}$$

Hence our purpose is to find a command T that satisfies (14). Command T must be independent of v, so the solution $[\![r := v\,;\, S]\!]$ is not adequate.

Remark. Formula (14) does not follow from (13). In fact, formula (14) is an equation in T that need not have solutions. For example, let $S = !(r = v0)$. Assume that V contains different elements $v0$ and $v1$. If $v = v1$, the righthand side of (14) does not terminate. Therefore, equation (14) implies that T does not terminate. This leads to a contradiction in the case that $v = v0$.

3. The command algebra approach

In this section we give a concise introduction to command algebras as introduced in [H1]. The command algebra together with the procedure declaration serves as an abstract syntax with a more flexible concept of equality. Equality in the command algebra is weaker than the strong requirement of syntactic equality, but in the presence of procedures it is stronger than semantic equivalence.

In [H1], a command algebra A is defined to be a set with constants $fail \in A$, $skip \in A$ and with binary operators ";" and "$[\![$" such that the following axioms are satisfied

$$
\begin{aligned}
(15) \qquad & a \, [\!] \, a = a \, , \\
& a \, [\!] \, b = b \, [\!] \, a \, , \\
& (a \, [\!] \, b) \, [\!] \, c = a \, [\!] \, (b \, [\!] \, c) \, , \\
& a \, [\!] \, fail = a \, , \\
& (a \, ; \, b) \, ; \, c = a \, ; \, (b \, ; \, c) \, , \\
& skip \, ; \, a = a \, ; \, skip = a \, , \\
& fail \, ; \, a = fail \, , \\
& (a \, [\!] \, b) \, ; \, c = a \, ; \, c \, [\!] \, b \, ; \, c \, , \\
& a \, ; \, (b \, [\!] \, c) = a \, ; \, b \, [\!] \, a \, ; \, c \, .
\end{aligned}
$$

A command algebra A is equipped with a partial order "$\leq$" given by

$$(16) \qquad a \leq b \; \equiv \; a = a \, [\!] \, b.$$

It turns out that $a \, [\!] \, b$ is the greatest lower bound of a and b with respect to the order. Therefore, it is natural to use the symbol $[\!]$ for arbitrary greatest lower bounds in A. So, if $E \subset A$ has a greatest lower bound in A, then that bound is denoted by $([\!] \, x \in E :: x)$. The algebra A is called *complete* if and only if every subset of A has a greatest lower bound.

Now we assume that all simple commands used are element of a given command algebra B. We regard the elements of B as straight-line commands. We assume that B is semantically separated (cf. [H1]) in the sense that

$$(17) \qquad (\forall c, d \in B :: c \cong d \; \equiv \; c = d).$$

Procedures and recursion are treated as follows. We introduce a set H of the occurring procedure names. We then form the polynomial algebra $B[H]$, which consists of the command algebra expressions in elements of B and H modulo the equalities induced by the axioms (15) and the identity relations of B and H, see [H1] section 3.1. The next step is to construct an embedding of algebra $B[H]$ into a complete command algebra $B[H]^*$, see [H2]. This completion satisfies the strong distributive law

$$(18) \qquad ([\!] \, p \in E, q \in F :: p \, ; \, q) = ([\!] \, p \in E :: p) \, ; \, ([\!] \, q \in F :: q)$$

for any pair of nonempty subsets E and F of $B[H]^*$. It turns out that a command $([\!] \, x \in E :: x)$ may be regarded as a nondeterminate choice between the commands $x \in E$.

A declaration of the procedures is a function $d : H \to B[H]^*$, where the body of procedure $h \in H$ is defined to be the element $d.h \in B[H]^*$. In this way, recursion and even mutual recursion is possible, and procedure bodies may contain unbounded choice.

4. The algebraic version of the program

An important special case where equation (14) can be solved is the case that $S = skip$. For in that case the assignment $T = [\![r := q]\!]$ solves (14) because of

(19) $(\forall v :: [\![r := q ; \ ?(q = v)]\!] = [\![r := v ; \ ?(q = v)]\!])$.

The formal verification of this formula is left to the reader. The operational argument is that the assignment always terminates and does not change the value of q. Therefore, if initially $q \neq v$, both sides of equation (19) fail. If $q = v$ initially, variable r gets the value v in either case.

We now specialise to command S as given in program (0). The translation to our formalism is done in two steps. We first give a recursive version of (0) in a syntax similar to Pascal. Then we introduce some abbreviations and give the algebraic version. The recursive version of (0) is

(20) $S = [\![\ read(p) ; \ Sr(p)]\!]$

where procedure Sr is given by

(21) **procedure** $Sr(\textbf{input} \ p)$:

     if $\neg b(p, q)$ **then** $skip$ **else**

     $[\![\quad q := f(p, q)$

     $; \quad r := g(p, r)$

     $; \quad read(p)$

     $; \quad Sr(p)]\!]$ **end** Sr.

As we shall need algebraic manipulation, we introduce the abbreviations

(22) $bq.i = b(i, q)$,

     $P = read(p)$,

     $Q.i = [\![q := f(i, q)]\!]$,

     $R.i = [\![r := g(i, r)]\!]$.

The identifiers P, Q and R are chosen to indicate that the commands update the variables p, q and r, respectively. Using (8) and (10) we get from (20), (21) and (22)

(23) $S = [\![P ; ([\![i :: ?(p = i) ; Sr.i)]\!]$

where $Sr.i$ is the procedure with body

(24) $d.(Sr.i) =$

     $(\ ?\neg bq.i \ [\!] \ ?bq.i ; \ Q.i ; \ R.i ; \ P ; \ ([\![j :: ?(p = j) ; \ Sr.j))$.

5. Commutation relations

At this point we need the observation that the assignment $r := v$ is a terminating command that is independent of variable p and therefore commutes with command P and the guards $?(p = i)$. Later on, we also need independence of variable q. Therefore, we give a more general statement.

Borrowing a term from algebra, let the commutator of a command c be defined as the subset $Z.c$ of algebra B given by

(25) $d \in Z.c \equiv c ; d = d ; c$.

Let Br be defined as the subset of B given by

(26) $c \in Br \equiv$

     $(\forall i, v :: P, ?(p = i), Q.i, ?(q = v), ?bq.i, ?\neg bq.i, abort \in Z.c)$.

Using (22), one easily verifies that

(27) $(\forall v :: [\![r := v]\!] \in Br) \quad \land \quad (\forall i :: R.i \in Br)$.

By (25) and (26), Br is a multiplictive subset of B in the sense that

(28) $skip \in Br \quad \land \quad (\forall c, d \in Br :: c\,; d \in Br)$.

Remark. Because of commutation with *abort*, all elements of Br are total. If there are at least two different values $v0$ and $v1$, the guards of $?(q = v0)$ and $?(q = v1)$ can be used to prove that all commands in Br terminate.

6. The introduction of parameters

We are looking for a solution T of equation (14), which must be independent of v. We observe that for any v

$$r := v\,; S\,; \ ?(q = v)$$
$$= \quad \{(23)\}$$
$$r := v\,; P\,; (\,[\!]\,i :: ?(p = i)\,; Sr.i)\,; \ ?(q = v)$$
$$\cong \quad \{(18), (25), (26), (27)\}$$
$$P\,; (\,[\!]\,i :: ?(p = i)\,; r := v\,; Sr.i\,; \ ?(q = v))$$
$$\cong \quad \{\text{use equation (29) below}\}$$
$$P\,; (\,[\!]\,i :: ?(p = i)\,; Tr.i\,; \ ?(q = v))$$
$$= \quad \{(18); \text{use definition (30) below}\}$$
$$T\,; \ ?(q = v).$$

This shows that if $Tr.i$ satisfies for all v

(29) $Tr.i\,; \ ?(q = v) \quad \cong \quad r := v\,; Sr.i\,; \ ?(q = v)$,

then a solution of (14) and hence of (13) is given by

(30) $T \ = \ P\,; (\,[\!]\,i :: ?(p = i)\,; Tr.i)$.

Up to this point we mainly used commutation and distributivity. In order to solve equation (29), however, we need the structure of the recursive procedure $Sr.i$. We solve (29) by introduction of a recursive procedure $Tf.i.K$ with a command parameter K that is a kind of preprocessor of variable r. So, we generalise equation (29) to

(31) $Tf.i.K\,; \ ?(q = v) \quad \cong \quad r := v\,; K\,; Sr.i\,; \ ?(q = v)$.

A solution Tf of (31) induces a solution of (29) in the form

(32) $Tr.i \ = \ Tf.i.skip$.

Therefore, a solution of (31) gives a solution T of (13) and (14) in

(33) $T \ = \ P\,; (\,[\!]\,i :: ?(p = i)\,; Tf.i.skip)$.

Formally speaking, the introduction of procedure Tf with its two parameters means that the set H of procedure names contains elements $Tf.i.K$ with

$$Tf.i.K = Tf.j.L \quad \equiv \quad i = j \land K = L.$$

7. The crucial calculation

Recall that function $d : H \to B[H]^*$ associates to a procedure name $h \in H$ its body $d.h$. Function d is extended to a function $d^* : B[H]^* \to B[H]^*$ such that $d^*.s$ is obtained from s by replacing every procedure in expression s by its body. Therefore, $d^*.s$ is called the unfolding of s.

A *congruence* on a complete command algebra is defined to be an equivalence relation $\sim$ such that for all commands p, q, r, and s

(34) $\qquad p \sim q \;\wedge\; r \sim s \;\Rightarrow\; p\,;r \sim q\,;s$

and that for all sets of commands E, F

(35) $\qquad (\forall p \in E :: (\exists q \in F :: p \sim q)) \;\wedge\; (\forall q \in F :: (\exists p \in E :: p \sim q))$
$\qquad\qquad \Rightarrow \; (\,\|\, p \in E :: p) \sim (\,\|\, q \in F :: q).$

In view of equation (31), we let $\sim$ be a congruence on commands such that for all values t and v and all commands $K \in Br$ we have

(36) $\qquad Tf.i.K\,;\; ?(q = v) \quad \sim \quad r := v\,;\, K\,;\, Sr.i\,;\; ?(q = v).$

Under this assumption, the unfoldings of both sides of (36) can be shown to satisfy a similar relation. Starting with the unfolding of the righthand side of (36), we have

(37) $\qquad d^*.(r := v\,;\, K\,;\, Sr.i\,;\; ?(q = v))$

$= \quad \{(24);\; K \in B\}$
$\qquad r := v\,;\, K\,;$
$\qquad (\,?\neg bq.i \;\|\; ?bq.i\,;\, Q.i\,;\, R.i\,;\, P\,;\, (\,\|\, j :: ?(p = j)\,;\, Sr.j))\,;\; ?(q = v)$

$= \quad \{(18);\; K \in Br,\; (26)\text{ and }(27)\}$
$\qquad (\,?\neg bq.i\,;\, r := v\,;\; ?(q = v)\,;\, K$
$\qquad \|\; ?bq.i\,;\, Q.i\,;\, P\,;\, (\,\|\, j :: ?(p = j)\,;\, r := v\,;\, K\,;\, R.i\,;\, Sr.j\,;\; ?(q = v)))$

$= \quad \{(19)\}$
$\qquad (\,?\neg bq.i\,;\, r := q\,;\; ?(q = v)\,;\, K$
$\qquad \|\; ?bq.i\,;\, Q.i\,;\, P\,;\, (\,\|\, j :: ?(p = j)\,;\, r := v\,;\, K\,;\, R.i\,;\, Sr.j\,;\; ?(q = v)))$

$\sim \quad \{K \in Br \text{ and } (26);\; (36) \text{ with } K := (K\,;\, R.i)\}$
$\qquad (\,?\neg bq.i\,;\, r := q\,;\, K\,;\; ?(q = v)$
$\qquad \|\; ?bq.i\,;\, Q.i\,;\, P\,;\, (\,\|\, j :: ?(p = j)\,;\, Tf.j.(K\,;\, R.i)\,;\; ?(q = v)))$

$= \quad \{\text{distribution and declaration (38) below}\}$
$\qquad d^*.(Tf.i.(K\,;\, R.i)\,;\; ?(q = v)).$

This calculation requires the declaration

(38) $\qquad d.(Tf.i.K) =$
$\qquad (\,?\neg bq.i\,;\, r := q\,;\, K$
$\qquad \|\; ?bq.i\,;\, Q.i\,;\, P\,;\, (\,\|\, j :: ?(p = j)\,;\, Tf.j.(K\,;\, R.i))).$

8. The conclusion

Let $da : B[H]^* \to B[H]^*$ be the function such that $da.s$ is obtained from expression s by substituting *abort* for every procedure name in expression s. In [H2], we introduce a certain subset Lia of $B[H]^*$. Let BU be the set of the commands in B that are of bounded nondeterminacy. The results 8(0) and 8(1) of [H2] imply

(39) $\qquad B \subset Lia \;\wedge\; (BU\,;\, H\,;\, B) \subset Lia$
$\qquad\qquad \wedge\; (\forall p, q \in Lia :: p \,\|\, q \in Lia).$

The main result of [H2] is a generalisation of the induction rule of De Bakker and Scott [M] theorem 5.5, [B] theorem 7.16). It reads

(40) **Theorem** ([H2] 7(14)). Let E be a set of pairs of elements of Lia such that
(41) $(\forall \langle x, y \rangle \in E :: da.x = da.y)$,
and that for every congruence $\sim$ on $B[H]^*$ we have
(42) $(\forall \langle x, y \rangle \in E :: x \sim y) \Rightarrow (\forall \langle x, y \rangle \in E :: d^*.x \sim d^*.y)$.
Then $x \cong y$ for all pairs $\langle x, y \rangle \in E$.

We apply this theorem to prove that declaration (38) is a solution of equation (31). We need the restriction that the procedure parameters K are elements of BU. By inspection of (38), however, we see that this holds. Since $skip \in BU$, the commands mentioned in (36) belong to the set $(BU \,;\, H \,;\, B)$, and hence to Lia by (39). Condition (42) is verified in calculation (37). Condition (41) follows from $K \in Br$ together with the definition of Br in (26). This verification may be left to the reader.

Our solution (33) with (38) can be translated into a more sugared version as the declaration

  procedure T :
   procedure $Tf($ **input** i , **procedure** $K)$:
    procedure L : $[\![K \,;\, r := g(i, r)]\!]$ **end** L
     ; **if** $\neg b(i, q)$ **then** $[\![r := q \,;\, K]\!]$ **else**
     $[\![\quad q := f(i, q); \;\; \text{read}(p)$
      ; $\;\; Tf(p, L)]\!]$ **end** Tf
    ; $[\![\quad \text{read}(p)$
    ; $\;\; Tf(p, skip)]\!]$ **end** T.

References

[B] J. de Bakker: Mathematical theory of program correctness. Prentice–Hall International, 1980.

[H0] W.H. Hesselink: An algebraic calculus of commands (WHH 13). Tech. Rep. CS 8808, Groningen University 1988.

[H1] W.H. Hesselink: Command algebras, recursion and program tranformation (WHH 36). Tech. Rep. CS 8812, Groningen University 1988.

[H2] W.H. Hesselink: Command algebras with unbounded choice (WHH 47). Draft, 1989.

[M] Z. Manna: Mathematical theory of computation. McGraw–Hill Book Company 1974.

A derivation of a systolic rank order filter with constant response time

Anne Kaldewaij and Martin Rem
Department of Mathematics and Computing Science
Eindhoven University of Technology
P.O. Box 513, 5600 MB Eindhoven
The Netherlands

Abstract

A design technique for systolic computations is explained by means of an example. The example is the derivation of a fast, parallel program for rank order filtering. The derivation proceeds in a calculational manner, originating from a formal specification and guided by performance considerations. The resulting solution is a linear systolic array of N cells, where N is the window size. It has constant response time and latency N.

1 Introduction

Solid design techniques are indispensable for the design of reliable and efficient programs. In this paper we explain a design technique for the derivation of parallel programs that we have found to be very effective in many different applications. We introduce the technique by means of a non-trivial example: we produce a fast, parallel program for a complicated non-linear filter. The derivation of this program proceeds in a calculational manner, originating from a formal specification and guided by performance considerations.

The filter we design consists of a linear network of cells, cf. Figure 1. The cells communicate with each other by exchanging messages. Communication can take place between neighbor cells only. The two outermost cells can communicate with the environment of the network: these are the only cells that are involved in the external input and output of the program. Such networks are often called systolic arrays [3]. Communications are performed along channels. As in CSP [2], these channels are directed and communications are distributed assignments. For channel

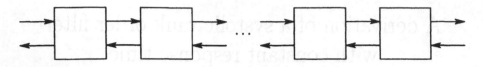

Figure 1: A linear network of cells

a from cell p to cell q the simultaneous execution of $a!E$ in cell p and $a?x$ in cell q performs assignment $x := E$.

Filters are mechanisms that transform streams of values into other streams of values. The output stream is a function of the input stream. Which function a filter should establish depends on its particular purpose. We consider rank order filters. These filters find application in digital image processing, where they are used to remove impulse noise from signals.

The idea of rank order filtering is to move a window of fixed size, say N, over the input stream and to output at each position of the window for fixed K, $0 \leq K < N$ the value that would occupy position K in the window if the values in the window were ordered ascendingly. For example, if $N = 3$ and $K = 1$ the median of every three consecutive inputs is output:

```
input   0  0  1  0  0  1  1  1  1  0  0  1  1  0  1  1
output  -  -  0  0  0  0  1  1  1  1  0  0  1  1  1  1
```

The isolated values are replaced by their neighbor values and all others remain unchanged. Thus, rank order filters remove sparkles while leaving edges intact. The particular values of N and K to be used depend on characteristics of the impulse noise. Filters with $N = 2K + 1$ are known as median filters.

Let us forget for a while the particular filter we want to design. Consider a program with input channel a and output channel b. The specification of such a program should capture the way in which the values communicated along b depend on those communicated along a. This dependence is called the i/o-relation. We let $a(i)$ for $i \geq 0$ denote the value of the ith communication along channel a. Thus sequence $a(j : j \geq 0)$ is the input stream and sequence $b(j : j \geq 0)$ the output stream. The i/o-relation is then a relation between these two sequences. An example of an i/o-relation is

$$b(i) = (\Sigma j : i \leq j < i+N : a(j)) \quad (i \geq 0) \tag{*}$$

The crux of our design technique is partitioning the i/o-relation into simpler ones, for example by splitting off a term:

$$b(i) = (\Sigma j : i \leq j < i+N-1 : a(j)) + a(i+N-1)$$

r, equivalently,

$$b(i) = c(i) + a(i+N-1)$$

here

$$c(i) = (\Sigma j : i \le j < i+N-1 : a(j))$$

The computation of sequence $c(j : j \ge 0)$ is similar to the original problem. We have ingled out one cell, which upon receiving $c(i)$ and $a(i+N-1)$ produces their sum (i). Thus, designing cells amounts to splitting off terms in the i/o-relation. Splitting off just one term of the summation yields solutions with fine-grained parallelism, which are very suitable for integration into VLSI circuits [5],[8]. We can obtain more coarse-grained parallelism by splitting off more terms simultaneously [7].

Thus far our design technique resembles that of functional programming [1]. A major distinction, however, is that we have to program all communications explicitly. The values that are required in cells have to be sent to them, and neighbor cells have to agree on the order in which they perform their mutual communications. In return or that we get the possibility of accurately controlling and analyzing the performance of our programs.

A good estimate for the space requirement of a program is the number of variables t contains. Cells receive values in variables. If they receive values along all input channels concurrently – as is often the case – they need at least one variable per input channel. It is our experience that the total number of variables in a program can be decreased by making the program more coarse-grained, but that usually slows down he computation.

For analyzing the speed of a computation we use sequence functions [6],[9]. A sequence function exhibits a possible execution order by assigning all communications o time slots. For sequence function σ natural number $\sigma(a, i)$ denotes the time slot to which the ith communication along channel a is assigned. We say that a program has constant response time if $\sigma(b, i)$ is a linear function of i. The latency of a program is

$$(\max i : i \ge 0 : \sigma(b, i) - \sigma(a, f(i)))$$

where $a(j : 0 \le j \le f(i))$ is the shortest prefix of $a(j : j \ge 0)$ that determines $b(i)$.

In this introduction we have skimmed over many problems. Most of these problems – and how they may be solved – will become apparent in the sequel. We discuss here he two problems that we already alluded to above: making required values available o cells, and matching the communications between neighbor cells.

We introduce an input channel to a cell for each sequence of values that the cell requires. Thus, auxiliary channels are introduced. Our rank order filter turns out to require six channels between every two neighbor cells. For each auxiliary channel the designer has to choose whether it comes from the left or from the right. In practise this is not a difficult choice: the i/o-relation often suggests the direction, and a wrong choice usually manifests itself rapidly.

We call the order in which a cell or a network of cells communicates with its environment its communication behavior. The i/o-relation restricts the possible communication behaviors: no value can be used before it is received. A communication behavior that conforms to i/o-relation (∗) is

$$a^{N-1} ; (a ; b)^*$$

First $N-1$ input values are received, after which input and output alternate. If the left-most cell performs the communication with the environment the above would be part of its communication behavior. But this cell also communicates with the second cell of the network; these communications must be added to obtain the complete behavior of the first cell. Let the channels between the first two cells be c and d, and suppose we extend the communication behavior of the first cell to

$$(a ; d)^{N-1} ; (a, c ; b, d)^*$$

where the comma denotes concurrency of the two communications it connects. Then

$$d^{N-1} ; (c ; d)^*$$

should agree with the communication behavior of the next cell. If that does not conform with its i/o-relation we can change the communication behaviors by delaying the production of outputs. To accomodate this buffering the cells require auxiliary variables. An example of this phenomenon can be found in the palindrome recognizer of [9]. In the design of the rank order filter the need for buffering does not arise.

2   Problem definition

Let $a(j : j \geq 0)$ be an infinite sequence of integers and let N be a fixed positive integer. For $i \geq 0$ sequence $a(j : i \leq j < i+N)$ is denoted by $a[i..i+N)$. It is called a *window* of sequence a. There are many interesting window computations, such as

- determining the minimum value of each window

- determining the median of each window

In general one may ask which value would occupy the Kth $(0 \leq K < N)$ position in window $a[i..i+N)$ if its values were ordered ascendingly. That value X is determined by

$$(\mathbf{N}\, k\colon i \leq k < i+N\colon a(k) < X) \leq K$$
$$\wedge\ (\mathbf{N}\, k\colon i \leq k < i+N\colon a(k) \leq X) > K$$

where **N** stands for "number of".

Producing these values X is known as rank order filtering. Thus, our design task is to construct a parallel program with input channel a and output channel b, both of type integer, which for fixed N and K, $0 \leq K < N$, has i/o-relation

$$(\mathbf{N}\, k\colon i \leq k < i+N\colon a(k) < b(i)) \leq K \qquad\qquad (i)$$
$$\wedge\ (\mathbf{N}\, k\colon i \leq k < i+N\colon a(k) \leq b(i)) > K$$

for $i \geq 0$.

3 Derivation

We derive our solution in a number of steps, the first one of which amounts to massaging the specification into a more manageable form.

3.1 Massaging the specification

From specification (i) we infer that $b(0)$ depends on the values in window $a[0..N)$. This gives rise to (external) communication behaviors in which $a(N-1)$ is received before $b(0)$ is produced, such as $a^N\,;(b\,;a)^*$. To obtain a simpler communication behavior, such as $(a\,;b)^*$, we let $b(i)$ depend on window $a(i-N..i]$ and change for $i \geq N-1$ the i/o-relation into

$$(\mathbf{N}\, k\colon i-N < k \leq i\colon a(k) < b(i)) \leq K \qquad\qquad (ii)$$
$$\wedge\ (\mathbf{N}\, k\colon i-N < k \leq i\colon a(k) \leq b(i)) > K$$

Then, however, nothing is specified about values $b(0)$ through $b(N-2)$. We extend relation (ii) to all natural i by defining $a(i) = a(0)$ for $i < 0$. This leads, as will turn out later, to relatively simple recurrence relations.

Given (ii), there is at least one n, $0 \leq n < N$, for which $b(i) = a(i-n)$. To single out a particular n we observe that, given (ii),

$$(\mathbf{N}\, k\colon i-N < k < i-n\colon a(k) < a(i-n)) \qquad\qquad (iii)$$
$$+ (\mathbf{N}\, k\colon i-n < k \leq i\colon a(k) \leq a(i-n))\ =\ K$$

implies $b(i) = a(i - n)$. This shows how our specification can be rewritten into a more manageable form. We generalize the left-hand side of (iii) from window $a(i-N..i]$ to window $a(p..q]$ by defining for $0 \leq n < q-p$ the rank of $q-n$ in $a(p..q]$ as follows

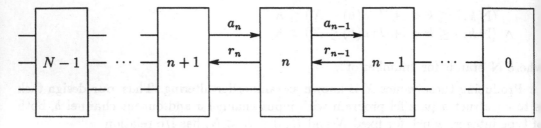

Figure 2: A network of N cells with cell n computing the rank of
$i - n$ in $a(i-N..i]$

$$rank(n, p, q) = (\mathbf{N} \, k: p < k < q{-}n: a(k) < a(q{-}n))$$
$$+ (\mathbf{N} \, k: q{-}n < k \leq q: a(k) \leq a(q{-}n))$$

For fixed p and q, rank is then a permutation of $[0..q{-}p)$, viz. one that orders window $a(p..q]$ ascendingly.

Relation (iii) may now be written as

$$rank(n, i{-}N, i) = K$$

For our design we aim at a network of N cells, cf. Figure 2. Cell n, $0 \leq n < N$, computes $rank(n, i{-}N, i)$. Whenever that equals K, we have $b(i) = a(i{-}n)$. We temporarily neglect the generation of output values and focus our attention on computing $rank(n, i{-}N, i)$.

3.2 Computing ranks

Channels between cell n and cell $n + 1$ will have subscript n, cf. Figure 2. Cell n, $0 \leq n < N$, has to compute $rank(n, i{-}N, i)$. We derive

$$rank(n, i{-}N, i)$$
$$= \quad \{ \text{definition of } rank \}$$
$$(\mathbf{N} \, k: i{-}N < k < i{-}n: a(k) < a(i{-}n))$$
$$+ (\mathbf{N} \, k: i{-}n < k \leq i: a(k) \leq a(i{-}n))$$
$$= \quad \{ \text{dummy change: } k := i{-}k \}$$
$$(\mathbf{N} \, k: n < k < N: a(i{-}k) < a(i{-}n))$$
$$+ (\mathbf{N} \, k: 0 \leq k < n: a(i{-}k) \leq a(i{-}n))$$

which yields as i/o-relation for output r_n

$$r_n(i) = (\mathbf{N} \, k: 0 \leq k < n: a(i{-}k) \leq a(i{-}n))$$
$$+ (\mathbf{N} \, k: n < k < N: a(i{-}k) < a(i{-}n))$$

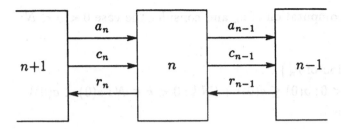

Figure 3: Cell n with inputs a_n, c_n, and r_{n-1} and outputs a_{n-1},
c_{n-1}, and r_n

Then, however, $r_n(0)$ would have value n. To have as little difference between the cells as possible, we replace in the domain of the quantifications n by $n \min i$, the minimum of n and i, and define for $i \geq 0$

$$r_n(i) = (\mathbf{N}\, k: 0 \leq k < n \min i: a(i{-}k) \leq a(i{-}n))$$
$$+\ (\mathbf{N}\, k: n \min i < k < N: a(i{-}k) < a(i{-}n))$$

Thus $r_n(i) = rank(n, i{-}N, i)$ for $i \geq N{-}1$. Cell n $(0 \leq n < N)$ has input a_n and output r_n. Sequence a_n equals input sequence a: $a_n(i) = a(i)$ for $i \geq 0$.

For $n = 0$ the definition of r_n yields

$$r_0(i) = (\mathbf{N}\, k: 0 < k < N: a(i{-}k) < a(i))$$

To make these values available to cell 0 we introduce auxiliary channel c. The i/o-relation for channel c_n is obtained by generalizing the expression above:

$$c_n(i) = (\mathbf{N}\, k: n < k < N: a(i{-}k) < a(i))$$

Then $r_0(i) = c_0(i)$. Cell n has c_n as input and, hence, c_{n-1} as output, cf. Figure 3. From its definition follows

$$c_{N-1}(i) = 0$$

and for $0 < n < N$

$$c_{n-1}(i) = c_n(i) + [a(i{-}n) < a(i)]$$

where $[B]$ is short for **if** $B \to 1 \,\|\, \neg B \to 0$ **fi**. By the definition of c_n, $c_n(0) = 0$ for all n. The relation for c_{n-1} may, consequently, be written as

$$c_{n-1}(0) = c_n(0)$$
$$c_{n-1}(i{+}1) = c_n(i{+}1) + [a(i{+}1{-}n) < a(i{+}1)]$$

We return to the computation of r_n and consider the case $0 < n < N$:

$r_n(0)$

$=$ { definition of r_n }

  $(\mathbf{N}\,k: 0 \leq k < 0: a(0) \leq a(0)) + (\mathbf{N}\,k: 0 < k < N: a(0) < a(0))$

$=$ { calculus }

  0

and

$r_n(i+1)$

$=$ { definition of r_n }

  $(\mathbf{N}\,k: 0 \leq k < n \min (i+1): a(i+1-k) \leq a(i+1-n))$
  $+ (\mathbf{N}\,k: n \min (i+1) < k < N: a(i+1-k) < a(i+1-n))$

$=$ { split off $k = 0$, add $k = N$ }

  $(\mathbf{N}\,k: 1 \leq k < n \min (i+1): a(i+1-k) \leq a(i+1-n))$
  $+ (\mathbf{N}\,k: n \min (i+1) < k < N+1: a(i+1-k) < a(i+1-n))$
  $+ [a(i+1) \leq a(i+1-n)] - [a(i+1-N) < a(i+1-n)]$

$=$ { dummy change: $k := k+1$ }

  $(\mathbf{N}\,k: 0 \leq k < (n-1) \min i: a(i-k) \leq a(i+1-n))$
  $+ (\mathbf{N}\,k: (n-1) \min i < k < N: a(i-k) < a(i+1-n))$
  $+ [a(i+1) \leq a(i+1-n)] - [a(i+1-N) < a(i+1-n)]$

$=$ { definition of r_n }

$r_{n-1}(i) + [a(i+1) \leq a(i+1-n)] - [a(i+1-N) < a(i+1-n)]$

We recapitulate the relations found:

cell 0:

$$r_0(i) = c_0(i) \tag{0}$$

cell n $(0 < n < N)$:

$$a_{n-1}(i) = a(i) \tag{1}$$

$$r_n(0) = 0 \tag{2}$$
$$r_n(i+1) = r_{n-1}(i) + [a(i+1) \leq a(i+1-n)]$$
$$\qquad\qquad - [a(i+1-N) < a(i+1-n)]$$

$$c_{n-1}(0) = c_n(0) \tag{3}$$
$$c_{n-1}(i+1) = c_n(i+1) + [a(i+1-n) < a(i+1)]$$

environment:

$$c_{N-1}(i) = 0 \tag{4}$$

To cope with expressions in which $a(i+1-n)$ and $a(i+1-N)$ occur, we introduce auxiliary channels. Since $a(i+1-n)$ depends on n and $i+1-n \leq i+1$, we decide to retrieve that value from cell $n-1$ and we introduce input channel d_{n-1} to cell n, satisfying

$$d_{n-1}(i) = a(i+1-n)$$

For output d_n we then have $d_n(i) = a(i-n)$, i.e.

$$d_0(i) = a(i) \tag{5}$$

and for $0 < n < N$:

$$d_n(0) = a(0) \tag{6}$$
$$d_n(i+1) = d_{n-1}(i)$$

Value $a(i+1-N)$ does not depend on n and we decide to retrieve that value from cell $n+1$ ("the environment") by introducing auxiliary input channel e_n to cell n, satisfying

$$e_n(i) = a(i+1-N)$$

Then $e_{n-1}(i) = a(i+1-N)$ as well, i.e.

$$e_{n-1}(i) = e_n(i) \tag{7}$$

The environment supplies e_{N-1} to the network. The environment receives d_{N-1} from cell $N - 1$, and we have

$$e_{N-1}(i) = a(i+1-N) = d_{N-1}(i) \tag{8}$$

Hence, the environment can satisfy the i/o-relation for e_{N-1} by simply returning the values received along d_{N-1}.

We now specify cell n, $0 < n < N$, in more detail. To that end we drop the subscripts of its channels: channel s_n is denoted by s and channel s_{n-1} is denoted by $\overline{s}$ (cf. Figure 4).

Cell n has input channels a, c, $\overline{d}$, e, and $\overline{r}$, and output channels $\overline{a}$, $\overline{c}$, d, $\overline{e}$, and r for which the following relations hold.

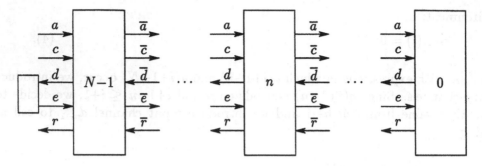

Figure 4: The network in which each cell determines its rank

$$\overline{a}(i) = a(i) \qquad \text{cf. (1)}$$

$$\overline{c}(0) = c(0) \qquad \text{cf. (3)}$$
$$\overline{c}(i+1) = c(i+1) + [\overline{d}(i) < a(i+1)]$$

$$d(0) = a(0) \qquad \text{cf. (6)}$$
$$d(i+1) = \overline{d}(i)$$

$$\overline{e}(i) = e(i) \qquad \text{cf. (7)}$$

$$r(0) = 0 \qquad \text{cf. (2)}$$
$$r(i+1) = \overline{r}(i) + [a(i+1) \le \overline{d}(i)] - [e(i) < \overline{d}(i)]$$

Cell 0 computes its results by $r(i) = c(i)$ and $d(i) = a(i)$, cf. (0) and (5). From (4) and (8) we conclude that cell $N-1$ is fed $c(i) = 0$ and $e(i) = d(i)$. For cell n $0 < n < N$, these relations give rise to the following communication behaviors:

$CB(\overline{a})$: $\quad (a \,; \overline{a})^*$
$CB(\overline{c})$: $\quad a, (c \,; \overline{c}) \,; (a, c, \overline{d} \,; \overline{c})^*$
$CB(d)$: $\quad a \,; d \,; (\overline{d} \,; d)^*$
$CB(\overline{e})$: $\quad (e \,; \overline{e})^*$
$CB(r)$: $\quad a, r \,; (a, \overline{d}, e, \overline{r} \,; r)^*$

These may be combined into

CB : $\quad a, c \,; \overline{a}, \overline{c}, d, r \,; (a, c, \overline{d}, e, \overline{r} \,; \overline{a}, \overline{c}, d, \overline{e}, r)^*$

We determine the projections of communication behavior CB on the channels to the left and on the channels to the right:

$$CB \upharpoonright \{a, c, d, e, r\} = a, c\,; (d, r\,; a, c, e)^*$$
and $CB \upharpoonright \{\overline{a}, \overline{c}, \overline{d}, \overline{e}, \overline{r}\} = \overline{a}, \overline{c}\,; (\overline{d}, \overline{r}\,; \overline{a}, \overline{c}, \overline{e})^*$

Thus, any two neighbor cells have matching behaviors, which guarantees (cf. [9]) the absence of deadlock. A possible sequence function for cell n $(0 < n < N)$ is

$$\sigma_n(a, i) = \sigma_n(c, i) = 2i + N - n - 1$$
$$\sigma_n(r, i) = \sigma_n(\overline{a}, i) = \sigma_n(\overline{c}, i) = \sigma_n(d, i) = 2i + N - n$$
$$\sigma_n(e, i) = \sigma_n(\overline{r}, i) = \sigma_n(\overline{d}, i) = 2i + N - n + 1$$
$$\sigma_n(\overline{e}, i) = 2i + N - n + 2$$

from which we infer that the rank computation has constant response time. In the following section we incorporate the generation of output b.

3.3 The solution

Cell n $(0 \le n < N)$ computes $rank(n, i - N, i)$. As observed in section 3.1, we have $b(i) = a(i - n)$, where n is (uniquely) determined by

$$rank(n, i - N, i) = K$$

Let $sel(i)$ be the solution for n in this equation:

$$0 \le sel(i) < N \wedge rank(sel(i), i - N, i) = K$$

The i/o-relation may then be written as

$$b(i) = a(i - sel(i))$$

We generalize this expresion to obtain the i/o-relation for output channel b_{n-1} of cell n $(0 \le n < N)$:

$$b_{n-1}(i) = \text{if } sel(i) \ge n \rightarrow a(i - sel(i)) \,\|\, sel(i) < n \rightarrow \text{``arbitrary''} \text{ fi}$$

Then $n = 0$ yields

$$b_{-1}(i) = a(i - sel(i))$$

The output is, consequently, produced by cell 0.

Since $rank(K, -N, 0) = K$, we have $sel(0) = K$. For $i = 0$ the i/o-relation of b_{n-1} therefore yields

$$b_{n-1}(0) = \text{if } K \geq n \rightarrow a(0) \parallel K < n \rightarrow \text{``arbitrary''} \text{ fi}$$

We implement this by

$$b_{n-1}(0) = a(0)$$

Furthermore

$$b_{n-1}(i+1)$$
$=$ $\{$ definition of $b_{n-1}\}$
    if $sel(i+1) \geq n \rightarrow a(i+1-sel(i+1)) \parallel sel(i+1) < n \rightarrow \text{``arbitrary''}$ fi
$=$ $\{$ calculus $\}$
    if $sel(i+1) = n \rightarrow a(i+1-n)$
    $\parallel sel(i+1) \neq n \rightarrow$ if $sel(i+1) \geq n+1 \rightarrow a(i+1-sel(i+1))$
                $\parallel sel(i+1) < n+1 \rightarrow \text{``arbitrary''}$
          fi
   fi
$=$ $\{$ definition of $b_{n-1}\}$
    if $sel(i+1) = n \rightarrow a(i+1-n) \parallel sel(i+1) \neq n \rightarrow b_n(i+1)$ fi
$=$ $\{$ $sel(i+1) = n$ is equivalent to $r_n(i+1) = K$, definition of $d_{n-1}\}$
    if $r_n(i+1) = K \rightarrow d_{n-1}(i) \parallel r_n(i+1) \neq K \rightarrow b_n(i+1)$ fi

In terms of b and $\bar{b}$ we have for cell n, $0 < n < N$,

$$\bar{b}(0) = a(0)$$
$$\bar{b}(i+1) = \text{if } r(i+1) = K \rightarrow \bar{d}(i) \parallel r(i+1) \neq K \rightarrow b(i+1) \text{ fi}$$

Since $sel(i) < N$, the environment should satisfy $b(i) = \text{``arbitrary''}$. The relation above yields for $\bar{b}$ communication behavior

$$CB(\bar{b}): \qquad a, b\,;(\bar{b}\,;b,\bar{d})^*$$

which is easily added to CB :

$$a, b, c\,;\bar{a}, \bar{b}, \bar{c}, d, r\,;(a, b, c, \bar{d}, e, \bar{r}\,;\bar{a}, \bar{b}, \bar{c}, d, \bar{e}, r)^*$$

Integration of the communication behavior and the i/o-relations yields the following programs. For $0 < n < N$:

cell n:

 [**var** pa, pb, pc, pd, pe, pr : integer;
  $a?pa, b?pb, c?pc$
 $;\overline{a}!pa, \overline{b}!pa, \overline{c}!pc, d!pa, r!0$
 $;(a?pa, b?pb, c?pc, \overline{d}?pd, e?pe, \overline{r}?pr$
  $;$**if** $pd < pa \rightarrow pc := pc+1 \ \| \ pd \geq pa \rightarrow pr := pr+1$ **fi**
  $;$**if** $pe < pd \rightarrow pr := pr-1 \ \| \ pe \geq pd \rightarrow$ skip **fi**
  $;$**if** $pr = K \rightarrow pb := pd \ \| \ pr \neq K \rightarrow$ skip **fi**
  $;\overline{a}!pa, \overline{b}!pb, \overline{c}!pc, d!pd, \overline{e}!pe, r!pr$
  $)^*$
 ]

For cell 0 we have

$$\overline{b}(i) = \textbf{if } r(i) = K \rightarrow a(i) \ \| \ r(i) \neq K \rightarrow b(i) \textbf{ fi}$$

Taking $a, b, c \ ;(\overline{b}, d, r \ ;a, b, c, e)^*$ as communication behavior yields the following program

cell 0:

 [**var** pa, pb, pc, pe : integer;
  $a?pa, b?pb, c?pc$
 $;($**if** $pc = K \rightarrow pb := pa \ \| \ pc \neq K \rightarrow$ skip **fi**
  $;\overline{b}!pb, d!pa, r!pc$
  $;a?pa, b?pb, c?pc, e?pe$
  $)^*$
 ]

Cell $N-1$ receives from its environment sequences a, b, c, and e. The latter three should satisfy

$$c(i) = 0$$
$$b(i) = \text{"arbitrary"}$$
$$e(i) = d(i)$$

Hence, connecting channels d and e by a one-place buffer, and feeding zeroes along channel c satisfies the requirements. Connecting channel r to a sink yields Figure 5, the ultimate network for specification (ii). The original specification (i) can be satisfied by having cell 0 suppress the production of its first $N-1$ outputs.

Consider cell 0. Output $\overline{b}(i)$ occurs in the same time slot as output $r(i)$. Since

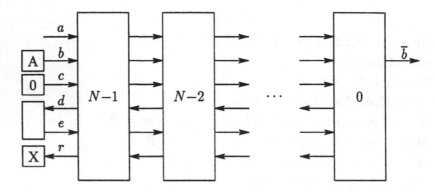

Figure 5: The ultimate rank order filter

$$\sigma_0(r, i) = 2i + N$$

we have constant response time: cell 0 produces an external output value in every other time slot. Value $\overline{b}(i)$ depends on $a(i-N..i]$. The latency is, consequently,

$$\sigma_0(r, i) - \sigma_{N-1}(a, i) = 2i + N - 2i = N$$

which is the best one can achieve in linear networks that have input and output at opposing sides.

The program we have derived bears resemblance to the systolic rank order filter in [4]. According to [4], however, our solution would not be called a systolic computation but a wave-front computation.

4 Concluding remarks

In a structured way we have derived a relatively simple solution for a complicated non-linear filter. We wrote "relatively simple", since the only data processing that occurs in the cells is test on equality and simple increments. As a consequence, our solution is very efficient: two outputs are separated only by the time required to perform three equality tests and an increment.

The communication behaviors of the cells are independent of the values that are communicated. Such programs are called data independent [6],[9]. To us it came as a (pleasant) surprise that rank order filtering, which at first sight seems to involve intricate data movements, can be performed in a data independent fashion.

The choice to define $a(i) = a(0)$ for $i < 0$ greatly simplified the derivations. Other possibilities were rejected, since they led to elaborate case analyses.

For the introduction of an auxiliary input channel there are in general two choices cell n receives the required value either from cell $n - 1$ or from cell $n + 1$. Making a wrong decision is in no way fatal: the way of deriving the relation for the corresponding output channel will reveal the bad choice.

We believe that we would not have been able to find this solution without a design discipline that allows one to reason about these programs in a non-operational way. Thus, the i/o-relations play a role in parallel program design that is very similar to that of invariants in the design of sequential programs.

5 Acknowledgements

Thanks are due to Berry Schoenmakers for his comments on an earlier design of the rank order filter. The Eindhoven Algorithm Club and the Eindhoven VLSI Club are gratefully acknowledged for scrutinizing a draft version of this paper.

References

[1] Bird, R., Wadler, P.
Introduction to Functional Programming
Prentice-Hall International, London, 1988

[2] Hoare, C.A.R.
Communicating Sequential Processes
Comm. of the ACM **21** (1978), 666-677

[3] Kung, H.T.
Let's design algorithms for VLSI systems
In *Proc 1st Caltech Conference on VLSI* (C.L. Seitz, ed.)
California Institute of Technology, Pasadena, 1979, 65-90

[4] Kung, S.Y.
VLSI Array Processors
Prentice-Hall, Englewood Cliffs, 1988

[5] Martin, A.J.
Compiling communicating processes into delay-insensitive VLSI circuits
Distributed Computing **1** (1986), 226-234

[6] Rem, M.
Trace theory and systolic computations
In *PARLE Parallel Architectures and Languages Europe Vol. 1*
(J.W. de Bakker et al., eds.)
Lecture Notes in Computer Science 258, Springer-Verlag, Berlin, 1987, 14-33

[7] Van Berkel, C.H., Rem, M., Saeijs, R.W.J.J.
VLSI programming
In *Proc. 1988 IEEE Int. Conf. on Computer Design*
IEEE Computer Society Press, Washington, 1988, 150-156

[8] Van Berkel, C.H., Saeijs, R.W.J.J.
Compilation of communicating processes into delay-insensitive circuits
In *Proc. 1988 IEEE Int. Conf. on Computer Design*
IEEE Computer Society Press, Washington, 1988, 157-162

[9] Zwaan, G.
Parallel Computations
Doctoral Dissertation, Eindhoven University of Technology, Eindhoven, 1989

Searching by Elimination

Anne Kaldewaij   Berry Schoenmakers

Dept. of Mathematics and Computing Science
Eindhoven University of Technology
P.O. Box 513, 5600 MB Eindhoven, Netherlands

Abstract

We present a way of program derivation that is applicable to a wide class of searching problems. Compared to more conventional approaches, this method yields very elegant programs. For a general problem specification, we derive a rather general program scheme. For the specific problem at hand, the general scheme is refined — depending on the mathematical properties of the objects involved — to a particular program. This is illustrated by some examples, varying from elementary problems to more advanced problems.

0   The program scheme

The general problem setting is as follows. We are given a finite set W and a boolean function S on W, such that $S.w$ holds for some $w \in W$. We are asked to derive a program that establishes for variable x postcondition

$R:\quad S.x$

where the dot denotes function application. We will freely switch between subsets of W and boolean functions on W. Hence, R may also be written as

$R:\quad x \in S$

Notice that "$S.w$ holds for some $w \in W$" can be expressed by $S \cap W \neq \emptyset$. Another way to formulate R is

$R:\quad S \cap \{x\} \neq \emptyset$

This characterization yields an invariant for a repetition that may be used to solve the problem. We introduce variable V and define invariant P by

$P:\quad S \cap V \neq \emptyset \;\wedge\; V \subseteq W$

From $P \wedge |V| = 1$ we infer that the unique element of V satifies R.

For the initialization of P there is not much choice. Since S might be equal to W, the only initialization of V that is independent of S is given by $V := W$. As a variant function we choose $|V|$. This leads to

> $V := W$
> ; **do** $|V| \neq 1 \rightarrow$ "decrease $|V|$ under invariance of P " **od**
> ; $x :\in V$

From $P \wedge |V| \neq 1$ we conclude that $|V| \geq 2$. Our strategy is based on the fact that at least one of each two elements of V may be removed from V without violating P. This yields the following approximation:

> $V := W$
> ; **do** $|V| \neq 1 \rightarrow$
> "choose a and b in V, such that $a \neq b$"
> $\{ a \in V \wedge b \in V \wedge a \neq b \wedge S \cap V \neq \emptyset \}$
> ; **if** $B0 \rightarrow V := V \setminus \{a\}$
> [] $B1 \rightarrow V := V \setminus \{b\}$
> **fi**
> **od**
> ; $x :\in V$

A candidate for $B0$ is $S \cap (V \setminus \{a\}) \neq \emptyset$, since this equivales the weakest precondition of $V := V \setminus \{a\}$ with respect to the first conjunct of P. Similarly, $S \cap (V \setminus \{b\}) \neq \emptyset$ is a candidate for $B1$. It is easily verified that $B0 \vee B1$ holds, if these candidates are chosen. However, in order to exploit the precondition of the selection statement, we choose sligthly stronger guards as follows. Evidently, $a \notin S \Rightarrow S \cap (V \setminus \{a\}) \neq \emptyset$, since $S \cap V \neq \emptyset$. Also, $b \in S \Rightarrow S \cap (V \setminus \{a\}) \neq \emptyset$, since $b \in V \wedge a \neq b$. Using the symmetry between a and b, we then obtain two guards whose disjunction is true. (Notice that V does not occur in these guards anymore.) The program scheme becomes:

> $V := W$
> ; **do** $|V| \neq 1 \rightarrow$
> "choose a and b in V, such that $a \neq b$"
> ; **if** $\neg S.a \vee S.b \rightarrow V := V \setminus \{a\}$
> [] $\neg S.b \vee S.a \rightarrow V := V \setminus \{b\}$
> **fi**
> **od**
> ; $x :\in V$

In the next section we shall use this scheme to solve problems with $W = [0..N]$, where $N \geq 0$. This enables us to represent set V in a succinct way: initially, $V = [0..N]$. Furthermore, assignment $a, b := min.V, max.V$ establishes $a \in V \wedge b \in V \wedge a \neq b$, since $|V| \geq 2$. Moreover, we observe that $V := V \setminus \{min.V\}$ as well as $V := V \setminus \{max.V\}$ maintain the property that V is an interval, i.e. $V = [min.V..max.V]$. Since an interval is completely specified by its extremes, our final scheme becomes:

```
    a, b := 0, N
  ; do a ≠ b  →
        if ¬S.a ∨ S.b → a := a + 1
        [] ¬S.b ∨ S.a → b := b - 1
        fi
    od
  ; x := a
```

with invariant

$$0 \leq a \leq b \leq N \ \land \ S \cap [a..b] \neq \emptyset$$

Under the precondition $S \neq \emptyset$ it establishes $S.x$.
So much for the program scheme.

1 Applications

In this section we derive programs for the following four problems: maxlocation, starting pit location, the celebrity problem and the bounded linear search problem.

The starting-point for each derivation is the program scheme of section 0. Therefore, S denotes a subset of $[0..N]$, and a, b and x denote elements of $[0..N]$ in each derivation, as in the program scheme. Furthermore, we use i, j and k as dummies ranging over $[0..N]$. Finally, we sometimes use that $a \neq b$, or even $a < b$, is implied by the precondition of the selection statement in the program scheme.

Another remark regarding the derivations is the following. In order to refine the guards in the program scheme, we first try to simplify $¬S.a$. Often, this also results in a refinement for $¬S.b$, because of symmetry. If the disjunction of these guards is *true*, we are done. Otherwise, we have to consider the disjuncts $S.a$ and $S.b$.

1.0 Maxlocation

The problem is to locate an occurrence of the maximum value in an array. The functional specification of *maxlocation* reads (cf. [0]):

```
|[N : int  { N ≥ 0 };
 f[0..N] : array of int;
 |[x : int;
   maxlocation
   { (Ai :: f.i ≤ f.x) }
 ]|
]|
```

In order to use our program scheme we instantiate S as follows

$$S.x \equiv (\mathbf{A}i :: f.i \leq f.x)$$

We compute:

$$\neg S.a$$
$$= \quad \{\text{definition of } S;\ \text{De Morgan}\}$$
$$(\mathbf{E}i :: f.i > f.a)$$
$$\Leftarrow \quad \{\text{predicate calculus}\}$$
$$f.b > f.a$$

Similarly, we have $f.a > f.b \Rightarrow \neg S.b$ as well. Furthermore,

$$f.a = f.b$$
$$\Leftarrow \quad \{\text{definition of } S \text{ and predicate calculus}\}$$
$$S.a \equiv S.b$$
$$= \quad \{\text{predicate calculus}\}$$
$$(\neg S.a \lor S.b) \land (\neg S.b \lor S.a)$$

Consequently, $f.b \geq f.a \Rightarrow \neg S.a \lor S.b$, and $f.a \geq f.b \Rightarrow \neg S.b \lor S.a$.
We thus arrive at the following solution for *maxlocation*:

```
|[ a, b : int;
   a, b := 0, N
 ; do a ≠ b →
      if f.b ≥ f.a  → a := a + 1
      [] f.a ≥ f.b  → b := b − 1
      fi
   od
 ; x := a
]|
```

In our opinion, this is a very elegant algorithm, and it is also new to us.

1.1 Starting pit location

Another nice result is our solution to the pit location problem. We do not know the origin of this problem. It can be found as an exercise in [0], and it reads as follows: there are $N + 1$ pits located along a circular race-track. The pits are numbered clockwise from 0 through N. At pit i, there are $p.i$ gallons of petrol available. To race from pit i to its clockwise neighbour one needs $q.i$ gallons of petrol. One is asked to determine a pit from which it is possible to race a complete lap, starting with an empty fuel tank. To guarantee the existence of such a starting pit it is given that:

$$(\mathbf{S}i :: p.i) = (\mathbf{S}i :: q.i) \tag{0}$$

In order to state the problem concisely, we introduce $D.i.j$ as the difference of the number of gallons provided and the number of gallons needed, when racing from pit i to j in clockwise direction. More formally:

$$D.i.j = (\mathbf{S}k : k \text{ between } i \text{ and } j \text{ (including } i) \text{ in clockwise order} : p.k - q.k)$$

The functional specification now reads:

$$
\begin{aligned}
&\|[N : \mathbf{int} \ \{ N \geq 0 \}; \\
&\quad p, q[0..N] : \mathbf{array \ of \ int} \ \{ (0) \}; \\
&\quad \|[x : \mathbf{int}; \\
&\quad \ \ \textit{starting pit location} \\
&\quad \ \ \{ (\mathbf{A}i :: D.x.i \geq 0) \} \\
&\quad]| \\
&]|
\end{aligned}
$$

As may be expected, we define S by:

$$S.x \equiv (\mathbf{A}i :: D.x.i \geq 0)$$

To begin with we have the following important property of D, which may be inferred from (0):

$$D.i.k = D.i.j + D.j.k \tag{1}$$

for all i, j, and k in $[0..N]$. Notice that (1) also gives $D.i.i = 0$ and $D.i.j + D.j.i = 0$, for all i and j in $[0..N]$.

In order to show that $S \neq \emptyset$, we derive:

$$
\begin{aligned}
&S.x \\
= \ \ &\{\text{definition of } S\} \\
&(\mathbf{A}i :: D.x.i \geq 0) \\
= \ \ &\{(1)\} \\
&(\mathbf{A}i :: D.x.0 + D.0.i \geq 0) \\
= \ \ &\{(1), \text{ hence } D.x.0 = -D.0.x\} \\
&(\mathbf{A}i :: D.0.i \geq D.0.x)
\end{aligned}
$$

expressing that x is a starting pit, whenever $D.0.x$ is minimal. Since $D.0.x$ is minimal for some x, we conclude that $S \neq \emptyset$.

Now, we may proceed as in the previous section:

$$
\begin{aligned}
&\neg S.a \\
= \ \ &\{\text{definition of } S; \text{ De Morgan}\} \\
&(\mathbf{E}i :: D.a.i < 0) \\
\Leftarrow \ \ &\{\text{predicate calculus}\}
\end{aligned}
$$

$$D.a.b < 0$$

Similarly, $D.b.a < 0 \Rightarrow \neg S.b$, and, since $D.b.a = -D.a.b$, this may be rewritten as $D.a.b > 0 \Rightarrow \neg S.b$. Furthermore, assuming $D.a.b = 0$, we have

$$
\begin{aligned}
& S.a \\
= \quad & \{\text{definition of } S\} \\
& (\mathbf{A}i :: D.a.i \geq 0) \\
= \quad & \{(1)\} \\
& (\mathbf{A}i :: D.a.b + D.b.i \geq 0) \\
= \quad & \{\text{assumption: } D.a.b = 0\} \\
& (\mathbf{A}i :: D.b.i \geq 0) \\
= \quad & \{\text{definition of } S\} \\
& S.b
\end{aligned}
$$

Hence, $D.a.b = 0 \Rightarrow (\neg S.a \lor S.b) \land (\neg S.b \lor S.a)$.

In order to obtain a linear program, we introduce variable d with additional invariant: $d = D.a.b$. Observe that d has to be initialized to $D.0.N$, which equals $-D.N.0$. Furthermore, $D.a.b = (\mathbf{S}k : a \leq k < b : p.k - q.k)$, since $a \leq b$. Our solution is:

```
|[ a, b, d : int;
    a, b, d := 0, N, q.N - p.N
  ; do a ≠ b →
       if d ≤ 0  → a, d := a + 1, d + q.a - p.a
       [] d ≥ 0  → b, d := b - 1, d + q.(b - 1) - p.(b - 1)
       fi
    od
  ; x := a
]|
```

1.2 The celebrity problem

This problem seems to be part of the folklore. It was posed to us a few months ago, and recently we found a treatment in [1]. We follow the description in [1]: among $N + 1$ persons, a celebrity is someone who is known by everyone, but does not know anyone. This relation between these persons is represented by a boolean matrix r as follows:

$$r.i.j \equiv \text{``person } i \text{ knows person } j\text{''}$$

For the sake of convenience we assume that such a celebrity exists among these persons. Our specification thus becomes:

```
|[ N : int  { N ≥ 0 };
  r[0..N]×[0..N] : array of bool  { (Ei :: A.i ∧ B.i) };
  |[ x : int;
     celebrity
     { A.x ∧ B.x }
  ]|
]|
```

here $A.x \equiv (\mathbf{A}i : i \neq x : r.i.x)$, and $B.x \equiv (\mathbf{A}j : x \neq j : \neg r.x.j)$.
We choose $S.x \equiv A.x \land B.x$, and derive:

$$\neg S.a$$
= {definition of S; De Morgan}
$$\neg A.a \lor \neg B.a$$
= {definition of A and B; De Morgan}
$$(\mathbf{E}i : i \neq a : \neg r.i.a) \lor (\mathbf{E}j : a \neq j : r.a.j)$$
⇐ {$a \neq b$, predicate calculus}
$$\neg r.b.a \lor r.a.b$$

Similarly, we have $\neg r.a.b \lor r.b.a \Rightarrow \neg S.b$.
Since $r.a.b \lor \neg r.a.b \equiv true$, we may strengthen the guards slightly, thereby destroying some of the symmetry:

```
|[ a, b : int;
   a, b := 0, N
 ; do a ≠ b  →
     if  r.a.b  → a := a + 1
     []  ¬r.a.b → b := b - 1
     fi
   od
 ; x := a
]|
```

To appreciate the above derivation the reader is invited to study the treatment in [1].

1.3 Bounded linear search

In [2] a nice solution is presented for the bounded linear search problem. Starting from our program scheme, we will derive the same solution. The problem is stated as follows. A boolean function d is defined on $[0..N-1]$, and one is asked to assign to variable x the least number i in $[0..N-1]$ such that $d.i$. If no such number exists, N has to be assigned to x.

By defining $d.N \equiv true$, the formal specification reads:

$$
\begin{aligned}
&|[\,N \,:\, \text{int } \{\, N \geq 0 \,\}; \\
&\quad d[0..N-1] \,:\, \textbf{array of } \text{bool}; \\
&\quad |[\,x \,:\, \text{int}; \\
&\qquad \textit{bounded linear search} \\
&\qquad \{\, (\textbf{A}i : i < x : \neg d.i) \,\wedge\, d.x \,\} \\
&\quad]| \\
&]|
\end{aligned}
$$

As before, we choose

$$
S.x \equiv (\textbf{A}i : i < x : \neg d.i) \,\wedge\, d.x
$$

Since the precondition of the selection statement in the program scheme implies $0 \leq a < b \leq N$, we may freely use $d.a$ in the guards, but $d.b$ should be avoided, since $b = N$ is not excluded. We derive:

$$
\begin{aligned}
&\quad \neg S.a \\
&= \quad \{\text{definition of } S;\ \text{De Morgan}\} \\
&\quad (\textbf{E}i : i < a : d.i) \,\vee\, \neg d.a \\
&\Leftarrow \quad \{\text{predicate calculus}\} \\
&\quad \neg d.a
\end{aligned}
$$

And, for the second alternative:

$$
\begin{aligned}
&\quad \neg S.b \\
&= \quad \{\text{definition of } S;\ \text{De Morgan}\} \\
&\quad (\textbf{E}i : i < b : d.i) \,\vee\, \neg d.b \\
&\Leftarrow \quad \{\text{``avoiding } d.b\text{''}\} \\
&\quad (\textbf{E}i : i < b : d.i) \\
&\Leftarrow \quad \{a < b,\ \text{predicate calculus}\} \\
&\quad d.a
\end{aligned}
$$

We obtain:

$$
\begin{aligned}
&|[\,a, b \,:\, \text{int}; \\
&\quad a, b := 0, N \\
&\quad ;\, \textbf{do } a \neq b \rightarrow \\
&\qquad \textbf{if } \neg d.a \rightarrow a := a + 1 \\
&\qquad []\quad d.a \rightarrow b := b - 1 \\
&\qquad \textbf{fi} \\
&\quad \textbf{od} \\
&\quad ;\, x := a \\
&]|
\end{aligned}
$$

This program differs slighty from the program in [2]: replacing $b := b - 1$ by $b := a$ removes the difference. This replacement is allowed, since $d.a$ is an invariant of the repetition.

2 Concluding remarks

We have shown that the "Searching by Elimination" approach yields very elegant algorithms. Even such an old problem as maxlocation turned out to be a nice illustration. We remark that it is not difficult to adapt the results of section 0 so that the requirement $S \neq \emptyset$ becomes superfluous. The invariant should be changed into

$$(S \neq \emptyset \Rightarrow S \cap V \neq \emptyset) \wedge \emptyset \subset V \subseteq W$$

and, accordingly, the postcondition becomes

$$S \neq \emptyset \Rightarrow S.x$$

Notice that the program at the end of section 0 is also valid for this case. The adapted scheme may be used to remove the assumption that there is a celebrity among the $N + 1$ persons (see section 1.2).

Finally, we would like to stress that the derivations in section 1 are fairly straightforward. The complications particular to a specific problem can be dealt with in isolation, if we use the program scheme. In all the examples, we started with the calculation of $\neg S.a$. Such a calculation gives rise to a candidate for the first guard in the selection statement. Due to symmetry, this often yields a candidate for the second guard as well. If these candidates do not guarantee the absence of abortion of the selection statement, $S.a$ and $S.b$ may be taken into account as well. In order to show that it is not always sensible to start with $\neg S.a$, we give as a final example a program that nondeterministically computes a number in the range $[0..N]$. The reader is invited to write such a program without using our scheme! We obtain, since $S.x \equiv true$, the following program:

```
|[ a, b : int;
    a, b := 0, N
 ; do a ≠ b →
       if true → a := a + 1
       [] true → b := b - 1
       fi
    od
 ; x := a
]|
```

References

[0] Dijkstra, E.W., Feijen, W.H.J.
     A method of programming.
     Addison-Wesley (1988)

[1] Manber, Udi
     Using induction to design algorithms.
     Communications of the ACM **31** (Nov. 1988) 1300-1313

[2] Dijkstra, E.W., Feijen, W.H.J.
     The linear search revisited.
     EWD1029, The University of Texas at Austin (1988)

THE PROJECTION OF SYSTOLIC PROGRAMS

C. LENGAUER[†,‡] AND J. W. SANDERS
PROGRAMMING RESEARCH GROUP
OXFORD UNIVERSITY COMPUTING LABORATORY
8–11 KEBLE ROAD, OXFORD, ENGLAND OX1 3QD

Abstract

A scheme is presented which transforms systolic programs with a two-dimensional structure to one dimension. The elementary steps of the transformation are justified by theorems in the theory of communicating sequential processes and the scheme is demonstrated with an example in occam: matrix composition/decomposition.

1 Introduction

We combine two types of formal refinement to transform a two-dimensional systolic program to one dimension. *Systolic arrays* are particularly regular distributed processor networks capable of processing large amounts of data quickly by accepting streams of input and producing streams of output [6]. Typical applications are to image or signal processing; ours is an algorithm which subsumes matrix composition and decomposition.

Systolic arrays are usually realized in hardware. We are interested in realizing them in *software*, because then they can run on one of the families of distributed computers (now plentiful) capable of emulating systolic arrays. We are led to express such software in a distributed programming language that provides constructs for process definition and communication. The production of that software is relatively straight-forward if the program's process and channel structure, which matches the processor and communication structure of the systolic array, also matches the distributed computer. That is not always the case. If the distributed computer does not offer the processor layout and interconnections that the systolic program prescribes, one has two options:

1. one can derive a systolic array that matches the limitations of the computer and derive a program from it, or

2. one can adjust the program derived from the ideal systolic array.

We pursue the second route, following the principle that real-world limitations should be imposed as late as possible in the design.

We consider one specific case: the processor layout of the machine has fewer dimensions than the process layout of the systolic program.[1] In this case, a *projection*, i.e., a transformation of

---

[†]On leave from the Department of Computer Sciences, The University of Texas at Austin, Taylor Hall 2.124, Austin, Texas 78712-1188.

[‡]Supported in part by the following funding agencies: through Oxford University by the Science and Engineering Research Council under Contract GR/E 63902; through the University of Texas at Austin by the Office of Naval Research under Contract N00014-86-K-0763, and by the National Science Foundation under Contract DCR-8610427.

[1]For work that explores the first option, see [7].

the process layout of the systolic program is required. We consider the transformation of two-dimensional systolic programs into one-dimensional systolic programs. There are programming environments that permit the specification of a mapping from software processes to hardware processors (e.g., for a Transputer network [4]), which makes explicit program projections unnecessary. We require this mapping to be the identity in order to avoid inefficiencies caused by the software simulation of channel communication.

The method we use to justify the projection from two to one dimension appears to be novel. It can be thought of as a variant of a hybrid of refinement techniques used in "formal methods". There, criteria for the refinement of *sequential* systems involve a relation between the states of the two systems [2,10]; criteria for the refinement of *concurrent* systems enable one system to be replaced by another in any environment [1,5]. We employ a technique of state relabelling which enables one system to replace another in any of a restricted class of environments. We hope this feature will be useful in other contexts. The refinement, as usual, makes a program more specific for the machine at hand: by postulating a one-dimensional systolic architecture, it leads from the ideal two-dimensional design to a one-dimensional implementation.

2 The Problem

We are given three matrices: A, B and C. Our goal is to establish that C is the matrix product of A and B:

$$(\forall\, i,j : 0 \leq i,j < n : \quad c_{i,j} = (\textstyle\sum k : 0 \leq k < n : a_{i,k} \cdot b_{k,j}))$$

That goal may be achieved in different ways, depending on which of the matrices are to be determined. We consider two possibilities. Because we wish to derive a systolic solution we shall assume that the matrices are distinct program objects, i.e., they do not share elements.

2.1 Matrix Composition

A and B are input and C is output. A and B uniquely determine C.

2.2 Matrix Decomposition

C is input and A and B are output. For A and B to be determined uniquely, we require them to be triangular matrices: A is one on the diagonal and zero above it; B is zero below the diagonal.

3 The Two-Dimensional occam Program

A two-dimensional systolic occam program that establishes the required relation between A, B and C is listed in Appendix A.1. The program has been obtained by formal methods that are documented elsewhere [3,8]; we shall not justify its correctness here. We note some limitations of the original version of occam [4]:

Full Parenthesization. Arithmetic expressions must be fully parenthesized.

One-Dimensional Arrays Only. We must represent an $n \times n$ matrix by an $n * n$ vector. Read index [(n*col)+row] as index pair [col,row].

No Floating-Point Arithmetic. We use a floating-point package. Read RealOp(z,x,Op,y) as z := x Op y.

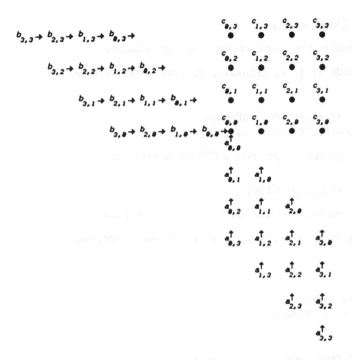

Figure 1: 4 × 4 Matrix Composition/Decomposition – The Two-Dimensional Systolic Array

A picture is helpful in understanding the structure of the program (see Fig. 1). Stream A moves through the processor array from bottom to top, stream B from left to right, and stream C is stationary during the computation (it must be loaded into the array before and recovered from it after the computation). The systolic program consists of three sets of processors (or cells):

Computation Cells. They first accept the stationary stream C from the left, then they execute the basic operations assigned to them, propagating streams A and B, and finally they eject stream C to the right.

Input Cells. Input cells on the left of the array inject first stream C and then stream B. Input cells on the bottom inject stream A.

Output Cells. Output cells on the right of the array extract first stream B and then stream C. Output cells on the top extract stream A.

Only the computation cells appear in Fig. 1, where they are represented by dots. The required channel connections can be inferred from the data flow. Fig. 1 indicates horizontal channels pointing right and vertical channels pointing up.

The program refers to a basic operation BasicOp. Its body differs for matrix composition and decomposition. We have not filled in the preprocessing and postprocessing phases. They also differ for matrix composition and decomposition. The following two subsections specify these individual refinements – for the sake of completeness. We shall not refer to them again.

3.1 Matrix Composition

For matrix composition, the basic operation is defined as follows:

```
PROC BasicOp(VALUE i, j, k, AElement, BElement, VAR CElement) =
  VAR tmp:
  SEQ
    RealOp(tmp, AElement, Mul, BElement)
    RealOp(CElement, CElement, Add, tmp) :
```

In the preprocessing phase, output matrix C is initialized to zero.

3.2 Matrix Decomposition

For matrix decomposition, the basic operation is defined as follows:

```
PROC BasicOp(VALUE i, j, k, VAR AElement, BElement, CElement) =
  VAR tmp:
  SEQ
    IF
      (i<=j) AND (i=k)
        BElement := CElement
      (i>j) AND (j=k)
        SEQ
          RealOp(tmp, One, Div, BElement)
          RealOp(AElement, CElement, Mul, tmp)
      (i>k) AND (j>k)
        SEQ
          RealOp(tmp, AElement, Mul, BElement)
          RealOp(CElement, CElement, Sub, tmp)
      TRUE
        SKIP :
```

In the preprocessing phase, the output matrices A and B are initialized to the identity and zero, respectively.

4 The Projection

We eliminate the vertical dimension by projecting horizontally. In accordance with Fig. 1, we shall refer to the three data streams as follows:

A is the *projected stream*. Its direction of flow is in the dimension that disappears in the projection. A is turned from a moving into a stationary stream.

B is the *moving stream*. It remains moving to the right.

C is the *stationary stream*. It remains stationary.

We perform the projection in two steps: we combine first the cells and then the channels of each column into one. Both steps result in startlingly simple program transformations as far as the moving and stationary streams are concerned. The cell projection of the handling of the projected stream is more complicated: it involves a conversion from moving to stationary and – more seriously – a redirection of the stream i/o. We provide first an informal account of the projection, then several transformation theorems and, finally, their application in the transformation. The reader may find it helpful to consult the appendix throughout the following subsections.

4.1 Informal Description

4.1.1 Cell Projection

The Moving and Stationary Streams

We replace the PAR loop over the dimension that is projected away by a SEQ loop. In our case, it is the dimension indexed by row (App. A.1, line 20 and App. A.2, line 30). This combines the computation processes for each column in increasing sequence rather than in parallel. We account similarly for the projection by replacing SEQ for PAR in the input and output loops on row (App. A.1, lines 13 and 44 and App. A.2, lines 13 and 59). Also, since variables BElement in each column of computation cells are now being accessed in sequence without overlap, we represent them by a single variable: we move the declaration of BElement from the loop on row out to the loop on col (App. A.1, line 21 and App. A.2, line 20).

The Projected Stream

For loading and recovery, we convert the flow direction of the stream from vertical to horizontal by commuting col and row in the input and output loops for the projected stream and replacing channels Up by channels Right (App. A.1, lines 10–12 and 50–52 and App. A.2, lines 10–12 and 65–67). We must also eliminate the communications on Up in the computation processes (App. A.1, lines 32 and 36). Then we account for the projection by replacing SEQ for PAR, now for the loop on row (App. A.2., lines 10 and 65). We also add a loading and recovery phase to the computation processes (App. A.2, lines 22–29 and 50–57). Each process must hold the stationary elements of one column of the array. We convert variable AElement into a vector and declare it per column of the array instead of per column and row (App. A.1, line 21 and App. A.2, line 20).

4.1.2 Channel Projection

We simply discard the dimension that is projected away – here it is row – from the channel array.

4.2 Theorems

We reason in a language $\mathcal{P}$, which lies midway between CSP [1] and the restricted subset of occam [11] used to express our programs. It includes those processes which engage in a finite number of inputs, outputs and assignments before terminating. From CSP, it inherits a calculus of communication traces and refusals; from occam, it inherits local variables. Since we do not consider infinite or divergent programs, we are able to reason using a drastically simplified semantics.

Each process P is described by

- a channel alphabet γP (those channels on which P may communicate),
- a variable alphabet νP (P's local program variables),

- communications (via P's failures; see [1, Chap. 3]), and

- the change in program variables (which we describe by using a predicate whose free variables consist of the vector x of P's variable values before execution and the vector x' of P's variable values after execution).

There are three types of basic process in $\mathcal{P}$. We now describe each informally and say how their variables change; it is implicit that a process cannot change variables outside its alphabet. For a description of their refusals, the reader is referred to [1, Chap. 3]. There, slightly different syntax is used: each basic process is regarded as an event and is converted to a process by postfixing it with *SKIP*. From [1, Chap. 1], we also adopt the notation P **sat** S, which means that process P satisfies condition S.

An input process $P = c?x$ inputs the value e communicated on channel c and assigns it to variable x. Its alphabet has $\gamma P = \{c\}$ and $\nu P = \{x\}$ and, regardless of its previous value, the final value x' of x equals e

$$P \text{ sat } x' = e.$$

An output process $P = c!e$ outputs the value of expression e on channel c. Its alphabet has $\gamma P = \{c\}$ and $\nu P = \{\,\}$, so it cannot alter any variables.

An assignment process $P = x{:=}e$ assigns the value of expression e to variable x. Its alphabet has $\gamma P = \{\,\}$ and $\nu P = \{x\}$; it achieves the same program state as the previous input process, but without any communications:

$$P \text{ sat } x' = e.$$

Processes are combined using sequential composition, denoted $\to$, and parallel composition, denoted $\|$. When a pair of processes is being composed, we use these symbols in infix; for the composition of a sequence $(i : 0 \leq i < n : P_i)$ of processes, we use the prefix notations $(\to i : 0 \leq i < n : P_i)$ and $(\| i : 0 \leq i < n : P_i)$. Again, we refer to [1] for laws satisfied by sequential and parallel composition (there, the semicolon is used for sequential composition; we reserve that symbol for forward composition of binary relations and predicates). As usual, we suppose that processes are only placed in parallel if none accesses a variable that another modifies, thus

$$\gamma(\| i : 0 \leq i < n : P_i) = (\cup\, i : 0 \leq i < n : \gamma P_i)$$

$$\nu(\| i : 0 \leq i < n : P_i) = (\cup\, i : 0 \leq i < n : \nu P_i)$$

and, if S_i is a predicate in the variables x and x' of P_i with

$$(\forall\, i : 0 \leq i < n : P_i \text{ sat } S_i),$$

then

$$(\| i : 0 \leq i < n : P_i) \text{ sat } (\forall\, i : 0 \leq i < n : S_i).$$

For sequential composition, no constraint on variable accesses applies, of course, thus

$$\gamma(\to i : 0 \leq i < n : P_i) = (\cup\, i : 0 \leq i < n : \gamma P_i)$$

$$\nu(\to i : 0 \leq i < n : P_i) = (\cup\, i : 0 \leq i < n : \nu P_i)$$

and, if S_i is a predicate in the variables of P_i with

$$(\forall\, i : 0 \leq i < n : P_i \text{ sat } S_i),$$

then

$$(\rightarrow i : 0 \leq i < n : P_i) \text{ sat } (; i : 0 \leq i < n : S_i).$$

For example, if P and Q are processes with

$$\nu P = \{x, y\} \quad \text{and} \quad \nu Q = \{y, z\}$$

such that

$$P \text{ sat } x' = f(x) \wedge y' = g(y)$$
$$Q \text{ sat } y' = h(y) \wedge z' = k(z)$$

then

$$\nu(P \rightarrow Q) = \{x, y, z\}$$
$$(P \rightarrow Q) \text{ sat } x' = f(x) \wedge y' = h(g(y)) \wedge z' = k(z).$$

When considering a parallel composition, we shall often stress one process by referring to the other(s) as its environment. When we say that P satisfies property S in environment Q, we mean

$$(P \parallel Q) \text{ sat } S.$$

Many of our transformations replace one process with another, in a given environment.

We shall use the law

$$((c!e \rightarrow P) \parallel (c?x \rightarrow Q)) = (c!e \rightarrow x:=e \rightarrow (P \parallel Q)). \tag{1}$$

Using this law, and those from [1,11], we reason in $\mathcal{P}$ about occam programs, just as one reasons in the language of guarded commands about Modula-2 programs. Down-coding is done by identifying the basic processes with occam programs (from [11, Sect. 2]):

$$c?x \qquad \text{with} \qquad \textbf{VAR } y :$$
$$\textbf{ALT } (c?y \quad x:=x[y/x])$$

$$c!e \qquad \text{with} \qquad \textbf{ALT } (c!e \quad x:=x)$$

$$x:=e \qquad \text{with} \qquad x:=x[e/x]$$

and by identifying $\parallel$ with $\textbf{PAR}$ and $\rightarrow$ with $\textbf{SEQ}$.

The final operation we require is that of concealment. If $E \subseteq \gamma P$, then $P \setminus E$ is a process which behaves like P but with all communications on channels in E concealed. Thus $\gamma(P \setminus E) = (\gamma P) \setminus E$ and $\nu(P \setminus E) = \nu P$, and no variables are altered by $P \setminus E$. For the failures of $P \setminus E$ and for the laws satisfied by concealment, see [1, Chap. 3].

In the following subsections, we justify all transformations except the movement of the declaration of variable BElement.

4.2.1 Cell Projection

We use three theorems. The first, the cell projection theorem, takes care of moving and stationary streams. Two more theorems, the stream projection and stream reflection theorem, address the treatment of projected streams.

The Moving and Stationary Streams

The cell projection theorem addresses two properties of a finite set of messages, which are communicated over separate channels:

1. Messages that are consumed in a total order may be produced in the same order or in any approximating (i.e., less defined) order.

2. Messages that are produced in some partial order may be consumed in that partial order or in any more defined order, provided the target variables are distinct.

For our purposes, a more restricted version of the cell projection theorem suffices: it takes for the approximating order the undefined order (which relates no elements at all) and for the approximated order a total order (which relates all elements).

Cell Projection Theorem:

Let c_i be distinct channels, e_i expressions and x_i distinct variables. The processes

$$(\parallel i : 0 \leq i < n : c_i?x_i) \quad \text{and} \quad (\rightarrow i : 0 \leq i < n : c_i?x_i)$$

both satisfy condition $S = (\forall i : 0 \leq i < n : x_i' = e_i)$ in either of the environments

$$(\parallel i : 0 \leq i < n : c_i!e_i) \quad \text{or} \quad (\rightarrow i : 0 \leq i < n : c_i!e_i).$$

Proof:

There are four processes to consider; we enumerate them for ease of reference (in fact, only the first three appear in our application). Even though their communication traces are not the same, the final state of all four processes are.

(a) $(\parallel i : 0 \leq i < n : c_i!e_i) \parallel (\parallel i : 0 \leq i < n : c_i?x_i)$
     $= \{\text{by } [1, \text{Sect. 4.3: L1}] \text{ and } (1)\}$
     $(\parallel i : 0 \leq i < n : c_i!e_i \rightarrow x_i := e_i)$
     sat
       $S.$

(b) $(\parallel i : 0 \leq i < n : c_i!e_i) \parallel (\rightarrow i : 0 \leq i < n : c_i?x_i)$
     $= \{\text{by } [1, \text{Sect. 2.3.1: L7, Sect. 4.3: L1}] \text{ and } (1)\}$
     $(\rightarrow i : 0 \leq i < n : c_i!e_i \rightarrow x_i := e_i)$
     sat
       $S.$

The proofs that

(c) $(\rightarrow i : 0 \leq i < n : c_i!e_i) \parallel (\rightarrow i : 0 \leq i < n : c_i?x_i)$ **sat** S

and

(d) $(\rightarrow i : 0 \leq i < n : c_i!e_i) \parallel (\parallel i : 0 \leq i < n : c_i?x_i)$ **sat** S

are identical to (b).

End of Proof.

The Projected Stream

Two things happen in the transformation of a projected stream:

1. "moving" is projected to "stationary"; this affects elements that are processed in sequence by one column,

2. "up" is reflected to "right"; this affects elements that are processed in parallel by different columns.

Stream Projection Theorem:

Let c_i be distinct channels, f_i expressions (i.e., functions) in one parameter, x_i distinct variables, x a variable and let $f = (; i : 0 \le i < n : f_i)$ denote the forward relational composition of the f_i. Then, condition $z' = f(e)$ is satisfied by both the processes

$$P = (\| i : 0 \le i < n : c_i?x_i \to x_i:=f_i(x_i) \to c_{i+1}!x_i)\backslash\{i : 0 < i < n : c_i\}$$

and

$$Q = c_0?x \to (\to i : 0 \le i < n : x:=f_i(x)) \to c_n!f(x)$$

in environment $c_0!e \to c_n?z$.

Proof:

In spite of the fact that P and Q have the same communication traces, they are not equal since they have different alphabets. However, by a repeated application of [1, Sect. 3.5.1: L5],

$$P = c_0?x_0 \to (\to i : 0 < i < n : x_{i+1}:=f_i(x_i)) \to c_n!x_n$$

hence

$$P \parallel (c_0!e \to c_n?z) \quad \textbf{sat} \quad z' = f(e).$$

The result for Q is immediate.

End of Proof.

The reflection is more intricate to express, because it is a conversion of the vertical-parallel i/o of stream values into a horizontal-sequenced i/o with loading and recovery.

Stream Reflection Theorem:

Let c_i and d_i be distinct channels, f_i expressions in one parameter and x_i, xin_i, $xout_i$ and $xtmp_i$ distinct variables. Condition $S = (\forall i : 0 \le i < n : xout_i' = f_i(xin_i))$ is satisfied by the following processes in their respective environments:

(a) by process

$$(\| i : 0 \le i < n : c_i?x_i \to x_i:=f_i(x_i) \to d_i!x_i)$$

in environment

$$(\| i : 0 \le i < n : c_i!xin_i) \parallel (\| i : 0 \le i < n : d_i?xout_i),$$

(b) by process

$$(\| \, i : 0 \leq i < n : \quad c_i?x_i$$
$$\rightarrow \quad (\rightarrow j : i < j < n : c_i?xtmp_i \rightarrow c_{i+1}!xtmp_i)$$
$$\rightarrow \quad x_i := f_i(x_i)$$
$$\rightarrow \quad (\rightarrow j : 0 \leq j < i : c_i?xtmp_i \rightarrow c_{i+1}!xtmp_i)$$
$$\rightarrow \quad c_{i+1}!x_i)$$

in environment

$$(\rightarrow i : 0 \leq i < n : c_0!xin_i) \, \| \, (\rightarrow i : 0 \leq i < n : c_n?xout_i).$$

Proof:

(a) By [1, Sect. 2.3.1: L7, Sect. 4.3: L1] and (1), this process simplifies to

$$(\| \, i : 0 \leq i < n : c_i!xin_i \rightarrow x_i := f_i(xin_i) \rightarrow d_i!f_i(xin_i) \rightarrow xout_i := f_i(xin_i)) \ \textbf{sat} \ S$$

(b) The resulting process cannot be simplified like the previous one (because of its communications) but nevertheless satisfies the condition (which involves only variables) by induction. In the case $n = 1$,

$$c_0!xin_0 \, \| \, (c_0?x_0 \rightarrow x_0 := f_0(x_0) \rightarrow c_1!x_0) \, \| \, c_1?xout_0$$
$$= \{\text{by [1, Sect. 2.3.1: L7, Sect. 4.3: L1] and (1)}\}$$
$$c_0!xin_0 \rightarrow x_0 := f_0(xin_0) \rightarrow c_1!f_0(xin_0) \rightarrow xout_0 := f_0(xin_0)$$
sat
$$xout_0' = f_0(xin_0).$$

For the induction step, assume the result for n. Then, for $n + 1$, the ith process satisfies, after $n + 1 - i$ inputs on channel c_i, $xtmp_i' = e$, where e is the $n + 1 - i^{th}$ value input on that channel. Thus, the process in its environment satisfies

$$(\forall i : 0 \leq i < n : xout_i' = f_i(xin_i)) \wedge xout_n' = f_n(xin_n)$$

as required.

End of Proof.

4.2.2 Channel Projection

The channel projection theorem states that successive communications on separate channels can be transmitted over a common channel.

Channel Projection Theorem:

Let c_i be distinct channels and c a channel, e_i expressions and x_i distinct variables. Condition $S = (\forall \, i : 0 \leq i < n : x_i' = e_i)$ is satisfied by the following processes in their respective environments:

(a) process $(\rightarrow i : 0 \leq i < n : c_i?x_i)$ in environment $(\rightarrow i : 0 \leq i < n : c_i!e_i)$,

(b) process $(\rightarrow i : 0 \leq i < n : c?x_i)$ in environment $(\rightarrow i : 0 \leq i < n : c!e_i)$.

Proof.

(a) Case (c) of cell projection.

(b) Simply replace c_i by c in the proof above since the condition is independent of channel names.

End of Proof.

4.3 Application

4.3.1 Cell Projection

The Moving and Stationary Streams

The cell projection theorem is applied recursively to each column of cells, right to left. As the base case, consider the output cells. A substitution of the PAR on row by SEQ (App. A.1, line 44 and App. A.2, line 59) is a conversion from (a) to (b) in the theorem. The induction hypothesis is that the input of stationary and moving streams in some column has been projected. Consider the column to its left. In the induction step, we project the output of the stationary and moving streams in that column by converting from (b) to (c), and the input of stationary and moving streams in that column by converting from (a) to (b) again. This means replacing the PAR on row that encases both the input and the output of stationary and moving streams by a SEQ (App. A.1, line 20 and App. A.2, line 30). This is done for a fixed iteration of the encasing PAR loop on col (App. A.1 and A.2, line 19). The induction is on col. Finally, we replace the PAR on row in the column of input cells by a SEQ (App. A.1 and A.2, line 13), converting once more from (b) to (c).

It is important to note that we apply the cell projection theorem in a benevolent environment: no communications other than the ones stated in the theorem are transmitted over the stated channels; in particular, there are no messages in the reverse direction, i.e., there is no feedback that could create circular dependencies.

We do not justify the projection of variable BElement formally. The theory of CSP, as presented in [1], does not provide for this kind of program transformation.

The Projected Stream

Initially, we had entertained the hope that we could split the cell projection of the treatment of stream A into two steps:

1. the reflection of the stream from horizontal to vertical and its treatment as stationary, and

2. the cell projection, as previously for stationary streams.

Unfortunately, the intermediate (still two-dimensional) program – the output of step 1 and input of step 2 – is not occam. It is dangerous to pretend that the projected stream is stationary in the two-dimensional array when it really is not. Since cells share the stream's elements, they update shared variables, which is illegal in occam.

The stream projection and stream reflection theorem split the projection of stream A up differently. We have to perform the cell projection first in order to avoid the ill-defined intermediate two-dimensional program. Our transformation proceeds as follows.

By appealing to the stream projection theorem, we eliminate lines 32 and 36 of the two-dimensional program. These communications on Up correspond to the communications on the middle channels $c_1, ..., c_{n-1}$ in the theorem. We apply the theorem by substituting Q for P. The transformation of the variables x_i in P to the single variable x in Q corresponds to the movement of the declaration of variable AElement from the PAR on row in the two-dimensional program (line 21) to the PAR loop on col in the one-dimensional program (line 20). AElement becomes a vector of variables as a result of an inductive application of the stream projection theorem.

By appealing to the stream reflection theorem, we frame the computation cell code with code portions for the loading and recovery of stationary stream A (App. A.2, lines 22–29 and 50–57). We convert from (a) to (b). The stream reflection theorem also covers the reflection of the input and output from channels Up in the two-dimensional program (App. A.1, lines 10–12 and 50–52) to channels Right in the one-dimensional program (App. A.2, lines 10–12 and 65–67).

4.3.2 Channel Projection

The channel projection theorem is also applied recursively, converting from (a) to (b). Each application collapses the set of channels between two columns (which have already been collapsed to single cells) to a single channel. At this point, there are only stationary and moving streams left; no distinction needs to be made between them.

5 Conclusions

We have formulated a general projection scheme of cells and channels in systolic programs and have applied it to a specific example. We have stated and proved the transformation theorems in a language $\mathcal{P}$, and our scheme applies to any distributed programming language that obeys $\mathcal{P}$'s laws. The program example is in one implemented programming language that obeys those laws: occam. At present, there is a gap between the theorems and their application; we have bridged it with English explanations. Making our transformations completely precise is possible but elaborate. It would be easier were we to replace the mechanical systolic design that produces our two-dimensional occam program by a derivation that relies more on the semantics of processes in $\mathcal{P}$ – future work. Such a derivation would also simplify adjustments like the elimination of the PAR on lines 31 and 35 in the two-dimensional program together with the Up communications on lines 33 and 36 (PARs with just one statement can be dropped).

Similar projection schemes can be applied to systolic programs with different stream movements. We have covered the three elementary cases: projected, moving and stationary streams. All of the required substitutions are static and can be easily incorporated into a compiler. We have tried to make the substitutions as simple as possible. The simplicity of the substitutions depends on the form of the program to be projected.[2] Luckily, our two-dimensional program is itself the product of a mechanical derivation [8]. Thus, we have the choice of imposing a derivation scheme that simplifies projections.

Our theorems are simplified by the fact that we distinguish the computation cells from the i/o cells, and that we reason about states rather than traces wherever possible. In the application of the theorems, we presume the absence of feedback between the computation and the i/o cells. Programs that are compiled from linear systolic designs [8] do not have feedback, but

---

[2] For example, letting computation cells during the loading of stationary streams propagate elements first and then keep their own element leads to an inversion of the column's index in the input loop, which complicates the projection of stream A.

feedback may arise when a linear systolic design is partitioned, i.e., transformed into a ring or toroid (e.g., [9]). Therefore, to keep the transformations simple, we suggest to project first and partition later.

6 Acknowledgements

The first author is indebted to Tony Hoare for the invitation to join PRG for a term, and to all members of PRG for making his stay a fruitful, enjoyable, and unforgettable one. Thanks go also to Richard Miller, Andrew Kay, and Geraint Jones, who assisted in the use of the occam language and compiler.

7 References

[1] C. A. R. Hoare, *Communicating Sequential Processes*, Series in Computer Science, Prentice-Hall Int., 1985.

[2] C. A. R. Hoare, He Jifeng and J. W. Sanders, "Prespecification in Data Refinement", *Information Processing Letters 25*, 2 (May 1987), 71–76.

[3] C. H. Huang and C. Lengauer, "The Derivation of Systolic Implementations of Programs", *Acta Informatica 24*, 6 (Nov. 1987), 595–632.

[4] INMOS Ltd., occam *Programming Manual*, Series in Computer Science, Prentice-Hall Int., 1984.

[5] J. L. Jacob, "On Shared Systems", D. Phil. Thesis, Programming Research Group, Oxford University Computing Laboratory, 1987.

[6] H. T. Kung and C. E. Leiserson, "Algorithms for VLSI Processor Arrays", in *Introduction to VLSI Systems*, C. Mead and L. Conway (eds.), Addison-Wesley, 1980, Sect. 8.3.

[7] P. Lee, Z. Kedem, "Synthesizing Linear Array Algorithms from Nested for Loop Algorithms", *IEEE Trans. on Computers TC-37*, 12 (Dec. 1988), 1578-1598.

[8] C. Lengauer, "Towards Systolizing Compilation: An Overview", Proc. *Conf. on Parallel Architectures and Languages Europe (PARLE 89)*, June 1989, to appear as Springer-Verlag Lecture Notes in Computer Science.

[9] D. I. Moldovan and J. A. B. Fortes, "Partitioning and Mapping Algorithms into Fixed-Size Systolic Arrays", *IEEE Trans. on Computers C-35*, 1 (Jan. 1986), 1–12.

[10] T. Nipkow, "Non-Determinstic Data Types", *Acta Informatica 22*, 6 (Mar. 1986), 629–661.

[11] A. W. Roscoe and C. A. R. Hoare, "The Laws of occam Programming", *Theoretical Computer Science 60*, 2 (1988), 177ff.

A   The occam Programs

A.1   The Two-Dimensional Program

```
1    VAR AIn[n*n], AOut[n*n],
2        BIn[n*n], BOut[n*n],
3        CIn[n*n], COut[n*n]:

4    CHAN Right[n*(n+1)]:           -- horizontal channels
5    CHAN Up[(n+1)*n]:              -- vertical channels

6    SEQ

         -- PREPROCESSING

7        "read in input matrices"
8        "initialize output matrices"

9        PAR

           -- INPUT CELLS

           -- vertical input: inject stream A

10         PAR col = [0 FOR n]
11           SEQ row = [0 FOR n]
12             Up[((n+1)*col)+0] ! AIn[(n*col)+row]

           -- horizontal input: load stream C and inject stream B

13         PAR row = [0 FOR n]
14           SEQ

15             SEQ col = [0 FOR n]
16               Right[(n*0)+row] ! CIn[(n*col)+row]

17             SEQ col = [0 FOR n]
18               Right[(n*0)+row] ! BIn[(n*col)+row]

           -- COMPUTATION CELLS

19         PAR col = [0 FOR n]
20           PAR row = [0 FOR n]

21               VAR AElement, BElement, CElement:
```

```
SEQ

   -- load stream C

   Right[(n*col)+row] ? CElement

   SEQ unused = [0 FOR (n-1)-col]
     VAR tmp:
     SEQ
       Right[(n*col)+row] ? tmp
       Right[(n*(col+1))+row] ! tmp

   -- do the computation

   SEQ k = [0 FOR n]
     SEQ

       PAR
         Up[((n+1)*col)+row] ? AElement
         Right[(n*col)+row] ? BElement

       BasicOp(col, row, k, AElement, BElement, CElement)

       PAR
         Up[((n+1)*col)+row+1] ! AElement
         Right[(n*(col+1))+row] ! BElement

   -- recover stream C

   SEQ k = [0 FOR col]
     VAR tmp:
     SEQ
       Right[(n*col)+row] ? tmp
       Right[(n*(col+1))+row] ! tmp

   Right[(n*(col+1))+row] ! CElement

-- OUTPUT CELLS

-- horizontal output: extract stream B and recover stream C

PAR row = [0 FOR n]
  SEQ

    SEQ col = [0 FOR n]
      Right[(n*n)+row] ? BOut[(n*col)+row]

    SEQ col = [0 FOR n]
      Right[(n*n)+row] ? COut[(n*col)+row]
```

```
                -- vertical output: extract stream A

50              PAR col = [0 FOR n]
51                SEQ row = [0 FOR n]
52                  Up[((n+1)*col)+n] ? AOut[(n*col)+row]


                -- POSTPROCESSING

53              "read out output matrices"
```

A.2 The One-Dimensional Program

```
1    VAR AIn[n*n], AOut[n*n],
2        BIn[n*n], BOut[n*n],
3        CIn[n*n], COut[n*n]:

4    CHAN Right[n+1]:

5    SEQ

            -- PREPROCESSING

6        "read in input matrices"
7        "initialize output matrices"

8        PAR

            -- INPUT CELLS

9            SEQ

                -- load stream A

10              SEQ row = [0 FOR n]
11                SEQ col = [0 FOR n]
12                  Right[0] ! AIn[(n*col)+row]

                -- load stream C and inject stream B

13              SEQ row = [0 FOR n]
14                SEQ

15                  SEQ col = [0 FOR n]
16                    Right[0] ! CIn[(n*col)+row]

17                  SEQ col = [0 FOR n]
18                    Right[0] ! BIn[(n*col)+row]
```

```
-- COMPUTATION CELLS

PAR col = [0 FOR n]

  VAR AElement[n], BElement:

  SEQ

    -- load stream A

    SEQ row = [0 FOR n]
      SEQ

        Right[col] ? AElement[row]

        SEQ unused = [0 FOR (n-1)-col]
          VAR tmp:
          SEQ
            Right[col] ? tmp
            Right[col+1] ! tmp

    SEQ row = [0 FOR n]
      VAR CElement:
      SEQ

        -- load stream C

        Right[col] ? CElement

        SEQ unused = [0 FOR (n-1)-col]
          VAR tmp:
          SEQ
            Right[col] ? tmp
            Right[col+1] ! tmp

        -- do the computation

        SEQ k = [0 FOR n]
          SEQ

            Right[col] ? BElement

            BasicOp(col, row, k, AElement[k], BElement, CElement)

            Right[col+1] ! BElement
```

```
                -- recover stream C

44            SEQ unused = [0 FOR col]
45              VAR tmp:
46              SEQ
47                Right[col] ? tmp
48                Right[col+1] ! tmp

49              Right[col+1] ! CElement

            -- recover stream A

50          SEQ row = [0 FOR n]
51            SEQ

52              SEQ unused = [0 FOR col]
53                VAR tmp:
54                SEQ
55                  Right[col] ? tmp
56                  Right[col+1] ! tmp

57              Right[col+1] ! AElement[row]

      -- OUTPUT CELLS

58      SEQ

          -- extract stream B and recover stream C

59        SEQ row = [0 FOR n]
60          SEQ

61            SEQ col = [0 FOR n]
62              Right[n] ? BOut[(n*col)+row]

63            SEQ col = [0 FOR n]
64              Right[n] ? COut[(n*col)+row]

          -- recover stream A

65        SEQ row = [0 FOR n]
66          SEQ col = [0 FOR n]
67            Right[n] ? AOut[(n*col)+row]

    -- POSTPROCESSING

68    "read out output matrices"
```

THE FORMAL CONSTRUCTION OF
A PARALLEL TRIANGULAR SYSTEM SOLVER

L. D. J. C. Loyens and R. H. Bisseling
Koninklijke/Shell-Laboratorium, Amsterdam (Shell Research B.V.)
P.O. Box 3003, 1003 AA Amsterdam, The Netherlands

Abstract. A parallel program for the solution of a triangular system of equations is formally derived. The program assumes the grid distribution of the $n \times n$ triangular matrix across $p = Q^2$ processes. The complexity is $n^2/p + O(n)$, both for a complete and for a square mesh communication network.

0. Introduction

Formal techniques are a powerful tool in the construction of parallel programs, as will be demonstrated by the following derivation of an efficient parallel algorithm for the solution of the triangular system

$$L x = b. \qquad (0)$$

Here $L(i, j : 0 \le i, j < n)$ is a given unit lower triangular matrix of size $n \times n$, $b(i : 0 \le i < n)$ is a given vector of length n, and $x(i : 0 \le i < n)$ is the unknown solution vector.

Triangular system solving is part of many direct and iterative methods for the solution of linear systems. The performance of a number of recently developed parallel algorithms [Eisenstat 88], [Heath 88], [Li 88], [Romine 88] indicates that triangular system solving is difficult to parallelise. Therefore, triangular system solving may become a sequential bottleneck in the parallel solution of linear systems. The data distribution scheme of these algorithms is based on either a row or a column distribution of the triangular matrix.

The *grid distribution* of matrices [van de Vorst 88], also called *scattered decomposition* [Fox 88] or *cyclic storage* [Johnsson 87], is the key to achieving high efficiency in many parallel linear algebra computations, such as e.g. LU- and QR-decomposition. However, to take full advantage of this distribution, care must be taken in the derivation of the algorithms. A grid based algorithm for the solution of a triangular system with multiple right-hand sides b is presented in [Fox 88]. For the present problem, with a single right-hand side, this algorithm achieves a maximal speedup of only $\sqrt{p}$, for p processes. On the other hand, the QWERTY algorithm [Bisseling 88], which is also grid based, achieves a maximal speedup of p. The focus of the present paper is the formal derivation of the QWERTY algorithm. (The name "QWERTY" was chosen for three reasons: (i) it emphasises the abstract reasoning as opposed to the operational or intuitive reasoning which can be very misleading in the construction of parallel algorithms; (ii) it competes in clarity with many existing acronyms for parallel triangular system solving algorithms; (iii) it requires a minimal effort to reproduce. The QWERTY algorithm should not be confused with the QWERTY keyboard, nor with the QWERTY programmer [Gries 81].)

The remainder of this paper is organised as follows. Section 1 presents the functional specification. Section 2 derives the QWERTY algorithm, and proves its absence of computational deadlock. A program text is given in Section 3. Section 4 discusses the complexity of the algorithm, and Section 5 draws the conclusions.

1. Functional specification

A major concern in the construction of parallel programs is the distribution of the variables across the processes, because of its influence on load balancing behaviour and communication overhead. Assume there are $p = Q^2$ processes, each identified by an ordered pair (s, t), $0 \leq s, t < Q$, which are connected by a complete communication network. For the sake of simplicity we assume that n is a multiple of Q. Since the grid distribution is very efficient for parallel linear algebra programs, we have adopted it as the standard distribution for matrices in all our programs, including triangular system solving. Vectors are distributed in a number of ways, but in the present case vectors of length n are distributed in the same way as the diagonal of an $n \times n$ matrix. The notation in this paper follows closely the conventions of [Gries 81].

Definition { G }

$G(a, r) = \{j : 0 \leq j < a \wedge j \bmod Q = r : j\}$, for all $a, r : a, r \geq 0$.

(End of Definition)

Property { G }

For all $s, t, k : 0 \leq s, t < Q \wedge k \geq 0 \wedge k \bmod Q = 0$:

$G(k+s, t) = G(k, t)$, for $s \leq t$,

$G(k+s, t) = G(k, t) \cup \{k+t\}$, for $s > t$,

$G(k+Q, t) = G(k, t) \cup \{k+t\}$.

(End of Property)

Definition { *distr* }

For every $n \times n$ matrix A : $distr(A) = $ grid $\equiv$

$(A\ s, t : 0 \leq s, t < Q$: process (s, t) owns all $A[i, j]$ with $(i, j) \in G(n, s) \times G(n, t))$.

For every $n \times 1$ vector y : $distr(y) = $ grid.diag $\equiv$

$(A\ s, t : 0 \leq s, t < Q : s \neq t \vee$ process (s, t) owns all $y[i]$ with $i \in G(n, s))$.

(End of Definition)

We are now able to give a functional specification,

$|[L(i, j : 0 \leq i, j < n)$: matrix of real;

$\quad b(i : 0 \leq i < n)$: vector of real;

$\quad \{n \geq 1 \wedge (A\ i, j : 0 \leq i < j < n : L[i, j] = 0) \wedge (A\ i : 0 \leq i < n : L[i, i] = 1) \wedge$

$\quad\quad p = Q^2 \wedge Q \geq 1 \wedge (n \bmod Q = 0) \wedge distr(L) = $ grid $\wedge distr(b) = $ grid.diag$\}$

$\quad |[x(i : 0 \leq i < n)$: vector of real;

$\quad$ QWERTY

$\quad\quad \{distr(x) = $ grid.diag $\wedge L\ x = b\ \}$

$\quad]|$

$]|$

In this notation, L and b are constants of QWERTY, and x a variable.

Definition { *sum* }

$sum(i) = (\sum j : 0 \le j < i : L[i, j]*x[j])$, for all $i : 0 \le i < n$.

End of Definition)

The postcondition in the functional specification is the starting point for the construction of the QWERTY algorithm. Using the unit lower triangularity of L and the definition of *sum*, the postcondition can be rewritten as

$$(A\ i : 0 \le i < n : x[i] = b[i] - sum(i)). \tag{1}$$

Taking into account the grid.diag distribution of b and x, the postcondition can be reformulated as the conjunction of $p = Q^2$ parameterised postconditions $R[s, t], 0 \le s, t < Q$,

$$R[s, t] : s \ne t \vee (A\ i : i \in G(n, s) : x[i] = b[i] - sum(i)). \tag{2}$$

2. Derivation

The QWERTY algorithm consists of the parallel composition of instances of a parameterised process. From the parameterised postcondition (2) a parameterised invariant can be obtained, which is used in the derivation and correctness proof of the algorithm. We propose two invariants $P0$ and $P1$ as a generalisation of the postcondition given by (2),

$$P0[s, t] : 0 \le k \le n \wedge k \bmod Q = 0, \tag{3}$$

$$P1[s, t] : s \ne t \vee (A\ i : i \in G(k, s) : x[i] = b[i] - sum(i)). \tag{4}$$

$P1$ is derived from R by replacing the constant n by the variable k, which is local to process (s, t). As a consequence of $P0$, process (s, t) contains a loop with initialisation $k := 0$, guard $k \ne n$, and increment $k := k+Q$.

$P1[s, t](k := k+Q)$

$\equiv$ { substitution }

$s \ne t \vee (A\ i : i \in G(k+Q, s) : x[i] = b[i] - sum(i))$

$\equiv$ { property G, range splitting }

$s \ne t \vee ((A\ i : i \in G(k, s) : x[i] = b[i] - sum(i)) \wedge x[k+s] = b[k+s] - sum(k+s))$

$\equiv$ { calculus, definition $P1$ }

$$P1[s, t] \wedge (s \ne t \vee x[k+s] = b[k+s] - sum(k+s)). \tag{5}$$

The value $x[k+s]$ has to be calculated by process (s, s) from the value of $sum(k+s)$. The term $sum(k+s)$ can be expressed as a sum of partial sums *psum*, such that each partial sum contains only elements of L that are local to one particular process (s, t); this obviates the need to communicate elements of L during the computation of a partial sum.

328

Definition { *psum* }

$psum(a, r, i) = (\sum j : j \in G(a, r) : L[i, j]*x[j])$,

for all $a, r, i : 0 \le a \le n \wedge 0 \le i < n \wedge 0 \le r < Q$.

(End of Definition)

Property { *psum* }

For all $s, t, k, i : 0 \le s, t < Q \wedge 0 \le k < n \wedge k \bmod Q = 0 \wedge 0 \le i < n$:

$psum(k+s, t, i) = psum(k, t, i)$, for $s \le t$,

$psum(k+s, t, i) = psum(k, t, i) + L[i, k+t]*x[k+t]$, for $s > t$,

$psum(k+Q, t, i) = psum(k, t, i) + L[i, k+t]*x[k+t]$.

(End of Property)

This property follows from property G and the definition of *psum*.

$sum(k+s)$

= { definition *sum* }

$\quad(\sum j : 0 \le j < k+s : L[k+s, j]*x[j])$

= { calculus }

$\quad(\sum t : 0 \le t < Q : (\sum j : j \in G(k+s, t) : L[k+s, j]*x[j]))$

= { definition *psum* }

$\quad(\sum t : 0 \le t < Q : psum(k+s, t, k+s))$.

= { range splitting }

$\quad(\sum t : 0 \le t < s : psum(k+s, t, k+s)) + (\sum t : s \le t < Q : psum(k+s, t, k+s))$

= { property *psum* }

$\quad(\sum t : 0 \le t < s : psum(k, t, k+s) + L[k+s, k+t]*x[k+t]) +$

$\quad(\sum t : s \le t < Q : psum(k, t, k+s))$. \hfill (6)

Eqn (6) suggests to introduce a third invariant $P2$, which expresses the fact that process (s, t) has accumulated locally the terms of its partial sum, into a variable w,

$$P2[s, t] : (A i : i \in G(n, s) : w[i, t] = psum(i \bmod k, t, i)). \hfill (7)$$

Using $P2[s, t]$, $sum(k+s)$ can be rewritten as

$sum(k+s)$

= { definition $w[k+s, t]$ in $P2[s, t]$ }

$\quad(\sum t : 0 \le t < s : w[k+s,t]+L[k+s,k+t]*x[k+t]) + (\sum t : s \le t < Q : w[k+s,t])$. \hfill (8)

The invariant $P1[s, s](k := k+Q)$ can be established using eqns (5) and (8). The guard $k \neq n$ and $P0[s, s]$ imply that $k+s < k+Q \leq n$, so that $k+s \in G(n, s)$. Because of the $P2[s, t]$, this implies that the $w[k+s, t]$ are available. The predicates $P1[t, t](k := k+Q)$ with $t < s$ imply that the $x[k+t]$ are available.

$P2[s, t](k := k+Q)$

$\equiv$ { substitution }

$(A\ i : i \in G(n, s) : w[i, t] = psum(i\ \textbf{min}\ (k+Q), t, i))$

$\equiv$ { range splitting, calculus }

$(A\ i : i \in G(n, s) \wedge i < k : w[i, t] = psum(i, t, i)) \wedge$

$(w[k+s, t] = psum(k+s, t, k+s)) \wedge$

$(A\ i : i \in G(n, s) \wedge i \geq k+Q : w[i, t] = psum(k+Q, t, i))$

$\equiv$ { calculus, property $psum$ }

$(A\ i : i \in G(n, s) \wedge i < k : w[i, t] = psum(i, t, i)) \wedge$

$((s \leq t \wedge w[k+s, t] = psum(k, t, k+s)) \vee$

$(s > t \wedge w[k+s, t] = psum(k, t, k+s) + L[k+s, k+t]*x[k+t])) \wedge$

$(A\ i : i \in G(n, s) \wedge i \geq k+Q : w[i, t] = psum(k, t, i) + L[i, k+t]*x[k+t]).$ (9)

The invariant $P2[s, t](k := k+Q)$ can be established using eqn (9). $P1[t, t](k := k+Q)$ implies that $x[k+t]$ is available; $P2[s, t]$ implies that the $w[i, t]$ and $w[k+s, t]$ are available.

The restoration procedure for the invariants $P1[s, s]$ and $P2[s, t]$ is based upon eqns (5), (8), and (9). (The invariants $P0[s, t]$ and the invariants $P1[s, t]$ with $s \neq t$ are trivially kept true.) Since the restoration procedure of an invariant assumes the validity of other invariants (with different s, t, or k), it is not *a priori* clear that there exists an order in which the invariants can be established. The situation in which there is no such order is called *computational deadlock*, to be distinguished from *communicational deadlock*, which may occur in the actual implementation of an algorithm.

The algorithm defines a set of invariants *Inv* and a precedence relation $\ll$. It is sufficient to find a ranking function on these invariants, in order to prove absence of computational deadlock of the algorithm.

Definition { *Inv* }

$Inv = \{s, k : 0 \leq s < Q \wedge 0 \leq k \leq n \wedge k\ \textbf{mod}\ Q = 0 : P1[s, s](k)\} \cup$

$\quad\quad \{s, t, k : 0 \leq s, t < Q \wedge 0 \leq k \leq n \wedge k\ \textbf{mod}\ Q = 0 : P2[s, t](k)\}.$

End of Definition)

Definition { $\ll$ }

For $I0, I1 \in Inv : \quad I0 \ll I1 \equiv \quad I0$ must be established before $I1$ can be established.

End of Definition)

The elements of the relation $<<$ are:

$P\,1[s,s](k)$ $<<$ $P\,1[s,s](k+Q)$ (see eqn (5)),

$P\,2[s,t](k)$ $<<$ $P\,1[s,s](k+Q)$ (see eqns (5),(8)),

$P\,1[t,t](k+Q)$ $<<$ $P\,1[s,s](k+Q)$ for $t<s$ (see eqns (5),(8)),

$P\,2[s,t](k)$ $<<$ $P\,2[s,t](k+Q)$ (see eqn (9)),

$P\,1[t,t](k)$ $<<$ $P\,2[s,t](k+Q)$ (see eqn (9)),

for all $s,t,k : 0 \le s,t < Q \wedge 0 \le k < n \wedge k \bmod Q = 0$.

Definition { $<<*$ }

$<<*$ is the transitive nonreflexive closure of $<<$.

(End of Definition)

Definition { *ranking function* }

A ranking function r is a function $Inv \rightarrow \mathbf{N}$, such that

$(\mathbf{A}\ I0, I1 : I0, I1 \in Inv \wedge I0 <<* I1 : r(I0) < r(I1))$.

(End of Definition)

Definition { *No computational deadlock* }

No computational deadlock $\equiv (\mathbf{E}\ r : r$ is a ranking function$)$.

(End of Definition)

Definition { f }

$f(P\,1[s,s](k)) = 2k + 2s + 1$,

$f(P\,2[s,t](k)) = 2k + 2s + 2$,

for all $s,t,k : 0 \le s,t < Q \wedge 0 \le k \le n \wedge k \bmod Q = 0$.

(End of Definition)

It can easily be verified that $f(I0) < f(I1)$, for all $I0, I1 \in Inv$ with $I0 << I1$, and hence for all $I0, I1$ with $I0 <<* I1$, because of the definition of $<<*$. This proves that f is a ranking function.

3. Program text

In order to present a program text of the QWERTY algorithm, a number of conventions regarding the process model and the communication primitives must be established. The process model we use is based on CSP [Hoare 85]. A parallel program is viewed as the parallel composition of a number of processes. Each process has its own set of local variables that cannot be shared with other processes. Parallel composition of processes $S0$ and $S1$ yields a process, denoted by **par** $S0, S1$ **rap**. The composite process is terminated when both processes $S0$ and $S1$ are terminated. A straightforward generalisation is the parallel composition of parameterised processes, denoted by **par** $i : i \in D : S(i)$ **rap**. If the index set D is empty, then the parallel composition is equivalent to *skip*.

Communication between processes is explicit, by use of input and output actions on channels. The communication mechanism may be either synchronous or asynchronous. The only assumptions are that messages are received in the same order as they were sent and that no messages get lost. Communication is denoted by $j \ ! \ e$, for output of the value of the expression e to process j, and $i \ ? \ x$, for input of a value from process i into the variable x. In the program text, assertions are used to state explicitly which values are communicated. If $\{e = \hat{e}\}$ holds prior to $j \ ! \ e$ in process i, then $\{x = \hat{e}\}$ holds after $i \ ? \ x$ in process j. Here $\hat{e}$ is an expression in terms of auxiliary variables, x is a local variable of process j and e is a local expression of process i.

Assertions about communicated values must be expressed in terms of auxiliary variables, because shared variables are not available. In particular, in the following program text an auxiliary variable $\hat{x}[i]$, $0 \le i < n$, is introduced to denote the solution element $\hat{x}[i] = (L^{-1}b)[i]$, to be distinguished from the variable $x[i]$. We may also use *psum* in assertions, as an expression in auxiliary variables, provided x is replaced by $\hat{x}$ in the definition of *psum*.

The program text is given on the next page.

4. Complexity

The time complexity of the QWERTY algorithm is derived under the following assumptions: the communication network is complete; multiplication and addition of reals takes one time unit; assignments and integer calculations are not counted; communication of one real from any process to any other process takes α time units; parallel communications are counted in parallel. The complexity of each part of the program is computed separately. The resulting partial complexities are combined, by adding them in the case of sequential composition, and by taking their maximum in the case of parallel composition. This procedure implicitly assumes synchronisation between processes at the start of separate parts, and therefore the total computed complexity is an upper bound on the actual complexity of the algorithm.

Every process (s, t) performs n/Q steps, each consisting of two parts, *RestoreP* 1 and *RestoreP* 2. The bulk of the computational work in step k is the **for all**-statement of *RestoreP* 2, which takes $2*(N \ i : i \in G(n, s) : i \ge k+Q) = 2(n-k)/Q - 2$ time units. The **if**-statement of *RestoreP* 2 is a broadcast of $\hat{x}[k+t]$, in α time units. (The value to be assigned to $w[k+s, t]$ for $s > t$ is already computed in *RestoreP* 1, and does not have to be recomputed.) The total complexity of *RestoreP* 2 in step k is $2(n-k)/Q - 2 + \alpha$.

The complexity of *RestoreP* 1 is obtained by a careful analysis of the critical path of the data flow. In order to obtain a low complexity, the program should be transformed, by rewriting the program text of *RestoreP* 1 for processes (s, t) with $s = t$. The resulting implementation of *RestoreP* 1 consists of two phases:

In the first phase, all processes (s, t) with $s \le t$ are active. The processes (s, s) perform the initialisation $x[k+s] := b[k+s]$. The processes with $s < t$ send their values $w[k+s, t]$ in parallel to process (s, s), in time α. These values and the local value $w[k+s, s]$ of process (s, s) are subtracted from $x[k+s]$, in at most Q time units. The total complexity of the first phase of *RestoreP* 1 in step k is $Q + \alpha$.

Program text of the QWERTY algorithm

QWERTY ::
|[$w(i, t : 0 \le i < n, 0 \le t < Q)$: matrix of real;
  par $s, t : 0 \le s, t < Q : (s, t)$ **rap**
]|

(s, t) ::
|[k : integer;
  $k := 0$;
  for all $i : i \in G(n, s) : w[i, t] := 0$ **lla rof**;
  {$Allinvariants : P0[s, t] \land P1[s, t] \land P2[s, t]$}
  do $k \ne n$
  $\rightarrow$ {$Allinvariants \land k \ne n$, hence $k+Q \le n$}
    |[y : real;
      $a(q : 0 \le q < Q)$: vector of real;
      $RestoreP1$; {$P1[s, t](k := k+Q)$}
      $RestoreP2$ {$P2[s, t](k := k+Q)$}
    ]|;
    $k := k+Q$ {$Allinvariants$}
  od
]|

$RestoreP1$ ::
if $s < t \rightarrow$ {$w[k+s, t] = psum(k+s, t, k+s)$} (s, s) ! $w[k+s, t]$
[] $s = t \rightarrow$ **par** $q : 0 \le q < Q \land q \ne t : (s, q)$? $a[q]$ {$a[q] = psum(k+s, q, k+s)$} **rap**;
          $a[t] := w[k+s, t]$; {$a[t] = psum(k+s, t, k+s)$}
          $x[k+s] := b[k+s] - (\sum q : 0 \le q < Q : a[q])$;
          par $q : t < q < Q : \{x[k+t] = \hat{x}[k+t]\}$ (q, t) ! $x[k+t]$ **rap**
[] $s > t \rightarrow (t, t)$? y; {$y = \hat{x}[k+t]$}
          {$w[k+s, t] + L[k+s, k+t]*y = psum(k+s, t, k+s)$}
          (s, s) ! $w[k+s, t] + L[k+s, k+t]*y$
fi

$RestoreP2$ ::
if $s < t \rightarrow (t, t)$? y {$y = \hat{x}[k+t]$}
[] $s = t \rightarrow y := x[k+t]$;
          par $q : 0 \le q < t : \{y = \hat{x}[k+t]\}$ (q, t) ! y **rap**
[] $s > t \rightarrow \{y = \hat{x}[k+t]\}$ $w[k+s, t] := w[k+s, t] + L[k+s, k+t]*y$
fi; {$y = \hat{x}[k+t]$}
for all $i : i \in G(n, s) \land i \ge k+Q : w[i, t] := w[i, t] + L[i, k+t]*y$ **lla rof**

In the second phase, all processes (s, t) with $s \geq t$ are active. In particular, the processes (s, s) receive the values $psum(k+s, t, k+s)$ with $t = 0, 1, \ldots, s-1$, in this order, and immediately subtract them from $x[k+s]$ (instead of first collecting the values and then subtracting them, which would cause a delay along the critical path of the data flow). The processes (s, t) with $s > t$ receive the value $\hat{x}[k+t]$ from process (t, t), then compute the value of $psum(k+s, t, k+s)$, and send the result to process (s, s).

The critical path of the second phase is the data flow from process $(0, 0)$, to $(1, 0)$, to $(1, 1), \ldots$, to $(Q-1, Q-1)$. A process (s, s) on this path receives a value from process $(s, s-1)$, subtracts it from the current value of $x[k+s]$, and sends the result $\hat{x}[k+s]$ to process $(s+1, s)$. This process in turn uses the result to compute the value of $psum(k+s+1, s, k+s+1)$, which is then sent to process $(s+1, s+1)$. The time of the critical path is at most $3Q + 2(Q-1)\alpha$, and this is the complexity of the second phase of $RestoreP\,1$ in step k.

An upper bound for the total time complexity of the QWERTY algorithm is obtained by summing over k,

$$T_p(n) \leq \frac{n^2}{p} + (2\alpha+4)n, \qquad \text{for a complete network.} \tag{10}$$

The time complexity for a square mesh can be obtained by a similar count,

$$T_p(n) \leq \frac{n^2}{p} + (4\alpha+5)n, \qquad \text{for a square mesh network.} \tag{11}$$

The complexity of the best sequential algorithm is

$$T_{seq}(n) = n^2 - n. \tag{12}$$

The theoretical time complexity has been verified by experiments on square meshes of up to $p = 36$ T800-20 Transputers [Bisseling 88]. An approximate formula for the measured time complexity is

$$T_p(n) \approx 1.89\,\frac{n^2}{p} + 38.0\,n \quad \mu s. \tag{13}$$

5. Conclusions

The aim of the present work was to give the formal construction of the grid based QWERTY algorithm for the solution of triangular systems. The algorithm was shown correct using predicate calculus, invariants, and a ranking function.

The choice of the grid distribution has resulted in a program with a low complexity, and an asymptotically maximal speedup. The communication cost $2\alpha n$ is of a lower order than the computation cost $n^2/p + O(n)$, and does not grow with the number of processes. The complexity of the resulting program is an *a posteriori* justification of the chosen grid distribution.

The communication complexities for a complete network and for a square mesh are of the same order. This implies that a square mesh communication network is sufficiently rich for an efficient implementation of the QWERTY algorithm.

Acknowledgement

We thank our colleague Hans van de Vorst for many interesting and stimulating discussions.

334

References

[Bisseling 88]   R. H. BISSELING AND J. G. G. VAN DE VORST, "Parallel Triangular System Solving on a Mesh Network of Transputers," submitted (1988).

[Eisenstat 88]   S. C. EISENSTAT, M. T. HEATH, C. S. HENKEL, AND C. H. ROMINE, "Modified Cyclic Algorithms for Solving Triangular Systems on Distributed-Memory Multiprocessors," *SIAM J. Sci. Statist. Comput.,* **9** (1988), pp. 589-600.

[Fox 88]   G. C. FOX, M. A. JOHNSON, G. A. LYZENGA, S. W. OTTO, J. K. SALMON, AND D. W. WALKER, "Solving Problems on Concurrent Processors," Vol. 1, Prentice-Hall, Inc., Englewood Cliffs, NJ, 1988.

[Gries 81]   D. GRIES, "The Science of Computer Programming," Springer-Verlag New York Inc., 1981.

[Heath 88]   M. T. HEATH AND C. H. ROMINE, "Parallel Solution of Triangular Systems on Distributed-Memory Multiprocessors," *SIAM J. Sci. Statist. Comput.,* **9** (1988), pp. 558-588.

[Hoare 85]   C. A. R. HOARE, "Communicating Sequential Processes," Prentice-Hall International, UK, Ltd., London, 1985.

[Johnsson 87]   S. L. JOHNSSON, "Communication Efficient Basic Linear Algebra Computations on Hypercube Architectures," *J. Parallel Distrib. Comput.,* **4** (1987), pp. 133-172.

[Li 88]   G. LI AND T. F. COLEMAN, "A Parallel Triangular Solver for a Distributed-Memory Multiprocessor," *SIAM J. Sci. Statist. Comput.,* **9** (1988), pp. 485-502.

[Romine 88]   C. H. ROMINE AND J. M. ORTEGA, "Parallel Solution of Triangular Systems of Equations," *Parallel Comput.,* **6** (1988), pp. 109-114.

[van de Vorst 88]   J. G. G. VAN DE VORST, "The Formal Development of a Parallel Program Performing LU-Decomposition," *Acta Inform.,* **26** (1988), pp. 1-17.

Homomorphisms and Promotability

Grant Malcolm

Department of Computing Science
Groningen University
P.O. Box 800
9700 AV Groningen
The Netherlands

Λίγα δέντρα καί λίγα
Βρεμένα χαλίκια

— Odysseus Elytis, Επέτειος.

Abstract

The construction of structure-preserving maps, or "homomorphisms," is described for an arbitrary data type: examples of these functions are given for list- and tree-like structures and types defined by mutual induction. From the definition of a data type it is also possible to infer a "promotion" theorem for proving equalities of homomorphisms.

1 Introduction

Our starting point in this paper is the "Bird-Meertens Formalism" currently being developed by Richard Bird at Oxford and Lambert Meertens at Amsterdam. This formalism comprises a concise functional notation and a very few, powerful theorems for proving equalities of functions. The conciseness of the notation is largely a result of concentrating attention upon two basic operations and — until recently — upon only one data structure: finite lists. Using the basic operations, it is possible to construct a large number of list manipulating functions; the basic nature of the operations ensures that the resultant functions are potentially both easily understood and grossly inefficient. Both comprehensibility and inefficiency can then be reduced in a process of program transformation which results in an equivalent and, ideally, more concise and efficient program.

It is in this process of program transformation that the advantage of concentrating upon only a few theorems for proving equalities becomes apparent. The ideal is to have only one theorem applicable at any given stage in the transformation, and to have that theorem's applicability be obvious. Such an ideal is unlikely to be realised, but the general principle is: the more trivial and mechanical the transformation process can be made, the better. For then the construction and implementation of tactics to handle the trivial steps is made easier, leaving one free to devote one's energies to those stages which require some degree of ingenuity.

Recent work by Bird and Meertens [3,8] has applied the formalism to other data structures such as binary trees, arrays and "rose trees." It turns out that the basic operations and theorems used in the work on finite lists have analogous operations and theorems which are applicable to those other data structures. So, rather than building "a theory of lists," "a theory of rose trees," and so on, might it not be possible to build a *polymorphic* theory of data structures, a theory applicable to any given data structure? The answer we give in this paper, albeit hesitantly, is "yes." We concentrate upon only one operation, which is polymorphic in that there is an analogous operation for every data structure: these operations are called "homomorphisms" by Bird (and "catamorphisms" by Meertens — we shall adopt the former term). Furthermore, we concentrate upon only one theorem for proving equalities of functions, which is a polymorphic theorem in the sense that there is a form of this theorem for every data structure and this form may be inferred in a uniform way. These theorems are called "promotion theorems" by Bird and Meertens; we shall adopt this term as well, although our theorems are more general.

The implication that there does not already exist a polymorphic theory of data structures might cause offence: such a theory is certainly implicit in Bird's and Meertens' recent work; the definition we give of homomorphism is similar to definitions of terms in the second-order polymorphic λ-calculus [5]; and should a category theorist happen to read this paper, his response would surely be "well yes, we knew that already."

There is a close connection between the results of this paper and certain basic notions in category theory. We shall have more to say on this connection in the concluding section, where we allow ourselves the luxury of speculation; for the present we simply note that we find the triviality of these basic category theoretical notions encouraging — as computing scientists we have already declared our interest in the trivial. The difficulty with respect to category theory lies in discovering which aspects of the theory are relevant to our own discipline. Recent work in this field has done much to clarify matters (see, for example, [6]), but there is still a long way to go.

As to the second-order polymorphic λ-calculus, while it was certainly a source of inspiration, it has the great drawback that one has to reason about its data structures indirectly, via a model. More general theories may be able to overcome this disadvantage, but more work has to be done in that area. In any case, we are not presenting here a formal theory of typed functions; rather, we hope to adumbrate what is common to all data structures. Constructive type theory presents a uniform mechanism for reasoning about data structures (see Backhouse [2]), and we should like to discover more such mechanisms.

Finally, we make no apology for making explicit that which previously was only implicit. The principles informing Bird's and Meertens' recent work are important enough to bear public expression, and it is our aim in the pages below to convince the reader of this.

1.1 notation

The notation we use is based on that of Bird and of Backhouse (see [4,1]). We denote the application of function f to argument a with an infix dot: $f.a$. For binary operators we use infix notation, writing $x \oplus y$ for the application of operator $\oplus$ to the pair of arguments x and y. If $\oplus$ is a binary operator, then we use $\tilde{\oplus}$ to denote its "reverse," i.e.,

$$x \tilde{\oplus} y = y \oplus x.$$

Also, we write $(x\oplus)$ for the function such that:

$$(x\oplus).y = x \oplus y.$$

The identity of operator $\oplus$ (if it exists) is written: $1_\oplus$. Thus, for all x,

$$1_\oplus \oplus x = x = x \oplus 1_\oplus.$$

We often include type information where we feel that it helps clarify an expression; if a function f takes arguments of type A into expressions of type B, we denote this by $f \in A \to B$. Cartesian product of two types A and B is denoted by $A \times B$. (Binary operators are thus considered to have type $A \times B \to C$ for some types A, B and C.) We use I for the polymorphic identity function, and let the reader infer its type from the context. We occasionally write $a = b \in A$ to denote that a and b are both objects of type A, and are equal under the equality of that type.

2 Homomorphisms and Join Lists

Central to this paper is the notion of homomorphism. The word, "homomorphism" comes from Bird (see, for example, [4]), who used it to describe a structure-preserving map from lists (an example of a monoid) to another monoid — hence the nomenclature. We use it in the more general sense of a structure-preserving map from one data structure to another, similar structure. Before giving a formal definition of homomorphisms, we exemplify the notion by considering homomorphisms over the type of join lists.

2.1 join lists

We denote the type of join lists whose elements are taken from a base type A by $JL(A)$. Join lists are constructed by means of three "constructors": the empty list $\square$,

$$\frac{}{\square \in JL(A)}$$

the singleton constructor $\lfloor \cdot \rfloor$,

$$\frac{a \in A}{\lfloor a \rfloor \in JL(A)}$$

and the associative concatenation operator $+\!\!+$,

$$\frac{\begin{array}{l} r \in JL(A) \\ s \in JL(A) \end{array}}{r +\!\!+ s \in JL(A).}$$

Moreover, $\square$ is the identity of $+\!\!+$; i.e., for all $x \in JL(A)$, $\square +\!\!+ x = x = x +\!\!+ \square$. Thus the type of join lists can be considered as the monoid: $\langle JL(A), +\!\!+, \square \rangle$. We define a homomorphism from this monoid to another, similar monoid, $\langle B, \oplus, 1_\oplus \rangle$, as a function of the form $(\!| e, f, \oplus |\!)$, where $e \in B$ is the identity of $\oplus$ (i.e., $e = 1_\oplus$), $f \in A \to B$, and $\oplus \in B \times B \to B$ is associative. The homomorphism is defined by:

$$\begin{aligned} (\!| e, f, \oplus |\!).\square &= e \\ (\!| e, f, \oplus |\!).\lfloor a \rfloor &= f.a \\ (\!| e, f, \oplus |\!).(r +\!\!+ s) &= ((\!| e, f, \oplus |\!).r) \oplus ((\!| e, f, \oplus |\!).s) \end{aligned}$$

When applied to a list of the form $\lfloor x_1 \rfloor +\!\!+ \cdots +\!\!+ \lfloor x_n \rfloor$, such a homomorphism produces a structure of the form $f.x_1 \oplus \cdots \oplus f.x_n$; the homomorphism replaces, as it were, all occurrences of $\square$ by e ($= 1_\oplus$), all occurrences of $\lfloor \cdot \rfloor$ by f, and all occurrences of $+\!\!+$ by $\oplus$. Thus the identity function on join lists is the homomorphism $(\!| \square, \lfloor \cdot \rfloor, +\!\!+ |\!)$, which assigns each constructor to itself.

Note that both the type $JL(A)$ and its homomorphisms are defined by the three constructors, $\square$, $\lfloor \cdot \rfloor$ and $+\!\!+$.

As an example of a homomorphism, we define the map operation:

Definition 2.1 (map) If $f \in A \to B$, then

$$f* \triangleq (\!| \square, \lfloor \cdot \rfloor \circ f, +\!\!+ |\!) \in JL(A) \to JL(B).$$

That is, $f*$ is the homomorphism from $\langle JL(A), +\!\!+, \square \rangle$ to the monoid $\langle JL(B), +\!\!+, \square \rangle$ which applies f to every element of a given list, but preserves the structure of that list. We treat $*$ as a binary operator, so that $f*$ is a function of type $JL(A) \to JL(B)$, and if $l \in JL(A)$, then $f * l$ denotes the list obtained by applying f to each element of l.

We can now prove a simple property of the map operation, namely that mapping the identity function is itself the identity function:

Theorem 2.2 $I* = I$.

Proof:

$$I*$$
$$= \quad \{ \text{ definition 2.1 } \}$$
$$(\![\, \square, \lfloor . \rfloor \circ I, +\!]\!)$$
$$= \quad \{ \text{ identity } \}$$
$$(\![\, \square, \lfloor . \rfloor, +\!]\!)$$
$$= \quad \{ \text{ identity homomorphism } \}$$
$$I$$

Q.E.D.

Our promotion theorem for homomorphisms on join lists is a generalisation of that given originally by Meertens in [7] and independently by Bird in [3] and by Backhouse in [1].

Theorem 2.3 (promotion) If $g.(x \oplus y) = g.x \otimes g.y$, then

$$g \circ (\![\, e, f, \oplus \!]\!) = (\![\, g.e, g \circ f, \otimes \!]\!).$$

Proof is by induction and is very similar to the proof given by Backhouse (loc. cit.).

The following corollary turns out to be very useful.

Corollary 2.4 (map distribution) $f* \circ g* = (f \circ g)*.$

Proof. Expanding $g*$ and $(f \circ g)*$ by definition 2.1, we have to prove:

$$f* \circ (\![\, \square, \lfloor . \rfloor \circ g, +\!]\!) = (\![\, \square, \lfloor . \rfloor \circ f \circ g, +\!]\!)$$

This follows by promotion if we can prove that $f*$ distributes over concatenation:

$$f * (x + y) = (f * x) + (f * y)$$

and that

$$f* \circ \lfloor . \rfloor \circ g = \lfloor . \rfloor \circ f \circ g$$

and

$$f * \square = \square.$$

All three equations are immediate from the definitions of map and homomorphisms, and so theorem 2.3 gives the desired equality. Q.E.D.

2.2 homomorphisms

In this section, we give the formal details of the construction of homomorphisms for an arbitrary data structure. This process was exemplified above for the case of join lists; the process is straightforward but the details cumbersome, so the reader who grasped the discussion above may prefer to skip this section and go on to the further examples in the following sections.

We consider an arbitrary type $T(\bar{A})$, where $\bar{A}$ is a sequence of type parameters (as A is a type parameter in $JL(A)$). As was the case with join lists, the type is defined by a number of constructors, $\tau_1, \ldots, \tau_m$, where each constructor has a type:

$$\tau_i \in E_{i_1} \times \cdots \times E_{i_{\rho(i)}} \to T(\bar{A})$$

for $0 < i \le m$ (if $\rho(i) = 0$, then $\tau_i \in T(\bar{A})$). Each E_{i_j} is either $T(\bar{A})$ itself or a type expression constructed from the variables of $\bar{A}$ using the type operators $\times$, $\to$, etc. (We could let E_{i_j} be a type expression built from the variables of $\bar{A}$ and $T(\bar{A})$, but then we should have to impose a restriction on such an expression — that it be positive in T, see Mendler [9] — but for the sake of simplicity we ignore the possibility here.) For join lists, the constructors are $\square$, $\lfloor . \rfloor$ and $+$; their types are:

$$\square \in JL(A)$$
$$\lfloor . \rfloor \in A \to JL(A)$$
$$+ \in JL(A) \times JL(A) \to JL(A)$$

The idea of a homomorphism is that it replaces each constructor in an object of $T(\bar{A})$ by some other function, mapping one structure to a similar structure, so we assume that we already have m functions of the appropriate types:

$$\phi_i \in E'_{i_1} \times \cdots \times E'_{i_{\rho(i)}} \to B$$

for $0 < i \leq m$; the expressions E'_{i_j} are constructed from the expressions E_{i_j} in a way which we explain below. Then homomorphisms over the type $T(\bar{A})$ are functions of the form:

$$([\phi_1, \ldots, \phi_m]) \in T(\bar{A}) \to B$$

The expressions E'_{i_j} are constructed as follows: if $E_{i_j} = T(\bar{A})$, then $E'_{i_j} = B$; if E_{i_j} is constructed from the variables of $\bar{A}$, then $E'_{i_j} = E_{i_j}$.

The homomorphism is defined by a set of equations:

$$([\phi_1, \ldots, \phi_m]).(\tau_i.(e_{i_1}, \ldots, e_{i_{\rho(i)}})) = \phi_i.(e'_{i_1}, \ldots, e'_{i_{\rho(i)}})$$

where $e_{i_j} \in E_{i_j}$ for $0 < j \leq k$, and if $E_{i_j} = T(\bar{A})$, then $e'_{i_j} = ([\phi_1, \ldots, \phi_m]).e_{i_j}$, and if E_{i_j} is built from the variables of $\bar{A}$, then $e'_{i_j} = e_{i_j}$.

Since a homomorphism $([\phi_1, \ldots, \phi_m])$ replaces each constructor τ_i by the function ϕ_i, the identity homomorphism is that which replaces each constructor by itself; i.e.,

$$\mathbf{I} = ([\tau_1, \ldots, \tau_m]).$$

The promotion theorem for type $T(\bar{A})$ is constructed as follows. Each constructor gives rise to a condition on the theorem: for each constructor

$$\tau_i \in E_{i_1} \times \cdots \times E_{i_{\rho(i)}} \to T(\bar{A}),$$

the corresponding condition on the theorem is,

"if $g.(\phi_i.(x_1, \ldots, x_{\rho(i)})) = \psi_i.(x'_1, \ldots, x'_{\rho(i)})$ for all $x_j \in E_{i_j}$,"

where $x'_j = g.x_j$ if $E_{i_j} = T(\bar{A})$ and $x'_j = x_j$ otherwise. The conclusion of the theorem is,

"then $g \circ ([\phi_1, \ldots, \phi_m]) = ([\psi_1, \ldots, \psi_m])$."

According to this construction, the promotion theorem for join lists reads:

"If $g.e = e'$, and $g.(f.x) = f'.x$ for all $x \in A$, and $g.(x \oplus y) = g.x \otimes g.y$, for all $x, y \in \mathrm{JL}(A)$, then $g \circ ([e, f, \oplus]) = ([e', f', \otimes])$."

In the actual statement of the theorem in the previous subsection, we omitted the first two conditions, replacing e' and f' by $g.e$ and $g \circ f$ respectively.

The validity of this general statement of the promotion theoerem for arbitrary type $T(\bar{A})$ can be proven by induction on the structure of the terms of that type; we shall not, therefore, prove the promotion theorems for particular types in the following sections. They are all instantiations of the general statement.

In the following sections, we present homomorphisms for a variety of data structures. We generally begin each section by presenting a number of rules which describe the constructors for that data structure, and we use the same notation for homomorphisms for each data structure: $([\ldots])$. To help the reader, the order of functions within a homomorphism follows the order in which the rules are presented; thus $([\phi_1, \ldots, \phi_m])$ replaces the constructor of the ith rule by ϕ_i.

3　Forward Lists

Forward lists are constructed by means of the empty list nil and the "cons" operator $\twoheadleftarrow$.

$$\frac{}{\mathrm{nil} \in \mathsf{L}(A)}$$

$$\frac{a \in A \quad m \in \mathsf{L}(A)}{a \twoheadleftarrow m \in \mathsf{L}(A)}$$

A homomorphism on forward lists is a function $(\![e, \oplus]\!)$, which replaces $\prec$ by $\oplus$ and nil by e:

$$(\![e, \oplus]\!).\text{nil} = e$$
$$(\![e, \oplus]\!).(a \prec m) = a \oplus ((\![e, \oplus]\!).m)$$

Thus the identity function on forward lists is the homomorphism $(\![\text{nil}, \prec]\!)$, which replaces each constructor by itself. (Note that what we write as $(\![e, \oplus]\!)$ is, in Bird's notation, $\oplus \!\!\not{/}_e$.)

An example of a homomorphism is seen in the append function, $@$:

Definition 3.1 (append) For $x, y \in L(A)$: $x @ y \triangleq (\![y, \prec]\!).x$.

It is straightforward to show that nil is the identity of $@$. To show that nil $@$ $x = x$:

$$nil @ x$$
$$= \qquad \{ \text{ definition 3.1 } \}$$
$$(\![x, \prec]\!).\text{nil}$$
$$= \qquad \{ \text{ homomorphism } \}$$
$$x$$

and to show that $x @ \text{nil} = x$:

$$x @ \text{nil}$$
$$= \qquad \{ \text{ definition 3.1 } \}$$
$$(\![\text{nil}, \prec]\!).x$$
$$= \qquad \{ \text{ identity homomorphism } \}$$
$$x$$

Q.E.D.

Following the construction of section 2.2, we obtain the following promotion theorem for forward lists.

Theorem 3.2 (promotion) If $g.(x \oplus y) = x \otimes g.y$ for all x and y, then:

$$g \circ (\![e, \oplus]\!) = (\![g.e, \otimes]\!).$$

Note that the map operator for forward lists can be defined in terms of a homomorphism; $f*$ is a function which applies f to each element of a given list.

Definition 3.3 (map) $f* \triangleq (\![\text{nil}, {}_f\!\prec]\!)$, where, for all binary operators $\oplus$ and functions g, the operator ${}_g\!\oplus$ is defined by:

$$x \, {}_g\!\oplus y = g.x \oplus y.$$

Note that ${}_I\!\oplus = \oplus$.

The following (generalised) property of maps is a corollary of the promotion theorem.

Corollary 3.4 $(\![d, \oplus]\!) \circ (\![e, {}_f\!\prec]\!) = (\![(\![d, \oplus]\!).e, {}_f\!\oplus]\!)$. In particular, when $e = \text{nil}$,

$$(\![d, \oplus]\!) \circ f* = (\![d, {}_f\!\oplus]\!).$$

Proof: we note that $(\![d, \oplus]\!).(f.x \prec y) = f.x \oplus ((\![d, \oplus]\!).y)$, by the definition of homomorphisms, so theorem 3.2 is applicable with $g := (\![d, \oplus]\!)$, $\oplus := ({}_f\!\prec)$, $e := e$ and $\otimes := ({}_f\!\oplus)$; the term $g.e$, therefore, becomes $(\![d, \oplus]\!).e$. We obtain, then, by theorem 3.2, the desired equality. Q.E.D.

We can use this corollary to prove the associativity of the append operator:

$$(x @ y) @ z$$
$$= \qquad \{ \text{ definition 3.1 } \}$$
$$(\![z, \prec]\!).((\![y, \prec]\!).x)$$
$$= \qquad \{ \text{ identity } \}$$
$$((\![z, \prec]\!) \circ (\![y, {}_I\!\prec]\!)).x$$
$$= \qquad \{ \text{ corollary 3.4 } \}$$
$$(\![(\![z, \prec]\!).y, {}_I\!\prec]\!).x$$
$$= \qquad \{ \text{ identity, definition 3.1 } \}$$
$$x @ (y @ z)$$

The following is also a corollary to the promotion theorem, and will be used below in examining the relationship between join and forward lists. It is a very simple statement about associativity.

Corollary 3.5 If $\oplus$ is associative, then $(([d, f\oplus]).m) \oplus e = [d \oplus e, f\oplus].m$.

Proof: the left-hand side can be re-expressed as $((e\tilde{\oplus}) \circ [d, f\oplus]).m$, so it suffices to show:

$$(e\tilde{\oplus}) \circ [d, f\oplus] = [d \oplus e, \oplus \circ f]$$

Since $(e\tilde{\oplus}).d = d \oplus e$, this follows immediately from theorem 3.2 if we can show that:

$$(e\tilde{\oplus}).(f.x \oplus y) = f.x \oplus ((e\tilde{\oplus}).y);$$

this, in turn, is shown by:

$$
\begin{aligned}
& (e\tilde{\oplus}).(f.x \oplus y) \\
=\ & \{ \triangle \sim \} \\
& (f.x \oplus y) \oplus e \\
=\ & \{ \oplus \text{ is associative} \} \\
& f.x \oplus (y \oplus e) \\
=\ & \{ \triangle \sim \} \\
& f.x \oplus ((e\tilde{\oplus}).y)
\end{aligned}
$$

Q.E.D.

3.1 example: join and forward lists

In this subsection, we show that join and forward lists are isomorphic in that there are bijections between the two types. That is, the two types can be considered equivalent in the sense that each join list can be expressed as a forward list and vice versa: the bijections "coerce" a list of the one type into a list of the other type. In the following subsection we give an example of how this equivalence may be used in transforming a homomorphism on join lists into an equivalent homomorphism on forward lists. In this subsection we prove that the coercion functions are indeed bijections: this is proven by showing that the two functions are inverses of each other.

The coercion homomorphism from join to forward lists is $[nil, (nil\tilde{\prec}), @]$. The coercion from forward lists to join lists is $[\square, {}_{\sqcup}+]$.

The following corollaries to theorem 3.2 state that the composition of the two coercion homomorphisms is the identity function from forward lists to forward lists (corollary 3.6), and from join lists to join lists (corollary 3.7).

Corollary 3.6 $[nil, (nil\tilde{\prec}), @] \circ [\square, {}_{\sqcup}+] = I \in L(A) \to L(A)$.

Proof: We introduce the abbreviation: $c_{jf} \triangleq [nil, (nil\tilde{\prec}), @]$. In order to apply theorem 3.2 on the left-hand side, we first show that

$$c_{jf}.(\lfloor x \rfloor + y) = x \oplus (c_{jf}.y)$$

for some operator $\oplus$. We find this $\oplus$ by direct calculation:

$$
\begin{aligned}
& c_{jf}.(\lfloor x \rfloor + y) \\
=\ & \{ \text{homomorphism}, \triangle \sim \} \\
& (x \prec nil) @ (c_{jf}.y) \\
=\ & \{ \text{definition 3.1} \} \\
& [c_{jf}.y, \prec].(x \prec nil) \\
=\ & \{ \text{homomorphism} \} \\
& x \prec (c_{jf}.y)
\end{aligned}
$$

So, we may take $\prec$ for $\oplus$ and apply theorem 3.2:

$$
\begin{aligned}
& [nil, (nil\tilde{\prec}), @] \circ [\square, {}_{\sqcup}+] \\
=\ & \{ \text{thm. 3.2} \} \\
& [([nil, (nil\tilde{\prec}), @].\square, \prec] \\
=\ & \{ \text{homomorphism} \} \\
& [nil, \prec] \\
=\ & \{ \text{identity homomorphism} \} \\
& I
\end{aligned}
$$

Q.E.D.

Corollary 3.7 $(\![\square, \sqcup + \!]) \circ (\![nil, (nil \tilde{\prec}), @\!]) = I \in JL(A) \to JL(A)$.

Proof: we use theorem 2.3 to show that the left-hand side is equal to the identity homomorphism $(\![\square, \sqcup, + \!])$. In order to do so, we have to show the distributivity property:

(1)
$$(\![\square, \sqcup + \!]).(x @ y) = ((\![\square, \sqcup + \!]).x) + ((\![\square, \sqcup + \!]).y)$$

and, further,

(2)
$$(\![\square, \sqcup + \!]) \circ (nil \tilde{\prec}) = \sqcup$$

and

(3)
$$(\![\square, \sqcup + \!]).nil = nil.$$

Now, (1) is shown as follows:

$$
\begin{aligned}
&(\![\square, \sqcup + \!]).(x @ y)\\
= \quad &\{ \triangleq @ \}\\
&((\![\square, \sqcup + \!]) \circ (\![y, \prec \!])).x\\
= \quad &\{ \text{corollary 3.4} \}\\
&((\![\square, \sqcup + \!]).y, \sqcup + \!]).x\\
= \quad &\{ \text{corollary 3.5} \}\\
&((\![\square, \sqcup + \!]).x) + ((\![\square, \sqcup + \!]).y).
\end{aligned}
$$

(2) is proven as follows; for all x,

$$
\begin{aligned}
&(\![\square, \sqcup + \!]).((nil \tilde{\prec}).x)\\
= \quad &\{ \triangleq \sim \}\\
&(\![\square, \sqcup + \!]).(x \prec nil)\\
= \quad &\{ \text{homomorphism} \}\\
&\lfloor x \rfloor + \square\\
= \quad &\{ \square = 1_{+} \}\\
&\lfloor x \rfloor
\end{aligned}
$$

which, by extensionality, proves (2). And, finally, (3) is immediate from the definition of homomorphisms.
To summarise,

$$
\begin{aligned}
&(\![\square, \sqcup + \!]) \circ (\![nil, (nil \tilde{\prec}), @\!])\\
= \quad &\{ (1), \text{theorem 2.3} \}\\
&((\![\square, \sqcup + \!]).\square, (\![\square, \sqcup + \!]) \circ (nil \tilde{\prec}), + \!])\\
= \quad &\{ (2),(3) \}\\
&(\![\square, \sqcup, + \!])\\
= \quad &\{ \text{identity homomorphism} \}\\
&I.
\end{aligned}
$$

Q.E.D.

3.2 example: reversing lists

The function which reverses the order of elements in a join list is the homomorphism

$$rev_j \triangleq (\![\square, \sqcup, \tilde{+} \!]) \in JL(A) \to JL(A).$$

We show that the function is its own inverse, i.e., composing the function with itself produces the identity homomorphism:

(4)
$$rev_j \circ rev_j = (\![\square, \sqcup, + \!]).$$

This follows from theorem 2.3 if we can prove the following equalities:

$$
\begin{aligned}
(\![\square, \sqcup, \tilde{+} \!]).\square &= \square\\
(\![\square, \sqcup, \tilde{+} \!]) \circ \sqcup &= \sqcup\\
(\![\square, \sqcup, \tilde{+} \!]).(x \tilde{+} y) &= (\![\square, \sqcup, \tilde{+} \!]).x + (\![\square, \sqcup, \tilde{+} \!]).y
\end{aligned}
$$

The first two of these equalities are immediate from the definition of homomorphisms, and the last is proven by:

$$
\begin{aligned}
& (\!(\square, \lfloor\cdot\rfloor, \tilde{\#})\!) . (x \mathbin{\tilde{\#}} y) \\
=\ & \{\ \triangle \sim\ \} \\
& (\!(\square, \lfloor\cdot\rfloor, \tilde{\#})\!) . (y \mathbin{\#} x) \\
=\ & \{\ \text{homomorphism}\ \} \\
& (\!(\square, \lfloor\cdot\rfloor, \tilde{\#})\!) . y \mathbin{\tilde{\#}} (\!(\square, \lfloor\cdot\rfloor, \tilde{\#})\!) . x \\
=\ & \{\ \triangle \sim\ \} \\
& (\!(\square, \lfloor\cdot\rfloor, \tilde{\#})\!) . x \mathbin{\#} (\!(\square, \lfloor\cdot\rfloor, \tilde{\#})\!) . y
\end{aligned}
$$

and so (4) follows by promotion.

Now define $c_{jf} \triangleq (\!(\text{nil}, (\text{nil} \mathbin{\overleftarrow{\kappa}}), @)\!)$, and $c_{fj} \triangleq (\!(\square, \lfloor\cdot\rfloor \#)\!)$, the two coercion homomorphisms. Then the function which reverses the order of elements in a forward list is the composition:

$$(5) \qquad\qquad rev_f \triangleq c_{jf} \circ rev_j \circ c_{fj} \in L(A) \to L(A).$$

Since $(c_{jf} \circ rev_j).\square = \text{nil}$ and $(c_{jf} \circ rev_j).(\lfloor x \rfloor \mathbin{\#} y) = (x \mathbin{\overleftarrow{\kappa}} \text{nil}) \mathbin{\tilde{@}} (c_{jf} \circ rev_j).y$, promotion gives that $rev_f = (\!(\text{nil}, {}_g\tilde{@})\!)$, where $g = (\text{nil}\mathbin{\overleftarrow{\kappa}})$. This function is also its own inverse, since

$$
\begin{aligned}
& rev_f \circ rev_f \\
=\ & \{\ (5)\ \} \\
& c_{jf} \circ rev_j \circ c_{fj} \circ c_{jf} \circ rev_j \circ c_{fj} \\
=\ & \{\ \text{corollary 3.7, identity}\ \} \\
& c_{jf} \circ rev_j \circ rev_j \circ c_{fj} \\
=\ & \{\ (4)\ \} \\
& c_{jf} \circ c_{fj} \\
=\ & \{\ \text{corollary 3.6}\ \} \\
& \text{I.}
\end{aligned}
$$

4   Arrays

The type of arrays we discuss in this section is that defined by Richard Bird in a series of lectures given at the 1988 Summer School in Marktoberdorf (see [3]).

For some base type A, the type of arrays of dimension $m \times n$ is denoted by: $A(m, n)$. That is, A is a family of types indexed by pairs of positive natural numbers (we exclude the empty array). Arrays are constructed by the singleton function, $[.]$:

$$\frac{a \in A}{[a] \in A(1,1)}$$

and inductively by the horizontal alignment operator $\ominus$ and the vertical alignment operator ϕ:

$$
\frac{\begin{array}{l} i,j,k \in \mathbb{N}^+ \\ a \in A(i,j) \\ b \in A(i,k) \end{array}}{a \ominus b \in A(i, j+k)}
\qquad\qquad
\frac{\begin{array}{l} i,j,k \in \mathbb{N}^+ \\ a \in A(j,i) \\ b \in A(k,i) \end{array}}{a \phi b \in A(j+k, i)}
$$

Both $\ominus$ and ϕ are associative, and satisfy the interchange rule:

$$(a \ominus b) \phi (c \ominus d) = (a \phi c) \ominus (b \phi d)$$

whenever both sides are well-formed, i.e., $a \in A(i,j)$, $b \in A(i,k)$, $c \in A(l,j)$ and $d \in A(l,k)$, for some $i, j, k, l \in \mathbb{N}^+$.

Homomorphisms on arrays are therefore functions of the form: $(\!(f, \oplus, \otimes)\!)$, where $\oplus$ and $\otimes$ are associative binary operators satisfying the interchange rule:

$$(a \oplus b) \otimes (c \oplus d) = (a \otimes c) \oplus (b \otimes d).$$

Homomorphisms are defined by:

$$([f, \oplus, \otimes]).[a] = f.a$$
$$([f, \oplus, \otimes]).(a \ominus b) = (([f, \oplus, \otimes]).a) \oplus (([f, \oplus, \otimes]).b)$$
$$([f, \oplus, \otimes]).(a \oslash b) = (([f, \oplus, \otimes]).a) \otimes (([f, \oplus, \otimes]).b)$$

The identity homomorphism is accordingly $([.], \ominus, \oslash)$.

The promotion theorem for arrays is:

Theorem 4.1 If $g.(x \oplus y) = g.x \odot g.y$ and $g.(x \otimes y) = g.x \oslash g.y$, then

$$g \circ ([f, \oplus, \otimes]) = ([g \circ f, \odot, \oslash]).$$

Proof is by induction on the structure of arrays, and similar to the proofs of the list promotion theorems.

Note that the four promotion theorems for arrays given by Bird (loc. cit.) are all corollaries to this promotion theorem.

5 Rose Trees

In this section we consider homomorphisms over a type defined by mutual induction: rose trees, presented by Lambert Meertens in [8]. Rose trees may be thought of as two mutually inductively defined types, bushes and faggots. Faggots are constructed by the empty faggot, □:

$$\frac{}{\square \in F(A)}$$

and the singleton constructor $\lfloor . \rfloor$, and the associative concatenation operator $+\!\!+$:

$$\frac{b \in B(A)}{\lfloor b \rfloor \in F(A)} \qquad \frac{\begin{array}{c} r \in F(A) \\ s \in F(A) \end{array}}{r +\!\!+ s \in F(A)}$$

Moreover, □ is the unit of $+\!\!+$.

Bushes are constructed by the rosary operator, τ, and the forking operator, π.

$$\frac{a \in A}{\tau.a \in B(A)} \qquad \frac{r \in F(A)}{\pi.r \in B(A)}$$

Thus faggots are list-like sequences of (sub)trees, and a bush is either a rose (of the form $\tau.a$) or branches into an arbitrary number of subtrees.

Homomorphisms on rose trees are therefore functions of the form:

$$([e, \phi, \oplus, \chi, \psi]),$$

where $e \in B$ is the unit of $\oplus$, $\phi \in C \to B$, $\oplus \in B \times B \to B$ is associative, $\chi \in A \to C$ and $\psi \in B \to C$. The homomorphism $([e, \phi, \oplus, \chi, \psi])$ has two types: $F(A) \to B$ and $B(A) \to C$. It is defined by:

$$([e, \phi, \oplus, \chi, \psi]).\square = e$$
$$([e, \phi, \oplus, \chi, \psi]).\lfloor b \rfloor = \phi.(([e, \phi, \oplus, \chi, \psi]).b)$$
$$([e, \phi, \oplus, \chi, \psi]).(r +\!\!+ s) = (([e, \phi, \oplus, \chi, \psi]).r) \oplus (([e, \phi, \oplus, \chi, \psi]).s)$$
$$([e, \phi, \oplus, \chi, \psi]).(\tau.a) = \chi.a$$
$$([e, \phi, \oplus, \chi, \psi]).(\pi.r) = \psi.(([e, \phi, \oplus, \chi, \psi]).r)$$

The identity homomorphism is therefore: $([\square, \lfloor . \rfloor, +\!\!+, \tau, \pi])$.

Promotion theorems for mutually recursive types are similar to those for other types; in this case, because we are considering two mutually recursive types, we consider composition of homomorphisms with two separate functions, g and h.

Theorem 5.1 Let $g \in C \to E$, $h \in B \to D$, $\alpha \in E \to D$, $\otimes \in D \times D \to D$ be associative, and $\beta \in D \to E$. If

$$g \circ \psi = \beta \circ h, \quad h \circ \phi = \alpha \circ g \quad \text{and} \quad h.(x \oplus y) = h.x \otimes h.y,$$

then

$$h \circ (\![e, \phi, \oplus, \chi, \psi]\!) = (\![h.e, \alpha, \otimes, g \circ \chi, \beta]\!) \in F(A) \to D$$

and

$$g \circ (\![e, \phi, \oplus, \chi, \psi]\!) = (\![h.e, \alpha, \otimes, g \circ \chi, \beta]\!) \in B(A) \to E.$$

As an example of the use of rose tree promotion, we prove map distribution. If $g \in A \to B$, then

Definition 5.2 (map) $g* \triangleq (\![\square, \lfloor . \rfloor, +\!\!+, \tau \circ g, \pi]\!)$.

The function $g*$ preserves the structure of a rose tree, changing only its roses. The homomorphism $g*$ has two types: $B(A) \to B(B)$ and $F(A) \to F(B)$. We shall show that, if $h \in B \to C$, then $h* \circ g* = (h \circ g)*$, i.e.,

$$h* \circ (\![\square, \lfloor . \rfloor, +\!\!+, \tau \circ g, \pi]\!) = (\![\square, \lfloor . \rfloor, +\!\!+, \tau \circ h \circ g, \pi]\!) \in \left\{ \begin{array}{l} B(A) \to B(C) \\ F(A) \to F(C) \end{array} \right.$$

In order to apply theorem 5.1 on the left-hand side of this equality, we have to show (instantiating theorem 5.1 with $g, h := h*$, $\otimes := +\!\!+$, $\beta := \pi$ and $\alpha := \lfloor . \rfloor$):

$$h* \circ \pi = \pi \circ h*$$
$$h* \circ \lfloor . \rfloor = \lfloor . \rfloor \circ h*$$
$$h * (x +\!\!+ y) = (h * x) +\!\!+ (h * y)$$

all three of which are immediate from the definitions of $*$ and homomorphisms. Thus we obtain

$$
\begin{array}{rl}
 & h* \circ g* \\
= & \quad \{ \text{ theorem 5.1 } \} \\
 & (\![h * \square, \lfloor . \rfloor, +\!\!+, h* \circ \tau \circ g, \pi]\!) \\
= & \quad \{ \triangleq *, \text{homomorphism} \} \\
 & (\![\square, \lfloor . \rfloor, +\!\!+, \tau \circ h \circ g, \pi]\!) \\
= & \quad \{ \triangleq * \} \\
 & (h \circ g)*
\end{array}
$$

Q.E.D.

6 Conclusion

As we said in the introduction, our starting point in this paper has been the work of Bird and Meertens. Our contribution, as we see it, is the generalisation of their work to other data structures in a uniform way. We proposed a uniform notion of homomorphism over arbitrary data structures, and derived promotion theorems for each type of homomorphism. These promotion theorems are more general than those given by Bird and Meertens, and moreover the promotion theorem for each data structure can be inferred from the definition of the data structure. One of the advantages of this generality is that certain properties, such as map distribution for list-like structures, are more easily proven; compare, for example, our proof of map distribution for rose trees in section 5 with that given by Meertens in [8]. Admittedly, our notation is more awkward (sometimes, at least) than that of Bird and Meertens, which enjoys a great clarity due to its concentration upon binary operators. It might, nevertheless, be profitable to deviate even further than we have done from a notation of binary operators. For example, we might consider those primitive recursive functions $f \in L(A) \to B$ that follow the paradigm:

$$f.\text{nil} = e$$
$$f.(a \prec m) = h.(a, m, f.m)$$

for some $e \in B$ and $h \in A \times L(A) \times B \rightarrow B$ We might denote such a function f as $[h, e]$, and obtain a new promotion theorem:

If $g.(h.(x, y, z)) = \phi.(x, y, g.z)$, then $g \circ [h, e] = [\phi, g.e]$.

Again, such functions and promotion theorems could be described in a uniform way for any data structure. This is a topic for further research.

Since we started to write this paper, it has been made increasingly clear to us that many of our results are fairly standard in category theory. In particular, it seems that our descriptions of homomorphisms and their promotability are closely related to the universal properties of the data structures that we have considered. We are no category theorists, so we shall not say much in this respect, but a general idea might be conveyed by considering the type of join lists. A category theorist might express the universal property of join lists as the following diagram, which says that given any function $f \in A \rightarrow B$, a binary operator $\oplus \in B \times B \rightarrow B$, and an "object" $e \in B$, there exists a unique function $h \in JL(A) \rightarrow B$ — this function is the homomorphism which we have written as $(\!|e, f, \oplus|\!)$ — such that the diagram commutes:

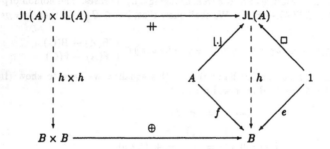

Furthermore, if there are also functions $g \in B \rightarrow C$ and $\otimes \in C \times C \rightarrow C$, then there is also a unique homomorphism $\phi \triangleq (\!|g.e, g \circ f, \otimes|\!)$ such that

$$(6) \qquad \phi \circ + \!\!\!+ \,= \otimes \circ (\phi \times \phi).$$

But if the following diagram commutes,

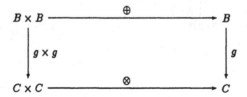

i.e., $g.(x \oplus y) = g.x \otimes g.y$, for all $x, y \in B$, then

$$
\begin{aligned}
& g \circ h \circ +\!\!\!+ \\
=\ & \{\text{ universal property of } h \} \\
& g \circ \oplus \circ (h \times h) \\
=\ & \{\text{ diagram }\} \\
& \otimes \circ (g \times g) \circ (h \times h) \\
=\ & \{\text{ property of } \times \} \\
& \otimes \circ ((g \circ h) \times (g \circ h)).
\end{aligned}
$$

So $g \circ h$ also has the property of (6); but since ϕ is the unique function with this property, we have that $g \circ h = \phi$. In our notation,

$$g \circ (\!|e, f, \oplus|\!) = (\!|g.e, g \circ f, \otimes|\!).$$

Which is the promotion theorem we gave in section 2.1.

The conciseness of category theory's descriptions of such notions as universal properties means that the promotion theorems of this paper are easily derived. Instead of proving the promotion theorems by induction over the structure of the data type, as we have done here, we should only have to prove that the data structures we consider have a universal property like that of join lists above. In fact, it is possible to prove that all data structures have such a universal property, provided that they are constructed from the type operators $\times$, $\rightarrow$, etc., and fixed points (in the sense that the type $JL(A)$ is the least fixed point in X of $1 + A + X \times X$; though here a monotonicity requirement is necessary). Finally, the notion of adjunction has been receiving a lot of attention recently (see [6,10]). Since adjunctions are closely related to universal properties, it would be interesting to examine how these relate to our promotion theorems.

Acknowledgements. Paul Chisholm and Roland Backhouse pointed out errors and suggested improvements.

References

[1] R.C. Backhouse. *An Exploration of the Bird-Meertens Formalism*. Technical Report CS8810, Department of Mathematics and Computing Science, University of Groningen, 1988.

[2] R.C. Backhouse. *On the Meaning and Construction of the Rules in Martin-Löf's Theory of Types*. Technical Report CS8606, Department of Mathematics and Computing Science, University of Groningen, 1986.

[3] R. S. Bird. Constructive functional programming. International Summer School on Constructive Methods in Computing Science, Marktoberdorf, 1988.

[4] R. S. Bird. An introduction to the theory of lists. In M. Broy, editor, *Logic of Programming and Calculi of Discrete Design*, Springer-Verslag, Berlin, 1987. NATO ASI Series ,volume F36.

[5] C. Böhm and A. Berarducci. Automatic synthesis of typed λ-programs on term algebras. *Theoretical Computer Science*, 39:135–154, 1985.

[6] C.A.R. Hoare. Approach to category theory for computer scientists. Lecture Notes, International Summer School on Constructive Methods in Computing Science, Marktoberdorf 1988.

[7] L. Meertens. Algorithmics – towards programming as a mathematical activity. In *Proceedings of the CWI Symposium on Mathematics and Computer Science*, pages 289–334, North-Holland, 1986.

[8] L. Meertens. First steps towards the theory of rose trees. in preparation, CWI, Amsterdam 1988.

[9] N.P. Mendler. *Inductive Definitions in Type Theory*. Ph.D. thesis, Cornell University, September 1987.

[10] M. Spivey. A Categorical Approach to the Theory of Lists. To appear, these proceedings.

APPLICATIVE ASSERTIONS

Bernhard Möller

Institut für Informatik, Technische Universität München
Postfach 20 24 20, D-8000 München 2, Fed. Rep. Germany

1 Introduction

We present a way of introducing and manipulating assertions in an applicative language, mainly for use in transformational program development. It turns out that this can be achieved wholly within the language itself. The advantage of this is twofold: One has the full power of the language in formulating the assertions, hence decreasing problems with expressiveness. Second, the algebraic laws of the language carry over to the assertions and allow a uniform way of manipulating programs together with assertions.

We represent assertions within applicative programs by Boolean expressions. Of course, the sub-language of Boolean expressions of the applicative language considered has to be quite rich, e.g., it has to include quantifiers. An example of such a language is CIP-L (cf. [Bauer et al. 89] for a survey; details are given in [Bauer et al. 85]). We are then free to use recursively defined predicates in assertions; this provides great flexibility.

The basic idea is that an expression E with assertion A is represented by another expression F: if E satisfies A, then F should be equivalent to E alone, whereas, if E fails to satisfy A, it should be equivalent to error. This can be realized by taking for F the conditional expression

$$\textsf{if } A \textsf{ then } E \textsf{ else error fi}$$

which we abbreviate to

$$A \triangleright E.$$

In this, both A and E may be non-determinate. However, usually we will use only determinate assertions A.

The main emphasis in this paper is placed on a formal calculus of such assertions and of their propagation. Such calculi have been proposed for logical frameworks (cf. [Monk 88]) and at the metalanguage level for applicative languages (cf. [Pepper 85, 87]). The idea here is to stay at the object language level as much as possible. Although we present a number of examples, we have to refer to the literature for really interesting uses of assertions during transformational program development (see e.g. [Partsch 86]); however, there the developments are usually not fully calculized.

2 The Algebra of Assertions

2.1 Preliminaries

We base the following developments on the semantics of the language CIP-L. In this section we briefly sketch the central notions of this semantics; the full formal details can be found in [Bauer et al. 85].

For an identifier x and expression E we write OCCURS$[x$ in $E]$ to express that x occurs free in E. By $E[F$ for $x]$ we denote the expression that results from E by replacing all free occurrences (if any) of x by F (with appropriate renaming of bound variables, if necessary).

We use the notation $E_1 \equiv E_2$ to express that E_1 and E_2 have the same sets of possible values (non-determinacy!). Such equivalences are also denoted in the form of transformation rules, viz. as

$$
\begin{array}{c}
E_1 \\
\text{------} \downarrow \text{------}\{\, C \\
E_2
\end{array}
$$

where C is a (possibly empty) list of applicability conditions, i.e., of conditions sufficient for the validity of the equivalence. The special value $\perp$ models nontermination as well as partialities of basic operations; the expression error has $\perp$ as its only possible value. The language uses the concept of the so-called *erratic* nondeterminism; hence e.g. $\{\perp, 0\}$, $\{0\}$, and $\{\perp\}$ are considered as different sets of possible values, i.e., neither is $\perp$ absorbed by defined values nor the other way around. Two important predicates about expressions E are

$$\text{DEFINED}[E] \quad \overset{\text{def}}{\Longleftrightarrow} \quad E \not\equiv \text{error}$$
$$\text{DETERMINATE}[E] \quad \overset{\text{def}}{\Longleftrightarrow} \quad E \text{ has only one possible value .}$$

Moreover, for expression F and identifier x we set

$$\text{STRICT}[F \text{ wrt } x] \overset{\text{def}}{\Longleftrightarrow} F[\text{error for } x] \equiv \text{error .}$$

CIP-L has a call-by-value, call-time-choice semantics (cf. [Hennessy, Ashcroft 76]). Hence the usual β-conversion is not unconditionally valid for CIP-L. We only have

$$
\begin{array}{c}
((m\ x)n : F)(E) \\
\text{------} \downarrow \text{------} \left[\begin{array}{l} (\text{STRICT}[F \text{ wrt } x] \lor \text{DEFINED}[E]) \land \\ (\text{SINGULAR}[F \text{ wrt } x] \lor \text{DETERMINATE}[E]) \end{array} \right. \\
F[E \text{ for } x]
\end{array}
$$

Here, SINGULAR$[F$ wrt $x]$ means that F contains at most one free occurrence of x.

The declaration of auxiliary identifiers is defined by the following rule: Let F be an expression of type n possibly containing free occurrences of the identifier x of type m, and let E be an expression of type m such that $\neg$ OCCURS$[x$ in $E]$. Then

$$\lceil\, m\ x \equiv E\ ;\ F\,\rfloor \overset{\text{def}}{\equiv} ((m\ x)n : F)(E) .$$

As a consequence, we have

$$(2.1) \qquad G(E) \equiv \lceil\, m\ x \equiv E\ ;\ G(x)\,\rfloor \text{ provided } \neg \text{ OCCURS}[x \text{ in } E, G].$$

An important construct is the choice

$$\text{some } m\ x : B$$

with a Boolean expression B possibly involving the identifier x. Its possible values are all those values u for which $B[u$ for $x]$ has true as a possible value (for convenience, values, too, are considered as expressions in the semantic description of CIP-L). If none such value exists or if $B[u$ for $x] \equiv$ error for some u, then $\perp$ is the only possible value. Assume now that $=$ is a (strict) equality test for objects of type m, i.e., that $=$ has type funct(m,m)bool. Then a characteristic property of the choice is

(2.2) (**some** m $x : x = E$) $\equiv E$
provided DETERMINATE$[\![E]\!] \wedge$ DEFINED$[\![E]\!]$.

Like any applicative language, CIP-L has a conditional expression. Two important properties of it are

(2.3) **if** B **then** E **else** F **fi** $\equiv$ **if** B **then** $E[\![\text{true forsome } B]\!]$ **else** $f[\![\text{false forsome } B]\!]$ **fi**
provided DETERMINATE$[\![B]\!]$.

(2.4) $E \equiv$ **if** B **then** E **else** E **fi** provided DEFINED$[\![B]\!]$.

Here, for expressions X, Y, Z we denote by $X[\![Y \text{ forsome } Z]\!]$ any expression that results from X by replacing some occurrences of Z by Y (with appropriate renaming of bound variables, if necessary).

In the sequel, in addition to the usual strict Boolean connectives $\wedge$, $\vee$, and $\Rightarrow$, we also use the sequential (or conditional) Boolean connectives $\wedge\!\!\!\wedge$, $\vee\!\!\!\vee$, and $\dot\Rightarrow$ defined by

$$
\begin{aligned}
B \wedge\!\!\!\wedge C &\stackrel{\text{def}}{\equiv} \textbf{if } B \textbf{ then } C \textbf{ else false fi} \\
(2.5) \qquad B \vee\!\!\!\vee C &\stackrel{\text{def}}{\equiv} \textbf{if } B \textbf{ then true else } C \textbf{ fi} \\
B \dot\Rightarrow C &\stackrel{\text{def}}{\equiv} \textbf{if } B \textbf{ then } C \textbf{ else true fi} .
\end{aligned}
$$

Their characteristic properties are

$$
(2.6) \quad
\begin{array}{lll}
\textbf{true} \wedge\!\!\!\wedge C \equiv C & \textbf{true} \vee\!\!\!\vee C \equiv \textbf{true} & \textbf{true} \dot\Rightarrow C \equiv C \\
\textbf{false} \wedge\!\!\!\wedge C \equiv \textbf{false} & \textbf{false} \vee\!\!\!\vee C \equiv C & \textbf{false} \dot\Rightarrow C \equiv \textbf{true} \\
\textbf{error} \wedge\!\!\!\wedge C \equiv \textbf{error} & \textbf{error} \vee\!\!\!\vee C \equiv \textbf{error} & \textbf{error} \dot\Rightarrow C \equiv \textbf{error} .
\end{array}
$$

2.2 Properties of Assertions

The following properties of assertions should be self-evident (indeed, in CIP-L they can be verified w.r.t the mathematical semantics of the language):

(2.7) $\textbf{true} \rhd E \equiv E$

(2.8) $\textbf{false} \rhd E \equiv \textbf{error}$

(2.9) $\textbf{error} \rhd E \equiv \textbf{error}$.

The next properties will allow the use of assertions in subexpressions of an expression. Let B, F, H be *determinate* expressions such that B is of type **bool** and F, G have equal type m. Assume moreover that $=$ is an equality test for objects of type m. Then we have

(2.10) $B \rhd E \equiv B \rhd E[\![\text{true forsome } B]\!]$

(2.11) $(F = H) \rhd E \equiv (F = H) \rhd E[\![H \text{ forsome } F]\!]$

provided no new bindings for the free variables of B resp. H and F surround the occurrences of B resp. F that are replaced.

Further useful properties of assertions are the following:

(2.12) $(B \wedge C) \triangleright E \equiv B \triangleright ((B \wedge C) \triangleright E)$ provided DETERMINATE$[\![B]\!]$.

(2.13) $(B \triangleright C) \triangleright E \equiv B \triangleright (C \triangleright E) \equiv (B \wedge C) \triangleright E \equiv (B \wedge C) \triangleright E$

(2.14) $B \triangleright E \equiv B \triangleright (B \triangleright E)$ provided DETERMINATE$[\![B]\!]$.

(2.15) $B \triangleright E \equiv B \triangleright (C \triangleright E)$ provided $B \overset{\cdot}{\Rightarrow} C \equiv$ true .

Moreover, if Q is a predicate and x is an identifier,

(2.16) $Q(x) \equiv$ true $\Leftrightarrow (Q(x) \triangleright x) \equiv x$.

Hence

(2.17) $Q(E) \equiv$ true $\Rightarrow$
$\lceil$ m $x \equiv E$; $F(x) \rfloor \equiv \lceil$ m $x \equiv E$; $Q(x) \triangleright F(x) \rfloor$
provided $\neg$ OCCURS$[\![x$ in $F]\!] \wedge$ STRICT$[\![F]\!]$.

More generally,

(2.18) $R \overset{\cdot}{\Rightarrow} Q(E) \equiv$ true $\Rightarrow$
$R \triangleright \lceil$ m $x \equiv E$; $F(x) \rfloor \equiv R \triangleright \lceil$ m $x \equiv E$; $Q(x) \triangleright F(x) \rfloor$
provided $\neg$ OCCURS$[\![x$ in $F]\!] \wedge$ STRICT$[\![F]\!]$.

The next few properties serve for propagating assertions into subexpressions of an expression.

(2.19) $B \triangleright f(E) \equiv f(B \triangleright E)$
provided STRICT$[\![f]\!] \vee$ DEFINED$[\![B]\!]$.

(2.20) $B \triangleright (E_1, \ldots, E_n) \equiv (B \triangleright E_1, \ldots, B \triangleright E_n)$
provided DETERMINATE$[\![B]\!]$.

(2.21) $B \triangleright f(E_1, \ldots, E_n) \equiv f(B \triangleright E_1, \ldots, B \triangleright E_n)$
provided (STRICT$[\![f]\!] \vee$ DEFINED$[\![B]\!]) \wedge$ DETERMINATE$[\![B]\!]$.

(2.22) if B then E else F fi $\equiv$
if B then $B \triangleright E$ else F fi $\equiv$
if B then E else $\neg B \triangleright F$ fi
provided DETERMINATE$[\![B]\!]$.

(2.23) $P \triangleright$ if B then E else F fi $\equiv$
$P \triangleright$ if B then $(P \wedge B) \triangleright E$ else F fi $\equiv$
$P \triangleright$ if B then E else $(P \wedge \neg B) \triangleright F$ fi $\equiv$
if B then $P \triangleright E$ else $P \triangleright F$ fi $\equiv$
if $P \wedge B$ then $P \triangleright E$ else $P \triangleright F$ fi $\equiv$
if $P \wedge B$ then $(P \wedge B) \triangleright E$ else $(P \wedge \neg B) \triangleright F$ fi
provided DETERMINATE$[\![P, B]\!]$.

(2.24) For $? \in \{\forall, \exists, \text{some}\}$ and Boolean expression Q,
$P \triangleright ?$ m $x : Q \equiv ?$ m $x : P \triangleright Q$
provided $\neg$ OCCURS$[\![x$ in $P]\!] \wedge$ DETERMINATE$[\![P]\!]$.

Two auxiliary properties for Boolean expressions are the following:

(2.25) $(F = H) \wedge B \equiv (F = H) \wedge B[\![H$ forsome $F]\!]$
provided no new bindings for the free variables of H and F surround the occurrences of F that are replaced.

(2.26) $B \equiv B \wedge C$ provided $B \Rightarrow C \equiv$ true .

3 Parameter restrictions

As a first example of assertions we describe parameter restrictions for functions (cf. [Bauer, Wössner 82, Bauer et al. 85]): Let R be a Boolean expression possibly involving the identifier x of type m. Then the declaration

$$\text{funct } f \equiv (mx : R) \; n : E$$

of function f with parameter x restricted by R and body E of result type n is by definition equivalent to

$$\text{funct } f \equiv (mx) \; n : R \triangleright E \;.$$

This means that f is undefined for all arguments x that violate the restriction R, or, in other words, that R is a precondition for definedness of f. If f is recursive, R has to hold also for the parameters of the recursive calls to ensure definedness; hence in this case R corresponds to what is known as an invariant at the procedural language level.

4 A Simple Example

In this section we want to demonstrate the use of the algebra of assertions in transformational program development. The problem to be treated consists in finding square roots of natural numbers. More precisely, the specification reads

> funct $sqrt \equiv (\text{nat } m)$ nat :
> some nat $k : k^2 \leq m \land (k+1)^2 > m$.

The first step in the development uses the technique of **embedding** or **generalization**: The original problem is embedded into a more general one, in this case via an additional parameter that provides a lower bound for the search space. The specification for the embedding function *esqrt* reads

> funct $esqrt \equiv (\text{nat } m, \text{nat } u : u^2 \leq m)$ nat :
> some nat $k : u \leq k \land k^2 \leq m \land (k+1)^2 > m$.

Thus the specification of *esqrt* consists of the one of *sqrt* together with the requirement that the result lie above the parameter u. Hence the old problem indeed is a special case of the new one; 0 is a trivial lower bound and thus

$$(4.1) \qquad sqrt(m) \equiv esqrt(m, 0) \text{ for all } m.$$

The next goal is now to use the additional degree of freedom gained by the parameter u to develop a recursive version of *esqrt* no longer containing any occurrences of the specification construct **some**. To achieve this, we use algebraic manipulations to derive a recursion equation for *esqrt* . In this calculation, a prominent role is played by the algebraic laws for assertions given in the previous section.

We calculate:

$esqrt(m, u)$

$\equiv$ (by definition of $esqrt$)

$(u^2 \leq m) \;\rhd\;$ some nat $k : u \leq k \wedge k^2 \leq m \wedge (k+1)^2 > m$

$\equiv$ (arithmetic)

$(u^2 \leq m) \;\rhd\;$ some nat $k : (u = k \vee u < k) \wedge k^2 \leq m \wedge (k+1)^2 > m$

$\equiv$ (distributivity of $\wedge$ over $\vee$)

$(u^2 \leq m) \;\rhd\;$ some nat $k : (u = k \wedge k^2 \leq m \wedge (k+1)^2 > m) \;\vee$
$\qquad\qquad\qquad\qquad\qquad (u < k \wedge k^2 \leq m \wedge (k+1)^2 > m)$

$\equiv$ (arithmetic)

$(u^2 \leq m) \;\rhd\;$ some nat $k : (u = k \wedge k^2 \leq m \wedge (k+1)^2 > m) \;\vee$
$\qquad\qquad\qquad\qquad\qquad (u + 1 \leq k \wedge k^2 \leq m \wedge (k+1)^2 > m)$

$\equiv$ (by (2.24))

some nat $k : (u^2 \leq m) \;\rhd\; ((u = k \wedge k^2 \leq m \wedge (k+1)^2 > m) \;\vee$
$\qquad\qquad\qquad\qquad\qquad (u + 1 \leq k \wedge k^2 \leq m \wedge (k+1)^2 > m))$

$\equiv$ (by (2.19) and (2.20))

some nat $k : ((u^2 \leq m) \;\rhd\; (u = k \wedge k^2 \leq m \wedge (k+1)^2 > m) \;\vee$
$\qquad\qquad (u^2 \leq m) \;\rhd\; (u + 1 \leq k \wedge k^2 \leq m \wedge (k+1)^2 > m))$

$\equiv$ (by (2.25))

some nat $k : ((u^2 \leq m) \;\rhd\; (u = k \wedge u^2 \leq m \wedge (k+1)^2 > m) \;\vee$
$\qquad\qquad (u^2 \leq m) \;\rhd\; (u + 1 \leq k \wedge k^2 \leq m \wedge (k+1)^2 > m))$

$\equiv$ (by (2.10))

some nat $k : ((u^2 \leq m) \;\rhd\; (u = k \wedge \text{true} \wedge (k+1)^2 > m) \;\vee$
$\qquad\qquad (u^2 \leq m) \;\rhd\; (u + 1 \leq k \wedge k^2 \leq m \wedge (k+1)^2 > m))$

$\equiv$ (neutrality of true w.r.t. $\wedge$)

some nat $k : ((u^2 \leq m) \;\rhd\; (u = k \wedge (k+1)^2 > m) \;\vee$
$\qquad\qquad (u^2 \leq m) \;\rhd\; (u + 1 \leq k \wedge k^2 \leq m \wedge (k+1)^2 > m))$

$\equiv$ (by (2.19), (2.20), (2.24))

$(u^2 \leq m) \;\rhd\;$ some nat $k : (u = k \wedge (k+1)^2 > m) \;\vee$
$\qquad\qquad\qquad\qquad\qquad (u + 1 \leq k \wedge k^2 \leq m \wedge (k+1)^2 > m)$

$\equiv$ (by (2.4))

$(u^2 \leq m) \;\rhd\;$
if $(u+1)^2 > m$
    then some nat $k : (u = k \wedge (u+1)^2 > m) \;\vee$
$\qquad\qquad\qquad\qquad\quad (u + 1 \leq k \wedge k^2 \leq m \wedge (k+1)^2 > m)$
    else some nat $k : (u = k \wedge (u+1)^2 > m) \;\vee$
$\qquad\qquad\qquad\qquad\quad (u + 1 \leq k \wedge k^2 \leq m \wedge (k+1)^2 > m)$ fi

$\equiv$ (by (2.26) and arithmetic)

$(u^2 \leq m) \;\rhd\;$
if $(u+1)^2 > m$
    then some nat $k : (u = k \wedge (u+1)^2 > m) \;\vee$
$\qquad\qquad\qquad\qquad\quad (u + 1 \leq k \wedge (u+1)^2 \leq k^2 \wedge k^2 \leq m \wedge (k+1)^2 > m)$
    else some nat $k : (u = k \wedge (u+1)^2 > m) \;\vee$
$\qquad\qquad\qquad\qquad\quad (u + 1 \leq k \wedge k^2 \leq m \wedge (k+1)^2 > m)$ fi

$\equiv$ (transitivity of $\leq$ and (2.26))

$(u^2 \leq m) \;\rhd\;$
if $(u+1)^2 > m$
    then some nat $k : (u = k \wedge (u+1)^2 > m) \;\vee$
$\qquad\qquad\qquad\quad (u + 1 \leq k \wedge (u+1)^2 \leq k^2 \wedge k^2 \leq m \wedge$
$\qquad\qquad\qquad\quad (u+1)^2 \leq m \wedge (k+1)^2 > m)$
    else some nat $k : (u = k \wedge (u+1)^2 > m) \;\vee$
$\qquad\qquad\qquad\qquad\quad (u + 1 \leq k \wedge k^2 \leq m \wedge (k+1)^2 > m)$ fi

$\equiv$ (arithmetic and (2.3))
$(u^2 \leq m)$ ▷
if $(u+1)^2 > m$
 then some nat $k : (u = k \wedge \text{true}) \vee$
          $(u+1 \leq k \wedge (u+1)^2 \leq k^2 \wedge k^2 \leq m \wedge \text{false} \wedge (k+1)^2 > m)$
 else some nat $k : (u = k \wedge \text{false}) \vee$
         $(u+1 \leq k \wedge k^2 \leq m \wedge (k+1)^2 > m)$ fi

$\equiv$ (Boolean algebra)
$(u^2 \leq m)$ ▷
if $(u+1)^2 > m$
 then some nat $k : u = k$
 else some nat $k : u+1 \leq k \wedge k^2 \leq m \wedge (k+1)^2 > m$ fi

$\equiv$ (by (2.2))
$(u^2 \leq m)$ ▷
if $(u+1)^2 > m$
 then u
 else some nat $k : u+1 \leq k \wedge k^2 \leq m \wedge (k+1)^2 > m$ fi

$\equiv$ (by (2.22) and arithmetic)
$(u^2 \leq m)$ ▷
if $(u+1)^2 > m$
 then u
 else $(u+1)^2 \leq m$ ▷ some nat $k : u+1 \leq k \wedge k^2 \leq m \wedge (k+1)^2 > m$ fi

$\equiv$ (by definition of *esqrt*)
$(u^2 \leq m)$ ▷
if $(u+1)^2 > m$ then u
    else $esqrt(m, u+1)$ fi .

Since termination of the obtained recursion is immediate (take $f(m, u) \stackrel{\text{def}}{\equiv} m - u^2$ as the "variant", i.e., as the termination function, cf. [Dijkstra 76], [Bauer, Wössner 82]), we may pass to the recursive definition

 funct *esqrt* $\equiv$ (nat m, nat $u : u^2 \leq m$) nat :
  if $(u+1)^2 > m$ then u
      else $esqrt(m, u+1)$ fi .

We have obtained a first operative solution of our problem. However, the repeated squaring in each of the incarnations makes the program rather inefficient. An ameliorated version is obtained by using an additional parameter that carries the square $(u+1)^2$ and is incremented properly from incarnation to incarnation. This technique, also called finite differencing [Paige, Koenig 82] or formal differentiation [Sharir 82], is a generalization of the well-known "strength reduction" in compiler construction. To apply it, we use another assertion that expresses the relation between the "old" and the "new" parameters. We define

 funct *esqrts* $\equiv$ (nat m, nat u, nat $v : u^2 \leq m \wedge v = (u+1)^2$) nat :
  $esqrt(m, u)$.

Based on the relation

 (4.2) $esqrt(m, u) \equiv esqrts(m, u, (u+1)^2)$

we calculate

$$esqrts(m, u, v)$$
$\equiv$ (by definition of esqrts)
$$u^2 \leq m \wedge v = (u+1)^2 \ \triangleright \ esqrt(m, u)$$
$\equiv$ (by definition of $esqrt$)
$$u^2 \leq m \wedge v = (u+1)^2 \ \triangleright$$
$$\text{if } (u+1)^2 > m \text{ then } u$$
$$\text{else } esqrt(m, u+1) \text{ fi}$$
$\equiv$ (by (2.13), (2.11), (4.2))
$$u^2 \leq m \wedge v = (u+1)^2 \ \triangleright$$
$$\text{if } v > m \text{ then } u$$
$$\text{else } esqrts(m, u+1, ((u+1)+1)^2) \text{ fi}$$
$\equiv$ (arithmetic)
$$u^2 \leq m \wedge v = (u+1)^2 \ \triangleright$$
$$\text{if } v > m \text{ then } u$$
$$\text{else } esqrts(m, u+1, (u+1)^2 + 2*(u+1)+1) \text{ fi}$$
$\equiv$ (by (2.13), (2.11) and arithmetic)
$$u^2 \leq m \wedge v = (u+1)^2 \ \triangleright$$
$$\text{if } v > m \text{ then } u$$
$$\text{else } esqrts(m, u+1, v + 2*u + 3) \text{ fi} .$$

The termination argument is still valid; hence we obtain

> **funct** $esqrts \equiv (\text{nat } m, \text{nat } u, \text{nat } v : u^2 \leq m \wedge v = (u+1)^2) \text{ nat} :$
> $\quad \text{if } v > m \text{ then } u$
> $\qquad \text{else } esqrts(m, u+1, v + 2*u + 3) \text{ fi} .$

Another transformation of this kind leaves us with

> **funct** $esqrto \equiv (\text{ nat } m, \text{nat } u, \text{nat } v, \text{nat } w :$
> $\qquad u^2 \leq m \wedge v = (u+1)^2 \wedge w = 2*u + 3) \text{ nat} :$
> $\quad \text{if } v > m \text{ then } u$
> $\qquad \text{else } esqrto(m, u+1, v + w, w + 2) \text{ fi}$

which satisfies the relation

$$(4.3) \qquad esqrts(m, u, v) \equiv esqrto(m, u, v, 2*u + 3)$$

and hence solves the square root problem according to

$$(4.4) \qquad sqrt(m) \equiv esqrt(m, 0) \equiv esqrts(m, 0, 1) \equiv esqrto(m, 0, 1, 3) .$$

To transform *esqrto* into iterative form we use the following general transformation rule (ITER) for passing from tail-recursion to a loop (NEW$[\![y]\!]$ requires y to be a fresh identifier):

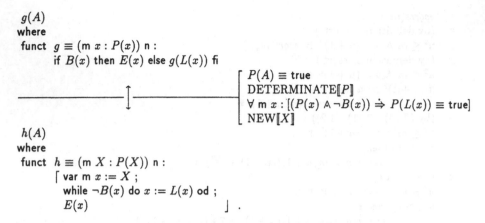

$g(A)$
where
funct $g \equiv (\text{m } x : P(x))$ n :
    if $B(x)$ **then** $E(x)$ **else** $g(L(x))$ **fi**

$\begin{array}{l} P(A) \equiv \text{true} \\ \text{DETERMINATE}[\![P]\!] \\ \forall \text{ m } x : [(P(x) \wedge \neg B(x)) \Rightarrow P(L(x)) \equiv \text{true}] \\ \text{NEW}[\![X]\!] \end{array}$

$h(A)$
where
funct $h \equiv (\text{m } X : P(X))$ n :
    ⌈ **var m** $x := X$;
      while $\neg B(x)$ **do** $x := L(x)$ **od** ;
      $E(x)$ ⌋ .

Here, NEW$[\![X]\!]$ requires X to be a fresh identifier.

Applying this to *esqrto* and unfolding the resulting function in *sqrt* we obtain finally

funct *sqrt* $\equiv$ (**nat** m) **nat** :
    ⌈ (**var nat** u, **var nat** v, **var nat** w) := $(0, 1, 3)$;
      while $v \leq m$ **do** $(u, v, w) := (u + 1, v + w, w + 2)$ **od** ;
      u ⌋ .

5   Strengthening and Weakening Assertions

Frequently, one has to strengthen an assertion to achieve a certain simplification. However, after
the simplification, one wants to get rid of the assertion again. A tool for this for the case of
linearly recursive functions is the following rule:

Theorem:
The following transformation rule is valid:

$g(A)$
where
funct $g \equiv (\text{m } x : P(x))$ n :
    if $B(x)$ **then** $E(x)$
        else $K(g(L(x)))$ **fi**

$\begin{array}{l} Q(A) \equiv \text{true} \\ \text{DETERMINATE}[\![Q]\!] \\ \text{DETERMINATE}[\![P]\!] \\ \forall \text{ m } x : [(((P(x) \wedge Q(x)) \wedge \neg B(x)) \\ \qquad\qquad\qquad \Rightarrow Q(L(x)) \equiv \text{true}] \\ \text{STRICT}[\![K]\!] \\ \neg \text{ OCCURS}[\![g, h \text{ in } L(x), K]\!] \end{array}$

$h(A)$
where
funct $h \equiv (\text{m } x : P(x) \wedge Q(x))$ n :
    if $B(x)$ **then** $E(x)$
        else $K(h(L(x)))$ **fi** .

Thus, g and h have the same recursion structure, but h has the stronger "invariant" $P(x) \wedge Q(x)$.

Proof:

We use computational induction (see e.g. [Manna 74]) to show $R[g, h]$ where the predicate R is given by

$$R[k, l] \stackrel{\text{def}}{\Leftrightarrow} \forall m x : [Q(x) \rhd k(x) \equiv Q(x) \rhd l(x)] .$$

The induction base $R[\Omega, \Omega]$ is trivial. For the induction step assume $R[k, l]$. Then we have to show $R[\tau_g[k], \tau_h[l]]$ where τ_g, τ_h are the functionals belonging to the recursive definitions of g and h. We calculate

$$
\begin{aligned}
&\quad Q(x) \rhd \tau_g[k](x) \\
&\equiv \text{ (by definition)} \\
&\quad Q(x) \rhd (P(x) \rhd \text{if } B(x) \text{ then } E(x) \text{ else } K(k(L(x))) \text{ fi}) \\
&\equiv \text{ (by (2.13))} \\
&\quad P(x) \wedge Q(x) \rhd \text{if } B(x) \text{ then } E(x) \text{ else } K(k(L(x))) \text{ fi} \\
&\equiv \text{ (by (2.23))} \\
&\quad P(x) \wedge Q(x) \rhd \text{if } P(x) \\
&\qquad\qquad\qquad\qquad \text{then } E(x) \\
&\qquad\qquad\qquad\qquad \text{else } P(x) \wedge Q(x) \wedge \neg B(x) \rhd K(k(L(x))) \text{ fi} \\
&\equiv \text{ (by (2.13))} \\
&\quad P(x) \wedge Q(x) \rhd \text{if } P(x) \\
&\qquad\qquad\qquad\qquad \text{then } E(x) \\
&\qquad\qquad\qquad\qquad \text{else } (P(x) \wedge Q(x)) \wedge \neg B(x) \rhd K(k(L(x))) \text{ fi} \\
&\equiv \text{ (by (2.19))} \\
&\quad P(x) \wedge Q(x) \rhd \text{if } P(x) \\
&\qquad\qquad\qquad\qquad \text{then } E(x) \\
&\qquad\qquad\qquad\qquad \text{else } K((P(x) \wedge Q(x)) \wedge \neg B(x) \rhd k(L(x))) \text{ fi} \\
&\equiv \text{ (by (2.1))} \\
&\quad P(x) \wedge Q(x) \rhd \text{if } P(x) \\
&\qquad\qquad\qquad\qquad \text{then } E(x) \\
&\qquad\qquad\qquad\qquad \text{else } K((P(x) \wedge Q(x)) \wedge \neg B(x) \rhd \\
&\qquad\qquad\qquad\qquad\qquad\qquad \lceil m\, y \equiv L(x) \,;\, k(y) \rfloor \qquad) \text{ fi} \\
&\equiv \text{ (by the fourth applicability condition and (2.18))} \\
&\quad P(x) \wedge Q(x) \rhd \text{if } P(x) \\
&\qquad\qquad\qquad\qquad \text{then } E(x) \\
&\qquad\qquad\qquad\qquad \text{else } K((P(x) \wedge Q(x)) \wedge \neg B(x) \rhd \\
&\qquad\qquad\qquad\qquad\qquad\qquad \lceil m\, y \equiv L(x) \,;\, Q(y) \rhd k(y) \rfloor) \text{ fi} \\
&\equiv \text{ (by the induction hypothesis)} \\
&\quad P(x) \wedge Q(x) \rhd \text{if } P(x) \\
&\qquad\qquad\qquad\qquad \text{then } E(x) \\
&\qquad\qquad\qquad\qquad \text{else } K((P(x) \wedge Q(x)) \wedge \neg B(x) \rhd \\
&\qquad\qquad\qquad\qquad\qquad\qquad \lceil m\, y \equiv L(x) \,;\, Q(y) \rhd l(y) \rfloor) \text{ fi} \\
&\equiv \text{ (by the fourth applicability condition and (2.18))} \\
&\quad P(x) \wedge Q(x) \rhd \text{if } P(x) \\
&\qquad\qquad\qquad\qquad \text{then } E(x) \\
&\qquad\qquad\qquad\qquad \text{else } K((P(x) \wedge Q(x)) \wedge \neg B(x) \rhd \\
&\qquad\qquad\qquad\qquad\qquad\qquad \lceil m\, y \equiv L(x) \,;\, l(y) \rfloor \qquad) \text{ fi}
\end{aligned}
$$

$$\equiv \quad \text{(by (2.1))}$$
$$P(x) \wedge Q(x) \; \triangleright \; \text{if} \; P(x)$$
$$\text{then} \; E(x)$$
$$\text{else} \; K((P(x) \wedge Q(x)) \wedge \neg B(x) \; \triangleright \; l(L(x))) \; \text{fi}$$

$$\equiv \quad \text{(by (2.19))}$$
$$P(x) \wedge Q(x) \; \triangleright \; \text{if} \; P(x)$$
$$\text{then} \; E(x)$$
$$\text{else} \; (P(x) \wedge Q(x)) \wedge \neg B(x) \; \triangleright \; K(l(L(x))) \; \text{fi}$$

$$\equiv \quad \text{(by (2.13) and (2.23))}$$
$$P(x) \wedge Q(x) \; \triangleright \; \text{if} \; B(x) \; \text{then} \; E(x) \; \text{else} \; K(l(L(x))) \; \text{fi}$$

$$\equiv \quad \text{(by (2.12))}$$
$$Q(x) \; \triangleright \; (P(x) \wedge Q(x) \; \triangleright \; \text{if} \; B(x) \; \text{then} \; E(x)$$
$$\text{else} \; K(l(L(x))) \; \text{fi})$$

$$\equiv \quad \text{(by definition)}$$
$$Q(x) \; \triangleright \; \tau_h[l](x) \; .$$

$\square$

In the case where $P(x) \equiv$ true this rule gives us the possibility of discarding the invariant $Q(x)$ from h by passing to g. Note that similar rules can be developed for more general kinds of recursion.

6 Applicative Updating

As an application of the previous theorem we want to develop an algorithm for rearranging the elements of an array. In doing so we will now make larger steps, since the detailed working of the assertion calculus has already been demonstrated.

We consider arrays to be partial mappings from a fixed finite set index to a set elem of array elements. A fairly general applicative specification of our problem reads as follows:

> funct $move \equiv$ (array a) array :
> some array $b : \forall$ index $i : b[i] = f(a, i)$.

Here, f may be any function of type funct(array,index)elem where elem is the type of the array elements. Define

$$\text{set index} \; all \equiv \{\text{index} \; i : \text{true}\} \; .$$

Then a tail-recursive solution of this problem (the derivation of which we omit) is

> funct $move \equiv$ (array a) array :
> $rmove(a, c, all)$
> where
> funct $rmove \equiv$ (array a, d, set index s) array :
> if $s = \emptyset$
> then d
> else index $i \equiv$ some index $j : j \in s$;
> $rmove(a, d[i \leftarrow f(a, i)], s \backslash \{i\})$ fi

Here, $d[i \leftarrow x]$ is the array that results from d by changing the i-th element to x. Note that the parameter c in the call $rmove(a, c, all)$ is a completely arbitrary value of type array. This will be the key to obtaining an applicative preparation of overwriting with selective updating.

Now we specialize the problem by assuming that the index set is linearly ordered by an order $\leq$. Then the choice of i above may be specialized to taking the minimum of s w.r.t. $\leq$:

```
funct  rmove ≡ (array a, d, set index s) array :
       if  s = ∅
           then d
           else index i ≡ min(s) ;
                rmove(a, d[i←f(a, i)], s\{i}) fi
```

Now the indices are processed in ascending order. If the function f is **oriented** w.r.t. $\leq$, i.e., if for all i the value $f(a, i)$ depends at most on values $a[j]$ with $j \geq i$, we can, at the procedural level, implement an assignment

$$a := move(a)$$

by selectively updating the elements $a[i]$ in ascending order. We want to prepare this step at the applicative level using again assertions.

To state formally when a function is oriented, we introduce some notation: Let, for index i,

$$\overset{\vee}{i} \overset{def}{\equiv} \{\text{index } j : i \leq j\},$$

i.e., the interval above i. Moreover, for an array a and a set $s \subseteq$ index we define the selection function

$$a|s : \begin{cases} s \to \text{elem} \\ i \mapsto a[i] . \end{cases}$$

Then we can define

$$\text{ORIENTED}[\![f \text{ wrt } \leq]\!] \overset{def}{\Leftrightarrow}$$
$$\forall \text{array } b, c, \text{index } i : [b|\overset{\vee}{i} = c|\overset{\vee}{i} \equiv \text{true} \Rightarrow f(b, i) \equiv f(c, i)] ;$$

here, $=$ is the equality test on finite mappings. Note that the function that sorts an array cannot be oriented w.r.t. any ordering at all.

We now apply the rule from the previous section to $move$. Here, $P(x) \equiv \text{true}$, and for $Q(x)$ we choose

$$a|s = d|s .$$

To satisfy the preconditions of our rule we first specialize the arbitrary parameter c to a, because then Q holds for the initial call. The second condition, viz.

$$(a|s = d|s \wedge s \neq \emptyset \overset{\cdot}{\Rightarrow} a|s = d[i \leftarrow a[i]]|t) \equiv \text{true}$$

for $i \equiv min(s), t \equiv s\setminus\{i\}$, holds, since $b|\overset{\vee}{i} = c|\overset{\vee}{i}$ implies $b|\overset{\vee}{j} = c|\overset{\vee}{j}$ for all $j \geq i$ by transitivity of $\leq$. Hence we obtain

```
funct  move ≡ (array a) array :
       srmove(a, a, all)
where
funct  srmove ≡ (array a, d, set index s : a|s = d|s) array :
       if  s = ∅
           then d
           else index i ≡ min(s) ;
                srmove(a, d[i←f(a, i)], s\{i}) fi
```

Using ORIENTED$[\![f \text{ wrt } \leq]\!]$ and the assertion this may now be transformed into

```
funct  move ≡ (array a) array :
       srmove(a, a, all)
where
funct  srmove ≡ (array a, d, set index s : s≠∅ ⇒ a|s = d|s) array :
       if  s = ∅
           then d
           else index i ≡ min(s) ;
                srmove(a, d[i←f(d, i)], s\{i}) fi .
```

Now the body of *srmove* has become independent of *a*—except for the assertion. By using the rule of weakening, however, we can eliminate the assertion and thus get rid of the parameter *a* altogether. This is the decisive step in getting an applicative variant of overwriting. The result reads

```
funct  move ≡ (array a) array :
       esrmove(a, all)
where
funct  esrmove ≡ (array d, set index s) array :
       if  s = ∅
           then d
           else index i ≡ min(s) ;
                esrmove(d[i←f(d, i)], s\{i}) fi
```

We now again apply the rule (ITER) from section 2 to transform *esrmove* into

```
funct  esrmove ≡ (array D, set index S) array :
       ⌈ (var array d, var set index s) := (D, S) ;
         while s≠∅
         do index i ≡ min(s) ;
            (d, s) := (d[i←f(d, i)], s\{i}) od ;
         d                                          ⌋
```

Finally, we can implement the assignment

$$a := move(a)$$

first by

$$a := esrmove(a, all)$$

and then reuse the variable *a* to obtain

```
⌈ var set index s := all ;
  while s≠∅
  do index i ≡ min(s) ;
     (a, s) := (a[i←f(a, i)], s\{i}) od ⌋
```

We omit the formal treatment of this last step, since it is independent of the use of assertions.

7 Calculating Parameters From Assertions

The development in the previous section depended on the property ORIENTED[f wrt $\leq$]. If this property does not hold for a given f, one can try to find another order $\preceq$ on index such that ORIENTED[f wrt $\preceq$] is satisfied. Let us demonstrate this with an example: Assume that

$$\mathsf{index} \equiv \mathsf{nat}\ i : i < N$$

for some constant N, and that

$$(7.1) \qquad f(a, i) = \begin{cases} c0 & \text{if } i = 0 \\ a[i-1] & \text{otherwise .} \end{cases}$$

The requirement on $\preceq$ then unfolds into

$\forall$ array b, c, index i :
$\quad [(\forall$ index $j : j \succeq i \Rightarrow b[j] = c[j]) \equiv$ true $\Rightarrow (i = 0 \lor b[i-1] = c[i-1]) \equiv$ true] .

Because of the premise, the conclusion is satisfied if

$$(i \neq 0 \overset{\Rightarrow}{\Rightarrow} i - 1 \succeq i) \equiv \mathsf{true} .$$

But then $\preceq$ is fixed, as is easily seen by induction, viz.

$$k \preceq l \equiv l \leq k .$$

Hence the array indices should be processed in decreasing order.

8 Discussion

We hope to have demonstrated that techniques known from the verification or verifying construction (see e.g. [Dijkstra 76]) of imperative programs can fruitfully be carried over to an applicative language style. In particular, this opens the possibility of using assertions in conjunction with transformation techniques applied to schematic programs; hence developments can be done once and for all for whole classes of problems. To make the approach practical, one must find more compact rules (best, semi-automatically applicable ones) for manipulating programs with assertions.

A second point concerns the issue of functional (i.e., combinator-oriented) versus applicative (λ-calculus-oriented) languages. Of course, all the rules in section 2 can be lifted to the functional level. However, the ones involving substitution get a bit more complicated. Consider, for instance, the expression $p \vartriangleright p \circ f$ with a Boolean function p and an arbitrary function f, both with the same argument type. If we write this in λ-notation, viz. as $\lambda x.\ p(x) \vartriangleright p(f(x))$, we see that we cannot replace the second occurrence of p by the everywhere true function, since $p(x)$ does not necessarily imply $p(f(x))$. To avoid the definition of a corresponding special mechanism (substitution only for occurrences not to the left of compositions) we have used an applicative rather than a functional language style.

Acknowledgment
This work has profited a great deal from discussions with F.L.Bauer, U. Berger, R. Berghammer, M. Broy, H. Ehler, M. Lichtmannegger, H. Partsch, and H. Schwichtenberg. Valuable comments were also provided by the referee.

9 References

[Bauer, Wössner 82]
F.L. Bauer, H. Wössner: Algorithmic language and program development. New York: Springer 1982

[Bauer et al. 85]
F.L. Bauer et al.: The Munich project CIP. Volume I: The wide spectrum language CIP-L. Lecture Notes in Computer Science **183**. New York: Springer 1985

[Bauer et al. 89]
F.L. Bauer et al.: Formal program construction by transformations—Computer-aided, Intuition-guided Programming. IEEE Trans. Software Eng. **15**, 165–180 (1989)

[Dikstra 76]
E.W. Dijkstra: A discipline of programming. Englewood Cliffs, N.J.: Prentice-Hall 1976

[Manna 74]
Z. Manna: Mathematical theory of computation. New York: McGraw-Hill 1974

[Monk 88]
L.G. Monk: Inference rules using local contexts. J. Automated Reasoning **4**, 445–462 (1988)

[Paige, Koenig 82]
R. Paige, S. Koenig: Finite differencing of computable expressions. ACM TOPLAS **4**, 402–454 (1982)

[Partsch 86]
H. Partsch: Transformational program development in a particular problem domain. Sci. Comput. Programming **7**, 99–241 (1986)

[Pepper 85]
P. Pepper: Modal logics for applicative programs. Habilitation Thesis, Technische Universität München, 1985

[Pepper 87]
P. Pepper: Application of modal logics to the reasoning about applicative programs. In L.G.L.T. Meertens (ed.): Program specification and transformation. Amsterdam: North-Holland 1987, 429–449

[Sharir 82]
M. Sharir: Some observations concerning formal differentiation of set theoretic expressions. ACM TOPLAS **4**, 196–226 (1982)

Types and invariants
in the refinement calculus

Carroll Morgan *

Abstract

A rigorous treatment of types as sets is given for the refinement calculus, a method of imperative program development. It is simple, supports existing practice, casts new light on type-checking, and suggests generalisations that might be of practical benefit.

1   Introduction

Program developments in the style of Dijkstra [2] rely on *implicit* typing of variables. One agrees beforehand that all variables have a certain type (say Z, the integers); then individual steps are justified by referring to that type, where necessary. For example, the truth of the entailment

$$a < b \Rightarrow wp(a := a + 1, a \leq b)$$

depends on a, b being integers. But that dependence is at present informal.

In the refinement calculus also [1, 10, 13], the dependence is informal; and the contribution of this paper is to make it rigorous. We make *typed* local variable declarations affect the meaning of commands within their scope, and allow development steps there to refer to that type information.

In fact, typing is a special kind of invariant: in the scope of the declaration **var** $n: N$, which introduces a new local variable n of type N (the natural numbers), the invariant is $n \in N$ and all commands preserve it. We allow the declaration of *local invariants* in general, and the rules for typing follow from that.

A surprising feature of our approach is that imposing an invariant does not increase the developer's proof obligations in the usual (prohibitive) way: it is not necessary to prove, during development, that the invariant is maintained. It is maintained automatically.

Thus even programs that appear to break the invariant actually maintain it: instead of being type-incorrect, they are miracles [9, 13, 14]. But miracles are still programs, and that allows a more uniform calculus of program refinement.

Nevertheless, a check is necessary to exclude miracles from the final program, since they cannot be executed. That check, like the type checking which it subsumes, is

---

*Programming Research Group, Oxford University, 8-11 Keble Road, Oxford, OX1 3QD, U.K.

$$
\begin{aligned}
wp_I(\textbf{skip}, \phi) &\;\triangleq\; I \wedge \phi \\
wp_I(\textbf{abort}, \phi) &\;\triangleq\; false \\
wp_I(x := E, \phi) &\;\triangleq\; I \wedge (I \Rightarrow \phi)[x \backslash E] \\
wp_I(P; Q, \phi) &\;\triangleq\; wp_I(P, wp_I(Q, \phi))
\end{aligned}
$$

$$
\begin{aligned}
wp_I(\textbf{if}\ (\|i \bullet G_i \to P_i)\ \textbf{fi}, \phi) \\
\triangleq\quad & (\vee i \bullet G_i) \\
\wedge\quad & (\wedge i \bullet G_i \Rightarrow wp_I(P_i, \phi))
\end{aligned}
$$

The substitution $[x \backslash E]$ replaces all free occurrences of x by E. Iteration $\textbf{do} \cdots \textbf{od}$, a special case of recursion, is dealt with in Section 8.3.

Figure 1: Invariant semantics for Dijkstra's language

often obvious and can in many cases be delegated to machine. When a machine cannot perform it, it is only because the program developer has used more general invariants than typing.

We believe that it is important to separate the use of an invariant (or type) from the proof that it is respected. Continual formal type-checking *during* development is impractical — and that has, so far, limited the rigorous use of types in imperative programs.

2 Invariant semantics

We retain Dijkstra's language, but now give its meaning relative to an invariant, which we call the *context*. Any formula over the program variables (even *false*) may be a context. We write $wp_I(P, \phi)$ for the weakest precondition in context I of a program P with respect to a postcondition ϕ, and give the resulting semantics of Dijkstra's language in Figure 1. Note that taking I to be *true* in Figure 1 gives the usual semantics: therefore we say that *true* is the default context.

These theorems support our choice of semantics in Figure 1:

Theorem 1 *Assume invariant.* No program P, in context I, is guaranteed to terminate unless I holds initially:
$$
wp_I(P, true) \Rightarrow I.
$$
Proof: Structural induction over P.
♡

Theorem 2 *Establish invariant.* Any program P, in context I, establishes I iff it establishes anything:
$$
wp_I(P, \phi) \equiv wp_I(P, I \wedge \phi).
$$
Proof: Structural induction over P.
♡

Note that $wp_I(P, \sqcup)$ is still monotonic over implication (in its second argument), and still distributes conjunction. Note also that, in the (typing) context $n \in \mathbb{N}$, the command $n := -1$ terminates, and hence (Theorem 2) reëstablishes the invariant! We return to that later.

3 The refinement calculus

The refinement calculus is based on an extended programming language, in which specifications can be written, and a relation of refinement between its programs such that implementations refine their specifications [1, 10, 13].

3.1 Language extensions

A *specification* is a list w of changing variables, called the *frame*, and a formula *post*, called the *postcondition*. It is defined as follows:

Definition 1 *Specification.*

$$wp_I(w : [post], \phi) \quad \hat{=} \quad I \wedge (\forall w \bullet I \wedge post \Rightarrow \phi).$$

$\heartsuit$

(Quantifications are written within parentheses $(\cdots)$, and the bound variable list is terminated by $\bullet$. Our precedence for propositional connectives is (highest) $\neg, \wedge, \vee, \Rightarrow,$ $\Leftrightarrow$ (lowest).)

In the special case of a specification with an empty list of changing variables, we have a *coercion*, whose definition is derived from Definition 1:

Definition 2 *Coercion.*

$$wp_I([post], \phi) \quad \hat{=} \quad I \wedge (post \Rightarrow \phi).$$

$\heartsuit$

An *assertion* is a single condition *pre*, written $\{pre\}$, and is defined as follows:

Definition 3 *Assertion.*

$$wp_I(\{pre\}, \phi) \quad \hat{=} \quad pre \wedge I \wedge \phi.$$

$\heartsuit$

Coercions and assertions are together known as *annotations*. We will omit the sequential composition operator ; whenever one or both of its arguments is an annotation.

Assertions and specifications often occur together; for example,

$$\{m > 0\}n : [n < m] \tag{1}$$

sets n below m provided m was positive to begin with. (Note that Definitions 1 and 3 differ slightly from the notation of [9], where Specification (1) would be written $n : [m > 0, n < m]$. The present notation agrees with [13]; but [1] remains substantially different.)

An untyped local variable x is introduced using the declaration **var** and scope brackets $|[\cdots]|$. It is defined

Definition 4 *Untyped local variable.* Provided neither I nor ϕ contains free x,

$$wp_I(\|[\text{ var } x \bullet P \,]\|, \phi) \quad \triangleq \quad \left(\forall x \bullet wp_I(P, \phi) \right).$$

♡

Definition 4 is standard; later, we extend it for typed local variables.

A local invariant J is introduced by the declaration **inv** and scope brackets. It is defined

Definition 5 *Local invariant.*

$$wp_I(\|[\text{ inv } J \bullet P \,]\|, \phi) \quad \triangleq \quad wp_{I \wedge J}(P, \phi).$$

♡

In $\|[\text{ inv } J \bullet P \,]\|$, the new invariant J is assumed initially, is maintained automatically by every command in P, and therefore is established finally.

Finally, typed local variables are a combination of the above: an untyped declaration, an initialisation, and a local invariant. We have

Definition 6 *Typed local variables.* For any set T and formula I,

$$\|[\text{ var } x\colon T \text{ and } I \bullet P \,]\|$$

$$\triangleq \quad \begin{aligned} &\|[\text{ var } x \bullet x\colon [x \in T \wedge I]; \\ &\qquad \|[\text{ inv } x \in T \wedge I \bullet P \,]\| \\ &\,]\|. \end{aligned}$$

♡

The "$: T$" gives the type of x; the "and I" gives an invariant to be imposed additionally. An invariant *true* may be omitted.

Invariants introduced by **inv** or **and** are *explicit*; invariants introduced by typing $x\colon T$ are *implicit*.

3.2 The refinement relation

The refinement relation $\sqsubseteq$ holds between programs P and Q if Q satisfies every specification that P does, in every context. This is its definition:

Definition 7 *Refinement.* For programs P and Q, we have $P \sqsubseteq Q$ iff for all contexts I and postconditions ϕ,

$$wp_I(P, \phi) \Rightarrow wp_I(Q, \phi).$$

♡

If a program fragment is contained within the scope of a local invariant I, we can take advantage of the invariant by exploiting a weaker refinement relation $\sqsubseteq_I$, defined as follows:

Definition 8 *Refinement in context.* For programs P and Q,

$$P \sqsubseteq_I Q \quad \triangleq \quad \|[\text{ inv } I \bullet P]\| \sqsubseteq \|[\text{ inv } I \bullet Q]\|.$$

♡

In Definition 8, the index I of $\sqsubseteq_I$ is the context in which the refinement is valid. For example, with $I \triangleq n \in \mathbb{N}$, we have

$$x: [x \geq 0] \sqsubseteq_I x := n.$$

That is, setting x to a natural number n refines setting it to any non-negative value. (Law 1 below supplies an easy proof.)

In practice, we use the following lemma to demonstrate refinements in context:

Lemma 1 *Refinement in context.* For programs P and Q, we have $P \sqsubseteq_I Q$ iff for all postconditions ϕ, and stronger contexts J with $J \Rightarrow I$,

$$wp_J(P, \phi) \Rightarrow wp_J(Q, \phi).$$

Proof: From Definitions 8, 7, and 5, $P \sqsubseteq_I Q$ iff for all postconditions ϕ and contexts K

$$wp_{I \wedge K}(P, \phi) \Rightarrow wp_{I \wedge K}(Q, \phi).$$

But the set of contexts "$I \wedge K$ for all K" is exactly the set of contexts "J with $J \Rightarrow I$", as required.

♡

An immediate consequence of Lemma 1 is that strengthening the context cannot invalidate a refinement:

Lemma 2 *Strengthen context.* If $P \sqsubseteq_I Q$ and $J \Rightarrow I$, then also $P \sqsubseteq_J Q$.

Proof: Trivial, since Lemma 1 treats all stronger J than I.

♡

4 A development method

We regard as our "programming" language all the constructions of Figure 1 (traditional) and Section 3.1 (novel). That includes abstract programs, like

$$x: \left[x^2 - 3x + 2 = 0 \right],$$

and it of course admits "ordinary" programs too, like $x := 1$ and $x := 2$ (both of which refine the above).

Though "programming" and "ordinary" we use informally, we do precisely identify a subset of the language, called *code*, that can be executed automatically by computer. It includes all of Figure 1, and Definitions 3 and 6 without **and** of Section 3.1. (But in the case of Definition 6, we do restrict the language — in code — with which the set T can be expressed.) Code does *not* include specifications, coercions, untyped local variables, or explicit invariants.

In the refinement calculus, the aim of development is to refine a given program into another one written entirely in code. For that we use refinement laws, one of which is shown in this section. We need not use *wp* directly — it is used only to prove the refinement laws themselves.

There are two necessary aspects of code: first, any program written in code must be executable; and second, it must be decidable whether or not any text *is* code. The first aspect is straightforward: the language of code was *designed* for execution. Specifications, however, were not — and, in general, they *are* not, because most of the types of interest do not have recursively axiomatizable theories. Assertions, however, are code because they are refined by skip.

The second aspect is straightforward, too, but requires "type checking". Consider this program:

$$\lVert\ \text{var}\ n{:}\mathsf{N} \bullet n{:}{=}\ -1\ \rVert. \tag{2}$$

Definitions 6, 4, 1, and 5 show that it does terminate in the default context *true*. But it establishes *false*:

$$
\begin{aligned}
&wp(\lVert\ \text{var}\ n{:}\mathsf{N} \bullet n{:}{=}\ -1\ \rVert, false) \\
\equiv\ &\big(\forall n \bullet wp(n{:}\,[n \in \mathsf{N}], wp_{n\,\in\,\mathsf{N}}(n{:}{=}\ -1, false))\big) \\
\equiv\ &(\forall n \bullet (\forall n \bullet n \in \mathsf{N} \Rightarrow n \in \mathsf{N} \wedge (-1 \in \mathsf{N} \Rightarrow false))) \\
\equiv\ &true.
\end{aligned}
$$

Thus Program (2) violates Dijkstra's *Law of the excluded miracle* [2, p.18], and it cannot, therefore, be code.

That program is not code because it is ill-typed; but we defer the recognition of code to Section 7. Assuming we *can* recognise code, the development method is this: given a program, find code that refines it. Instrumental in that process are laws of refinement such as the following:

Law 1 *Assignment.* Provided $I \wedge pre \Rrightarrow post[w\backslash E]$,

$$\{pre\}w{:}\,[post] \sqsubseteq_I w{:}{=}\ E.$$

Proof: We use Lemma 1: let $J \Rrightarrow I$. Then

$$
\begin{aligned}
&wp_J(\{pre\}w{:}\,[post], \phi) \\
\equiv\ &J \wedge pre \wedge J \wedge (\forall w \bullet J \wedge post \Rightarrow \phi) \\
\Rrightarrow\ &J \wedge pre \wedge (J[w\backslash E] \wedge post[w\backslash E] \Rightarrow \phi[w\backslash E]) \\
\Rrightarrow\ &\text{"assumptions"} \\
&J \wedge (J \Rightarrow \phi)[w\backslash E] \\
\equiv\ &wp_J(w{:}{=}\ E, \phi).
\end{aligned}
$$

♡

Note that, in Law 1, the context *I* plays a *constructive* role: the stronger it is, the more likely is the refinement to be valid. That is an example of Lemma 2, and is an important practical point: one need not examine *all* invariant declarations in order to apply a particular law.

Also, Law 1 illustrates the general coding process: it replaces a non-executable construct, the specification, with code. Similar laws for the remaining constructs (but without invariants) can be found in [1, 10, 13].

5 Laws for local invariants

Local invariants are introduced with this law, whose proof uses Lemma 3 following.

Law 2 *Local invariant.* For any I, J, and P,

$$\{J\}P[J] \sqsubseteq_I \;\|[\; \text{inv } J \bullet P \;]\|.$$

Proof: Let $K \Rightarrow I$. Then

$$
\begin{aligned}
&wp_K(\{J\}P[J], \phi)\\
\equiv\quad& J \wedge wp_K(P[J], \phi)\\
\equiv\quad& J \wedge wp_K(P, K \wedge (J \Rightarrow \phi))\\
\equiv\quad& \text{``Theorem 2''}\\
& J \wedge wp_K(P, J \Rightarrow \phi)\\
\Rightarrow\quad& \text{``Lemma 3''}\\
& wp_{K \wedge J}(P, \phi)\\
\equiv\quad& wp_K(\|[\; \text{inv } J \bullet P \;]\|, \phi).
\end{aligned}
$$

$\heartsuit$

Lemma 3 *Maintain invariant.*

$$J \wedge wp_I(P, J \Rightarrow \phi) \Rightarrow wp_{I \wedge J}(P, \phi).$$

Proof: Structural induction over P; in fact equivalence $\equiv$ holds in every case except sequential composition.

$\heartsuit$

Note that in Law 2 the left-hand side assumes J before P and establishes it after P; the right-hand side maintains it within P as well.

Local invariants can also be introduced implicitly, within typed local variable declarations:

Law 3 *Introduce local block.* Provided x is a fresh local variable, not occurring in T or *post*,

$$w: [post] \quad \sqsubseteq_I \quad \|[\; \text{var } x\colon T \text{ and } J \bullet w, x: [post] \;]\|.$$

Proof: Let $K \Rightarrow I$, and assume x is a fresh variable. We introduce the abbreviation $\Phi \triangleq x \in T \wedge J$, and proceed

$$
\begin{aligned}
&wp_K(w: [post], \phi)\\
\equiv\quad& K \wedge (\forall w \bullet K \wedge post \Rightarrow \phi)\\
\equiv\quad& \text{``}x\text{ is fresh''}\\
& (\forall x \bullet K \wedge (\forall w, x \bullet K \wedge post \Rightarrow \phi))\\
\Rightarrow\quad& (\forall x \bullet K \wedge (\forall x \bullet K \wedge \Phi \Rightarrow K \wedge \Phi \wedge (\forall w, x \bullet K \wedge \Phi \wedge post \Rightarrow \phi)))\\
\equiv\quad& (\forall x \bullet wp_K(x: [\Phi], wp_{K \wedge \Phi}(w, x: [post], \phi)))\\
\equiv\quad& \text{``Definition 6''}\\
& wp_K(\|[\; \text{var } x\colon T \text{ and } J \bullet w, x: [post] \;]\|, \phi).
\end{aligned}
$$

♡

Theorem 3 below justifies *stepwise refinement* in context: refining a part of a program in context I refines the whole program in that context:

Theorem 3 *Monotonicity.* Let C be a program scheme containing the program name p, and let $C(X)$ be the result of replacing all occurrences of p in C by the program X. Then for any programs P, Q, if $P \sqsubseteq_I Q$, then also $C(P) \sqsubseteq_I C(Q)$.

Proof: Structural induction over C. The only novel case is local invariants: suppose $P \sqsubseteq_I Q$. If $J \Rightarrow I$, then

$$
\begin{aligned}
& wp_J(|[\ \text{inv}\ K \bullet P\ ]|, \phi) \\
\equiv\ & wp_{J \wedge K}(P, \phi) \\
\Rightarrow\ & \text{``Lemma 1 and assumption, since } J \wedge K \Rightarrow I\text{''} \\
& wp_{J \wedge K}(Q, \phi) \\
\equiv\ & wp_J(|[\ \text{inv}\ K \bullet Q\ ]|, \phi).
\end{aligned}
$$

♡

Theorem 4 does better: it is *the* reason for introducing a local invariant, since within its scope we can use the refinement relation $\sqsubseteq_{I \wedge J}$, easier to establish than $\sqsubseteq_I$.

Theorem 4 *Use local invariant.* Let C be as before. If $P \sqsubseteq_{I \wedge J} Q$, then

$$
|[\ \text{inv}\ J \bullet C(P)\ ]| \sqsubseteq_I |[\ \text{inv}\ J \bullet C(Q)\ ]|.
$$

Proof: From Theorem 3, $C(P) \sqsubseteq_{I \wedge J} C(Q)$. The result follows from Definitions 8 and 5.

♡

Note that the stronger hypothesis $P \sqsubseteq_I Q$ would be enough in Theorem 4: we may use the new invariant J, but are not obliged to do so.

Although local invariants make refinement easier, there is a price to pay later. After the refinement, still the **inv** remains — and it is not code. The next section deals with its elimination.

6 Eliminating local invariants

An implicit invariant, introduced by Law 3, need not be eliminated — because in that special case it *is* code. But explicit invariants (Law 2, or **and** in Law 3) must be removed, and that requires laws like these:

Law 4 *Invariant distribution through sequential composition.* For any context J,

$$
|[\ \text{inv}\ I \bullet P; Q\ ]| \quad \sqsubseteq_J \quad |[\ \text{inv}\ I \bullet P\ ]|; |[\ \text{inv}\ I \bullet Q\ ]|.
$$

Proof: Direct from Definition 5 and Figure 1. (In fact, the two programs are equal.)

♡

Law 5 *Invariant distribution through alternation.* For any context J, suppose that $J \wedge I \Rightarrow (G_i \Leftrightarrow G'_i)$ for each branch i of the alternation. Then

$$\|[\text{ inv } I \bullet \text{if } ([]i \bullet G_i \rightarrow P_i) \text{ fi }]\|$$

$$\sqsubseteq_J \quad \text{if } ([]i \bullet G'_i \rightarrow \|[\text{ inv } I \bullet P_i]\|) \text{ fi.}$$

Proof: Let $K \Rightarrow J$. Then

$\quad wp_K(lhs, \phi)$

$\equiv \quad (\bigvee i \bullet G_i) \wedge (\bigwedge i \bullet G_i \Rightarrow wp_{I \wedge K}(P_i, \phi))$

$\Rightarrow \quad \text{"assumptions, Theorem 1"}$

$\quad (\bigvee i \bullet G'_i) \wedge (\bigwedge i \bullet G'_i \Rightarrow wp_{I \wedge K}(P_i, \phi))$

$\equiv \quad wp_K(rhs, \phi).$

♡

Law 6 *Invariant elimination for assignment.* For any context J, provided $J \wedge I \Rightarrow I[w \backslash E]$,

$$\|[\text{ inv } I \bullet w := E]\| \sqsubseteq_J w := E.$$

Proof: Let $K \Rightarrow J$. Then

$\quad wp_K(\|[\text{ inv } I \bullet w := E]\|, \phi)$

$\equiv \quad wp_{I \wedge K}(w := E, \phi)$

$\equiv \quad I \wedge K \wedge (I \wedge K \Rightarrow \phi)[w \backslash E]$

$\Rightarrow \quad \text{"assumptions"}$

$\quad K \wedge (K \Rightarrow \phi)[w \backslash E]$

$\equiv \quad wp_K(w := E, \phi).$

♡

Law 7 *Invariant elimination for* **skip**. For any context J,

$$\|[\text{ inv } I \bullet \text{skip}]\| \sqsubseteq_J \text{skip}.$$

Proof: Trivial.

♡

We see in Section 8.2 a law that distributes **inv** over recursion; and there are analogs of Laws 6 and 7 that deal with **abort**, annotations, and specifications. All of those, together, allow **inv** to be eliminated by first distributing it towards the atomic statements of a program, then discharging certain proof obligations at each separately. That last step, of which Law 6 is an example, is like type-checking, to which finally we turn.

7 Type-checking

Type-checking is the automated application, say by a complier, of the procedure described in Section 6 — but in the special case of implicit invariants for typed local variables.

If the types can be made only in certain ways (for example, enumeration, Cartesian product, disjoint union, *etc.*), and the expressions E in assignments are restricted similarly, then it is decidable whether an expression E is of type T, given that we know the types of the constituents of E. Consider, for example, the typing context

$$a, b, c \in Z, \tag{3}$$

and the assignment $a := b + c$. For the elimination of the invariant (3), we require by Law 6

$$a, b, c \in Z \Rrightarrow b + c, b, c \in Z.$$

And that follows from $b, c \in Z \Rrightarrow b + c \in Z$, which can be built in to a compiler.

But now consider a more interesting case: let the invariant be $I \triangleq m, n \in N$. By Law 1 (taking *pre* to be *true*), we have

$$n: [n = m - 1] \quad \sqsubseteq_I \quad n := m - 1.$$

And so by Definition 6 and Theorems 4, 3, we have

$$|[\textbf{ var } m, n: N \bullet n: [n = m - 1] \,]|$$

$$\sqsubseteq \; |[\textbf{ var } m, n: N \bullet n := m - 1 \,]|.$$

To the experienced programmer, that looks unlikely: if the value of m is zero, surely the assignment will abort — yet the specification does not abort! And we are not saved either by (decidable) type checking, unless *all* such assignments are ill-typed: a type checker cannot know the actual value of m.

In fact, all such assignments are all ill-typed. Natural number subtraction is not integer subtraction: it differs exactly in the case where the result would be negative. Using $\ominus$ for natural number subtraction, the assignment $n := m \ominus 1$ is well typed, but the earlier refinement fails:

$$n: [n = m - 1] \quad \not\sqsubseteq_I \quad n := m \ominus 1.$$

And that is where it should fail.

Suppose, then, that we know m is positive. We must show

$$\{m > 0\} n: [n = m - 1] \quad \sqsubseteq_I \quad n := m \ominus 1,$$

and that follows from Law 1 provided

$$I \wedge m > 0 \Rrightarrow m - 1 = m \ominus 1.$$

The proviso is clearly true.

Fortunately, most operators can still be overloaded; we needn't distinguish natural and integer addition, for example. And some of the distinctions are already in widespread use: compare / and div.

Note further that Definition 6 introduces an initialising specification. That can be refined to an assignment, provided the type is non-empty — which, therefore, we require.

Thus, within the above constraints, we can view type-checking as the elimination of a specific kind of local invariant, and it can be done automatically by a compiler.

8 Recursion

8.1 Syntax and semantics

A recursive program is written

$$\text{mu } p \bullet C \text{ um,} \tag{4}$$

where p is a program name and C a program scheme probably containing p. For its meaning, we must understand C as a function from programs to programs: the application of C to the program X is just $C(X)$, the program left when p is replaced in C by X. The meaning of (4) is the least fixed-point of that function.

It is not the meanings of programs that must be monotonic for such least fixed points to exist; and indeed those meanings are not monotonic in their context argument. For example, from Figure 1 we have

$$wp_{false}(x := 0, x \neq 0) \equiv false$$
$$wp_{x \neq 0}(x := 0, x \neq 0) \equiv true$$
$$wp_{true}(x := 0, x \neq 0) \equiv false.$$

It is the program constructors that must be monotonic over programs; and their monotonicity is stated in Theorem 3. (The monotonicity of mu $\cdots$ um follows from the monotonicity of fix, the least fixed-point operator itself.)

8.2 Eliminating local invariants

We must extend Section 6 with a law that allows inv to be eliminated when it surrounds a recursion. This is the law:

Law 8 *Invariant elimination for recursion.* Let C and D be two program schemes, and for any program X let $C(X)$ and $D(X)$ be the programs resulting when the program name p is replaced by X. Suppose that for any program X,

$$\lvert[\text{ inv } I \bullet C(X) \,]\rvert \sqsubseteq_J D(\lvert[\text{ inv } I \bullet X \,]\rvert).$$

Then we may eliminate a surrounding invariant as follows:

$$\lvert[\text{ inv } I \bullet \text{mu } p \bullet C \text{ um }]\rvert \sqsubseteq_J \text{mu } p \bullet D \text{ um.}$$

Proof: Let $K \Rightarrow J$. Then

$$wp_K\,(\lVert\,\text{inv }I\bullet\text{mu }p\bullet C\text{ um }\rVert,\phi)$$
$$\equiv\quad wp_{K\,\wedge\,I}(\text{mu }p\bullet C\text{ um},\phi)$$
$$\equiv\quad \textit{fix }C\ (K\wedge I)\ \phi,$$

where we use C also for the *meaning* of the program scheme. (A more exact treatment would use semantic functions with environments, in the style of [17].) Since C is monotonic, we can continue

$$\equiv\quad \text{``for some ordinal }\beta\text{''}$$
$$(\bigvee_{\alpha<\beta} C^\alpha\text{ abort }(K\wedge I)\ \phi)$$
$$\equiv\quad (\bigvee_{\alpha<\beta} \lVert\,\text{inv }I\bullet C^\alpha\text{ abort }\rVert\ K\ \phi)$$
$$\Rightarrow\quad \text{``assumption, and transfinite induction over }\alpha\text{''}$$
$$(\bigvee_{\alpha<\beta} D^\alpha\,\lVert\,\text{inv }I\bullet\text{ abort }\rVert\ K\ \phi)$$
$$\equiv\quad (\bigvee_{\alpha<\beta} D^\alpha\text{ abort }K\ \phi)$$
$$\Rightarrow\quad wp_K(\text{mu }p\bullet D\text{ um},\phi).$$

$\heartsuit$

Given a program scheme C, in practice the D required by Law 8 is found as before: $\lVert\,\text{inv}\cdots\rVert$ is distributed inwards until it reaches the recursive call p; then it is removed. What results is D. An example is given in the next section.

8.3 Iteration

Iteration, written do $(\lVert i\bullet G_i\to P_i)$ od, is just an abbreviation for this recursion:

$$\begin{aligned}
&\text{mu }p\bullet\\
&\quad\text{if }(\lVert i\bullet G_i\to P_i;\ p)\\
&\quad\rVert\ \neg(\vee i\bullet G_i)\to\textbf{skip}\\
&\quad\textbf{fi}\\
&\text{um.}
\end{aligned}$$

That completes Figure 1 for Dijkstra'a original language. Now by Laws 5, 4, 7, we have that for any context J and program X, the program

$$\begin{aligned}
&\lVert\,\text{inv }I\bullet\\
&\quad\text{if }(\lVert i\bullet G_i\to P_i;\ X)\\
&\quad\rVert\ \neg(\vee i\bullet G_i)\to\textbf{skip}\\
&\quad\textbf{fi}\\
&\rVert
\end{aligned}$$

is refined under $\sqsubseteq_J$ by

$$\begin{aligned}
&\text{if }(\lVert i\bullet G_i'\to\lVert\,\text{inv }I\bullet P_i\,\rVert;\ \lVert\,\text{inv }I\bullet X\,\rVert)\\
&\rVert\ \neg(\vee i\bullet G_i')\to\textbf{skip}\\
&\textbf{fi},
\end{aligned}$$

provided that, for each i, $J \wedge I \Rightarrow (G_i \Leftrightarrow G_i')$. Law 8 then gives immediately that

$$\| [\text{ inv } I \bullet \text{do } ([]i \bullet G_i \to P_i) \text{ od}] \|$$
$$\sqsubseteq_J \quad \text{do } ([]i \bullet G_i' \to \| [\text{ inv } I \bullet P_i] \|) \text{ od},$$

under the same assumptions.

9 A discussion of motives

The definition of $wp_I(\sqcup, \sqcup)$ was suggested by a certain kind of data refinement. Let $P \leq P'$ mean that P is data-refined to P' under the transformation

(no abstract variables, no concrete variables, coupling invariant I).

Such data refinements are described in [7]. From the definitions there, we have that if $P \leq P'$ then for all ϕ,

$$I \wedge wp(P, \phi) \Rightarrow wp(P', I \wedge \phi).$$

It can be shown that the least-refined such P' is defined by

$$wp(P', \phi) \quad = \quad I \wedge wp(P, I \Rightarrow \phi), \tag{5}$$

and that is the motivation for Lemma 3. (Incidentally, there is a corresponding formula for data refinements in general: it is

$$(\exists a \bullet I \wedge wp(P, (\forall c \bullet I \Rightarrow \phi))).$$

We have just taken the special case in which the lists a and c of abstract and concrete variables are both empty.)

Equation (5) is where the definitions of Figure 1 and Section 3.1 come from, and it is the uniform application of that which gives an invariant-breaking assignment its miraculous semantics, just as ill-advised data refinements lead to miracles [8].

We know that data refinement has nice distribution properties, and that is why $\| [\text{ inv } I \bullet \cdots] \|$ does too. One can see

$$\| [\text{ inv } I \bullet P] \|$$

as the program got by distributing the data refinement, above, through P. And that is why Lemma 3 is true: such distribution can only refine the program.

10 Related work

The refinement calculus, first proposed by Back [1], has in fact been invented twice more [9, 13]. At Oxford it was made specifically for the rigorous development of programs from Z specifications [4, 16].

A prominent feature of Z specifications is the *schema* which, when used to describe abstract operations, carries an invariant around with it that includes type information and is maintained automatically. That is where we started.

Where we have finished is very similar to work by Lamport and Schneider [6]. Their **constraints** clause and our **and** declaration have the same effect; their *Constraint strengthening rule* is like our Law 2. Lamport and Schneider use *partial* correctness, however, and do not write specifications within their programs. Their constructions are defined within temporal logic; ours are defined by weakest preconditions.

Lamport and Schneider's use of partial correctness identifies aborting and miraculous behaviour, leading them to say that invariant-breaking assignments abort. For them, such programs establish *false* if they terminate — therefore they don't terminate. Ours "damn the torpedoes" and terminate anyway. Section 11 explains why.

Within our refinement calculus, Lamport and Schneider's constraint $x \perp y$ — "x and y are independent" — would be expressed instead as a dependency (their **may alias**). That dependency would in Definition 1 link the variables in the frame to the bound variables in its meaning, allowing a more general relationship than our present equality. The frame would be expanded, according to the aliasing dependencies, before being applied as a universal quantification. Finally, their proposed extension to generalised assignments $exp := exp'$ is already neatly done with specifications.

Invariants are used also by Reynolds [15], called *general invariants*, and are true from their point of occurrence to the end of the smallest enclosing block. But the *specification logic* does not give them a meaning, nor are they connected with type information. The temporary falsification of a general invariant is allowed, however, and we have not discussed that here: there are several approaches to pursue. Like Lamport and Schneider, Reynolds uses partial correctness.

11 Conclusions

Although the traditional $wp(\sqcup,\sqcup)$ is our $wp_{true}(\sqcup,\sqcup)$, the traditional $\sqsubseteq$ [1, 5, 9, 13] is *not* our $\sqsubseteq$. That is because Definition 7 insists that the implication hold for all contexts.

What have we lost? Not much. Here is an example; with our definition of refinement,

$$n := -1; \ n := 0 \quad \not\sqsubseteq \quad n := 0.$$

Just take the context $n \in \mathbb{N}$, and the left-hand side becomes miraculous: it cannot refine to code. But most refinement laws have *atomic* left-hand sides — after all, they are there to introduce structure, not remove it. And when the left-hand side is atomic, we do preserve the traditional refinement relation — because that is true for any data-refinement [3, 12, 1]. Thus most existing refinement laws remain valid. For example (the left-hand side is atomic), we still have

$$n := 0 \sqsubseteq n := -1; \ n := 0.$$

But the price of the miraculous assignment, when it appears to break the invariant, is the final type-checking. The "obvious" alternative is the operationally-motivated alternative definition

$$wp_I(x := E, \phi) \quad \hat{=} \quad I \wedge (I \wedge \phi)[x \backslash E].$$

All that does, however, is add the type-checking to Law 1, and we lose, *formally* at least, the ability to delay such checking until the final test for feasibility. More significant, however, is that using the above definition would not allow the refinement

$$x: [x = E] \quad \sqsubseteq \quad x := E.$$

(We assume that E contains no x.) For if that refinement were valid, then by Lemma 2 it would be valid in the context $x \neq E$ as well. But it can't be: in that context, the left-hand side is a miracle but, with the alternative definition of assignment, the right-hand side would abort.

The ability to factor "details" like feasibility, and hence type-checking, is essential in a practical method. Experienced programmers will only be impeded by continual checking of types: their programs tend to be well-typed anyway. And in cases of error, the compiler acts at the last minute, catching the mistake. Because they are experienced, that will happen rarely.

Inexperienced programmers, however, will waste a lot of time by leaving their feasibility and type checks till later. When eventually the check is made, and fails, all the intervening development must be discarded. Because they are inexperienced, that will happen often.

But we cannot exploit experience by allowing those having it to apply "only some of the rules". All programmers, experienced or not, must apply all of the rules; but for each, the set of rules to which "all" applies may be different. The high-performance rules are those from which all feasibility and type checks have been removed; the training rules have all the checks built in, and performance suffers. A mathematical factorisation is necessary to make that distinction reliably; the one we have chosen is close to what people do already.

Acknowledgement

I thank Paul Gardiner for his pervasive influence on this work, and Ian Hayes for his helpful comments.

References

[1] R.-J. Back. Correctness preserving program refinements: Proof theory and applications. Tract 131, Mathematisch Centrum, Amsterdam, 1980.

[2] E.W. Dijkstra. *A Discipline of Programming.* Prentice-Hall, Englewood Cliffs, 1976.

[3] P.H.B. Gardiner and C.C. Morgan. Data refinement of predicate transformers. Accepted by *Theoretical Computer Science.* Reprinted in [11].

[4] I.J. Hayes. *Specification Case Studies.* Prentice-Hall, London, 1987.

[5] E.C.R. Hehner. *The Logic of Programming.* Prentice-Hall, London, 1984.

[6] L. Lamport and F.B. Schneider. Constraints: a uniform approach to aliasing and typing. In *12th ACM Symposium on Principles of Programming Languages*, pages 205–216, New Orleans, January 1985.

[7] C.C. Morgan. Auxiliary variables in data refinement. *Inf. Proc. Lett.*, 29(6):293–296, December 1988. Reprinted in [11].

[8] C.C. Morgan. Data refinement using miracles. *Inf. Proc. Lett.*, 26(5):243–246, January 1988. Reprinted in [11].

[9] C.C. Morgan. The specification statement. *Trans. Prog. Lang. Sys.*, 10(3), July 1988. Reprinted in [11].

[10] C.C. Morgan and K.A. Robinson. Specification statements and refinement. *IBM Jnl. Res. Dev.*, 31(5), September 1987. Reprinted in [11].

[11] C.C. Morgan, K.A. Robinson, and P.H.B. Gardiner. On the refinement calculus. Technical Report PRG–70, Programming Research Group, 1988.

[12] J.M. Morris. Laws of data refinement. Accepted by *Acta Informatica*.

[13] J.M. Morris. A theoretical basis for stepwise refinement and the programming calculus. *Science of Computer Programming*, 9(3):298–306, December 1987.

[14] G. Nelson. A generalization of Dijkstra's calculus. Technical Report 16, Digital Systems Research Center, April 1987.

[15] J.C. Reynolds. *The Craft of Programming*. Prentice-Hall, London, 1981.

[16] J.M. Spivey. *The Z Notation: A Reference Manual*. Prentice-Hall, London, 1989.

[17] J.E. Stoy. *Denotational Semantics: the Scott-Strachey Approach to Programming Language Theory*. MIT Press, 1977.

Algorithm Theories and Design Tactics

Douglas R. Smith and Michael R. Lowry
Kestrel Institute
1801 Page Mill Road
Palo Alto, California 94304-1216 USA

Abstract

Algorithm theories represent the structure common to a class of algorithms, such as divide-and-conquer or backtrack. An algorithm theory for a class $\mathcal{A}$ provides the basis for design tactics - specialized methods for designing $\mathcal{A}$-algorithms from formal problem specifications. We illustrate this approach with recent work on the theory of global search algorithms and briefly mention several others. Several design tactics have been implemented in the KIDS/CYPRESS system and have been used to semiautomatically derive many algorithms.

1 Introduction

We describe an approach to the formal derivation of algorithms that is based on the notion of an *algorithm theory* which represents the structure common to a class of algorithms, such as divide-and-conquer or backtrack. Algorithm theories abstract away concerns about control strategy, target programming language, and, to some extent, the target architecture. These and other concerns can be factored in separately, thereby giving rise to a tree of alternative implementations. This separation of concerns reduces the problem of algorithm derivation to that of constructing an algorithm theory for a given problem. Furthermore, constructing an algorithm theory for a given problem is reduced to constructing a theory morphism from an abstract algorithm theory to the concrete domain theory. In this manner, we reuse the structure common to a class in the design process, only adding in the structure necessary for the particular problem. We have developed specialized construction methods, called *design tactics*, for various algorithm theories. We illustrate this approach with recent work on the theory of global search algorithms [18] and briefly mention theories of divide-and-conquer [16], local search [8, 9], and other classes of algorithms. We have implemented several of these design methods in the KIDS/CYPRESS system [19] and used them to semiautomatically derive many algorithms.

There are several advantages to representing the structure of a class of algorithms as a theory. Firstly, it abstracts away concerns about programming language and style (e.g., functional vs. logical vs. imperative, recursive vs. iterative), control strategy (e.g., top-down vs. bottom-up), and, to some extent, target architecture (e.g., sequential vs. parallel). These concerns can be factored in as later decisions in the design process. Secondly, once and for all we can derive abstract programs (schemes) as theorems in the abstract theory and then apply them to concrete problems. This allows us to reduce the problem of constructing a correct concrete algorithm to constructing an algorithm theory for a given problem. Thirdly, we can develop a generic and thus highly-reusable design tactics on the basis of the abstract theory. Those design steps that are common to all instances of the class can be done just once in the abstract theory. The tactics that we have developed to date are sound, well-motivated, and mostly automatic in their implemented form. Fourth, our approach has much in common with current approaches to abstract data types and algebraic specifications which provides opportunities for fruitful interactions in the future. For example, the concept of global search underlies a number of well-known data structures such as binary search trees, quad-trees, and B-trees. In the expanded setting of data structure design, the global search concept provides a way to structure and access a dictionary (a set plus access operation). Finally, algorithmic theories can be combined to allow the inference of hybrid algorithms.

Several well-known program derivation methodologies, e.g. [3, 10], are based on inference rules for various programming language constructs - rules for infering statement sequences, conditionals, loops, etc. Our complementary approach can be viewed as providing inference rules for various problem-solving methods or algorithmic paradigms. In a related approach, Bird [2] advocates a calculus of functional programs which exploits theorems relating problem structure to program structure.

Problems can be specified by means of a problem theory (Section 2). Designing an algorithm for a problem is mainly a matter of constructing an algorithm theory (Section 3). There are two ways to view this construction. From the point of view of the problem theory, the algorithm theory is an extension that provides just enough structure to support the construction of a concrete algorithm (Section 4). From the point of view of an abstract algorithm theory $\mathcal{A}$, the construction is a theory morphism or interpretation [8, 20]. These two points of views are tied together in the categorical concept of a pushout (Section 5). Constructing an algorithm theory for a given problem is accomplished by specialized design tactics (Section 5). These concepts are illustrated by application to the problem of enumerating cyclic difference sets [1].

2 Problem Theories and Extensions

We briefly review some concepts based on the abstract data type literature. A *theory* is a structure $\langle S, \Sigma, A \rangle$ consisting of sorts S, operations over those sorts Σ, and axioms A to constrain the meaning of the operations. A *theory morphism* maps from the sorts and operations of one theory to the sorts and expressions over the operations of another theory such that the image of each source theory axiom is valid in the target theory. A *parameterized theory* has formal parameters that are themselves theories [5]. The binding of actual values to formal parameters is accomplished by a theory morphism. Theory $T_2 = \langle S_2, \Sigma_2, A_2 \rangle$ *extends* (or is an *extension* of) theory $T_1 = \langle S_1, \Sigma_1, A_1 \rangle$ if $S_1 \subseteq S_2$, $\Sigma_1 \subseteq \Sigma_2$, and $E_1 \subseteq E_2$. An exension can be represented by a special theory morphism called an *inclusion* that takes each takes each sort and operation symbol to itself in the target theory. A category of theories can be formed by taking theories as objects, theory morphisms as arrows, and map composition as arrow composition.

Problem theories define a problem by specifying a domain of problem instances or inputs and the notion of what constitutes a solution to a given problem instance. Formally, a *problem theory* B has the following structure.

Sorts	D, R
Operations	$I : D \to Boolean$
	$O : D \times R \to Boolean$

The *input condition* $I(x)$ constrains the input domain D. The *output condition* $O(x, z)$ describes the conditions under which output domain value $z \in R$ is a *feasible solution* with respect to input $x \in D$. Theories of booleans and sets are implicitly imported. Problems of finding optimal feasible solutions can be treated as extensions of problem theory by adding a cost domain, cost function, and ordering on the cost domain (see [8, 18] for examples).

As a running example we use the problem of enumerating Cyclic Difference Sets (CDSs) [1, 14]. They are relatively rare sets that are somewhat analogous to primes in the natural numbers. The problem can be defined as follows. Given a modulus v, a set size k, and a constant ℓ, a $\langle v, k, \ell \rangle$-cyclic difference set C is a subset of $\{0..v-1\}$ that has size k. Furthermore, if we consider "rotating" C by adding an arbitrary constant i, where $i \bmod v \neq 0$, to each element yielding a new set D, then C and D have exactly ℓ elements in common. For example, the simplest CDS is the $\langle 7, 3, 1 \rangle$-cds $\{0,1,3\}$. It has the property that for any $i \in \{1..6\}$ that

$$size(\{0,1,3\} \cap \{i + j \bmod 6 \mid j \in \{0,1,3\}\}) = 1,$$

for example, for $i = 4$ we have $size(\{0,1,3\} \cap \{4,5,1\}) = 1$.

Cyclic difference sets have been used for coding satellite communications, creating masks for X-ray telescopes, and other applications. Baumert [1] list all known CDSs where $k \leq 100$. These known CDSs were found purely by mathematical construction. Below we describe the derivation of a program to enumerate CDSs. We have used this program to discover a previously unknown CDS: the $\langle 13, 4, 1 \rangle$-CDS: $\{0,1,4,6\}$.

The problem of enumerating cyclic difference sets can be specified via a theory morphism $\mathcal{B} \mapsto \mathcal{B}_{CDS}$.

$$
\begin{aligned}
\mathbf{D} &\mapsto Nat \times Nat \times Nat \\
\mathbf{I} &\mapsto \lambda \langle v, k, \ell \rangle.\, 1 \leq \ell \leq k < v \\
\mathbf{R} &\mapsto set(Nat) \\
\mathbf{O} &\mapsto \lambda \langle v, k, \ell \rangle, sub.\, sub \subseteq \{0..v-1\} \wedge size(sub) = k \\
&\qquad \wedge \forall (i)(\, i \in \{1..v-1\} \implies self\_overlap\_under\_rotation(i, v, sub) = \ell)\}.
\end{aligned}
$$

where we define

$$self\_overlap\_under\_rotation(i, v, S) = size(S \cap \{\, (a + i) \bmod v \mid a \in S \,\}).$$

Derived laws in $\mathcal{B}_{CDS}$ include

$$self\_overlap\_under\_rotation(i, v, \{\}) = 0$$

$$self\_overlap\_under\_rotation(i, v, \{0..v-1\}) = v$$

$$S \subseteq T \implies self\_overlap\_under\_rotation(i, v, S) \leq self\_overlap\_under\_rotation(i, v, T).$$

3   Algorithm Theories

An *algorithm theory* represents the essential structure of a certain class of algorithms. Algorithm theory $\mathcal{A}$ extends problem theory $\mathcal{B}$ with any additional sorts, operators, and axioms needed to support the correct construction of an $\mathcal{A}$ algorithm for the given problem. Algorithms theories can be arranged in a refinement hierarchy as in Figure 1. Below each algorithm theory in this hierarchy are listed various well-known classes of algorithms or computational paradigms that are based on it. In this section we present a theory for the class of global search algorithms.

Global search generalizes the computational paradigms of binary search, backtracking, branch-and-bound, constraint satisfaction, heuristic search, and others. The basic idea of global search is to represent and manipulate sets of candidate solutions. The principal operations are to **Extract** candidate solutions from a set and to **Split** a set into subsets. Derived operations include various *filters* which are used to eliminate sets containing no feasible or optimal solutions. Global search algorithms work as follows: starting from an initial set that contains all solutions to the given problem instance, the algorithm repeatedly extracts candidates, splits sets, and eliminates sets via filters until no sets remain to be split. The process is often described as a tree (or DAG) search in which a node represents a set of candidates and an arc represents the split relationship between set and subset. The filters serve to prune off branches of the tree that cannot lead to solutions.

The sets of candidate solutions are often infinite and even when finite they are rarely represented extensionally. Thus the intuitive notion of global search can be formalized as the extension of problem theory with an abstract data type of intensional representations called *descriptors*. In addition to the extraction and splitting operations mentioned above, the type also includes a *satisfaction* predicate that determines when a candidate solution is in the set denoted by a descriptor. For the sake of simplifying the presentation we will use the term *space* (or *subspace*) to denote both the descriptor and the set that it denotes. It should be clear from context which meaning is intended.

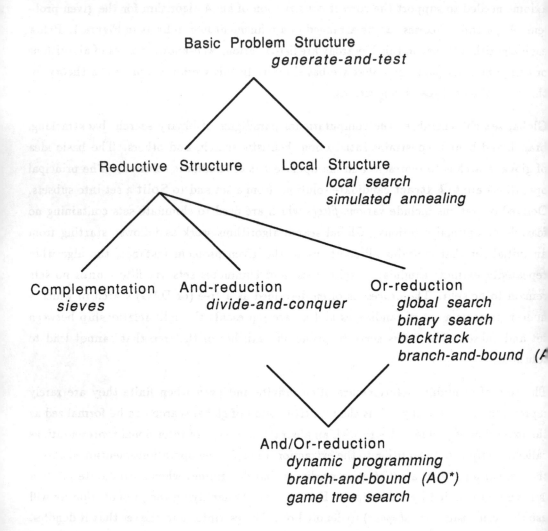

Figure 1: Refinement Hierarchy of Algorithm Theories

Formally, $gs-theory$ $\mathcal{G}$ consists of the following structure:

Sorts $\mathbf{D}, \mathbf{R}, \hat{\mathbf{R}}$
Operations
$\quad$ $\mathbf{I} : \mathbf{D} \to Boolean$
$\quad$ $\mathbf{O} : \mathbf{D} \times \mathbf{R} \to Boolean$
$\quad$ $\hat{\mathbf{r}}_0 : \mathbf{D} \to \hat{\mathbf{R}}$
$\quad$ $\mathbf{Satisfies} : \mathbf{R} \times \hat{\mathbf{R}} \to Boolean$
$\quad$ $\mathbf{Split} : \mathbf{D} \times \hat{\mathbf{R}} \times \hat{\mathbf{R}} \to Boolean$
$\quad$ $\mathbf{Extract} : \mathbf{R} \times \hat{\mathbf{R}} \to Boolean$

Axioms
$\quad$ GS1. $\quad \mathbf{O}(\mathbf{x}, \mathbf{z}) \implies \mathbf{Satisfies}(\mathbf{z}, \hat{\mathbf{r}}_0(\mathbf{x}))$
$\quad$ GS2. $\quad \mathbf{Satisfies}(\mathbf{z}, \hat{\mathbf{r}}) \iff \exists k \in Nat \; \exists \hat{\mathbf{s}} \in \hat{\mathbf{R}} \, [\, \mathbf{Split}^k(\mathbf{x}, \hat{\mathbf{r}}, \hat{\mathbf{s}}) \land \mathbf{Extract}(\mathbf{z}, \hat{\mathbf{s}}) \,]$

where $\hat{\mathbf{R}}$ is the domain of meaningful descriptors, $\hat{\mathbf{r}}$, $\hat{\mathbf{s}}$, and $\hat{\mathbf{t}}$ vary over descriptors, $\hat{\mathbf{r}}_0(\mathbf{x})$ is the descriptor of the initial set of candidate solutions, $\mathbf{Satisfies}(\mathbf{z}, \hat{\mathbf{r}})$ means that $\mathbf{z}$ is in the set denoted by descriptor $\hat{\mathbf{r}}$ or that $\mathbf{z}$ satisfies the constraints that $\hat{\mathbf{r}}$ represents, $\mathbf{Split}(\mathbf{x}, \hat{\mathbf{r}}, \hat{\mathbf{s}})$ means that $\hat{\mathbf{s}}$ is a subspace of $\hat{\mathbf{r}}$ with respect to input $\mathbf{x}$, and $\mathbf{Extract}(\mathbf{z}, \hat{\mathbf{r}})$ means that $\mathbf{z}$ is directly extractable from $\hat{\mathbf{r}}$. Axiom GS1 gives the denotation of the initial descriptor — all feasible solutions are contained in the initial space. Axiom GS2 gives the denotation of an arbitrary descriptor $\hat{\mathbf{r}}$ — an output object $\mathbf{z}$ is in the set denoted by $\hat{\mathbf{r}}$ if and only if $\mathbf{z}$ can be extracted after finitely many applications of $\mathbf{Split}$ to $\hat{\mathbf{r}}$ where

$$\mathbf{Split}^0(\mathbf{x}, \hat{\mathbf{r}}, \hat{\mathbf{t}}) \iff \hat{\mathbf{r}} = \hat{\mathbf{t}}$$

and for all $k \in Nat$

$$\mathbf{Split}^{k+1}(\mathbf{x}, \hat{\mathbf{r}}, \hat{\mathbf{t}}) \iff \exists \hat{\mathbf{s}} \in \hat{\mathbf{R}} \, [\, \mathbf{Split}(\mathbf{x}, \hat{\mathbf{r}}, \hat{\mathbf{s}}) \land \mathbf{Split}^k(\mathbf{x}, \hat{\mathbf{s}}, \hat{\mathbf{t}}) \,].$$

Note that all variables are assumed to be universally quantified unless explicitly specified otherwise.

Example: Enumerating Subsets

Consider the problem of enumerating subsets of a given finite set S. A space can be described by a pair $\langle U, V \rangle$ of disjoint sets that denotes the set of all subsets of $U \uplus V$ that extend U. The descriptor for the initial space is just $\langle \{ \, \}, S \rangle$. Formally, the descriptor $\langle U, V \rangle$ denotes the set

$$\{T \mid U \subseteq T \; \land \; T \subseteq V \uplus U\}.$$

Splitting is accomplished by either adding or not adding an arbitrary element $a \in V$ to U. If V is empty then the subset U can be extracted as a solution. This global search theory for enumerating subsets $\mathcal{G}_{subsets}$ can be presented via a theory morphism from abstract gs-theory $\mathcal{G}$.

$$
\begin{array}{rcl}
\mathbf{D} & \mapsto & set(\alpha) \\
\mathbf{R} & \mapsto & set(\alpha) \\
\mathbf{I} & \mapsto & \lambda S.true \\
\mathbf{O} & \mapsto & \lambda S, T.\ T \subseteq S \\
\mathbf{\hat{R}} & \mapsto & \lambda S.\ \{\langle U, V \rangle \mid U \uplus V \subseteq S \wedge U \cap V = \{\}\} \\
\mathbf{Satisfies} & \mapsto & \lambda T.\langle U, V \rangle.\ U \subseteq T \ \wedge\ T \subseteq V \uplus U \\
\mathbf{\hat{r}_0} & \mapsto & \lambda S.\ \langle emptyset, S \rangle \\
\mathbf{Split} & \mapsto & \lambda S.\langle U, V \rangle, \langle U', V' \rangle.\ V \neq \{\} \ \wedge\ a = arb(V) \\
& & \quad \wedge\ (\langle U', V' \rangle = \langle U, V - a \rangle \ \vee\ \langle U', V' \rangle = \langle U + a, V - a \rangle) \\
\mathbf{Extract} & \mapsto & \lambda T.\langle U, V \rangle.\ empty(V) \ \wedge\ T = U
\end{array}
$$

The descriptor type is dependent on input values in this theory.
End of Example.

In addition to the above components of global search theory, there are various derived operations which may play a role in producing an efficient algorithm. Filters, described next, are crucial to the efficiency of a global search algorithm. Filters correspond to the notion of pruning branches in backtrack algorithms and to pruning via lower bounds and dominance relations in branch-and-bound. A *feasibility filter* $\psi : \mathbf{D} \times \mathbf{\hat{R}} \to Boolean$ is used to eliminate spaces from further processing. The *ideal feasibility filter* decides the question "Does there exist a feasible solution in space $\mathbf{\hat{r}}$?", or, to be more precise,

$$\exists \mathbf{z} \in \mathbf{R} \ [\ \mathbf{Satisfies(z, \hat{r})} \ \wedge \ \mathbf{O(x, z)}\ ]. \tag{1}$$

However, to use (1) directly as a filter would usually be too expensive, so instead we use various approximations to it. These approximations can be classified as either

1. *necessary feasibility filters* where $(1) \implies \psi(\mathbf{x}, \mathbf{\hat{r}})$;

2. *sufficient feasibility filters* where $\psi(\mathbf{x}, \mathbf{\hat{r}}) \implies (1)$;

3. *heuristic feasibility filters* which bear other relationships to (1).

Necessary filters only eliminate spaces that do not contain solutions, so they are generally useful. Sufficient filters are mainly used when only one solution is desired. Heuristic filters offer no guarantees, but a fast heuristic approximation to (1) may have the best performance in practice.

4 Program Theories

A program theory represents an executable program and its properties such as invariants, termination, and correctness with respect to a problem theory. Formally, a *program theory* $\mathcal{P}$ is parameterized with an algorithm theory or, more generally, an extended problem theory. The sort and operator symbols of the theory parameter can be used in defining programs in $\mathcal{P}$. Parameter instantiation, which is expressed as a theory morphism from the parameter theory, results in the replacement of each sort and operator symbol in $\mathcal{P}$ by its image under the theory morphism. The program theory introduces operator symbols for various functions and defines them and their correctness conditions via axioms. The main function would be defined as follows in the case where all feasible solutions are desired.

> **Operations** $\mathbf{F} : \mathbf{D} \rightarrow set(\mathbf{R})$
>
> $\cdots$
>
> **Axioms** $\forall \mathbf{x} \in \mathbf{D} \, [\, I(\mathbf{x}) \implies \mathbf{F}(\mathbf{x}) = \{ \mathbf{z} \mid O(\mathbf{x}, \mathbf{z}) \} \,]$
>
> $\forall \mathbf{x} \in \mathbf{D} \, [\, I(\mathbf{x}) \implies \mathbf{F}(\mathbf{x}) = Body(\mathbf{x}) \,]$
>
> $\cdots$

where *Body* is code that can be executed to compute **F**. In order to express *Body* it is generally necessary to import a programming language and extend it with specification language features. In this paper we assume a straightforward mathematical language that uses set-theoretic data types and operators and serves both as specification and program language. Consistency of the program theory entails that the function computed by the code (*Body*) must return all feasible solutions. The axioms for other functions would be similar.

Program theories can be expressed in a more conventional format:

```
function  F (x : D) : set(R)
   where  I(x)
   returns  {z | O(x, z)}
   = Body(x)
```

Depending on choices of control strategy and programming language, a range of abstract programs can be inferred in abstract global search theory [18]. We are interested in those program theories whose consistency can be established for all possible input theories; that is, those program theories whose consistency can be established solely on the basis of the parameter theory. One such theory is presented below. Given a global search theory, the following theorem shows how to infer a correct program for enumerating all feasible solutions. In this theorem the auxiliary function $F\_gs(x, \hat{r})$ computes the set of all feasible solutions z in space $\hat{r}$.

Theorem 4.1 *Let $\mathcal{G}$ be a global search theory. If Φ is a necessary feasibility filter then the following program specification is consistent*

> **function** $F(x : D) : set(R)$
> **where** $I(x)$
> **returns** $\{z \mid O(x, z)\}$
> $= \{z \mid \Phi(x, \hat{r}_0(x)) \wedge z \in F\_gs(x, \hat{r}_0(x))\}$

> **function** $F\_gs(x : D, \hat{r} : \hat{R}) : set(R)$
> **where** $I(x) \wedge \Phi(x, \hat{r})$
> **returns** $\{z \mid \text{Satisfies}(z, \hat{r}) \wedge O(x, z)\}$
> $= \{z \mid \text{Extract}(z, \hat{r}) \wedge O(x, z)\}$
> $\cup \, reduce(\cup, \{ F\_gs(x, \hat{s}) \mid \text{Split}(x, \hat{r}, \hat{s}) \wedge \Phi(x, \hat{s})\}).$

The proof may be found in [18]. In words, the abstract global search program works as follows. On input x the program F calls F_gs with the initial space $\hat{r}_0(x)$ if the filter holds (otherwise there are no feasible solutions and the set-former evaluates to the emptyset). The program $F\_gs(x, \hat{r})$ unions together two sets; (1) all solutions that can be directly extracted from the space $\hat{r}$, and (2) the union of all solutions found recursively in spaces $\hat{s}$ that are obtained by splitting $\hat{r}$ and that survive the filter. Note that Φ becomes an input invariant in F_gs.

5   Design Tactics

Theorem 4.1 and its analogues reduce the problem of constructing a program to the problem of constructing an algorithm theory for a given problem F. The task of constructing an $\mathcal{A}$-algorithm theory for F is described by the following commutative diagram (a pushout in the category of theories).

$$
\begin{array}{ccc}
\mathcal{B} & \xrightarrow{\;m\;} & \mathcal{B}_F \\
\downarrow{\scriptstyle e} & & \downarrow{\scriptstyle e'} \\
\mathcal{A} & \xrightarrow{\;m'\;} & \mathcal{A}_F
\end{array}
$$

where e and e' are inclusions (theory extensions) and m and m' are theory morphisms. That is, the construction of an $\mathcal{A}$-theory for F can be viewed both as an extension of $\mathcal{B}_F$ and as a theory morphism $\mathcal{A} \mapsto \mathcal{A}_F$.

For each of several algorithm theories that we have explored we have developed specialized design tactics. An $\mathcal{A}$-design tactic constructs an $\mathcal{A}$-algorithm theory for a given problem theory. Our tactic for designing global search algorithms relies on a deductive inference system and a knowledge base of standard gs-theories for common domains. The steps of the tactic are (1) to select and specialize a standard gs-theory, (2) to infer various filters, (3) to infer a concrete program, and (4) to perform program optimizations.

We describe first how to specialize a gs-theory to a given problem theory. Let $\mathcal{G}_G$ be a gs-theory whose components are denoted $\mathbf{D}_G, \mathbf{R}_G, \mathbf{O}_G, \mathbf{Satisfies}_G$, etc., and let $\mathcal{B}_F$ be a given problem theory with components $\mathbf{D}_F, \mathbf{R}_F, \mathbf{I}_F, \mathbf{O}_F$. The problem theory $\mathcal{B}_G$ generalizes $\mathcal{B}_F$ if for every input x to F there is an input y to G such that the set of feasible solutions $G(y)$ is a superset of $F(x)$; formally

$$\forall \mathbf{x} \in \mathbf{D}_F \, \exists \mathbf{y} \in \mathbf{D}_G \, \forall \mathbf{z} \in \mathbf{R}_F \, [\mathbf{R}_F \subseteq \mathbf{R}_G \, \wedge \, (\mathbf{O}_F(\mathbf{x}, \mathbf{z}) \Rightarrow \mathbf{O}_G(\mathbf{y}, \mathbf{z}))] \qquad (2)$$

Verifying (2) provides a substitution θ for the input variables of $\mathcal{B}_G$ in terms of the input variables of F. The type and number of input variables can differ between $\mathcal{B}_G$ and $\mathcal{B}_F$, as in the example below. The gs-theory $\mathcal{G}_F$ is obtained by applying substitution θ across $\mathcal{G}_G$. To see that the axioms GS1 and GS2 hold for $\mathcal{G}_F$ note that we have replaced the input variables of $\mathcal{G}_G$ with terms which take on a subset of their previous values.

Example: Cyclic Difference Sets.

The gs-theory $\mathcal{G}_{subsets}$ generalizes the CDS specification. To see this, first instantiate (2)

$\forall \langle v, k, \ell \rangle \in \{ \langle v, k, \ell \rangle \mid 1 \leq \ell \leq k < v \}$
$\exists S \in set(Nat)$
$\forall Sub \in set(Nat)$
  $[Sub \subseteq \{0..v-1\} \, \wedge \, size(sub) = k$
  $\wedge \, \forall(i)(\, i \in \{1..v-1\} \implies self\_overlap\_under\_rotation(i, v, sub) = \ell)$
  $\implies Sub \subseteq S]$

The proof is trivial and yields the substitution

$$\theta = \{ S \mapsto \{0..v-1\} \}.$$

This substitution is a critical translation between the problem theory $\mathcal{B}_{subsets}$, which takes a single set-valued argument S, and $\mathcal{B}_{CDS}$, which takes three arguments v, k, ℓ. After applying these substitutions to $\mathcal{G}_{subsets}$, we obtain the following specialized gs-theory $\mathcal{G}_{CDS}$ for cyclic difference sets.

$$
\begin{aligned}
\mathbf{D} &\mapsto Nat \times Nat \times Nat \\
\mathbf{I} &\mapsto \lambda\langle v, k, \ell\rangle. \, 1 \leq \ell \leq k < v \\
\mathbf{R} &\mapsto set(Nat) \\
\mathbf{O} &\mapsto \lambda\langle v, k, \ell\rangle, sub. \, Sub \subseteq \{0..v-1\} \\
&\qquad \wedge \, size(Sub) = k \\
&\qquad \wedge \, \forall(i)(\, i \in \{1..v-1\} \implies self\_overlap\_under\_rotation(i, v, sub) \\
\mathbf{\hat{R}} &\mapsto \lambda\langle v, k, \ell\rangle. \{\langle U, V\rangle \mid U \uplus V \subseteq \{0..v-1\} \wedge U \cap V = \{\}\} \\
\mathbf{Satisfies} &\mapsto \lambda Sub, \langle U, V\rangle. \, U \subseteq Sub \, \wedge \, Sub \subseteq V \uplus U \\
\mathbf{\hat{r}_0} &\mapsto \lambda\langle v, k, \ell\rangle. \langle emptyset, \{0..v-1\}\rangle \\
\mathbf{Split} &\mapsto \lambda\langle v, k, \ell\rangle, \langle U, V\rangle, \langle U', V'\rangle. \, V \neq \{\} \, \wedge \, a = arb(V) \\
&\qquad \wedge \, (\langle U', V'\rangle = \langle U, V - a\rangle \, \vee \, \langle U', V'\rangle = \langle U + a, V - a\rangle) \\
\mathbf{Extract} &\mapsto \lambda Sub, \langle U, V\rangle. \, empty(V) \, \wedge \, Sub = U
\end{aligned}
$$

The next step in constructing a global search theory is to derive filters. For this step we need an inference system capable of deriving necessary or sufficient conditions.

Example: Cyclic Difference Sets.
We can obtain a feasibility filter for *CDS* by deriving a necessary condition of the expression

$$
\begin{aligned}
&U \subseteq Sub \subseteq V \uplus U \\
&\wedge \, Sub \subseteq \{0..v-1\} \, \wedge \, size(Sub) = k \\
&\wedge \, \forall(i)(\, i \in \{1..v-1\} \implies self\_overlap\_under\_rotation(i, v, sub) = \ell)
\end{aligned}
$$

which is obtained by instantiating (1). Furthermore we are only interested in necessary conditions expressed over the variables $\{v, k, \ell, U, V\}$. The inference process may exploit the assumptions $1 \leq \ell \leq k < v$ and $U \uplus V \subseteq \{0..v-1\}$ (the input conditions **I** and the data type invariants of $\mathbf{\hat{R}}$).

The derivation of the filters exploits two montonicity laws. One,

$$
S \subseteq T \implies size(S) \leq size(T)
$$

is from the domain of set theory, and the other

$$
S \subseteq T \implies self\_overlap\_under\_rotation(i, v, S) \leq self\_overlap\_under\_rotation(i, v, T)
$$

is from the domain theory of the CDS problem. Inference proceeds as follows.

$U \subseteq Sub \subseteq V \uplus U$

$\implies size(U) \leq size(Sub) \leq size(V \uplus U)$ (by monotonicity of $size$)

$\iff size(U) \leq k \leq size(V) + size(U)$ using $k = size(Sub)$.

Thus we obtain $size(U) \leq k \leq size(V) + size(U)$ as one necessary feasibility filter. In words, the partial set being incrementally constructed (U) must have at most k elements, but there must be at least k elements between U and the pool of remaining elements V. Another filter can be derived as follows.

$U \subseteq Sub \subseteq V \uplus U$

$\implies \forall(i)(\ i \in \{1..v - 1\} \implies$
$\quad self\_overlap\_under\_rotation(i, v, U)$
$\quad \leq self\_overlap\_under\_rotation(i, v, Sub)$
$\quad \leq self\_overlap\_under\_rotation(i, v, V \uplus U))$
$\qquad$ (by monotonicity of $self\_overlap\_under\_rotation$)

$\iff \forall(i)(\ i \in \{1..v - 1\} \implies$
$\quad self\_overlap\_under\_rotation(i, v, U)$
$\quad \leq \ell \leq self\_overlap\_under\_rotation(i, v, V \uplus U))$

Thus we obtain

$\forall(i)(\ i \in \{1..v - 1\} \implies$
$\quad self\_overlap\_under\_rotation(i, v, U)$
$\quad \leq \ell \leq self\_overlap\_under\_rotation(i, v, V \uplus U))$

as another necessary feasibility filter. In words, the partial solution U must have a self-overlap of at most ℓ and the combined set $U \uplus V$ must have a self-overlap of at most ℓ.

Applying Theorem 4.1 we obtain the consistent program specification in Figure 2. Note that this program specification includes not only the input and output conditions of the function, but also invariants that characterize the meaning of all data structures. These invariants are crucial to later optimizations.
End of example.

---

function $CDS(v, k, \ell)$
   where $1 \le \ell \le k < v$
   returns $\{sub \mid sub \subseteq \{0..v - 1\} \;\wedge\; size(sub) = k$
        $\wedge \; \forall(i)(\; i \in \{1..v - 1\} \implies self\_overlap\_under\_rotation(i, v, sub) = \ell)\}$
$= \;\; \{sub \mid size(\{\,\}) \le k \le size(\{\,\}) + size(\{0..v - 1\})$
        $\wedge \; \forall(i)(\; i \in \{1..v - 1\} \implies self\_overlap\_under\_rotation(i, v, \{\,\}) \le \ell$
            $\wedge \; \ell \le self\_overlap\_under\_rotation(i, v, \{\,\} \uplus \{0..v - 1\}))$
        $\wedge \; CDS\_gs(v, k, \ell, \{\,\}, \{0..v - 1\}))\}$

function $CDS\_gs(v, k, \ell, U, V)$
   where $1 \le \ell \le k < v \;\wedge\; V \uplus U \subseteq \{0..v - 1\}$
     $\wedge \; size(U) \le k \le size(U) + size(V)$
     $\wedge \; \forall(i)(\; i \in \{1..v - 1\} \implies self\_overlap\_under\_rotation(i, v, U) \le \ell$
            $\wedge \; \ell \le self\_overlap\_under\_rotation(i, v, U \uplus V))$
   returns $\{\; sub \mid U \subseteq sub \subseteq V \uplus U \;\wedge\; size(sub) = k$
        $\wedge \; \forall(i)(\; i \in \{1..v - 1\} \implies self\_overlap\_under\_rotation(i, v, sub) = \ell)\}$
$= \{sub \mid empty(V) \;\wedge\;\; sub = U$
      $\wedge \; sub \subseteq \{0..v - 1\}$
      $\wedge \; size(sub) = k$
      $\wedge \; \forall(i)(\; i \in \{1..v - 1\} \implies self\_overlap\_under\_rotation(i, v, sub) = \ell)\}$
   $\cup \; reduce(\cup, \; \{CDS\_gs(v, k, \ell, U', V') \mid$
          $V \ne \{\,\} \;\wedge\; a = arb(V)$
             $\wedge \; (\langle U', V' \rangle = \langle U, V - a \rangle \;\vee\; \langle U', V' \rangle = \langle U + a, V - a \rangle)$
             $\wedge \; size(U') \le k \le size(U') + size(V')$
        $\wedge \; \forall(i)(\; i \in \{1..v - 1\} \implies self\_overlap\_under\_rotation(i, v, U') \le \ell$
             $\wedge \; \ell \le self\_overlap\_under\_rotation(i, v, U' \uplus V'))\}).$

Figure 2: Cyclic Difference Set Algorithm

The filter Φ will often dramatically reduce the amount of work needed to enumerate the feasible space. One feature of necessary filters is that one, *true*, is immediately available; stronger filters are obtained with more investment of computational resource at design-time.

Following the production of a concrete global search program, there are typically many opportunities for program optimization. These tend to follow a stereotypic order: simplifying the body of programs with respect to their input assumptions/data structure invariants, applying finite differencing, partial evaluation, data structure refinement, and compilation. For example, in *CDS* the expression

$$self\_overlap\_under\_rotation(i, v, \{\ \}) \leq \ell \leq self\_overlap\_under\_rotation(i, v, \{0..v-1\})$$

simplifies to *true* using the laws

$$self\_overlap\_under\_rotation(i, v, \{\ \}) = 0$$

and

$$self\_overlap\_under\_rotation(i, v, \{0..v-1\}) = v$$

and the input condition $1 \leq \ell \leq v$. For another example, in *CDS_gs* the expressions

$$self\_overlap\_under\_rotation(i, v, U')$$

and

$$self\_overlap\_under\_rotation(i, v, U' \uplus V')$$

can be maintained incrementally using the technique of finite differencing [13]. Examples of derivations that present various optimizations in more detail may be found in [18, 19].

6 KIDS

We have implemented the global search design tactic and various optimization techniques in the KIDS/CYPRESS system [18, 19] and used it to design dozens of algorithms.

Implementation serves to check on the effectiveness of our derivations and to uncover issues that might be overlooked when doing derivations on paper. We have been able to derive a wide variety of algorithms without having to rely on the programmer supplying invariants, generalizations, or other such "eureka" steps. All interaction with the system during design and optimization involves the use of a mouse to select program expressions or items from a machine-generated menu. We hope to demonstrate that interaction at this level can be natural enough to pose successful explanations of the derivation process and that the tactics can be made both efficient enough and comprehensive enough to be useful for routine programming.

The user goes through the following steps in using KIDS for algorithm design.

1. *Define terms* - The user builds up a domain theory by defining appropriate terms. In this paper we defined the term *self_overlap_under_rotation*.

2. *Provide laws* - The user currently must provide derived laws that allow reasoning about the derived terms at a high level. Our experience has been that distributive and monotonicity laws provide almost all of the laws that are needed to support design and optimization.

3. *Create a specification* - The user enters a specification in a general but stylized format that is easily converted to a problem theory.

4. *Apply a design tactic* - The user selects a design tactic from a menu and applies to a specification by pointing to it with a mouse. Subsequent steps describe the global search design tactic.

5. *Specialize a known gs-theory* - The system presents a menu of gs-theories that are currently in its library and the user selects one. It is automatically matched (by instantiating and verifying (2)) and specialized to the given problem.

6. *Derive filters* - The tactic then automatically derives filters by exhaustively searching to a fixed inference depth all necessary conditions of (1). The user is then presented with a menu of candidate filters and must select a subset (any subset will yield a correct algorithm). The user also has the option of having the search for necessary conditions continue to greater depths. Generally the stronger the filter the better, although one has to trade off filtering power with the cost of executing the filter. Currently this step takes the bulk of the design time - about 10 minutes for the CDS problem. Mechanisms for automating the selection of strongest filters are known and would make use of dependency-tracking in the inference system.

7. *Instantiate a program* - The user is presented with a menu of program theories (schemes) that embody different control strategies and possibly different languages. Having selected one, the resulting programs and their problem theories and invariants are displayed.

8. *Apply optimizations and compile* - The KIDS system allows the application of optimization techniques such as simplification, finite differencing, partial evaluation, loop fusion, iterator inversion, and others. The user selects an optimization method from a menu and applies it by pointing at a program expression. Each of the optimization methods are fully automatic and, with the exception of simplification (which is arbitrarily hard) return instantly. Compilation is performed by the same mechanism.

We have run the partially optimized CDS program on a number of inputs, and were surprised to discover a cyclic difference set that was previously unknown (according to [ ]): the $\langle 13, 4, 1\rangle$-CDS: $\{0,1,4,6\}$. Other problems treated by specializing the subset theory $\mathcal{G}_{subsets}$ include set covers, binary knapsack, k-clique, vertex covers, and k-subset problems. As of early 1989 over two dozen global search algorithms have been designed and optimized using the KIDS system.

Other Algorithm Theories

A divide-and-conquer algorithm can be treated as a homomorphism from a decomposition algebra on the input domain of a problem to a composition algebra on its output domain [15]. One tactic for designing a divide-and-conquer algorithm involves selecting a simple or standard decomposition algebra from a library and then using the homomorphism condition to derive a specification for the corresponding composition algebra on the output domain. Another useful tactic is to select a simple composition algebra and derive a specification for a decomposition algebra on the input domain. We have implemented these tactics and used them to derive dozens of algorithms [16], including recently one that was previously unknown and substantially faster than previously known algorithms [7].

Local search algorithms are based on a discrete neighborhood structure that is imposed on the output domain. Examples include steepest ascent algorithms, simulated annealing, and many network flow algorithms. We have developed a theory of local search and a design tactic based on it [8, 9]. The implemented tactic has been used to derive a variant of the classic simplex algorithm for linear programming.

Other examples of theories that relate problem structure to algorithm structure can be found in the literature, although only recently has there been much interest in using these theories as a basis for formal derivation of algorithms as opposed to analysis or verification. Bellman's principle of optimality, if suitably formalized, is a sufficient condition for solution by dynamic programming [7]. Various theories of branch-and-bound algorithms have been presented [6, 11, 12]. Matroids [4] provide sufficient structure for an optimization problem to be solved by a greedy algorithm. Bird [2] presents algorithm theorems for special cases of greedy and dynamic programming algorithms and applies them to a coding problem.

8 Concluding Remarks

Algorithm design can be treated as the construction of an algorithm theory which extends a problem theory with the structure of a certain class of algorithms. We presented one special design tactic for constructing global search theories and used it to derive an algorithm for enumerating cyclic difference sets. Theorem 4.1 and its analogues mediate the transition from an algorithm theory to a concrete program by factoring in commitments to control strategy and target language.

Our specialized design tactics should be useful in many formal approaches to programming. For those algorithms that can be derived via tactics the resulting derivations are shorter, simpler, and more motivated than they would be if derived from first principles or in a more general-purpose calculus of programs. We cannot now claim that all algorithms can be naturally derived as instances of various well-known programming paradigms. Therefore one might want to embed the tactics in a more general derivation methodology.

Acknowledgements

This paper benefited from helpful comments by Richard Bird on an earlier draft and from discussions with Joseph Goguen. This research was supported in part by the Office of Naval Research under Contract N00014-87-K-0550 and in part by the Air Force Office of Scientific Research under Contract F49620-85-C-0015.

References

[1] BAUMERT, L. D. *Cyclic Difference Sets*. Springer-Verlag, Berlin, 1971. Lecture Notes in Mathematics, Vol. 182.

[2] BIRD, R. *A Calculus of Functions for Program Derivation*. Tech. Rep. PRG-64, Oxford University, Programming Research Group, December 1987.

[3] DIJKSTRA, E. W. *A Discipline of Programming*. Prentice-Hall, Englewood Cliffs, NJ, 1976.

[4] EDMONDS, J. Matroids and the greedy algorithm. *Mathematical Programming 1* (1971), 127–136.

[5] GOGUEN, J. A., AND WINKLER, T. *Introducing OBJ3*. Tech. Rep. SRI-CSL-88-9, SRI International, Menlo Park, California, 1988.

[6] IBARAKI, T. Branch-and-bound procedures and state space representation of combinatorial optimization problems. *Information and Control 36* (1978), 1–36.

[7] KARP, R., AND HELD, M. Finite state processes and dynamic programming. *SIAM Journal of Applied Mathematics 15* (1967), 693–718.

[8] LOWRY, M. R. Algorithm synthesis through problem reformulation. In *Proceedings of the 1987 National Conference on Artificial Intelligence* (Seattle, WA, July 13–17, 1987). Technical Report KES.U.87.10, Kestrel Institute, August 1987.

[9] LOWRY, M. R. *Algorithm Synthesis Through Problem Reformulation*. PhD thesis, Stanford University, 1989.

[10] MANNA, Z., AND WALDINGER, R. A deductive approach to program synthesis. *ACM Transactions on Programming Languages and Systems 2*, 1 (January 1980), 90–121.

[11] MITTEN, L. G., AND WARBURTON, A. R. *Implicit Enumeration Procedures*. Tech. Rep. Working Paper 251, University of British Columbia, 1973.

[12] NAU, D., KUMAR, V., AND KANAL, L. General branch and bound and its relation to A* and AO*. *Artificial Intelligence 23*, 1 (May 1984), 29–58.

[13] PAIGE, R., AND KOENIG, S. Finite differencing of computable expressions. *ACM Transactions on Programming Languages and Systems 4*, 3 (July 1982), 402–454.

[14] SKINNER, G. K. X-ray imaging with coded masks. *Scientific American 259*, 2 (August 1988), 84–89.

[15] SMITH, D. R. *The Structure of Divide-and-Conquer Algorithms*. Tech. Rep. NPS52-83-002, Naval Postgraduate School, Monterey, CA, March 1983.

[16] SMITH, D. R. Top-down synthesis of divide-and-conquer algorithms. *Artificial Intelligence 27*, 1 (September 1985), 43–96. (Reprinted in *Readings in Artificial Intelligence and Software Engineering*, C. Rich and R. Waters, Eds., Los Altos, CA, Morgan Kaufmann, 1986.).

[17] SMITH, D. R. Applications of a strategy for designing divide-and-conquer algorithms. *Science of Computer Programming 8*, 3 (June 1987), 213–229. Technical Report KES.U.85.2, Kestrel Institute, March 1985.

[18] SMITH, D. R. *Structure and Design of Global Search Algorithms.* Tech. Rep. KES.U.87.12, Kestrel Institute, November 1987.

[19] SMITH, D. R. KIDS – a knowledge-based software development system. In *Proceedings of the Workshop on Automating Software Design* (St. Paul, MN, August 25, 1988). Technical Report KES.U.88.7, Kestrel Institute, October 1988.

[20] VELOSO, P. A. Problem solving by interpretation of theories. In *Contemporary Mathematics*, American Mathematical Society, Providence, Rhode Island, 1988, pp. 241–250.

A Categorical Approach to the Theory of Lists

Mike Spivey

Programming Research Group
Oxford University Computing Laboratory
11, Keble Road, Oxford, OX1 3QD, England

Abstract

Many of the laws in Bird's 'theory of lists' [1, 2] are precisely the conditions for various constructions to be functors, natural transformations, adjunctions, and so on. In this paper, I explore this categorical background to the theory, and – by generalizing one law and adding another – establish a completeness result for part of the theory. In the final section of the paper, I indicate how a theory of expression trees could be compiled along similar lines.

None of the mathematical results in this paper are new; instead, its contribution is in showing how category theory can be used to organize a complete set of laws for program transformation. I hope, too, that the paper will provide a readable introduction to category theory for those already acquainted with functional programming.

1   Types and functions

Functional programming is concerned with functions from one type to another. Although there are various ways of understanding in full generality what these functions and types are, it will be enough for us to consider the types to be certain sets, and the functions to be ordinary mathematical functions between these sets.

For each type α, there is an identity function $id_\alpha : \alpha \to \alpha$. It will suit our purposes to make explicit in the name id_α the dependence on the type α; we are considering a family of functions indexed by a type, rather than a single 'polymorphic' identity function.

If $f : \alpha \to \beta$ and $g : \beta \to \gamma$ are functions, we can form their composition $g \cdot f$, a function in $\alpha \to \gamma$. Familiar laws of mathematics state that composition is associative:

$$(h \cdot g) \cdot f = h \cdot (g \cdot f),$$

and that the identify functions id_α and id_β are right and left identities for composition with $f : \alpha \to \beta$:

$$f \cdot id_\alpha = f = id_\beta \cdot f.$$

In category theory, these properties of id and $\cdot$ are summarized by saying that types and functions form a *category*.

2 Lists

If α is a type, we can form the type $\alpha*$: its elements are *lists* of elements of α. Also, if $f : \alpha \to \beta$ is a function, we can form the function $f* : \alpha* \to \beta*$ which maps f over the elements of its argument: it is the function *mapcar* of LISP.

The notation $*$ is used here for both the operation which takes a type α to the type of lists of elements of α, and the operation which takes a function f to the function that applies f uniformly to each member of a list. This choice of notation may seem like an attack of the Computing Science disease – that of an unhealthy preoccupation with notational issues – but it is justified by the patterns it reveals in the laws of the theory of lists.

Two laws show how $*$ interacts with the identity function and composition:

$$id_\alpha* = id_{\alpha*},$$
$$(g \cdot f)* = g* \cdot f*.$$

So $*$ takes identity functions to identity functions and the composition of two functions to the result of composing their images under $*$. In categorical language, we say $*$ is a *functor* from types to types.

3 Flatten

Many families of functions can be defined uniformly for any type. These families of functions obey laws which follow a certain pattern.

For a first example, consider the "flatten" function $+\!\!+/_\alpha : \alpha** \to \alpha*$, defined for any type α. This function takes a list of lists and forms a list by concatenating all the members of its argument. If $f : \alpha \to \beta$ is a function, then we can form the functions

$$f* : \alpha* \to \beta*,$$
$$f** : \alpha** \to \beta**.$$

The family of flatten functions also gives us the two functions

$$+\!\!+/_\alpha : \alpha** \to \alpha*,$$
$$+\!\!+/_\beta : \beta** \to \beta*,$$

and these four functions can be made into the following picture:

$$
\begin{array}{ccc}
\alpha** & \xrightarrow{f**} & \beta** \\
{\scriptstyle +\!\!+/_\alpha}\Big\downarrow & & \Big\downarrow{\scriptstyle +\!\!+/_\beta} \\
\alpha* & \xrightarrow{f*} & \beta*
\end{array}
$$

A law in the thory of lists states that

$$f* \cdot +\!\!+/_\alpha = +\!\!+/_\beta \cdot f**.$$

n other words, the function we obtain by composing the bottom and the left-hand side of the square is the same as the one we obtain by composing the right-hand side and the top. Speaking categorically, we say the square *commutes*.

This picture is an instance of a general picture we shall meet several times:

$$
\begin{array}{ccc}
G\,\alpha & \xrightarrow{\ Gf\ } & G\,\beta \\
\theta_\alpha \downarrow & & \downarrow \theta_\beta \\
H\,\alpha & \xrightarrow{\ Hf\ } & H\,\beta
\end{array}
$$

The top left corner of this picture is obtained by applying a functor G to the type α (in this instance, G is the functor $**$). In the top right corner is G applied to another type β, and connecting them is the function

$$Gf : G\,\alpha \to G\,\beta.$$

The bottom part of the picture differs in that G has been replaced by a functor H (in this instance, H is $*$). The top and bottom are connected by two members of a family θ of functions: on the left is $\theta_\alpha : G\,\alpha \to H\,\alpha$ (in this instance, $+\!+/_\alpha : \alpha** \to \alpha*$) and on the right is $\theta_\beta : G\,\beta \to H\,\beta$. We say the square commutes if the following equation holds:

$$Hf \cdot \theta_\alpha = \theta_\beta \cdot Gf.$$

If this equation is true for every function $f : \alpha \to \beta$, then we say the family θ is a *natural transformation* and write $\theta : G \overset{\cdot}{\to} H$ (in this instance, $+\!+/ : ** \overset{\cdot}{\to} *$).

4 Singleton

Another example of a natural transformation is the function which takes any element x of type α to the singleton list $[x]$ of type $\alpha*$; this is written $[\cdot]_\alpha : \alpha \to \alpha*$. To draw the picture, we take $G\,\alpha = \alpha$ and $H\,\alpha = \alpha*$:

$$
\begin{array}{ccc}
\alpha & \xrightarrow{\ f\ } & \beta \\
[\cdot]_\alpha \downarrow & & \downarrow [\cdot]_\beta \\
\alpha* & \xrightarrow{\ f*\ } & \beta*
\end{array}
$$

For the square to commute, the equation which must hold is

$$f* \cdot [\cdot]_\alpha = [\cdot]_\beta \cdot f,$$

or – applying both sides to an arbitrary object x –

$$f * [x] = [f\,x].$$

So $[\cdot]$ is another natural transformation and we write $[\cdot] : Id \overset{\cdot}{\to} *$. In this expression, Id is the identity functor used as G in the picture.

5 Concatenation

To see the concatenation function $+\!\!+_\alpha$ in the same way, we need to introduce a new functor $\_^2$. If α is a type, then $\alpha^2 = \alpha \times \alpha$, and if $f : \alpha \to \beta$ is a function, then $f^2 : \alpha^2 \to \beta^2$ is defined by

$$f^2\,(x, y) = (f\,x, f\,y).$$

This really is a functor, because for any $x, y : \alpha$,

$$\begin{aligned}
id_\alpha^2\,(x, y) &= (id_\alpha\,x, id_\alpha\,y) \\
&= (x, y) \\
&= id_{\alpha^2}\,(x, y),
\end{aligned}$$

and if $f : \alpha \to \beta$ and $g : \beta \to \gamma$ then

$$\begin{aligned}
(g \cdot f)^2\,(x, y) &= ((g \cdot f)\,x, (g \cdot f)\,y) \\
&= (g\,(f\,x), g\,(f\,y)) \\
&= g^2\,(f\,x, f\,y) \\
&= g^2\,(f^2\,(x, y)) \\
&= (g^2 \cdot f^2)\,(x, y).
\end{aligned}$$

Now $+\!\!+_\alpha : \alpha* \times \alpha* \to \alpha*$ can be viewed as a function in $\alpha*^2 \to \alpha*$ and we can draw the following picture, choosing G to be the functor $*^2$ and H to be the functor $*$:

$$\begin{array}{ccc}
\alpha*^2 & \xrightarrow{\ f*^2\ } & \beta*^2 \\
{\scriptstyle +\!\!+_\alpha}\Big\downarrow & & \Big\downarrow{\scriptstyle +\!\!+_\beta} \\
\alpha* & \xrightarrow{\ f*\ } & \beta*
\end{array}$$

The fact that this picture commutes is expressed by the following law:

$$f* \cdot +\!\!+_\alpha = +\!\!+_\beta \cdot f*^2,$$

or – applying both sides to a pair of lists (a, b) –

$$f * (a +\!\!+ b) = (f * a) +\!\!+ (f * b).$$

Again, this is a familiar law from the theory of lists; in categorical notation, we write i $+\!\!+ : *^2 \xrightarrow{\ \bullet\ } *$.

6 Empty list

For any type α, the empty list $[\,]_\alpha$ is an object of type $\alpha*$. To draw one of our pictures we need to view it as a function, and we can do this using a standard trick of category theory.

Let *unit* be a type with the single element $(\,)$, and for any type α, define $[\,]_\alpha^\circ : unit \to \alpha*$ by $[\,]_\alpha^\circ(\,) = [\,]_\alpha$. Categorically speaking, *unit* is a *terminal object* in the category of types

This function $[\,]^{\circ}_{\alpha}$ picks out $[\,]_{\alpha}$ as the image of $(\,)$: in fact, for any type β, the functions from *unit* to β are in one-to-one correspondence with the elements of β.

Next, for any type γ, we define a functor K_{γ} from types to types: it is the constant functor such that $K_{\gamma}\,\alpha = \gamma$, and if $f : \alpha \to \beta$ then $K_{\gamma}\,f = id_{\gamma}$. With this definition, we can view $[\,]^{\circ}_{\alpha}$ as a function from $K_{unit}\,\alpha$ to $\alpha*$, and draw the picture

$$
\begin{array}{ccc}
K_{unit}\,\alpha & \xrightarrow{\ K_{unit}\,f\ } & K_{unit}\,\beta \\[4pt]
{\scriptstyle[\,]^{\circ}_{\alpha}}\Big\downarrow & & \Big\downarrow{\scriptstyle[\,]^{\circ}_{\beta}} \\[4pt]
\alpha* & \xrightarrow[\ f*\ ]{} & \beta*
\end{array}
$$

What law must be true for this square to commute? By definition, it is the equation

$$f* \cdot [\,]^{\circ}_{\alpha} = [\,]^{\circ}_{\beta} \cdot K_{unit}\,f.$$

But $[\,]^{\circ}_{\beta} \cdot K_{unit}\,f = [\,]^{\circ}_{\beta} \cdot id_{unit} = [\,]^{\circ}_{\beta}$, so this equation is equivalent to

$$f* \cdot [\,]^{\circ}_{\alpha} = [\,]^{\circ}_{\beta},$$

or – applying both sides to $(\,)$ – to

$$f * [\,]_{\alpha} = [\,]_{\beta}.$$

This is another familiar law. We write $[\,]^{\circ} : K_{unit} \overset{\cdot}{\to} *$ to express the fact that $[\,]^{\circ}$ is a natural transformation from K_{unit} to $*$.

The theme of the first part of the paper is that many functions like $+\!\!+/_{\alpha}$ which are defined uniformly for any type α can be viewed as natural transformations because of the laws they satisfy.

7 Reduction

The reduction $\oplus/ : \alpha* \to \alpha$ is fully defined only if $\oplus : \alpha \times \alpha \to \alpha$ is an associative operation with an identity element e. In this case, we say that the triple $(\alpha, \oplus, e)$ is a *monoid*. If $(\alpha, \oplus, e)$ and $(\beta, \otimes, d)$ are two monoids, we shall be especially interested in functions $h : \alpha \to \beta$ which 'respect the monoid structure' on α and β – that is, such that

$$h\,e = d,$$

and

$$h\,(x \oplus y) = (h\,x) \otimes (h\,y)$$

for all x and y in α. Such functions are called *homomorphisms* and we write

$$h : (\alpha, \oplus, e) \overset{m}{\to} (\beta, \otimes, d).$$

Two important facts are that id_{α} is a homomorphism, and that the composition of two homomorphisms is also a homomorphism. In symbols,

$$id_{\alpha} : (\alpha, \oplus, e) \overset{m}{\to} (\alpha, \oplus, e),$$

and if $f : (\alpha, \oplus, e) \overset{m}{\to} (\beta, \otimes, d)$ and $g : (\beta, \otimes, d) \overset{m}{\to} (\gamma, \odot, c)$, then

$$g \cdot f : (\alpha, \oplus, e) \overset{m}{\to} (\gamma, \odot, c).$$

These two facts are summarized by saying that monoids form a category, in which the arrows are homomorphisms.

For any type α, we can form the *list monoid* $(\alpha*, +\!\!+_\alpha, [\,]_\alpha)$, which we shall write $F \alpha$. The reduction $\oplus/$ – which we shall sometimes write pedantically as $\epsilon_{(\alpha, \oplus, e)}$ – is a homomorphism

$$\epsilon_{(\alpha, \oplus, e)} = \oplus/ : (\alpha*, +\!\!+_\alpha, [\,]_\alpha) \overset{m}{\to} (\alpha, \oplus, e).$$

Also, if $f : \alpha \to \beta$ is any function, then $f*$ is a homomorphism from $F \alpha$ to $F \beta$: we define

$$F f = f* : F \alpha \overset{m}{\to} F \beta.$$

If $h : (\alpha, \oplus, e) \overset{m}{\to} (\beta, \otimes, d)$ is any homomorphism, we can form the square

$$
\begin{array}{ccc}
F \alpha = (\alpha*, +\!\!+_\alpha, [\,]_\alpha) & \overset{F h = h*}{\longrightarrow} & (\beta*, +\!\!+_\beta, [\,]_\beta) = F \beta \\
\epsilon_{(\alpha, \oplus, e)} = \oplus/ \downarrow & & \downarrow \otimes/ = \epsilon_{(\beta, \otimes, d)} \\
(\alpha, \oplus, e) & \overset{h}{\longrightarrow} & (\beta, \otimes, d)
\end{array}
$$

The fact that this square commutes is expressed by the law

$$h \cdot \oplus/ = \otimes/ \cdot h*.$$

This law is a generalization of the law (7) of Richard Bird's paper [2], in which the arbitrary homomorphism h is replaced by the special case $\otimes/ : (\beta*, +\!\!+_\beta, [\,]_\beta) \overset{m}{\to} (\beta, \otimes, d)$. Here is the picture which results:

$$
\begin{array}{ccc}
F (\beta*) = (\beta**, +\!\!+_{\beta*}, [\,]_{\beta*}) & \overset{F (\otimes/) = (\otimes/)*}{\longrightarrow} & (\beta*, +\!\!+_\beta, [\,]_\beta) = F \beta \\
\epsilon_{(\beta*, +\!\!+_\beta, [\,]_\beta)} = +\!\!+/ \downarrow & & \downarrow \otimes/ = \epsilon_{(\beta, \otimes, d)} \\
(\beta*, +\!\!+_\beta, [\,]_\beta) & \overset{\otimes/}{\longrightarrow} & (\beta, \otimes, d)
\end{array}
$$

The equation is

$$\otimes/ \cdot +\!\!+/ = \otimes/ \cdot (\otimes/)*.$$

Categorically speaking, ϵ is a natural transformation $\epsilon : F \cdot U \overset{\cdot}{\to} Id$, where U is the functor which "forgets" the structure of a monoid, leaving just a type.

8 The homomorphism theorem

There is a close relationship between reductions $\oplus/$ and the unit-list function $[\cdot]_\alpha$, as shown by the two laws

$$\oplus/ \cdot [\cdot]_\alpha = id_\alpha,$$
$$+\!\!+/_\alpha \cdot [\cdot]_\alpha* = id_{\alpha*}.$$

The second of these laws is absent from [2], but it is needed below. Together, the two laws state that the natural transformations $[\cdot]$ and ϵ form an *adjunction*.

The close relationship between $[\cdot]$ and ϵ manifests itself in two other ways: first, if $(\beta, \otimes, d)$ is a monoid and $f : \alpha \to \beta$, then there is exactly one homomorphism $h : (\alpha*, ++_\alpha, [\,]_\alpha) \overset{m}{\to} (\beta, \otimes, d)$ such that $f = h \cdot [\cdot]_\alpha$: it is given by $h = \otimes/ \cdot f*$. To see that $f = h \cdot [\cdot]_\alpha$, we calculate

$$
\begin{aligned}
h \cdot [\cdot]_\alpha &= \otimes/ \cdot f* \cdot [\cdot]_\alpha \\
&= \otimes/ \cdot [\cdot]_\beta \cdot f \\
&= id_\beta \cdot f \\
&= f.
\end{aligned}
$$

Also, if $f = h' \cdot [\cdot]_\alpha$ with $h' : (\alpha*, ++_\alpha, [\,]_\alpha) \overset{m}{\to} (\beta, \otimes, d)$, then

$$
\begin{aligned}
h &= \otimes/ \cdot f* \\
&= \otimes/ \cdot (h' \cdot [\cdot]_\alpha)* \\
&= \otimes/ \cdot h'* \cdot [\cdot]_\alpha* \\
&= h' \cdot ++/_\alpha \cdot [\cdot]_\alpha* \\
&= h' \cdot id_{\alpha*} \\
&= h'.
\end{aligned}
$$

This result shows how any function f defines a unique homomorphism h. The second result, called the "homomorphism theorem" in [2], is that any homomorphism $h : (\alpha*, ++, [\,]) \overset{m}{\to} (\beta, \otimes, d)$ can be defined in this way: specifically that there is a unique $f : \alpha \to \beta$ such that $h = \otimes/ \cdot f*$. This function is given by $f = h \cdot [\cdot]_\alpha$. We calculate:

$$
\begin{aligned}
\otimes/ \cdot f* &= \otimes/ \cdot (h \cdot [\cdot]_\alpha)* \\
&= \otimes/ \cdot h* \cdot [\cdot]_\alpha* \\
&= h \cdot ++/_\alpha \cdot [\cdot]_\alpha* \\
&= h \cdot id_{\alpha*} \\
&= h.
\end{aligned}
$$

To see that f is unique, suppose $h = \otimes/ \cdot f'*$. Then

$$
\begin{aligned}
f &= h \cdot [\cdot]_\alpha \\
&= \otimes/ \cdot f' * \cdot [\cdot]_\alpha \\
&= \otimes/ \cdot [\cdot]_\beta \cdot f' \\
&= id_\beta \cdot f' \\
&= f'.
\end{aligned}
$$

A theorem of category theory, part of the proof of which is reproduced here, says that each of these three ways of viewing the adjunction – the pair of laws and the two results about representing homomorphisms – is equivalent to the others.

9 Completeness

The homomorphism theorem provides a kind of completeness result for our theory of lists, because it gives a normal form for homomorphisms with the list monoid $F\alpha = (\alpha*, +\!\!+_\alpha, [\,]_\alpha)$ as their source. To show two such homomorphisms equal, we need only check that they act the same on singletons. This is often a convenient way of framing what amounts to induction on lists.

Another kind of completeness result follows from a theorem about uniqueness of adjunctions. The properties of $[\cdot]$ and ϵ we have examined are enough to determine the list monoid $F\alpha$ up to isomorphism. This means that any algebraic property of our list-processing operations is a consequence of the laws we have listed. This completeness of our set of transformation rules should give us a fresh confidence in tackling programming problems: if we cannot perform a desired transformation, this must be because it depends on some as-yet-unstated property of our programming problem, rather than because it requires some new property of lists.

10 Expression trees

Let us see how this idea of using category theory as the framework for the theory of a data type works out in another example, that of 'expression trees'. An expression tree over a type α of 'variables' is either simply an element of α, or the result of applying an operator (of type op) to a list of expression trees:

$$exp\,\alpha ::= Var_\alpha\,\alpha$$
$$\mid Apply_\alpha\,op\,((exp\,\alpha)*)$$

Following our practice with lists, let us write $\alpha\diamond$ for the type $exp\,\alpha$, and look for a function $f\diamond : \alpha\diamond \to \beta\diamond$ corresponding to each function $f : \alpha \to \beta$. The function $f\diamond$ acts on expression trees by copying the shape of its argument, but applying f to each variable. Here is a recursive definition:

$$f\diamond(Var_\alpha\,x) = Var_\beta\,(f\,x)$$
$$f\diamond(Apply_\alpha\,\omega\,a) = Apply_\beta\,\omega\,((f\diamond)*a).$$

But notice this: these two equations are exactly the conditions for Var and $Apply\,\omega$ (for $\omega : op$) to be natural transformations

$$Var : Id \overset{\cdot}{\to} \diamond$$
$$Apply\,\omega : \diamond* \overset{\cdot}{\to} \diamond.$$

In studying lists, we used the category of monoids. Here we use the category of tree algebras. A *tree algebra* is a pair (α, f) where α is a type, and $f : op \to \alpha* \to \alpha$, and a morphism

$$h : (\alpha, f) \overset{\iota}{\to} (\beta, g)$$

of tree algebras is a function $h : \alpha \to \beta$ such that, for each $\omega : op$, the following diagram commutes:

$$
\begin{array}{ccc}
\alpha* & \xrightarrow{\;h*\;} & \beta* \\[2pt]
{\scriptstyle f\omega}\downarrow & & \downarrow{\scriptstyle g\omega} \\[2pt]
\alpha & \xrightarrow{\;h\;} & \beta
\end{array}
$$

In symbols,

$$g\,\omega \cdot h* = h \cdot f\,\omega.$$

In place of the singleton function $[\cdot]_\alpha$, we have the constructor $Var_\alpha : \alpha \to \alpha\diamond$, and in place of the reduction

$$\oplus/ : (\alpha*, +\!+_\alpha, [\,]_\alpha) \xrightarrow{m} (\alpha, \oplus, e)$$

is a function

$$eval_\alpha\, f : (\alpha\diamond, Apply_\alpha) \xrightarrow{t} (\alpha, f)$$

called *evaluation in* (α, f). As before, these functions are natural transformations, and like $[\cdot]$ and $\oplus/$, they are related by a pair of equations:

$$eval_\alpha\, f \cdot Var_\alpha = id_\alpha$$
$$eval_{\alpha\diamond}\, Apply\alpha \cdot Var_\alpha\diamond = id_{\alpha\diamond}.$$

An analogue of the homomorphism theorem is the following: every morphism

$$h : (\alpha\diamond, Apply_\alpha) \xrightarrow{t} (\beta, g)$$

of tree algebras can be written as $h = eval_\beta\, g \cdot f\diamond$ for a unique $f : \alpha \to \beta$ given by $f = h \cdot Var_\alpha$.

As a closing example, consider the function which applies a substitution $s : \alpha \to \beta\diamond$ to an expression tree in $\alpha\diamond$. This is a morphism

$$subst\, s : (\alpha\diamond, Apply_\alpha) \xrightarrow{t} (\beta\diamond, Apply_\beta),$$

so the homomorphism theorem lets us write it as

$$subst\, s = eval_{\beta\diamond}\, Apply_\beta \cdot f\diamond$$

where $f = subst\, s \cdot Var_\alpha = s$. Thus substitution can be seen as a two-stage process: first replace each variable with its image under the substitution, then graft these images into the expression tree using $eval_{\beta\diamond}\, Apply_\beta$.

11 Conclusion

We have taken some of the laws from the theory of lists and shown that they fit into patterns suggested by category theory. In particular, many of the standard operations on lists can be seen as natural transformations, and this fact determines the way they interact with the mapping operation ∗. We have also seen how the homomorphism theorem for lists follows from the existence of a certain adjunction, and we have touched on the way completeness results for sets of laws can be derived from uniqueness theorems in category theory. Finally, we have sketched how a theory of expression trees can be constructed along the same lines as the theory of lists.

Categorical methods can assist in the development of theories for other data types: for example, lazy evaluation makes it possible to implement an exception mechanism as a collection of operations on 'lifted' types. In the paper [3], I develop a small categorical theory of exceptions and apply it to the derivation of term-rewriting strategies.

Many questions remain open for further investigation. It would be nice to find applications in programming for some of the deeper results of category theory as well as the conceptual language exploited in this paper. The theory of monads seems especially promising in this connexion, as Beck's theorem on classification of algebras provides further 'homomorphism theorems' for many algebraic data types: for example, in the theory of lists, any function $f : \alpha* \to \alpha$ which satisifes the equation

$$f \cdot f* = f \cdot +\!\!\!+/$$

is a homomorphism.

There is more to polymorphism than the simple view taken in this paper, and one might ask what view of polymorphism would lead to the best theories of data types.

Acknowledgements

The research reported in this paper was carried out partly under a Junior Research Fellowship at Oriel College, Oxford sponsored by Rank Xerox (U.K.) Ltd., and partly under an Atlas Research Fellowship at the Rutherford Appleton Laboratory of the Science and Engineering Research Council of Great Britain.

References

[1] R. S. Bird. 'An introduction to the theory of lists'. In *Logic of Programming and Calculi of Descrete Design*, M. Broy (ed.), Springer-Verlag, 1986, pp. 5–42.

[2] R. S. Bird. 'A calculus of functions for program derivation'. Technical monograph PRG–64, Programming Research Group, Oxford University Computing Laboratory, 1987. 21pp.

[3] J. M. Spivey. 'Term-rewriting without exceptions'. Submitted to *Science of Computer Programming*, 1988.

Rabbitcount := Rabbitcount − 1

Jaap van der Woude

TUE, Eindhoven.

§ 0

Programming is often regarded as problem solving requiring (unstructered) ingenious inventions. At the other end of the spectrum are those that advocate algorithm construction by formal manipulation only, such that machines can do the job.

Although the middle of the road is seldom paved with yellow bricks, we like to lend good things from both. Inventions? Yes, but they should be structured and triggered by the formalism, hence tamed to heuristics. Formal manipulation? Yes, but driven by the heuristics. So we regard programming as a human activity benefitting from suitable modelling and calculation.

To that end one should develop a formalism that reflects the properties of the objects under consideration. It should be concise, with limited manipulative choice. The development strategy should be guided by the derivation techniques, manipulative possibilities and by educated guesses about what may be accomplished. The details are to be fully calculational, and representation should enter the picture at the very last stage.

> We shall demonstrate this by a problem thrown at the audience in Marktoberdorf by R.S. Bird. (We return to that in the last section.)

The title above may be misleading: we don't kill rabbits, we try to avoid them. We confess to like rabbits a lot, provided ... they are welltrained enough to pop up at the appropriate stages in the derivations. Beauty loses its splendour if it is all over the place. Therefore we plea for rabbit anti-conception.

§ 1. Example

The problem we use to illustrate some derivation principles with is called:

> "the largest rectangle under a histogram"

There are several ways to state it, depending on the chosen formalism and point of view (cf [B], [E]):

- transform the following function on lists of naturals

$$\uparrow / \ \text{area} * \text{segs} \quad \text{where} \quad \text{area} \, x = (\#x) \times \downarrow / x$$

to an expression that can be computed in linear time.

- find a linear algorithm that establishes

$$b = (\underline{\text{MAX}} \, p, q : 0 \le p \le q \le N : (q - p) * (\underline{\text{MIN}} \, i : p \le i < q : X \cdot i))$$

where X is an array of naturals.

Instead of introducing heaps (cf [B]) or performing a lot of quantifier juggling (cf [E]), we rephraze the problem in terms of the "relevant concepts": histograms and rectangles.

Let I be a finite segment of the integers.

A <u>histogram</u> <u>on</u> <u>domain</u> I is a natural function on I. Histograms on I are ordered pointwise, i.e.

(0) $$X \le Y \equiv (\underline{A} \, i : i \in I : X \cdot i \le Y \cdot i)$$

Unless the domain of a histogram is understood, we provide it: $X[m, n)$ stands for histogram X on the finite segment $\{i \in \text{int} \mid m \le i < n\}$.

A constant histogram with value c is denoted by the value in boldface, e.g. $\mathbf{c}[m, n)$.

Histograms can be catenated or restricted:

Let $X[m, q)$ and $Y[q, r)$ be histograms and $m \le q \le r$, then
$X[m, q) \# Y[q, r)$ is a histogram on $[m \, r)$ (catenation)
for $m \le n \le p \le q$, $X[n, p)$ is a histogram (restriction of X to $[n, p)$).
A <u>rectangle</u> on $[m, q)$ is a histogram of the form (for some c in nat)

$$\mathbf{0}[m, n) \# \mathbf{c}[n, p) \# \mathbf{0}[p, q) .$$

X being a rectangle is expressed by: $\text{rect} \cdot X$.

Our specification of the problem:

$$\llbracket \ N : \text{nat} ; X : \text{histogram on } [0, N) ;$$
$$\llbracket \ b : \text{nat} ;$$
$$S$$
$$\{ b = \text{MRA} \cdot X \}$$
$$\rrbracket$$
$$\rrbracket$$

where the maximal rectangular area $\text{MRA} \cdot X$ under X is defined by

(1) $\qquad \text{MRA} \cdot X = (\underline{\text{MAX}} Z : Z \leq X \;\wedge\; \text{rect} \cdot Z : \square \cdot Z)$

(where $\square \cdot Z$ = area of Z; for now, only $\square \cdot Z \geq 0$ is relevant)

The problem is easily solved for constant histograms and for monotonic ones. Therefore, we try to gradually reduce the problem to histograms of a more monotonic shape. The proposed reduction corresponds to the choice for invariant

$P_0 \qquad b \; \underline{\max} \; \text{MRA} \cdot Y = \text{MRA} \cdot X$

This is an example of the standard strategy "replacement of a constant by a variable", where the invisible constant 0 in the postcondition

$$b \; \underline{\max} \; \text{MRA} \cdot 0 = \text{MRA} \cdot X$$

is replaced by the histogram variable Y. (The variable b is sometimes called an accumulation variable.)

Initialization of P_0 is forced: $\quad b, Y := 0, X$. For the guard of the repetition we may take "$Y \neq 0$", or the stronger, "Y is not monotonic". Since, by P_0, the requirement $Y \leq X$ is almost unavoidable, we don't have to choose between the two possibilities for the guard if we assume that X has value 0 at both ends of its domain. For, under assumption of

(2) $\qquad N \geq 1 \;\wedge\; X \cdot 0 = 0 \;\wedge\; X \cdot (N-1) = 0$

we have

(3) $\qquad Y = 0 \;\equiv\; Y \leq X \;\wedge\; Y$ is monotonic .

From now on, (2) is assumed for the problem at hand.

The above discussion and the wish to investigate X in some orderly fashion lead to the following sweetly reasonable invariants:

$P_1 \qquad Y[0, n) \leq X[0, n) \;\wedge\; Y[n, N) = \dot{X}[n, N)$

$P_2 \qquad Y[0, n)$ is ascending

$P_3 \qquad 1 \leq n \leq N$

(The choice for ascendingness in P_2 is forced by P_1: since we start with $Y \cdot 0 = 0$, descendingness is too restrictive!)

Since under assumption of $P_{0..3}$

$$n = N$$
$$\Rightarrow \{P_1, P_2\}$$
$$Y \leq X \; \wedge \; Y \text{ is monotonic}$$
$$= \{(3)\}$$
$$Y = 0$$
$$\Rightarrow \{P_0 \;, \; \text{MRA} \cdot 0 = 0\}$$
$$b = \text{MRA} \cdot X,$$

the following skeleton for S results:

$$b, Y, n := 0, X, 1 \quad \{P_{0..3}\}$$
$$; \underline{\text{do}} \; n \neq N$$
$$\rightarrow \{P_{0..3} \; \wedge \; n \neq N\}$$
$$S_0$$
$$\{P_{0..3} \, [n := n+1]\}$$
$$; n := n + 1$$
$$\underline{\text{od}}$$
$$\{P_{0..3} \; \wedge \; n = N, \text{ hence } b = \text{MRA} \cdot X\}$$

$$* \quad * \quad *$$

Next we solve S_0:
Since, for $n \neq N$,

$$P_{0..3} \; \wedge \; X \cdot n \geq Y \cdot (n-1) \Rightarrow P_{0..3} \, [n := n+1]$$

we are led to a repetition for S_0, with invariant $P_{0..3}$ and guard

(4) $X \cdot n < Y \cdot (n-1)$.

Because X is fixed, gradual falsification of the guard (4) can only be established by decreasing Y, especially $Y \cdot (n-1)$. The desired invariance of P_2 tells us to decrease "the whole $Y \cdot (n-1)$-level", i.e. to decrease $Y[k, n)$, where

(5) $k = (\underline{\text{MIN}} \, i : 0 \leq i < n \; \wedge \; Y \cdot i = Y \cdot (n-1) : i)$

Observe that, by (4) and $Y \cdot 0 = 0$, $k > 0$. Hence by (5):

(6) $Y \cdot (k-1) < Y \cdot k \; \wedge \; Y \cdot k = Y \cdot (n-1)$.

The choice for a suitable decrement of Y, i.e. the choice for histogram Y' with $Y' < Y$, is gouverned by three "strategic" considerations:

- Simplicity: only decrease $Y[k, n)$ and decrease it to a constant. So, let

(7) $$Y' = Y[0, k) \#\!\!+ c[k, n) \#\!\!+ X[n, N)$$

for a suitable $c < Y \cdot k$. The decrement should be strictly necessary, so it is reasonable to require $c \geq X \cdot n$.

- Monotonicity of Y' (P_2): c should be chosen such that $Y \cdot (k-1) \leq c$.

  Since by (4) and (6) $X \cdot n \underline{\max} Y \cdot (k-1) < Y \cdot k$, this leads us to $X \cdot n \underline{\max} Y \cdot (k-1)$ as a good candidate for c.

- Easy expressibility of MRA$\cdot Y$ in MRA$\cdot Y'$: we show that our candidate is indeed a good choice:

Firstly:

$$\text{MRA} \cdot Y$$

$$= \{(1), \text{domainsplit} ; Y' < Y\}$$

(8) $$\text{MRA} \cdot Y' \underline{\max} (\underline{\text{MAX}} Z : Z \leq Y \wedge \neg Z \leq Y' \wedge \text{rect} \cdot Z : \square \cdot Z)$$

Secondly, we calculate the righthand argument of $\underline{\max}$ in (8) for our candidate Y' (as in (7) with $c = X \cdot n \underline{\max} Y \cdot (k-1)$).
Let Z be a rectangle, say

(9) $$Z = 0[0, p) \#\!\!+ h[p, q) \#\!\!+ 0[q, N) .$$

Then $Z \leq Y \wedge \neg Z \leq Y' \equiv k \leq p < q \leq n \wedge c + 1 \leq h \leq Y \cdot k$, for

$$Z \leq Y \wedge \neg Z \leq Y'$$
$$= \{(7), (0)\}$$
$$Z \leq Y \wedge \neg Z[k, n) \leq c[k, n)$$
$$= \{(9), Y \cdot i \geq 0 \text{ and } c \geq 0\}$$
$$h[p, q) \leq Y[p, q) \wedge \neg h((p, q) \cap [k, n)) \leq c((p, q) \cap [k, n))$$
$$= \{(0) \text{ take negation }\}$$
$$h[p, q) \leq Y[p, q) \wedge [p, q) \cap [k, n) \neq \varnothing \wedge c < h$$
$$= \{Y \text{ const. on } [k, n) \ (5) ; \ c < h \equiv c + 1 \leq h\}$$
$$h[p, q) \leq Y[p, q) \wedge [p, q) \cap [k, n) \neq \varnothing \wedge c + 1 \leq h \leq Y \cdot k$$
$$\Rightarrow \{ \text{transitivity} \}$$
$$c + 1[p, q) \leq Y[p, q) \wedge [p, q) \cap [k, n) \neq \varnothing \wedge c + 1 \leq h \leq Y \cdot k.$$

$\Rightarrow$ { choice for c ; so $c + 1 > X \cdot n = Y \cdot n \ \land \ c + 1 > Y \cdot k - 1$}

$\quad n \notin [p, q) \ \land \ k - 1 \notin [p, q) \ \land \ [p, q) \cap [k, n) \neq \varnothing \ \land \ c + 1 \leq h \leq Y \cdot k$

$= \{$ calculus $\}$

$\quad k \leq p < q \leq n \ \land \ c + 1 \leq h \leq Y \cdot k$

$\Rightarrow \{(5)\}$

$\quad \mathbf{h}[p, q) \leq Y[p, q) \ \land \ p \in [k, n) \ \land \ c < h$

$\Rightarrow \{(0), (9)\}$

$\quad Z \leq Y \ \land \ \neg Z[k, n) \leq \mathbf{c}[k, n).$

Hence, with $\square \cdot Z = (q - p) * h$ for rectangle Z as in (9):
(only here the definition of $\square \cdot Z$ is relevant.)

$$(\underline{MAX} Z : Z \leq Y \ \land \ \neg Z \leq Y' \ \land \ \text{rect} \cdot Z : \square \cdot Z)$$

$= \{$ above $\}$

$$(\underline{MAX} p, q, h : k \leq p < q \leq n \ \land \ c + 1 \leq h \leq Y \cdot k : (q - p) * h)$$

$= \{k < n, c < Y \cdot k \text{ ; calc}\}$

$$(n - k) * Y \cdot k$$

So with $c = X \cdot n \ \underline{max} \ Y \cdot (k - 1)$ and Y' as in (7) the easy expression we longed for is:

$$\text{MRA} \cdot Y = \text{MRA} \cdot Y' \ \underline{max} \ (n - k) * Y \cdot k \ .$$

We derived and proved the following approximation for S_0:

$\quad$ "calculate k" $\{(5) \ \land \ Y \cdot k = Y \cdot (n - 1) \ \land \ P_{0.3}\}$

$\quad ; \underline{do} \ X \cdot n < Y \cdot k$

$\quad \rightarrow \{k > 0\}$

$\qquad b := b \ \underline{max} \ (n - k) * Y \cdot k \ \{P_0[Y := Y']\}$

$\qquad ; c := X \cdot n \ \underline{max} \ Y \cdot (k - 1)$

$\qquad ; Y[k, n) := \mathbf{c}[k, n) \ \{P_{0.3}\}$

$\qquad ;$ "calculate k " $\{(5)\}$

$\quad \underline{od}$

$\{X \cdot n \geq Y \cdot k \ \land \ Y \cdot k = Y \cdot (n - 1) ; \text{ hence } P_{0.3}[n := n + 1]\}$

$$* \quad * \quad *$$

For the design we should worry about "calculate k". A linear search would be fatal for the efficiency. Another thing to worry about is the representation and the implementation of $Y[k, n) := \mathbf{c}[k, n)$ (i.e. $Y := Y'$). Since in the development until now we only used the "levels" of $Y[0, n)$, we may combine the two remaining worries:

Represent the ascending (P_2) histogram $Y[0, n)$ by its values and their first occurrences, preferably in increasing order (i.e. represent $Y[0, n)$ by its stepfunction).

In doing so we get "calculate k" for free!

So we introduce

s : nat; y , l $(i : 0 \leq i \leq N)$: <u>array</u> <u>of</u> nat;

and define y , $l[0, s] = \text{Step} \cdot Y[0, n)$ by

(10) $\quad \begin{cases} \quad y\ [0, s]\ \text{and}\ l[0, s]\ \text{are increasing} \\ \wedge Y\ [0, n) = (+ i : 0 \leq i < s : \mathbf{y} \cdot \mathbf{i}[l \cdot i,\ l \cdot (i+1)) + \mathbf{y} \cdot \mathbf{s}[l \cdot s,\ n) \end{cases}$

The two worries above are translated into a representation invariant (strengthening of P_2):

$P_4 \qquad y, l[0, s] = \text{Step} \cdot Y[0, n)$

Initialization of P_4 : $\ s, y \cdot 0, l \cdot 0 := 0, 0, 0.$

"Calculate k" in the approximation of S_0 is superfluous, since k (as defined in (5)) is just $l \cdot s$. $Y \cdot k$ is represented by $y \cdot s$ and, assuming $X \cdot n < y \cdot s$, $Y \cdot (k-1)$ is found in $y \cdot (s-1)$.

The statement list

$$c := X \cdot n\ \underline{\max}\ Y \cdot (k-1)$$

$$; Y[k, n) := \mathbf{c}[k, n)$$

should be translated in terms of the representation such that P_4 is maintained;

$\underline{\text{if}}\ X \cdot n \leq y \cdot (s-1) \rightarrow \{c := y \cdot (s-1);\}\ s := s - 1$
$[]\ X \cdot n > y \cdot (s-1) \rightarrow \{c := X \cdot n;\}\ y \cdot s := X \cdot n$
$\underline{\text{fi}}$

As follows (the second alternative is left to the reader):
assume $X \cdot n \leq y \cdot (s-1)$ then

$\qquad Y'[0, n)$
$= \{(7), P_4\}$
$\qquad (+ i : 0 \leq i < s : \mathbf{y} \cdot \mathbf{i}[l \cdot i, l(i+1)) + \mathbf{c}[l \cdot s, n)$
$= \{\text{split off}\ s - 1\ ;\ c = y \cdot (s-1)\ ;\ +\}$
$\qquad (+ i : 0 \leq i < s - 1 : \mathbf{y} \cdot \mathbf{i}[l \cdot i, l \cdot (i+1))) + \mathbf{y} \cdot (\mathbf{s-1})\ [l \cdot (s-1), n)$

Finally, immediately after S_0 and before $n := n + 1$, we have to insert "establish $P_4 [n := n+1]$" :

$$\underline{if}\, X \cdot n = y \cdot s \to skip$$
$$[]\, X \cdot n > y \cdot s \to s := s + 1 ; y \cdot s , l \cdot s := X \cdot n , n$$
$$\underline{fi}$$

This results in the final algorithm, which is linear with variant function : $2N - 2n + s$

```
[  n, s : nat ;
   y, l(i : 0 ≤ i ≤ N) : array of nat ;
   n , b , s , y· 0 , l· 0 := 1 , 0 , 0 , 0 , 0  {P₀.₄}
 ; do n ≠ N
   →  do X· n < y· s
      →  b := b max (n − l· s) * y· s
       ; if X· n ≤ y· (s−1) → s := s − 1
         [] X· n > y· (s−1) → y· s := X· n
         fi
      od
      {X· n ≥ y· s, hence P₀.₃ [n := n+1]}
    ; if X· n = y· s → skip
      [] X· n > y· s → s := s + 1 ; y· s , l· s := X· n , n
      fi {P₄[n := n+1]}
    ; n := n + 1  {P₀.₄}
   od
   {P₀.₄  ∧  n = N,  hence b = MRA· X}
]
```

Although the code above may be optimized, we won't bother. As it is, it shows the development more clearly.

§ 2 Application

Let I and J be finite segments of the naturals. A <u>matrix</u> <u>on</u> $I \times J$ is a natural function on $I \times J$. We adopt a notation similar to that of histograms:

$X\,I\,J$ is short for the matrix X on $I \times J$.

Note that for subsegments I' and J' of I and J (notation: $I'\ ss\ I$, $J'\ ss\ J$) and for $i \in I$

- $X\,I'\,J'$ is a matrix on $I' \times J'$, a submatrix of $X\,I\,J$.
- $X\,i\,J$ is a histogram on J.

We consider the following programmming exercise:
Given a matrix $X\,[0, M)\,[0, N)$ for natural M and N. Find the maximal area of any constant zero submatrix. More precisely: solve for T in

$$\llbracket\ M, N : \text{nat};$$
$$\quad X : \text{matrix on } [0, M) \times [0, N);$$
$$\quad \llbracket\ r : \text{nat};$$
$$\qquad T$$
$$\qquad \{r = \mu \cdot 0\}$$
$$\quad \rrbracket$$
$$\rrbracket$$

Where

(11) $\qquad \mu \cdot n = (\text{MAX}\,I, J : I\ ss\ [0, M)\ \wedge\ J\ ss\ [n, N)\ \wedge\ X\,I\,J = 0\,I\,J : \square \cdot I \times J)$

The definition of $\mu \cdot n$ already reflects a choice for one of the four constants to be generalized; any other would do perfectly well.
The invariants that go with this choice are:

$Q_0 \qquad r = \mu \cdot n$

$Q_1 \qquad 0 \le n \le N$

Since area is natural valued, the invariants hold after initialization: $n, r := N, 0$.
The resulting solution scheme for T is

$$n, r := N, 0\ \{Q_0 \wedge Q_1\}$$
$$;\ \underline{do}\ n \ne 0$$
$$\quad \rightarrow T_0$$
$$\qquad \{(Q_0 \wedge Q_1)\,[n := n-1]\}$$
$$\quad ;\ n := n-1$$
$$\underline{od}$$
$$\{Q_0\ \wedge\ n = 0,\ \text{hence}\ r = \mu \cdot 0\}$$

In order to derive T_0 we calculate for $n : 0 < n \le N$

$\quad \mu \cdot (n-1)$

$= \{(11), \text{domain split}\}$

$\quad \mu \cdot n \underline{\max}$

(12) $\qquad (\underline{\text{MAX}}\, I, J : I \text{ ss } [0, M) \ \wedge\ J \text{ iss } [n-1, N) \ \wedge\ X I J = 0 I J : \square \cdot I \times J))$

where $J \text{ iss } [n-1, N)$ means: J is an initial subsegment of $[n-1, N)$.

It seems useful to study the third conjunct in the domain of (12). so for $i \in [0, M)$:

$\quad X i J = 0 i J$

$= \{ \text{calculus} \}$

$\quad |J| \le (\underline{\text{MAX}}\, J' : J' \text{ iss } [n-1, N) \ \wedge\ X i J' = 0 i J' : |J'|)$

$= \{ \text{definition below} \}$

$\quad |J| \le \alpha_{n-1} \cdot i$

where

$$\alpha_{n-1} \cdot i = (\underline{\text{MAX}}\, J' : J' \text{ iss } [n-1, N) \ \wedge\ X i J' = 0 i J' : |J'|)$$

Note that α_{n-1} is a histogram on $[0, M)$, hence for $I = [q, r)$ with histogram notation:

$\quad X I J = 0 I J$

$= \{ \text{above} \}$

$\quad (\underline{A}\, i : i \in I : |J| \le \alpha_{n-1} \cdot i)$

$= \{ (0) \}$

$\quad |\mathbf{J}| \, I \le \alpha_{n-1} \cdot I$

$= \{ I = [q, r) \}$

$\quad 0[0, q) + |\mathbf{J}| \, [q, r) + 0[r, M) \le \alpha_{n-1}$

this reduces (12) to

$\quad (\underline{\text{MAX}}\, Z : Z \le \alpha_{n-1} \ \wedge\ \text{rect}. Z : \square \cdot Z)$

We derived the next approximation for T_0.

$\quad T_1$

$\quad \{ A = \alpha_{n-1} \}$

$\quad ; LRUH(A)$

$\quad \{ b = \text{MRA} \cdot A \ \wedge\ A = \alpha_{n-1} \}$

$\quad ; r := r \underline{\max} b$

$\quad \{ (Q_0 \wedge Q_1) [n := n-1) \}$

where LRUH (A) is the program we derived in the previous section, including the augmentation in order to satisfy (2). The final task, construction of T_1, is standard:

Strengthen invariant Q by adding

Q_3 $\quad A = \alpha_n$

with initialization : $A := 0$.

Then T_1 may be derived to be

$\quad\quad m := 0 \quad \{U\}$

$\quad\quad ; \underline{\text{do}}\ m \neq M$

$\quad\quad\quad \rightarrow \underline{\text{if}}\ X \cdot m \cdot (n-1) = 0 \rightarrow A \cdot m := A \cdot m + 1$

$\quad\quad\quad \,[\!]\ X \cdot m \cdot (n-1) \neq 0 \rightarrow A \cdot m := 0$

$\quad\quad\quad \underline{\text{fi}}$

$\quad\quad\quad ; m := m + 1$

$\quad\quad \underline{\text{od}}$

$\quad\quad\quad \{U\ \wedge\ m = M\ , \text{ hence } Q_3\,[n := n-1]\ \}$

where invariant U is given by

U $\quad\quad A[0, m) = \alpha_{n-1}[0, m)\ \wedge\ A[m, M) = \alpha_n[m, M)\ \wedge\ 0 \le m \le M$

This concludes the derivation of T, which is linear in the size of the matrix $X[0, M)\,[0, N)$.

§ 3 Final remarks

We stress that it was not the algorithm we were after, but merely it genesis as an example of fairly general derivation principles.

One of the disadvantages, felt with derivations as in the former sections, is that it is a stream of thoughts caught in a bunch of blueprints rather than application of unambiguous theorems with formalized conditions for applicability. Indeed, much of it seems to be apprehensible only by osmosis and experience. This is, however, also an advantage: situations, not (yet) covered by theorems do have a chance to be tackled. As such these derivations may even be seen as a first stage in the development of theorems. (Besides, the diversity of problems may lead to an unbridled growth of theorems, such that picking the right theorem may suffer from the same disadvantage.) We do favour the idea of eventually replacing blueprints by theorems if it doesn't deprive the programmer of his derivation skills.

The choice for the problem, we have exemplified some derivation principles with, was not arbitrary. It resulted from the challenge to present a derivation of the algorithm for the maximal all-one block (all-zero matrix here) that was presented by R.S. Bird in Marktoberdorf ([B]). He used it to illustrate several aspects of the Bird-Meertens method "in two dimensions". One of those aspects was the heap-concept, which was applied to the largest-rectangle-under-a-histogram subproblem. In his "rabbitcount" this heap introduction gave an increment 2. Since the heap reflects the "inherent recursion" structure, it is doubtful that it is a rabbit at all. But, the necessary heuristics not been developed yet, we do consider it as a rabbit (for now). In our derivation (of an iterative solution) that heap does not occur, but the representation invariant P_4 may be viewed as a projection of it.

Time flies ....

In [E] solutions to this and similar other problems are derived with one blueprint, be it with more quantifier juggling. Very recently, a theorem emerged for recursive solutions of those problems and the like ([Z]). Another solution is given using a derivation method for recursion based on refinements ([M]).

Again, don't worry about the solution itself, the derivation is what this was all about.

We like to thank many people for their encouragements and remarks, in particular Wim Feijen.

References

[B] Bird, R.S., Constructive functional programming, Working material for the international summer school on constructive methods in computing science, Marktoberdorf, 1988.

[E] Eijnde, J.P.H.W. van den, Left bottom and right top segments, preprint.

[M] Morris, J.M., Private communication.

[Z] Zantema, H., Private communication.

AUTHORS' INDEX

. 324: M.P. Chytil, L. Janiga, V. Koubek (Eds.), Mathematical undations of Computer Science 1988. Proceedings. IX, 562 jes. 1988.

. 325: G. Brassard, Modern Cryptology. VI, 107 pages. 1988.

. 326: M. Gyssens, J. Paredaens, D. Van Gucht (Eds.), ICDT '88. d International Conference on Database Theory. Proceedings, 38. VI, 409 pages. 1988.

. 327: G.A. Ford (Ed.), Software Engineering Education. Proceed-s, 1988. V, 207 pages. 1988.

. 328: R. Bloomfield, L. Marshall, R. Jones (Eds.), VDM '88. M – The Way Ahead. Proceedings, 1988. IX, 499 pages. 1988.

. 329: E. Börger, H. Kleine Büning, M.M. Richter (Eds.), CSL '87. Workshop on Computer Science Logic. Proceedings, 1987. VI, 6 pages. 1988.

. 330: C.G. Günther (Ed.), Advances in Cryptology – EURO-RYPT '88. Proceedings, 1988. XI, 473 pages. 1988.

. 331: M. Joseph (Ed.), Formal Techniques in Real-Time and Fault-lerant Systems. Proceedings. VI, 229 pages. 1988.

. 332: D. Sannella, A. Tarlecki (Eds.), Recent Trends in Data Type ecification. V, 259 pages. 1988.

. 333: H. Noltemeier (Ed.), Computational Geometry and its plications. Proceedings, 1988. VI, 252 pages. 1988.

. 334: K.R. Dittrich (Ed.), Advances in Object-Oriented Database stems. Proceedings, 1988. VII, 373 pages. 1988.

. 335: F.A. Vogt (Ed.), CONCURRENCY 88. Proceedings, 1988. 401 pages. 1988.

. 336: B.R. Donald, Error Detection and Recovery in Robotics. V, 314 pages. 1989.

. 337: O. Günther, Efficient Structures for Geometric Data Man-ement. XI, 135 pages. 1988.

. 338: K.V. Nori, S. Kumar (Eds.), Foundations of Software chnology and Theoretical Computer Science. Proceedings, 1988. 520 pages. 1988.

. 339: M. Rafanelli, J.C. Klensin, P. Svensson (Eds.), Statistical d Scientific Database Management. Proceedings, 1988. IX, 454 jes. 1989.

. 340: G. Rozenberg (Ed.), Advances in Petri Nets 1988. VI, 439 jes. 1988.

. 341: S. Bittanti (Ed.), Software Reliability Modelling and Identifi-ion. VII, 209 pages. 1988.

. 342: G. Wolf, T. Legendi, U. Schendel (Eds.), Parcella '88. ceedings, 1988. 380 pages. 1989.

. 343: J. Grabowski, P. Lescanne, W. Wechler (Eds.), Algebraic d Logic Programming. Proceedings, 1988. 278 pages. 1988.

. 344: J. van Leeuwen, Graph-Theoretic Concepts in Computer ence. Proceedings, 1988. VII, 459 pages. 1989.

. 345: R.T. Nossum (Ed.), Advanced Topics in Artificial Intelli-nce. VII, 233 pages. 1988 (Subseries LNAI).

. 346: M. Reinfrank, J. de Kleer, M.L. Ginsberg, E. Sandewall ds.), Non-Monotonic Reasoning. Proceedings, 1988. XIV, 237 jes. 1989 (Subseries LNAI).

. 347: K. Morik (Ed.), Knowledge Representation and Organization Machine Learning. XV, 319 pages. 1989 (Subseries LNAI).

. 348: P. Deransart, B. Lorho, J. Małuszyński (Eds.), Programming nguages Implementation and Logic Programming. Proceedings, 38. VI, 299 pages. 1989.

. 349: B. Monien, R. Cori (Eds.), STACS 89. Proceedings, 1989. , 544 pages. 1989.

. 350: A. Törn, A. Žilinskas, Global Optimization. X, 255 pages. 39.

. 351: J. Díaz, F. Orejas (Eds.), TAPSOFT '89. Volume 1. Pro-dings, 1989. X, 383 pages. 1989.

. 352: J. Díaz, F. Orejas (Eds.), TAPSOFT '89. Volume 2. Pro-dings, 1989. X, 389 pages. 1989.

Vol. 354: J.W. de Bakker, W.-P. de Roever, G. Rozenberg (Eds.), Linear Time, Branching Time and Partial Order in Logics and Models for Concurrency. VIII, 713 pages. 1989.

Vol. 355: N. Dershowitz (Ed.), Rewriting Techniques and Applica-tions. Proceedings, 1989. VII, 579 pages. 1989.

Vol. 356: L. Huguet (Ed.), Applied Algebra, Algebraic Algorithms and Error-Correcting Codes. Proceedings, 1987. VI, 417 pages. 1989.

Vol. 357: T. Mora (Ed.), Applied Algebra, Algebraic Algorithms and Error-Correcting Codes. Proceedings, 1988. IX, 481 pages. 1989.

Vol. 358: P. Gianni (Ed.), Symbolic and Algebraic Computation. Proceedings, 1988. XI, 545 pages. 1989.

Vol. 359: D. Gawlick, M. Haynie, A. Reuter (Eds.), High Performance Transaction Systems. Proceedings, 1987. XII, 329 pages. 1989.

Vol. 360: H. Maurer (Ed.), Computer Assisted Learning – ICCAL '89. Proceedings, 1989. VII, 642 pages. 1989.

Vol. 361: S. Abiteboul, P.C. Fischer, H.-J. Schek (Eds.), Nested Relations and Complex Objects in Databases. VI, 323 pages. 1989.

Vol. 362: B. Lisper, Synthesizing Synchronous Systems by Static Scheduling in Space-Time. VI, 263 pages. 1989.

Vol. 363: A.R. Meyer, M.A. Taitslin (Eds.), Logic at Botik '89. Proceedings, 1989. X, 289 pages. 1989.

Vol. 364: J. Demetrovics, B. Thalheim (Eds.), MFDBS 89. Proceed-ings, 1989. VI, 428 pages. 1989.

Vol. 365: E. Odijk, M. Rem, J.-C. Syre (Eds.), PARLE '89. Parallel Architectures and Languages Europe. Volume I. Proceedings, 1989. XIII, 478 pages. 1989.

Vol. 366: E. Odijk, M. Rem, J.-C. Syre (Eds.), PARLE '89. Parallel Architectures and Languages Europe. Volume II. Proceedings, 1989. XIII, 442 pages. 1989.

Vol. 367: W. Litwin, H.-J. Schek (Eds.), Foundations of Data Organi-zation and Algorithms. Proceedings, 1989. VIII, 531 pages. 1989.

Vol. 368: H. Boral, P. Faudemay (Eds.), IWDM '89, Database Machi-nes. Proceedings, 1989. VI, 388 pages. 1989.

Vol. 375: J.L.A. van de Snepscheut (Ed.), Mathematics of Program Construction. Proceedings, 1989. VI, 421 pages. 1989.

This series reports new developments in computer science research and teaching – quickly, informally and at a high level. The type of material considered for publication includes preliminary drafts of original papers and monographs, technical reports of high quality and broad interest advanced level lectures, reports of meetings, provided they are of exceptional interest and focused on a single topic. The timeliness of a manuscript is more important than its form which may be unfinished or tentative. If possible, a subject index should be included. Publication of Lecture Notes is intended as a service to the international computer science community, in that a commercial publisher, Springer-Verlag, can offer a wide distribution of documents which would otherwise have a restricted readership. Once published and copyrighted, they can be documented in the scientific literature.

Manuscripts

Manuscripts should be no less than 100 and preferably no more than 500 pages in length.
They are reproduced by a photographic process and therefore must be typed with extreme care. Symbol not on the typewriter should be inserted by hand in indelible black ink. Corrections to the typescrip should be made by pasting in the new text or painting out errors with white correction fluid. Authors receiv 75 free copies and are free to use the material in other publications. The typescript is reduced slightly i size during reproduction; best results will not be obtained unless the text on any one page is kept withi the overall limit of 18 x 26.5 cm (7 x 10½ inches). On request, the publisher will supply special paper wit the typing area outlined.
Manuscripts should be sent to Prof. G. Goos, GMD Forschungsstelle an der Universität Karlsruhe, Haid- un Neu-Str. 7, 7500 Karlsruhe 1, Germany, Prof. J. Hartmanis, Cornell University, Dept. of Computer Science, Ithaca NY/USA 14850, or directly to Springer-Verlag Heidelberg.

Springer-Verlag, Heidelberger Platz 3, D-1000 Berlin 33
Springer-Verlag, Tiergartenstraße 17, D-6900 Heidelberg 1
Springer-Verlag, 175 Fifth Avenue, New York, NY 10010/USA
Springer-Verlag, 37-3, Hongo 3-chome, Bunkyo-ku, Tokyo 113, Japan

ISBN 3-540-51305-1
ISBN 0-387-51305-1